CIMA

MANAGERIAL
PAPER **P2**
MANAGEMENT ACCOUNTING – DECISION MANAGEMENT

In this edition we:

- Discuss the **best strategies** for studying for CIMA exams

- Highlight the **most important elements** in the syllabus and the **key skills** you will need

- **Signpost** how each chapter links to the syllabus and the learning outcomes

- Provide lots of **exam focus points** demonstrating what the examiner will want you to do

- Emphasise key points in regular **fast forward summaries**

- Test your knowledge of what you've studied in **quick quizzes**

- Examine your understanding in our **exam question bank**

- Reference all the important topics in our **full index**

BPP Learning Media's **i-Learn** and **i-Pass** products also support this paper.

FOR EXAMS IN NOVEMBER 2007 AND MAY 2008

LEARNING MEDIA

First edition 2004
Fourth edition May 2007

ISBN 9780 7517 4212 1
(previous edition 0 7517 2638 9)

British Library Cataloguing-in-Publication Data
A catalogue record for this book
is available from the British Library

Published by

BPP Learning Media Ltd
BPP House, Aldine Place
London W12 8AA

www.bpp.com/learningmedia

Printed in Great Britain by
W M Print
45-47 Frederick Street
Walsall, West Midlands
WS2 9NE

Your learning materials, published by BPP Learning
Media Ltd, are printed on paper sourced from
sustainable, managed forests.

We are grateful to the Chartered Institute of Management
Accountants for permission to reproduce past
examination questions. The suggested solutions in the
exam answer bank have been prepared by BPP Learning
Media Ltd.

Contents

CONTENTS

The BPP Learning Media Effective Study Package

Distance Learning from BPP Professional Education

You can access our exam-focused interactive e-learning materials over the **Internet**, via BPP Learn Online, hosted by BPP Professional Education.

BPP Learn Online offers **comprehensive tutor support**, **revision guidance** and **exam tips**.

Visit www.bpp.com/cima/learnonline for further details.

Learning to Learn Accountancy

BPP Learning Media's ground-breaking **Learning to Learn Accountancy** book is designed to be used both at the outset of your CIMA studies and throughout the process of learning accountancy. It challenges you to consider how you study and gives you helpful hints about how to approach the various types of paper which you will encounter. It can help you **focus your studies on the subject and exam**, enabling you to **acquire knowledge, practise and revise efficiently and effectively**.

How the BPP Learning Media Study Text can help you pass

LEARNING MEDIA

How the BPP Learning Media Study Text can help you pass

Tackling studying

We know that studying for a number of exams can seem daunting, particularly when you have other commitments as well.

- We therefore provide guidance on **what you need to study efficiently and effectively** – to use the limited time you have in the best way possible.

- We explain the **purposes** of the **different features** in the Study Text, demonstrating how they help you and improve your chances of passing.

Developing exam awareness

We never forget that you're aiming to pass your exams, and our Texts are completely focused on helping you do this.

- In the section **Studying P2** we introduce the key themes of the syllabus, describe the skills you need and summarise how to succeed.

- The **Introduction** to each chapter of this Study Text sets the chapter in the context of the syllabus and exam.

- We provide specific tips, **Exam focus points**, on what you can expect in the exam and what to do (and not to do!) when answering questions.

And our Study Text is **comprehensive**. It covers the syllabus content. No more, no less.

Using the Learning outcomes and Syllabus

We set out the Learning outcomes and Syllabus in full.

- Reading the **Learning outcomes** will show you what **capabilities** (skills) you'll have to demonstrate.

- The topics listed in the **Syllabus** are the **key topics** in this exam. By quickly looking through the Syllabus, you can see the breadth of the paper. Reading the Syllabus will also highlight topics to look out for when you're reading newspapers or *Financial Management* magazine.

- Don't worry if the Syllabus seems large when you look through it; the Study Text will **carefully guide you** through it all.

- Remember the Study Text shows, at the start of every chapter, which **Learning outcomes** and **Syllabus areas** are covered in the chapter.

Testing what you can do

Testing yourself helps you develop the skills you need to pass the exam and also confirms that you can recall what you have learnt.

- We include **Questions** within chapters, and the **Exam Question Bank** provides lots more practice.

- Our **Quick Quizzes** test whether you have enough knowledge of the contents of each chapter.

Example chapter

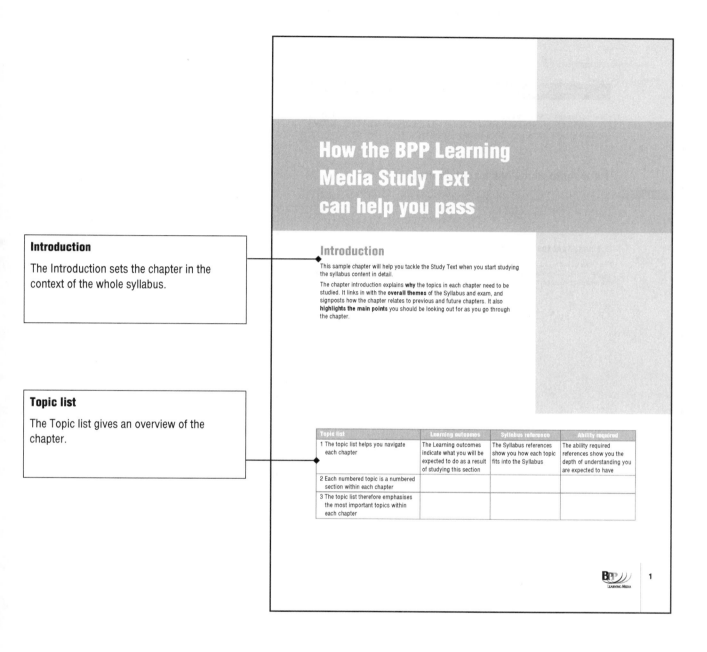

Introduction

The Introduction sets the chapter in the context of the whole syllabus.

Topic list

The Topic list gives an overview of the chapter.

How the BPP Learning Media Study Text can help you pass

Introduction

This sample chapter will help you tackle the Study Text when you start studying the syllabus content in detail.

The chapter introduction explains **why** the topics in each chapter need to be studied. It links in with the **overall themes** of the Syllabus and exam, and signposts how the chapter relates to previous and future chapters. It also **highlights the main points** you should be looking out for as you go through the chapter.

Topic list	Learning outcomes	Syllabus reference	Ability required
1 The topic list helps you navigate each chapter	The Learning outcomes indicate what you will be expected to do as a result of studying this section	The Syllabus references show you how each topic fits into the Syllabus	The ability required references show you the depth of understanding you are expected to have
2 Each numbered topic is a numbered section within each chapter			
3 The topic list therefore emphasises the most important topics within each chapter			

HOW THE BPP LEARNING MEDIA STUDY TEXT CAN HELP YOU PASS

Knowledge brought forward from earlier studies

Knowledge brought forward boxes summarise information and techniques that you are **assumed to know** from your earlier studies. As the exam may test your knowledge of these areas, you should **revise** your previous study material if you are unsure about them.

1 Key topic which has a section devoted to it

FAST FORWARD Fast forwards give you a **summary** of the content of each of the main chapter sections. They are listed together in the roundup at the end of each chapter to allow you to review each chapter quickly.

1.1 Important topic within section

The headings within chapters give you a good idea of the **importance** of the topics covered. The larger the header, the more important the topic is. The headers will help you navigate through the chapter and locate the areas that have been highlighted as important in the front pages or in the chapter introduction.

Knowledge brought forward

Knowledge brought forward shows you what you need to remember from previous exams.

Fast forward

Fast forwards allow you to preview and review each section easily.

Example

Examples show you how theory is put into practice.

Key term

Key terms are the core vocabulary.

Exam focus point

Exam focus points provide specific links to the exam.

Formula to learn

You must remember these formulae in the exam.

Question

Questions provide vital practice of what you've learnt.

Case Study

Case Studies link what you've learnt with the business environment.

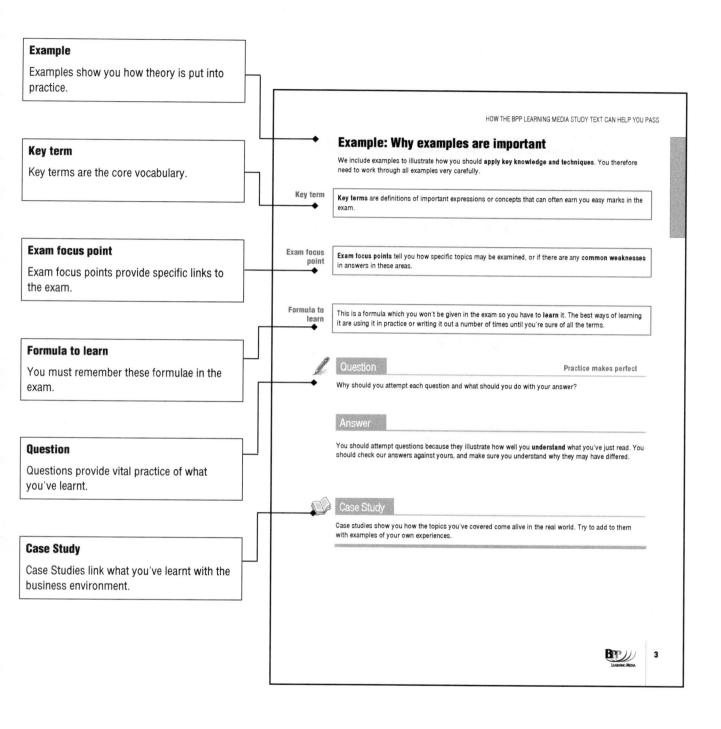

HOW THE BPP LEARNING MEDIA STUDY TEXT CAN HELP YOU PASS

Example: Why examples are important

We include examples to illustrate how you should **apply key knowledge and techniques**. You therefore need to work through all examples very carefully.

Key term

> **Key terms** are definitions of important expressions or concepts that can often earn you easy marks in the exam.

Exam focus point

> **Exam focus points** tell you how specific topics may be examined, or if there are any **common weaknesses** in answers in these areas.

Formula to learn

> This is a formula which you won't be given in the exam so you have to **learn** it. The best ways of learning it are using it in practice or writing it out a number of times until you're sure of all the terms.

Question | Practice makes perfect

Why should you attempt each question and what should you do with your answer?

Answer

You should attempt questions because they illustrate how well you **understand** what you've just read. You should check our answers against yours, and make sure you understand why they may have differed.

Case Study

Case studies show you how the topics you've covered come alive in the real world. Try to add to them with examples of your own experiences.

BPP LEARNING MEDIA   3

Chapter Roundup

- Fast forwards give you a **summary** of the content of each of the main chapter sections. They are listed together in the roundup at the end of each chapter to allow you to review each chapter quickly.

Quick Quiz

1   What are the main purposes of the Quick Quiz?

2   What should you do if you get Quick Quiz questions wrong?

    A   Nothing as you now know where you went wrong
    B   Note the correct answer and go on to the next chapter
    C   Practise full questions on this topic when you revise
    D   Go back and look through the topic again to ensure you know it

Answers to Quick Quiz

1   The main purposes of the Quick Quiz are to check how much you've remembered of the topics covered and to practise questions in a variety of formats.

2   D   Go back and look through the topic again to ensure that you know it.

Now try the questions below from the Exam Question Bank

Number	Level	Marks	Time
Questions that give you practice of what you've learnt in each chapter	Examination	25	45 mins

Chapter Roundup

The Chapter Roundup lists all the Fast forwards.

Quick Quiz

The Quick Quiz speedily tests your knowledge.

Exam Question Bank

Each chapter cross-references to further question practice.

Learning styles

BPP Learning Media's guide to studying, *Learning to Learn Accountancy*, provides guidance on identifying how you learn and the variety of intelligences that you have. We shall summarise some of the material in *Learning to Learn Accountancy*, as it will help you understand how to you are likely to approach the Study Text:

If you like	Then you might focus on	How the Study Text helps you
Word games, crosswords, poetry	Going through the detail in the Text	Chapter introductions, Fast forwards and Key terms help you determine the detail that's most significant
Number puzzles, Sudoku, Cluedo	Understanding the Text as a logical sequence of knowledge and ideas	Chapter introductions and headers help you follow the flow of material
Drawing, cartoons, films	Seeing how the ways material is presented show what it means and how important it is	The different features and the emphasis given by headers and emboldening help you see quickly what you have to know
Attending concerts, playing a musical instrument, dancing	Identifying patterns in the Text	The sequence of features within each chapter helps you understand what material is really crucial
Sport, craftwork, hands on experience	Learning practical skills such as preparing a set of accounts	Examples and question practice help you develop the practical skills you need

If you want to learn more about developing some or all of your intelligences, *Learning to Learn Accountancy* shows you plenty of ways in which you can do so.

Studying efficiently and effectively

What you need to study efficiently and effectively

Positive attitude

Yes there is a lot to learn. But look at the most recent CIMA pass list. See how many people have passed. They've made it; you can too. Focus on all the **benefits** that passing the exam will bring you.

Exam focus

Keep the exam firmly in your sights throughout your studies.

- Remember there's lots of **helpful guidance** about P2 in this first part of the Study Text.
- Look out for the **exam references** in the Study Text, particularly the types of question you'll be asked.

Organisation

Before you start studying you must organise yourself properly.

- We show you how to **timetable** your study so that you can ensure you have enough time to cover all of the syllabus – and revise it.
- Think carefully about the way you take **notes**. You needn't copy out too much, but if you can summarise key areas, that shows you understand them.
- Choose the notes **format** that's most helpful to you; lists, diagrams, mindmaps.
- Consider the **order** in which you tackle each chapter. If you prefer to get to grips with a theory before seeing how it's applied, you should read the explanations first. If you prefer to see how things work in practice, read the examples and questions first.

Active brain

There are various ways in which you can keep your brain active when studying and hence improve your **understanding** and **recall** of material.

- Keep asking yourself how the topic you're studying fits into the **whole picture** of this exam. If you're not sure, look back at the chapter introductions and Study Text front pages.
- Go carefully through every **example** and try every **question** in the Study Text and in the Exam Question Bank. You will be thinking deeply about the syllabus and increasing your understanding.

Review, review, review

Regularly reviewing the topics you've studied will help fix them in your memory. Your BPP Learning Media Texts help you review in many ways.

- Important points are emphasised **in bold**.
- **Chapter Roundups** summarise the **Fast forward** key points in each chapter.
- **Quick Quizzes** test your grasp of the essentials.

BPP Learning Media Passcards present summaries of topics in different visual formats to enhance your chances of remembering them.

Timetabling your studies

As your time is limited, it's vital that you calculate how much time you can allocate to each chapter. Following the approach below will help you do this.

Step 1   Calculate how much time you have

Work out the time you have available per week, given the following.

- The standard you have set yourself

- The time you need to set aside for work on the Practice & Revision Kit, Passcards, i-Learn and i-Pass

- The other exam(s) you are sitting

- Practical matters such as work, travel, exercise, sleep and social life

Hours

Note your time available in box A.   A [   ]

Step 2   Allocate your time

- Take the time you have available per week for this Study Text shown in box A, multiply it by the number of weeks available and insert the result in box B.   B [   ]

- Divide the figure in box B by the number of chapters in this Study Text and insert the result in box C.   C [   ]

Remember that this is only a rough guide. Some of the chapters in this Study Text are longer and more complicated than others, and you will find some subjects easier to understand than others.

Step 3   Implement your plan

Set about studying each chapter in the time shown in box C. You'll find that once you've established a timetable, you're much more likely to study systematically.

Short of time: Skim study technique

You may find you simply do not have the time available to follow all the key study steps for each chapter, however you adapt them for your particular learning style. If this is the case, follow the **Skim study technique** below.

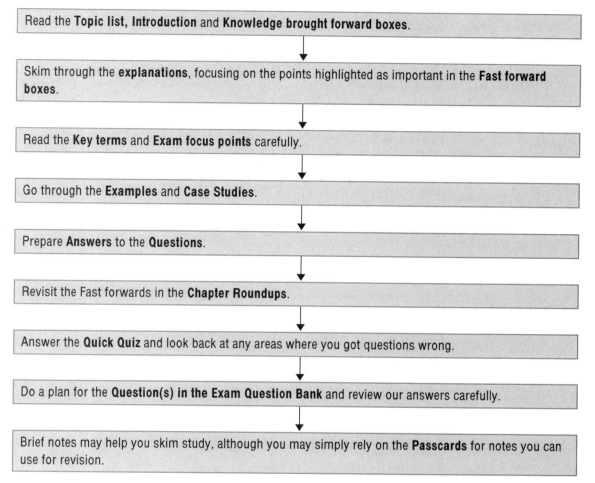

Read the **Topic list, Introduction** and **Knowledge brought forward boxes**.

Skim through the **explanations**, focusing on the points highlighted as important in the **Fast forward boxes**.

Read the **Key terms** and **Exam focus points** carefully.

Go through the **Examples** and **Case Studies**.

Prepare **Answers** to the **Questions**.

Revisit the Fast forwards in the **Chapter Roundups**.

Answer the **Quick Quiz** and look back at any areas where you got questions wrong.

Do a plan for the **Question(s) in the Exam Question Bank** and review our answers carefully.

Brief notes may help you skim study, although you may simply rely on the **Passcards** for notes you can use for revision.

Revision

When you are ready to start revising, you should still refer back to this Study Text.

- As a source of **reference** (you should find the index particularly helpful for this)
- As a way to **review** (the Fast forwards, Exam focus points, Chapter Roundups and Quick Quizzes help you here)

Remember to keep careful hold of this Study Text – you will find it invaluable in your work.

Learning to Learn Accountancy

BPP Learning Media's guide to studying for accountancy exams, **Learning to Learn Accountancy**, challenges you to think about how you can study effectively and gives you lots and lots of vital tips on studying, revising and taking the exams.

Approaching P2

Studying P2

1 What P2 is about

This Managerial level paper is the second in the Management Accounting pillar of the current CIMA syllabus. It develops topics introduced in P1 *Management Accounting Fundamentals* and leads on to P3 *Management Accounting Risk and Control* at Strategic level. It aims to test your ability to apply a range of management accounting techniques and decision-making tools in the context of the modern business environment.

It is expected that you will use these tools at some stage in your professional career if you haven't already encountered them. The syllabus covers core areas of knowledge for a management accountant including costing and decision making and CIMA considers cost accounting core to the qualification.

There is assumed prior knowledge of Certificate paper C1, *Fundamentals of Management Accounting* but not of paper P1.

The syllabus covers four distinct areas:

- The treatment of uncertainty in decision making
- Financial information for short-term decision making
- Financial information for long-term decision making
- Cost planning and analysis for competitive advantage

1.1 Uncertainty and decision making

The paper looks at techniques for measuring risk and evaluating uncertainty. These include expected values, sensitivity analysis and decision trees. You need to be familiar with the techniques and their application across a variety of decision-making tools such as relevant cash flows, DCF and CVP analysis.

1.2 Financial information for short-term decision making

This part of the syllabus focuses on the short term so decisions being made cover the near future. You will need to understand and apply relevant cash flows, marginal and full costing, pricing strategies, joint costs, variable and fixed costs and multiple product situations with resource constraints.

1.3 Financial information for long-term decision making

You are expected to understand and apply techniques for evaluating long-term proposals. Thus, identifying relevant cash flows, using investment appraisal techniques including DCF and ARR and factoring in inflation and taxation, ranking of projects and applying sensitivity analysis.

1.4 Cost planning and analysis for competitive advantage

In this section of the syllabus are a range of techniques for measuring cost and looking at the external influences on the organisation. Therefore you will expect to cover JIT, TQM, TOC, ABM, Pareto, target costs, learning curves, continuous improvement, kaizen costing, value and functional costs, lifecycle costing, value chain and gain sharing arrangements.

2 What's required

2.1 Application

This exam is looking at **application** in addition to knowledge, which is assumed at this level. Eighty percent of the marks available in the exam consist of longer questions looking for application of knowledge to various scenarios. The examiner wants to see how you would apply your knowledge to the scenario he has outlined in the exam questions. The examiner stated recently that common problems with the paper included the following.

- Lack of detail in answering questions. Remember the two questions in Section C are worth 25 marks each so expect to write at least two pages in the exam for each

- Not answering all of the requirements of the question

- Not answering written questions in the context of the scenario provided

- An inability to put forward well constructed answers to the discursive questions

2.2 Knowledge including brought forward knowledge

Well, you couldn't pass the exam without actually knowing what you were talking about so the remaining twenty percent [Section A questions] of the marks test your knowledge of certain techniques. Here are some more reasons the examiner has given for people not passing the paper.

- Lack of basic knowledge. He also made a general point that some fundamental topics were poorly answered. He commented that this reflects an unfamiliarity with topics covered at lower levels. Make sure that you read Chapter 1 which is a revision chapter and also any knowledge brought forward sections elsewhere in the Text. They are all examinable still.

- Not showing clear workings to enable method marks to be awarded

3 Passing P2

The examiner has also offered some advice on improving performance:

3.1 Study ALL of the syllabus

Yes, we all know that examiners have their favourite subjects but the examiner is free to test anything on the syllabus so it is not safe to leave out large chunks of material. Remember he thinks that you love his subject so much you have read everything available on it. He would be hurt if this wasn't the case. By all means concentrate on core techniques and knowledge but be prepared for anything. Read the text through once if you can and use the passcards as a reminder.

3.2 Practise

Just like playing the piano, if you want to get anywhere you have to practise. Accountancy is a **practical** skill and an **applied** skill. Use the question bank at the back of this text. Try questions from the BPP Learning Media Practice and Revision kit. Read the guidance later in the introduction on answering OT questions and the top tips advice contained within the answers to longer questions in the study material.

The examiner has pointed out the importance of showing workings in answers to questions as these are given credit even if the final answer is wrong. So when you are doing your question practice, learn the habit of writing down workings neatly and in order. It could mean a pass rather than a fail!

Practise written questions so that you can learn to develop arguments and explanations in the time allotted to the question.

3.3 Develop time management skills

One key piece of advice from the examiner is to attempt all parts of questions. You need to work out before you start tackling the questions just how much time you will spend on each and stick to this guide.

3.4 Develop business awareness

You are being assessed on your suitability as a professional practitioner of accountancy. You are expected to read the financial press and relevant industry journals. This awareness of business will enable you to apply your knowledge in **context when you come to answer questions. The examiner has noted this as a top tip for improving candidate performance in the exam.**

4 And finally..

The UK pass rate for this paper was 50% in the November 2006 sitting. Pass rates have improved over the last two sittings which is encouraging as this has a reputation as a difficult paper. You can considerably improve your chances by following the advice given above which, after all, comes straight from the examiner.

Learning outcomes and Syllabus

Paper P2 Management Accounting Decision Management

The syllabus comprises:

Topic and Study Weighting

A	Financial Information for Short-term Decision Making	30%
B	Financial Information for Long-term Decision Making	25%
C	The Treatment of Uncertainty in Decision Making	15%
D	Cost Planning and Analysis for Competitive Advantage	30%

Learning aims

Students should be able to:

- Separate costs into their fixed and variable components and use these in break-even analysis and in decision-making under multiple constraints

- Establish relevant cash flows for decision making and apply these principles in a variety of contexts including process/product viability and pricing including evaluation of the tension between short-term, 'contribution based' pricing and long-term 'return on investment' pricing

- Develop relevant cash flows for long-term projects taking account of inflation and taxation where appropriate, evaluate projects using discounting and traditional methods, critically assess alternative methods of evaluation and place evaluation techniques in the context of the whole process of investment decision making

- Apply learning curves in forecasting future costs and the techniques of activity-based management, target costing and value analysis in managing future costs and evaluate the actual and potential impacts of contemporary techniques such as JIT, TOC and TQM on efficiency, inventory and cost

- Undertake sensitivity analysis and assess the impact of risk in decision models using probability analysis, expected value tables and decision trees as appropriate

- Discuss externally oriented management accounting techniques and apply these techniques to the value chain, 'gain sharing' arrangements and customer/channel profitability analysis

Learning outcomes and Syllabus content

A – Financial Information for Short-term Decision Making – 30%

Learning outcomes

On completion of their studies students should be able to:

(i)   Discuss the principles of decision making including the identification of relevant cash flows and their use alongside non-quantifiable factors in making rounded judgements

(ii) Explain the particular issues that arise in pricing decisions and the conflict between 'marginal cost' principles and the need for full recovery of all costs incurred

(iii) Apply an approach to pricing based on profit maximisation in imperfect markets and evaluate the financial consequences of alternative pricing strategies

(iv) Explain the possible conflicts between cost accounting for profit reporting and stock valuation and the convenient availability of information for decision-making

(v) Explain why joint costs must be allocated to final products for financial reporting purposes, but why this is unhelpful when decisions concerning process and product viability have to be taken

(vi) Discuss the usefulness of dividing costs into variable and fixed components in the context of short-term decision making

(vii) Apply variable/fixed cost analysis in multiple product contexts to break-even analysis and product mix decision making, including circumstances where there are multiple constraints and linear programming methods are needed to reach 'optimal' solutions

(viii) Discuss the meaning of 'optimal' solutions and show how linear programming methods can be employed for profit maximising, revenue maximising and satisfying objectives

Syllabus content

(1) Relevant cash flows and their use in short-term decisions, typically concerning acceptance/rejection of contract, pricing and cost/benefit comparisons

(2) The importance of strategic, intangible and non-financial judgements in decision-making

(3) Pricing decisions for profit maximising in imperfect markets. (Note: tabular methods of solution are acceptable)

(4) Pricing strategies and the financial consequences of market skimming, premium pricing, penetration pricing, loss leaders, product bundling/optional extras and product differentiation to appeal to different market segments

(5) The allocation of joint costs and decisions concerning process and product viability based on relevant costs and revenues

(6) Multi-product break-even analysis including break-even and profit/volume charts, contribution/sales ratio, margin of safety etc

(7) Simple product mix analysis in situations where there are limitations on product/service demand and one other production constraint

(8) Linear programming for more complex situations involving multiple constraints. Solution by graphical methods of two variable problems, together with understanding of the mechanics of simplex solution, shadow prices etc. (Note: questions requiring the full application of the simplex algorithm will not be set although candidates should be able to formulate an initial tableau, interpret a final simplex tableau and apply the information it contained in a final tableau.)

B – Financial Information for Long-term Decision Making – 25 %

Learning outcomes

On completion of their studies students should be able to:

(i) Explain the processes involved in making long-term decisions

(ii) Apply the principles of relevant cash flow analysis to long-term projects that continue for several years

(iii) Calculate project cash flows, accounting for tax and inflation, and apply perpetuities to derive 'end of project' value where appropriate

(iv) Apply activity-based costing techniques to derive approximate 'long-run' product or service costs appropriate for use in strategic decision making

(v) Explain the financial consequences of dealing with long-term projects, in particular the importance of accounting for the 'time value of money'

(vi) Evaluate project proposals using the techniques of investment appraisal

(vii) Compare, contrast and evaluate the alternative techniques of investment appraisal

(viii) Evaluate and rank projects that might be mutually exclusive, involve unequal lives and/or be subject to capital rationing

(ix)   Apply sensitivity analysis to cash flow parameters to identify those to which net present value is particularly sensitive

(x)   Produce decision support information for management, integrating financial and non-financial considerations

Syllabus content

(1)   The process of investment decision making, including origination of proposals, creation of capital budgets, go/no go decisions on individual projects (where judgements on qualitative issues interact with financial analysis), and post audit of completed projects

(2)   Generation of relevant project cash flows taking account of inflation, tax, and 'final' project value where appropriate

(3)   Activity-based costing to derive approximate 'long-run' costs appropriate for use in strategic decision making

(4)   The techniques of investment appraisal: payback, discounted payback, accounting rate of return, net present value and internal rate of return

(5)   Application of the techniques of investment appraisal to project cash flows and evaluation of the strengths and weaknesses of the techniques

(6)   Sensitivity analysis to identify the input variables that most effect the chosen measure of project worth (payback, ARR, NPV or IRR)

(7)   Methods of dealing with particular problems: the use of annuities in comparing projects with unequal lives and the profitability index in capital rationing situations

C – The Treatment of Uncertainty in Decision Making – 15%

Learning outcomes

On completion of their studies students should be able to:

(i)   Evaluate the impact of uncertainty and risk on decision models that may be based on CVP analysis, relevant cash flows, learning curves, discounting techniques etc

(ii)   Apply sensitivity analysis on both short and long-run decision models to identify variables that might have significant impacts on project outcomes

(iii) Analyse risk and uncertainty by calculating expected values and standard deviations together with probability tables and histograms

(iv)   Prepare expected value tables and ascertain the value of information

(v)   Prepare and apply decision trees

Syllabus content

(1)   The nature of risk and uncertainty

(2)   Sensitivity analysis in decision modelling and the use of computer software for 'what if' analysis

(3)   Assignment of probabilities to key variables in decision models

(4)   Analysis of probabilistic models and interpretation of distributions of project outcomes

(5)   Expected value tables and the value of information

(6)   Decision trees for multi-stage decision problems

D – Cost Planning and Analysis for Competitive Advantage – 30%

Learning outcomes

On completion of their studies students should be able to:

(i) Compare and contrast value analysis and functional cost analysis

(ii) Evaluate the impacts of just-in-time production, the theory of constraints and total quality management on efficiency, inventory and cost

(iii) Explain the concepts of continuous improvement and Kaizen costing that are central to total quality management and prepare cost of quality reports

(iv) Explain and apply learning and experience curves to estimate time and cost for new products and services

(v) Apply the techniques of activity-based management in identifying cost drivers/activities and explain how process re-engineering can be used to eliminate non-value adding activities and reduce activity costs

(vi) Explain how target costs can be derived from target prices and describe the relationship between target costs and standard costs

(vii) Explain the concept of life cycle costing and how life cycle costs interact with marketing strategies at each stage of the life cycle

(viii) Explain the concept of the value chain and discuss the management of contribution/profit generated throughout the chain

(ix) Discuss gain sharing arrangements whereby contractors and customers benefit if contract targets for cost, delivery etc are beaten

(x) Apply activity-based costing ideas to analyse direct customer profitability and extend this analysis to distribution channel profitability

(xi) Apply Pareto analysis as a convenient technique for identifying key elements of data and in presenting the results of other analyses, such as activity-based profitability calculations

Syllabus content

(1) Value analysis and quality function deployment

(2) The benefits of just-in-time production, total quality management and theory of constraints and the implications of these methods for decision-making in the 'new manufacturing environment'

(3) Kaizen costing, continuous improvement and cost of quality reporting

(4) Learning curves and their use in predicting product/service costs, including derivation of the learning rate and the learning index

(5) Activity-based management in the analysis of overhead and its use in improving the efficiency of repetitive overhead activities

(6) Target costing

(7) Life cycle costing and implications for marketing strategies

(8) The value chain and supply chain management, including the trend to outsource manufacturing operations to Eastern Europe and the Far East

(9) Gain sharing arrangements in situations where, because of the size of the project, a limited number of contractors or security issues (eg in defence work), normal competitive pressures do not apply

(10) The use of direct and activity-based cost methods in tracing cost to 'cost objects', such as customers or distribution channels, and the comparison of such costs with appropriate revenues to establish 'tiered' contribution levels, as in the activity-based cost hierarchy

(11) Pareto analysis

31

The exam paper

Format of the paper

		Number of marks
Section A:	Up to 10 multiple choice and other objective test questions, 2-4 marks each	20
Section B:	3 compulsory questions, 10 marks each	30
Section C:	2 out of 3 questions, 25 marks each	50
		100

Time allowed: 3 hours, with 20 minutes reading time before the exam begins.

Question weighting will reflect syllabus weighting.

Section A will always contain some multiple choice questions but will not consist solely of multiple choice questions. Section A may contain types of objective test questions that are different from those included in the pilot paper.

Further guidance on objective test questions and multiple choice questions is included on pages 36-38.

Section B may include a short scenario that could relate to several of the questions.

Section C questions are likely to be scenario-based and include sub questions.

November 2006

Section A

1.1   Further processing decision
1.2   Relevant costing
1.3   Investment appraisal, profitability index
1.4   Payback period
1.5   Perpetuities and NPV
1.6   Limiting factor
1.7   Optimum selling price
1.8   Contribution/Sales ratio

Section B

2   Value chain analysis
3   Lifecycle costing
4   Decision-making with price and cost analysis

Section C

5   Absorption costing, ABC costing and price setting
6   EV, Two-way data tables, VOPI
7   NPV, IRR, real and money rates or return

May 2006

Section A

1.1 Relevant costing
1.2 Relevant costing
1.3 C/S ratio
1.4 Make or buy decision
1.5 Payback method
1.6 Discounted payback
1.7 IRR
1.8 Learning curves

Section B

2 Sensitivity analysis
3 Value analysis
4 Quality costs

Section C

5 Rates of learning, profit maximising selling price, standard and target costs
6 Decision tress, investment decisions, non-financial considerations
7 Relevant contribution, limiting factor, C/S ratios, multi-product PV chart

November 2005

Section A

1.1 Investment appraisal (2 marks)
1.2 EV calculation (2 marks)
1.3 EV calculation (2 marks)
1.4 Learning curves (2 marks)
1.5 Investment appraisal – capital rationing (2 marks)
1.6 Investment appraisal – IRR (3 marks)
1.7 Learning curves (3 marks)
1.8 Minimax regret (4 marks)

Section B

2 Investment appraisal – inflation and lowest common multiple method
3 Absorption and marginal costing
4 Costing

Section C

5 Investment appraisal including expected values and simulation
6 Throughput accounting, decision making with limiting factors and linear programming
7 Activity based costing, for customer profitability analysis and pricing

May 2005

Section A

1.1	Limiting factor analysis (2 marks)
1.2	Multi-product CVP analysis (2 marks)
1.3	Relevant costing (2 marks)
1.4	Calculation of IRR (2 marks)
1.5	Investment appraisal with inflation (2 marks)
1.6	Learning curves (3 marks)
1.7	EVs and probabilities (3 marks)
1.8	Profit maximisation (4 marks)

Section B

2	JIT
3	Lease v buy decision (including taxation)
4	Joint cost apportionment and further processing decision

Section C

5	Investment appraisal including taxation and sensitivity analysis
6	Relevant costing; two-way data tables
7	The product life-cycle and pricing policies; optimum pricing including learning curves; target profit calculation

Pilot paper

Section A

1.1	Limiting factor analysis (2 marks)
1.2	Linear programming (2 marks)
1.3	Relevant costs (2 marks)
1.4	EV calculation (2 marks)
1.5	Value of perfect information (3 marks)
1.6	Throughput accounting (3 marks)
1.7	Learning curves (3 marks)
1.8	Transfer pricing (3 marks)

Section B

2	JIT
3	Investment appraisal and taxation
4	Investment appraisal and when-to-replace decision

Section C

5	Investment appraisal including taxation and sensitivity analysis
6	Relevant costing; use of two-way data tables
7	Pricing

What the examiner means

The table below has been prepared by CIMA to help you interpret exam questions.

Learning objective	Verbs used	Definition
1 Knowledge What you are expected to know	• List • State • Define	• Make a list of • Express, fully or clearly, the details of/facts of • Give the exact meaning of
2 Comprehension What you are expected to understand	• Describe • Distinguish • Explain • Identify • Illustrate	• Communicate the key features of • Highlight the differences between • Make clear or intelligible/state the meaning of • Recognise, establish or select after consideration • Use an example to describe or explain something
3 Application How you are expected to apply your knowledge	• Apply • Calculate/ compute • Demonstrate • Prepare • Reconcile • Solve • Tabulate	• Put to practical use • Ascertain or reckon mathematically • Prove with certainty or to exhibit by practical means • Make or get ready for use • Make or prove consistent/compatible • Find an answer to • Arrange in a table
4 Analysis How you are expected to analyse the detail of what you have learned	• Analyse • Categorise • Compare and contrast • Construct • Discuss • Interpret • Produce	• Examine in detail the structure of • Place into a defined class or division • Show the similarities and/or differences between • Build up or compile • Examine in detail by argument • Translate into intelligible or familiar terms • Create or bring into existence
5 Evaluation How you are expected to use your learning to evaluate, make decisions or recommendations	• Advise • Evaluate • Recommend	• Counsel, inform or notify • Appraise or assess the value of • Advise on a course of action

Tackling multiple choice questions

The MCQs in your exam will contain four or five possible answers. You have to **choose the option that best answers the question**. The three or four incorrect options are called distracters. There is a skill in answering MCQs quickly and correctly. By practising MCQs you can develop this skill, giving yourself a better chance of passing the exam.

You may wish to follow the approach outlined below, or you may prefer to adapt it.

Step 1   Skim read all the MCQs and identify which appear to be the easier questions and which questions you will not need a calculator to answer.

Step 2   Remember that the examiner will not expect you to spend an equal amount of time on each MCQ; some can be answered instantly but others will take time to work out.

Step 3   Attempt each question **The questions** identified in Step 1 are questions which you should be able to answer during the 20 minutes reading time. Read the question thoroughly. You may prefer to work out the answer before looking at the options, or you may prefer to look at the options at the beginning. Adopt the method that works best for you.

               You may find that you recognise a question when you sit the exam. Be aware that the detail and/or requirement may be different. If the question seems familiar, read the requirement and options carefully – do not assume that it is identical.

Step 4   Read the five options and see if one matches your own answer. Be careful with numerical questions, as the distracters are designed to match answers that incorporate **common errors**. Check that your calculation is correct. Have you followed the requirement exactly? Have you included every stage of the calculation?

Step 5   You may find that none of the options matches your answer.

- Re-read the question to ensure that you understand it and are answering the requirement
- Eliminate any obviously wrong answers
- Consider which of the remaining answers is the most likely to be correct and select that option

Step 6   If you are still unsure, make a note and continue to the next question. Likewise if you are nowhere near working out which option is correct, leave the question and come back to it later.

Step 7   Revisit unanswered questions. When you come back to a question after a break, you often find you can answer it correctly straightaway. If you are still unsure, have a guess. You are not penalised for incorrect answers, so **never leave a question unanswered!**

Step 8   **Rule off answers** to each MCQ in the answer booklet.

Tackling objective test questions

What is an objective test question?

An objective test (**OT**) question is made up of some form of **stimulus**, usually a question, and a **requirement** to do something.

- **MCQs.** Read through the information on page 36 about MCQs and how to tackle them.

- **True or false.** You will be asked if a statement is true or false.

- **Data entry**. This type of OT requires you to provide figures such as the answer to a calculation, words to fill in a blank, single word answers to questions, or to identify numbers and words to complete a format.

- **Word-limited answers**. You may be asked to state, define or explain things in no more than a certain number of words or within a single line in the answer booklet.

- **Hot spots**. This question format may ask you to identify specific points on a graph or diagram.

- **Interpretation.** You may be asked to interpret or analyse graphical data.

- **Multiple response.** These questions provide you with a number of options and you have to identify those that fulfil certain criteria.

- **Listing**. You may be asked to list items in rank order.

- **Matching.** This OT question format could ask you to classify particular costs into one of a range of cost classifications provided, to match descriptions of variances with one of a number of variances listed, and so on.

OT questions in your exam

Section A of your exam will contain different types of OT questions. It is not certain how many questions in your exam will be MCQs and how many will be other types of OT, nor what types of OT you will encounter in your exam. Practising different types of OTs will prepare you well for whatever questions come up in your exam.

Dealing with OT questions

Again you may wish to follow the approach we suggest, or you may be prepared to adapt it.

Step 1 Work out **how long** you should allocate to each OT, taking into account the marks allocated to it. Remember that you will not be expected to spend an equal amount of time on each one; some can be answered instantly but others will take time to work out.

Step 2 **Jot down answers, workings or ideas** for as many OTs as possible on the question paper during the 20 minutes reading time.

Step 3 **Attempt each question**. Read the question thoroughly, and note in particular what the question says about the **format** of your answer and whether there are any **restrictions** placed on it (for example the number of words you can use).

You may find that you recognise a question when you sit the exam. Be aware that the detail and/or requirement may be different. If the question seems familiar read the requirement and options carefully – do not assume that it is identical.

Step 4 Read any options you are given and select which ones are appropriate. Check that your calculations are correct. Have you followed the requirement exactly? Have you included every stage of the calculation?

Step 5 You may find that you are unsure of the answer.

- Re-read the question to ensure that you understand it and are answering the requirement
- Eliminate any obviously wrong options if you are given a number of options from which to choose

Step 6 If you are still unsure, **continue to the next question**.

Step 7 Revisit questions you are uncertain about. When you come back to a question after a break you often find you are able to answer it correctly straightaway. If you are still unsure have a guess. You are not penalised for incorrect answers, so **never leave a question unanswered!**

Step 8 Make sure you show your **workings** clearly on calculation OTs, as you may gain some credit for workings even if your final answer is incorrect.

Step 9 Rule off answers to each OT in the answer booklet.

Tackling the rest of the paper

General comments

The examiner has recommended that candidates don't spot questions but try to cover the whole syllabus if possible.

Of course, certain topics lend themselves more to the indepth questions in Section C.

Thus, investment decision making is likely to appear at least once in the paper probably with sensitivity and/or tax features if a longer question. Some examination of pricing is also likely in Section C based on previous exams.

Also possibly a question on modern management accounting techniques could appear.

Section B could also feature modern management accounting techniques in a discursive or calculation question. A written question could require a discussion of pricing, investment appraisal or uncertainty.

The objective test questions in Section A could cover any part of the syllabus so it is not wise to try to spot these. Nonetheless, it is worth practising learning curves and optimal pricing as these are examiner perennials.

Reading time/Order of tackling paper

The 20 minutes reading time should be spent reading Section C. You have to choose two out of three questions so use 10 minutes to read the three questions thoroughly. Make sure you concentrate on all requirements. With 10 minutes taken to choose which questions you'll attempt, you can spend the remaining 10 minutes picking out the relevant data from the questions, setting up working layouts and brainstorming ideas for discussion requirements.

Leave the objective questions until the last 40 minutes of answering time. As most of these are three or four marks, little is gained from duplicating workings which cannot go on the answer paper until the actual exam begins.

Easy marks

Examples of suggestions for scoring easy marks are contained in the Answer Section of the kit. They include in Question 35 answering the written part in (d) which is pure knowledge. Ensuring that you can answer the main part of longer mark questions as in Question 41(b) or shorthand, but correct methods as in Question 24.

It is always a good idea to layout clear formats especially where calculating NPVs and to clearly set out steps taken in a linear programming question. These examples both have clear and consistent approaches so ensure you are familiar with these and use them in the exam.

Approach to questions

You'll improve your chances by following a step-by-step approach to 10 and 25 mark scenarios along the following lines.

Step 1 Read the requirements first to identify the knowledge areas being tested and see if there are links between them. This helps with focusing on what's important in the scenario. Ensure you can define technical terms used so that you know what the question is about.

Step 2 Identify the action verbs in the requirement because this conveys the level of skill you need to exhibit (e.g. define, illustrate, evaluate require quite different skills see 'What the examiner means' list.

Step 3 Identify the parts to the question. For example a requirement with 'and' implies two parts to the question that may be linked.

Step 4 Check mark allocation of each section. This shows you the depth anticipated and helps allocate time

Step 5 Read scenario/preamble and put key points under headings related to requirements (e.g. by marginal notes, highlighting or jotting down on page).

Step 6 Scribble a plan answer (just a few words jotted untidly under the key requirements not a summary that someone else could write the answer from. Perhaps a brainstorm or spider diagram/mindmap).

Step 7 Write answer.

The examiner

The examiner examined this paper under the previous syllabus.

- **Flexible thinking**. Questions will often not spell out the techniques you can use. You will need to select the appropriate techniques yourself. Often, more than one technique is valid, and there may be no single right answer. (Remember this last point when you review our answers: if your answer is different from ours, it does not necessarily mean that it is wrong.)

- **Strategic awareness**. You will be tested in different questions on your ability to **understand strategic implications** of problems you are faced with, and you will be asked to draft reports explaining and evaluating the financial consequences of strategic decisions.

- **Knowledge of current issues**. Be prepared for topical questions on **recent events** in the global environment, eg developments on the Euro; corporate governance; World Trade Organisation.

- **Evaluation** of past and future performance using information provided.

You will improve your chances significantly by practising questions in all of the key areas of the paper (see the Learning Outcomes and Syllabus). You need to be comfortable with advanced techniques such DCF including uncertainty, and also current thought on management accounting techniques.

Discursive parts of questions are also important, as there will be sub-sections within longer questions asking for discussion.

Pilot paper

CIMA – Managerial Level

Paper P2

Management Accounting – Decision Management

Pilot paper

Instructions to candidates:

You are allowed three hours to answer this question paper.
In the real exam, you are allowed 20 minutes reading time before the examination begins during which you should read the question paper, and if you wish, make annotations on the question paper. However, you will **not** be allowed, **under any circumstances**, to open the answer book and start writing or use your calculator during this reading time.
You are strongly advised to carefully read the question requirement before attempting the question concerned.
Answer the ONE compulsory question in Section A. This is comprised of sub-questions
Answer ALL THREE compulsory sub-questions in Section B.
Answer TWO of the THREE questions in Section C.

DO NOT OPEN THIS PAPER UNTIL YOU ARE READY TO START UNDER EXAMINATION CONDITIONS

SECTION A – 20 marks

Answer ALL EIGHT sub-questions

Each of the sub-questions numbered from 1.1 to 1.8 inclusive, given below, has ONE correct answer.

Question 1

1.1 The following details relate to three services provided by JHN.

	J	H	N
Service	$	$	$
Fee charged to customers for each unit of service	84	122	145
Unit service costs			
Direct materials	12	23	22
Direct labour	15	20	25
Variable overhead	12	16	20
Fixed overhead	20	42	40

All three services use the same type of labour which is paid at $30 per hour.

In a period when the availability of the direct labour is limited, the most and least profitable use of the direct labour are:

	Most profitable	Least profitable
A	H	J
B	H	N
C	N	J
D	N	H

(2 marks)

1.2 The following equations have been taken from the plans of DX for the year ending 31 December 20X5.

Contribution (in dollars) = $12 x_1 + 5 x_2 + 8 x_3$

$2 x_1 + 3 x_2 + 4 x_3 + s_1 = 12{,}000$ kilos
$6 x_1 + 4 x_2 + 3 x_3 + s_2 = 8{,}000$ machine hours

0	x_1	2,000
100	x_2	500
5	x_3	200

where: x_1, x_2 and x_3 are the number of units of products produced and sold,
s_1 is raw material still available, and
s_2 is machine hours still available

If an unlimited supply of raw material s_1 could be obtained at the current price, the product mix that maximises the value of DX's contribution is:

	x_1	x_2	x_3
A	1,333	0	0
B	1,233	0	200
C	1,166	100	200
D	1,241	100	50

(2 marks)

1.3 An organisation is considering the costs to be incurred in respect of a special order opportunity. The order would require 1,250 kgs of material D. This is a material that is readily available and regularly used by the organisation on its normal products. There are 265 kgs of material D in stock which cost $795 last week. The current market price is $3.24 per kg.

Material D is normally used to make product X. Each unit of X requires 3 kgs of material D, and if material D is costed at $3 per kg, each unit of X yields a contribution of $15.

The relevant cost of material D to be included in the costing of the special order is nearest to:

A $3,990
B $4,050
C $10,000
D $10,300   **(2 marks)**

The following data relates to questions 1.4 and 1.5

TX Ltd can choose from five mutually exclusive projects. The projects will each last for one year only and their net cash inflows will be determined by the prevailing market conditions. The forecast net cash inflows and their associated probabilities are shown below.

Market conditions	Poor	Good	Excellent
Probability	0.20	0.50	0.30
	$'000	$'000	$'000
Project L	500	470	550
Project M	400	550	570
Project N	450	400	475
Project O	360	400	420
Project P	600	500	425

1.4 Based on the expected value of the net cash inflows, which project should be undertaken?

(Write your answer in the space provided in the answer sheet.)   **(2 marks)**

1.5 The value of perfect information about the state of the market is calculated as:

(Write your answer in the space provided in the answer sheet.)   **(3 marks)**

1.6 An organisation manufactures four products – J, K, L and M. The products use a series of different machines but there is a common machine, X, which causes a bottleneck.

The standard selling price and standard cost per unit for each product for the forthcoming year are as follows.

	J £/unit	K £/unit	L £/unit	M £/unit
Selling price	2,000	1,500	1,500	1,750
Cost				
Direct materials	410	200	300	400
Labour	300	200	360	275
Variable overheads	250	200	300	175
Fixed overheads	360	300	210	330
Profit	680	600	330	570
Machine X – minutes per unit	120	100	70	110

Direct materials is the only unit-level manufacturing cost.

Using a throughput accounting approach, the ranking of the products would be:

(Write your answer in the space provided in the answer sheet.) **(3 marks)**

1.7 BG has recently developed a new product. The nature of BG's work is repetitive, and it is usual for there to be an 80% learning effect when a new product is developed. The time taken for the first unit was 22 minutes. Assuming that an 80% learning effect applies, the time to be taken for the fourth unit is:

(Write your answer in the space provided in the answer sheet.) **(3 marks)**

1.8 XJ, a manufacturing company, has two divisions: Division A and Division B. Division A produces one type of product, Prod X, which it transfers to Division B and also sells externally. Division B has been approached by another company which has offered to supply 2,500 units of Prod X for $35 each.

The following details for Division A are available.

	$'000
Sales revenue	
Sales to Division B @ $40 per unit	400
External sales @ $45 per unit	270
Less	
Variable cost @ $22 per unit	352
Fixed costs	100
Profit	218

If Division B decides to buy from the other company, the impact of the decision on the profits of Division A and XJ, assuming external sales of Prod X cannot be increased, will be:

(Write your answer in the space provided in the answer sheet.) **(3 marks)**

(Total for Section A = 20 marks)

SECTION B – 30 marks

Answer ALL THREE questions

Question 2

SW is a member of the SWAL Group of companies. SW manufactures cleaning liquid using chemicals that it buys from a number of suppliers. In the past SW has used a periodic review stock control system with maximum, minimum and re-order levels to control the purchase of the chemicals and the economic order quantity model to minimise its costs.

The managing director of SW is considering a change by introducing a just-in-time (JIT) system.

Required

As management accountant, prepare a report to the managing director that explains how a JIT system differs from the system presently being used and the extent to which its introduction would require a review of SW's quality control procedures.

(10 marks)

Question 3

RAD Enterprises (RAD) has signed a contract with LPC to supply accounting packages. However, there has been a fire in one of the software manufacturing departments and a machine has been seriously damaged and requires urgent replacement.

The replacement machine will cost £1 million and RAD is considering whether to lease or buy the machine. A lease could be arranged under which RAD would pay £300,000 per annum for four years with each payment being made annually in advance. The lease payments would be an allowable expense for taxation purposes.

Corporation tax is payable at the rate of 30% of profits in two equal instalments: one in the year that profits are earned and the other in the following year. Writing-down allowances are available at 25% each year on a reducing balance basis. It is anticipated that the machine will have a useful economic life of four years, at the end of which there will be no residual value.

The after-tax cost of capital is 12%.

Required

Evaluate the lease or buy considerations for acquiring the new machine from a financial viewpoint, assuming that RAD has sufficient profits to claim all available tax reliefs.

(10 marks)

Question 4

A hypermarket now delivers to a significant number of customers that place their orders via the Internet and this requires a fleet of delivery vehicles that is under the control of local management. The cost of the fleet is now significant and management is trying to determine the optimum replacement policy for the vehicle fleet. The total purchase price of the fleet is $220,000.

The running costs for each year and the scrap values of the fleet at the end of each year are:

	Year 1 $'000	Year 2 $'000	Year 3 $'000	Year 4 $'000	Year 5 $'000
Running costs	110	132	154	165	176
Scrap value	121	88	66	55	25

The hypermarket's cost of capital is 12% per annum.

Ignore tax and inflation.

Required

Prepare calculations that demonstrate when the hypermarket should replace its fleet of delivery vehicles from a financial perspective.

(10 marks)

(Total for Section B = 30 marks)

SECTION C – 50 marks

Answer TWO questions

Question 5

CH Limited (Ltd) is a swimming club. Potential exists to expand the business by providing a gymnasium as part of the facilities at the club. The directors believe that this will stimulate additional membership of the club.

The expansion project would require an initial expenditure of £550,000. The project is expected to have a disposal value at the end of five years which is equal to 10% of the initial expenditure.

The following schedule reflects a recent market research survey regarding the estimated annual sales revenue from additional memberships over the project's five-year life.

Level of demand	£'000	Probability
High	800	0.25
Medium	560	0.50
Low	448	0.25

It is expected that the contribution to sales ratio will be 55%. Additional expenditure on fixed overheads is expected to be £90,000 per annum.

CH Ltd incurs a 30% tax rate on corporate profits. Corporation tax is to be paid in two equal instalments: one in the year that profits are earned and the other in the following year.

CH Ltd's after-tax nominal (money) discount rate is 15.5% per annum. A uniform inflation rate of 5% per annum will apply to all costs and revenues during the life of the project.

All of the values above have been expressed in terms of current prices. You can assume that all cash flows occur at the end of each year and that the initial investment does not qualify for capital allowances.

Required

(a)   Evaluate the proposed expansion from a financial perspective.   **(13 marks)**

(b)   Calculate and then demonstrate the sensitivity of the project to changes in the expected annual contribution.   **(5 marks)**

You have now been advised that the capital cost of the expansion will qualify for writing down allowances at the rate of 25% per annum on a reducing balance basis. Also, at the end of the project's life, a balancing charge or allowance will arise equal to the difference between the scrap proceeds and the tax written down value.

Required

(c)   Calculate the financial impact of these allowances.   **(7 marks)**

(Total = 25 marks)

Question 6

You have received a request from EXE to provide a quotation for the manufacture of a specialised piece of equipment. This would be a one-off order, in excess of normal budgeted production. The following cost estimate has already been prepared.

		Note	$
Direct materials			
Steel	10m² @ $5.00 per m²	1	50
Brass fittings		2	20
Direct labour			
Skilled	25 hours @ $8.00 per hour	3	200
Semi-skilled	10 hours @ $5.00 per hour	4	50
Overhead	35 hours @ $10.00 per hour	5	350
Estimating time		6	100
			770
Administration overhead @ 20% of production cost		7	154
			924
Profit @ 25% of total cost		8	231
Selling price			1,155

Notes

1   The steel is regularly used, and has a current stock value of $5.00 per square metre. There are currently 100 square metres in stock. The steel is readily available at a price of $5.50 per square metre.

2   The brass fittings would have to be bought specifically for this job; a supplier has quoted the price of $20 for the fittings required.

3   The skilled labour is currently employed by your company and paid at a rate of $8.00 per hour. If this job were undertaken it would be necessary either to work 25 hours' overtime, which would be paid at time plus one half, OR in order to carry out the work in normal time, reduce production of another product that earns a contribution of $13.00 per hour.

4   The semi-skilled labour currently has sufficient paid idle time to be able to complete this work.

5   The overhead absorption rate includes power costs which are directly related to machine usage. If this job were undertaken, it is estimated that the machine time required would be ten hours. The machines incur power costs of $0.75 per hour. There are no further overhead costs that can be specifically identified with this job.

6   The cost of the estimating time is that attributed to the four hours taken by the engineers to analyse the drawings and determine the cost estimate given above.

7   It is company policy to add 20% to the production cost as an allowance for administration costs associated with the jobs accepted.

8   This is the standard profit added by your company as part of its pricing policy.

Required

(a)   Prepare on a relevant cost basis, the lowest cost estimate that could be used as the basis for a quotation. Explain briefly your reasons for using EACH of the values in your estimate.

(12 marks)

(b)   Now that the cost estimate has been prepared, the engineers have considered the skilled labour rate and hourly power costs that have been used. They have now realised that the following alternative values may occur and they have estimated the probabilities of each value.

	Skilled labour		Power costs	
$/hour	Probability		$/hour	Probability
10	0.3		0.90	0.25
8	0.6		0.75	0.55
7	0.1		0.65	0.20

The following two-way data table shows the effects of these possible changes on the lowest cost estimate (all values in $).

Skilled labour rate (per hour)	Power costs (per hour)		
	0.90	0.75	0.65
10	+76.50	+75.00	+74.00
8	+1.50	0.00	−1.00
7	−36.00	−37.50	−38.50

Required

Demonstrate and explain how the two-way data table may be used to assist the company in making a decision concerning the contract.

(13 marks)

(Total = 25 marks)

Question 7

(a) TQ manufactures and retails second generation mobile (cell) phones. The following details relate to one model of phone.

	$/unit
Budgeted selling price	60
Budgeted variable cost	25
Budgeted fixed cost	10

Period	1	2	3
Budgeted production and sales (units)	520	590	660
Fixed overhead volume variance	$1,200 (A)	$1,900 (A)	$2,600 (A)

There was no change in the level of stock during any of periods 1 to 3.

The board of directors had expected sales to keep on growing but, instead, they appeared to have stabilised. This has led to the adverse fixed overhead volume variances. It is now the start of period 4 and the board of directors is concerned at the large variances that have occurred during the first three periods of the year. The sales and marketing director has confirmed that the past trend of sales is likely to continue unless changes are made to the selling price of the product. Further analysis of the market for the mobile phone suggests that demand would be zero if the selling price was raised to $100 or more.

Required

(i) Calculate the price that TQ should have charged for the phone assuming that it wished to maximise the contribution from this product.

Note. If price $= a - bx$
then marginal revenue $= a - 2bx$ **(7 marks)**

(ii) Calculate the difference between the contribution that would have been earned at the optimal price and the actual contribution earned during period 3, assuming the variable costs per unit were as budgeted. **(3 marks)**

(b)   TQ is currently developing a third generation mobile phone. It is a 'state of the art' new handheld derive that acts as a mobile phone, personal assistant, digital camera (pictures and video) and music player. The board of directors seeks your advice as to the pricing strategy that it should adopt for such a product.

The company has incurred a significant level of development costs and recognises that the technology for these products is advancing rapidly and that the life cycle for the product is relatively short.

Required

Prepare a report, addressed to the board of directors, that discusses the alternative pricing strategies available to TQ.

(15 marks)

(Total = 25 marks)

(Total for Section C = 50 marks)

Part A
Revision

Cost accounting concepts and techniques

Introduction

We're going to break you in gently to your Paper 2 studies so we begin this text with something easy: a brief reminder of the fundamentals of cost accounting that were introduced at Certificate level and which provide the foundation for many of the topics included in the Paper P2 syllabus (although they do not relate to specific syllabus topics).

Section 1 summarises what you should have covered on the subject of cost classification and cost behaviour – all pretty basic stuff really.

The remainder of the chapter is concerned with two alternative approaches to dealing with overheads. First we look at absorption costing **(Sections 3 and 4)**, then at marginal costing **(Section 5)** and then compare the two **(Sections 6 and 7)**. We've included summaries of those areas you have covered at Certificate level before we go on to consider some more in-depth issues. In particular you need to pay close attention to under and over absorption **(Section 4)**, profit reconciliation **(Section 6)** and the comparison of the two approaches **(Section 7)**.

The examiner has set recent questions asking students to explain absorption and marginal costing, to calculate full cost using absorption costing and to comment on marginal cost pricing. If you feel a bit rusty on any of this chapter's topics, read over your Certificate level notes, or take a look through a copy of BPP Passcards.

Topic list	Learning outcomes	Syllabus references	Ability required
1 Some basic cost accounting concepts	A (iv)(vi)	–	Analysis/comprehension
2 The problem of overheads	A (iv)(vi)	–	Analysis/comprehension
3 A revision of absorption costing	A (iv)(vi)	–	Analysis/comprehension
4 Overhead absorption	A (iv)(vi)	–	Analysis/comprehension
5 A revision of marginal costing	A (iv)(vi)	–	Analysis/comprehension
6 Reconciling profit figures	A (iv)(vi)	–	Analysis/comprehension
7 Absorption costing and marginal costing compared	A (iv)(vi)	–	Analysis/comprehension

1 Some basic cost accounting concepts

- **Costs** can be **classified** according to their **nature** or according to their **purpose** (inventory valuation/profit measurement, decision making, control).
- **Costs** can **behave** in **variable, fixed, semi-variable/semi-fixed/mixed** or **stepped** fashion in relation to changes in activity level.
- **Semi-variable costs** can be **analysed** using the **high-low** or **scattergraph methods**.

Knowledge brought forward from earlier studies

Exam focus point

It may surprise you but the examiner set a ten-mark question testing the material in this section in the November 2006 exam. So he will test knowledge that he expects you to have **already** as well as that you will learn in your studies of P2.

Cost units and cost centres

Cost unit

- Anything that is measurable and useful for cost control purposes
- Can be tangible (such as a tonne of coal) or intangible (such as an hour of accountant's time)
- Composite cost units are made up of two parts (such as the passenger/kilometre (the cost of transporting one passenger for one kilometre) for a bus company)

Cost centre

- Act as collecting places for costs before they are analysed further
- Examples: A production department, a service location such as the canteen, a function such as a sales representative, an activity such as quality control or an item of equipment such as a key production machine

Cost classification

According to their nature

- Into materials, labour, expenses and then further subdivided (such as raw materials, components, consumables)

According to their purpose

- For **inventory valuation and profit measurement**, costs might be classified as **product costs and period costs, direct costs and indirect costs/overheads**, or they might be **classified by function** (production/manufacturing, administration, marketing/selling and distribution)
- For **decision making**, costs are **classified by behaviour** (see below) or as **relevant and non-relevant** (a concept covered in Chapter 2)
- **Classification for control** involves dividing costs into those that are **controllable** and those that are **uncontrollable,** or into **normal and abnormal costs**

Cost behaviour

Variable costs

- Tend to **vary directly with the level of output** (so that there is a **linear relationship** between **variable cost per unit and output**)

- Variable cost per unit is the **same amount for each unit produced** but **total variable cost increases as volume of output increases**

- Example: materials

Fixed costs

- Tend to be **unaffected by increases or decreases in the level of output**

- Relate to a span of time and so are a **period charge** (as the **time span increases so too will the cost**)

- Only **constant** at all levels of output **within the relevant range** of output (the range of output at which the organisation has had experience of operating in the past and for which cost information is available)

- Examples: local government taxes for commercial properties (rates) and UK road fund licence

Semi-variable (or semi-fixed or mixed) costs

- Made up of a **fixed cost element** and a **variable cost element** and so **partly affected by changes in the level of activity**

- Can be **analysed** using the **high-low method** or the **scattergraph method**

Stepped costs

- **Behave like fixed costs within certain ranges of activity**

- Example: rent (of an organisation's one factory) may be a fixed cost if production remains below 1,000 units a month, but if production exceeds 1,000 units a second factory may be required and the cost of rent (on two factories) would go up a step

- Do not behave like variable costs and so, continuing the example above, if monthly output is 1,500 units, two factories are required – not 1.5 factories

1.1 Are you struggling?

If you were unsure about the meaning of any of the terms or concepts mentioned above, it might be a good idea to reread the relevant sections of your Certificate level Study Text or Passcards to refresh your memory.

Question

Scattergraph method

Learning outcome: A(vi)

The intersection of the line of best fit on the vertical axis of a scattergraph is $3,750. A point on the line of best fit represents output of 4,500 units at a total cost of $5,100. What is the variable cost per unit?

Answer

Variable cost per unit = $(5,100 − 3,750)/4,500 = $0.30

2 The problem of overheads

The traditional approach to dealing with overheads is **absorption costing**. It is recommended in financial accounting, but in some situations the **information it provides can be misleading**.

2.1 Using absorption costing to deal with the problem of overheads

Traditionally, the view has been that a fair share of overheads should be added to the cost of units produced. This fair share will **include a portion of all production overhead expenditure** and possibly administration and marketing overheads too. This is the view embodied in the principles of **absorption costing.**

The **theoretical justification** for using absorption costing is that all production overheads are incurred in the production of the organisation's output and so each unit of the product receives some benefit from these costs. Each unit of output should therefore be charged with some of the overhead costs.

2.1.1 Practical reasons for using absorption costing

(a)   **Inventory valuations**

Inventory in hand must be valued for two reasons.

(i)   For the closing inventory figure in the balance sheet
(ii)   For the cost of sales figure in the income statement

The valuation of inventories will affect profitability during a period because of the way in which the cost of sales is calculated.

	The cost of goods produced
+	the value of opening inventories
−	the value of closing inventories
=	the cost of goods sold.

(b)   **Pricing decisions**

Many companies attempt to set selling prices **by calculating the full cost of production or sales** of each product, and then adding a margin for profit. 'Full cost plus pricing' can be particularly useful for companies which do jobbing or contract work, where each job or contract is different, so that a standard unit sales price cannot be fixed. Without using absorption costing, a full cost is difficult to ascertain.

(c)   **Establishing the profitability of different products**

This argument in favour of absorption costing states that if a company sells more than one product, it will be difficult to judge **how profitable each individual product is**, unless overhead costs are shared on a fair basis and charged to the cost of sales of each product.

Of these three arguments, the problem of valuing inventories is perhaps the most significant. **Absorption costing is recommended in financial accounting** by the *Statement of standard accounting practice* on inventories and long-term contracts (SSAP 9). SSAP 9 deals with financial accounting systems and not with cost accounting systems. The cost accountant is (in theory) free to value inventories by whatever method seems best, but where companies integrate their financial accounting and cost accounting systems into a single system of accounting records, the valuation of closing inventories will be determined by SSAP 9.

SSAP 9 states that costs of all inventories should comprise those costs which have been incurred in the normal course of business in **bringing the product to its 'present location and condition'**. These costs incurred will include all related production overheads, even though these overheads may accrue on a time basis. In other words, in financial accounting, closing inventories should be valued at full factory cost, and it may therefore be convenient and appropriate to value inventories by the same method in the cost accounting system.

For many purposes absorption costing is, however, less useful as a costing method than marginal costing. In some situations, **absorption costing can be misleading** in the information it supplies.

2.2 Using marginal costing to deal with the problem of overheads

Advocates of **marginal costing** take the view that only the variable costs of making and selling a product or service should be identified. **Fixed costs should be dealt with separately** and treated as a cost of the accounting period rather than shared out somehow between units produced. Some overhead costs are, however, variable costs which increase as the total level of activity rises and so the marginal cost of production and sales should include an amount for variable overheads.

3 A revision of absorption costing

FAST FORWARD

The three stages of absorption costing are **allocation**, **apportionment** and **absorption**.

You should have covered absorption costing in your earlier studies. We will therefore summarise the simpler points of the topic but will go into some detail on the more complex areas to refresh your memory.

Key term

Absorption costing is 'A method of costing that, in addition to direct costs, assigns all, or a proportion of, production overhead costs to cost units by means of one or a number of overhead absorption rates'.

(CIMA *Official Terminology*)

Knowledge brought forward from earlier studies

Absorption costing

- Product costs are built up using absorption costing by a process of **allocation**, **apportionment** and **overhead absorption**.

- **Allocation** is the process by which whole cost items are charged directly to a cost unit or cost centre. **Direct costs are allocated directly to cost units. Overheads clearly identifiable with cost centres are allocated to those cost centres** but costs which **cannot be identified with one particular cost centre** are **allocated to general overhead cost centres**. The cost of a warehouse security guard would therefore be charged to the warehouse cost centre but heating and lighting costs would be charged to a general overhead cost centre.

- The **first stage of overhead apportionment** involves sharing out (or apportioning) the overheads within **general overhead cost centres** between the other cost centres using a fair basis of apportionment (such as floor area occupied by each cost centre for heating and lighting costs).

- The **second stage of overhead apportionment** is to apportion the costs of **service cost centres** (both directly allocated and apportioned costs) to production cost centres.

- The **final stage** in absorption costing is the **absorption into product costs** (using overhead absorption rates) of the overheads which have been allocated and apportioned to the production cost centres.

- Costs allocated and apportioned to non-production cost centres are usually deducted from the full cost of production to arrive at the cost of sales.

Elements of an absorption costing system

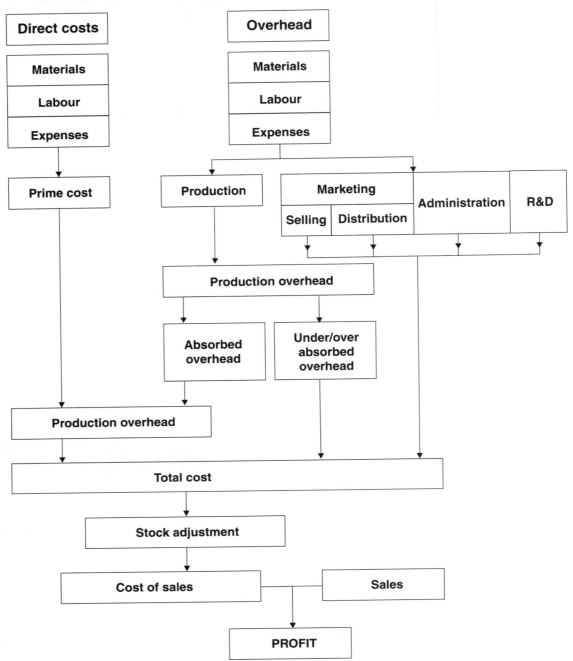

Notes

1   The above chart is based on the absorption costing principle.
2   In the case of marginal costing, the amount of production overhead absorbed would relate to
    the variable element only.
3   The relative sizes of the boxes are of no significance.

(CIMA *Official Terminology*)

Question

Apportionment

Learning outcome: A(iv)

A company is preparing its production overhead budgets and determining the apportionment of those overheads to products. Cost centre expenses and related information have been budgeted as follows.

	Total $	Machine shop A $	Machine shop B $	Assembly $	Canteen $	Maintenance $
Indirect wages	78,560	8,586	9,190	15,674	29,650	15,460
Consumable materials	16,900	6,400	8,700	1,200	600	–
Rent and rates	16,700					
Buildings insurance	2,400					
Power	8,600					
Heat and light	3,400					
Depreciation (machinery)	40,200					
Value of machinery	402,000	201,000	179,000	22,000	–	–
Power usage (%)	100	55	40	3	–	2
Direct labour (hours)	35,000	8,000	6,200	20,800	–	–
Machine usage (hours)	25,200	7,200	18,000	–	–	–
Area (sq ft)	45,000	10,000	12,000	15,000	6,000	2,000

Required

Using the direct apportionment to production departments method and bases of apportionment which you consider most appropriate from the information provided, calculate overhead totals for the three production departments.

Answer

	Total $	A $	B $	Assembly $	Canteen $	Maintenance $	Basis of apportionment
Indirect wages	78,560	8,586	9,190	15,674	29,650	15,460	Actual
Consumable materials	16,900	6,400	8,700	1,200	600	–	Actual
Rent and rates	16,700	3,711	4,453	5,567	2,227	742	Area
Insurance	2,400	533	640	800	320	107	Area
Power	8,600	4,730	3,440	258	–	172	Usage
Heat and light	3,400	756	907	1,133	453	151	Area
Depreciation	40,200	20,100	17,900	2,200	–	–	Val of mach
	166,760	44,816	45,230	26,832	33,250	16,632	
Reallocate	–	7,600	5,890	19,760	(33,250)	–	Direct labour
Reallocate	–	4,752	11,880	–	–	(16,632)	Mach usage
Totals	166,760	57,168	63,000	46,592	–	–	

4 Overhead absorption

Having allocated and/or apportioned all **overheads**, the next stage in absorption costing is to **add them to, or absorb them into**, the cost of production or sales.

Key term

> **Absorbed overhead** is 'Overhead attached to products or services by means of absorption rates'.
> (CIMA *Official Terminology*)

4.1 Use of a predetermined absorption rate

FAST FORWARD

> After apportionment, overheads are absorbed into products using an appropriate **absorption rate based on budgeted costs and budgeted activity levels**.

Key term

> **Overhead absorption rate** is 'A means of attributing overhead to a product or service, based for example on direct labour hours, direct labour cost or machine hours'.   (CIMA *Official Terminology*)

Overheads are not **absorbed** on the basis of the actual overheads incurred but on the **basis of estimated or budgeted figures** (calculated prior to the beginning of the period). The rate at which overheads are included in cost of sales (**absorption rate**) is predetermined before the accounting period actually begins for a number of reasons.

(a)   Goods are produced and sold throughout the year, but many actual overheads are not known until the end of the year. It would be **inconvenient to wait until the year end** in order to decide what overhead costs should be.

(b)   An attempt to calculate overhead costs more regularly (such as each month) is possible, although estimated costs must be added for occasional expenditures such as rent and rates (incurred once or twice a year). The difficulty with this approach would be that **actual overheads from month to month would fluctuate randomly**; therefore, overhead costs charged to production would depend on a certain extent on random events and changes. A unit made in one week might be charged with $4 of overhead, in a subsequent week with $5, and in a third week with $4.50. Only units made in winter would be charged with the heating overhead. Such charges are considered **misleading** for costing purposes and **administratively and clerically inconvenient** to deal with.

(c)   Similarly, **production output might vary each month**. For example actual overhead costs might be $20,000 per month and output might vary from, say, 1,000 units to 20,000 units per month. The unit rate for overhead would be $20 and $1 per unit respectively, which would again lead to administration and control problems.

Knowledge brought forward from earlier studies

Step 1   The overhead likely to be incurred during the coming year is estimated.

Step 2   The total hours, units or direct costs on which the overhead absorption rates are based (activity levels) are estimated.

Step 3   Absorption rate = estimated overhead ÷ budgeted activity level

4.2 Choosing the appropriate absorption base

The choice of an absorption basis is a **matter of judgement and common sense**. There are no strict rules or formulae involved. The ease of collecting the data required for the chosen rate is a major factor. But the basis should realistically reflect the characteristics of a given cost centre, avoid undue anomalies and be 'fair'. It is generally accepted **time-based bases** should be used if possible as many overheads, such as rent and rates, increase with time The **choice will be significant in determining the cost of individual products, but the total cost of production overheads is the budgeted overhead expenditure, no matter what basis of absorption is selected**. It is the relative share of overhead costs borne by individual products and jobs which is affected.

Question

Bases of absorption

Learning outcome: A(iv)

List as many possible bases of absorption (or 'overhead recovery rates') that you can think of, and give their advantages and disadvantages.

Answer

(a) **Percentage of direct materials cost.** It is safe to assume that the overhead costs for producing brass screws, say, are similar to those for producing steel screws. The cost of brass is, however, very much greater than that of steel. Consequently, the overhead charge for brass screws would be too high and that for steel screws too low, if a percentage of cost of materials rate were to be used.

(b) Using **prime cost** as the absorption base would lead to anomalies because of the inclusion of the cost of material, as outlined above.

(c) **Percentage of direct labour cost.** If the overhead actually attributable to units was incurred on, say a time basis, but one highly-paid employee was engaged on producing one item, while a lower-paid employee was producing another item, the overhead charged to the first item using a percentage of wages rate might be too high while the amount absorbed by the second item might be too low. This method should therefore only be used if similar wage rates are paid to all direct employees in a production department. A direct labour hour rate might be considered 'fairer'.

(d) It is for this reason that many organisations use a **direct labour hour rate** or **machine hour rate** in preference to a rate based on a percentage of direct materials cost, wages or prime cost.

    (i) A **direct labour** hour basis is most appropriate in a **labour intensive** environment.

    (ii) A **machine hour** rate would be used in departments where production is controlled or dictated by **machines**. This basis is becoming more appropriate as factories become more heavily automated.

(e) A **rate per unit** would be effective only if all units were identical.

Question

Learning outcome: A(iv)

Using the information in and the results of **Question: apportionment** (in Section 3), determine budgeted overhead absorption rates for each of the production departments using appropriate bases of absorption.

Answer

Machine shop A:	$57,168/7,200 = $7.94 per machine hour
Machine shop B:	$63,000/18,000 = $3.50 per machine hour
Assembly:	$46,592/20,800 = $2.24 per direct labour hour

4.3 Over and under absorption of overheads

FAST FORWARD

Under-/over-absorbed overhead occurs when overheads incurred do not equal overheads absorbed.

The rate of overhead absorption is based on estimates (of both numerator and denominator) and it is quite likely that either one or both of the estimates will not agree with what actually occurs. Actual overheads incurred will probably be either greater than or less than overheads absorbed into the cost of production, and so it is almost inevitable that at the end of the accounting year there will have been an over absorption or under absorption of the overhead actually incurred.

- **Over absorption** means that the **overheads charged to the cost of sales are greater than the overheads actually incurred**.

- **Under absorption** means that **insufficient overheads have been included in the cost of sales**.

Key term

> **Under- or over-absorbed overhead** (or **under- or over-recovered overhead**) is 'The difference between overhead incurred and overhead absorbed, using an estimated rate, in a given period'.
> (CIMA *Official Terminology*)

Suppose that the budgeted overhead in a production department is $80,000 and the budgeted activity is 40,000 direct labour hours, the overhead recovery rate (using a direct labour hour basis) would be $2 per direct labour hour. Actual overheads in the period are, say $84,000 and 45,000 direct labour hours are worked.

	$
Overhead incurred (actual)	84,000
Overhead absorbed (45,000 × $2)	90,000
Over-absorption of overhead	6,000

In this example, the cost of production has been charged with $6,000 more than was actually spent and so the cost that is recorded will be too high. The over-absorbed overhead will be an adjustment to the income statement at the end of the accounting period to reconcile the overheads charged to the actual overhead.

Question | Under and over **absorption**

Learning outcome: A(iv)

The total production overhead expenditure of the company in **Question: apportionment** and **Question: absorption rates** (in Sections 3 and 4) was $176,533 and its actual activity was as follows.

	Machine shop A	Machine shop B	Assembly
Direct labour hours	8,200	6,500	21,900
Machine usage hours	7,300	18,700	–

Required

Using the information in and results of the two questions mentioned above, what is the under or over absorption of overheads?

A $4,065 under absorbed
B $4,065 over absorbed
C $39,619 under absorbed
D $39,619 over absorbed

Answer

The correct answer is A.

		$	$
Actual expenditure			176,533
Overhead absorbed			
Machine shop A	7,300 hrs × $7.94	57,962	
Machine shop B	18,700 hrs × $3.50	65,450	
Assembly	21,900 hrs × $2.24	49,056	
			172,468
Under-absorbed overhead			4,065

Option B is incorrect because actual expenditure was greater than overhead absorbed. Not enough overhead was therefore absorbed.

Options C and D are based on absorption using direct labour hours for the two machine shops. Their overheads are incurred in line with machine hours.

4.3.1 The reasons for under- /over-absorbed overhead

The overhead absorption rate is predetermined from budget estimates of overhead cost and activity level. Under or over recovery of overhead will occur in the following circumstances.

- Actual overhead costs are different from budgeted overheads.
- The actual activity level is different from the budgeted activity level.
- Actual overhead costs **and** actual activity level differ from those budgeted.

Question   Reasons for under/over absorption

Learning outcome: A(iv)

Elsewhere Ltd has a budgeted production overhead of $180,000 and a budgeted activity of 45,000 machine hours.

Required

Fill in the blanks and choose the correct terms from those highlighted in the following statements.

(a)   If actual overheads cost $170,000 and 45,000 machine hours were worked, **under-absorbed/over-absorbed** overhead will be $ .... because ....
....

(b)   If actual overheads cost $180,000 and 40,000 machine hours were worked, **under-absorbed/over-absorbed** overhead will be $ .... because ....
....

(c)   If actual overheads cost $170,000 and 40,000 machine hours were worked, **under-absorbed/over-absorbed** overhead will be $ .... because ....
....

Answer

The overhead recovery rate is $180,000/45,000 = $4 per machine hour.

		$
(a)	Actual overhead	170,000
	Absorbed overhead (45,000 × $4)	180,000
	Over-absorbed overhead	10,000

Reason: Actual and budgeted machine hours are the same but actual overheads cost less than expected.

		$
(b)	Actual overhead	180,000
	Absorbed overhead (40,000 × $4)	160,000
	Under-absorbed overhead	20,000

Reason: Budgeted and actual overhead costs were the same but fewer machine hours were worked than expected.

		$
(c)	Actual overhead	170,000
	Absorbed overhead (40,000 × $4)	160,000
	Under-absorbed overhead	10,000

Reason: A combination of the reasons in (a) and (b).

Exam focus point

In November 2006, there were four marks available in a Section C question for the calculation of full cost per unit using absorption costing.

5 A revision of marginal costing

FAST FORWARD

In **marginal costing**, **inventories** are **valued** at **variable production cost** whereas in **absorption costing** they are valued at their **full production cost**.

If **opening and closing inventory levels differ**, **profit** reported under the two methods will be **different**.

In the **long run**, **total profit** will be the **same** whatever method is used.

Key terms

Marginal cost is 'The part of the cost of one unit of a product or service which would be avoided if that unit were not produced, or which would increase if one extra unit were produced'.

Contribution is 'Sales value less variable cost of sales'.

Marginal costing is 'The accounting system in which variable costs are charged to cost units and fixed costs of the period are written off in full against the aggregate contribution. Its special value is in recognising cost behaviour, and hence assisting in decision-making.' (CIMA *Official Terminology*)

Knowledge brought forward from earlier studies

Marginal costing

- In **marginal costing**, closing **inventories are valued at marginal (variable) production cost** whereas, in **absorption costing**, inventories are **valued at their full production cost** which includes absorbed fixed production overhead.

- If the opening and closing inventory levels differ, the **profit reported** for the accounting period **under the two costing systems will therefore be different**.

- But **in the long run, total profit for a company will be the same** whichever is used because, in the long run, total costs will be the same by either method of accounting. Different accounting conventions merely affect the profit of individual periods.

Profit statements

- **Absorption costing**

	£	£
Sales		X
Opening stock (at full cost)	X	
Full production cost	X	
Less closing stock (at full cost)	X	
Cost of sales	X	
Under-/over-absorbed overhead	X	
Total cost		X
Gross profit		X
Less non-manufacturing costs		X
Net profit		X

- **Marginal costing**

	£	£
Sales		X
Opening stock (at variable cost)	X	
Production cost (variable costs)	X	
Less closing stock (at variable cost)	X	
Cost of sales		X
Contribution		X
Less fixed production costs		X
Gross profit		X
Less non-manufacturing fixed costs		X
Net profit		X

Question

Learning outcome: A(iv)

RH makes and sells one product, which has the following standard production cost.

		$
Direct labour	3 hours at $6 per hour	18
Direct materials	4 kilograms at $7 per kg	28
Production overhead	Variable	3
	Fixed	20
Standard production cost per unit		69

Normal output is 16,000 units per annum. Variable selling, distribution and administration costs are 20 per cent of sales value. Fixed costs are $180,000 per annum. There are no units in finished goods inventory at 1 October 20X2. The fixed overhead expenditure is spread evenly throughout the year. The selling price per unit is $140. Production and sales budgets are as follows.

	Six months ending 31 March 20X3	Six months ending 30 September 20X3
Production	8,500	7,000
Sales	7,000	8,000

Required

Prepare profit statements for each of the six-monthly periods, using the following methods of costing.

(a)   Marginal costing
(b)   Absorption costing

Answer

(a)   **Profit statements for the year ending 30 September 20X3**
      Marginal costing basis

	Six months ending 31 March 20X3		Six months ending 30 September 20X3	
	$'000	$'000	$'000	$'000
Sales at $140 per unit		980		1,120
Opening inventory	–		73.5	
Std. variable prod. cost (at $49 per unit)	416.5		343.0	
	416.5		416.5	
Closing inventory (W1)	73.5		24.5	
Cost of sales		343		392
		637		728
Variable selling and so on costs		196		224
Contribution		441		504
Fixed costs: production (W2)		160		160
Gross profit		281		344
Fixed costs: selling and so on		90		90
Net profit		191		254

(b) **Profit statements for the year ending 30 September 20X3**
Absorption costing basis

	Six months ending 31 March 20X3		Six months ending 30 September 20X3	
	$'000	$'000	$'000	$'000
Sales at $140 per unit		980		1,120
Opening inventory	–		103.5	
Std. cost of prod. (at $69 per unit)	586.5		483.0	
	586.5		586.5	
Closing inventory (W1)	103.5		34.5	
Cost of sales	483.0		552.0	
(Over-)/under-absorbed overhead (W3)	(10.0)		20.0	
Total costs		473		572
Gross profit		507		548
Selling and so on costs				
Variable	196		224	
Fixed	90		90	
		286		314
Net profit		221		234

Workings

1

	Six months ending 31 March 20X3	Six months ending 30 September 20X3
	Units	Units
Opening inventory	–	1,500
Production	8,500	7,000
	8,500	8,500
Sales	7,000	8,000
Closing inventory	1,500	500
Marginal cost valuation (× $49)	$73,500	$24,500
Absorption cost valuation (× $69)	$103,500	$34,500

2   Budgeted fixed production o/hd = 16,000 units × $20 = $320,000 pa = $160,000 per six months

3

	Six months ending 31 March 20X3		Six months ending 30 September 20X3	
Normal output (16,000 ÷ 2)	8,000	units	8,000	Units
Budgeted output	8,500	units	7,000	Units
Difference	500	units	1,000	Units
× std. fixed prod. o/hd per unit	× $20		× $20	
(Over-)/under-absorbed overhead	($10,000)		$20,000	

6 Reconciling profit figures

6.1 Reconciling the profit figures given by the two methods

The **difference in profits** reported using marginal costing and absorption costing is **due to** the **different inventory valuation methods** used.

(a) **If inventory levels increase** between the beginning and end of a period, **absorption costing will report the higher profit** because some of the fixed production overhead incurred during the period will be carried forward in closing **inventory** (which reduces cost of sales) to be set against sales revenue in the following period instead of being written off in full against profit in the period concerned.

(b) **If inventory levels decrease, absorption costing will report the lower profit** because as well as the fixed overhead incurred, fixed production overhead which had been carried forward in opening **inventory** is released and is also included in cost of sales.

6.1.1 Example: reconciling profits

The profits reported for the six months ending 31 March 20X3 in the previous question would be reconciled as follows.

	$'000
Marginal costing profit	191
Adjust for fixed overhead in inventory (inventory increase of 1,500 units × $20 per unit)	30
Absorption costing profit	221

Question   Profit reconciliation

Learning outcomes: A(iv)

Reconcile the profits reported for the six months ending 30 September 20X3 in **Question: marginal costing and absorption costing**.

Answer

	$
Marginal costing profit	254
Adjust for fixed overhead in inventory (inventory decrease of 1,000 units × $20 per unit)	(20)
Absorption costing profit	234

Question   Difference between absorption costing and marginal costing profits

Learning outcomes: A(iv)

D&M report an absorption costing profit of $112,500 for the year to 31 December 19X0. Opening inventory consisted of 58,000 units, closing inventory 43,000 units. The fixed overhead absorbed per unit is $19.50.

Required

Fill in the blank in the following statement.

The marginal costing profit for the period would be $ ....

Answer

The correct answer is $405,000.

	$
Absorption costing profit	112,500
Adjust for fixed overhead in inventory	
(inventory decrease of 15,000 × $19.50 per unit)	292,500
Marginal costing profit	405,000

6.2 Reconciling the profits for different periods

When **marginal costing** is used, **differences in profits in different periods** are **due to changes in sales volume**. When **absorption costing** is used differences are **due to changes in sales volumes and adjustments made for over-/under-absorbed overhead.**

Look back at the information in **Question: marginal costing and absorption costing**.

6.2.1 For marginal costing

Selling prices, variable costs per unit and fixed costs are the same in both periods, so the only factor that could have **caused the difference in the profits of the two periods** is **sales volume**. The higher sales volume in the second six months resulted in a higher contribution and therefore a higher profit (as fixed costs remained constant).

Contribution per unit

	$
Selling price	140
Less direct labour	(18)
direct materials	(28)
variable production overhead	(3)
variable selling and other costs (20% × $140)	(28)
Contribution	63

The **marginal costing profit figures** can be reconciled as follows.

	$'000
Marginal costing profit for six months to 31 March 20X3	191
Increase in contribution in second six-month period due to increase in sales volume	
((8,000 – 7,000) × $63)	63
Marginal costing profit for six months to 30 September 20X3	254

6.2.2 For absorption costing

The **major part of the difference** in profits is caused by the **change in sales volumes**, but a **further difference** is due to the **adjustments** made in the two periods for **under and over absorption** of fixed production overheads.

Profit per unit

	$
Selling price	140
Less standard production cost	(69)
variable selling and so on costs	(28)
Profit	43

The **absorption costing profit figures** can be reconciled as follows.

	$'000
Absorption costing profit for six months to 31 March 20X3	221
Increase in profit in second six-month period due to increase in sales volume ((8,000 – 7,000) × $43)	43
Adjustments for under/over absorption	
Six months to 31 March 20X3	(10)
Six months to 30 September 20X3	(20)
Absorption costing profit for six months to 30 September 20X3	234

The over absorption in the first six months must be deducted in the reconciliation because it made that period's profit higher (and we are reconciling from the first six months' figure to the second six months'). The under absorption in the second six months must also be deducted, however, as it made that period's profits lower than the first six months'.

This is a bit confusing so go over the paragraph above until you have the reasoning clear in your mind. Then try the following question.

Question	Reconciliation of profits for different periods

Learning outcome: A(iv)

In a reconciliation of the absorption costing profits of 20X0 to those of 20X1, there was under absorption of fixed production overhead in both periods. How should the under absorbed overhead figures be dealt with in the reconciliation?

	20X0 figure	20X1 figure
A	Add	Add
B	Deduct	Add
C	Add	Deduct
D	Deduct	Deduct

Answer

The correct answer is C.

The under absorption in 20X0 made the 20X0 profit lower and so it should be added. The under absorption in 20X1 made the 20X1 profit lower than the 20X0 profit and so it should be deducted.

7 Absorption costing and marginal costing compared

Exam focus point

The November 2005 exam tested candidates' knowledge of absorption and marginal costing as they are used in pricing in a 10 mark Section B written question. This topic was revisited in the November 2006 exam where candidates were asked to discuss marginal cost and full cost plus pricing as part of a Section C question.

So it is worthwhile rehearsing your knowledge of both costing approaches and linking this to pricing which is explained in the later chapters in pricing approaches.

Attention!

Remember that if **opening inventory** values are **greater than closing inventory** values, **marginal** costing shows the **greater profit**.

7.1 Marginal versus absorption costing: reporting to management

FAST FORWARD

Profit can be **manipulated** if absorption costing is used.

We know that the reported profit in any period is likely to differ according to the costing method used, but does one method provide a more reliable guide to management about the organisation's profit position.

With marginal costing, contribution varies in direct proportion to the volume of units sold. Profits will increase as sales volume rises, by the amount of extra contribution earned. Since fixed cost expenditure does not alter, marginal costing gives an accurate picture of how a firm's cash flows and profits are affected by changes in sales volumes.

With absorption costing, in contrast, **there is no clear relationship between profit and sales volume**, and as sales volume rises the total profit will rise by the sum of the gross profit per unit plus the amount of overhead absorbed per unit. Arguably this is a confusing and unsatisfactory method of monitoring profitability.

If sales volumes are the same from period to period, marginal costing reports the same profit each period (given no change in prices or costs). In contrast, using absorption costing, profits can vary with the volume of production, even when the volume of sales is constant. **Using absorption costing there is therefore the possibility of manipulating profit, simply by changing output and inventory levels.** Fixed overheads can be carried forward in closing inventory levels, to be charged against a future period's profit, whereas all fixed overhead incurred in a period has to be charged in that period when marginal costing is used.

Marginal costing is not so useful when sales fluctuate from month to month because of seasonal variations in sales demand, but production per month is held constant in order to arrange for an even flow of output (and thereby prevent the cost of idle resources in periods of low demand and overtime in periods of high demand) as the resulting fluctuations in profitability can be misleading.

7.1.1 Other arguments in favour of absorption costing for internal profit reporting

(a) **Marginal costing fails to recognise the importance of working to full capacity**. With absorption costing, the effect of higher production volumes is to reduce unit costs (because the fixed cost per unit is lower) and if sales prices are based on the 'cost-plus' method, the relevance of output capacity to cost/price/sales demand should be clear.

(b) **Selling prices based on marginal costing** might enable the firm to make a contribution on each unit of product it sells, but the **total contribution earned might be insufficient to cover all fixed costs**.

(c) **In the long run, all costs are variable**, and inventory values based on **absorption costing will give recognition to these long-run variable costs**.

7.1.2 Arguments in favour of marginal costing for internal profit reporting

(a)   **Fixed costs** (such as depreciation, rent or salaries) **relate to a period of time and should be charged against the revenues of the period in which they are incurred**.

(b)   Marginal costing profits are a **better indicator of cash flow** than absorption costing profits. Marginal costing accounts for all fixed overheads in the period in which they are incurred, rather than carrying some forward in closing inventory values (as happens with absorption costing). This is a more accurate reflection of how costs are actually paid.

7.2 Marginal versus absorption costing: external reporting

It **might be argued that absorption costing is preferable** to marginal costing in management accounting, **in order to be consistent with the requirement of SSAP 9** to include production overhead in inventory values in published accounts. This argument might be especially relevant when a firm has an integrated or combined accounting system for its financial and management accounts.

The argument is, however, an unimportant one because it is quite easy for a firm to maintain its accounts on a marginal costing basis, and when financial accounts are prepared, to convert its inventory values into fully absorbed costs.

7.3 Marginal versus absorption costing: decision-making information

FAST FORWARD

> **Absorption costing information** about unit profits is **irrelevant in short-run decisions**.

Suppose that a sales manager has an item of product which he is having difficulty in selling. Its historical full cost is $80, made up of variable costs of $50 and fixed costs of $30. A customer offers $60 for it.

(a)   If there is no other customer for the product, **$60 would be better than nothing** and the product should be sold to improve income and profit by this amount.

(b)   If the company has spare production capacity which would otherwise not be used, it would be profitable to continue making more of the same product, if customers are willing to pay $60 for each extra unit made. This is because the additional costs are only $50 so that the profit would be increased marginally by $10 per unit produced.

(c)   In **absorption costing terms**, the **product makes a loss of $20**, which would **discourage the sales manager from accepting a price of $60**. His decision would be a bad one.

   (i)   If the product is **not sold** for $60, it will presumably be scrapped eventually, so the **choice** is really between making a **loss in absorption costing terms of $20, or a loss of $80 when the inventory is written off**, whenever this happens.

   (ii)   If there is **demand** for some extra units at $60 each, the absorption costing loss would be $20 per unit, but at the end of the year there would be an **additional contribution** to overheads and profit of $10 per unit. The under-absorbed overhead would be reduced by $30 (the fixed cost part of the product's full cost) for each extra unit made and sold.

Absorption costing information about unit profits is therefore **irrelevant in short-run decisions in which fixed costs do not change**. In such circumstances the decision rule is to choose the alternative which maximises contribution.

7.4 Summary

Although any technique can be used for internal purposes, absorption costing must be used for external reporting. The use of marginal costing in an organisation for cost accumulation appears to be rare. But this does not mean that marginal costing techniques are unimportant. An understanding of the behaviour of cost and the implications of contribution is vital for accountants and managers, and the use of marginal costing for planning and decision making is universal.

Chapter roundup

- **Costs** can be **classified** according to their **nature** or according to their **purpose** (**inventory** valuation/profit measurement, decision making, control).

- **Costs** can **behave in variable, fixed, semi-variable/semi-fixed/mixed or stepped** fashion in relation to changes in activity level.

- **Semi-variable costs** can be **analysed** using the **high-low** or **scattergraph methods**.

- The traditional approach to dealing with overheads is **absorption costing**. It is recommended in financial accounting, but in some situations the **information it provides can be misleading**.

- The three stages of absorption costing are **allocation, apportionment** and **absorption**.

- After apportionment, overheads are absorbed into products using an appropriate **absorption rate based on budgeted costs and budgeted activity levels**.

- **Under-/over-absorbed overhead** occurs when overheads incurred do not equal overheads absorbed.

- In **marginal costing**, inventories are **valued** at **variable production cost** whereas in **absorption costing** they are valued at their **full production cost**.

- If **opening and closing inventory levels differ**, **profit** reported under the two methods will be **different**.

- In the **long run**, total profit will be the **same** whatever method is used.

- The **difference in profits** reported using marginal costing and absorption costing is **due** to the **different inventory valuation methods** used.

- When **marginal costing** is used, **differences in profits in different periods** are **due to changes in sales volume**. When **absorption costing** is used differences are **due to changes in sales volumes and adjustments made for over-/under-absorbed overhead.**

- Profit can be **manipulated** if absorption costing is used.

- **Absorption costing information** about unit profits is **irrelevant** in **short-run decisions**.

Quick quiz

1   The behaviour of fixed costs depends on whether marginal costing or absorption costing is used. *True or false?*

2   How is an overhead absorption rate calculated?

   A   Estimated overhead ÷ actual activity level
   B   Estimated overhead ÷ budgeted activity level
   C   Actual overhead ÷ actual activity level
   D   Actual overhead ÷ budgeted activity level

3   Over absorption means that the overheads charged to the cost of sales are greater than the overheads actually incurred. *True or false?*

4   *Fill in the blanks in the statements about marginal costing and absorption costing below.*

   (a)   If **inventory** levels .... between the beginning and end of a period, absorption costing will report the higher profit.

   (b)   If **inventory** levels decrease, ... costing will report the lower profit.

5   *Fill in the following blanks with either 'marginal' or 'absorption'.*

   (a)   Using .... costing, profits can be manipulated simply by changing output and **inventory** levels.

   (b)   Fixed costs are charged in full against the profit of the period in which they are incurred when .... costing is used.

   (c)   .... costing fails to recognise the importance of working to full capacity.

   (d)   .... costing could be argued to be preferable to .... costing in management accounting in order to be consistent with the requirements of SSAP 9.

   (e)   .... costing should not be used when decision-making information is required.

6   What are the three practical reasons cited in the chapter for using absorption costing?

   (a)   ....
   (b)   ....
   (c)   ....

7   Draw up proforma profit statements for absorption costing and marginal costing.

Answers to quick quiz

1   False. The behaviour of fixed costs remains the same regardless of the costing system being used.

2   B. Actual figures are *not* used.

3   True

4   (a)   Increase
     (b)   Absorption

5   (a)   absorption
     (b)   marginal
     (c)   marginal
     (d)   absorption, marginal
     (e)   absorption

6   (a)   Inventory valuation
     (b)   Pricing decisions
     (c)   Establishing profitability of different products

7   *Absorption costing*

	£	£
Sales		X
Opening stock (at full cost)	X	
Full production cost	X	
Less closing stock (at full cost)	X	
Cost of sales	X̄	
Under-/over-absorbed overhead	X	
Total cost		X
Gross profit		X̄
Less non-manufacturing costs		X
Net profit		X̄

Marginal costing

	£	£
Sales		X
Opening stock (at variable cost)	X	
Production cost (variable costs)	X	
Less closing stock (at variable cost)	X̄	
Cost of sales		X
Contribution		X̄
Less fixed production costs		X
Gross profit		X̄
Less non-manufacturing fixed costs		X
Net profit		X̄

Now try the question below from the Exam Question Bank

Number	Level	Marks	Time
Q1	Exam standard	10	18 mins

Part B
Financial information for short-term decision making

Relevant cash flows for decisions

Introduction

The topics covered in this chapter underpin many of the techniques covered in this text and so this is a key chapter.

The chapter begins with an **introduction** to decision making (**Sections 1 and 2**) and provides some general information about the decision-making process.

In **Sections 3 to 5** of this chapter you will learn how to identify the **relevant costs and revenues** in decisions, so that management time is not wasted in considering information that is not relevant to the decision. You will also learn about the importance of considering the **non-quantifiable factors** in every decision (in **Section 7**) and about the **assumptions** underlying the relevant costing approach to decision making (**Section 6**). These are topics that you looked at in your Certificate level studies, so they won't be completely new to you.

Once you have worked through this chapter you should be able to **identify and discuss relevant costs and revenues** and **non-quantifiable issues**.

As mentioned above, the topics herein underlie many more advanced techniques and are expected knowledge in the exam. Thus all of the past exams in the new syllabus have examined relevant costs either in Section A or as part of a longer Section B or C question.

The November 2005 exam in particular asked candidates to consider traditional cost classifications as fixed and variable costs and how these would be affected by modern manufacturing methods.

Topic list	Learning outcomes	Syllabus references	Ability required
1 Decisions	A(i)	A1	Analysis
2 Information for decision making	A(i), (iv), (vi)	A1	Comprehension/ Analysis
3 Relevant and non-relevant costs and revenues	A(i)	A1	Analysis
4 Some rules for identifying relevant costs	A(i)	A1	Analysis
5 The relevant cost of scarce resources	A(i)	A1	Analysis
6 The assumptions in relevant costing	A(i)	A1	Analysis
7 Non-quantifiable factors in decision making	A(i)	A2	Analysis

1 Decisions

FAST FORWARD **Most decisions** can be categorised as one of two types, **accept or reject** decisions or **ranking** decisions.

1.1 Accept or reject decisions

These decisions are taken on the **merits of a particular opportunity** under consideration, **without the need to compare** that opportunity to other available opportunities (although alternative uses for the resources that will be needed if the opportunity is accepted have to be taken into account).

If a decision is taken to go ahead with a particular course of action (the **'accept'** option), the organisation will **still be free to consider and take on any other opportunities** presented.

One example of this type of decision is whether or not to go ahead with a one-off contract or order that is outside the normal trading framework. The decision would be made on the basis of the merits of the contract/order (will it increase contribution? could it lead to more orders in the future?) rather than on how the contract/order compares to other opportunities available.

We will be looking at accept/reject decisions later in this chapter.

1.2 Ranking decisions

These decisions involve a **choice between one or more competing opportunities**, and so the different opportunities have to be **compared**. They tend to arise for one of two reasons.

(a) Because there are not enough resources to pursue all the available opportunities. For instance, an organisation may have to decide on what components it will make in house and what components it will have to buy-in because of a shortage of labour.

(b) The opportunities offer different means to the same or similar ends. In a decision whether a new regional office should be located in city A or city B, for example, both opportunities are different means towards the same end of the choice of an office location.

In this chapter and the ones that follow we will be looking at how to make these types of decision.

2 Information for decision making

2.1 Cost accounting versus information for decision making

FAST FORWARD There is a **conflict** between cost accounting for **profit reporting** and **inventory valuation** and the convenient availability of information for **decision making**.

As we saw in the previous chapter, information derived from **cost accounting data** accumulation systems is **totally misleading** for **decision-making purposes**.

Attention!

> For once-only decisions or decisions affecting the use of marginal spare capacity, absorption costing information about unit profits is irrelevant and misleading. On the other hand, since total contribution must be sufficient to cover the fixed costs of the business, marginal costing would be unsuitable as a basis for establishing long-term sales prices for all output.

2.2 Fixed and variable costs and information for short-term decision making

FAST FORWARD

The division of **costs** into their **variable and fixed components** is **useful** in the context of **short-term decision making**.

Exam focus point

A 10-mark question in the November 2005 exam asked candidates to explain how the changing nature of cost structures in the modern manufacturing environment would affect inventory valuation and short-term decision making. This meant the candidates had to look at how fixed and variable costs have changed as manufacturing has become less labour driven and more mechanised. So you need to understand cost structures but also apply you knowledge to a specific scenario!

2.2.1 Costs that vary with activity levels

A large proportion of **short-term decisions require information** about how **costs and revenues vary with activity** so that the alternative options of each decision can be evaluated. Here are some examples.

(a) At what level should budgeted output be set?
(b) Should selling prices be lowered to increase sales volumes?
(c) Should additional factory capacity be purchased so that output can be increased?
(d) Should component X be manufactured internally or purchased from a supplier?
(e) Should a one-off special order be accepted?

For each of these decisions, **management require estimates of costs at different levels of activity of the alternative courses of action**. An organisation might decide to accept a one-off order without understanding that the extra work will mean taking on new staff. Fulfilling the order at the agreed price might therefore result in an overall loss for the organisation.

For short-term decision making, costs should therefore be **divided** into:

(a) **Purely variable costs**, such as direct materials, which can be easily attributed to products, services, customers and so on.

(b) **Variable costs** that are **fixed in the short term** and which **cannot be directly attributed to cost objects, but** which are **avoidable** if the product is not produced, the service not provided and so on. Decisions about the level of such costs are often made when the budget is set (on the basis of anticipated levels of activity), rather than on a daily basis. An example is the costs incurred by a warehouse. Warehouse staff cannot be dismissed or taken on on a daily basis and so it is vital that the correct level of activity is determined to enable effective cost management. Such costs are attached to cost objects using an absorption rate, traditionally based on labour or machine hours (which is only acceptable if there is a causal link between time and the level of cost).

(c) **Fixed costs**, which become **variable in the longer term**, or if activity levels change **significantly**. They tend to be **incurred because of strategic decisions** rather than because of particular products, customers and so on. They are **not relevant to short-term decision making** based on marginal costing principles as they do not change in the short term. They are **relevant to long-run decisions**, however, if **long-run average costs** are required, and because they may be avoidable in the long term.

By classifying costs in this way, it is then **possible to predict total costs** at different levels of output.

2.2.2 Marginal costing concepts

Short-term decisions are those that seek to make the best use of existing facilities. **Typically, in the short run, fixed costs remain unchanged, which means that the marginal cost, revenue and contribution of each decision option are relevant.**

The **selection of the option which maximises contribution is the correct decision option** in such circumstances. Such an approach cannot be taken unless costs have been split into their fixed and variable elements, however.

Even if fixed costs do change, the division of costs into their fixed and variable components is still needed so as to take this fact into account.

Many of the decision-making topics covered in this part of the Study Text rely on the analysis of costs into their fixed and variable components.

3 Relevant and non-relevant costs and revenues

3.1 Relevant costs

The costs which should be **used for decision making** are often referred to as relevant costs.

Key term

> In its *Official Terminology*, CIMA defines **relevant costs** as 'Costs appropriate to a specific management decision. These are represented by future cash flows whose magnitude will vary depending upon the outcome of the management decision made'.

FAST FORWARD

Relevant costs are **future, incremental cash flows**.

(a) Relevant costs are **future costs**.

   (i) A decision is about the future; it cannot alter what has been done already. A cost that has been incurred in the past is totally irrelevant to any decision that is being made 'now'. Such costs are **past costs** or **sunk costs.**

   (ii) Costs that have been incurred include not only costs that have already been paid, but also costs that are the subject of legally binding contracts, even if payments due under the contract have not yet been made. (These are known as **committed costs**.)

(b) Relevant costs are **cash flows**. This means that costs or charges such as the following, which do not reflect additional cash spending, should be ignored for the purpose of decision making.

   (i) **Depreciation**, as a fixed overhead incurred.

   (ii) **Notional rent or interest**, as a fixed overhead incurred.

   (iii) **All overheads absorbed**. Fixed overhead absorption is always irrelevant since it is overheads **to be incurred** which affect decisions.

(c) Relevant costs are **incremental costs**. For example, if an employee is expected to have no other work to do during the next week, but will be paid his basic wage (of, say, $100 per week) for attending work and doing nothing, his manager might decide to give him a job which earns only $40. The **net relevant benefit** is $40 and the $100 is irrelevant to the decision because although it is a future cash flow, it will be incurred anyway whether the employee is given work or not.

3.2 Differential costs, avoidable costs and opportunity costs

Other terms are used to describe relevant costs.

Key term

> The CIMA *Official Terminology* defines **incremental** or **differential costs** as 'The difference in total cost between alternatives; calculated to assist decision-making'.

Differential costs are relevant costs which are simply the additional costs incurred as a consequence of a decision.

Key term

> **Avoidable costs** are defined as 'The specific costs of an activity or sector of a business which would be avoided if that activity or sector did not exist'.   (CIMA *Official Terminology*)

Avoidable costs is a term usually associated with shutdown or disinvestment decisions, but it can be applied to control decisions too.

Key term

> **Opportunity cost** is 'The value of a benefit sacrificed when one course of action is chosen, in preference to an alternative. The opportunity cost is represented by the forgone potential benefit from the best rejected course of action'.   (CIMA *Official Terminology*).

FAST FORWARD

An **opportunity cost** is the benefit forgone by choosing one opportunity instead of the next best alternative.

Opportunity cost is a useful concept when there are a number of possible uses for a scarce resource.

Question

Relevant costs

Learning outcome: A(i)

An information technology consultancy firm has been asked to do an urgent job by a client, for which a price of $2,500 has been offered. The job would require the following.

(a) 30 hours' work from one member of staff, who is paid on an hourly basis, at a rate of $20 per hour, but who would normally be employed on work for clients where the charge-out rate is $45 per hour. No other member of staff is able to do the member of staff in question's work.

(b) The use of 5 hours of mainframe computer time, which the firm normally charges out to external users at a rate of $50 per hour. Mainframe computer time is currently used 24 hours a day, 7 days a week.

(c) Supplies and incidental expenses of $200.

Required

Fill in the blank in the sentence below.

The relevant cost or opportunity cost of the job is $........ .

Answer

The correct answer is $1,800.

The relevant cost or opportunity cost of the job would be calculated as follows.

	$
Labour (30 hours × $45)	1,350
Computer time opportunity cost (5 hours × $50)	250
Supplies and expenses	200
	1,800

Exam focus point

An MCQ in the May 2005 exam required knowledge of opportunity costs as relevant costs.

3.3 Non-relevant costs

A number of terms are used to describe costs that are **irrelevant** for decision making because they are either not future cash flows or they are costs which will be incurred anyway, regardless of the decision that is taken.

FAST FORWARD Non-relevant costs include **sunk costs**, **committed costs**, **notional costs** and **historical costs**.

3.3.1 Sunk costs

Key term

A **sunk cost** is 'Cost that has been irreversibly incurred or committed and cannot therefore be considered relevant to a decision. Sunk cost costs may also be deemed **irrecoverable** costs.'

CIMA *Official Terminology)*

Here are some examples of sunk costs

(a)   **Dedicated non-current assets**. Suppose a company purchased an item of computer equipment two years ago for $20,000. It has been depreciated to a net book value of $7,000 already, but in fact it already has no resale value because of developments in computer technology. The equipment can be used for its existing purpose for at least another year, but the company is considering whether or not to purchase more modern equipment with additional facilities and so scrap the existing equipment now.

In terms of decision making and relevant costs the existing equipment, which initially cost $20,000 but now has a net book value of $7,000, is a sunk cost. The money has been spent and the asset has no alternative use. 'Writing off' the asset and incurring a 'paper' loss on disposal of $7,000 would be irrelevant to the decision under consideration.

(b)   **Development costs already incurred**. Suppose that a company has spent $250,000 in developing a new service for customers, but the marketing department's most recent findings are that the service might not gain customer acceptance and could be a commercial failure. The decision whether or not to abandon the development of the new service would have to be taken, but the $250,000 spent so far should be ignored by the decision makers because it is a sunk cost.

3.3.2 Committed costs

A committed cost is a **future cash outflow** that will be **incurred anyway, whatever decision is taken now** about alternative opportunities. Committed costs may exist because of contracts already entered into by the organisation, which it cannot now avoid.

3.3.3 Notional costs

Key term

> The CIMA *Official Terminology* definition of a **notional cost** is 'A cost used in product evaluation, decision-making and performance measurement to reflect the use of resources which have no "**actual** (observable) cost".

Examples of notional costs in cost accounting systems

(a)   **Notional rent**, such as that charged to a subsidiary, cost centre or profit centre of an organisation for the use of accommodation which the organisation owns.

(b)   **Notional interest charges on capital employed**, sometimes made against a profit centre or cost centre.

3.3.4 Historical costs

Although historical costs are irrelevant for decision making, historical cost data will **often** provide the **best available basis for predicting future costs**.

3.4 Fixed and variable costs

FAST FORWARD

> Unless you are given an indication to the contrary, you should assume that **variable costs** will be **relevant** costs and that **fixed costs** are **irrelevant** to a decision.

The assumption in the 'Fast Forward' above need not be the case, however, and you should analyse variable and fixed cost data carefully. Do not forget that 'fixed' costs may only be fixed in the short term.

3.4.1 Non-relevant variable costs

There might be occasions when a variable cost is in fact a sunk cost. For example, suppose that a company holds some units of raw material. They have been paid for already, and originally cost $2,000. They are now obsolete and are no longer used in regular production, and they have no scrap value. However, they could be used in a special job which the company is trying to decide whether to undertake. The special job is a 'one-off' customer order, and would use up all the materials currently held.

In deciding whether the job should be undertaken, the relevant cost of the materials to the special job is nil. Their **original cost** of $2,000 is a **sunk cost**, and should be ignored in the decision.

However, if the materials did have a **scrap value** of, say, $300, then their relevant cost to the job would be the **opportunity cost** of being unable to sell them for scrap, ie $300.

3.4.2 Attributable fixed costs

Attention!

> There might be occasions when a fixed cost is a relevant cost, and you must be aware of the distinction between 'specific' or 'directly attributable' fixed costs, and general overheads.

(a)   **Directly attributable fixed costs** are those costs which, although fixed within a relevant range of activity level are relevant to a decision for either of the following reasons.

(i) They would increase if certain extra activities were undertaken. For example, it may be necessary to employ an extra supervisor if a particular order is accepted. The extra salary would be an attributable fixed cost.

(ii) They would decrease or be eliminated entirely if a decision were taken either to reduce the scale of operations or shut down entirely.

(b) **General fixed overheads** are those fixed overheads which will be unaffected by decisions to increase or decrease the scale of operations, perhaps because they are an apportioned share of the fixed costs of items which would be completely unaffected by the decisions. An apportioned share of head office charges is an example of general fixed overheads for a local office or department. General fixed overheads are not relevant in decision making.

Attention!

> Fixed costs are assumed to be irrelevant in decision making (unless given an indication to the contrary). In ABC (covered in Chapter 16), however, the crucial assumption is that many so-called 'fixed' costs are actually variable with business complexity given a long enough period of time.

3.5 Relevant revenues

Relevant revenues are also **future, incremental cash flows**.

(a) (i) Revenue **received in the past** is totally **irrelevant** to any decision that is being made now. A progress payment already received from a customer for a contract under consideration is therefore totally irrelevant to any decision about whether to continue with that project.

(ii) Revenue that has **not yet been received but will be received regardless of the decision made** is **not relevant**. A fee that a customer is contractually obliged to pay irrespective of whether or not a contract is to continue is therefore not relevant.

(b) Relevant revenues are **cash flows**. The book profit on the sale of a non-current asset is therefore not relevant to a decision on whether or not to sell that asset, whereas the cash received for the asset is.

(c) Relevant revenues are **incremental revenues**. If project A earns revenue of $1,000 and project B earns revenue of $2,500, the relevant revenue in a decision about whether to choose project B instead of project A is $(2,500 − 1,000) = $1,500.

3.6 Minimum price quotations for special orders

The total relevant cost of an order represents the minimum price that the company should charge for an order if they wish to make neither a profit or a loss.

Therefore this gives management a **starting point** for their pricing decision as a baseline price before any profit margin. They can compare this to prices tendered by other supplied to make a decision on whether it is worth making the order.

4 Some rules for identifying relevant costs

4.1 The relevant cost of materials

FAST FORWARD

> The **relevant cost of raw materials** is generally their current replacement cost unless the materials have already been purchased and will not be replaced, in which case the relevant cost of using them is the higher of their current resale value and the value they would obtain if they were put to an alternative use.

If the materials have no resale value and no other possible use, then the relevant cost of using them for the opportunity under consideration would be nil.

You should test your knowledge of the relevant cost of materials by attempting the following question.

Question

Relevant cost of materials

Learning outcome: A(i)

DLN has been approached by a customer who would like a special job to be done for him, and who is willing to pay $22,000 for it. The job would require the following materials.

Material	Total units required	Units already held	Book value of units held $/unit	Realisable value $/unit	Replacement cost $/unit
A	1,000	0	–	–	6.00
B	1,000	600	2.00	2.50	5.00
C	1,000	700	3.00	2.50	4.00
D	200	200	4.00	6.00	9.00

Material B is used regularly by DLN, and if units of B are required for this job, they would need to be replaced to meet other production demand.

Materials C and D are held as the result of previous over buying, and they have a restricted use. No other use could be found for material C, but the units of material D could be used in another job as substitute for 300 units of material E, which currently costs $5 per unit (and of which the company holds no units at the moment).

Required

Fill in the blank in the sentence below.

The relevant cost of material for deciding whether or not to accept the contract is $ ....

Answer

The correct answer is $15,450.

(a)   **Material A** is not yet owned. It would have to be bought in full at the replacement cost of $6 per unit.

(b)   **Material B** is used regularly by the company. There is existing inventory (600 units) but if these are used on the contract under review a further 600 units would be bought to replace them. Relevant costs are therefore 1,000 units at the replacement cost of $5 per unit.

(c)   1,000 units of **material C** are needed and 700 are already held. If used for the contract, a further 300 units must be bought at $4 each. The existing inventory of 700 will not be replaced. If they are used for the contract, they could not be sold at $2.50 each. The realisable value of these 700 units is an opportunity cost of sales revenue forgone.

(d)   The required units of **material D** are already held and will not be replaced. There is an opportunity cost of using D in the contract because there are alternative opportunities either to sell the existing inventory for $6 per unit ($1,200 in total) or avoid other purchases (of material E), which would cost 300 x $5 = $1,500. Since substitution for E is more beneficial, $1,500 is the opportunity cost.

(e) **Summary of relevant costs**

	$
Material A (1,000 × $6)	6,000
Material B (1,000 × $5)	5,000
Material C (300 × $4) plus (700 × $2.50)	2,950
Material D	1,500
Total	15,450

Exam focus point

MCQ questions on the relevant cost of materials have featured in most exams since May 2005 when the new syllabus was first examined. The November 2005 exam Section C required candidates to consider relevant costs in the context of investment appraisement. Relevant costing is a key topic and underpins short-term decision making.

4.2 The relevant cost of using machines

FAST FORWARD

Using **machinery** will involve some **incremental costs**.

- Repair costs arising from use
- Hire charges
- Any fall in resale value of owned assets which results from their use

Depreciation is **not** a relevant cost.

4.2.1 Example: the relevant cost of using machines

An organisation is considering whether to undertake some contract work for a customer. The machinery required for the contract would be as follows.

(a) A special cutting machine will have to be hired for three months for the work (the length of the contract). Hire charges for this machine are $75 per month, with a minimum hire charge of $300.

(b) All other machinery required in the production for the contract has already been purchased by the organisation on hire purchase terms. The monthly hire purchase payments for this machinery are $500. This consists of $450 for capital repayment and $50 as an interest charge. The last hire purchase payment is to be made in two months' time. The cash price of this machinery was $9,000 two years ago. It is being depreciated on a straight line basis at the rate of $200 per month. However, it still has a useful life which will enable it to be operated for another 36 months.

The machinery is highly specialised and is unlikely to be required for other, more profitable jobs over the period during which the contract work would be carried out. Although there is no immediate market for selling this machine, it is expected that a customer might be found in the future. It is further estimated that the machine would lose $200 in its eventual sale value if it is used for the contract work.

Required

Calculate the relevant cost of machinery for the contract.

Solution

(a) The cutting machine will incur an incremental cost of $300, the minimum hire charge.

(b) The historical cost of the other machinery is irrelevant as a past cost; depreciation is irrelevant as a non-cash cost; and future hire purchase repayments are irrelevant because they are committed costs. The only relevant cost is the loss of resale value of the machinery, estimated at $200 through use. This user cost will not arise until the machinery is eventually resold and the $200 should be discounted to allow for the time value of money. However, discounting is ignored here.

(c) **Summary of relevant costs**

	$
Incremental hire costs	300
User cost of other machinery	200
	500

Question

Relevant cost of using machines

Learning outcome: A(i)

A machine which originally cost $12,000 has an estimated life of ten years and is depreciated at the rate of $1,200 a year. It has been unused for some time, however, as expected production orders did not materialise.

A special order has now been received which would require the use of the machine for two months.

The current net realisable value of the machine is $8,000. If it is used for the job, its value is expected to fall to $7,500. The net book value of the machine is $8,400.

Routine maintenance of the machine currently costs $40 a month. With use, the cost of maintenance and repairs would increase to $60 a month for the months that the machine is being used.

Ignore the time value of money.

What is the relevant cost of using the machine for the order?

A $240
B $520
C $540
D $620

Answer

The correct answer is C.

	$
Loss in net realisable value of the machine through using it on the order $(8,000 – 7,500)	500
Costs in excess of existing routine maintenance costs $(120 – 80)	40
Total marginal user cost	540

If you selected **option A** you incorrectly included the depreciation cost. Depreciation is not relevant because it is not a future cash flow.

Option B is incorrect because it allows for only one month's increased maintenance cost. The special order will take two months.

Option D is incorrect because it includes all of the maintenance cost to be incurred. $40 per month would be incurred anyway so it is only the incremental $20 that is relevant.

5 The relevant cost of scarce resources

The **relevant cost of a scarce resource** is the sum of the contribution/incremental profit forgone from the next-best opportunity for using the scarce resource and the variable cost of the scarce resource.

5.1 Scarce resources and opportunity costs

When a decision maker is faced with an opportunity which would call for the **use of a scarce resource**, the total **incremental cost** of using the resource will be **higher than the direct cash cost of purchasing it**. This is because the resource could be used for other purposes, and so by using it in one way, the benefits obtainable from using it another way must be forgone.

A numerical example may help to clarify this point. Suppose that your company is considering a contract. The work would involve the use of certain equipment for five hours and its running costs would be $2 per hour. However, your company faces heavy demand for usage of the equipment which earns a contribution of $7 per hour from this other work. If the contract is undertaken, some of this work would have to be forgone.

The contribution obtainable from putting the scarce resource to its alternative use is its **opportunity cost**. Since the equipment can earn $7 per hour in an alternative use, the contract under consideration should also be expected to earn at least the same amount. This can be accounted for by charging the $7 per hour as an opportunity cost to the contract and the total relevant cost of 5 hours of equipment time would be as follows.

	$
Running costs (5 × $2)	10
Internal opportunity cost (5 × $7)	35
Relevant cost	45

It is important to notice that the variable running costs of the equipment are included in the total relevant cost.

5.2 Example: relevant costs of labour and variable overheads

A company has been offered $21,000 by a prospective customer to make some purpose-built equipment. The extra costs of the machine would be $3,000 for materials. There would also be a requirement for 2,000 labour hours. Labour wages are $4 per hour, variable overhead is $2 per hour and fixed overhead is absorbed at the rate of $4 per hour.

Labour, however, is in limited supply, and if the job is accepted, workers would have to be diverted from other work which is expected to earn a contribution of $5 per hour towards fixed overheads and profit.

Required

Assess whether the contract should be undertaken.

Solution

The relevant costs of the scarce resource, labour, are the sum of the following.

- The variable costs of the labour and associated variable overheads
- The contribution forgone from not being able to put it to its alternative use

Fixed costs are ignored because there is no incremental fixed cost expenditure.

	$
Materials	3,000
Labour (2,000 hours at $4 per hour)	8,000
Variable overhead (2,000 hours at $2 per hour)	4,000
	15,000
Opportunity cost:	
Contribution forgone from other work (2,000 hours × $5 per hour)	10,000
Total costs	25,000
Revenue	21,000
Net loss on contract	(4,000)

The contract should not be undertaken.

It is worth thinking carefully about labour costs. The labour force will be paid $8,000 for 2,000 hours work, and variable overheads of $4,000 will be incurred no matter whether the workers are employed on the new job or on other work. Relevant costs are future cash flows arising as a direct consequence of a decision, and the decision here will not affect the total wages paid. If this money is going to be spent anyway, should it not therefore be ignored as an irrelevant cost?

The answer to this crucial question is 'no'. The labour wages and variable overheads are relevant costs even though they will be incurred whatever happens. The reason for this is that the other work earns a contribution of $5 per hour **after having covered** labour and variable overhead costs. Work on the purpose-built equipment ought therefore to do at least the same.

Question

More relevant costing

Learning outcome: A(i)

LAM is involved in a project that requires 100kg of material J. The company holds 50kg of material J. It purchased this material, which has a standard cost of $10 per kg, six months ago for $12 per kg. Material J can currently be purchased for $9 per kg. If the 50kg of material J held is not used, it could be sold for $8 per kg.

The relevant cost of the material J required for the project is $900. *True or false?*

Answer

The correct answer is $850 and so the statement is false.

	$
Material already held, relevant cost = 50kg × $8 =	400
Material to be purchased, relevant cost = 50kg × $9 =	450
	850

$900 is incorrect because the material held should be valued at its realisable value of $8.

6 The assumptions in relevant costing

Relevant costs are future costs. Whenever anyone tries to predict what will happen in the future, the predictions could well be wrong. Cost accountants have to make the best forecasts of relevant income and costs that they can, and at the same time recognise the assumptions on which their estimates are based. A variety of assumptions will be made, and you ought to be aware of them.

Attention!

> In particular, if you make an assumption in answering an examination question and you are not sure that the examiner or marker will appreciate or recognise the assumption you are making, you should explain it in narrative in your solution.

FAST FORWARD

There are a number of **assumptions** typically made in relevant costing.

(a)   **Cost behaviour patterns are known**; if a department closes down, for example, the attributable fixed cost savings would be known.

This is not necessarily so, and it is always important to question assumptions of this nature. For example, if you are told in an examination question that a factory intends to increase production by 50%, and you are invited to assume in your number work that fixed costs and unit variable costs would be unaffected, it is important to challenge this assumption as a footnote to your solution, making the following points.

(i)   Is it clear that the factory could handle such a large increase in output?

(ii)   If so, fixed costs would probably change dramatically, and there might also be a shift in unit variable costs.

(b)   **The amount of fixed costs, unit variable costs, sales price and sales demand are known with certainty**. However, it is possible to apply risk and uncertainty analysis to decisions and so recognise that what will happen in the future is not certain. You will cover such techniques in Chapter 14 of this text.

(c)   **The objective of decision making in the short run is to maximise 'satisfaction'**, which is often regarded as 'short-term profit'. However, there are many qualitative factors or financial considerations, other than those of profit, which may influence a final decision: again a footnote may be called for.

(d)   **The information on which a decision is based is complete and reliable.** This is obviously unrealistic and decision makers must be made aware of any inadequacies of the information that they are using for their decisions.

7 Non-quantifiable factors in decision making

Non-quantifiable factors in decision making are factors which might influence the eventual decisions but which have not been quantified in terms of relevant costs or benefits. They may stem from **two sources**.

(a)   Non-financial objectives

(b)   Factors which might be quantifiable in **money terms**, but which have not been quantified, perhaps because there is **insufficient information to make reliable estimates.** Such factors tend to focus on the **long-term implications** of decisions.

FAST FORWARD

Non-quantifiable factors should **always be considered** alongside the quantitative data in a decision.

Attention!

> Decision making questions in the exam often ask you to detail 'other factors that should be considered' after you have completed the figurework for the decision. However, even if the question does not invite you to do so, it is a good idea to get into the habit of adding a few notes concerning 'other factors'. This applies especially if you feel that you have made any assumptions that could be challenged.

7.1 Examples of non-quantifiable factors

Non-quantifiable factors in decision making will vary with the circumstances and nature of the opportunity being considered. Here are some examples.

Factors	Details
The **availability of cash**	An opportunity may be profitable, but there must be sufficient cash to finance any purchases of equipment and build-up of working capital.
Inflation	The effect of inflation on the prices of various items may need to be considered, especially where a fixed price contract is involved in the decision: if the income from an opportunity is fixed by contract, but the costs might increase with inflation, the contract's profitability would be over-stated unless inflation is taken into account.
Employees	Any decision involving the shutdown of a plant, creation of a new work shift, or changes in work procedures or location will require acceptance by employees, and ought to have regard to employee welfare.
Customers	Decisions about new products or product closures, the quality of output or after-sales service will inevitably affect customer loyalty and customer demand. It is also important to remember that a decision involving one product may have repercussions on customer attitudes towards a range of products. For example, a company which sells a range of garden tools and equipment under a single brand name should consider the effects on demand for the entire brand range if one product (for example a garden rake) is deleted, or a new product of poor quality is added.
Competitors	In a competitive market, some decisions may stimulate a response from rival companies. For example, the decision to reduce selling prices in order to raise demand may not be successful if all competitors take similar action.
Timing factors	There might be a choice in deciding when to take up an opportunity. The choice would not be 'accept or reject'; there would be three choices. • Accept an opportunity now • Do not accept the opportunity now, but wait before doing so • Reject the opportunity Other choices which may need to be made (a) If a department is shut down, will the closure be permanent, or temporary? Temporary closure may be a viable proposition during a period of slack demand. (b) If a decision is taken to sell goods at a low price where the contribution earned will be relatively small, it is important to consider the duration of the low price promotion. If it is a long-term feature of selling, and if demand for the product increases, the company's total contribution may sink to a level where it fails even to cover fixed costs.
Suppliers	Some decisions will affect suppliers, whose long-term goodwill may be damaged by a decision to close a product line temporarily. Decisions to change the specifications for purchased components, or change inventory policies so as to create patchy, uneven demand might also put a strain on suppliers. In some cases, where a company is the supplier's main customer, a decision to reduce demand or delay payments for goods received might drive the supplier out of business.

Factors	Details
Feasibility	A proposal may look good in financial terms, but technical experts or departmental managers may have some reservations about their ability to carry it out. For example, a decision may be required to buy some computer equipment, but the departmental manager might have reservations about the willingness of his staff to accept the proposal, the possibility of implementing the scheme by the planned date, and even whether the proposed scheme will actually do the job intended.
Flexibility and internal control	Decisions to subcontract work, or to enter into a long-term contract have the disadvantages of inflexibility and lack of controllability. Where requirements may be changeable, it would be preferable to build flexibility into the organisation of operations.
Unquantified opportunity costs	Even where no opportunity costs are specified, it is probable that other opportunities would be available for using the resources to earn profit. It may be useful to qualify a recommendation by stating that a given project would appear to be viable on the assumption that there are no other more profitable opportunities available.
Political pressures	Some large companies may suffer political pressures applied by the government to influence their investment or disinvestment decisions.
Legal constraints	A decision might occasionally be rejected because of doubts about the legality of the proposed action.

Attention!

> Although the various decision-making scenarios you will encounter in the next chapter are known as short-term decisions, in reality **no decision has just short-term implications**. All decisions have longer-term implications because they usually allow certain options for future action while disallowing others.

Question

Using relevant costs

Learning outcome: A(i)

An organisation in the civil engineering industry with headquarters located 22 miles from London undertakes contracts anywhere in the United Kingdom.

The organisation has had its tender for a job in north-east England accepted at $288,000 and work is due to begin in March 20X3. However, the organisation has also been asked to undertake a contract on the south coast of England. The price offered for this contract is $352,000. Both of the contracts cannot be taken simultaneously because of constraints on staff site management personnel and on plant available. An escape clause enables the organisation to withdraw from the contract in the north-east, provided notice is given before the end of November and an agreed penalty of $28,000 is paid.

BPP)))
LEARNING MEDIA

The following estimates have been submitted by the organisation's quantity surveyor.

COST ESTIMATES

		North-east $	South Coast $
Materials:	Held at original cost, Material X	21,600	·
	Held at original cost, Material Y		24,800
	Firm orders placed at original cost, Material X	30,400	
	Not yet ordered – current cost, Material X	60,000	
	Not yet ordered – current cost, Material Z		71,200
Labour – hired locally		86,000	110,000
Site management		34,000	34,000
Staff accommodation and travel for site management		6,800	5,600
Plant on site – depreciation		9,600	12,800
Interest on capital, 8%		5,120	6,400
Total local contract costs		253,520	264,800
Headquarters costs allocated at rate of 5% on total contract costs		12,676	13,240
		266,196	278,040
Contract price		288,000	352,000
Estimated profit		21,804	73,960

Notes

(a) X, Y and Z are three building materials. Material X is not in common use and would not realise much money if re-sold; however, it could be used on other contracts but only as a substitute for another material currently quoted at 10% less than the original cost of X. The price of Y, a material in common use, has doubled since it was purchased; its net realisable value if re-sold would be its new price less 15% to cover disposal costs. Alternatively it could be kept for use on other contracts in the following financial year.

(b) With the construction industry not yet recovered from a recent recession, the organisation is confident that manual labour, both skilled and unskilled, could be hired locally on a sub-contracting basis to meet the needs of each of the contracts.

(c) The plant which would be needed for the south coast contract has been owned for some years and $12,800 is the year's depreciation on a straight-line basis. If the north-east contract is undertaken, less plant will be required but the surplus plant will be hired out for the period of the contract at a rental of $6,000.

(d) It is the organisation's policy to charge all contracts with notional interest at 8% on the estimated working capital involved in contracts. Progress payments would be receivable from the contractee.

(e) Salaries and general costs of operating the small headquarters amount to about $108,000 each year. There are usually ten contracts being supervised at the same time.

(f) Each of the two contracts is expected to last from March 20X3 to February 20X4 which, coincidentally, is the company's financial year.

(g) Site management is treated as a fixed cost.

Required

As the management accountant to the organisation, do the following.

(a) Present comparative statements to show the net benefit to the organisation of undertaking the more advantageous of the two contracts.

(b) Explain the reasoning behind the inclusion in (or omission from) your comparative financial statements of each item given in the cost estimates and the notes relating thereto.

Answer

One way of determining which is the more advantageous of the two contracts is to calculate the net cost or benefit of cancelling the north-east contract in favour of the work on the south cost. We are asked to present comparative statements, however, and so our approach will be to prepare statements of the relevant costs of each contract.

Did you read note (c) properly? Rent receivable is *not* an expense. Make sure that the explanations you give in part (b) do not differ from the treatment of items in part (a).

(a)   **Statements of the relevant costs of each contract**

	Note	North-East $	South Coast $
Material X held ($21,600 × 90%)	1	19,440	
Material Y held ($24,800 × 2)	2		49,600
Material X on order ($30,400 × 90%)	1	27,360	
Material X not yet ordered	3	60,000	
Material Z not yet ordered	3		71,200
Labour	4	86,000	110,000
Site management	5	–	–
Staff accommodation and travel	6	6,800	5,600
Plant for north-east contract	7	(6,000)	
Plant for south coast contract	8	–	–
Interest on capital	9	–	–
Headquarters' costs	10	–	–
Penalty payment	11		28,000
Total relevant costs		193,600	264,400
Contract price		288,000	352,000
Net benefit		94,400	87,600

The **north-east** contract is therefore the **more advantageous**, with a net benefit to the organisation of $94,400.

(b)   The **reasoning** behind the treatment of each cost item is given in the following notes.

Notes

1   The relevant cost of the material X held and on order is the **opportunity cost** of the saving which is forgone by not using X as a substitute material.

2   Ignoring the time value of money and the cost of storing the material, it would not be worth selling material Y and then repurchasing it next year. In fact the cost of borrowing is 8%, which is much less than the 15% cost of disposing of the material. The relevant cost of using material Y is the **replacement cost** which would have to be paid to obtain more material for next year's contracts.

3   Since this material has not yet been ordered, the **current cost** is the relevant cost of a decision to proceed with each contract.

4   The labour costs are the **incremental costs** which would have to be incurred if the contract goes ahead. They are therefore relevant costs of both contracts.

5   The statement that site management is treated as a fixed cost is assumed to mean that it is a **committed cost** which will be incurred irrespective of the decision concerning these contracts.

6   It is assumed that these are **incremental costs** which will only be incurred if the contracts go ahead.

7   If the north-east contract is undertaken, the **rental value received** will be $6,000. The **depreciation cost is not relevant** (see note 8).

8   It is assumed that the depreciation cost is an accounting book entry and that the **value of the plant will not be affected** by using it on either contract.

9   Although there would probably be some incremental **working capital financing costs** as a result of the contracts, we have **no way of knowing** how much they would be. They would be somewhat reduced by the effect of the progress payments received from the contractee.

10   It is assumed that the total amount of headquarters' costs **would not be affected** by the decision to undertake either contract. This is therefore not a relevant cost.

11   The penalty payment is a **relevant cost of cancelling the north-east contract in order to proceed with the south coast contract**.

Chapter Roundup

- Most decisions can be categorised as one of two types, **accept or reject** decisions or **ranking** decisions.

- There is a **conflict** between cost accounting for **profit reporting** and **inventory valuation** and the convenient availability of information for **decision making**.

- The division of **costs** into their **variable and fixed components** is **useful** in the context of **short-term decision making**.

- Relevant costs are **future, incremental cash flows**.

- An **opportunity cost** is the benefit forgone by choosing one opportunity instead of the next best alternative.

- Non-relevant costs include **sunk costs, committed costs, notional costs** and **historical costs**.

- Unless you are given an indication to the contrary, you should assume that **variable costs** will be **relevant** costs and that **fixed costs** will be **irrelevant** to a decision.

- The **relevant cost of raw materials** is generally their current replacement cost unless the materials have already been purchased and will not be replaced, in which case the relevant cost of using them is the higher of their current resale value and the value they would obtain if they were put to an alternative use.

- Using **machinery** will involve some **incremental costs**.

  - Repair costs arising from use
  - Hire charges
  - Any fall in resale value of owned assets which results from their use

  Depreciation is **not** a relevant cost.

- The **relevant cost of a scarce resource** is the sum of the contribution/incremental profit forgone from the next-best opportunity for using the scarce resource and the variable cost of the scarce resource.

- There are a number of **assumptions** typically made in relevant costing.

- **Non-quantifiable factors** should **always be considered** alongside the quantitative data in a decision.

Quick Quiz

1   Tick the correct box for each of these types of cost.

	Relevant cost	Non-relevant cost
Incremental cost	☐	☐
Sunk cost	☐	☐
Committed cost	☐	☐

2   An attributable fixed cost is never a relevant cost. *True or false*?

3   The total relevant cost of a scarce resource is equal to the sum of the variable cost of the scarce resource and

   A   the price that the resource would sell for in the open market
   B   the fixed cost absorbed by a unit of the scarce resource
   C   the contribution forgone from the next-best opportunity for using the scarce resource
   D   the price that would have to be paid to replace the scarce resource

4   *Fill in the boxes in the diagram below about determining the relevant cost of materials.*

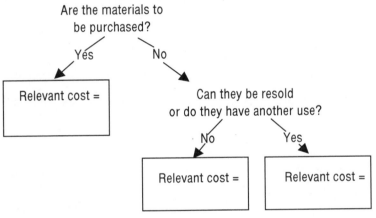

5   Which of the following is not an assumption typically made in relevant costing?

   A   Cost behaviour patterns are known.
   B   The amount of fixed costs, unit variable costs, sales prices and sales demand are known with certainty.
   C   The objective of decision making in the short run is to maximise satisfaction.
   D   There is no scarcity of resources.

6   What are the six steps in the decision-making process?

   Step 1   ....
   Step 2   ....
   Step 3   ....
   Step 4   ....
   Step 5   ....
   Step 6   ....

7   We detailed 12 non-quantifiable factors in decision making. List ten of them.

8   *Choose the correct words from those highlighted.*

Opportunity cost is the **value/cost** of a **benefit/cost** which is **sacrificed/purchased** when one course of action is chosen, in preference to an alternative. The opportunity cost is represented by the forgone **potential/expected/net realisable value** benefit from the **best/worst** rejected course of action.

Answers to Quick Quiz

1   Relevant; non-relevant; non-relevant

2   False. It is relevant to a decision because it is a fixed cost that would be affected by the decision being taken.

3   C. It is a common mistake to forget to include the opportunity cost.

4
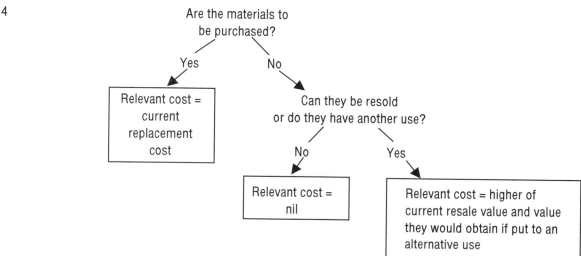

5   D. This is *not* an assumption in relevant costing.

6   **Step 1**   Identify objectives

Step 2   Search for alternative courses of action

Step 3   Collect data about the alternative courses of action

Step 4   Select the appropriate course of action

Step 5   Implement the decision

Step 6   Compare actual and planned outcomes and take any necessary corrective action if the planned results have not been achieved

7   Here are all 12.

- The availability of cash
- Inflation
- Employees
- Customers

- Competitors
- Timing factors
- Suppliers
- Feasibility

- Flexibility and internal control
- Unquantified opportunity costs
- Political pressures
- Legal constraints

8   Opportunity cost is the value of a benefit which is sacrificed when one course of action is chosen, in preference to an alternative. The opportunity cost is represented by the forgone potential benefit from the best rejected course of action.

Now try the questions below from the Exam Question Bank

Number	Level	Marks	Time
Q2	Examination	25	45 mins

BPP
LEARNING MEDIA

Short-term decisions

Introduction

In this chapter we will be continuing our study of relevant cash flows and short-term decision making.

Sections 1 to 7 cover a **range of short-term decision-making scenarios**. Any scenario you encounter in the exam might not fall neatly into one of the categories described in this chapter. It might comprise a number of features from more than one scenario (for example an accept/reject decision might be linked with a make or buy decision) and/or a different type of scenario might be presented. Whatever the scenario, however, you simply need to take account of the relevant cash flows of the decision under consideration.

Take note of the advice we give on presentation and workings. In an exam, careful layout can earn you valuable marks.

We end in **Section 8** with a topic that you covered briefly at Certificate level, that of **joint cost allocation**. We look at the methods of allocation and then move on to **joint cost decisions**.

Some of the topics in this chapter have appeared in the exams under the current syllabus. These include make or buy decisions and joint costs.

However, all of the scenarios here are equally valid for examination so ensure you read and understand them!

Topic list	Learning outcomes	Syllabus references	Ability required
1 Acceptance/rejection of contracts	A(i)	A(1), (2)	Analysis
2 Minimum pricing	A(i)	A(1), (2)	Analysis
3 Extra shift decisions and overtime	A(i)	A(1), (2)	Analysis
4 Make or buy decisions	A(i)	A(1), (2)	Analysis
5 Either/or problems	A(i)	A(1), (2)	Analysis
6 Shutdown problems	A(i)	A(1), (2)	Analysis
7 Choosing between options	A(i)	A(1), (2)	Analysis
8 Allocation of joint costs	A(v)	A(5)	Comprehension

1 Acceptance/rejection of contracts

FAST FORWARD

In general terms, a **contract** will probably be **accepted** if it **increases contribution** and profit, and rejected if it reduces profit.

If an organisation has **spare capacity** (which means that it would *not* have to turn away existing business), a 'special' (one-off) contract (which is normally (in the exam) at a price below the normal price of the product) should be **accepted if the price offered makes some contribution to fixed costs and profit**. In other words, the variable cost of the contract needs to be less than the price offered. Fixed costs are irrelevant to such a decision since they will be incurred regardless of whether or not the contract is accepted. Additional fixed costs incurred as a result of accepting the contract must be taken into account, however.

FAST FORWARD

If an organisation **does not have sufficient spare capacity, existing business** should only be **turned away if the contribution from the contract is greater than the contribution from the business which must be sacrificed.**

1.1 Example: accepting or rejecting contracts

HP makes a single product which sells for $20, and for which there is great demand. It has a variable cost of $12, made up as follows.

	$
Direct material	4
Direct labour (2 hrs)	6
Variable overhead	2
	12

The labour force is currently working at full capacity producing a product that earns a contribution of $4 per labour hour. A customer has approached the company with a request for the manufacture of a special contract for which he is willing to pay $5,500. The costs of the contract would be $2,000 for direct materials, and 500 labour hours will be required.

Decide whether the contract should be accepted.

Solution

(a) The labour force is working at full capacity. By accepting the contract, work would have to be diverted away from the standard product, and contribution will be lost, that is, there is an **opportunity cost** of accepting the new contract, which is the contribution forgone by being unable to make the standard product.

(b) Direct labour pay costs $3 per hour, but it is also usually assumed that variable production overhead varies with hours worked, and must therefore be spent in addition to the wages cost of the 500 hours.

(c)

	$	$
Value of contract		5,500
Cost of contract		
Direct materials	2,000	
Direct labour (500 hrs × $3)	1,500	
Variable overhead (500 hrs × $1)	500	
Opportunity cost (500 hrs × $4) (contribution forgone)	2,000	
Relevant cost of the contract		6,000
Loss incurred by accepting the contract		(500)

Although accepting the contract would earn a contribution of $1,500 ($5,500 – $4,000), the lost production of the standard product would reduce contribution earned elsewhere by $2,000 and so the contract should not be accepted.

Other considerations must also be taken into account, however.

(a)   Will **relationships with existing customers**, or prices that can be commanded in the market, be affected if the contract is accepted?

(b)   As a loss leader, could it create **further business opportunities**?

(c)   Should existing business be turned away in order to fulfil a one-off enquiry or could a **long-term contract** be established?

Question
Accept or reject

Learning outcome: A(i)

A company has been making a machine to order for a customer, but the customer has since gone into liquidation, and there is no prospect that any money will be obtained from the winding up of the company.

Costs incurred to date in manufacturing the machine are $50,000 and progress payments of $15,000 had been received from the customer prior to the liquidation.

The sales department has found another company willing to buy the machine for $34,000 once it has been completed.

To complete the work, the following costs would be incurred.

(a)   Materials: these have been bought at a cost of $6,000. They have no other use, and if the machine is not finished, they would be sold for scrap for $2,000.

(b)   Further labour costs would be $8,000. Labour is in short supply, and if the machine is not finished, the work force would be switched to another job, which would earn $30,000 in revenue, and incur direct costs of $12,000 and absorbed (fixed) overhead of $8,000.

(c)   Consultancy fees $4,000. If the work is not completed, the consultant's contract would be cancelled at a cost of $1,500.

(d)   General overheads of $8,000 would be added to the cost of the additional work.

The new customer's offer should be accepted. *True or false?*

Answer

The offer should be accepted and so the statement is true.

(a)   Costs incurred in the past, or revenue received in the past are not relevant because they cannot affect a decision about what is best for the future. **Costs incurred to date of $50,000** and **revenue received** of $15,000 are 'water under the bridge' and should be **ignored**.

(b)   Similarly, the **price paid in the past for the materials** is **irrelevant**. The only relevant cost of materials affecting the decision is the opportunity cost of the revenue from scrap which would be forgone – $2,000.

(c) **Labour costs**

	$
Labour costs required to complete work	8,000
Opportunity costs: contribution forgone by losing	
other work $(30,000 – 12,000)	18,000
Relevant cost of labour	26,000

(d) The **incremental cost of consultancy from completing the work** is $2,500.

	$
Cost of completing work	4,000
Cost of cancelling contract	1,500
Incremental cost of completing work	2,500

(e) **Absorbed overhead** is a notional accounting cost and should be **ignored**. **Actual overhead incurred** is the only overhead cost to **consider**. **General overhead** costs (and the absorbed overhead of the alternative work for the labour force) should be **ignored**.

(f) **Relevant costs** may be summarised as follows.

	$	$
Revenue from completing work		34,000
Relevant costs		
Materials: opportunity cost	2,000	
Labour: basic pay	8,000	
opportunity cost	18,000	
Incremental cost of consultant	2,500	
		30,500
Extra profit to be earned by accepting the completion order		3,500

2 Minimum pricing

 FAST FORWARD

> The **minimum price** for a one-off product or service contract is its total relevant costs: this is the price at which the company would make no incremental profit and no incremental loss from undertaking the work, but would just achieve an incremental cost breakeven point.

The following example will illustrate the technique.

2.1 Example: minimum price using an opportunity cost approach

Minimax has just completed production of an item of special equipment for a customer, only to be notified that this customer has now gone into liquidation.

After much effort, the sales manager has been able to interest a potential buyer who might buy the machine if certain conversion work could first be carried out.

(a) The sales price of the machine to the original buyer had been fixed at $138,600 and had included an estimated normal profit mark-up of 10% on total costs. The costs incurred in the manufacture of the machine were as follows.

	$
Direct materials	49,000
Direct labour	36,000
Variable overhead	9,000
Fixed production overhead	24,000
Fixed sales and distribution overhead	8,000
	126,000

(b)   If the machine is converted, the production manager estimates that the cost of the extra work required would be as follows.

Direct materials (at cost) $9,600
Direct labour
  Department X: 6 workers for 4 weeks at $210 per worker per week
  Department Y: 2 workers for 4 weeks at $160 per worker per week

(c)   Variable overhead would be 20% of direct labour cost, and fixed production overhead would be absorbed as follows.

Department X: 83.33% of direct labour cost
Department Y: 25% of direct labour cost

(d)   Additional information is available as follows.

    (i)   In the original machine, there are three types of material.

        (1)   Type A could be sold for scrap for $8,000.

        (2)   Type B could be sold for scrap for $2,400 but it would take 120 hours of casual labour paid at $3.50 per hour to put it into a condition in which it would be suitable for sale.

        (3)   Type C would need to be scrapped, at a cost to Minimax of $1,100.

    (ii)   The direct materials required for the conversion are already in inventory. If not needed for the conversion they would be used in the production of another machine in place of materials that would otherwise need to be purchased, and that would currently cost $8,800.

    (iii)   The conversion work would be carried out in two departments, X and Y. Department X is currently extremely busy and working at full capacity; it is estimated that its contribution to fixed overhead and profits is $2.50 per $1 of labour.

Department Y, on the other hand, is short of work but for organisational reasons its labour force, which at the moment has a workload of only 40% of its standard capacity, cannot be reduced below its current level of eight employees, all of whom are paid a wage of $160 per week.

    (iv)   The designs and specifications of the original machine could be sold to an overseas customer for $4,500 if the machine is scrapped.

    (v)   If conversion work is undertaken, a temporary supervisor would need to be employed for four weeks at a total cost of $1,500. It is normal company practice to charge supervision costs to fixed overhead.

    (vi)   The original customer has already paid a non-returnable deposit to Minimax of 12.5% of the selling price.

Required

Calculate the minimum price that Minimax should accept from the new customer for the converted machine. Explain clearly how you have reached this figure.

Solution

The minimum price is the price which reflects the relevant costs (opportunity costs) of the work. These are established as follows.

(a)   **Past costs are not relevant**, and the $126,000 of cost incurred should be excluded from the minimum price calculation. It is necessary, however, to consider the alternative use of the direct materials which would be forgone if the conversion work is carried out.

	$
Type A Revenue from sales as scrap (note (i))	8,000
Type B Revenue from sales as scrap, minus the additional cash costs necessary to to prepare it for sale ($2,400 − (120 × $3.50)) (note (i))	1,980
Type C Cost of disposal if the machine is not converted (a negative opportunity cost) (note (ii)) Total opportunity cost of materials types A, B and C	(1,100) 8,880

By agreeing to the conversion of the machine, Minimax would therefore lose a net revenue of $8,880 from the alternative use of these materials.

Notes

(i)   Scrap sales would be lost if the conversion work goes ahead.

(ii)   These costs would be incurred unless the work goes ahead.

(b)   The cost of additional **direct materials for conversion** is $9,600, but this is an historical cost. The relevant cost of these materials is the **$8,800** which would be spent on new purchases if the conversion is carried out. If the conversion work goes ahead, the materials held would be unavailable for production of the other machine mentioned in item (d)(ii) of the question and so the extra purchases of $8,800 would then be needed.

(c)   **Direct labour** in departments X and Y is a fixed cost and the labour force will be paid regardless of the work they do or do not do. The cost of labour for conversion in **department Y is not a relevant cost** because the work could be done without any extra cost to the company.

In **department X**, however, acceptance of the conversion work would oblige the company to divert production from other profitable jobs. The minimum contribution required from using department X labour must be sufficient to cover the cost of the labour and variable overheads and then make an additional $2.50 in contribution per direct labour hour.

Department X: costs for direct labour hours spent on conversion

6 workers × 4 weeks × $210 = $5,040

Variable overhead cost $5,040 × 20% = $1,008

Contribution forgone by diverting labour from other work
  $2.50 per $1 of labour cost = $5,040 × 250% = $12,600

(d)   **Variable overheads** in department Y are **relevant** costs because they will only be incurred if production work is carried out. (It is assumed that if the workforce is idle, no variable overheads would be incurred.)

Department Y   20% of (2 workers × 4 weeks × $160) = $256

(e)   If the machine is converted, the company cannot sell the **designs and specifications** to the overseas company. $4,500 is a **relevant** (opportunity) cost of accepting the conversion order.

(f)   **Fixed overheads**, being mainly unchanged regardless of what the company decides to do, should be ignored because they are **not relevant** (incremental) costs. The additional cost of **supervision** should, however, be included as a **relevant** cost of the order because the $1,500 will not be spent unless the conversion work is done.

(g) The **non-refundable deposit** received should be **ignored** and should not be deducted in the calculation of the minimum price. Just as costs incurred in the past are not relevant to a current decision about what to do in the future, revenues collected in the past are also irrelevant.

Estimate of minimum price for the converted machine

	$	$
Opportunity cost of using the direct materials types A, B and C		8,880
Opportunity cost of additional materials for conversion		8,800
Opportunity cost of work in department X		
Labour	5,040	
Variable overhead	1,008	
Contribution forgone	12,600	
		18,648
Opportunity cost: sale of designs and specifications		4,500
Incremental costs		
Variable production overheads in department Y		256
Fixed production overheads (additional supervision)		1,500
Minimum price		42,584

Exam focus point

Relevant costing is a highly-examinable topic. One of the 25-mark Section C questions in the pilot paper required you to calculate, for 12 marks, the lowest cost estimate (on a relevant cost basis) that could be used for a quotation for a one-off order, and to give reasons for the values used in the estimate. In the May 2005 exam, the relevant cost of a contract had to be calculated, and reasons given both for values included and costs excluded. This was worth ten marks.

3 Extra shift decisions and overtime

Extra shift decisions are another type of decision problem. They are concerned with whether or not it is worth opening up an extra shift for operations.

FAST FORWARD

The decision to work an **extra shift** should be taken on the basis of whether the costs of the shift are exceeded by the benefits to be obtained.

Qualitative factors in extra shift decisions include the following.

(a) **Would the work force be willing** to work the shift hours, and if so, what overtime or shift work premium over their basic pay might they expect to receive?

(b) **Do extra hours have to be worked just to remain competitive**? Banks might decide to open on Saturdays just to match what competitors are doing and so keep customers.

(c) Would extra hours result in **more sales revenue, or would there merely be a change in the demand pattern**? For example, if a shop were trying to decide whether to open on Sundays, one consideration would be whether the customers it would get on Sunday would simply be customers who would otherwise have done their shopping on another day of the week instead, or whether they would be additional customers.

When a business expands, the management is often faced with the problems of whether to acquire larger premises and more plant and machinery and whether to persuade existing personnel to work longer hours (on an overtime basis) or to engage extra staff who would use the existing equipment but at a different time (on a shift basis).

If the management decide to **incur additional expenditure on premises** and plant, that expenditure is a **fixed cost**. It will therefore be necessary to determine how much additional contribution will be required from the anticipated increased production to cover the extra fixed cost.

If it is decided to use the existing non-current assets, but for a longer period each day, the choice of shift working or overtime will also involve a marginal costing consideration.

(a)   If **overtime** is selected, the **direct wages cost per unit produced will be increased** because the wages paid to workers on overtime are a basic rate plus an overtime bonus.

(b)   If the management opt for **shift working** the shift premium may not be as expensive as the overtime premium so the **direct wages cost may be relatively lower**. On the other hand, there may be **an increase in fixed (or semi-fixed) costs** such as lighting, heating and canteen facilities.

4 Make or buy decisions

Exam focus point

A short two-mark Section A question covering a make-or-buy decision appeared in the May 2006 exam.

A make or buy problem involves a decision by an organisation about whether it should make a product or carry out an activity with its own internal resources, or whether it should pay another organisation to make the product or carry out the activity. Examples include whether a company should manufacture its own components, or else buy the components from an outside supplier.

The **'make' option** should give management **more direct control** over the work, but the **'buy' option** often has the benefit that the external organisation has a **specialist skill and expertise** in the work. Make or buy decisions should certainly not be based exclusively on cost considerations.

(a)   How can spare capacity freed up by subcontracting be used most profitably?

(b)   Could the decision to use an outside supplier cause an industrial dispute?

(c)   Would the subcontractor be reliable with delivery times and product quality?

(d)   Does the company wish to be flexible and maintain better control over operations by making everything itself?

FAST FORWARD

If an organisation has the freedom of choice about whether to **make internally or buy externally and has no scarce resources** that put a restriction on what it can do itself, the relevant costs for the decision will be the differential costs between the two options.

The **variable cost of buying** is likely to be **higher than the variable cost of making in-house**, but **savings in directly attributable fixed costs by using an outside supplier also need to be considered.**

4.1 Example: make or buy

An organisation makes four components, W, X, Y and Z, for which costs in the forthcoming year are expected to be as follows.

	W	X	Y	Z
Production (units)	1,000	2,000	4,000	3,000
Unit marginal costs	$	$	$	$
Direct materials	4	5	2	4
Direct labour	8	9	4	6
Variable production overheads	2	3	1	2
	14	17	7	12

Directly attributable fixed costs per annum and committed fixed costs are as follows.

	$
Incurred as a direct consequence of making W	1,000
Incurred as a direct consequence of making X	5,000
Incurred as a direct consequence of making Y	6,000
Incurred as a direct consequence of making Z	8,000
Other fixed costs (committed)	30,000
	50,000

A subcontractor can supply units of W, X, Y and Z for $12, $21, $10 and $14 respectively.

Required

Decide whether the organisation should make or buy the components.

Solution and discussion

(a) The relevant costs are the differential costs between making and buying, and they consist of differences in unit variable costs plus differences in directly attributable fixed costs. Subcontracting will result in some fixed cost savings.

	W	X	Y	Z
	$	$	$	$
Unit variable cost of making	14	17	7	12
Unit variable cost of buying	12	21	10	14
	$(2)	$4	$3	$2
Annual requirements (units)	1,000	2,000	4,000	3,000
Extra variable cost of buying (per annum)	(2,000)	8,000	12,000	6,000
Fixed costs saved by buying	1,000	5,000	6,000	8,000
Extra total cost of buying	(3,000)	3,000	6,000	(2,000)

(b) The company would save $3,000 pa by subcontracting component W (where the purchase cost would be less than the marginal cost per unit to make internally) and would save $2,000 pa by subcontracting component Z (because of the saving in fixed costs of $8,000).

(c) Important **further considerations** would be as follows.

(i) If components W and Z are subcontracted, the company will have spare capacity. How should that **spare capacity be profitably used**? Are there **hidden benefits** to be obtained from subcontracting? Would the company's workforce resent the loss of work to an outside subcontractor, and might such a decision cause an **industrial dispute**?

(ii) Would the subcontractor be **reliable with delivery times**, and would he supply components of the same **quality** as those manufactured internally?

(iii) Does the company wish to be **flexible** and **maintain better control** over operations by making everything itself?

(iv) Are the **estimates** of fixed cost savings **reliable**? In the case of product W, buying is clearly cheaper than making in-house. In the case of product Z, the decision to buy rather than make would only be financially beneficial if the fixed cost savings of $8,000 could really be 'delivered' by management

5 Either/or problems

The next example shows you how to lay out an answer to the more complicated type of relevant costs question that you could encounter in Paper 2.

5.1 Example: do now or do later?

MM currently carries out Process B the output from which can be sold for $20 per unit and has variable unit costs of $7.50 per unit. Process B has directly attributable fixed operating costs of $40,000 per annum. MM also carries out Process C by using equipment that has running costs of $25,000 per annum. The equipment could be sold *now* for $50,000 (but this would incur dismantling costs of $7,500) or in one year's time for $45,000 with dismantling costs of $8,750.

Process B could be adapted so that it incorporated Process C.

(a)   The existing Process B machinery would have to be removed, either now at a dismantling cost of $12,500 and with the sale of the machinery for $100,000, or in one year's time for $75,000 with dismantling costs of $13,750.

(b)   Alternative Process B machinery would have to be leased. This would cost $10,000 per annum and have annual fixed running costs of $30,000.

The existing Process B machinery originally cost $250,000 when bought five years ago. It is being depreciated at 10% per annum.

Required

Prepare an analysis on an incremental opportunity cost basis to decide on financial grounds whether to adopt Process B immediately or to delay it for one year. *Ignore the time value of money.*

Solution

 FAST FORWARD

The best approach to a complex **either/or problem** is to draw up a three-column table with columns for the first option (say, adapt now) and the second (say, adapt later), and a third column for the differences between the options (Column 1 minus Column 2).

	Adapt Now $	Adapt in one year $	Net (savings) /costs $
Savings			
Sale of Process C equipment	(50,000)	(45,000)	(5,000)
Sale of Process B machinery	(100,000)	(75,000)	(25,000)
Costs			
Fixed operating costs	0	40,000	(40,000)
Removal of Process B machinery	12,500	13,750	(1,250)
Process C – running costs	0	25,000	(25,000)
Process C – dismantling costs	7,500	8,750	(1,250)
Leased Process B equipment running costs	30,000	0	30,000
Leasing costs	10,000	0	10,000
Net (savings) less costs			(57,500)

Conclusion. Adapting now will bring savings of $57,500 more than adapting in one year.

There are lessons to be learned here about extracting information from complex Paper 2 questions. Note the following points.

(a)   You should do **savings and costs separately** and put **one type in brackets** (it doesn't matter which way round you do this as long as you are consistent within the question: we have put savings in brackets in keeping with the accounting convention that they are credits). This is important because it is easy to get the signs wrong when you come to work out the differences.

(b)   Subtract column 2 from column 1 taking **care with the minus signs**. For instance:

$$-50,000 - (-45,000) = -5,000$$

(c)   Adapting now means that the fixed operating costs of $40,000 will not be incurred so a **nought** goes in the Now column. Adapting in one year means that fixed operating costs of $40,000 will have to be paid for another year. The net benefit of adapting now is therefore a saving of $40,000.

(d)   There are some **red herrings** in the information given. Unit selling prices and costs are not relevant, since they do not change, whenever Process B is adapted. Original cost and depreciation are not relevant because they are not future cash flows.

6 Shutdown problems

FAST FORWARD

Non-quantifiable factors in shutdown problems include the impact on employees, customers, competitors and suppliers.

Decisions to be made in shutdown or discontinuance problems

- Whether or not to close down a product line, department or other activity.
- If the decision is to shut down, whether the closure should be permanent or temporary.
- If there is a choice about the timing of the closure, when should it take place.

Read our four step guide method in 6.1 when you come to work through these decisions.

6.1 Financial considerations

The basic method is to use short-run relevant costs to calculate contributions and profits or losses.

1   Calculate what is earned by the process at present (perhaps in comparison with others).

2   Calculate what will be the financial consequences of closing down (selling machines, redundancy costs etc).

3   Compare the results and act accordingly.

4   Bear in mind that some fixed costs may no longer be incurred if the decision is to shut down and they are therefore relevant to the decision.

Bear these in mind as you read through the example below.

6.2 Example: adding or deleting products

An organisation manufactures three products, Pawns, Rooks and Bishops. The present net annual income from these is:

	Pawns $	Rooks $	Bishops $	Total $
Sales	50,000	40,000	60,000	150,000
Variable costs	30,000	25,000	35,000	90,000
Contribution	20,000	15,000	25,000	60,000
Fixed costs	17,000	18,000	20,000	55,000
Profit/loss	3,000	(3,000)	5,000	5,000

The organisation is concerned about its poor profit performance, and is considering whether or not to cease selling Rooks. It is felt that selling prices cannot be raised or reduced without adversely affecting net income. $5,000 of the fixed costs of Rooks are direct fixed costs which would be saved if production ceased. All other fixed costs, it is considered, would remain the same.

Solution

By stopping production of Rooks, the consequences would be a $10,000 fall in profits:

	$
Loss of contribution	(15,000)
Savings in fixed costs	5,000
Incremental loss	(10,000)

Suppose, however, it were possible to use the resources realised by stopping production of Rooks and switch to producing a new item, Crowners, which would sell for $50,000 and incur variable costs of $30,000 and extra direct fixed costs of $6,000. A new decision is now required:

	Rooks	Crowners
	$	$
Sales	40,000	50,000
Less variable costs	25,000	30,000
	15,000	20,000
Less direct fixed costs	5,000	6,000
Contribution to shared fixed costs and profit	10,000	14,000

It would be more profitable to shut down production of Rooks and switch resources to making Crowners, in order to boost profits by $4,000 to $9,000.

6.3 Non-quantifiable considerations

As usual the decision is not merely a matter of choosing the best financial option.

(a) A product may be retained if it is providing a contribution, albeit a small one. Retaining a wide range of **low volume/low contribution products** would add to the **complexity** and hence costs of manufacture, however, but very little to overall profit. Low volume/low contribution products should therefore be examined on a regular basis.

(b) The **effect on demand for other products** if a particular product is no longer produced should be taken into account.

(c) The extent to which demand for **other products** (existing or new) can expand to **use** the **capacity** vacated by the product being deleted is an issue.

(d) **Pricing policy**. Is the product a **loss leader?** Is the product in the introductory stage of its **life cycle** and consequently priced low to help it to become accepted and hence maximise its long-term market share **(penetration pricing).** (These are issues you will cover in Chapter 9.)

Question

Deleting products

Learning outcome: A(i)

A company's product range includes product F, on which the following data (relating to a year's production) are available.

	$
Revenue	200,000
Materials cost	157,000
Machine power cost	14,000
Overheads: type A	28,000
type B	56,000

Type A overheads would be avoided if production of product F ceased, but type B overheads would not be. Both types of overheads are absorbed in direct proportion to machine power cost, and that cost is a purely variable cost.

Production of product F should be ended. *True or false?*

Answer

Production of product F should continue and so the statement is false.

	$	$
Revenue		200,000
Less: materials cost	157,000	
machine power cost	14,000	
type A overheads	28,000	
		199,000
Contribution		1,000

Production of product F should be continued, because it makes a contribution of $1,000 a year.

6.4 Relative profitability

The relative profitability of products can be judged by **calculation** of their contribution to sales **(C/S) ratios**. Suppose an organisation produces three products A, B and C, and that production capacity is limited. If product A has a C/S ratio of 22%, product B a C/S ratio of 27% and product C a C/S ratio of 25%, given unlimited demand for the three products the organisation should concentrate on producing product B.

6.5 Example: shutdown decisions

You may consider by now that you understand the basic principles of selecting relevant cash flows for decision making and it may therefore be useful at this stage to test your understanding with a more advanced example. Attempt your own solution before reading on.

Ayeco, with a head office in Ayetown, has three manufacturing units. One is in Beetown, the second in Ceetown and the third in Deetown. The company manufactures and sells an air-conditioner under the brand-name of Ayecool at a price of $200. It is unable to utilise fully its manufacturing capacity.

Summarised income statements for the year are shown below.

	Beetown $'000	Ceetown $'000	Deetown $'000	Total $'000
Costs				
Direct materials	200	800	400	1,400
Direct wages	200	900	350	1,450
Production overhead: variable	50	300	150	500
fixed	200	600	300	1,100
Sub-total	650	2,600	1,200	4,450
Selling overhead: variable	25	200	100	325
fixed	75	250	150	475
Administration overhead	100	450	200	750
Sub-total	850	3,500	1,650	6,000
Head office costs	50	200	100	350
Total	900	3,700	1,750	6,350
Profit	100	300	250	650
Sales	1,000	4,000	2,000	7,000

The management of the company has to decide whether or not to renew the lease of the property at Beetown, which expires next year. The company has been offered an extension to the lease at an additional cost of $50,000 per annum. This situation concerning the lease has been known for some time, so the accountant has collected relevant information to aid the decision. It is estimated that the cost of closing down Beetown would be offset by the surplus obtained by the sale of plant, machinery and inventories.

If Ayeco does not renew the lease of the Beetown property it has two alternatives.

(a) Accept an offer from Zeeco, a competitor, to take over the manufacture and sales in the Beetown area and pay to Ayeco a commission of $3 for each unit sold.

(b) Transfer the output at present made in Beetown to either Ceetown or Deetown. Each of these units has sufficient plant capacity to undertake the Beetown output but additional costs in supervision, salaries, storage and maintenance would be incurred. These additional costs are estimated as amounting yearly to $250,000 at Ceetown and to $200,000 at Deetown.

  If the Beetown sales are transferred to either Ceetown or Deetown, it is estimated that additional transport costs would be incurred in delivering to customers in the region of Beetown, and that these would amount to $15 per unit and $20 per unit respectively.

Required

Present a statement to the board of directors of Ayeco to show the estimated annual profit which would arise from the following alternative courses of action.

(a) Continuing production at all three sites
(b) Closing down production at Beetown and accepting the offer from Zeeco
(c) Transferring Beetown sales to Ceetown
(d) Transferring Beetown sales to Deetown

Comment on your statement, indicating any problems which may arise from the various decisions which the board may decide to take.

Solution

The main difficulty in answering this question is to decide what happens to fixed cost expenditure if the Beetown factory is closed, and what would be the variable costs of production and sales at Ceetown or Deetown if work was transferred from Beetown.

Fixed costs

It should be assumed that the direct fixed costs of the Beetown factory will be saved when shutdown occurs. These costs will include rent, depreciation of machinery, salaries of administrative staff and so on and it is therefore probably correct to assume that savings on shutdown will include all fixed costs charged to Beetown with the exception of the apportioned head office costs.

Variable cost of production

The variable cost of production at Ceetown or Deetown is more tricky, because the variable cost/sales ratio and the contribution/sales ratio differs at each factory.

	Beetown	Ceetown	Deetown
	%	%	%
Direct materials/sales	20.0	20.0	20.0
Direct wages/sales	20.0	22.5	17.5
Variable production overhead/sales	5.0	7.5	7.5
Variable selling overhead/sales	2.5	5.0	5.0
Total variable costs/sales	47.5	55.0	50.0
Contribution/sales	52.5	45.0	50.0

Labour appears to be less efficient at Ceetown and more efficient at Deetown, but variable overheads are more costly at both Ceetown and Deetown than at Beetown. It is probably reasonably accurate to assume that the variable cost/sales ratio of work transferred from Beetown will change to the ratio which is current at the factory to which the work is transferred. Transport costs would then be added as an additional cost item.

Statement of estimated annual profit

Option 1 Continuing production at all three sites

	$
Profit before rent increase on lease	650,000
Increase in annual cost of lease	50,000
Revised estimate of annual profit	600,000

Option 2 Accepting the offer from Zeeco

	$	$
Current estimate of total profit		650,000
Less revenue lost from closing Beetown	(1,000,000)	
Direct costs saved at Beetown	850,000	
	(150,000)	
Commission from Zeeco* (5,000 × $3)	15,000	
Net loss from closure		(135,000)
Revised estimate of total profit		515,000

* Number of units = $1,000,000 ÷ $200 per unit = 5,000 units.

Option 3 Transfer work to Ceetown

	$	$	$
Current estimate of total profit			650,000
Direct costs saved by closing Beetown		850,000	
Extra costs at Ceetown			
Variable costs (55% of $1,000,000)	(550,000)		
Extra costs of supervision etc	(250,000)		
Extra costs of transport (5,000 units × $15)	(75,000)		
		(875,000)	
Net extra costs of transfer			(25,000)
Revised estimate of total profit			625,000

Option 4 Transfer work to Deetown

	$	$	$
Current estimate of total profit			650,000
Direct costs saved by closing Beetown		850,000	
Extra costs at Deetown			
Variable costs (50% of $1,000,000)	(500,000)		
Extra costs of supervision etc	(200,000)		
Extra costs of transport (5,000 units × $20)	(100,000)		
		(800,000)	
Net savings from transfer			50,000
Revised estimate of total profit			700,000

Conclusion. The preferred option should be to transfer production from Beetown to Deetown, since profits would rise to $700,000, and would be $75,000 higher than profits obtainable from the next most profitable option (option 3).

6.5.1 Comments on the example

The previous example illustrates how accounting information for decision making can often be presented in a concise form, without the need to reproduce a complete table of revenues, costs and profits for each option. You should study the presentation of the figures above, and note how they show only the relevant costs or benefits arising as a direct consequence of each decision option.

The eventual management decision may not be to transfer to Deetown, because other **non-quantifiable factors** might influence the final decision.

(a) Concern for employees at Beetown and the wish to avoid redundancies.

(b) Problems in recruiting additional staff at Deetown.

(c) The possibility that the extra workload at Deetown might reduce labour efficiency there, making costs of production higher than those estimated in the statement.

(d) Difficulties in assembling and organising a transport fleet might persuade management to reject options 3 and 4.

6.6 When to close

As well as being able to deal with 'whether to close' situations you may also be required to handle 'when to close' situations. This is similar to the 'do now or do later' example.

6.6.1 Example: when to close

Daisy currently publish, print and distribute a range of catalogues and instruction manuals. The management have now decided to discontinue printing and distribution and concentrate solely on publishing. Stem will print and distribute the range of catalogues and instruction manuals on behalf of Daisy commencing either at 30 June 20X0 or 30 November 20X0. Stem will receive $65,000 per month for a contract which will commence either at 30 June 20X0 or 30 November 20X0.

The results of Daisy for a typical month are as follows.

	Publishing	Printing	Distribution
	$'000	$'000	$'000
Salaries and wages	28.0	18.0	4.0
Materials and supplies	5.5	31.0	1.1
Occupancy costs	7.0	8.5	1.2
Depreciation	0.8	4.2	0.7

Other information has been gathered relating to the possible closure proposals.

(a) Two specialist staff from printing will be retained at their present salary of $1,500 each per month in order to fulfil a link function with Stem. One further staff member will be transferred to publishing to fill a staff vacancy through staff turnover, anticipated in July. This staff member will be paid at his present salary of $1,400 per month which is $100 more than that of the staff member who is expected to leave. On closure all other printing and distribution staff will be made redundant and paid an average of two months redundancy pay.

(b) The printing department has a supply of materials (already paid for) which cost $18,000 and which will be sold to Stem for $10,000 if closure takes place on 30 June 20X0. Otherwise the material will be used as part of the July 20X0 printing requirements. The distribution department has a contract to purchase pallets at a cost of $500 per month for July and August 20X0. A cancellation clause allows for non-delivery of the pallets for July and August for a one-off payment of $300. Non-delivery for August only will require a payment of $100. If the pallets are taken from the supplier, Stem has agreed to purchase them at a price of $380 for each month's supply which is available. Pallet costs are included in the distribution materials and supplies cost stated for a typical month.

(c) Company expenditure on apportioned occupancy costs to printing and distribution will be reduced by 15% per month if printing and distribution departments are closed. At present, 30% of printing and 25%

of distribution occupancy costs are directly attributable costs which are avoidable on closure, whilst the remainder are apportioned costs.

(d)   Closure of the printing and distribution departments will make it possible to sub-let part of the building for a monthly fee of $2,500 when space is available.

(e)   Printing plant and machinery has an estimated net book value of $48,000 at 30 June 20X0. It is anticipated that it will be sold at a loss of $21,000 on 30 June 20X0. If sold on 30 November 20X0 the prospective buyer will pay $25,000.

(f)   The net book value of distribution vehicles at 30 June 20X0 is estimated as $80,000. They could be sold to the original supplier at $48,000 on 30 June 20X0. The original supplier would purchase the vehicles on 30 November 20X0 for a price of $44,000.

Required

Using the above information, prepare a summary to show whether Daisy should close the printing and distribution departments on financial grounds on 30 June 20X0 or on 30 November 20X0. Explanatory notes and calculations should be shown.

Solution

		Handover 30.6.X0 $	Handover 30.11.X0 $	Net savings/ (costs) of 30.6.X0 handover $
Relevant inflows				
Inventory (W2)		10,000		10,000
Pallet sale (W3)		380		380
Rent	(5 × $2,500)	12,500		12,500
Non-current asset sales				
Printing		27,000	25,000	2,000
Distribution		48,000	44,000	4,000
Total inflows		97,880	69,000	28,880
Relevant outflows				
Salaries and wages (W1)		15,500	110,000	(94,500)
Materials and supplies (W2)			142,500	(142,500)
Pallets (W3)		600		600
Occupancy costs (W4)				
Apportioned		29,112	34,250	(5,138)
Direct			14,250	(14,250)
Stem fee	(5 × $65,000)	325,000		325,000
Total outflows		370,212	301,000	69,212
Net inflow/(outflow)		(272,332)	(232,000)	(40,332)

Conclusion. The operation should be kept open until 30.11.20X0.

Workings

1   *Salaries and wages*

	Printing $	Distribution $	Total $
Costs if 30.6.X0 handover			
2 × $1,500 × 5 months	15,000	–	15,000
$100 × 5 months		500	500
			15,500
Costs if 30.11.X0 handover			
5 months usual costs	90,000	20,000	110,000

2   *Inventory*

The $18,000 cost of production is a sunk cost from previous periods. Therefore only the income is recorded. Also, the $10,000 income could be seen as one of the opportunity costs of continuing production.

			$
Therefore materials costs are	printing:	($31,000 × 5 – $18,000) =	137,000
	distribution:	($1,100 × 5) =	5,500
			142,500

3   *Pallets*

The alternative flows can be estimated as follows.

Take both deliveries

	$
Payment (2 × $500) =	1,000
Resale (2 × $380) =	760
Net flow	240

Take one delivery (ie July)

	$
Payment	500
Cancellation fee (August)	100
	600
Sale to Stem	380
Net flow	220

Take no deliveries

Cancellation fee	$300

Only the July delivery should be taken.

4   *Site costs*

	Printing $	Distribution $	Total $
Total occupancy costs (5 months)	42,500	6,000	48,500
of which directly attributable (30%/25%)	(12,750)	(1,500)	(14,250)
∴ Apportioned costs	29,750	4,500	34,250
Reduction in apportioned costs (15%)	(4,463)	(675)	(5,138)
Apportioned costs after closure	25,287	3,825	29,112

6.6.2 Temporary closure

The decision whether to shut down temporarily should take into account the following factors.

(a)   The **impact on the organisation's other products** and the product in question
(b)   Problems of **recruitment** of skilled labour when production begins again
(c)   Possibility of **plant obsolescence**
(d)   Problems of closing down and **restarting production** in some industries
(e)   Expenditure on disconnection of services, start up costs and so on

If contribution is only just covering fixed costs but improved trading conditions in the future seem likely it may be worth continuing the business.

Attention!

> Be very careful when setting out any relevant cost evaluation. **Do not** incorporate in the same analysis both the incremental costs and revenues that would apply if the decision proceeded (such as continuing with a product) *and* the avoidable costs if it did not (deleting the product). This is an easy mistake to make. You should consider first a decision to continue with the product and then compare it with a decision to delete the product.

6.7 Idle production capacity

If an organisation does decide to shut down a factory, department, product line or other activity, it may well be faced with a decision about what to do with the resulting idle production capacity.

(a) **Marketing strategies** could be used to increase demand for existing products.

(b) **Idle plant and machinery could be moved to another department** or factory, thereby reducing expenditure on new plant and machinery and/or interest charges.

(c) **Special orders could be accepted**, providing that the contribution generated is either greater than any reduction in fixed overheads which would occur if the idle capacity was not used or greater than any increase in fixed overheads if the idle capacity were to be used.

(d) **Space could be sub-let** to a third party.

Such considerations are particularly important if the closure is only temporary.

7 Choosing between options

The **key point** in decision-making questions is that you **let the marker see** what you are doing. This is simply a matter of **layout and labelling**. Every examiner, in every subject, for every professional body, always complains about the layout and labelling of students' answers. Get wise to this!

In this section we look at an alternative choice type question, which is basically a matter of comparing relevant costs and revenues.

The example we have chosen is one where there is a strong temptation to just tap away on a calculator and write down the final answer. This will not earn you any marks if you happen to tap the wrong figure, because nobody will know what you did wrong. In other words the main issue in this section is the value of **good presentation.**

7.1 Example: options available

AA has three options for Machine A.

Option 1 Dispose of Machine A in one year's time for $8,750

Option 2 Modify Machine A now at a cost of $6,250. This choice is being considered in conjunction with another decision, Decision A.

Decision A would mean that production output would increase by 25,000 units per annum except in the first year when 25% of the production enhancement would be lost due to running in. Production units sell for $20 per unit and have variable costs of $7.50 per unit.

The modification will mean that Machine A can only be sold for $5,000 in one year's time. However, it will reduce the production enhancement loss from 25% to 15%.

Option 3 Modify Machine A now at a cost of $2,500, which will mean that the company does not have to hire an alternative machine at a cost of $7,500. This modification would mean that Machine A will have a disposal cost of $625 in one year's time.

Required

Determine what the company should do with Machine A. *Ignore the time value of money.*

Solution: easy marks if you're a prize winner

Here is how to lay out a **summary** of your answer that would instantly put you in the running for **Best Overall Answer**.

Summary final answer

	(Saving)/Cost	Reference
Option 1	$(8,750)	W1
Option 2	$(30,000)	W2
Option 3	$(4,375)	W3

Conclusion. Option 2 is clearly the best because it gives the highest revenue.

Solution: easy marks if you're keen to get on

Here, on the other hand, is how good **pass-standard** students should **lay out** the **workings** that markers would scrutinise if the overall answer happened not to be right.

Workings for Question X (a)

1   **Option 1**

The revenue from **Option 1** is given in the question: $8,750.

2   **Option 2**

	$
Reduction in impact of production losses(25,000 × (25-15)% × $(20 −7.50))	(31,250)
Modification (given)	6,250
Sales value after one year (given)	(5,000)
Saving	(30,000)

3   **Option 3**

	$
Modification (given)	2,500
Hire costs avoided (given)	(7,500)
Disposal cost (given)	625
Saving	(4,375)

Wording

The 'double negative' **wording of Option 2** may have confused you. The enhancement is 25,000 units × $12.50 contribution = $312,500. Decision A reduces this enhancement **by 25%** to $234,375. Use of machine A only reduces it **by 15%** to $265,625 and therefore *saves* $31,250.

7.2 The importance of showing workings

If the marker can **see** from your workings that you have **read the question**, extracted the **right information**, and had a good go at **using the techniques** that you should know about, having studied for this paper, there is a good chance that you will get through the exam quite comfortably.

(a)   **Number your workings** consecutively. You may end up with workings 1 to 50 if you are not quite sure how to proceed at the outset, and experiment with the numbers a bit, or just workings 1 to 3 if you sorted out exactly how to do the question from the start. It does not matter **how many** workings you do. Only **layout, labelling** and **cross-referencing** matter in the exam.

(b)   Always **label your workings** and tables with headings and sub-headings, and show units used ($, kg, units, etc). (Note the extent of the labelling in the workings shown above, in spite of the fact that most of the figures are given.)

(c)   As you go along, **do a summary** on a separate clean page of whatever you expect to be your **final figures** and **state your conclusion** if it is not immediately clear.

(d)   Without fail your summary **must be cross-referenced** to your **workings**, because you will get marks for sensible workings, even if the answer is wrong.

Attention!

Many of the decision scenarios covered in this chapter could be described as **cost/benefit comparisons** because you need to compare the costs and benefits associated with the decision in order to determine what action to take.

8 Allocation of joint costs

In your earlier studies you covered the techniques of process costing, which is the costing method which applies when goods or services are produced in a sequence of continuous processes. Here we look at the methods of accounting for **joint products** and **by-products** which arise as a result of a continuous process and the various decision problems that can occur.

8.1 Joint products and by-products

Key term

Joint products are defined in CIMA *Official Terminology* as 'Two or more products produced by the same process and separated in processing, each having a sufficiently high saleable value to merit recognition as a main product'.

FAST FORWARD

Features of joint products

(a)   They are produced in the same process.
(b)   They are indistinguishable from each other until the separation point.
(c)   They each have a substantial sales value (after further processing, if necessary).
(d)   They may require further processing after the separation point.

For example in the oil refining industry the following joint products all arise from the same process.

(a)   Diesel fuel
(b)   Petrol
(c)   Paraffin
(d)   Lubricants

Key term

A **by-product** is defined in CIMA *Official Terminology* as 'Output of some value produced incidentally in manufacturing something else (main product)'.

FAST FORWARD

A **by-product** is a product which is similarly produced at the same time and from the same common process as the 'main product' or joint products. The distinguishing feature of a by-product is its relatively low sales value in comparison to the main product. In the timber industry, for example, by-products include sawdust, small offcuts and bark.

What exactly distinguishes a joint product from a by-product?

The answer lies in management attitudes to their products, which in turn is reflected in the cost accounting system.

(a)   A **joint product** is regarded as an important saleable item, and so it should be **separately costed**. The profitability of each joint product should be assessed in the cost accounts.

(b)   A **by-product** is not important as a saleable item, and whatever revenue it earns is a 'bonus' for the organisation. It is not worth costing by-products separately, because of their relative insignificance. It is therefore equally irrelevant to consider a by-product's profitability. The only question is how to account for the 'bonus' net revenue that a by-product earns.

8.2 Problems in accounting for joint products

Joint products are not separately identifiable until a certain stage is reached in the processing operations. This stage is the **'split-off point'**, sometimes referred to as the **separation point**.

Costs incurred prior to this point of separation are **common or joint costs**, and these need to be allocated (apportioned) in some manner to each of the joint products. In the following sketched example, there are two different split-off points.

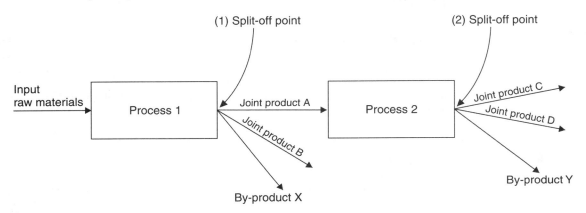

The special problems in accounting for joint products are basically of two different sorts.

(a)   How joint costs should be apportioned between products.

(b)   Whether it is more profitable to sell a joint product at one stage of processing, or to process the product further and sell it at a later stage. In the above diagram, product A has been processed further but product B has been sold at the split-off point.

We will return to the second problem later in this section. Let us for now consider the first problem.

8.3 Apportioning joint costs to joint products

The problem of costing for joint products concerns **joint costs**, that is those common processing costs shared between the units of eventual output up to their 'split-off point'. Some method needs to be devised for sharing the joint costs between the individual joint products for the following reasons.

(a)   **To put a value to inventory held at the period end** of each joint product for **financial reporting purposes** in particular, but also for management reports. For external reporting it is necessary that inventory valuation includes an apportionment of the common costs of production, as well as any directly attributable costs of further processing.

(b)   **To record the costs and therefore the profit from each joint product**. This is of **limited value** however, because the costs and therefore profit from one joint product are influenced by the share of costs assigned to the other joint products. Management decisions would be based on the apparent relative profitability of the products which has arisen due to the arbitrary apportionment of the joint costs.

(c)   Perhaps to assist in **pricing decisions**.

8.3.1 Some examples of the joint costs problem

(a)   How to spread the joint costs of oil refining between the joint products made (petrol, naphtha, kerosene and so on).

(b)   How to spread the joint costs of running the telephone network between telephone calls in peak rate times and cheap rate times, or between local calls and long-distance calls.

FAST FORWARD

Methods used to apportion joint costs to joint products

(a)   Physical measurement

(b)   Relative sales value apportionment method 1; sales value at split-off point

(c)   Relative sales value apportionment method 2; sales value of end product less further processing costs after split-off point

(d)   A weighted average method

Exam focus point

There were five marks available in the May 2005 exam for a discussion about the suitability of a particular apportionment method and the need to apportion joint costs. This illustrates the importance of studying the entire syllabus, as this is quite a small topic area but it appeared in a compulsory question.

The November 2006 exam included a two-mark MCQ question testing knowledge of further processing.

8.4 Dealing with joint costs: physical measurement

With physical measurement, the joint cost is apportioned to the joint products on the basis of the proportion that the output of each product bears by weight or volume to the total output. An example of this would be the case where two products, product 1 and product 2, incur joint costs to the point of separation of $3,000 and the output of each product is 600 tons and 1,200 tons respectively.

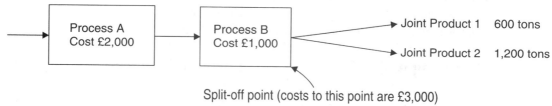

Split-off point (costs to this point are £3,000)

Product 1 sells for $4 per ton and product 2 for $2 per ton.

The division of the joint costs ($3,000) between product 1 and product 2 could be based on the tonnage of output.

	Product 1	Product 2	Total
Output	600 tons	1,200 tons	1,800 tons
Proportion of joint cost	$\frac{600}{1,800}$	$\frac{1,200}{1,800}$	
	$	$	$
Apportioned cost	1,000	2,000	3,000
Sales	2,400	2,400	4,800
Profit	1,400	400	1,800
Profit/sales ratio	58.3%	16.7%	37.5%

This method is unsuitable where the products separate during the processes into **different states**, for example where one product is a gas and another is a liquid. Furthermore, this method does not take into account the **relative income-earning potentials of the individual products**, with the result that one product might appear very profitable and another appear to be incurring losses.

8.5 Dealing with joint costs: sales value at split-off point

With relative sales value apportionment of joint cost, the cost is **apportioned according to the product's ability to produce income**. This method is most widely used because the assumption that some profit margin should be attained for all products under normal marketing conditions is satisfied. The joint cost is apportioned to each product in the proportion that the sales value of that product bears to the sales value of the total output from the particular processes concerned. Using the previous example where the sales price per ton is $4 for product 1 and $2 for product 2.

(a)   Joint costs of processes to split-off point $3,000
(b)   Sales value of product 1 at $4 per ton $2,400
(c)   Sales value of product 2 at $2 per ton $2,400

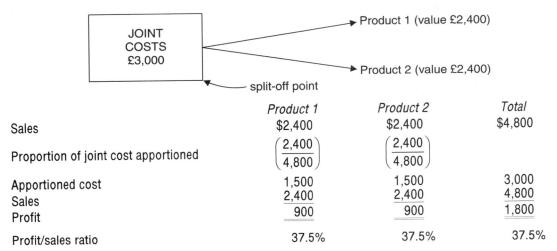

	Product 1	Product 2	Total
Sales	$2,400	$2,400	$4,800
Proportion of joint cost apportioned	$\left(\dfrac{2,400}{4,800}\right)$	$\left(\dfrac{2,400}{4,800}\right)$	
Apportioned cost	1,500	1,500	3,000
Sales	2,400	2,400	4,800
Profit	900	900	1,800
Profit/sales ratio	37.5%	37.5%	37.5%

A comparison of the different gross profit margins resulting from the application of the above methods for allocating joint costs will illustrate the greater acceptability of the relative sales value apportionment method. Physical measurement gives a higher profit margin to product 1, not necessarily because product 1 is highly profitable, but because it has been given a smaller share of joint costs.

8.6 Dealing with joint costs: sales value minus further processing costs

Joint products may have no known market value at the point of separation, because they need further separate processing to make them ready for sale. The allocation of joint costs should be accomplished as follows.

(a)   Ideally, by determining a **relative sales value at the split off point** for each product.

(b)   If a relative sales value cannot be found, a residual sales value at the split-off point can be determined.

(i)   Take the final sales value of each joint product
(ii)   Deduct the further processing costs for each product

This residual sales value is sometimes referred to as the **notional** or **proxy sales value** of a joint product.

8.6.1 Example: sales value minus further processing costs

JT has a factory where four products are originated in a common process.

During period 4, the costs of the common process were $16,000. Output was as follows.

	Units made	Units sold	Sales value per unit
Product P1	600		
Product Q1	400		
Product R	500	400	$7
Product S	600	450	$10

Products P1 and Q1 are further processed, separately, to make end-products P2 and Q2.

	Units processed	Units sold	Cost of further processing	Sales value per unit
Product P1/P2	600	600	$1,000	$10 (P2)
Product Q1/Q2	400	300	$2,500	$20 (Q2)

Required

Calculate the costs of each joint product and the profit from each of them in period 4. There was no inventory at the beginning of the period.

Solution

(a)   It is helpful to begin a solution to joint product problems with a diagram of the process.

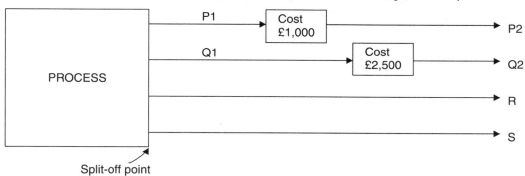

(b)   Next we calculate the notional sales values of P1 and Q1 at the split-off point.

	P2 $	Q2 $
Sales value of production	6,000	8,000
Less further processing costs	1,000	2,500
Notional sales value, P1, Q1	5,000 (P1)	5,500 (Q1)

(c)   Now we can apply sales values to apportion joint costs.

Joint product	Sales value of production $	%	Apportionment of joint costs $
P1	5,000	25	4,000
Q1	5,500	27 1/2	4,400
R	3,500	17 1/2	2,800
S	6,000	30	4,800
	20,000	100	16,000

(d)   We can now draw up the profit statement.

	P1/2	Q1/2	R	S	Total
	$	$	$	$	$
Joint costs	4,000	4,400	2,800	4,800	16,000
Further processing	1,000	2,500	–	–	3,500
Cost of production	5,000	6,900	2,800	4,800	19,500
Less inventory at period end	0	1,725	560	1,200	3,485
Cost of sales	5,000	5,175	2,240	3,600	16,015
Sales	6,000	6,000	2,800	4,500	19,300
Profit	1,000	825	560	900	3,285
Profit/sales ratio	17%	14%	20%	20%	17%

Question	Units method of splitting common costs

Learning outcome: A(v)

Refer back to the example above and fill in the blanks in the sentence below.

The profit for the period is $................ and the value of the inventory held at period end is $......... if joint costs are apportioned using the units method.

Answer

Learning outcome: A(v)

The correct answers are $3,091 and $3,291.

Joint product	Units produced		Apportionment of common costs
		%	$
P1	600	28.6	4,576
Q1	400	19.0	3,040
R	500	23.8	3,808
S	600	28.6	4,576
	2,100	100.0	16,000

Profit statement

	P1/2	Q1/2	R	S	Total
	$	$	$	$	$
Joint costs of production	4,576	3,040	3,808	4,576	16,000
Further processing	1,000	2,500	–	–	3,500
Cost of production	5,576	5,540	3,808	4,576	19,500
Less closing inventory	0	1,385	762	1,144	3,291
Cost of sales	5,576	4,155	3,046	3,432	16,209
Sales	6,000	6,000	2,800	4,500	19,300
Profit/(loss)	424	1,845	(246)	1,068	3,091
Profit/sales ratio	7%	31%	–	24%	16%

8.7 Dealing with joint costs: weighted average method

The weighted average method of joint cost apportionment is a development of the units method of apportionment. Since units of joint product may not be comparable in physical resemblance or physical weight (they may be gases, liquids or solids) units of each joint product may be multiplied by a weighting factor, and **'weighted units'** would provide a basis for apportioning the joint costs.

8.7.1 Example: weighted average method

MG manufactures four products which emerge from a joint processing operation. In April, the costs of the joint production process were as follows.

	$
Direct materials	24,000
Direct labour	2,000
	26,000

Production overheads are added using an absorption rate of 400% of direct labour costs. Output from the process during April was as follows.

Joint product	Output
D	600 litres
W	400 litres
F	400 kilograms
G	500 kilograms

Units of output of D, W, F and G are to be given weightings of 3, 5, 8 and 3 respectively for apportioning joint costs.

Required

Apportion the joint costs.

Solution

Total costs are $26,000 for direct costs plus $8,000 overhead. The costs would be $34,000, apportioned as follows.

Joint product	Output units	Weighting	Weighted units
D	600	3	1,800
W	400	5	2,000
F	400	8	3,200
G	500	3	1,500
			8,500

The costs are therefore apportioned at a rate of $34,000/8,500 = $4 per weighted unit.

Joint product	Apportionment of common cost
	$
D	7,200
W	8,000
F	12,800
G	6,000
	34,000

FAST FORWARD

You should be able to appreciate the **arbitrary nature of joint cost allocation**. The resulting product costs should never be used as a basis for decisions concerning process or product viability because the apparent relative profitability of the products has arisen due to the arbitrary apportionment of the joint costs.

8.8 The further processing decision

A different type of decision making problem with joint products occurs when there is a **choice between selling part-finished output or processing it further**. This decision problem is best explained by a simple example.

8.8.1 Example: further processing

An organisation manufactures two joint products, A and B. The costs of common processing are $15,000 per batch, and output per batch is 100 units of A and 150 units of B. The sales value of A at split-off point is $90 per unit, and the sales value of B is $60 per unit. An opportunity exists to process product A further, at an extra cost of $2,000 per batch, to produce product C. One unit of joint product A is sufficient to make one unit of C which has a sales value of $120 per unit.

Should the organisation sell product A, or should it process A and sell product C?

Solution

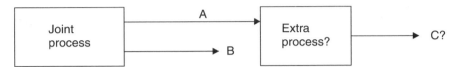

The problem is resolved on the basis that product C should be sold if the sales value of C minus its further processing costs exceeds the sales value of A.

	$
Sales value of C, per batch (100 × $120)	12,000
Sales value of A, per batch (100 × $90)	9,000
Incremental revenue from further processing	3,000
Further processing cost	2,000
Benefit from further processing in order to sell C	1,000 per batch

If the further processing cost had exceeded the incremental revenue from further processing, it would have been unprofitable to make and sell C. It is worth noting that the **apportionment of joint processing costs between A and B is irrelevant to the decision**, because the total extra profit from making C will be $1,000 per batch whichever method of apportionment is used.

FAST FORWARD

When there is a **choice between processing part-finished output further or selling it**, the further processing is worthwhile if the further processing cost is less than the incremental revenue gained from further processing.

Exam focus point

The further processing decision is the most important part of Section 8 and the area most likely to be examined. You must be able to apportion joint costs using the four methods illustrated, however – hence our full explanation and examples.

Question   **Joint products decision**

Learning outcome: A(v)

PCC produces two joint products, Pee and Cee, from the same process. Joint processing costs of $150,000 are incurred up to split-off point, when 100,000 units of Pee and 50,000 units of Cee are produced. The selling prices at split-off point are $1.25 per unit for Pee and $2.00 per unit for Cee.

The units of Pee could be processed further to produce 60,000 units of a new chemical, Peeplus, but at an extra fixed cost of $20,000 and variable cost of 30p per unit of input. The selling price of Peeplus would be $3.25 per unit.

Required

Choose the correct words from those highlighted.

The organisation **should convert/should not convert** Pee to Peeplus.

Answer

The correct answer is 'should convert'.

The only relevant costs/incomes are those which compare selling Pee against selling Peeplus. Every other cost is irrelevant: they will be incurred regardless of what the decision is.

		Pee			Peeplus
Selling price per unit		$1.25			$3.25
		$		$	$
Total sales		125,000			195,000
Post-separation processing costs	–		Fixed	20,000	
	–		Variable	30,000	50,000
Sales minus post-separation (further processing) costs		125,000			145,000

It is $20,000 more profitable to convert Pee into Peeplus.

Exam focus point

Five marks were available in one of the ten-mark compulsory questions of the May 2005 exam for evaluating the viability and determining the optimal solution of a further processing scenario.

8.9 Costing by-products

A by-product is a supplementary or secondary product (arising as the result of a process) whose **value is small relative to that of the principal product**. Nevertheless the by-product has some commercial value, and has to be accounted for.

FAST FORWARD

The usual method of **accounting for a by-product** is to deduct its net realisable value from the cost of production of the main product.

Question

Accounting for by-products

Learning outcome: A(v)

Randolph manufactures two joint products, J and K, in a common process. A by-product X is also produced. Data for the month of December 20X2 were as follows.

Opening inventory		nil	
Costs of processing	direct materials	$25,500	
	direct labour	$10,000	

Production overheads are absorbed at the rate of 300% of direct labour costs.

		Production Units	Sales Units
Output and sales consisted of:	product J	8,000	7,000
	product K	8,000	6,000
	by-product X	1,000	1,000

The sales value per unit of J, K and X is $4, $6 and $0.50 respectively. The net realisable value of the by-product is deducted from process costs before apportioning costs to each joint product. Costs of the common processing are apportioned between product J and product K on the basis of sales value of production.

Required

Fill in the blanks in the sentences below.

The profit for December 20X2 is $ .... The profit attributable to product J is $ ...., while that attributable to product K is $ ....

Answer

The correct answers are $12,000, $5,250 and $6,750.

The **sales value of production** was $80,000.

		$
Product J (8,000 × $4)		32,000 (40%)
Product K (8,000 × $6)		48,000 (60%)
		80,000

The **costs of production** were as follows.	$
Direct materials	25,500
Direct labour	10,000
Overhead (300% of $10,000)	30,000
	65,500
Less NRV of by-product (1,000 × 50p)	500
Net production costs	65,000

The **profit statement** would appear as follows (nil opening inventory).

		Product J		Product K	Total
		$		$	$
Production costs	(40%)	26,000	(60%)	39,000	65,000
Less closing inventory	(1,000 units)	3,250	(2,000 units)	9,750	13,000
Cost of sales		22,750		29,250	52,000
Sales	(7,000 units)	28,000	(6,000 units)	36,000	64,000
Profit		5,250		6,750	12,000

Question

Another joint products decision

Learning outcome: A(v)

Ruffage manufactures two products, T42 and 24T. These products are made jointly in process A, and then processed further, separately, with the manufacture of T42 completed in process B and 24T in process C. Costs and revenues for September were as follows.

2,000 tonnes of material (costing $36,000) were input to process A, 500 tonnes (costing $5,000) were added in process B and 1,000 tonnes (costing $8,000) were added in process C. Labour and overhead were $24,000 in process A, $20,000 in process B and $25,000 in process C.

Output from process A was 1,000 tonnes of part-finished T42 and 1,000 tonnes of part-finished 24T. At this stage in processing the sales value of T42 is $26 per tonne and of 24T is $39 per tonne. All completed output of T42 (1,500 tonnes) was sold in the month for $66,000 and all completed output of 24T (2,000 tonnes) was sold for $66,000.

Required

(a)   Calculate the profitability of each product in the month, assuming that joint costs in process A are apportioned using the following methods.

(i)   On a physical units basis
(ii)   On the basis of sales value at the point of separation

(b)   Comment on what these figures suggest about the following.

(i)   Whether either product makes losses and ought not to be manufactured

(ii)   Whether either product should be sold partially-finished as output from process A, instead of processed further in process B or C

Answer

(a)   (i)   **Units basis of apportionment**

	Product T42 $	Product 24T $	Total $
Process A costs (apportioned 1:1)	30,000	30,000	60,000
Process B costs	25,000	–	25,000
Process C costs	–	33,000	33,000
Total costs	55,000	63,000	118,000
Revenue	66,000	66,000	132,000
Profit	11,000	3,000	14,000

(ii)   **Sales revenue basis of apportionment**

	Product T42 $	Product 24T $	Total $
Process A costs (apportioned 26:39)	24,000	36,000	60,000
Process B costs	25,000		25,000
Process C costs	–	33,000	33,000
Total costs	49,000	69,000	118,000
Revenue	66,000	66,000	132,000
Profit	17,000	(3,000)	14,000

(b)   (i)   Product 24T makes a loss when the sales revenue basis of apportionment is used, but not when the units basis of apportionment is used. The difference between income statement is due simply to how the common costs in Process A are shared between the two products.

Although product 24T **makes a loss by one method**, it would be **wrong to conclude that it should not be made at all**. If the company continues to make T42, it has got to make 24T as well, at least in process A, since the products are output jointly from a common process. And if product 24T does **make some contribution** towards covering fixed overheads, it is **worth making and selling**, if no better alternative exists.

(ii)   In this situation, there is some **choice**. Product 24T can either be sold as part-finished output from process A, for $39 per tonne, or processed further in process C. The **relevant analysis** of this decision would be:

	$
Revenue from process C output	66,000
Revenue obtainable from sale of process A output (1,000 × 39)	39,000
Extra revenue from further processing	27,000
Costs of process C	33,000
Possible loss in process C	(6,000)

Not all of the $33,000 of process C costs might be **avoidable**. If there are some fixed and unavoidable costs charged to process C, there would be a smaller loss incurred by operating process C instead of selling part-finished product 24T. It might even be profitable to run process C, for example if avoidable costs were only $25,000, say, out of the $33,000 total costs for process C.

Even so, the possibility ought to be drawn to management's attention that it **might be more profitable to close down process C and sell product 24T in its part-complete form**. Neither method of cost apportionment that we used brings out this information for management's attention, and so both methods of costing are **inadequate** in this respect.

Chapter Roundup

- In general terms, a **contract** will probably be **accepted** if it **increases contribution** and profit, and rejected if it reduces profit.

- If an organisation **does not have sufficient spare capacity**, existing business should only be **turned away if the contribution from the contract is greater than the contribution from the business which must be sacrificed**.

- The **minimum price** for a one-off product or service contract is its total relevant costs: this is the price at which the company would make no incremental profit and no incremental loss from undertaking the work, but would just achieve an incremental cost breakeven point.

- The decision to work an **extra shift** should be taken on the basis of whether the costs of the shift are exceeded by the benefits to be obtained.

- If an organisation has the freedom of choice about whether to **make internally or buy externally and has no scarce resources** that put a restriction on what it can do itself, the relevant costs for the decision will be the differential costs between the two options.

- The best approach to a complex **either/or problem** is to draw up a three-column table with columns for the first option (say, adapt now) and the second (say, adapt later), and a third column for the differences between the options (Column 1 minus Column 2).

- **Non-quantifiable factors** in **shutdown problems** include the impact on employees, customers, competitors and suppliers.

- The **key point** in decision-making questions is that you **let the marker see** what you are doing. This is simply a matter of **layout and labelling**. Every examiner, in every subject, for every professional body, always complains about the layout and labelling of students' answers. Get wise to this!

- **Features of joint products**

    - They are produced in the same process.
    - They are indistinguishable from each other until the separation point.
    - They each have a substantial sales value (after further processing, if necessary).
    - They may require further processing after the separation point.

- A **by-product** is a product which is similarly produced at the same time and from the same common process as the 'main product' or joint products. The distinguishing feature of a by-product is its relatively low sales value in comparison to the main product. In the timber industry, for example, by-products include sawdust, small offcuts and bark.

Chapter Roundup (cont'd)

- Joint products are not separately identifiable until a certain stage is reached in the processing operations. This stage is the **'split-off point'**, sometimes referred to as the **separation point**.

- **Methods used to apportion joint costs to joint products**

  - Physical measurement

  - Relative sales value apportionment method 1; sales value at split-off point

  - Relative sales value apportionment method 2; sales value of end product less further processing costs after split-off point

  - A weighted average method

- You should be able to appreciate the **arbitrary nature of joint cost allocation**. The resulting product costs should never be used as a basis for decisions concerning process or product viability because the apparent relative profitability of the products has arisen due to the arbitrary apportionment of the joint costs.

- When there is a **choice between processing part-finished output further or selling it**, the further processing is worthwhile if the further processing cost is less than the incremental revenue gained from further processing.

- The usual method of **accounting for a by-product** is to deduct its net realisable value from the cost of production of the main product.

Quick Quiz

1   Fixed costs should never be taken into account in an accept/reject decision. *True or false?*

2   What are the relevant costs in a make or buy decision?

    A   The sum of the relevant costs of the two options
    B   The opportunity costs associated with the decision
    C   The differential costs between the two options
    D   The incremental costs of the two options

3   *Choose the correct words from those highlighted.*

In a situation where a company must sub-contract work to make up a shortfall in its own in-house capabilities, its total costs will be minimised if those units bought have the **lowest/highest** extra **variable/fixed** cost of **buying/making** per unit of scarce resource.

4   *Fill in the blank.*

An organisation produces four products for which there is unlimited demand. Production capacity is limited. The organisation should concentrate on producing the product with the .... C/S ratio.

5   Sunny plc manufactures both work and leisure clothing. The company is considering whether to cease production of leisure clothing. List the **costs, which are relevant** to the decision to cease production.

6   Joint cost allocations are essential for the purposes of determining relative product profitability. *True or false?*

7   When deciding, purely on financial grounds, whether or not to process a joint product further, the information required is:

(i)   the value of the joint process costs;
(ii)   the method of apportioning the joint costs between the joint products;
(iii) the sales value of the joint product at the separation point;
(iv)   the final sales value of the joint product;
(v)   the further processing cost of the joint product.

Which of the above statements are correct?

A   (i), (ii) and (iii) only
B   (iii), (iv) and (v) only
C   (iv) and (v) only
D   (i), (ii), (iv) and (v) only

8   *Choose the correct words from those highlighted.*

A joint product should be processed further if **post-separation/pre-separation** costs are **greater than/ less than** the **increase in revenue/additional fixed costs**.

9   *Fill in the blanks.*

The accounting treatment of a by-product usually consists of deducting the .... of the by-product from the .... of the main product.

Answers to Quick Quiz

1   False. Additional fixed costs incurred as a result of accepting the order must be taken into account.

2   C. You need to know the difference in cost between the two options.

3   lowest, variable, buying

4   highest

5   Those costs which will be saved if production of leisure clothing ceases (that is, all variable costs plus any fixed costs which are specific to producing and selling leisure clothing (such as advertising))

•   Any closure costs such as the cost of equipment disposal and staff redundancies

•   **Opportunity costs** such as the loss of any contribution which would have been earned from the continued manufacture and sale of leisure clothing

•   The **opportunity costs** of continuing to produce leisure clothing such as the potential contribution which could be earned from using the capacity released to produce work clothing (although these costs will only occur if work clothing production has capacity constraints)

Any fixed costs, which will continue whether or not leisure clothing ceases are not relevant.

6   False

7   B. Any costs incurred up to the point of separation are irrelevant.

8   post separation, less than, increase in revenue

9   net realisable value, cost of production

Number	Level	Marks	Time
Q3	Examination	25	45 mins

Now try the question below from the Exam Question Bank

Multi-product breakeven analysis

4

Introduction

This is the first of four chapters that looks at the **application of the analysis of total cost into its fixed and variable components.**

You will have **already encountered breakeven (or CVP) analysis** in your earlier studies so you should not be surprised by the terminology or basic techniques that you meet in this chapter. But in case your memory needs refreshing we have included a brief reminder of the material you covered at the beginning of the chapter, and a question on simple breakeven analysis. You could still be asked to carry out straightforward breakeven analysis in the exam so make sure that you are perfectly happy with the basic stuff before moving on to the higher-level Managerial material.

You should remember that one of the **major assumptions** underpinning breakeven analysis is that it can **only be applied to one product or to a constant (fixed proportions) mix of products.** So far you will only have studied single product breakeven analysis but as most organisations produce and sell a range of products we are going to look at what is known as multi-product breakeven analysis. We will see how to perform the various calculations you covered at Certificate level but for multiple products, as well as how to draw breakeven and P/V charts.

Multi-product breakeven analysis has been examined in Sections A and C of the exam paper. It has been examined in most sittings so far in a Section A question, and in May 2006 in a Section C question. That's not to say that one of the medium questions won't incorporate it, of course!

Topic list	Learning outcomes	Syllabus references	Ability required
1 Breakeven analysis in a multi-product environment	A(vii)	A(6)	Application
2 Breakeven point for multiple products	A(vii)	A(6)	Application
3 Contribution to sales (C/S) ratio for multiple products	A(vii)	A(6)	Application
4 Sales/product mix decisions	A(vii)	A(6)	Application
5 Target profits for multiple products	A(vii)	A(6)	Application
6 Margin of safety for multiple products	A(vii)	A(6)	Application
7 Multi-product breakeven charts	A(vii)	A(6)	Application
8 Further aspects of breakeven analysis	A(vii)	A(2),(6)	Application
9 Sensitivity analysis	A(vii), C(i),(ii)	A(6),C(2)	Application/Evaluation

Key term

Breakeven analysis or **cost-volume-profit analysis (CVP)** is 'The study of the effects on future profit of changes in fixed cost, variable cost, sales price, quantity and mix'.   (CIMA *Official Terminology*)

FAST FORWARD

You should have covered the basics of breakeven analysis in your earlier studies. Flick through the relevant chapters of the BPP Study Text or Passcards if your memory needs refreshing.

Knowledge brought forward from earlier studies

Breakeven analysis

- Contribution per unit = unit selling price – unit variable costs

- Profit = (sales volume × contribution per unit) – fixed costs

- Breakeven point   = activity level at which there is neither profit nor loss

$$= \frac{\text{total fixed costs}}{\text{contribution per unit}} = \frac{\text{contribution required to breakeven}}{\text{contribution per unit}}$$

- Contribution/sales (C/S) ratio = profit/volume (P/V) ratio = (contribution/sales) × 100%

- Sales revenue at breakeven point = fixed costs ÷ C/S ratio

- Margin of safety (in units)   = budgeted sales units – breakeven sales units

- Margin of safety (as %) $= \dfrac{\text{budgeted sales} - \text{breakeven sales}}{\text{budgeted sales}} \times 100\%$

- Sales volume to achieve a target profit $= \dfrac{\text{fixed cost} + \text{target profit}}{\text{contribution per unit}}$

- Assumptions
    - Can only apply to one product or constant mix
    - Fixed costs same in total and unit variable costs same at all levels of output
    - Sales prices constant at all levels of activity
    - Production = sales

Breakeven, contribution and P/V charts

- Breakeven chart   •   Contribution (contribution breakeven) chart

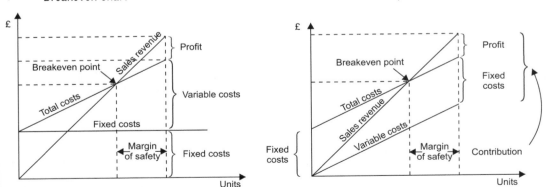

Knowledge brought forward from earlier studies (continued)

- Profit/volume (P/V) chart

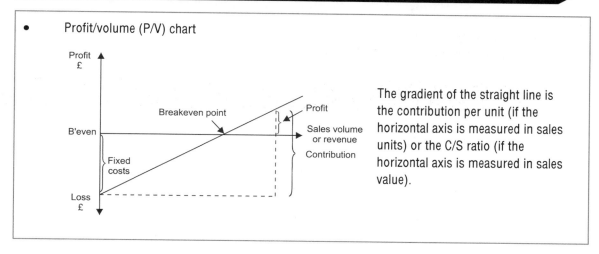

The gradient of the straight line is the contribution per unit (if the horizontal axis is measured in sales units) or the C/S ratio (if the horizontal axis is measured in sales value).

Question

Basic breakeven analysis

Learning outcome: A(vii)

A summary of a manufacturing organisation's budgeted profit statement for its next financial year, when it expects to be operating at 75% of capacity, is given below.

	$	$
Sales 9,000 units at $32		288,000
Less: direct materials	54,000	
direct wages	72,000	
production overhead: fixed	42,000	
variable	18,000	
		186,000
Gross profit		102,000
Less: Administration, selling and distribution costs:		
fixed	36,000	
varying with sales volume	27,000	
		63,000
Net profit		39,000

Required

(a) (i) Calculate the breakeven point in units and in value.
   (ii) Draw a contribution volume (profit volume) graph.
   (iii) Calculate the profit that could be expected if the company operated at full capacity.

(b) It has been estimated that:

   (i) if the selling price per unit were reduced to $28, the increased demand would utilise 90% of the company's capacity without any additional advertising expenditure; and

   (ii) to attract sufficient demand to utilise full capacity would require a 15% reduction in the current selling price and a $5,000 special advertising campaign.

Present a statement showing the effect of the two alternatives compared with the original budget and advise management which of the three possible plans ought to be adopted (the original budget plan or (i) above or (ii) above).

(c) An independent market research study shows that by spending $15,000 on a special advertising campaign, the company could operate at full capacity and maintain the selling price at $32 per unit.

    (i)   Advise management whether this proposal should be adopted.

    (ii)   State any reservations you might have.

Answer

(a) (i)

		$'000	$'000
Sales			288
Variable costs:	direct materials	54	
	direct wages	72	
	Production overhead	18	
	variable administration costs, etc	27	
			171
Contribution			117

Contribution per unit = $117,000/9,000 = $13

Breakeven point   = Fixed costs/contribution per unit = ($42,000 + $36,000)/$13

                  = **6,000 units**

6,000 units × $32   = **$192,000 sales value**

(ii)

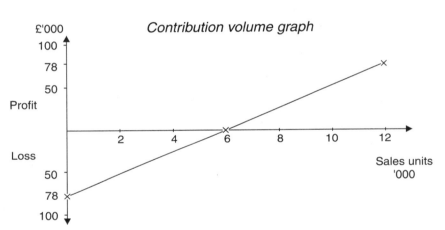

Contribution volume graph

(iii) Assuming that cost behaviour patterns remain the same if activity increases to 100% capacity, a profit of $78,000 can be expected.

	$'000
Contribution (12,000 × $13)	156
Less: fixed production overhead	42
fixed administration costs, etc	36
Profit	78

(b) **Alternative (i)**

	$'000
Sales ($28 × 10,800 units)	302.4
Variable costs ($171,000 × $\frac{90}{75}$)	205.2
Contribution	97.2
Fixed costs	78.0
Profit	19.2

Alternative (ii)

	$'000	$'000
Sales ($27.20 × 12,000 units)		326.4
Variable costs ($171,000 × $\frac{100}{75}$)		228.0
Contribution		98.4
Fixed costs – budgeted	78.0	
– special advertising	5.0	
		83.0
Profit		15.4

A **unit price of $32**, as suggested in the original budget plan, **should be adopted**, as it produces the highest profit of $39,000.

(c) (i)

	$'000	$'000
Sales ($32 × 12,000 units)		384
Variable costs (as (b)(ii))		228
Contribution		156
Fixed costs: budgeted	78	
advertising	15	
		93
Profit		63

The **proposed advertising campaign** generates a considerable increase in profit and **should be adopted**.

(ii) **Reservations** about the recommendation are as follows.

(1) The advertising expenditure has to be incurred before results are known. This increases the risk involved and raises the breakeven point.

(2) How reliable is the market research information?

(3) Does the company have any contingency plans in case the campaign generates more demand than the company can satisfy?

1 Breakeven analysis in a multi-product environment

FAST FORWARD

To perform breakeven analysis in a multi-product organisation, a **constant product sales mix** must be **assumed**, or all products must have the **same C/S ratio**.

1.1 A major assumption

Organisations typically produce and sell a variety of products and services. To perform breakeven analysis in a multi-product organisation, however, a **constant product sales mix must be assumed**. In other words, we have to assume that whenever x units of product A are sold, y units of product B and z units of product C are also sold.

Such an assumption allows us to **calculate** a **weighted average contribution per mix**, the weighting being on the basis of the quantities of each product in the constant mix. This means that the unit contribution of the product that makes up the largest proportion of the mix has the greatest impact on the average contribution per mix.

The only situation when the mix of products does not affect the analysis is when **all of the products have the same ratio of contribution to sales (C/S ratio)**.

2 Breakeven point for multiple products

> **Breakeven point** is 'The level of activity at which there is neither profit nor loss.'
>
> (CIMA *Official Terminology*)

This calculation is exactly the same as that for single products but the single product is the standard mix. Let's look at an example.

FAST FORWARD

> The **breakeven point (in number of mixes)** for a standard mix of products is calculated as fixed costs/contribution per mix.

2.1 Example: breakeven point for multiple products

Suppose that PL produces and sells two products. The M sells for $7 per unit and has a total variable cost of $2.94 per unit, while the N sells for $15 per unit and has a total variable cost of $4.50 per unit. The marketing department has estimated that for every five units of M sold, one unit of N will be sold. The organisation's fixed costs total $36,000.

Solution

We calculate the breakeven point as follows.

Step 1   Calculate **contribution per unit**

	M	N
	$ per unit	$ per unit
Selling price	7.00	15.00
Variable cost	2.94	4.50
Contribution	4.06	10.50

Step 2   Calculate **contribution per mix**

= ($4.06 × 5) + ($10.50 × 1) = $30.80

Step 3   Calculate the **breakeven point** in terms of the number of mixes

= fixed costs/contribution per mix = $36,000/$30.80
= 1,169 mixes (rounded)

Step 4   Calculate the **breakeven point** in terms of the **number of units of the products**

= (1,169 × 5) 5,845 units of M and (1,169 × 1) 1,169 units of N (rounded)

Step 5   Calculate the **breakeven point** in terms of **revenue**

= (5,845 × $7) + (1,169 × $15)
= $40,915 of M and $17,535 of N = $58,450 in total

It is important to note that the breakeven point is not $58,450 of revenue, whatever the mix of products. The breakeven point is $58,450 provided that the sales mix remains 5:1. Likewise the breakeven point is not at a production/sales level of (5,845 + 1,169) 7,014 units. Rather, it is when 5,845 units of M and 1,169 units of N are sold, assuming a sales mix of 5:1.

> An MCQ in the May 2005 exam required the use of this approach.

Question

Learning outcome: A(vii)

Alpha manufactures and sells three products, the beta, the gamma and the delta. Relevant information is as follows.

	Beta $ per unit	Gamma $ per unit	Delta $ per unit
Selling price	135.00	165.00	220.00
Variable cost	73.50	58.90	146.20

Total fixed costs are $950,000.

An analysis of past trading patterns indicates that the products are sold in the ratio 3:4:5.

Required

Fill in the blanks in the sentence below.

Alpha's breakeven point in terms of revenue of the three products is ………….................. of Beta, ……….................. of Gamma and ……….............….….... of Delta, making …….….….…........ in total.

Answer

The correct answer is $393,660 of Beta, $641,520 of Gamma and $1,069,200 of Delta, making $2,104,380 in total.

Step 1   Calculate **contribution per unit**

	Beta $ per unit	Gamma $ per unit	Delta $ per unit
Selling price	135.00	165.00	220.00
Variable cost	73.50	58.90	146.20
Contribution	61.50	106.10	73.80

Step 2   Calculate **contribution per mix**

= ($61.50 × 3) + ($106.10 × 4) + ($73.80 × 5)
= $977.90

Step 3   Calculate the **breakeven point** in terms of the **number of mixes**

= fixed costs/contribution per mix
= $950,000/$977.90 = 972 mixes (rounded up)

Step 4   Calculate the **breakeven point** in terms of the **number of units of the products**

= (972 × 3) 2,916 units of Beta, (972 × 4) 3,888 units of Gamma and (972 × 5) 4,860 units of Delta (rounded)

Step 5   Calculate the **breakeven point** in terms of **revenue**

= (2,916 × $135) + (3,888 × $165) + (4,860 × $220)
= $393,660 of Beta, $641,520 of Gamma and $1,069,200 of Delta = $2,104,380 in total

3 Contribution to sales (C/S) ratio for multiple products

The **breakeven point in terms of sales revenue** can be calculated as fixed costs/average C/S ratio.

3.1 Calculating the ratio

An alternative way of **calculating the breakeven point** is to use the **average contribution to sales (C/S) ratio** for the standard mix.

As you should already know, the C/S ratio is sometimes called the **profit/volume ratio** or **P/V ratio**.

We can calculate the breakeven point of PL (see Section 2.1) as follows.

Step 1   Calculate **revenue per mix**
$= (5 \times \$7) + (1 \times \$15) = \$50$

Step 2   Calculate **contribution per mix**
$= \$30.80$ (see Section 2.1)

Step 3   Calculate **average C/S ratio**
$= (\$30.80/\$50.00) \times 100\% = 61.6\%$

Step 4   Calculate **breakeven point** (total)
$=$ fixed costs $\div$ C/S ratio
$= \$36,000/0.616 = \$58,442$ (rounded)

Step 5   Calculate **revenue ratio of mix**
$= 35:15$, or $7:3$

Step 6   **Calculate breakeven sales**
Breakeven sales of M $= \$58,442 \times 7/10 = \$40,909$ rounded
Breakeven sales of N $= \$58,442 \times 3/10 = \$17,533$ rounded

Question   **C/S ratio for multiple products**

Learning outcome: A(vii)

Calculate the breakeven sales revenue of product Beta, Gamma and Delta (see the question above) using the approach shown in Section 3.1.

Answer

Step 1   Calculate revenue per mix
$= (3 \times \$135) + (4 \times \$165) + (5 \times \$220)$
$= \$2,165$

Step 2   Calculate contribution per mix
$= \$977.90$ (from Question: breakeven point for multiple products)

Step 3   Calculate average C/S ratio
$= (\$977.90/\$2,165) \times 100\%$
$= 45.17\%$

Step 4   Calculate breakeven point (total)
$=$ fixed costs $\div$ C/S ratio
$= \$950,000/0.4517$
$= \$2,103,166$ (rounded)

Step 5 Calculate revenue ratio of mix
= 405:660:1,100, or 81:132:220

Step 6 Calculate breakeven sales

Breakeven sales of Beta   = 81/433 × $2,103,166 = $393,433
Breakeven sales of Gamma   = 132/433 × $2,103,166 = $641,150
Breakeven sales of Delta   = 220/433 × $2,103,166 = $1,068,583

Alternatively you might be provided with the individual C/S ratios of a number of products. For example if an organisation sells two products (A and B) in the **ratio 2:5** and if the C/S ratio of A is **10%** whereas that of B is **50%**, the average C/S ratio is calculated as follows.

Average C/S ratio $= \dfrac{(2\times10\%)+(5\times50\%)}{2+5} = 38.6\%$

Question		Average C/S ratio

Learning outcome: A(vii)

TIM produces and sells two products, the MK and the KL. The organisation expects to sell 1 MK for every 2 KLs and have monthly sales revenue of $150,000. The MK has a C/S ratio of 20% whereas the KL has a C/S ratio of 40%. Budgeted monthly fixed costs are $30,000.

What is the budgeted breakeven sales revenue?

A $150,000
B $300,000
C $90,000
D $50,000

Answer

The correct answer is C.

Average C/S ratio $= \dfrac{(20\%\times1)+(40\%\times2)}{3} = 33^1/_3\%$

Sales revenue at the breakeven point $= \dfrac{\text{fixed costs}}{\text{C / S ratio}} = \dfrac{£30,000}{0.333} = \$90,000$

The C/S ratio is a measure of how much contribution is earned from each $1 of sales of the standard mix. The **C/S ratio of 33¹/₃%** in the question above means that for every $1 of sales of the standard mix of products, a contribution of 33.33p is earned. To **earn a total contribution of, say, $20,000, sales revenue from the standard mix** must therefore be

$\dfrac{£1}{33.33p} \times \$20,000 = \$60,006$

Question _____

Learning outcome: A(vii)

Refer back to the information in the paragraph following Question: C/S ratio for multiple products. Suppose the organisation in question has fixed costs of $100,000, and wishes to earn total contribution of $200,000.

What level of revenue must be achieved?

A $459,067
B $518,135
C $618,135
D $777,202

Answer _____

The correct answer is B.

Sales revenue must be $\dfrac{£1}{38.6p} \times \$200,000 = \$518,135$

3.2 Points to bear in mind

Any change in the proportions of products in the mix will change the contribution per mix and the average C/S ratio and hence the breakeven point.

(a)   If the mix shifts towards products with lower contribution margins, the breakeven point (in units) will increase and profits will fall unless there is a corresponding increase in total revenue.

(b)   A shift towards products with higher contribution margins without a corresponding decrease in revenues will cause an increase in profits and a lower breakeven point.

(c)   If sales are at the specified level but not in the specified mix, there will be either a profit or a loss depending on whether the mix shifts towards products with higher or lower contribution margins.

Exam focus point

C/S ratios were examined in May 2006 and November 2006 in short Section A questions

4 Sales/product mix decisions

One use of the methodology we have been looking at is to **determine the most profitable sales mix option** of a number open to management.

FAST FORWARD

If an organisation sells a number of products, the **total C/S ratio is the sum of the individual weighted (by market share) C/S ratios**.

4.1 Example: sales mix decisions

JM makes and sells two products, the J and the M. The budgeted selling price of the J is $60 and that of the M, $72. Variable costs associated with producing and selling the J are $30 and, with the M, $60. Annual fixed production and selling costs of JM are $3,369,600.

JM has two production/sales options. The J and the M can be sold either in the ratio two Js to three Ms or in the ratio one J to two Ms.

We can decide on the optimal mix by looking at breakeven points. We need to begin by determining contribution per unit.

	J	M
	$ per unit	$ per unit
Selling price	60	72
Variable cost	30	60
Contribution	30	12

Mix 1

Contribution per 5 units sold = ($30 × 2) + ($12 × 3) = $96

Breakeven point = $\dfrac{£3,369,600}{£96}$ = 35,100 sets of five units

	J		M	
Breakeven point:				
in units	(35,100 × 2)	70,200	(35,100 × 3)	105,300
in $	(70,200 × $60)	$4,212,000	(105,300× $72)	$7,581,600

'Total' breakeven point = $11,793,600

Mix 2

Contribution per 3 units sold = ($30 × 1) + ($12 × 2) = $54

Breakeven point = $\dfrac{£3,369,600}{£54}$ = 62,400 sets of three units.

	J		M	
Breakeven point:				
in units	(62,400 × 1)	62,400	(62,400 × 2)	124,800
in $	(62,400 × $60)	$3,744,000	(124,800× $72)	$8,985,600

'Total' breakeven point = $12,729,600

Ignoring commercial considerations, mix 1 is preferable to mix 2. This is because it results in a lower level of sales to break even (because of the higher average contribution per unit sold). The average contribution for mix 1 is $19.20 ($96 ÷ 5). In mix 2 it is $18 ($54 ÷ 3). Mix 1 contains a higher proportion (40% as opposed to $33^{1}/_{3}$%) of the more profitable product.

The following question looks at the **effect on the overall C/S ratio of changing a product/sales mix.**

4.2 Question: changing the product mix

AL sells three products - Exe, Why and Zed - in equal quantities and at the same selling price per unit. The C/S ratio for the Exe is 50%, that of the Why is 60% and the total C/S ratio is 55%. Suppose the product mix is changed to Exe 20%, Why 50% and Zed 30%.

Required

Calculate the revised total contribution/total sales ratio.

Solution

Original proportions

	Exe	Why	Zed	Total
C/S ratio	0.5	0.6	0.549(W2)	
Market share	× 1/3	× 1/3	× 1/3	
	0.167	0.200	0.183(W1)	0.55

Workings

1   The total C/S ratio is the sum of the weighted C/S ratios and so this figure is calculated as $0.55 - 0.167 - 0.2 = 0.183$

2   This figure is then calculated as $0.183 ÷ 1/3 = 0.549$

Revised proportions

	Exe	Why	Zed	Total
C/S ratio (as above)	0.5	0.6	0.549	
Market share	× 0.2	× 0.5	× 0.3	
	0.1	0.3	0.1647	0.5647

The total C/S ratio will increase because of the inclusion in the mix of proportionately more of Why, which has the highest C/S ratio.

Question

Sales mix decision

Learning outcome: A(vii)

LL currently sells three products U, C and Y at the same selling price per unit.

Current product mix	U – 25%	C – 35%	Y – 40%
Current P/V ratio	Total – 43.5%	C – 45%	Y – 35%
LL decides to change the product mix to	U – 30%	C – 40%	Y – 30%

The revised total contribution/total sales ratio is 43.5%. *True or false?*

Answer

The correct answer is 45% and so the statement is false.

	U	C	Y	Total
P/V ratio	0.55*	0.45	0.35	
Market share	× 0.25	× 0.35	× 0.40	
	0.1375	0.1575	0.140	0.435

* 0.1375/0.25

With revised proportions:

	U	C	Y	Total
P/V ratio	0.55	0.45	0.35	
Market share	× 0.30	× 0.40	× 0.30	
	0.165	0.18	0.105	0.45

5 Target profits for multiple products

At **breakeven point**, sales revenue (S) is equal to variable costs plus fixed costs (V+F), and there is no profit:

S = V+F

Suppose an organisation wishes to achieve a certain level of profit (P) during a period. To achieve this profit, sales must cover all costs and leave the required profit:

S = V + F + P
∴ S − V = F + P

So total contribution required = F + P

Once we know the total contribution required we can calculate the sales revenue of each product needed to achieve a target profit. The method is similar to the method used to calculate the breakeven point.

FAST FORWARD

The number of mixes of products required to be sold to achieve a **target profit** is calculated as (fixed costs + required profit)/contribution per mix.

5.1 Example: target profits for multiple products

An organisation makes and sells three products, F, G and H. The products are sold in the proportions F:G:H = 2:1:3. The organisation's fixed costs are $80,000 per month and details of the products are as follows.

Product	Selling price $ per unit	Variable cost $ per unit
F	22	16
G	15	12
H	19	13

The organisation wishes to earn a profit of $52,000 next month. Calculate the required sales value of each product in order to achieve this target profit.

Solution

Step 1   Calculate **contribution per unit**

	F $ per unit	G $ per unit	H $ per unit
Selling price	22	15	19
Variable cost	16	12	13
Contribution	6	3	6

Step 2   Calculate **contribution per mix**

= ($6 × 2) + ($3 × 1) + ($6 × 3) = $33

Step 3   Calculate the **required number of mixes**

= (Fixed costs + required profit)/contribution per mix
= ($80,000 + $52,000)/$33
= 4,000 mixes

Step 4   Calculate the required sales in terms of the number of units of the products and sales revenue of each product

Product		Units	Selling price $ per unit	Sales revenue required $
F	4,000 × 2	8,000	22	176,000
G	4,000 × 1	4,000	15	60,000
H	4,000 × 3	12,000	19	228,000
Total				464,000

The sales revenue of $464,000 will generate a profit of $52,000 if the products are sold in the mix 2:1:3.

Alternatively the C/S ratio could be used to determine the required sales revenue for a profit of $52,000. The method is again similar to that demonstrated earlier when calculating the breakeven point.

5.2 Example: using the C/S ratio to determine the required sales

We'll use the data from Section 5.1.

Step 1   **Calculate revenue per mix**
= (2 × $22) + (1 × $15) + (3 × $19)
= $116

Step 2   **Calculate contribution per mix**
= $33 (from Solution in Section 5.1)

Step 3   **Calculate average C/S ratio**
= ($33/$116) × 100%
= 28.45%

Step 4   **Calculate required total revenue**
= required contribution ÷ C/S ratio
= ($80,000 + $52,000) ÷ 0.2845
= $463,972

Step 5   **Calculate revenue ratio of mix**
= (2 × $22) : (1 × $15) : (3 × $19)
= 44:15:57

Step 6   **Calculate required sales**
Required sales of F   = 44/116 × $463,972 = $175,989
Required sales of G   = 15/116 × $463,972 = $59,996
Required sales of H   = 57/116 × $463,972 = $227,986

Which, allowing for roundings, is the same answer as calculated in Section 5.1.

6 Margin of safety for multiple products

It should not surprise you to learn that the calculation of the margin of safety for multiple products is exactly the same as for single products, but the single product is the standard mix. The easiest way to see how it's done is to look at an example.

FAST FORWARD

The **margin of safety** for a multi-product organisation is equal to the budgeted sales in the standard mix less the breakeven sales in the standard mix. It may be expressed as a percentage of the budgeted sales.

6.1 Example: margin of safety for multiple products

BA produces and sells two products. The W sells for $8 per unit and has a total variable cost of $3.80 per unit, while the R sells for $14 per unit and has a total variable cost of $4.20. For every five units of W sold, six units of R are sold. BA's fixed costs are $43,890 per period.

Budgeted sales revenue for next period is $74,400, in the standard mix.

Solution

To calculate the margin of safety we must first determine the **breakeven point.**

Step 1   Calculate **contribution per unit**

	W	R
	$ per unit	$ per unit
Selling price	8.00	14.00
Variable cost	3.80	4.20
Contribution	4.20	9.80

Step 2   Calculate **contribution per mix**

= ($4.20 × 5) + ($9.80 × 6) = $79.80

Step 3   Calculate the **breakeven point** in terms of the **number of mixes**

= fixed costs/contribution per mix = $43,890/$79.80
= 550 mixes

Step 4   Calculate the **breakeven point** in terms of the **number of units of the products**

= (550 × 5) 2,750 units of W and (550 × 6) 3,300 units of R

Step 5   Calculate the **breakeven point** in terms of **revenue**

= (2,750 × $8) + (3,300 × $14)
= $22,000 of W and $46,200 of R = $68,200 in total

Step 6   Calculate the **margin of safety**

= budgeted sales − breakeven sales
= $74,400 − $68,200
= $6,200 sales in total, in the standard mix

Or, as a percentage

= ($74,400 − $68,200)/$74,400 × 100%
= 8.3% of budgeted sales

7 Multi-product breakeven charts

xam focus
oint

The May 2006 exam included up to 12 marks in a Section C question for sketching a multi-product profit volume chart and explaining its use.

7.1 Breakeven charts

ey term

A **breakeven chart** is 'A chart which indicates approximate profit or loss at different levels of sales volume within a limited range'.

(CIMA *Official Terminology*)

A very serious limitation of breakeven charts is that they can show the costs, revenues, profits and margins of safety for a single product only, or at best for a **single 'sales mix' of products.**

Breakeven charts for multiple products can be drawn if a constant product sales mix is assumed.

For example suppose that FA sells three products, X, Y and Z which have variable unit costs of $3, $4 and $5 respectively. The sales price of X is $8, the price of Y is $6 and the price of Z is $6. Fixed costs per annum are $10,000.

A breakeven chart cannot be drawn, because we do not know the proportions of X, Y and Z in the sales mix.

Attention!

> If you are not sure about this point, you should try to draw a breakeven chart with the information given. It should not be possible.

There are a number of ways in which we can overcome this problem, however.

7.1.1 Approach 1: output in $ sales and a constant product mix

Assume that budgeted sales are 2,000 units of X, 4,000 units of Y and 3,000 units of Z. A breakeven chart would make the assumption that output and sales of X, Y and Z are in the proportions 2,000: 4,000: 3,000 at all levels of activity, in other words that the sales mix is 'fixed' in these proportions.

We begin by carrying out some calculations.

Budgeted costs		*Costs*		*Revenue*
		$		$
Variable costs of X	(2,000 × $3)	6,000	X (2,000 × $8)	16,000
Variable costs of Y	(4,000 × $4)	16,000	Y (4,000 × $6)	24,000
Variable costs of Z	(3,000 × $5)	15,000	Z (3,000 × $6)	18,000
Total variable costs		37,000	Budgeted revenue	58,000
Fixed costs		10,000		
Total budgeted costs		47,000		

The **breakeven chart** can now be drawn.

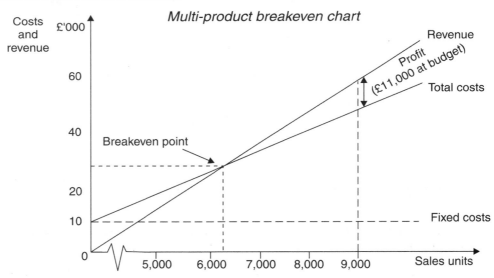

Multi-product breakeven chart

The **breakeven point** is approximately $27,500 of sales revenue. This may either be **read from the chart or computed mathematically**.

(a)   The budgeted C/S ratio for all three products together is contribution/sales = $(58,000 − 37,000)/$58,000 = 36.21%.

(b)   The required contribution to break even is $10,000, the amount of fixed costs. The breakeven point is $10,000/36.21% = $27,500 (approx) in sales revenue.

The margin of safety is approximately $(58,000 − 27,500) = $30,500.

7.1.2 Approach 2: products in sequence

The products could be plotted in a particular sequence (say X first, then Y, then Z).

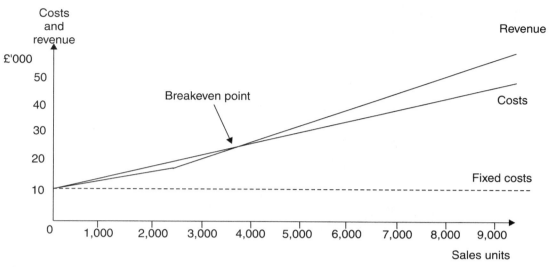

In this case the breakeven point occurs at about 3,800 units of sales (2,000 units of product X and 1,800 units of product Y) and the margin of safety is roughly 2,200 units of Y and 3,000 units of Z.

7.1.3 Approach 3: output in terms of % of forecast sales and a constant product mix

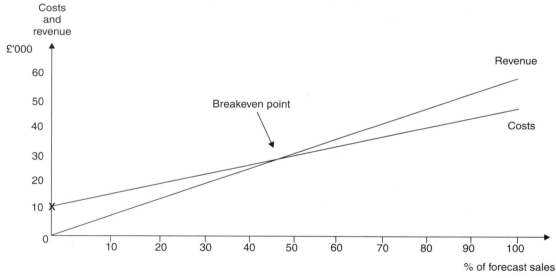

The breakeven point can be read from the graph as approximately 48% of forecast sales ($30,000 of revenue).

Alternatively, with contribution of $(58,000 − 37,000) = $21,000, one percent of forecast sales is associated with $21,000/100 = $210 contribution.

Breakeven point (%) = fixed costs/contribution per 1%
= $10,000/$210 = 47.62%

∴ Margin of safety = (100 − 47.62) = 52.38%

Attention!

> The general point of setting out these three approaches is to demonstrate that output can be viewed in several different ways.

7.2 Multi-product P/V charts

FAST FORWARD

> The **P/V chart** can show information about each product individually.

The same information could be shown on a **P/V chart**, as follows.

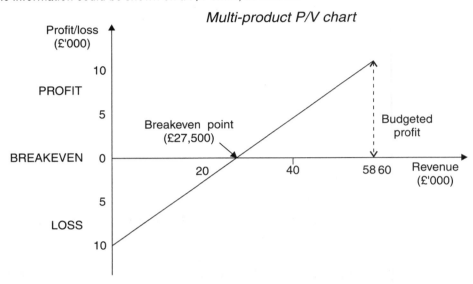

Multi-product P/V chart

An **addition** to the chart would **show further information about the contribution earned by each product individually**, so that their performance and profitability can be compared.

	Contribution	Sales	C/S ratio
	$	$	%
Product X	10,000	16,000	62.50
Product Y	8,000	24,000	33.33
Product Z	3,000	18,000	16.67
Total	21,000	58,000	36.21

By convention, the **products are shown individually** on a P/V chart from **left to right**, in **order of the size of their C/S ratio**. In this example, product X will be plotted first, then product Y and finally product Z. A **dotted line** is used to show the **cumulative profit/loss and the cumulative sales** as each product's sales and contribution in turn are added to the sales mix.

Product	Cumulative sales		Cumulative profit
	$		$
X	16,000	($10,000 – $10,000)	–
X and Y	40,000		8,000
X, Y and Z	58,000		11,000

You will see on the graph which follows that these three pairs of data are used to plot the dotted line, to indicate the contribution from each product. The **solid line** which joins the two ends of this dotted line **indicates the average profit** which will be earned from sales of the three products in this mix.

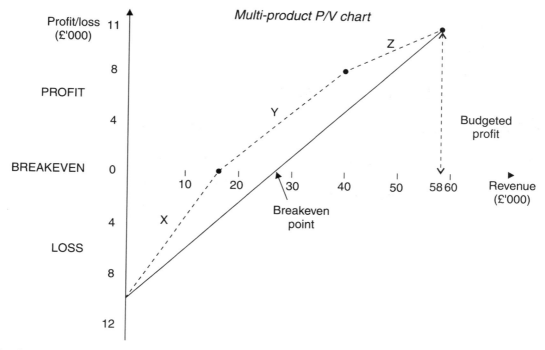

Multi-product P/V chart

The diagram **highlights** the following points.

(a)   Since X is the most profitable in terms of C/S ratio, it might be worth considering an increase in the sales of X, even if there is a consequent fall in the sales of Z.

(b)   Alternatively, the pricing structure of the products should be reviewed and a decision made as to whether the price of product Z should be raised so as to increase its C/S ratio (although an increase is likely to result in some fall in sales volume).

The **multi-product P/V chart** therefore helps to **identify** the following.

(a)   The overall company breakeven point.

(b)   Which products should be expanded in output and which, if any, should be discontinued.

(c)   What effect changes in selling price and sales volume will have on the company's breakeven point and profit.

| Question | Multi-product P/V chart |

Learning outcome: A(vii)

A company sells three products, X, Y and Z. Cost and sales data for one period are as follows.

	X	Y	Z
Sales volume	2,000 units	2,000 units	5,000 units
Sales price per unit	$3	$4	$2
Variable cost per unit	$2.25	$3.50	$1.25
Total fixed costs	$3,250		

Required

Construct a multi-product P/V chart based on the above information on the axes below.

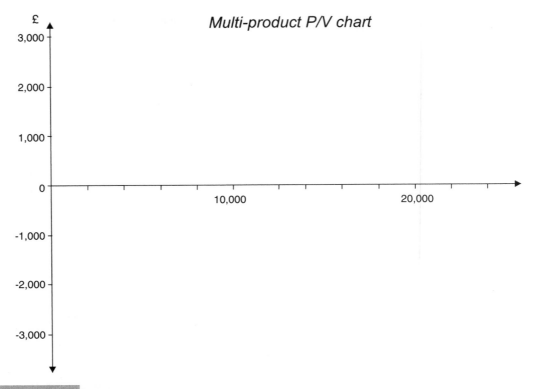

Multi-product P/V chart

Answer

	X	Y	Z	Total
				$
Contribution per unit	$0.75	$0.50	$0.75	
Budgeted contribution (total)	$1,500	$1,000	$3,750	6,250
Fixed costs				3,250
Budgeted profit				3,000

Product	Cumulative sales $		Cumulative profit $
Z	10,000	($3,750 – $3,250)	500
Z and X	16,000		2,000
Z, X and Y	24,000		3,000

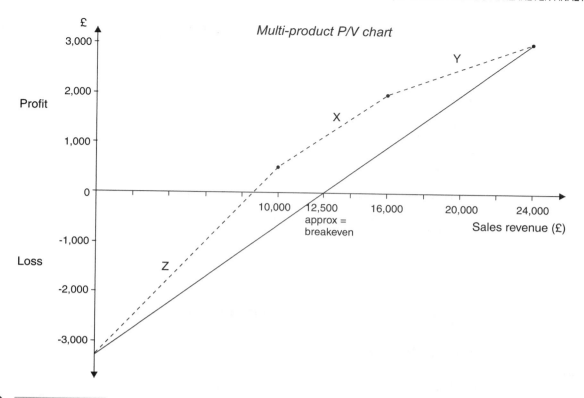

Multi-product P/V chart

Question

Breakeven point and sales value constraints

Learning outcome: A(vii)

Sutton produces four products. Relevant data is shown below for period 2.

	Product M	Product A	Product R	Product P
C/S ratio	5%	10%	15%	20%
Maximum sales value	$200,000	$120,000	$200,000	$180,000
Minimum sales value	$50,000	$50,000	$20,000	$10,000

The fixed costs for period 2 are budgeted at $60,000.

Required

Fill in the blank in the sentence below.

The lowest breakeven sales value, subject to meeting the minimum sales value constraints, is $............. .

Answer

The correct answer is $390,000

Breakeven point occurs when contribution = fixed costs

∴ Minimum breakeven point occurs when contribution is $60,000.

Contribution achieved from minimum sales value

		$
M	5% × $50,000	2,500
A	10% × $50,000	5,000
R	15% × $20,000	3,000
P	20% × $10,000	2,000
		12,500

Product P has the highest C/S ratio and so should be produced first (as it earns more contribution per $ of revenue than the others).

Contribution from sales of P between minimum and maximum points = $170,000 × 20% = $34,000

∴ Required contribution from Product R (which has the next highest C/S ratio)

$$= \$(60,000 - 12,500 - 34,000)$$
$$= \$13,500$$

Revenue from Product R of $13,500/0.15 = $90,000 will produce $13,500 of contribution.

∴ Lowest breakeven sales

$$= \$130,000 \text{ (minimum sales)} + \$170,000 \text{ (from P)} + \$90,000 \text{ (from R)}$$
$$= \$390,000$$

8 Further aspects of breakeven analysis

8.1 Limitations and advantages

FAST FORWARD ⟩⟩ The **limitations** of breakeven analysis are often raised, but the technique does have **advantages** too.

8.1.1 Limitations

(a) It is **assumed** that **fixed costs** are the **same in total** and **variable costs** are the **same per unit at all levels of output**. This assumption is a great **simplification**.

  (i) Fixed costs will change if output falls or increases substantially (most fixed costs are step costs).

  (ii) The variable cost per unit will decrease where economies of scale are made at higher output volumes, but the variable cost per unit will also eventually rise when diseconomies of scale begin to appear at even higher volumes of output (for example the extra cost of labour in overtime working).

  The **assumption** is only **correct within** a normal range or **relevant range of output**. It is generally assumed that both the budgeted output and the breakeven point lie within this relevant range.

(b) It is **assumed** that **sales prices** will be **constant** at **all levels of activity**. This may not be true, especially at higher volumes of output, where the price may have to be reduced to win the extra sales.

(c) **Production** and **sales** are **assumed** to be the **same**, so that the consequences of any increase in inventory levels or of 'de-stocking' are ignored.

(d) **Uncertainty** in the estimates of fixed costs and unit variable costs is often **ignored**.

8.1.2 Advantages

(a) **Graphical representation** of cost and revenue data (breakeven charts) can be **more easily understood by non-financial managers**.

(b) A breakeven model enables **profit or loss at any level of activity** within the range for which the model is valid to be **determined**, and the C/S ratio can indicate the **relative profitability of different products**.

(c)   Highlighting the breakeven point and the margin of safety gives managers some **indication** of the level of **risk** involved.

8.2 Accounting and economic models of breakeven analysis and the relevant range

FAST FORWARD

Within the **relevant range**, the **economists'** and **accountants' breakeven charts** are **not too different.**

A **fundamental assumption** of breakeven analysis is that **costs can be divided into a constant variable cost per unit and a constant total fixed cost.** However, there is a good **argument** that the **variable cost per unit**, which is the marginal cost per unit in the language of economics, **changes with the level of output.** This is because until a factory is working at a level approaching that for which it was designed it will be inefficient and the variable cost will be higher than it could be. Once it starts operating at a level beyond that for which it was designed it will become inefficient again and the variable cost will once more start to rise.

For the **economist**, therefore, the **marginal cost per unit** should be graphed as follows.

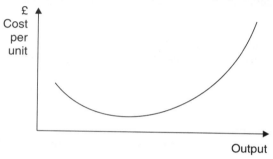

Total costs would therefore appear as a curved line as follows.

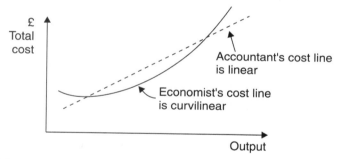

A **second fundamental assumption** of breakeven analysis is that the **selling price is constant**, no matter how many units are sold. To the **economist** this is quite **inaccurate**, because in order to achieve higher sales it is usually necessary to charge lower selling prices. For the economist, therefore **total revenue** also stands in a **curvilinear** relationship to volume.

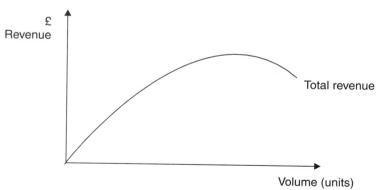

The **economist's breakeven chart therefore differs from the accountant's.**

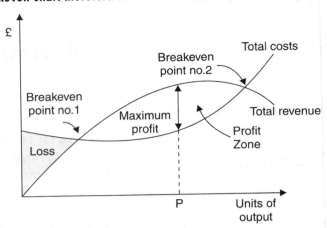

The shape of the total costs and total revenue lines means that there are **two breakeven points**. At the second, decreasing total revenue equals increasing total costs. The first is similar to the single breakeven point shown on an accountant's breakeven chart.

The accountant's breakeven chart is not intended to provide an accurate representation of total costs and total revenue behaviour in all ranges of output but rather to represent behaviour over the relevant range.

Key term

> **Relevant range.** 'Activity levels within which assumptions about cost behaviour in breakeven analysis remain valid.'
>
> *(CIMA official Terminology)*

Within the relevant range the **economist's and accountant's charts are not too different**. The two types of chart are superimposed below.

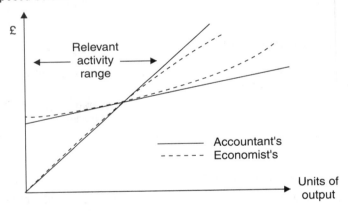

Fixed costs are also **assumed** to be **constant at all levels of output,** so that if there is no output at all, there will be a loss equal to the amount of fixed costs. It might be tempting to assume that this is true, but it could be a seriously **misleading assumption** because many **'fixed cost' items are step costs** in nature over a wide range of activity. **Fixed cost** estimates should therefore only **apply within the relevant range** of activity.

9 Sensitivity analysis

Sensitivity analysis is a term used to describe any technique whereby decision options are tested for their vulnerability to changes in any variable.

Sensitivity analysis can be applied to many areas of management accounting and you will encounter it in a number of chapters throughout this text in relation to specific techniques, as well as in Chapter 14, which deals with uncertainty in decision making.

9.1 Sensitivity analysis and breakeven analysis

The output from a breakeven model is only as good as the data used as input. Breakeven analysis is based on assumptions about sales mix, total fixed costs, variable costs and unit selling prices. Obviously estimates of the values of these **variables** will be **subject to varying degrees of uncertainty**.

But one way of **analysing the effects of changes in the values of these variables** is **sensitivity analysis**. Sensitivity analysis focuses on how a result will alter if estimates of values of variables or underlying assumptions change. It therefore provides answers to the following types of question.

- By how much will profit change if the sales mix changes from that originally predicted?

- By how much will profit change if fixed costs fall by 5% and variable costs increase by 10%?

It can **highlight the risks that an existing cost structure poses** for an organisation, and hence may lead managers to consider alternative cost structures.

Question	Sensitivity analysis

Learning outcomes: A(vii), C(i),(ii)

The directors of a family-owned retail department store were shocked to receive the following profit statement for the year ended 31 January 20X0.

	$'000	$'000	$'000
Sales		5,000	
Less cost of sales		3,398	
			1,602
Wages: departments	357		
office	70		
restaurant	26		
		453	
Delivery costs		200	
Departmental expenses		116	
Salaries: directors and management		100	
Directors' fees		20	
Sales promotion and advertising		120	
Store capacity costs (rent, rates and energy)		488	
Interest on bank overdraft		20	
Discounts allowed		25	
Bad debts		15	
Miscellaneous expenses		75	
		1,632	
Net loss		(30)	

Management accounting techniques have not been employed but the following breakdown has been extracted from the financial records.

	Ladies' wear	*Men's wear*	*General*	*Toys*	*Restaurant*
			Departments		
	$'000	$'000	$'000	$'000	$'000
Sales	800	400	2,200	1,400	200
Purchases	506	220	1,290	1,276	167
Opening inventory	90	70	200	100	5
Closing inventory	100	50	170	200	6
Wages	96	47	155	59	26
Departmental expenses	38	13	35	20	10
Sales promotion and advertising	10	5	30	75	-
Floor space occupied	20%	15%	20%	35%	10%

The directors are considering reducing selling prices on ladies' wear and men's wear by 5% in the hope of boosting sales.

Required

(a) Present the information for the year to 31 January 20X0 in a more meaningful way to aid decision making. Include any statistics or indicators of performance which you consider to be useful.

(b) Show for the ladies wear and menswear departments, if selling prices are reduced by 5% and unit costs remain the same:

(i) the increase in sales value (to the nearest thousand pounds) that would be required for a full year to maintain the gross profits, in $s, earned by each of these departments;

(ii) the increase in (i) above expressed as a percentage of the sales for each department to 31 January 20X0.

(c) State your views on the proposal being considered by the directors and recommend any alternative action you think appropriate.

Answer

(a) **Results for the year ended 31 January 20X0**

	Ladies' wear		*Men's wear*		*General*		*Toys*		*Restaurant*		*Total*	
	$'000	%	$'000	%	$'000	%	$'000	%	$'000	%	$'000	%
Sales	800	100	400	100	2,200	100	1,400	100	200	100	5,000	100
Cost of sales (W1)	496	62	240	60	1,320	60	1,176	84	166	83	3,398	68
Contribution	304	38	160	40	880	40	224	16	34	17	1,602	32
Wages	96		47		155		59		26		383	
Expenses	38		13		35		20		10		116	
Sales promotion and advertising	10		5		30		75		-		120	
	144	18	65	16	220	10	154	11	36	18	619	12
Gross profit/(loss)	160	20	95	24	660	30	70	5	(2)	(1)	983	20

	Total	
	$'000	$'000
Gross profit		983
Indirect costs		
Office wages	70	
Delivery costs	200	
Salaries: directors and management	100	
Directors' fees	20	
Store capacity costs	488	
Interest on bank overdraft	20	
Discounts allowed	25	
Bad debts	15	
Miscellaneous expenses	75	
		1,013
Net loss		(30)

	Ladies' wear	Men's wear	General	Toys	Restaurant
Contribution per 1% of floor space	$15,200	$10,667	$44,000	$6,400	$3,400
Gross profit per 1% of floor space	$8,000	$6,333	$33,000	$2,000	($200)
No of days inventory (W2)	74	76	47	62	13

Workings

1

	Ladies' wear	Men's wear	General	Toys	Restaurant
	$'000	$'000	$'000	$'000	$'000
Opening inventory	90	70	200	100	5
Purchases	506	220	1,290	1,276	167
	596	290	1,490	1,376	172
Closing inventory	100	50	170	200	6
Cost of sales	496	240	1,320	1,176	166

2	(i)	Cost of sales per day (÷ 365)	1.36	0.66	3.62	3.22	0.45
	(ii)	Closing inventory	100	50	170	200	6
		∴ (ii) ÷ (i)	74	76	47	62	13

(b) *Assumption.* Wages, departmental expenses and sales promotion and advertising expenses are fixed costs which would not be affected by any changes in sales.

	Ladies' wear		Men's wear	
	$'000	%	$'000	%
Revised sales value (95%)	760		380	
Cost of sales	496		240	
Revised contribution	264	34.74	140	36.84
Contribution required	304		160	
∴ Sales required (÷ 0.3474)	875	(÷ 0.3684)	434	
(i) Sales increase required compared to current sales	75		34	
(ii) Percentage increase		9.4		8.5

(c)   The calculations in part (b) show that **sales of ladies' wear and men's wear would have to increase** by 9.4% and 8.5% respectively to maintain profits if prices were reduced by 5%. The directors' decision will depend on their assessment of the likelihood of sales increasing by more than these amounts so that profits would increase. The lower prices could attract more people into the store so that the sales of other departments might also increase.

The only area showing a **negative gross profit** is the **restaurant**. However, before taking a decision to close the restaurant the directors should consider whether this will reduce the number of people entering the store and therefore reduce sales in the store as a whole. A review of restaurant prices should be carried out to attempt to improve profitability.

Inventory levels in the **ladies' wear and men's wear departments** are **high compared to the level of sales**. This can be costly in terms of interest charges on the bank overdraft and may lead to large inventory write-offs if fashions change rapidly. A review of the policy over inventory held may help to reduce costs.

9.2 Sensitivity analysis and breakeven charts

Breakeven charts can be used in a form of sensitivity analysis to show variations in the possible sales price, variable costs or fixed costs and the resulting effects on the breakeven point and the margin of safety.

9.2.1 Example: sensitivity analysis

Suppose that an organisation sells a product which has a variable cost of $2 per unit. Fixed costs are $15,000. It has been estimated that if the sales price is set at $4.40 per unit, the expected sales volume would be 7,500 units; whereas if the sales price is lower, at $4 per unit, the expected sales volume would be 10,000 units.

Required

Draw a breakeven chart to show the budgeted profit, the breakeven point and the margin of safety at each of the possible sales prices.

Solution

Workings	*Sales price $4.40 per unit* $		*Sales price $4 per unit* $
Fixed costs	15,000		15,000
Variable costs (7,500 × $2.00)	15,000	(10,000 × $2.00)	20,000
Total costs	30,000		35,000
Budgeted revenue (7,500 × $4.40)	33,000	(10,000 × $4.00)	40,000

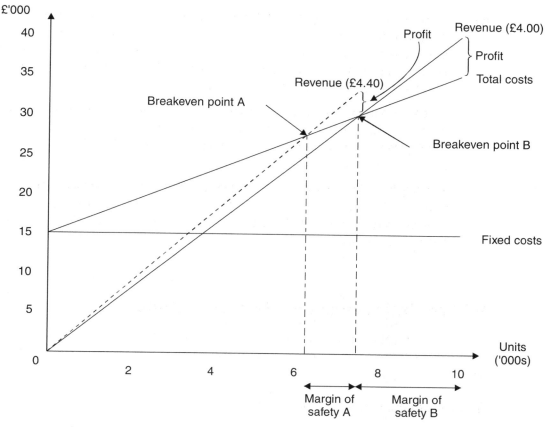

(a) **Breakeven point A** is the breakeven point at a sales price of $4.40 per unit, which is 6,250 units or $27,500 in costs and revenues.

$$\left(\text{check: } \frac{\text{required contribution to breakeven}}{\text{contribution per unit}} = \frac{£15,000}{£2.40 \text{ per unit}} = 6,250 \text{ units}\right)$$

The **margin of safety (A)** is 7,500 units – 6,250 units = 1,250 units or 16.7% of expected sales.

(b) **Breakeven point B** is the breakeven point at a sales price of $4 per unit which is 7,500 units or $30,000 in costs and revenues.

$$\left(\text{check: } \frac{\text{required contribution to breakeven}}{\text{contribution per unit}} = \frac{£15,000}{£2 \text{ per unit}} = 7,500 \text{ units}\right)$$

The **margin of safety (B)** = 10,000 units – 7,500 units = 2,500 units or 25% of expected sales.

Since a **price of $4** per unit gives a higher expected profit and a wider margin of safety, this price will probably be **preferred** even though the breakeven point is higher than at a sales price of $4.40 per unit.

9.3 Sensitivity analysis and the P/V chart

Just as breakeven charts can be used to show how variations in sales price, variable costs and fixed costs affect the breakeven point and the margin of safety, so too can P/V charts. Two circumstances can be considered.

(a) **Fixed cost changes** do not alter the slope of the P/V line but change the point of intersection and therefore the breakeven point.

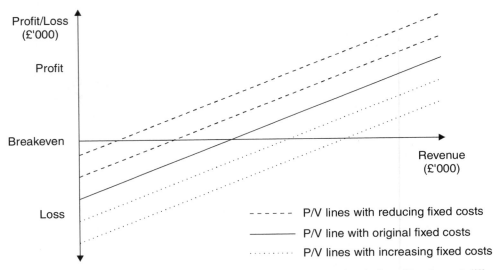

Such a diagram shows how the breakeven point and the level of profit or loss at different levels of revenue will change depending on the level of fixed costs.

(b)   **Variable cost and sales price changes** alter the slope of the line and hence the breakeven point and the profit or loss.

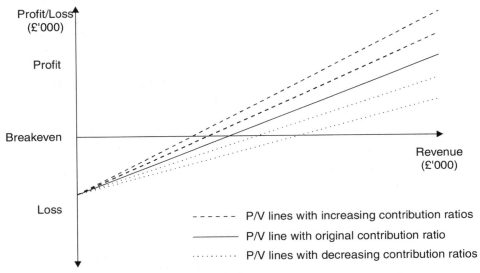

Such a diagram shows how the breakeven point and the level of profit or loss at different levels of revenue will change depending on the contribution ratio.

9.3.1 Example: sensitivity analysis and P/V chart

The budgeted annual output of a factory is 120,000 units. The budgeted fixed overheads amount to $40,000 and the budgeted variable costs are 50p per unit. The budgeted sales price is $1 per unit.

Contribution will be 120,000 × $(1.00 − 0.50) = $60,000 and total profit will be $20,000 (fixed costs being $40,000). The breakeven point is shown on the diagram below (breakeven point 1).

Suppose the budgeted selling price is increased to $1.20, with the result that demand drops to 105,000 units despite additional fixed costs of $10,000 being spent on advertising.

At a sales level of 105,000 units, contribution will be 105,000 × $(1.20 − 0.50) = $73,500 and total profit will be $23,500 (fixed costs being $50,000). The breakeven point is shown on the diagram below (breakeven point 2).

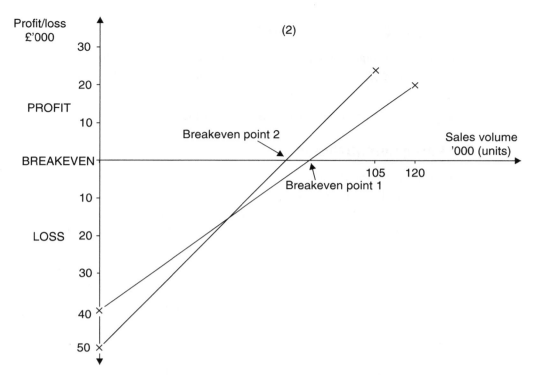

The diagram shows that if the selling price is increased, the breakeven point occurs at a lower level of sales revenue (71,429 units instead of 80,000 units), although this is not a particularly large increase when viewed in the context of the projected sales volume. It is also possible to see that for sales above 50,000 units, the profit achieved will be higher (and the loss achieved lower) if the price is $1.20. For sales volumes below 50,000 units the first option will yield lower losses.

Changes in the variable cost per unit or in fixed costs at certain activity levels can also be easily incorporated into a P/V chart. The profit or loss at each point where the cost structure changes should be calculated and plotted on the graph so that the profit/volume line becomes a series of straight lines.

Suppose that at sales levels in excess of 120,000 units (when the selling price is $1) the variable cost per unit increases to $0.60, perhaps because of overtime premiums that are incurred when production exceeds a certain level. The resulting P/V chart is shown below.

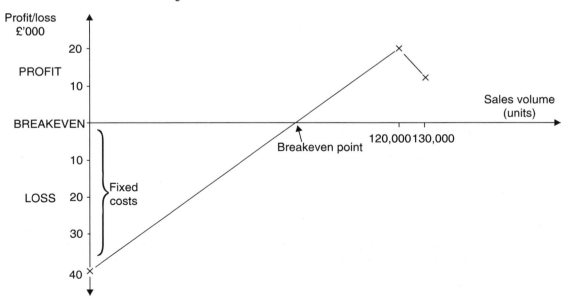

9.4 More complex situations

For **particularly complex situations**, for example if variables are extremely uncertain and/or if the values of some variables are dependent on the outcome of other variables, **Monte Carlo simulations** may be appropriate. This is covered in Chapter 14.

For **slightly less complex situations**, however, **spreadsheets** can be used.

9.5 Using spreadsheets

Because breakeven analysis is based on a number of straightforward mathematical equations and because of the widespread use of spreadsheet packages that do not require programming expertise, **computerised breakeven models to carry out sensitivity analysis** are often developed by management accountants. These models enable managers to consider alternative plans by keying different variable values into a PC, which will then quickly show the resulting changes both graphically and numerically. Managers can study the impact of various changes in selling prices, fixed costs, variable costs and product mix and can react quickly without waiting for formal reports from the management accountant.

For example, suppose a manager wanted to know the **sales level** required at three different **fixed cost levels** and three different **variable cost levels** (or corresponding contribution levels) to reach three different **profit levels**.

A **spreadsheet model** could be used to calculate the twenty-seven different sales levels quickly, without error, as shown below.

Any values for fixed costs, variable costs, contribution or profit could be inserted and the model will calculate the required sales level.

	A	B	C	D	E	F	G
1		VARIABLE		SALES REVENUE NEEDED TO EARN			
2	FIXED	COSTS	CONTRIBUTION		PROFIT OF		
3	COSTS	AS A % OF SALES	MARGIN %	£10,000	£20,000	£30,000	
4							
5	£20,000	40%	60%	£50,000	£66,667	£83,333	
6	£20,000	45%	55%	£54,545	£72,727	£90,909	
7	£20,000	50%	50%	£60,000	£80,000	£100,000	
8	£30,000	40%	60%	£66,667	£83,333	£100,000	
9	£30,000	45%	55%	£72,727	£90,909	£109,091	
10	£30,000	50%	50%	£80,000	£100,000	£120,000	
11	£40,000	40%	60%	£83,333	£100,000	£116,667	
12	£40,000	45%	55%	£90,909	£109,091	£127,273	
13	£40,000	50%	50%	£100,000	£120,000	£140,000	
14							
15							
16							
17							
18							
19							
20							
21							
22							
23							

In addition to speed and convenience, use of software packages allows a more sophisticated approach to breakeven analysis than is covered in this chapter. Models could incorporate multiple cost drivers, non-linear relationships and various sales mixes. Moreover, analysis need not be restricted to the relevant range.

10 Further reading

There is an article in the September 2006 edition of *Financial Management* which looks at **operational gearing**.

The article explains how a company's mix of fixed and variable costs relate to risk and the decisions management can then take based on the level of risk.

Read the article as useful background to how management would make decisions.

Chapter Roundup

- You should have covered the basics of breakeven analysis in your earlier studies. Flick through the relevant chapters of the BPP Study Text or Passcards if your memory needs refreshing.

- To perform breakeven analysis in a multi-product organisation, a **constant product sales mix** must be **assumed**, or all products must have the **same C/S ratio.**

- The **breakeven point (in number of mixes)** for a standard mix of products is calculated as fixed costs/contribution per mix.

- The **breakeven point in terms of sales revenue** can be calculated as fixed costs/average C/S ratio.

- If an organisation sells a number of products, the **total C/S ratio is the sum of the individual weighted** (by market share) **C/S ratios.**

- The number of mixes of products required to be sold to achieve a **target profit** is calculated as (fixed costs + required profit)/contribution per mix.

- The **margin of safety** for a multi-product organisation is equal to the budgeted sales in the standard mix less the breakeven sales in the standard mix. It may be expressed as a percentage of the budgeted sales.

- **Breakeven charts** for multiple products can be drawn if a constant product sales mix is assumed.

- The **P/V chart** can show information about each product individually.

- The **limitations** of breakeven analysis are often raised, but the technique does have **advantages** too.

- Within the **relevant range**, the **economists'** and **accountants' breakeven charts** are **not too different.**

- **Sensitivity analysis** is a term used to describe any technique whereby decision options are tested for their vulnerability to changes in any variable.

Quick Quiz

1   *Fill in the blanks.*

$$\text{Breakeven point} = \frac{\rule{3cm}{0.4pt}}{\text{Contribution per mix}} = \frac{\rule{3cm}{0.4pt}}{\text{Contribution per mix}}$$

2   C/S ratio = P/V ratio × 100. *True or false?*

3   *Fill in the blanks.*

$$\text{Margin of safety (as \%)} = \left(\frac{\text{.................... sales} - \text{.................... sales}}{\text{.................... sales}} \right) \times 100\%$$

4   Mark the following on the breakeven chart below.

- Profit
- Sales revenue
- Total costs
- Margin of safety

- Variable costs
- Fixed costs
- Breakeven point

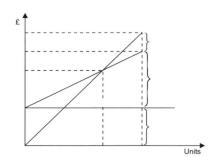

5   *Mark the following on the P/V chart below.*

- Breakeven point
- Fixed costs

- Contribution
- Profit

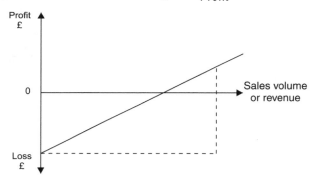

6   Which of the following is not a major assumption of breakeven analysis?

A   It can only apply to one product or a constant mix.
B   Fixed costs are the same in total and unit variable costs are the same at all levels of output.
C   Sales prices vary in line with levels of activity.
D   Production level is equal to sales level.

7   *Choose the appropriate words from those highlighted and fill in the blanks.*

When showing multiple products individually on a P/V chart, the products are shown from **left to right/right to left**, in order of **increasing/decreasing** size of C/S ratio. The line joining the two ends of the dotted line (which shows ....) indicates

....

8   *Choose the appropriate word from those highlighted.*

When choosing between two possible sales mix options, the mix with the **higher/lower** level of sales to break even should be selected.

9   An organisation which sells a number of products in fixed proportions wishes to earn a profit of $P. Its fixed costs are $F. The revenue per mix of products is $R, the contribution per mix $C. What revenue must it achieve to earn profit of $P?

A $R
B   ($F + $P) ÷ ($C/$R)
C $F + $P
D   ($F + $P) ÷ $R/$C

10   *Choose the appropriate words from those highlighted.*

The assumption in breakeven analysis that variable cost is the same per unit at all levels of output is a great simplification. The variable cost per unit will decrease where (1) **economies/diseconomies** of scale are made at higher volumes of output, but will also eventually rise where (2) **economies/diseconomies** of scale begin to appear at even (3) **higher/lower** volumes of output.

Answers to Quick Quiz

1   Breakeven point = $\dfrac{\text{Total fixed costs}}{\text{Contribution per unit}}$ = $\dfrac{\text{Contribution required to breakeven}}{\text{Contribution per unit}}$

2   False. The C/S ratio is another name for the P/V ratio.

3   Margin of safety (as %) = $\left(\dfrac{\text{Budgeted sales} - \text{breakeven sales}}{\text{Budgeted sales}}\right)$ x 100%

4

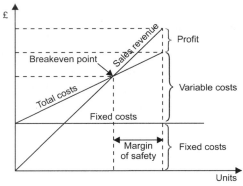

5

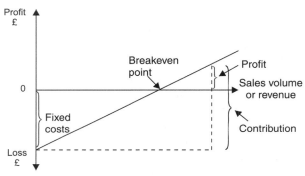

6   C. Sales prices *are constant* at all levels of activity.

7   When showing multiple products individually on a P/V chart, the products are shown from left to right, in order of decreasing size of C/S ratio. The line joining the two ends of the dotted line (which shows the cumulative profit/loss and the cumulative sales) indicates the average profit which will be earned from sales of the products in the mix.

8   lower

9   B. This is required contribution ÷ C/S ratio

10   (1)   economies
      (2)   diseconomies
      (3)   higher

Now try the question below from the Exam Question Bank			
Number	**Level**	**Marks**	**Time**
Q4	Examination	25	45 mins

Limiting factor analysis

Introduction

You have **already encountered limiting factor analysis** in your earlier studies and so we have included at the beginning of this chapter a reminder of the key concepts and basic techniques involved in this approach to allocating resources. Work through the examples and do the questions in **Section 1** to ensure that you are perfectly happy with the basics.

You need to build on this knowledge, however, and deal with situations in which organisations have **'restricted freedom of action'**. This type of problem is covered in **Section 2**.

In **Section 3** we will be considering the approach to take if an organisation has to buy in some of its products because it **cannot make in-house enough** to meet demand.

Shadow prices are covered in **Section 4**. Some students find it quite difficult to get their head around the concept so go over the material a number of times if necessary until you really understand it.

We end the chapter by looking at the issues to bear in mind when **using limiting factor analysis**.

Limiting factor analysis provides an ideal topic for objective test questions and appeared in a longer 25 mark question in both the November 2005 and May 2006 exams.

Limiting factor analysis can only be used if there is one limiting factor. If there are **two or more limiting factors**, a technique known as linear programming must be applied. This is covered in **Chapters 6 and 7**.

Topic list	Learning outcomes	Syllabus references	Ability required
1 Limiting factors	A(vii)	A(7)	Application
2 Limiting factor analysis and restricted freedom of action	A(vii)	A(7)	Application
3 Make or buy decisions and scarce resources	A(vii)	A(7)	Application
4 Limiting factors and shadow prices	A(vii)	A(7)	Application
5 Using limiting factor analysis	A(vii)	A(2), A(7)	Application

1 Limiting factors

FAST FORWARD

A **scarce resource** is a resource of which there is a limited supply. Once a scarce resource affects the ability of an organisation to earn profits, a scarce resource becomes known as a **limiting factor**.

Key term

A **limiting factor** or **key factor** is 'Anything which limits the activity of an entity. An entity seeks to optimise the benefit it obtains from the limiting factor'.   (CIMA *Official Terminology*)

Knowledge brought forward from earlier studies

Limiting factor analysis

- An organisation might be faced with just one limiting factor (other than maximum sales demand) but there might also be several scarce resources, with two or more of them putting an effective limit on the level of activity that can be achieved.

- Examples of limiting factors include sales demand and production constraints.

    – Labour. The limit may be either in terms of total quantity or of particular skills.

    – Materials. There may be insufficient available materials to produce enough units to satisfy sales demand.

    – Manufacturing capacity. There may not be sufficient machine capacity for the production required to meet sales demand.

- It is assumed in limiting factor analysis that management would make a product mix decision or service mix decision based on the option that would maximise profit and that profit is maximised when contribution is maximised (given no change in fixed cost expenditure incurred). **In other words, marginal costing ideas are applied.**

    – Contribution will be maximised by earning the biggest possible contribution per unit of limiting factor. For example if grade A labour is the limiting factor, contribution will be maximised by earning the biggest contribution per hour of grade A labour worked.

    – The limiting factor decision therefore involves the determination of the contribution earned per unit of limiting factor by each different product.

    – If the sales demand is limited, the profit-maximising decision will be to produce the top-ranked product(s) up to the sales demand limit.

- In limiting factor decisions, we generally assume that fixed costs are the same whatever product or service mix is selected, so that the only relevant costs are variable costs.

- When there is just one limiting factor, the technique for establishing the contribution-maximising product mix or service mix is to rank the products or services in order of contribution-earning ability per unit of limiting factor.

FAST FORWARD

If resources are limiting factors, **contribution** will be **maximised** by earning the biggest possible contribution per unit of limiting factor.

Where there is just one limiting factor, the technique for establishing the contribution-maximising product or service mix is to rank the products or services in order of contribution-earning ability per unit of limiting factor.

1.1 Example: limiting factor decision

Sausage makes two products, the Mash and the Sauce. Unit variable costs are as follows.

	Mash	Sauce
	$	$
Direct materials	1	3
Direct labour ($3 per hour)	6	3
Variable overhead	1	1
	8	7

The sales price per unit is $14 per Mash and $11 per Sauce. During July the available direct labour is limited to 8,000 hours. Sales demand in July is expected to be as follows.

Mash	3,000 units
Sauce	5,000 units

Required

Determine the production budget that will maximise profit, assuming that fixed costs per month are $20,000 and that there is no opening inventory of finished goods or work in progress.

Solution

Step 1   Confirm that the limiting factor is something other than sales demand.

	Mash	Sauces	Total
Labour hours per unit	2 hrs	1 hr	
Sales demand	3,000 units	5,000 units	
Labour hours needed	6,000 hrs	5,000 hrs	11,000 hrs
Labour hours available			8,000 hrs
Shortfall			3,000 hrs

Labour is the limiting factor on production.

Step 2   Identify the contribution earned by each product per unit of scarce resource, that is, per labour hour worked.

	Mash	Sauce
	$	$
Sales price	14	11
Variable cost	8	7
Unit contribution	6	4
Labour hours per unit	2 hrs	1 hr
Contribution per labour hour (= per unit of limiting factor)	$3	$4

Although Mashes have a higher unit contribution than Sauces, two Sauces can be made in the time it takes to make one Mash. Because labour is in short supply it is more profitable to make Sauces than Mashes.

Step 3   Determine the budgeted production and sales. Sufficient Sauces will be made to meet the full sales demand, and the remaining labour hours available will then be used to make Mashes.

(a)

Product	Demand	Hours required	Hours available	Priority for manufacture
Sauces	5,000	5,000	5,000	1st
Mashes	3,000	6,000	3,000 (bal)	2nd
		11,000	8,000	

(b)

Product	Units	Hours needed	Contribution per unit $	Total $
Sauces	5,000	5,000	4	20,000
Mashes (balance)	1,500	3,000	6	9,000
		8,000		29,000
Less fixed costs				20,000
Profit				9,000

Conclusion

(a) Unit contribution is *not* the correct way to decide priorities.

(b) Labour hours are the scarce resource, therefore **contribution per labour hour** is the correct way to decide priorities.

(c) The Sauce earns $4 contribution per labour hour, and the Mash earns $3 contribution per labour hour. Sauces therefore make more profitable use of the scarce resource, and should be manufactured first.

Question   Limiting factor decision

Learning outcome: A(vii)

Twickers makes two products, widgets and splodgets, for which there is unlimited demand at the budgeted selling prices. A widget takes three hours to make, and has a variable cost of $18 and a selling price of $30. A splodget takes two hours to make, and has a variable cost of $10 and a selling price of $20. Both products use the same type of labour, which is in short supply.

Required

Determine the product which should be made to maximise profits, and describe in detail the other considerations which might alter your decision.

Answer

We must **rank** the products in order of **contribution earning capability per labour hour**.

	Widgets per unit $	Splodgets per unit $
Sales price	30	20
Variable costs	18	10
Contribution	12	10
Hours per unit	3	2
Contribution per labour hour	$4	$5

Although widgets have the higher unit contribution, splodgets are more profitable because they make a greater contribution per labour hour. Three splodgets (worth 3 x $10 = $30) can be made in the same time as two widgets (worth only 2 x $12 = $24).

A profit-maximising decision would therefore be to produce splodgets only, given the assumptions made. It is important to remember, however, that **other considerations**, so far excluded from the problem, might alter the decision.

(a) Can the selling price of either product be raised, thereby increasing unit contribution, and the contribution per labour hour, and also reducing demand? Since demand is apparently unlimited, it would be reasonable to suspect that both products are underpriced.

(b) Would a decision to make and sell only splodgets have a harmful effect on customer loyalty and demand? To what extent are sales of each product interdependent? For example, a manufacturer of knives and forks could not expect to cease production of knives without affecting demand for forks.

(c) Would a decision to cease production of widgets have no effect on fixed costs? The assumption that fixed costs are unaffected by limiting factor decisions is not always valid, and closure of either the widgets or the splodgets production line might result in fixed cost savings. These savings would need to be considered when making the product mix decision.

(d) Will the decision affect the long-term plans of the company as well as the short term? If widgets are not produced, it is likely that competitors will take over the markets vacated by Twickers. Labour skilled in the manufacture of widgets will be lost, and a decision at a later date to re-open manufacture of widgets might not be possible.

Exam focus point

Limiting factor analysis is clearly a key exam technique that you must be able to use. There were MCQs very similar to the one above in the pilot paper, the May 2005 paper and the November 2006 paper.

There was also a limiting factor analysis required to rank products in a throughput accounting question in the November 2005 exam.

The May 2006 exam tested limiting factors in a Section C question. Candidates needed to assess the optimum production plan where a limiting factor existed and there was a risk of a financial penalty.

1.2 Two potentially limiting factors

You may be asked to deal with situations where two limiting factors are **potentially** limiting (and there are also product/service demand limitations). The approach in these situations is to find out which factor (if any) prevents the business from fulfilling maximum demand.

FAST FORWARD

Where there is a **maximum potential sales demand** for an organisation's products or services, they should still be ranked in order of contribution-earning ability per unit of the limiting factor. The contribution-maximising decision, however, will be to produce the top-ranked products (or to provide the top-ranked services) up to the sales demand limit.

1.2.1 Example: two potentially limiting factors

Lucky manufactures and sells three products, X, Y and Z, for which budgeted sales demand, unit selling prices and unit variable costs are as follows.

		X		Y		Z	
Budgeted sales demand		550 units		500 units		400 units	
		$	$	$	$	$	$
Unit sales price			16		18		14
Variable costs:	materials	8		6		2	
	labour	4		6		9	
			12		12		11
Unit contribution			4		6		3

The organisation has existing inventory of 250 units of X and 200 units of Z, which it is quite willing to use up to meet sales demand. All three products use the same direct materials and the same type of direct labour. In the next year, the available supply of materials will be restricted to $4,800 (at cost) and the available supply of labour to $6,600 (at cost).

Required

Determine what product mix and sales mix would maximise the organisation's profits in the next year.

Solution

There **appear to be two scarce resources**, direct materials and direct labour. This is not certain, however, and because there is a limited sales demand as well, either of the following might apply.

- There is **no limiting factor at all**, except sales demand.
- There is **only one scarce resource** that prevents the full potential sales demand being achieved.

Step 1   **Establish which of the resources, if any, is scarce.**

	X	Y	Z
	Units	Units	Units
Budgeted sales	550	500	400
Inventory in hand	250	0	200
Minimum production to meet demand	300	500	200

	Minimum production to meet sales demand	Required materials at cost	Required labour at cost
	Units	$	$
X	300	2,400	1,200
Y	500	3,000	3,000
Z	200	400	1,800
Total required		5,800	6,000
Total available		4,800	6,600
(Shortfall)/Surplus		(1,000)	600

Materials are a limiting factor, but labour is not.

Step 2   **Rank** X, Y and Z in order of contribution earned per $1 of direct materials consumed.

	X	Y	Z
	$	$	$
Unit contribution	4	6	3
Cost of materials	8	6	2
Contribution per $1 materials	$0.50	$1.00	$1.50
Ranking	3rd	2nd	1st

Step 3   **Determine a production plan.** Z should be manufactured up to the limit where units produced plus units held in inventory will meet sales demand, then Y second and X third, until all the available materials are used up.

Ranking	Product	Sales demand less units held Units	Production quantity Units		Materials cost $
1st	Z	200	200	(× $2)	400
2nd	Y	500	500	(× $6)	3,000
3rd	X	300	175	(× $8)	*1,400
		Total available			4,800

* Balancing amount using up total available.

Step 4   **Draw up a budget.** The profit-maximising budget is as follows.

	X	Y	Z
	Units	Units	Units
Opening inventory	250	0	200
Add production	175	500	200
Sales	425	500	400

	X	Y	Z	Total
	$	$	$	$
Revenue	6,800	9,000	5,600	21,400
Variable costs	5,100	6,000	4,400	15,500
Contribution	1,700	3,000	1,200	5,900

2 Limiting factor analysis and restricted freedom of action

In certain circumstances an organisation faced with a limiting factor on production and sales **might not be able to produce the profit-maximising product mix** because the mix and/or volume of products that can be produced and sold is also restricted by a factor other than a scarce resource.

(a)   A contract to **supply a certain number of products** to a customer

(b)   Production/sales of a minimum quantity of one or more products to **provide a complete product range and/or to maintain customer goodwill**

(c)   Maintenance of a **certain market share** of one or more products

In each of these cases, the organisation might have to **produce more of a particular product or products than the level established by ranking** according to contribution per unit of limiting factor.

FAST FORWARD

If an organisation has to **produce more of a particular product or products than the level established by ranking** according to contribution per unit of limiting factor, the products should be ranked in the normal way but the optimum production plan must first take into account the minimum production requirements. The remaining resource must then be allocated according to the ranking.

2.1 Example: restricted freedom of action

Harvey is currently preparing its budget for the year ending 30 September 20X2. The company manufactures and sells three products, Beta, Delta and Gamma.

The unit selling price and cost structure of each product is budgeted as follows.

	Beta	Delta	Gamma
	$	$	$
Selling price	100	124	32
Variable costs:			
Labour	24	48	6
Materials	26	7	8
Overhead	10	5	6
	60	60	20

Direct labour rate is budgeted at $6 per hour, and fixed costs at $1,300,000 per annum. The company has a maximum production capacity of 228,000 direct labour hours.

A meeting of the board of directors has been convened to discuss the budget and to resolve the problem as to the quantity of each product which should be made and sold. The sales director presented the results of a recent market survey which reveals that market demand for the company's products will be as follows.

Product	Units
Beta	24,000
Delta	12,000
Gamma	60,000

The production director proposes that since Gamma only contributes $12 per unit, the product should no longer be produced, and the surplus capacity transferred to produce additional quantities of Beta and Delta. The sales director does not agree with the proposal. Gamma is considered necessary to complement the product range and to maintain customer goodwill. If Gamma is not offered, the sales director believes that sales of Beta and Delta will be seriously affected. After further discussion the board decided that a minimum of 10,000 units of each product should be produced. The remaining production capacity would then be allocated so as to achieve the maximum profit possible.

Required

Prepare a budget statement which clearly shows the maximum profit which could be achieved in the year ending 30 September 20X2.

Solution

Step 1 **Ascertain whether labour hours are a scarce resource.**

	Units demanded	Labour hours per unit	Total labour hours
Beta	24,000	4 ($24/$6)	96,000
Delta	12,000	8 ($48/$6)	96,000
Gamma	60,000	1 ($6/$6)	60,000
			252,000

Step 2 **Rank the products.**
Since only 228,000 hours are available we need to establish which product earns the greatest contribution per labour hour.

	Beta	Delta	Gamma
Contribution ($)	40	64	12
Labour hours	4	8	1
Contribution per labour hour	$10	$8	$12
Ranking	2nd	3rd	1st

Step 3 **Determine a production plan.**
The optimum production plan must take into account the requirement that 10,000 units of each product are produced, and then allocate the remaining hours according to the above ranking.

		Hours
Beta	10,000 units × 4 hours	40,000
Delta	10,000 units × 8 hours	80,000
Gamma	10,000 units × 1 hour	10,000
		130,000
Gamma	50,000 units × 1 hour (full demand)	50,000
Beta	12,000 units × 4 hours (balance)	48,000
		228,000

Step 4 Draw up a budget.

BUDGET STATEMENT

	$
Contribution	
Beta (22,000 units × $40)	880,000
Delta (10,000 units × $64)	640,000
Gamma (60,000 units × $12)	720,000
	2,240,000
Fixed costs	1,300,000
Profit	940,000

Question

Learning outcome: A(vii)

JJ makes two products, the K and the L. The K sells for $50 per unit, the L for $70 per unit. The variable cost per unit of the K is $35, that of the L $40. Each unit of K uses 2 kgs of raw material. Each unit of L uses 3 kgs of material.

In the forthcoming period the availability of raw material is limited to 2,000 kgs. JJ is contracted to supply 500 units of K. Maximum demand for the L is 250 units. Demand for the K is unlimited.

What is the profit-maximising product mix?

	K	L
A	250 units	625 units
B	1,250 units	750 units
C	625 units	250 units
D	750 units	1,250 units

Answer

The correct answer is C.

	K	L
Contribution per unit	$15	$30
Contribution per unit of limiting factor	$15/2 = $7.50	$30/3 = $10
Ranking	2	1

Production plan	Raw material used kg
Contracted supply of K (500 x 2 kg)	1,000
Meet demand for L (250 x 3 kg)	750
Remainder of resource for K (125 x 2 kg)	250
	2,000

3 Make or buy decisions and scarce resources

An organisation might **want to do more things than it has the resources for**, and so its alternatives would be as follows.

(a) Make the best use of the available resources and ignore the opportunities to buy help from outside

(b) Combine internal resources with buying externally so as to do more and increase profitability

Buying help from outside is justifiable if it adds to profits. A further decision is then required on how to split the work between internal and external effort. What parts of the work should be given to suppliers or sub-contractors so as to maximise profitability?

FAST FORWARD

In a situation where a company must **sub-contract work to make up a shortfall in its own in-house capabilities**, its total costs will be minimised if those units bought have the lowest extra variable cost of buying per unit of scarce resource saved by buying.

3.1 Example: make or buy decision with scarce resources

MM manufactures three components, S, A and T using the same machines for each. The budget for the next year calls for the production and assembly of 4,000 of each component. The variable production cost per unit of the final product is as follows.

	Machine hours	Variable cost
		$
1 unit of S	3	20
1 unit of A	2	36
1 unit of T	4	24
Assembly		20
		100

Only 24,000 hours of machine time will be available during the year, and a sub-contractor has quoted the following unit prices for supplying components: S $29; A $40; T $34.

Required

Advise MM.

Solution

The organisation's budget calls for 36,000 hours of machine time, if all the components are to be produced in-house. Only 24,000 hours are available, and so there is a shortfall of 12,000 hours of machine time, which is therefore a limiting factor. The shortage can be overcome by subcontracting the equivalent of 12,000 machine hours' output to the subcontractor.

The assembly costs are not relevant costs because they are unaffected by the decision.

The decision rule is to **minimise the extra variable costs of sub-contracting per unit of scarce resource saved** (that is, per machine hour saved).

	S	A	T
	$	$	$
Variable cost of making	20	36	24
Variable cost of buying	29	40	34
Extra variable cost of buying	9	4	10
Machine hours saved by buying	3 hrs	2 hrs	4 hrs
Extra variable cost of buying per hour saved	$3	$2	$2.50

This analysis shows that it is **cheaper to buy A than to buy T** and it is **most expensive to buy S**. The **priority for making** the components in-house will be in the **reverse order**: S, then T, then A. There are enough machine hours to make all 4,000 units of S (12,000 hours) and to produce 3,000 units of T (another 12,000 hours). 12,000 hours' production of T and A must be sub-contracted.

The cost-minimising and so profit-maximising make and buy schedule is as follows.

Component	Machine hours used/saved	Number of units	Unit variable cost	Total variable cost
			$	$
Make: S	12,000	4,000	20	80,000
T	12,000	3,000	24	72,000
	24,000			152,000
Buy: T	4,000	1,000	34	34,000
A	8,000	4,000	40	160,000
	12,000			346,000

Total variable cost of components, excluding assembly costs

Question

Learning outcome: A(vii)

TW manufactures two products, the D and the E, using the same material for each. Annual demand for the D is 9,000 units, while demand for the E is 12,000 units. The variable production cost per unit of the D is $10, that of the E $15. The D requires 3.5 kgs of raw material per unit, the E requires 8 kgs of raw material per unit. Supply of raw material will be limited to 87,500 kgs during the year.

A sub contractor has quoted prices of $17 per unit for the D and $25 per unit for the E to supply the product. How many of each product should TW manufacture in order to maximise profits?

Required

Fill in the blanks in the sentence below.

TW should manufacture .... units of D and .... units of E to maximise profits.

Answer

The correct answer is: **TW should manufacture 9,000 units of D and 7,000 units of E.**

	D	E
	$ per unit	$ per unit
Variable cost of making	10	15
Variable cost of buying	17	25
Extra variable cost of buying	7	10
Raw material saved by buying	3.5 kgs	8 kgs
Extra variable cost of buying per kg saved	$2	$1.25
Priority for internal manufacture	1	2

Production plan

	Material used kgs
∴ Make D (9,000 × 3.5 kgs)	31,500
E (7,000 × 8 kgs)	56,000
	87,500

The remaining 5,000 units of E should be purchased from the contractor.

Question

Learning outcome A(vii)

B has insufficient workshop capacity to carry out all the repair work currently required on its fleet of delivery vehicles. In such circumstances certain repair jobs will be sub-contracted to local garages.

Set out below are the routine repair jobs scheduled for the coming week.

Job:	A	B	C	D	E	F
Cost of parts	$1,200	$1,375	$1,450	$550	$375	$690
Labour-hours	150	100	200	50	150	100
Equipment-hours	170	30	70	30	70	70
Sub-contract cost (including parts)	$3,950	$2,700	$4,900	$1,800	$2,700	$2,400

Labour is paid $6 per hour. Overtime is not worked on routine jobs. Labour-related variable overheads are $2 per labour hour. Equipment-related variable overheads are $1 per equipment-hour. Depreciation on workshop equipment is $960 per week. Other workshop fixed overheads are $1,540 per week.

Required

Which of the above jobs should be sub-contracted:

(a)   if the amount of workshop labour available in the week is fixed at 400 hours and there is no restriction on equipment availability;

(b)   if equipment capacity in the week is restricted to 200 hours, but there is no restriction on workshop labour?

Answer

(a)

	A	B	C	D	E	F
Additional cost of subcontracting (W)	$1,380	$495	$1,780	$820	$1,055	$840
Labour hours required	150	100	200	50	150	100
Cost per labour hour saved by subcontracting	$9.20	$4.95	$8.90	$16.40	$7.03	$8.40
Ranking of jobs to subcontract	5	1*	4	6	*2	*3

* Sub-contracted jobs

As labour capacity is restricted to 400 hours per week there is only enough capacity for jobs C, A and D. Jobs B, E and F should therefore be sub-contracted as they have the lowest incremental cost per labour hour saved.

(b)

	A	B	C	D	E	F
Additional cost of subcontracting (W)	$1,380	$495	$1,780	$820	$1,055	$840
Equipment hours required	170	30	70	30	70	70
Cost per equipment hour saved	$8.12	$16.50	$25.43	$27.33	$15.07	$12.00
Ranking of jobs to subcontract	*1	4	5	6	3	*2

* Sub-contracted jobs

As equipment capacity is restricted to 200 hours per week there is only enough capacity for jobs E, B, C and D. Jobs A and F should therefore be sub-contracted as they have the lowest incremental cost per equipment hour saved.

Working

Job	A	B	C	D	E	F
	$	$	$	$	$	$
Cost of doing work in-house						
Parts	1,200	1,375	1,450	550	375	690
Labour (labour hours × $6 per hour)	900	600	1,200	300	900	600
Labour-related overhead (labour hours × $2 per hour)	300	200	400	100	300	200
Equipment-related overhead (equipment hours × $1 per hour)	170	30	70	30	70	70
Total cost of doing work in-house	2,570	2,205	3,120	980	1,645	1,560
Cost of subcontracting (including parts)	3,950	2,700	4,900	1,800	2,700	2,400
Additional cost of subcontracting	1,380	495	1,780	820	1,055	840

4 Limiting factors and shadow prices

Whenever there are limiting factors, there will be **opportunity costs**. As you know, these are the **benefits forgone by using a limiting factor in one way instead of in the next most profitable way.**

For example, suppose that an organisation provides two services X and Y, which earn a contribution of $24 and $18 per unit respectively. Service X requires 4 labour hours, and service Y 2 hours. Only 5,000 labour hours are available, and potential demand is for 1,000 of each of X and Y.

Labour hours would be a limiting factor, and with X earning $6 per hour and Y earning $9 per hour, the profit-maximising decision would be as follows.

	Services	Hours	Contribution $
Y	1,000	2,000	18,000
X (balance)	750	3,000	18,000
		5,000	36,000

Priority is given to Y because the **opportunity cost** of providing Y instead of more of X is $6 per hour (X's contribution per labour hour), and since Y earns $9 per hour, the incremental benefit of providing Y instead of X would be $3 per hour.

If extra labour hours could be made available, more X (up to 1,000) would be provided, and an extra contribution of $6 per hour could be earned. Similarly, if fewer labour hours were available, the decision would be to provide fewer X and to keep provision of Y at 1,000, and so the loss of labour hours would cost the organisation $6 per hour in lost contribution. This $6 per hour, the **marginal contribution-earning potential of the limiting factor at the profit-maximising output level**, is referred to as the **shadow price** (or **dual price**) of the limiting factor.

FAST FORWARD

> The **shadow price** or **dual price** of a limiting factor is the increase in value which would be created by having one additional unit of the limiting factor at the original cost.

ey term

> A **shadow price** is 'An increase in value which would be created by having available one additional unit of a limiting resource at the original cost'.
> (CIMA *Official Terminology*)

Note that the shadow price only applies while the extra unit of resource can be obtained at its normal variable cost. The shadow price also indicates the amount by which contribution could fall if an organisation is deprived of one unit of the resource.

The shadow price of a resource is its **internal opportunity cost.** This is the marginal contribution towards fixed costs and profit that can be earned for each unit of the limiting factor that is available. A knowledge of the shadow price of a resource will help managers to decide how much it is worth paying to acquire another unit of the resource.

5 Using limiting factor analysis

am focus int

> Don't ignore this wordy session – if you were to get a full limiting factor analysis question in the exam there would undoubtedly be marks for discussion of pertinent non-quantifiable issues.

Limiting factor analysis provides us with a profit-maximising product mix, within the assumptions made. It is important to remember, however, that other considerations, so far not fully considered in our examples, might entirely alter the decision reached.

5.1 Non-quantifiable factors

Non-quantifiable factors, such as effect on customer goodwill, ability to restart production and reasons for a resource being a limiting factor, should also be borne in mind in product mix decisions.

Factor	Examples
Demand	Will the decision reached (perhaps to make and sell just one product rather than two) have a harmful effect on customer loyalty and sales demand? For example, a manufacturer of knives and forks could not expect to cease production of knives without affecting sales demand for the forks.
Long-term effects	Is the decision going to affect the long-term as well as the short-term plans of the organisation? If a particular product is not produced, or produced at a level below sales demand, is it likely that competitors will take over vacated markets? Labour skilled in the manufacture of the product may be lost and a decision to reopen or expand production of the product in the future may not be possible.
Labour	If labour is a limiting factor, is it because the skills required are difficult to obtain, perhaps because the organisation is using very old-fashioned production methods, or is the organisation a high-tech newcomer in a low-tech area? Or perhaps the conditions of work are so unappealing that people simply do not want to work for the organisation.
Other limiting factors	The same sort of questions should be asked whatever the limiting factor. If machine hours are in short supply is this because more machines are needed, or newer, more reliable and efficient machines? If materials are in short supply, what are competitors doing? Have they found an equivalent or better substitute? Is it time to redesign the product?

5.2 Assumptions in limiting factor analysis

Various **assumptions** are made in limiting factor analysis.

–   Fixed costs remain the same regardless of the decision taken.
–   Unit variable cost is constant regardless of the decision taken.
–   Estimates of sales demand and resources required are known with certainty.
–   Units of output are divisible.

In the examples covered in the chapter, certain assumptions were made. If any of the assumptions are not valid, then the profit-maximising decision might be different. These assumptions are as follows.

(a)   **Fixed costs will be the same** regardless of the decision that is taken, and so the profit-maximising and contribution-maximising output level will be the same.

This will not necessarily be true, since some fixed costs might be directly attributable to a product or service. A decision to reduce or cease altogether activity on a product or service might therefore result in some fixed cost savings, which would have to be taken into account.

(b)   **The unit variable cost is constant,** regardless of the output quantity of a product or service. This implies the following.

(i)   The price of resources will be unchanged regardless of quantity; for example, there will be no bulk purchase discount of raw materials.

(ii)   Efficiency and productivity levels will be unchanged; regardless of output quantity the direct labour productivity, the machine time per unit, and the materials consumption per unit will remain the same.

(c)   **The estimates of sales demand** for each product, and the **resources required** to make each product, **are known with certainty**.

In the example in Section 1.2.1, there were estimates of the budgeted sales demand for each of three products, and these estimates were used to establish the profit-maximising product mix. Suppose the estimates were wrong? The product mix finally chosen would then either mean that some sales demand of the most profitable item would be unsatisfied, or that production would exceed sales demand, leaving some inventory unsold. Clearly, once a profit-maximising output decision is reached, management will have to keep their decision under continual review, and adjust their decision as appropriate in the light of actual results.

(d)   **Units of output are divisible**, and a profit-maximising solution might include fractions of units as the optimum output level.

Where fractional answers are not realistic, some rounding of the figures will be necessary.

am focus
int

An examination problem might present you with a situation in which there is a limiting factor, without specifically stating that this is so, and you will have the task of recognising what the situation is. You may be given a hint with the wording of the question.

(a)   'It is possible that the main raw material used in manufacturing the products will be difficult to obtain in the next year.'

(b)   'The company employs a fixed number of employees who work a maximum overtime of eight hours on top of the basic 36 hour week. The company has also agreed that no more staff will be recruited next year.'

In (a) there is a hint that raw materials might be a limiting factor. In (b), perhaps less obviously, a maximum limit is placed on the available labour hours, and so the possibility should occur to you that perhaps labour is a limiting factor.

If you suspect the existence of a limiting factor, some quick computations should confirm your suspicions.

(a)   Calculate the amount of the scarce resource (material quantities, labour hours, machine hours and so on) needed to meet the potential sales demand.

(b)   Calculate the amount of the scarce resource available (for example number of employees multiplied by maximum working hours per employee).

(c)   Compare the two figures. Obviously, if the resources needed exceed the resources available, there is a limiting factor on output and sales.

Chapter Roundup

- A **scarce resource** is a resource of which there is a limited supply. Once a scarce resource affects the ability of an organisation to earn profits, a scarce resource becomes known as **a limiting factor**.

- If resources are limiting factors, **contribution** will be **maximised** by earning the biggest possible contribution per unit of limiting factor.

- **Where there is just one limiting factor**, the technique for establishing the contribution-maximising product or service mix is to rank the products or services in order of contribution-earning ability per unit of limiting factor.

- Where there is a **maximum potential sales demand** for an organisation's products or services, they should still be ranked in order of contribution-earning ability per unit of the limiting factor. The contribution-maximising decision, however, will be to produce the top-ranked products (or to provide the top-ranked services) up to the sales demand limit.

- If an organisation has to **produce more of a particular product or products than the level established by ranking** according to contribution per unit of limiting factor, the products should be ranked in the normal way but the optimum production plan must first take into account the minimum production requirements. The remaining resource must then be allocated according to the ranking.

- In a situation where an organisation must **subcontract work to make up a shortfall in its own in-house capabilities**, its total costs will be minimised if the units bought have the lowest extra variable cost of buying per unit of scarce resource saved by buying.

- The **shadow price** or **dual price** of a limiting factor is the increase in value which would be created by having one additional unit of the limiting factor at the original cost.

- **Non-quantifiable factors**, such as effect on customer goodwill, ability to restart production and reasons for a resource being a limiting factor, should also be borne in mind in product mix decisions.

- Various **assumptions** are made in limiting factor analysis.

    - Fixed costs remain the same regardless of the decision taken.
    - Unit variable cost is constant regardless of the decision taken.
    - Estimates of sales demand and resources required are known with certainty.
    - Units of output are divisible.

Quick Quiz

1   *Choose the correct word from those highlighted.*

When there is just one limiting factor, the product with the **biggest/smallest** contribution earning ability per unit of limiting factor should be produced first.

2   Which of the following is not an example of a limiting factor?

    A   Sales demand
    B   Materials
    C   Machine time
    D   Profit

3   Marginal costing ideas are applied in limiting factor analysis. *True or false?*

4   *Put the following in the correct order of approach to adopt when dealing with limiting factor analysis and limited freedom of action.*

    (a)   Allocate resource according to ranking
    (b)   Rank the products
    (c)   Take into account minimum production requirements

5   *Choose the correct words from those highlighted.*

If an organisation has to subcontract work to make up a shortfall in its own in-house capabilities, its total costs will be minimised if those units bought have the **highest/lowest** extra **variable cost/resource requirement** of buying per **unit of scarce resource/$** saved.

6   *Fill in the blanks.*

The shadow price of a scarce resource indicates the amount by which contribution would .... if an organisation were deprived of one unit of the resource. The shadow price only applies while the extra unit of resource can be obtained at its .... cost.

7   *Use the words listed below to fill in the blanks in the following statements about the assumptions in limiting factor analysis.*

Missing words: units of output; sales demand and resources required per unit; unit variable cost; fixed costs.

    (a)   .... will be the same regardless of the decision taken.
    (b)   The .... is constant, regardless of the output quantity.
    (c)   The estimates of .... are known with certainty.
    (d)   .... are divisible.

8   The following details relate to three services offered by DSF.

	V	A	L
	$ per service	$ per service	$ per service
Selling price of service	120	170	176
Direct labour	20	30	20
Variable overhead	40	56	80
Fixed overhead	20	32	40
	80	118	140
Profit	40	52	36

All three services use the same direct labour, but in different quantities.

In a period when the labour used on these services is in short supply, the most and least profitable use of the labour is:

	Most profitable	Least profitable
A	L	V
B	L	A
C	V	A
D	A	L

Answers to Quick Quiz

1   biggest

2   D. Limiting factors are resources or demand.

3   True

4   (b), (c), (a)

5   Lowest
     Variable cost
     Unit of scarce resource

6   fall
     normal variable

7   (a)   Fixed costs
     (b)   Unit variable cost
     (c)   Sales demand and resources required per unit
     (d)   Units of output

8   B

	V	*A*	*L*
	$	$	$
Selling price per service	120	170	176
Variable cost per service	60	86	100
Contribution per service	60	84	76
Labour cost per service	$20	$30	$20
Contribution per $ of labour	$3	$2.80	$3.80
Ranking	2	3	1

Now try the questions below from the Exam Question Bank

Number	Level	Marks	Time
Q5	Examination	10	18 mins
Q6	Examination	10	18 mins

BPP
LEARNING MEDIA

Linear programming: the graphical method

Introduction

In the previous chapter we saw how to determine the profit-maximising allocation of resources when an organisation is faced with just one resource constraint. When there is **more than one resource constraint**, the technique of **linear programming** can be used. This technique can be applied to problems with the following features.

- There is a **single objective**, which is to **maximise** or **minimise the value of a certain function**. The objective in commercial decision making is usually to **maximise contribution** and **thus maximise profit.**

- There are **several constraints**, typically scarce resources, that limit the value of the objective function.

There are two linear programming techniques. The **graphical method** is used for problems involving **two products**. The **simplex method** is used if the problem involves **more than two products.**

We will be looking at the graphical method in this chapter. The simplex method is covered in the next chapter.

Section 1 provides a **detailed step-by-step approach** to graphical linear programming. Make sure that you really understand how to carry out each step before you move on to the next.

Since the new syllabus was first examined in May 2005, the examiner hasn't tested this area. However, it remains on the syllabus and so you will still need to be prepared to answer exam questions if they are set.

Topic list	Learning outcomes	Syllabus references	Ability required
1 The graphical method	A(vii),(viii)	A(8)	Application/Analysis
2 The graphical method using simultaneous equations	A(vii),(viii)	A(8)	Application/Analysis
3 Different objectives	A(vii),(viii)	A(8)	Application/Analysis
4 Sensitivity analysis	A(vii), C(ii)	A(8), C(2)	Application

1 The graphical method

The **graphical method** of linear programming is used for problems involving two products.

1.1 Formulating the problem

Let us suppose that WX manufactures two products, A and B. Both products pass through two production departments, mixing and shaping. The organisation's objective is to maximise contribution to fixed costs.

Product A is sold for $1.50 whereas product B is priced at $2.00. There is unlimited demand for product A but demand for B is limited to 13,000 units per annum. The machine hours available in each department are restricted to 2,400 per annum. Other relevant data are as follows.

Machine hours required	Mixing Hrs	Shaping Hrs
Product A	0.06	0.04
Product B	0.08	0.12

Variable cost per unit	$
Product A	1.30
Product B	1.70

Before we work through the steps involved in solving this constraints problem using the graphical approach to linear programming, it is worth reading the CIMA *Official Terminology* definition of linear programming to get a glimpse of what we will be doing.

Key term

> **Linear programming** is 'The use of a series of linear equations to construct a mathematical model. The objective is to obtain an optimal solution to a complex operational problem, which may involve the production of a number of products in an environment in which there are many constraints'.
>
> (CIMA *Official Terminology*)

Question   Constraints

Learning outcomes: A(vii), (viii)

What are the constraints in the situation facing WX?

(i)   Machine hours in each department
(ii)   Labour hours in each department
(iii)   Sales demand for product B
(iv)   Selling price of product A

A   (i) and (iii)
B   (i) only
C   (ii) and (iv)
D   (i), (ii) and (iii)

Answer

The correct answer is A. There is no restriction on the availability of labour hours. Selling price cannot be a constraint.

FAST FORWARD

The **steps in the graphical method** are as follows.

- Define variables.
- Establish objective function.
- Establish constraints.
- Draw a graph of the constraints.
- Establish the feasible region.
- Determine the optimal product mix.

Let's start solving WX's problem.

Step 1 **Define variables**

What are the **quantities that WX can vary**? Obviously not the number of machine hours or the demand for product B. The only things which it can vary are the **number of units of each type of product produced**. It is those numbers which the company has to determine in such a way as to obtain the maximum possible profit. Our variables (which are usually products being produced) will therefore be as follows.

Let x = number of units of product A produced.
Let y = number of units of product B produced.

Step 2 **Establish objective function**

ey term

> The **objective function** is a quantified statement of the aim of a resource allocation decision.

We now need to introduce the question of contribution or profit. We know that the **contribution on each type of product** is as follows.

		$ per unit
Product A	$(1.50 − 1.30) =	0.20
Product B	$(2.00 − 1.70) =	0.30

The **objective of the company is to maximise contribution** and so the **objective function to be maximised** is as follows.

Contribution (C) = 0.2x + 0.3y

Step 3 **Establish constraints**

ey term

> A **constraint** is 'An activity, resource or policy that limits the ability to achieve objectives'.
>
> (CIMA *Official Terminology*)

The **value of the objective function** (the maximum contribution achievable from producing products A and B) is **limited by the constraints** facing WX, however. To incorporate this into the problem we need to **translate the constraints into inequalities involving the variables** defined in Step 1. An inequality is an equation taking the form 'greater than or equal to' or 'less than or equal to'.

(a) Consider the **mixing department machine hours** constraint.

   (i) **Each unit of product A** requires 0.06 hours of machine time. Producing five units therefore requires 5×0.06 hours of machine time and, more generally, **producing x units will require 0.06x hours**.

   (ii) Likewise producing **y units of product B will require 0.08y hours.**

   (iii) The total machine hours needed in the mixing department to make x units of product A and y units of product B is 0.06x + 0.08y.

(iv) We know that this **cannot be greater than 2,400 hours** and so we arrive at the following inequality.

0.06x + 0.08y ≤ 2,400

Question

Learning outcomes: A(vii), (viii)

How can the constraint facing the shaping department be written as an inequality?

A $0.4x + 0.012y \geq 2,400$
B $0.04x + 0.12y \leq 2,400$
C $0.4x + 0.012y \leq 2,400$
D $0.04x + 0.12y \geq 2,400$

Answer

The correct answer is B. The constraint has to be a 'less than equal to' inequality, because the amount of resource used (0.04x + 0.12y) has to be 'less than equal to' the amount available of 2,400 hours.

(b) The final inequality is easier to obtain. The **number of units of product B produced and sold is y** but this has to be **less than or equal to 13,000**. Our inequality is therefore as follows.

y ≤ 13,000

(c) We also need to add **non-negativity constraints** (x ≥ 0, y ≥ 0) since negative numbers of products cannot be produced. (Linear programming is simply a mathematical tool and so there is nothing in this method which guarantees that the answer will 'make sense'. An unprofitable product may produce an answer which is negative. This is mathematically correct but nonsense in operational terms. Always remember to include the non-negativity constraints. The examiner will not appreciate 'impossible' solutions.)

The **problem** has now been **reduced** to the following **four inequalities** and **one equation**.

Maximise contribution (C) = 0.2x + 0.3y, subject to the following constraints:

$$0.06x + 0.08y \leq 2,400$$
$$0.04x + 0.12y \leq 2,400$$
$$0 \leq y \leq 13,000$$
$$0 \leq x$$

Question

Learning outcomes: A(vii), (viii)

An organisation makes two products, X and Y. Product X has a contribution of $124 per unit and product Y $80 per unit. Both products pass through two departments for processing and the times in minutes per unit are as follows.

	Product X	Product Y
Department 1	150	90
Department 2	100	120

Currently there is a maximum of 225 hours per week available in department 1 and 200 hours in department 2. The organisation can sell all it can produce of X but EU quotas restrict the sale of Y to a maximum of 75 units per week. The organisation, which wishes to maximise contribution, currently makes and sells 30 units of X and 75 units of Y per week.

Required

Assume x and y are the number of units of X and Y produced per week. Formulate a linear programming model of this problem, filling in the blanks in (a) and (b) below.

(a)   The objective function is to maximise weekly contribution, given by C = ...

(b)   The constraints are:

Department 1 .... EU quota ....

Department 2 .... Non-negativity ....

Answer

(a)   The objective function is to maximise weekly contribution, given by C = 124x + 80y.

(b)   The constraints are:

Department 1	$150x + 90y$	$\leq$	225×60 minutes
Department 2	$100x + 120y$	$\leq$	200×60 minutes
EU quota	y	$\leq$	75
Non-negativity	x, y	$\geq$	0

These constraints can be simplified to:

Department 1	$15x + 9y$	$\leq$	1,350
Department 2	$10x + 12y$	$\leq$	1,200
EU quota	y	$\leq$	75
Non-negativity	x, y	$\geq$	0

1.2 Graphing the problem

A **graphical solution** is **only possible** when there are **two variables** in the problem. One variable is represented by the **x axis** of the graph and one by the **y axis**. Since non-negative values are not usually allowed, the graph shows **only zero and positive values of x and y**.

1.2.1 Graphing equations and constraints

A **linear equation with one or two variables** is shown as a **straight line on a graph**. Thus y = 6 would be shown as follows.

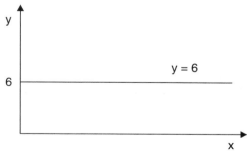

If the problem included a **constraint that y could not exceed 6**, the **inequality y ≤ 6** would be represented by the **shaded area of the graph below**.

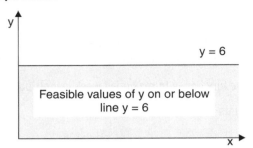

The equation 4x + 3y = 24 is also a straight line on a graph. To **draw any straight line**, we **need only to plot two points and join them up**. The easiest points to plot are the following.

- x = 0 (in this example, if x = 0, 3y = 24, y = 8)
- y = 0 (in this example, if y = 0, 4x = 24, x = 6)

By plotting the points, (0, 8) and (6, 0) on a graph, and joining them up, we have the line for 4x + 3y = 24.

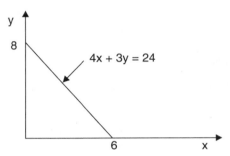

Any combination of values for x and y on the line satisfies the equation. Thus at a point where x = 3 and y = 4, 4x + 3y = 24. Similarly, at a point where x = 4.5 and y = 2, 4x + 3y = 24.

If we had a **constraint 4x + 3y ≤ 24**, **any combined value of x and y within the shaded area below (on or below the line)** would satisfy the constraint.

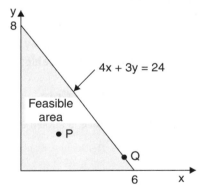

Consider point P which has coordinates of (2, 2). Here 4x + 3y = 14, which is less than 24; and at point Q where x = 5½, y = 2/3, 4x + 3y = 24. **Both P and Q lie within the feasible area** or **feasible region. A feasible area enclosed on all sides may also be called a feasible polygon.**

Key term

> A **feasible region** is 'The area contained within all of the constraint lines shown on a graphical depiction of a linear programming problem. All feasible combinations of output are contained within or located on the boundaries of the feasible region'.
> (CIMA *Official Terminology*)

When there are **several constraints**, the **feasible area** of combinations of values of x and y must be an area **where all the inequalities are satisfied**. Thus, if **y ≤ 6 and 4x + 3y ≤ 24** the **feasible area** would be the **shaded area** in the following graph.

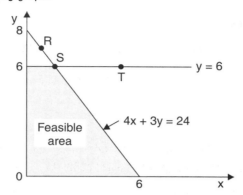

(a)   Point R (x = 0.75, y = 7) is not in the feasible area because although it satisfies the inequality 4x + 3y ≤ 24, it does not satisfy y ≤ 6.

(b)   Point T (x = 5, y = 6) is not in the feasible area, because although it satisfies the inequality y ≤ 6, it does not satisfy 4x + 3y ≤ 24.

(c)   Point S (x = 1.5, y = 6) satisfies both inequalities and lies just on the boundary of the feasible area since y = 6 exactly, and 4x + 3y = 24. Point S is thus at the intersection of the two lines.

Similarly, if y ≥ 6 and 4x + 3y ≥ 24 but x is ≤ 6, the feasible area would be the shaded area in the graph below.

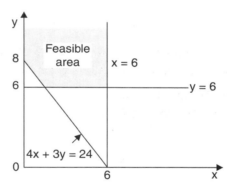

Learning outcomes: A(vii), (viii)

Draw the feasible region which arises from the constraints facing WX on the graph below.

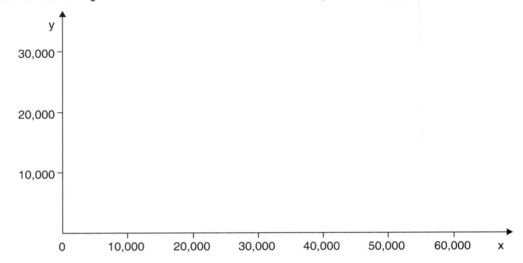

Answer

If $0.06x + 0.08y = 2,400$, then if $x = 0$, $y = 30,000$ and if $y = 0$, $x = 40,000$.
If $0.04x + 0.12y = 2,400$, then if $x = 0$, $y = 20,000$ and if $y = 0$, $x = 60,000$.

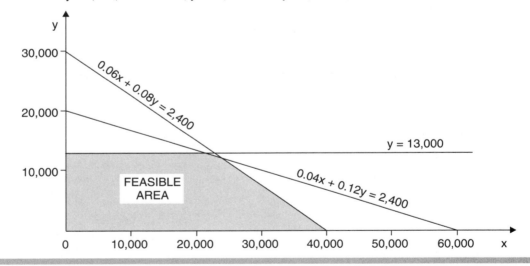

1.3 Finding the optimum allocation of resources

FAST FORWARD

> The **optimal solution** can be found by 'sliding the iso-contribution (or profit) line out'.

Having found the feasible region (which includes all the possible solutions to the problem) we need to **find which of these possible solutions is 'best'** or **optimal** in the sense that it yields the maximum possible contribution.

Look at the feasible region of the problem faced by WX (see the solution to the question above). Even in such a simple problem as this, there are a **great many possible solution points within the feasible area.** Even to write them all down would be a time-consuming process and also an unnecessary one, as we shall see.

Here is the graph of WX's problem.

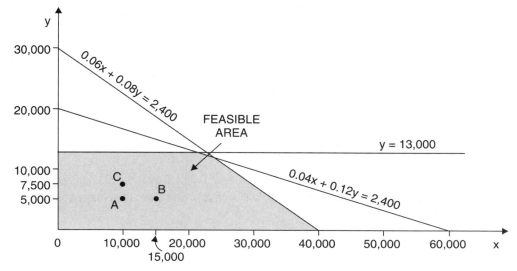

(a)   Consider point A at which 10,000 units of product A and 5,000 units of product B are being manufactured. This will yield a contribution of (10,000 × $0.20) + (5,000 × $0.30) = $3,500.

(b)   We would clearly get more contribution at point B, where the same number of units of product B are being produced but where the number of units of product A has increased by 5,000.

(c)   We would also get more contribution at point C where the number of units of product A is the same but 2,500 more units of product B are being produced.

This argument suggests that the **'best' solution** is going to be at a **point on the edge of the feasible area** rather than in the middle of it.

This still leaves us with quite a few points to look at but there is a way in which we can **narrow down still further the likely points at which the best solution will be found.** Suppose that WX wishes to earn contribution of $3,000. The company could sell the following combinations of the two products.

(a)   15,000 units of A, no B.
(b)   No A, 10,000 units of B.
(c)   A suitable mix of the two, such as 7,500 A and 5,000 B.

The **possible combinations required to earn contribution of $3,000** could be **shown by the straight line $0.2x + 0.3y = 3,000$.**

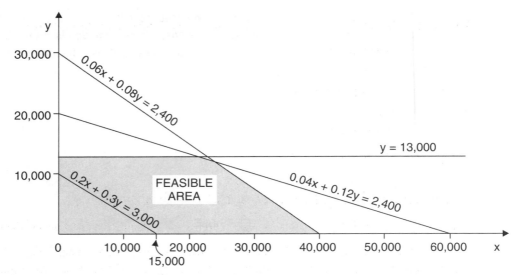

Likewise for profits of $6,000 and $1,500, lines of 0.2x + 0.3y = 6,000 and 0.2x + 0.3y = 1,500 could be drawn **showing the combination of the two products** which would **achieve contribution of $6,000 or $1,500.**

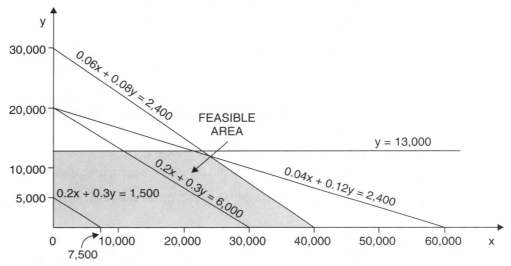

The **contribution lines are all parallel**. (They are called **iso-contribution lines**, 'iso' meaning equal.) A similar line drawn for any other total contribution would also be parallel to the three lines shown here. **Bigger contribution is shown by lines further from the origin** (0.2x + 0.3y = 6,000), smaller contribution by lines closer to the origin (0.2x + 0.3y = 1,500). As WX tries to increase possible contribution, we need to 'slide' any contribution line outwards from the origin, while always keeping it parallel to the other contribution lines.

As we do this there will come a point at which, if we were to **move the contribution line out any further, it would cease to lie in the feasible region**. Greater contribution could not be achieved, because of the constraints. In our example concerning WX this will happen, as you should test for yourself, where the contribution line just passes through the intersection of 0.06x + 0.08y = 2,400 and 0.04x + 0.12y = 2,400 (at coordinates (24,000, 12,000)). The point (24,000, 12,000) will therefore give us the optimal allocation of resources (to produce 24,000 units of A and 12,000 units of B).

We can usefully summarise the graphical approach to linear programming as follows.

Step 1   Define variables.

Step 2   Establish objective function.

Step 3   Establish constraints.

Step 4   Graph the problem.

Step 5   Define feasible area.

Step 6   Determine optimal solution.

1.4 Example: the graphical solution with a twist

This example shows that it is not always necessarily easy to identify the decision variables in a problem.

DCC operates a small plant for the manufacture of two joint chemical products X and Y. The production of these chemicals requires two raw materials, A and B, which cost $5 and $8 per litre respectively. The maximum available supply per week is 2,700 litres of A and 2,000 litres of B.

The plant can operate using either of two processes, which have differing operating costs and raw materials requirements for the production of X and Y, as follows.

Process	Raw materials consumed Litres per processing hour		Output Litres per hour		Cost $ per hour
	A	B	X	Y	
1	20	10	15	20	500
2	30	20	20	10	230

The plant can run for 120 hours per week in total, but for safety reasons, process 2 cannot be operated for more than 80 hours per week.

X sells for $18 per litre, Y for $24 per litre.

Required

Formulate a linear programming model, and then solve it, to determine how the plant should be operated each week.

Solution

Step 1   **Define variables**

You might decide that there are two decision variables in the problem, the quantity of X and the quantity of Y to make each week. If so, begin by letting these be x and y respectively.

You might also readily recognise that the aim should be to maximise the total weekly contribution, and so the objective function should be expressed in terms of maximising the total contribution from X and Y.

The contribution per litre from X and Y cannot be calculated because the operating costs are expressed in terms of processing hours.

	Process 1			Process 2	
	$ per hour	$ per hour		$ per hour	$ per hour
Costs:					
Material A		100			150
Material B		80			160
Operating cost		500			230
		680			540
Revenue:					
X $(15 \times \$18)$	270		$(20 \times \$18)$	360	
Y $(20 \times \$24)$	480		$(10 \times \$24)$	240	
		750			600
Contribution		70			60

The **decision variables** should be **processing hours in each process**, rather than litres of X and Y. If we let the processing hours per week for process 1 be P_1 and the processing hours per week for process 2 be P_2 we can now formulate an objective function, and constraints, as follows.

Step 2   **Establish objective function**

Maximise $70P_1 + 60P_2$ (total contribution) subject to the constraints below

Step 3   **Establish constraints**

$$20P_1 + 30P_2 \leq 2,700 \quad \text{(material A supply)}$$
$$10P_1 + 20P_2 \leq 2,000 \quad \text{(material B supply)}$$
$$P_2 \leq 80 \quad \text{(maximum time for } P_2\text{)}$$
$$P_1 + P_2 \leq 120 \quad \text{(total maximum time)}$$
$$P_1, P_2 \geq 0$$

Step 4   **Graph the problem**

The graphical solution looks like this.

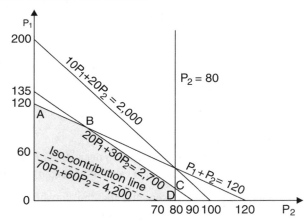

Step 5   **Define feasible area**

The material B constraint is not critical, and the feasible area for a solution is shown as ABCDO on the graph.

Step 6   **Determine optimal solution**

The optimal solution, determined using the iso-contribution line $70P_1 + 60P_2 = 4,200$, is at point A, where $P_1 = 120$ and $P_2 = 0$.

Production would be (120×15) 1,800 litres of X and (120×20) 2,400 litres of Y.

Total contribution would be $(120 \times \$70) = \$8,400$ per week.

Question

Learning outcomes: A(vii), (viii)

On 20 days of every month GS makes two products, the Crete and the Corfu. Production is carried out in three departments – tanning, plunging and watering. Relevant information is as follows.

	Crete	Corfu
Contribution per unit	$75	$50
Minutes in tanning department per unit	10	12
Minutes in plunging department per unit	15	10
Minutes in watering department per unit	6	15
Maximum monthly sales (due to government quota restrictions)	3,500	4,000

	Tanning	Plunging	Watering
Number of employees	7	10	5
Hours at work per day per employee	7	6	10
Number of idle hours per day per employee	0.5	1	0.25

Due to union restrictions, employees cannot be at work for longer than the hours detailed above.

Required

Use the graphical method of linear programming to determine the optimum monthly production of Cretes and Corfus and the monthly contribution if GS's objective is to maximise contribution.

Answer

Calculate the number of productive hours worked in each department each month

Number of employees x number of productive hours worked each day x number of days each month.

Tanning = $7 \times (7 - 0.5) \times 20 = 910$ hours
Plunging = $10 \times (6 - 1) \times 20 = 1,000$ hours
Watering = $5 \times (10 - 0.25) \times 20 = 975$ hours

Step 1   **Define variables**
Let the number of Cretes produced each month = x and the number of Corfus produced each month = y.

Step 2   **Establish objective function**
The contribution is $75 per Crete and $50 per Corfu. The objective function is therefore maximise C = 75x + 50y subject to the constraints below.

Step 3   **Establish constraints**
Tanning	$x/6 + y/5 \leq 910$
Plunging	$x/4 + y/6 \leq 1,000$
Watering	$x/10 + y/4 \leq 975$
Monthly sales units	$x \leq 3,500, y \leq 4,000$
Non negativity	$x \geq 0, y \geq 0$

Step 4   **Graph the problem**
The problem can be solved using the following graph which includes a sample contribution line 75x + 50y = 150,000.

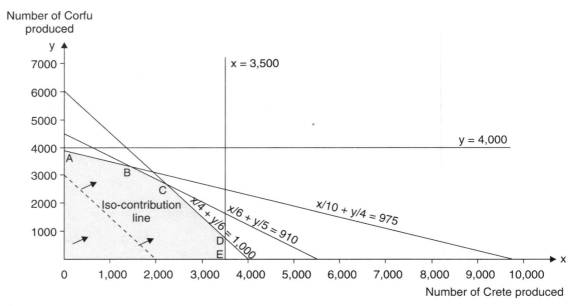

Step 5 Define the feasible area

The feasible region for a solution is OABCDE.

Step 6 Determine the optimal solution

Moving the sample contribution line across the feasible region it can be seen that the optimum solution is at any point along the line $x/4 + y/6 = 1,000$ between C and D (as the sample contribution line has the same gradient as the plunging constraint). The coordinates of point C are (2,175, 2,737.5) while those of point D are (3,500, 750).

The contribution from any of these solutions is $((75 \times 3,500) + (50 \times 750)) = \$300,000$ (using the coordinates of D).

2 The graphical method using simultaneous equations

Instead of a 'sliding the contribution line out' approach, **simultaneous equations** can be used to determine the optimal allocation of resources, as shown in the following example.

> **FAST FORWARD**
>
> The optimal solution can also be found using **simultaneous equations**.

2.1 Example: using simultaneous equations

An organisation manufactures plastic-covered steel fencing in two qualities: standard and heavy gauge. Both products pass through the same processes involving steel forming and plastic bonding.

The standard gauge sells at $15 a roll and the heavy gauge at $20 a roll. There is an unlimited market for the standard gauge but outlets for the heavy gauge are limited to 13,000 rolls a year. The factory operations of each process are limited to 2,400 hours a year. Other relevant data is given below.

Variable costs per roll

	Direct material	*Direct wages*	*Direct expense*
	$	$	$
Standard	5	7	1
Heavy	7	8	2

Processing hours per 100 rolls

	Steel forming Hours	Plastic bonding Hours
Standard	6	4
Heavy	8	12

Required

Calculate the allocation of resources and hence the production mix which will maximise total contribution.

Solution

Step 1   **Define variables**
Let the number of rolls of standard gauge to be produced be x and the number of rolls of heavy gauge be y.

Step 2   **Establish objective function**
Standard gauge produces a contribution of \$2 per roll (\$15 − \$(5 + 7 + 1)) and heavy gauge a contribution of \$3 (\$20 − \$(7 + 8 + 2)).

Therefore the objective is to maximise contribution (C) = 2x + 3y subject to the constraints below.

Step 3   **Establish constraints**
The constraints are as follows.

$$0.06x + 0.08y \leq 2,400 \qquad \text{(steel forming hours)}$$
$$0.04x + 0.12y \leq 2,400 \qquad \text{(plastic bonding hours)}$$
$$y \leq 13,000 \qquad \text{(demand for heavy gauge)}$$
$$x, y \geq 0 \qquad \text{(non-negativity)}$$

Step 4   **Graph problem**
The graph of the problem can now be drawn.

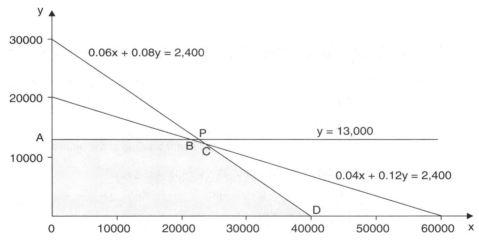

Step 5   **Define feasible area**
The combinations of x and y that satisfy all three constraints are represented by the area OABCD.

Step 6   **Determine optimal solution**
Which combination will maximise contribution? Obviously, the more units of x and y, the bigger the contribution will be, and the optimal solution will be at point B, C or D. It will not be at A, since at A, y = 13,000 and x = 0, whereas at B, y = 13,000 (the same) and x is greater than zero.

Using simultaneous equations to calculate the value of x and y at each of points B, C and D, and then working out total contribution at each point from this, we can establish the contribution-maximising product mix.

Point B

$$
\begin{aligned}
y &= 13,000 &&(1)\\
0.04x + 0.12y &= 2,400 &&(2)\\
0.12y &= 1,560 &&(3)\ ((1) \times 0.12)\\
0.04x &= 840 &&(4)\ ((2) - (3))\\
x &= 21,000 &&(5)
\end{aligned}
$$

Total contribution = $(21,000 \times \$2) + (13,000 \times \$3) = \$81,000$.

Point C

$$
\begin{aligned}
0.06x + 0.08y &= 2,400 &&(1)\\
0.04x + 0.12y &= 2,400 &&(2)\\
0.12x + 0.16y &= 4,800 &&(3)\ ((1) \times 2)\\
0.12x + 0.36y &= 7,200 &&(4)\ ((2) \times 3)\\
0.2y &= 2,400 &&(5)\ ((4) - (3))\\
y &= 12,000 &&(6)\\
0.06x + 960 &= 2,400 &&(7)\ (\text{substitute in (1)})\\
x &= 24,000 &&(8)
\end{aligned}
$$

Total contribution = $(24,000 \times \$2) + (12,000 \times \$3) = \$84,000$.

Point D

Total contribution = $40,000 \times \$2 = \$80,000$.

Comparing B, C and D, we can see that contribution is maximised at C, by making 24,000 rolls of standard gauge and 12,000 rolls of heavy gauge, to earn a contribution of $84,000.

2.2 Slack and surplus

Slack occurs when maximum availability of a resource is not used. **Surplus** occurs when more than a minimum requirement is used.

If, at the optimal solution, the resource used equals the resource available there is **no spare capacity** of a resource and so there is **no slack.**

If a resource which has a **maximum availability** is **not binding** at the optimal solution, there will be **slack**.

In the example above, the optimal solution is x = 24,000, y = 12,000.

If we substitute these values into the inequalities representing the constraints, we can determine whether the constraints are binding or whether there is slack.

Steel forming hours: $(0.06 \times 24,000) + (0.08 \times 12,000) = 2,400 = $ availability
Constraint is **binding.**

Plastic bonding hours: $(0.04 \times 24,000) + (0.12 \times 12,000) = 2,400 = $ availability
Constraint is **binding.**

Demand: Demand of $12,000 \le$ maximum demand of 13,000
There is **slack**.

Note that because we had already determined the optimal solution to be at the intersection of the steel forming hours and plastic bonding hours constraints, we knew that they were binding!

If a minimum quantity of a resource must be used and, at the optimal solution, **more than that quantity is used**, there is a **surplus** on the minimum requirement.

For example, suppose in a particular scenario a minimum of 8,000 grade A labour hours had to be worked in the production of products x and y, such that (say) $3x + 2y \geq 8,000$. If 10,000 hours are used to produce the optimal solution, there is a **surplus** of 2,000 hours.

We will be looking at this form of constraint in the next section.

3 Different objectives

So far the objective in the problems we have been looking at has been to maximise contribution. But linear programming can be used to allocate scarce resources between competing activities, products and so on in order to **maximise or minimise a range of numerical quantities including contribution.**

For example, problems might include determining the mix of ingredients to minimise costs, the mix of products to maximise revenue or the portfolio of investments to maximise worth. It can also be used for transport routing, production scheduling and personnel resource planning, the objective being to minimise costs.

Whatever the objective, the **optimal solution** is the one that yields the **largest value for the objective in the case of a maximisation problem**, the **smallest value in the case of a minimisation problem.**

FAST FORWARD

In a **minimisation problem** (minimise costs), the optimal solution is the point at which the total cost line touches the feasible polygon at a tangent as close to the origin as possible.

3.1 Minimisation problem

Although decision problems concerned with resource constraints usually involve the maximisation of contribution, there may be a **requirement to minimise costs.** The approach is similar to the one we have been looking at, with the exception that instead of finding a contribution line touching the feasible polygon at a tangent as far away from the origin as possible, we **look for a total cost line touching the feasible polygon at a tangent as close to the origin as possible.**

3.2 Example: minimising costs

BS has undertaken a contract to supply a customer with at least 260 units in total of two products, X and Y, during the next month. At least 50% of the total output must be units of X. The products are each made by two grades of labour, as follows.

	X Hrs	Y Hrs
Grade A labour	4	6
Grade B labour	4	2

Although additional labour can be made available at short notice, the company wishes to make use of 1,200 hours of grade A labour and 800 hours of grade B labour which have already been assigned to working on the contract next month. The total variable cost per unit is $120 for X and $100 for Y.

BS wishes to minimise expenditure on the contract next month.

Required

Calculate the number of units of X and Y that should be supplied in order to meet the terms of the contract.

Solution

Step 1 **Define variables**
Let the number of units of X supplied be x, and the number of units of Y supplied be y.

Step 2 **Define objective function**
Minimise 120x + 100y (costs) subject to the constraints below.

Step 3 **Establish constraints**

$$
\begin{aligned}
x + y &\geq 260 &&\text{(supply total)}\\
x &\geq 0.5\,(x + y) &&\text{(proportion of x in total)}\\
4x + 6y &\geq 1{,}200 &&\text{(grade A labour)}\\
4x + 2y &\geq 800 &&\text{(grade B labour)}\\
x, y &\geq 0
\end{aligned}
$$

The constraint $x \geq 0.5\,(x + y)$ needs simplifying further.

If	x	$\geq \ 0.5\,(x + y)$
then	$2x$	$\geq \ x + y$
and	x	$\geq \ y$

Steps 4 and 5 **Graph the problem and define the feasible area**

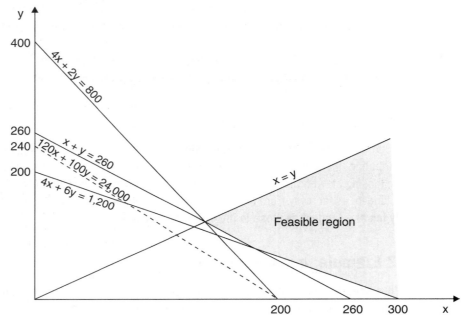

Step 6 **Determine the optimal solution**
The cost line 120x + 100y = 24,000 has been drawn to show the slope of every cost line 120x + 100y. Costs are minimised where a cost line touches the feasible region at a tangent, as close as possible to the origin of the graph. This occurs where the constraints line 4x + 2y = 800 crosses the line x + y = 260. At this point

	x + y = 260	.... (1)
	4x + 2y = 800	.... (2)
Divide (2) by 2	2x + y = 400	.... (3)
Subtract (1) from (3)	x = 140	
Substitute in (1)	y = 120	

Costs will be minimised by supplying the following output.

	Unit cost	Total cost
	$	$
140 units of X	120	16,800
120 units of Y	100	12,000
		28,800

The proportion of units of X in the total would exceed 50%, and demand for grade A labour would exceed the 1,200 hours minimum.

4 Sensitivity analysis

Once a graphical linear programming solution has been found, it should be possible to provide further information by interpreting the graph more fully to see what would happen if certain values in the scenario were to change.

(a) What if the contribution from one product was $1 lower than expected?
(b) What if the sales price of another product was raised by $2?
(c) What would happen if less or more of a limiting factor were available, such as material?

Sensitivity analysis with linear programming can be carried out in one of two ways.

(a) By **considering the value of each limiting factor or binding resource constraint**
(b) By **considering sale prices (or the contribution per unit)**

4.1 Limiting factor sensitivity analysis

We use the shadow price to carry out sensitivity analysis on the availability of a limiting factor.

4.1.1 Shadow prices

FAST FORWARD

The **shadow price** of a resource which is a limiting factor on production is the amount by which total contribution would fall if the organisation were deprived of one unit of the resource. The shadow price also indicates the amount by which total contribution would rise if the organisation were able to obtain one extra unit of the resource, provided that the resource remains an effective constraint on production and provided also that the extra unit of resource can be obtained at its normal variable cost.

We encountered the concept of shadow prices in Chapter 5 so you should have no problem in getting the following question correct.

Question   Shadow prices

Learning outcomes: A(vii), (viii)

Choose the correct words from those highlighted.

A shadow price is the **increase/decrease** in **contribution/revenue** created by the availability of an extra unit of a **resource/limiting resource** at **its original cost/a premium price**.

Answer

The correct answer is: A shadow price is the **increase** in **contribution** created by the availability of an extra unit of a **limiting resource** at its **original cost**.

So in terms of linear programming, the shadow price is the **extra contribution or profit that may be earned by relaxing by one unit a binding resource constraint**.

Suppose the availability of materials is a binding constraint. If one extra kilogram becomes available so that an alternative production mix becomes optimal, with a resulting increase over the original production mix contribution of $2, the shadow price of a kilogram of material is $2.

Note, however, that this increase in contribution of $2 per extra kilogram of material made available is calculated on the **assumption** that the **extra kilogram would cost the normal variable amount**.

Note the following points.

(a)   The shadow price therefore represents the maximum **premium** above the basic rate that an organisation should be **willing to pay for one extra unit** of a resource.

(b)   Since shadow prices indicate the effect of a one unit change in a constraint, they provide a measure of the **sensitivity** of the result.

(c)   The **shadow price** of a constraint that is **not binding** at the optimal solution is **zero**.

(d)   Shadow prices are **only valid for a small range** before the constraint becomes non-binding or different resources become critical.

Depending on the resource in question, shadow prices enable management to make **better informed decisions** about the payment of overtime premiums, bonuses, premiums on small orders of raw materials and so on.

4.1.2 Calculating shadow prices

In the earlier example of WX, the availability of time in both departments are limiting factors because both are used up fully in the optimal product mix. Let us therefore calculate the effect if **one extra hour of shaping department machine time** was made available so that 2,401 hours were available.

The **new optimal product mix would be at the intersection of the two constraint lines** $0.06x + 0.08y = 2,400$ and $0.04x + 0.12y = 2,401$.

Solution by simultaneous equations gives $x = 23,980$ and $y = 12,015$.

(You should solve the problem yourself if you are doubtful about the derivation of the solution.)

Product	Units	Contribution per unit $	Total contribution $
A	23,980	0.20	4,796.0
B	12,015	0.30	3,604.5
			8,400.5

Contribution in original problem ((24,000 × $0.20) + (12,000 × $0.30))	8,400.0
Increase in contribution from one extra hour of shaping time	0.5

The **shadow price of an hour of machining time in the shaping department is therefore $0.50.**

The **shadow price** of a limiting factor also shows by **how much contribution would fall if the availability of a limiting resource fell by one unit**. The **shadow price** (also called **dual price**) of an hour of machine time in the shaping department would again be calculated as $0.50. This is the **opportunity cost** of deciding to put an hour of shaping department time to an alternative use.

We can now make the following points.

(a)   The management of WX should be prepared to **pay up to $0.50 extra per hour** (ie $0.50 over and above the normal price) of shaping department machine time to obtain more machine hours.

(b)   This **value** of machine time **only applies as long as shaping machine time is a limiting factor.** If more and more machine hours become available, there will eventually be so much machine time that it is no longer a limiting factor.

Question

Shadow prices

Learning outcomes: A(vii), (viii)

What is the shadow price of one hour of machine time in the mixing department?

A $3
B $7
C $10.50
D $1,193

Answer

The correct answer is A.

If we assume one **less** hour of machine time in the mixing department is available, the new optimal solution is at the intersection of $0.06x + 0.08y = 2,399$ and $0.04x + 0.12y = 2,400$

Solution by simultaneous equations gives $x = 23,970$, $y = 12,010$

Product	Units	Contribution per unit $	Total contribution $
A	23,970	0.20	4,794
B	12,010	0.30	3,603
			8,397
Contribution in original problem			8,400
Reduction in contribution			3

∴ Shadow price of one hour of machine time in the mixing department is $3.

4.1.3 Ranges for limiting factors

We can calculate **how many hours will be available before machine time in the shaping department ceases to be a limiting factor.**

Look back at the third graph in Section 1.3. As more hours become available the constraint line moves out away from the origin. It ceases to be a limiting factor when it passes through the intersection of the sales constraint and the mixing department machine time constraint which is at the point (22,667, 13,000).

So, if $x = 22,667$ and $y = 13,000$, our new constraint would be $0.04x + 0.12y = H$ (hours) where $H = (0.04 \times 22,667) + (0.12 \times 13,000) = 2,466.68$ hours.

The shadow price of shaping department machine time is therefore $0.50 but only up to a maximum supply of 2,466.68 hours (that is 66.68 hours more than the original 2,400 hours). Extra availability of machine time above 2,466.68 hours would not have any use, and the two limiting factors would become sales demand for product B and machine time in the mixing department.

4.2 Sales price sensitivity analysis

FAST FORWARD

Sales price sensitivity analysis is carried out by changing the slope of the 'iso-contribution' line.

The optimal solution in our WX example was to make 24,000 units of product A and 12,000 units of product B. Would this solution change if the **unit sales price of A increased by 10p?**

The **contribution would increase** to 0.3x + 0.3y (in place of 0.2x + 0.3y). The **iso-contribution lines would now have a steeper slope** than previously, parallel (for example) to 0.3x + 0.3y = 3,000.

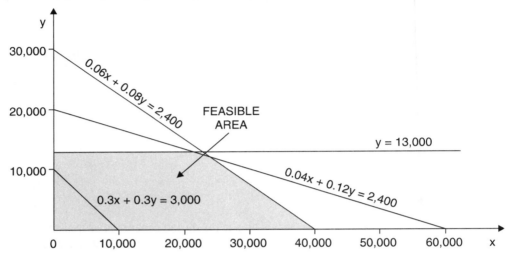

If you were to place a ruler along the iso-contribution line and move it away from the origin as usual, you would find its **last point within the feasible region** was the point (40,000, 0).

Therefore if the sales price of A is raised by 10p, WX's contribution-maximising product mix would be to produce 40,000 units of A and none of B.

4.2.1 Example: sensitivity analysis

SW makes two products, X and Y, which each earn a contribution of $8 per unit. Each unit of X requires four labour hours and three machine hours. Each unit of Y requires three labour hours and five machine hours.

Total weekly capacity is 1,200 labour hours and 1,725 machine hours. There is a standing weekly order for 100 units of X which must be met. In addition, for technical reasons, it is necessary to produce at least twice as many units of Y as units of X.

Required

(a)   Determine the contribution-maximising production plan each week.

(b)   Calculate the shadow price of the following.

    (i)   Machine hours
    (ii)   Labour hours
    (iii)   The minimum weekly demand for X of 100 units

Solution (a): production plan

The linear programming problem may be formulated as follows.

Step 1   **Define variables**

Let x = number of units of X produced and y = number of units of Y produced.

Step 2   **Establish objective function**

Maximise contribution (c) = 8x + 8y subject to the constraints below.

Step 3   **Establish constraints**

$$4x + 3y \leq 1{,}200 \quad \text{(labour hours)}$$
$$3x + 5y \leq 1{,}725 \quad \text{(machine hours)}$$
$$x \geq 100 \quad \text{(minimum demand)}$$
$$y \geq 2x \quad \text{(technical constraint)}$$
$$y \geq 0 \quad \text{(non-negativity)}$$

Step 4   **Graph the problem**

The graph of this problem would be drawn as follows, using 8x + 8y = 2,400 as an iso-contribution line.

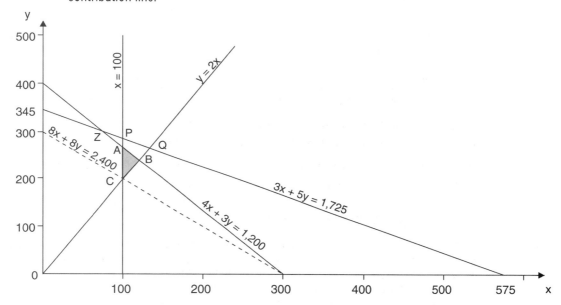

Step 5   **Establish feasible polygon**

The feasible polygon is ABC. Using the slope of the iso-contribution line, we can measure that the contribution-maximising point is point A.

Step 6   **Determine optimal solution**

At point A, the effective constraints are x = 100 and 4x + 3y = 1,200.

∴ If x = 100, (4 × 100) + 3y = 1,200
∴ 3y = 1,200 − 400 and so y = $266^2/_3$

It is important to be aware that in linear programming, the optimal solution is likely to give values to the decision variables which are in fractions of a unit. In this example, contribution will be maximised by making $266^2/_3$ units of Y.

	Contribution
	$
Make 100 units of X	800.00
$266^2/_3$ units of Y	2,133.33
Total weekly contribution	2,933.33

Solution (b): sensitivity analysis

(i)   **Machine hours** are not fully utilised in the optimal solution. 100 units of X and $266^2/_3$ units of Y need $(300 + 1,333.33) = 1,633.33$ machine hours, leaving 91.67 **machine hours unused**. Machine hours, not being an effective constraint in the optimal solution, have a **shadow price of $0**. Obtaining one extra machine hour would add nothing to the contribution.

(ii)   The shadow price of **labour hours** would be obtained by calculating the total weekly contribution if the labour hours constraint were 1,201 hours. It should be possible to see fairly easily that the **new optimal solution** would be where $x = 100$ and $4x + 3y = 1,201$. Therefore $x = 100$, $y = 267$ and total weekly contribution would be $(100 + 267) \times \$8 = \$2,936$.

Since contribution with 1,200 labour hours as the constraint was $2,933.33, the shadow price of labour hours is $(2,936 − 2,933.33) = \$2.67$ per hour. This is the amount by which total contribution would rise if one extra labour hour per week were made available.

Note that there is a limitation to the number of extra labour hours that could be used to earn extra contribution. As more and more labour hours are added, the constraint line will move further and further away from the origin. For example if we added 800 labour hours capacity each week, the constraint $4x + 3y \le (1,200 + 800)$ (ie $4x + 3y \le 2,000$) would be so much further away from the origin that it would no longer be an effective constraint. Machine hours would now help to impose limitations on production, and the profit-maximising output would be at point P on the graph.

Labour hours could only be added to earn more contribution up to point P, after which they would cease to be an effective constraint. At point P, $x = 100$ and $3x + 5y = 1,725$. Therefore $y = 285$.

The labour hours required to make 100 units of X and 285 units of Y are $(4 \times 100) + (3 \times 285) = 1,255$ hours, which is 55 hours more than the initial constraint limit.

Total contribution at point P $= (100 + 285) \times \$8 = \$3,080$. Since total contribution at point A, where labour hours were limited to 1,200 hours, was $2,933.33, the extra contribution from the 55 extra labour hours would be $(3,080 − 2,933.33)/55 = \$2.67$ per hour (as calculated previously).

Thus, the shadow price of labour hours is $2.67 per hour, for a maximum of 55 extra hours per week, after which additional labour hours would add nothing to the weekly contribution.

(iii)   The shadow price of the **minimum weekly demand for X** may be obtained by calculating the weekly contribution if the minimum demand is reduced by one unit to 99, so that $x \ge 99$, given no change in the other original constraints in the problem.

The new optimal solution would occur where $x = 99$ and $4x + 3y = 1,200$. Therefore $y = 268$.

Total contribution per week when $x = 99$ and $y = 268$ is $(99 + 268) \times \$8 = \$2,936$. Since the contribution when $x \ge 100$ was $2,933.33, the **shadow price** of the minimum demand for X is $(2,936 − 2,933.33) = \textbf{\$2.67 per unit}$. In other words, by reducing the minimum demand for X, the weekly contribution can be raised by $2.67 for each unit by which the minimum demand is reduced below 100 per week.

As with the constraint on labour hours, this shadow price is **only applicable up to a certain amount.** If you refer back to the graph of the problem, you should be able to see that if the minimum constraint on X is reduced beyond point Z, it will cease to be an effective constraint in the optimal solution, because at point Z the machine hours limitation will begin to apply.

Question

Learning outcomes: A(vii), (viii)

By how many units per week can the minimum demand be reduced before the shadow price of $2.67 per unit referred to above ceases to apply?

A   300 units
B   100 units
C   75 units
D   25 units

Answer

The correct answer is D.

At point Z:	$4x + 3y = 1,200$	.... (1)
	$3x + 5y = 1,725$	.... (2)
Multiply (1) by 3	$12x + 9y = 3,600$	.... (3)
Multiply (2) by 4	$12x + 20y = 6,900$	.... (4)
Subtract (3) from (4)	$11y = 3,300$	
	$y = 300$	
Substituting in (1)	$4x + 900 = 1,200$	
	$4x = 300$	
	$x = 75$	

The shadow price of the minimum demand for X is $2.67 per unit demanded, but only up to a total reduction in the minimum demand of (100 − 75) = 25 units per week.

Exam focus point

The graphical approach to linear programming has not made an appearance in the paper so far, but the question in the Exam Question Bank at the end of this Text gives you an idea of the sort of question you could encounter.

Chapter Roundup

- The **graphical method** of linear programming is used for problems involving two products.

- The **steps in the graphical method** are as follows.

  - Define variables.
  - Establish objective function.
  - Establish constraints.
  - Draw a graph of the constraints.
  - Establish the feasible region.
  - Determine the optimal product mix.

- The **optimal solution** can be found by 'sliding the iso-contribution (or profit) line out'.

- The optimal solution can also be found using **simultaneous equations**.

- **Slack** occurs when maximum availability of a resource is not used. **Surplus** occurs when more than a minimum requirement is used.

- In a **minimisation problem** (minimise costs), the optimal solution is the point at which the total cost line touches the feasible polygon at a tangent as close to the origin as possible.

- The **shadow price** of a resource which is a limiting factor on production is the amount by which total contribution would fall if the organisation were deprived of one unit of the resource. The shadow price also indicates the amount by which total contribution would rise if the organisation were able to obtain one extra unit of the resource, provided that the resource remains an effective constraint on production and provided also that the extra unit of resource can be obtained at its normal variable cost.

- **Sales price sensitivity analysis** is carried out by changing the slope of the 'iso-contribution' line.

Quick Quiz

1   *Fill in the blanks in the statements below with one of the following terms.*

Objective function; decision variable; constraint; inequality; non-negativity constraints.

(a)   .... should be included when formulating linear programming solutions to ensure that the answer makes sense in operational terms.

(b)   An .... is an equation taking the form 'greater than or equal to' or 'less than or equal to'.

(c)   An .... is a quantified statement of the aim of a resource allocation decision.

2   *Choose the correct words from those highlighted.*

A feasible **polygon/area** enclosed on all sides is known as a feasible **polygon/area.**

3   *Put the following steps in the graphical approach to linear programming in the correct order.*

Draw a graph of the constraints
Define variables
Establish the feasible region
Establish constraints
Establish objective function
Determine optimal product mix

4   *Choose the correct words from those highlighted.*

When dealing with a problem in which there is a requirement to minimise costs, we look for a total cost line touching the feasible area at a tangent **as close to/as far from** the origin as possible.

5   The shadow price of a scarce resource is not the same as its dual price. *True or false?*

6   In what circumstances does slack arise?

A   At the optimal solution, when the resource used equals the resource available

B   At the optimal solution, when a minimum quantity of a resource must be used, and more than that quantity is used

C   At the optimal solution, when the resource used is less than the resource available

D   At the optimal solution, when a minimum quantity of resource is used

7   Draw the feasibility polygon for the following inequalities.

$2x + 3y \leq 12$
$y \geq 2x$
$x \geq 0, y \geq 0$

8   *Choose the correct words from those highlighted.*

If a **maximum/minimum** quantity of a resource must be used and, at the optimal solution, **more than/less than** that quantity is used, there is a surplus on the **minimum/maximum** requirement.

Answers to Quick Quiz

1 (a) Non-negativity constraints
   (b) Inequality
   (c) Objective function

2 area
   polygon

3 Define variables
   Establish objective function
   Establish constraints
   Draw a graph of the constraints
   Establish the feasible region
   Determine optimal product mix

4 as close to

5 False

6 C. If a resource has a maximum availability and it's not binding at the optimal solution, there will be slack.

7 Start with the inequality $y \geq 2x$. The equation $y = 2x$ is a straight line, and you need to plot two points to draw it, such as (0, 0) and (2, 4).

Since $y \geq 2x$, feasible combinations of x and y lie above this line (for example if x = 2, y must be 4 or more).

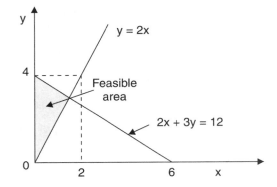

8 minimum
   more than
   minimum

Now try the question below from the Exam Question Bank			
Number	**Level**	**Marks**	**Time**
Q7	Examination	25	45 mins
Q8	Examination	10	18 mins

BPP
LEARNING MEDIA

7

Linear programming: the simplex method

Introduction

The graphical method of linear programming, covered in Chapter 6, can only be used for decision problems with a maximum of two decision variables. For more complex problems the **simplex** method is needed as it can deal with **two or more decision variables**.

Section 1 covers the **main principles** of the method and shows you how to formulate a problem and interpret a solution. Whether the solution is presented in what is known as a tableau (**Section 1**) or as computer output (**Section 3**), **sensitivity analysis** can be carried out on the results (**Section 2**). Any exam question on simplex is more than likely going to require some form of sensitivity analysis.

Section 4 covers **issues** that you might need to raise to answer a **discursive** question or part question on simplex.

Once you have worked through this chapter you should be able to formulate an initial simplex tableau, interpret a final simplex tableau and apply the information contained in that final tableau.

In the November 2005 exam, there was a nine-mark question as part of a larger 25-mark question covering the interpretation of values generated by the simplex method.

Topic list	Learning outcomes	Syllabus references	Ability required
1 The principles of the simplex method	A(vii)	A(8)	Application
2 Sensitivity analysis	A(vii), C(ii)	A(8), C(2)	Application
3 Using computer packages	A(vii)	A(8)	Application
4 Using linear programming	A(vii)	A(8)	Application

1 The principles of the simplex method

Key term

The **simplex method** is a method of solving linear programming problems with two or more decision variables.

FAST FORWARD

The formulation of the problem using the **simplex method** is similar to that required when the graphical method is used but **slack variables** must be incorporated into the constraints and the objective function.

1.1 General points about the simplex method

FAST FORWARD

A **slack variable** represents the amount of a constraint that is unused.

In any feasible solution, if a problem involves n constraints and m variables (decision plus slack), n variables will have a positive value and (m–n) variables will have a value of zero.

Feasible solutions to a problem are shown in a **tableau**.

Before introducing an example to explain the technique, we will make a few introductory points. Don't worry if you get confused, working through the example will make things clearer.

(a) The simplex method involves **testing one feasible solution after another**, in a **succession of tables or tableaux, until the optimal solution is found**. It can be used for problems with **any number of decision variables, from two upwards**.

(b) In addition to the decision variables, the method introduces additional variables, known as **slack variables** or **surplus variables**. There will be **one slack (or surplus) variable for each constraint in the problem (excluding non-negativity constraints)**.

For example, if a linear programming problem has three decision variables and four constraints, there will be four slack variables. With the three decision variables, there will therefore be a total of seven variables and four constraints in the problem.

(c) The technique is a **repetitive, step-by-step process**, with each step having the following **purposes**.

(i) To **establish a feasible solution** (in other words, a feasible combination of decision variable values and slack variable values) and the **value of the objective function** for that solution.

(ii) To **establish** whether that particular **solution** is one that **optimises** the value of the objective function.

(d) Each feasible solution is tested by drawing up a **matrix** or **tableau** with the following rows and columns.

(i) **One row per constraint, plus a solution row**
(ii) **One column per decision variable and per slack variable, plus a solution column**

(e) **Every variable**, whether a decision variable, slack variable or surplus variable, **must be ≥ 0 in any feasible solution**.

(f) A feature of the simplex method is that if there are **n constraints**, there will be **n variables with a value greater than 0 in any feasible solution**. Thus, if there are seven variables in a problem, and four constraints, there will be four variables with a positive value in the solution, and three variables with a value equal to 0.

Keep these points in mind as we work through an example.

Note that you do not need to be able to test solutions in the exam. You simply need to be able to prepare the appropriate formulae and formulate the appropriate initial tableau, interpret the final (optimal solution) tableau and apply the information contained in that optimal solution. The November 2005 exam included a nine part question requiring the interpretation of values in a final Simplex solution.

1.2 Example: the simplex method

An organisation produces and sells two products, X and Y. Relevant information is as follows.

	Materials units	Labour hours	Machine time hours	Contribution per unit $
X, per unit	5	1	3	20
Y, per unit	2	3	2	16
Total available, each week	3,000	1,750	2,100	

Required

Use the simplex method to determine the profit-maximising product mix.

1.3 Formulating the problem

We have just two decision variables in this problem, but we can still use the simplex method to solve it.

Step 1 **Define variables**

Let x be the number of units of X that should be produced and sold.
Let y be the number of units of Y that should be produced and sold.

Step 2 **Establish objective function**

Maximum contribution (C) = 20x + 16y subject to the constraints below.

Step 3 **Establish constraints**

The constraints are as follows.

Materials	$5x + 2y \leq 3,000$	Machine time	$3x + 2y \leq 2,100$
Labour	$x + 3y \leq 1,750$	Non-negativity	$x \geq 0, y \geq 0$

Step 4 **Introduce slack variables**

Begin by turning each constraint (ignoring the non-negativity constraints now) into an equation. This is done by introducing slack variables.

Let a be the quantity of unused materials, b be the number of unused labour hours and c be the number of unused machine hours.

Slack variable. 'Amount of each resource which will be unused if a specific linear programming solution is implemented.'

(CIMA Official Terminology)

Question

Learning outcome: A(vii)

A problem to be solved using linear programming has three decision variables, six constraints (including two non-negativity constraints) and one objective function.

How many slack variables will be required if the simplex method is used?

A   3
B   4
C   5
D   6

Answer

The correct answer is B.

A slack variable is required for each constraint (ignoring non-negativity constraints). There are $6 - 2 = 4$ such constraints.

We can now express the original constraints as equations.

$$5x + 2y + a = 3,000$$
$$x + 3y + b = 1,750$$
$$3x + 2y + c = 2,100$$

The slack variables a, b and c will be equal to 0 in the final solution only if the combined production of X and Y uses up all the available materials, labour hours and machine hours.

Step 5   **Values of variables – non-negative or zero?**
In this example, there are **five variables** (x, y, a, b and c) and **three equations**, and so in any **feasible solution** that is tested, **three variables** will have a **non-negative value** (since there are three equations) which means that **two variables** will have a value of **zero**.

Question

Learning outcome: A(vii)

A problem to be solved using linear programming has seven variables and four equations based on the original constraints.

How many variables will have a value of zero in any feasible solution determined using the simplex method?

A   7
B   5
C   4
D   3

Answer

The correct answer is D.

Four variables will have a non-negative value (since there are four equations), which means that $7 - 4 = 3$ variables will have a value of zero.

Step 6

Express objective function as an equation

It is usual to express the objective function as an equation with the right hand side equal to zero. In order to keep the problem consistent, the slack (or surplus) variables are inserted into the objective function equation, but as the quantities they represent should have no effect on the objective function they are given zero coefficients. In our example, the objective function will be expressed as follows.

Maximise contribution (C) given by $C - 20x - 16y + 0a + 0b + 0c = 0$.

Exam focus point

| The pilot paper contained an MCQ which merges limiting factor analysis and simplex terminology. |

1.4 Drawing up the initial tableau and testing the initial feasible solution

Attention!

| You will not be required to do this in the exam but seeing how the initial tableau is drawn up will give you additional insight into the technique. |

We begin by testing a solution that **all the decision variables have a zero value**, and **all the slack variables have a non-negative value.**

Obviously, this is **not going to be the optimal solution**, but it gives us a starting point from which we can develop other feasible solutions.

Simplex tableaux can be **drawn in several different ways,** and if you are asked to interpret a given tableau in an examination question, you may need to adapt your understanding of the tableau format in this Study Text to the format in the question. The following points apply to all tableaux, however.

(a) There should be a **column for each variable** and also a **solution column.**

(b) It helps to add a **further column on the left**, to **indicate the variable which is in the solution to which the corresponding value in the solution column relates.**

(c) There is a **row for each equation** in the problem, and a **solution row.**

Here is the initial matrix for our problem. Information on how it has been derived is given below.

Variables in solution	x	y	a	b	c	Solution
A	5	2	1	0	0	3,000
B	1	3	0	1	0	1,750
C	3	2	0	0	1	2,100
Solution	−20	−16	0	0	0	0

(a) The **figures in each** row correspond with the **coefficients of the variables in each of the initial constraints**. The bottom row or **solution row** holds the **coefficients of the objective function**. For example the materials constraint $5x + 2y + a = 3,000$ gives us the first row, 5 (number of x's), 2 (number of y's), 1 (number of a's), then zeros in the b and c columns (since these do not feature in the constraint equation) and finally 3,000 in the solution column.

(b) The **variables in the solution are a, b and c** (the unused resources).

(i) The **value of each variable is shown in the solution column.** We are testing a solution that all decision variables have a zero value, so there is no production and hence no resources are used. The total resource available is therefore unused.

(ii) The **column values** for each variable in the solution are as follows.

    — 1 in the variable's own solution row
    — 0 in every other row, including the solution row.

(c)   The **contribution per unit obtainable from x and y** is given in the **solution row.** These are the **dual prices** or **shadow prices** of the products X and Y. The minus signs are of no particular significance, except that in the solution given here they have the following meanings.

(i)   A **minus shadow price** indicates that the **value of the objective function can be increased by the amount of the shadow price per unit** of the variable that is introduced into the solution, given no change in the current objective function or existing constraints.

(ii)   A **positive shadow price** indicates the amount by which the **value of the objective function would be decreased** per unit of the variable introduced into the solution, given no change in the current objective function or the existing constraints.

1.5 Interpreting the tableau and testing for improvement

We can see that the **solution is testing a = 3,000, b = 1,750 and c = 2,100, contribution = 0. The co-efficients for the variables not in this solution, x and y, are the dual prices or shadow prices** of these variables, given the solution being tested. A **negative value** to a dual price means that the **objective function can be increased;** therefore the **solution in the tableau is not the optimal solution.**

The **shadow prices** in the initial solution (tableau) **indicate** the following.

(a)   The profit would be increased by $20 for every extra unit of x produced (because the shadow price of x is $20 per unit).

(b)   Similarly, the profit would be increased by $16 for every extra unit of y produced (because its shadow price is $16 per unit).

Since the **solution is not optimal,** the **contribution may be improved by introducing either x or y into the solution.**

1.6 The next step

The next step is to **test another feasible solution.** We do this by **introducing one variable into the solution, in the place of one variable that is now removed.** In our example, we **introduce x or y in place of a, b or c.**

The simplex technique continues in this way, producing a feasible solution in each successive tableau, until the optimal solution is reached.

1.7 Interpreting the final tableau

FAST FORWARD

If the **shadow prices** on the bottom (solution) row of a tableau are all positive, the tableau shows the optimal solution.

- The solution column shows the optimal production levels and the units of unused resource.

- The figure at the bottom of the solution column/right-hand side of the solution row shows the value of the objective function.

- The figures in the solution row indicate the shadow prices of resources.

After a number of iterations, the following tableau is produced.

Variables in solution	x	y	a	b	c	Solution column
X	1	0	0	−0.2857	0.4286	400
A	0	0	1	0.5714	−1.8571	100
y	0	1	0	0.4286	−0.1429	450
Solution row	0	0	0	1.1428	6.2858	15,200

This can be interpreted as follows.

(a) The solution in this tableau is the **optimal** one, because the **shadow prices on the bottom row are all positive.**

(b) The optimal solution is to **make and sell 400 units of X** and **450 units of Y, to earn a contribution of $15,200.**

(c) The solution will leave **100 units of material unused,** but will use up all available labour and machine time.

(d) The **shadow price of labour time (b) is $1.1428 per hour,** which **indicates the amount by which contribution could be increased if more labour time could be made available at its normal variable cost.**

(e) The **shadow price of machine time (c) is $6.2858 per hour,** which **indicates the amount by which contribution could be increased if more machine time could be made available, at its normal variable cost.**

(f) The **shadow price of materials is nil,** because there are 100 units of **unused** materials in the solution.

Question

Formulation of problem

Learning outcome: A(vii)

TDS manufactures two products, X and Y, which earn a contribution of $8 and $14 per unit respectively. At current selling prices, there is no limit to sales demand for Y, but maximum demand for X would be 1,200 units. The company aims to maximise its annual profits, and fixed costs are $15,000 per annum.

In the year to 30 June 20X2, the company expects to have a limited availability of resources and estimates of availability are as follows.

Skilled labour	maximum 9,000 hours
Machine time	maximum 4,000 hours
Material M	maximum 1,000 tonnes

The usage of these resources per unit of product are as follows.

	X	Y
Skilled labour time	3 hours	4 hours
Machine time	1 hour	2 hours
Material M	½ tonne	¼ tonne

Required

(a) Formulate the problem using the simplex method of linear programming.

(b) Determine how many variables will have a positive value and how many a value of zero in any feasible solution.

Answer

(a) The linear programming problem would be formulated as follows.

Define variables

Let x and y be the number of units made and sold of product X and product Y respectively.

Establish objective function

Maximise contribution (C) = 8x + 14y subject to the constraints below.

Establish constraints

3x + 4y	≤	9,000	(skilled labour)*
x + 2y	≤	4,000	(machine time)
0.5x + 0.25y	≤	1,000	(material M)
x	≤	1,200	(demand for X)
x, y	≥	0	

* This constraint is that skilled labour hours cannot exceed 9,000 hours, and since a unit of X needs 3 hours and a unit of Y needs 4 hours, 3x + 4y cannot exceed 9,000. The other constraints are formulated in a similar way.

Introduce slack variables

Introduce a slack variable into each constraint, to turn the inequality into an equation.

Let	a	=	the number of unused skilled labour hours
	b	=	the number of unused machine hours
	c	=	the number of unused tonnes of material M
	d	=	the amount by which demand for X falls short of 1,200 units

Then

3x + 4y + a	=	9,000 (labour hours)
x + 2y + b	=	4,000 (machine hours)
0.5x + 0.25y + c	=	1,000 (tonnes of M)
x + d	=	1,200 (demand for X)

and maximise contribution (C) given by C − 8x − 14y + 0a + 0b + 0c + 0d = 0

(b) There are six variables (x, y, a, b, c, d) and four equations. In any feasible solution four variables will have a non-negative value (as there are four equations), while two variables will have a value of zero.

Question

Interpretation of final tableau

Learning outcome: A(vii)

The final tableau to the problem in **Question: formulation of problem** is shown below.

Required

Interpret the tableau.

Variables in the solution	x	y	a	b	c	d	Solution column
x	1	0	0	−2	0	0	1,000
y	0	1	−0.5	1.5	0	0	1,500
c	0	0	−0.375	0.625	1	0	125
d	0	0	−1	2	0	1	200
Solution row	0	0	1	5	0	0	29,000

Answer

There is a column in the tableau for every variable, including the slack variables, but the important parts of the tableau are the 'variables in the solution' column, the solution row, and the solution column. These tell us a number of things.

Identifying the variables in the solution

The variables in the solution are x, y, c and d. It follows that a and b have zero values. To be the variable in the solution on a particular row of the table, a value of 1 must appear in the **column** for that variable, with zero values in every other row of that column. For example, x is the variable in the solution for the row which has 1 in the x column. There are zeros in every other row in the x column.

The value of the variables

The solution **column** gives the value of each variable.

x	1,000	(units made of X)
y	1,500	(units made of Y)
c	125	(unused material M)
d	200	(amount below the 1,200 maximum of demand for X)

This means that contribution will be maximised by making and selling 1,000 units of X and 1,500 units of Y. This will leave 125 unused tonnes of material M, and production and sales of X will be 200 units below the limit of sales demand. Since a and b are both zero, there is no unused labour and machine time; in other words, all the available labour and machine hours will be fully utilised.

The total contribution

The value of the objective function – here, the total contribution – is in both the solution row and the solution column. Here it is $29,000.

Shadow prices

The solution **row** gives the **shadow prices** of each variable. Here, the shadow price of a is $1 per labour hour and that for b is $5 per machine hour.

This means that if more labour hours could be made available **at their normal variable cost per hour**, total contribution could be increased by $1 per extra labour hour. Similarly, if more machine time could be made available, **at its normal variable cost**, total contribution could be increased by $5 per extra machine hour.

Question

Learning outcome: A(vii)

Here is the final tableau of a problem involving the production of products X and Y solved using the simplex method of linear programming.

Variables in solution	x	y	a	b	c	d	e	Solution column
x	1	0	−2.0	0	3.0	0	0	550
y	0	1	−0.8	0	0.5	0	0	720
b	0	0	1.5	1	1.0	0	0	95
d	0	0	0.7	0	−1.1	1	0	50
e	0	0	2.0	0	1.8	0	1	104
Solution row	0	0	7.0	0	4.0	0	0	14,110

Required

Draw a ring around the column or row which shows the variables in the solution.

Answer

Variables in solution	x	y	a	b	c	d	e	Solution column
x	1	0	−2.0	0	3.0	0	0	550
y	0	1	−0.8	0	0.5	0	0	720
b	0	0	1.5	1	1.0	0	0	95
d	0	0	0.7	0	−1.1	1	0	50
e	0	0	2.0	0	1.8	0	1	104
Solution row	0	0	7.0	0	4.0	0	0	14,110

To be a variable in the solution, a value of 1 must appear in the column for the variable, with zero values in every other row.

Question

Learning outcome: A(vii)

Refer to the tableau in **Question: identification of variables**.

What is the profit-maximising product mix?

A   Make 95 units of B, 50 units of D and 104 units of E
B   Make 550 units of X and 720 units of Y
C   Make 4 units of C and 7 units of A
D   None of the above

Answer

The correct answer is B. The answer can be found in the solution column in the rows for x and y.

Question

Unused resources

Learning outcome: A(vii)

Refer to the tableau in **Question: identification of variables**. Suppose that variables a to e refer to the unused quantity of resources A to E.

Required

Fill in the blank in the sentence below.

.... units of resource A will be unused.

Answer

The correct answer is that 0 units of A will be unused. A has a zero value in the solution column and so resource A is fully used.

Question

Shadow prices

Learning outcome: A(vii)

Refer to the tableau in **Question: identification of variables**. **The shadow price of resource C is $3**. *True or false*?

Answer

The correct answer is $4, so the statement is false.

The solution row gives the shadow price of each variable.

2 Sensitivity analysis

You might be asked to carry out some **sensitivity analysis** on a simplex tableau giving the optimal solution to a linear programming problem. This could involve the following.

(a) Testing **how the optimal solution** would change if there were either **more or less of a scarce resource**.

(b) Testing whether it would be **worthwhile obtaining more of a scarce resource by paying a premium** for the additional resources, for example by paying an overtime premium for extra labour hours, or by paying a supplier a higher price for extra raw materials.

2.1 The effect of having more or less of a scarce resource

FAST FORWARD

Sensitivity analysis can be applied to the final tableau to determine the effect of having more or less of a scarce resource (indicated by figures in the column for the resource's slack variable).

LEARNING MEDIA

The optimal solution to a linear programming problem is based on the assumption that the constraints are known with certainty, and fixed in quantity. Sensitivity analysis enables us to test how the solution would alter if the quantity of a scarce resource (the size of a constraint) were to change.

2.1.1 Example: the effect of having more or less of a scarce resource

Return to our previous example, and the optimal solution in Section 1.7, in which both labour hours and machine hours are fully used. How would the solution change if more labour hours (variable b) were available?

Solution

The simplex tableau, and in particular the **figures in the b column,** provide the following information for each extra labour hour that is available.

(a)   The **contribution** would **increase** by $1.1428
(b)   The value of **x** would **fall by 0.2857 units**
(c)   The value of **a** (unused materials) would **increase by 0.5714 units**
(d)   The value of **y** would **increase by 0.4286 units**

In other words, we would be able to make 0.4286 units of Y extra, to earn contribution of ($\times$ $16) $6.8576, but we would make 0.2857 units less of X and so lose contribution of ($\times$ $20) $5.714, leaving a net increase in contribution of $(6.8576 – 5.714) = $1.1436. Allowing for rounding errors of $0.0008, this is the figure already given above for the increase in contribution.

Since x = 400 in the optimal tableau, and extra labour hours would lead to a reduction of 0.2857 units of x, there is a **limit to the number of extra labour hours that would earn an extra $1.1428**. This limit is calculated as 400/0.2857 = 1,400 extra labour hours.

In other words, the **shadow price** of $1.1428 per hour for labour is **only valid for about 1,400 extra labour hours** on top of the given constraint in the initial problem, which was 1,750 hours, (that is up to a **total limit of 3,150 hours**).

If there were **fewer labour hours available**, the same sort of analysis would apply, but in reverse.

(a)   The contribution would fall by $1.1428 per hour unavailable
(b)   The value of x would increase by 0.2857 units
(c)   The value of a would fall by 0.5714 units
(d)   The value of y would fall by 0.4286 units

2.2 Example: obtaining extra resources at a premium on cost

FAST FORWARD

> Sensitivity analysis can also be applied to test whether or not it would be **worthwhile to obtain more of a scarce resource** by paying a premium for additional supplies (only if the shadow price is greater than the additional cost).

Suppose we are given the following additional information about our example.

(a)   The normal variable cost of labour hours (variable b) is $4 per hour, but extra labour hours could be worked in overtime, when the rate of pay would be time-and-a-half.

(b)   The normal variable cost of machine time is $1.50 per hour, but some extra machine time could be made available by renting another machine for 40 hours per week, at a rental cost of $160. Variable running costs of this machine would be $1.50 per hour.

Would it be worth obtaining the extra resources?

Solution

We know that the shadow price of labour hours is $1.1428 and of machine hours is $6.2858. We can therefore deduce the following.

(a) **Paying an overtime premium** of $2 per hour for labour **would not be worthwhile**, because the extra contribution of $1.1428 per hour would be more than offset by the cost of the premium, leaving the company worse off by $0.8572 per hour worked in overtime.

(b) **Renting the extra machine would be worthwhile**, but only by $91.43 (which is perhaps too small an amount to bother with).

	$
Extra contribution from 40 hours of machine time ($\times$ $6.2858)	251.43
Rental cost	160.00
Net increase in profit	91.43

Note that the variable running costs do not enter into this calculation since they are identical to the normal variable costs of machine time. We are **concerned here only with the additional costs.**

Question	Formulation

Learning outcome: A(vii)

An organisation manufactures three products, tanks, trays and tubs, each of which passes through three processes, X, Y and Z.

| | Process hours per unit | | | Total process |
Process	Tanks	Trays	Tubs	hours available
X	5	2	4	12,000
Y	4	5	6	24,000
Z	3	5	4	18,000

The contribution to profit of each product are $2 for each tank, $3 per tray and $4 per tub.

Required

Fill in the blanks in (a) and (b) below, which relate to the formulation of the above data into a simplex linear programming model. Use the following notation.

Let   a be the number of units of tanks produced
b be the number of units of trays produced
c be the number of units of tubs produced
x = quantity of unused process X hours
y = quantity of unused process Y hours
z = quantity of unused process Z hours

(a) Maximise contribution (C) given by .... subject to the following constraints in (b).

(b) .... (process X hours)
.... (process Y hours)
.... (process Z hours)

Answer

(a)   C is given by C − 2a − 3b − 4c + 0x + 0y + 0z

(b)   Constraint for process X hours: 5a + 2b + 4c + x = 12,000
       Constraint for process Y hours: 4a + 5b + 6c + y = 24,000
       Constraint for process Z hours: 3a + 5b + 4c + z = 18,000

Question

Interpretation

Learning outcome: A(vii)

The final simplex tableau, based on the data in the question above, looks like this.

Variables in solution	a	b	c	x	y	z	Solution column
c	1.583	0	1	0.417	0	−0.167	2,000
y	−2.167	0	0	−0.833	1	−0.667	2,000
b	−0.667	1	0	−0.333	0	0.333	2,000
Solution row	2.333	0	0	0.667	0	0.333	14,000

Required

(a)   Determine how many of each product should be produced and the maximum contribution. Calculate how much slack time, if any, is available in the processes.

(b)   Explain how your solution would vary if an extra 3,000 hours of process X time could be made available.

(c)   Describe what would happen to the production schedule and budgeted contribution if an order were received for 300 units of tanks which the company felt that it had to accept, because of the importance of the customer. **Ignore** the increase of process X time in part (b) above.

Answer

(a)   **Contribution is maximised at $14,000** by making **2,000 units of tubs** and **2,000 units of trays**. **No tanks** would be made.

There will be **2,000 slack hours in process Y**. Process X and process Z hours will be fully utilised.

(b)   The shadow price of process X time is $0.667 per hour, and for every extra hour of process X time that can be made available (at its normal variable cost), the production quantities could be altered in such a way that the following would happen.

   (i)   **Contribution would go up by $0.667 per extra process X** hour used.
   (ii)   c (the quantity of tubs) would **go up by 0.417 units**.
   (iii)   b (the quantity of trays) would **go down by 0.333 units**.
   (iv)   y (unused process Y time) would **fall by 0.833 hours**.

This is **only true up to the point** where so many extra process X hours have been made available that either b or y reaches 0 in value. This will be at the following points.

   (i)   For y, after $\dfrac{2,000}{0.833}$ = 2,400 extra process X hours

   (ii)   For b, after $\dfrac{2,000}{0.333}$ = 6,000 extra process X hours

2,400 is the lowest of these two limits.

The shadow price is therefore **valid only for up to 2,400 extra process X hours,** so that the full 3,000 available would not be required.

The **new optimal solution** would therefore be to make and sell the following.

c   2,000 + (2,400 × 0.417) = 3,000 units
b   2,000 − (2,400 × 0.333) = 1,200 units

These would require a total of 14,400 hours in process X, 24,000 hours in process Y and 18,000 hours in process Z.

Contribution would be as follows.

		$
Tubs	3,000 × $4	12,000
Trays	1,200 × $3	3,600
		15,600
Contribution in initial solution		14,000
Increase in contribution (2,400 × $0.667)		1,600

(c)   Going back to the original solution, if an order is received for 300 units of tanks, the production schedule would be re-arranged so that **for each unit of tank made the following would happen.**

(i)   **Contribution would fall** by $2.333.
(ii)   1.583 **units less of tubs** (variable c) would be made.
(iii)   0.667 **units more of trays** (variable b) would be made.
(iv)   **Unused process Y time would increase** by 2.167 hours.

The new production and contribution budget would be as follows.

Product		Process X time	Process Y time	Process Z time	Contribution
	Units	Hours	Hours	Hours	$
Tanks (a)	300	1,500	1,200	900	600
Trays (b)	2,200*	4,400	11,000	11,000	6,600
Tubs (c)	1,525**	6,100	9,150	6,100	6,100
		12,000	21,350	18,000	13,300

*   2,000 + (300 × 0.667)
**   2,000 − (300 × 1.583)

The contribution is $700 lower than in the original optimal solution (which represents 300 tanks × $2.333).

Unused process Y time is 2,650 hours, which is 650 more than in the original solution (which represents 300 × 2.167)

3 Using computer packages

FAST FORWARD

Spreadsheet packages can be used to solve linear programming problems.

- The **slack/surplus** columns provide information about the slack values of ≤ constraints and the surplus values of any ≥ constraints.

- The **worth** column shows the positive shadow price of resources.

- The **relative loss** shows by how much contribution (usually) would fall if extra units of particular decision variables were produced.

Nowadays, modern spreadsheet packages can be used to solve linear programming problems.

Suppose an organisation produces three products, X and Y and Z, subject to four constraints (1, 2, 3, 4).

(a) **Constraints 1 and 2** are **'less than or equal to' resource constraints**.

(b) **Constraint 3 provides a limit on the number of X** that can be produced.

(c) **Constraint 4** is a **'greater than or equal to' constraint** and provides for a **minimum number of Z** to be produced (400).

The organisation wishes to maximise contribution.

Typical output from a spreadsheet package for such a problem is shown below.

Objective function (c)		137,500
Variable	Value	Relative loss
x	475.000	0.000
y	0.000	105.000
z	610.000	0.000
Constraint	Slack/surplus	Worth
1	17.000	0.000
2	0.000	290.000
3	0.000	1,150.000
4	210.000	0.000

3.1 Interpretation

(a) Total optimal **contribution (c)** will be $137,500.

(b) The **variable** and **value columns** mean that x = 475, y = 0 and z = 610.

To maximise contribution, 475 units of X and 610 units of Z should therefore be produced. No units of Y should be produced.

(c) The **constraint** and **slack/surplus** columns provide information about the slack values of 'less than or equal to' constraints and the surplus values for any 'greater than or equal to' constraints.

(i) **Constraint 1** is a 'less than or equal to' resource constraint. The slack is 17 and so 17 units of resource 1 will be unused in the optimal solution.

(ii) **Constraint 2** is a 'less than or equal to' resource constraint. The slack is zero, indicating that all available resource 2 will be used in the optimal solution.

(iii) **Constraint 3** provides a limit on x. The slack is zero, showing that the limit has been met.

(iv) **Constraint 4** provides for a minimum z. The surplus is 210, meaning 400 + 210 = 610 units of Z are made.

(d) **Worth**. This column shows the positive shadow price of resources (the amount that contribution (or, in general terms, c) alters if the availability of the resource is changed by one unit).

    (i) Contribution would increase by $290 if one extra unit of resource 2 were made available.

    (ii) Contribution would increase by $1,150 if the limit on the minimum number of Z to be produced altered by 1.

    (iii) Resource 1 has a worth of 0 because 17 units of the resource are unused in the optimal solution.

Attention!

> **In general**, any constraint with a slack of zero has a positive worth figure, while any constraint with a positive slack figure will have a worth of zero.

(e) **Relative loss.** This indicates that if one unit of Y were produced, total contribution (or generally c) would fall by $105. A relative loss of $105 would therefore be made for every unit of Y made. Units of Y should only be made if unit contribution of Y increases by $105.

X and Z have relative losses of zero, indicating that they should be made.

Attention!

> **In general**, only those decision variables with a relative loss of zero will have a positive value in the optimal solution.

3.2 Using Solver

Let's now take a look at how to use a specific package for solving linear programming problems. You'll need to have the Excel Add-In Solver installed on your PC if you actually want to use the package yourself.

3.2.1 Example: a computer model

Suppose that Austen makes two products, X and Y, which make a unit contribution of $20 and $16 respectively. Sales demand is unlimited at current selling prices, but there is a potential shortage of labour, materials and machine time.

The constraints, ignoring the expected sales demands, are:

Materials	$5x + 2y \leq 3,000$	Machine time	$3x + 2y \leq 2,100$
Labour hours	$x + 3y \leq 1,750$	Non-negativity	$x \geq 0, y \geq 0$

where x and y are the quantities of product X and product Y respectively.

Using Microsoft Excel, set up the problem on one sheet of an Excel **workbook**. (It **is** important that you use a workbook.)

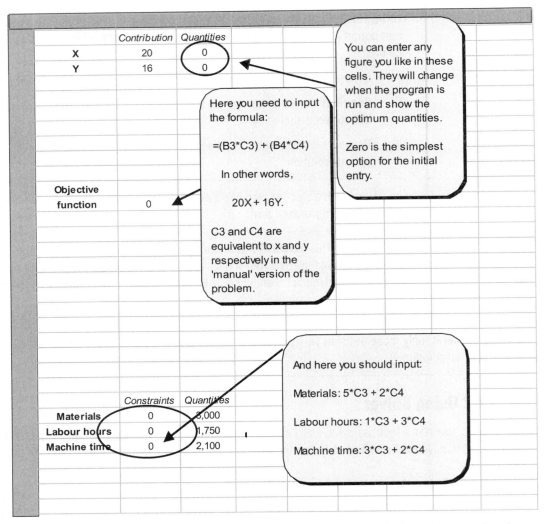

Note that you need to **insert formulae for the objective function and constraints**, not zero values!

Once you have done this, click on the cell containing the objective function (B13 in our example) so that it is highlighted. Then run Excel's analysis tool called 'Solver'. You will find Solver under 'Tools'. It throws up the following menu.

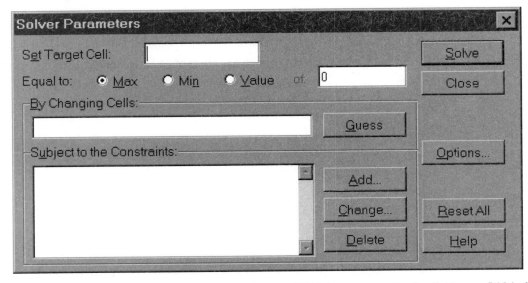

(a)   The **target cell** is the objective function - cell B13 in our example. By clicking on B13 before running Solver, $B$13 is automatically shown in the target cell area.

(b) You want to maximise the objective function so you click with your mouse on the **Max** button.

(c) The values you can change (**changing cells**) are the quantities of X and Y you produce. These values will appear in cells C3 and C4. Highlight C3:C4 and the information is automatically shown in 'By Changing Cells'.

(d) Now you need to set up the **constraints**, putting them into 'spreadsheet style'. For example $5x + 2y \leq 3,000$ is, in terms of the spreadsheet, $B27 \leq C27$. Each constraint, plus the negativity constraints, are added in turn by clicking on the **Add** button and entering the cell references or highlighting the relevant cells. The $ signs are included automatically, you do not need to worry about them. You can select the type of relationship you need ($\leq$, $\geq$, =) from the drop down menu. Click ok to return to the main 'Solver Parameters' menu.

(e) Finally, click on **Options,** which gives you another menu so that you can (amongst other things) instruct the computer that it should assume the model is linear. You don't need to do anything else to this menu.

Your completed menu should look like the one below.

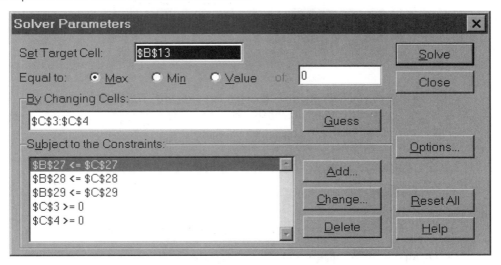

If you now click the **Solve** button the optimum solution is found in about five seconds.

The **solution** is **provided** on your **initial spreadsheet**.

This shows that the optimal solution is to produce 400 X and 450 Y, with a resulting contribution of $15,200, leaving 100 units of unused materials. All labour hours and machine time will be used.

	A	B	C	D
1				
2		*Contribution*	*Quantities*	
3	X	20	400	
4	Y	16	450	
5				
6				
7				
8				
9				
10				
11				
12	Objective			
13	function	15200		
14				
15				
16				
17				
18				
19				
20				
21				
22				
23				
24				
25				
26		*Constraints*	*Quantities*	
27	Materials	2900	3000	
28	Labour hours	1750	1750	
29	Machine time	2100	2100	
30				

Solver also gives you the option of obtaining **three reports**. To obtain a report, click on it and it will be saved to a worksheet in your workbook. After producing each report you need to go back to Solver via the Tools menu, click 'Solve' and obtain the next report.

3.2.2 Computer output: the limits report

The **limits report** basically shows the same information as provided in the solution spreadsheet.

Cell	Target Name	Value
$B$13	function Contribution	15200

Cell	Adjustable Name	Value	Lower Limit	Target Result	Upper Limit	Target Result
$C$3	X Quantities	400	0	7200	400	15200
$C$4	Y Quantities	450	0	8000	450	15200

3.2.3 Computer output: the sensitivity report

The **sensitivity report** tells you the final values of X, Y and the resources used as before but it also provides the following information.

(a)   The amounts by which **contribution** from X and Y could increase or decrease before the optimum production quantities would change (the **allowable increase**). For example, if the contribution from X were $23 it would still be best to produce 400 units of X and 450 of Y. If it were $25, the optimal solution would change. If Y's contribution were $60 (16 + 44), the optimal solution would again change.

(b) The amounts by which the various **constraints** could increase or decrease before the optimum solution would change (**allowable increase** column).

(c) The **shadow prices** of the labour and machine hour constraints (the materials constraint is not binding - there are spare materials left).

(*Note.* **R H Side** simply means the right hand side of the equation. The allowable increase for materials (1E + 30 = 10^{30}) is effectively infinity, because we already have more than enough materials.)

Changing Cells

Cell	Name	Final Value	Reduced Cost	Objective Coefficient	Allowable Increase	Allowable Decrease
$C$3	X Quantities	400	0	20	4	14.66666667
$C$4	Y Quantities	450	0	16	44	2.666666667

Constraints

Cell	Name	Final Value	Shadow Price	Constraint R.H. Side	Allowable Increase	Allowable Decrease
$B$27	Materials Constraints	2900	0	3000	1E+30	100
$B$28	Labour hours Constraints	1750	1.142857143	1750	1400	175
$B$29	Machine time Constraints	2100	6.285714286	2100	53.84615385	933.3333333

3.2.4 Computer output: the answer report

The third report is called an **answer report**, which summarises the problem and the solution.

Target Cell (Max)

Cell	Name	Original Value	Final Value
$B$13	function Contribution	0	15200

Adjustable Cells

Cell	Name	Original Value	Final Value
$C$3	X Quantities	0	400
$C$4	Y Quantities	0	450

Constraints

Cell	Name	Cell Value	Formula	Status	Slack
$B$27	Materials Constraints	2900	$B$27<=$C$27	Not Binding	100
$B$28	Labour hours Constraints	1750	$B$28<=$C$28	Binding	0
$B$29	Machine time Constraints	2100	$B$29<=$C$29	Binding	0
$C$3	X Quantities	400	$C$3>=0	Not Binding	400
$C$4	Y Quantities	450	$C$4>=0	Not Binding	450

3.2.5 Do-it-yourself!

If you have access to a modern spreadsheet package you may wish to set up the problem we have described and experiment with different values for the variables.

Computer tools such as Microsoft Excel's Solver can also be used to find the answers to highly complex 'What if?' problems with **hundreds of constraints** and variables.

4 Using linear programming

> There are a number of **assumptions** and **practical difficulties** in the use of linear programming.

The considerations, non-quantifiable factors and assumptions in limiting factor analysis that we looked at in Chapter 5 apply equally to linear programming.

4.1 Further assumptions

In addition, there are **further assumptions** if we are dealing with product mix decisions involving several limiting factors.

(a) The **total amount available of each scarce resource is known with accuracy**.

(b) There is **no interdependence between the demand** for the different products or services, so that there is a completely free choice in the product or service mix without having to consider the consequences for demand or selling prices per unit.

In spite of these assumptions, linear programming is a useful technique in practice. Some statistical studies have been carried out suggesting that linear cost functions do apply over fairly wide ranges of output, and so the assumptions underlying linear programming may be valid.

4.2 Uses of linear programming

(a) **Budgeting**. If scarce resources are ignored when a budget is prepared, the budget is unattainable and is of little use for planning and control. When there is more than one scarce resource, linear programming can be used to identify the most profitable use of resources.

(b) **Calculation of relevant costs**. The calculation of relevant costs is essential for decision making. The **relevant cost** of a **scarce resource** is calculated as **acquisition cost of the resource plus opportunity cost**. When **more than one scarce resource** exists, the **opportunity cost** (or **shadow price**) should be established using linear programming techniques.

(c) **Selling different products.** Suppose that an organisation faced with resource constraints manufactures products X and Y and linear programming has been used to determine the shadow prices of the scarce resources. If the organisation now wishes to manufacture and sell a modified version of product X (Z), requiring inputs of the scarce resources, the relevant costs of these scarce resources can be determined (see above) to ascertain whether the production of X and Y should be restricted in order to produce Z.

(d) **Maximum payment for additional scarce resources**. This use of shadow prices has been covered in this chapter.

(e) **Control.** Opportunity costs are also important for cost control: standard costing can be improved by incorporating opportunity costs into variance calculations. For example, adverse material usage variances can be an indication of material wastage. Such variances should be valued at the standard cost of the material plus the opportunity cost of the loss of one scarce unit of material. Such an approach highlights the true cost of the inefficient use of scarce resources and encourages managers of responsibility centres to pay special attention to the control of scarce factors of production. For organisations using an optimised production technology (OPT) strategy, this approach is particularly useful because variances arising from bottleneck operations will be reported in terms of opportunity cost rather than purchase cost.

(f)   **Capital budgeting**. Linear programming can be used to determine the combination of investment proposals that should be selected if investment funds are restricted in more than one period.

4.3 Practical difficulties with using linear programming

Difficulties with applying the linear programming technique in practice include the following.

(a)   It may be **difficult to identify** which **resources** are likely to be **in short supply** and **what the amount of their availability will be**.

With linear programming, the profit-maximising product mix and the shadow price of each limiting factor depend on the total estimated availability of each scarce resource. So it is not sufficient to know that labour hours and machine hours will be in short supply, it is also necessary to guess how many labour hours and machine hours will be available. Estimates of future availability will inevitably be prone to inaccuracy and any such inaccuracies will invalidate the profit-maximising product mix derived from the use of linear programming.

(b.)   Management may **not make product mix decisions which are profit-maximising**. They may be more concerned to develop a production/sales plan which has the following features.

(i)   Realistic
(ii)   Acceptable to the individual managers throughout the organisation
(iii)   Acceptable to the rest of the workforce
(iv)   Promises a 'satisfactory' profit and accounting return

In other words, management might look for a **satisfactory product mix** which achieves a satisfactory return, sales revenue and market share whilst at the same time plans operations and targets of achievement which employees can accept as realistic, not too demanding and unreasonable, and not too threatening to their job security.

If a 'satisfactory' output decision is adopted, the product mix or service mix **recommended by the linear programming** (profit-maximising) technique will inevitably be **'watered down', amended or ignored**.

(c)   The **assumption of linearity may be totally invalid except over smaller ranges**. For example, in a profit maximisation problem, it may well be found that there are substantial changes in unit variable costs arising from increasing or decreasing returns to scale.

(d)   The linear programming model is essentially **static** and is therefore not really suitable for analysing in detail the effects of changes in the various parameters, for example over time.

(e)   In some circumstances, a practical solution derived from a linear programming model may be of **limited use** as, for example, where the variables may only take on **integer values**. A solution must then be found by a combination of rounding up and trial and error.

(f)   The **shadow price** of a scarce resource **only applies up to a certain limit**.

Chapter Roundup

- The formulation of the problem using the **simplex method** is similar to that required when the graphical method is used but **slack variables** must be incorporated into the constraints and the objective function.

- A **slack variable** represents the amount of a constraint that is unused.

- In any feasible solution, if a problem involves n constraints and m variables (decision plus slack), n variables will have a positive value and (m–n) variables will have a value of zero.

- Feasible solutions to a problem are shown in a **tableau**.

- If the **shadow prices** on the bottom (solution) row of a tableau are all positive, the tableau shows the optimal solution.
    - The solution column shows the optimal production levels and the units of unused resource.
    - The figure at the bottom of the solution column/right-hand side of the solution row shows the value of the objective function.
    - The figures in the solution row indicate the shadow prices of resources.

- **Sensitivity analysis** can be applied to the final tableau to determine the effect of having more or less of a scarce resource (indicated by figures in the column for the resource's slack variable).

- Sensitivity analysis can also be applied to test whether or not it would be **worthwhile to obtain more of a scarce resource** by paying a premium for additional supplies (only if the shadow price is greater than the additional cost).

- **Spreadsheet packages** can be used to solve linear programming problems.
    - The **slack/surplus** columns provide information about the slack values of ≤ constraints and the surplus values of any ≥ constraints.
    - The **worth** column shows the positive shadow price of resources.
    - The **relative loss** shows by how much contribution (usually) would fall if extra units of particular decision variables were produced.

- There are a number of **assumptions** and **practical difficulties** in the use of linear programming.

Quick Quiz

1   *Choose the correct words from those highlighted.*

    The simplex method can be used for problems with **one / two / three / more than three / any number of** decision variables.

2   *Fill in the blanks.*

    If a linear programming problem has four decision variables and five constraints (excluding non-negativity constraints), there will be .... slack variables and a total of .... variables. Each feasible solution matrix will have .... rows and .... columns. There will be .... variables with a value greater than 0 in any feasible solution.

3   A slack variable represents the amount of constraining resource that is used. *True or false?*

4   What is the general form of an objective function to maximise contribution (C) for a problem with two decision variables (x and y, with coefficients n and m) and four slack variables (a to d)?

    A $C + nx + my + a + b + c + d = 0$

    B $C - nx - my + 0a + 0b + 0c + 0d = 0$

    C $C - nx - my + a + b + c + d = 0$

    D $C + nx + my - 0a - 0b - 0c - 0d = 0$

5   *Choose the correct words from those highlighted.*

If, in a simplex tableau, shadow prices have a negative value, the objective function can be **increased/decreased** and the tableau **shows the optimal solution/does not show the optimal solution.**

6   In an optimal simplex tableau, the figure in the row for decision variable x (product X) and column for slack variable a (resource A) is –1.35. What does this indicate?

    A   For each extra unit of X produced, the usage of resource A would fall by 1.35 units

    B   For each extra unit of X produced, the usage of resource A would rise by 1.35 units

    C   For each extra unit of resource A available, the number of units of X would rise by 1.35 units

    D   For each extra unit of resource A available, the number of units of X would fall by 1.35 units

7   If a resource constraint has a worth of 356.92 in a spreadsheet package solution to a linear programming problem, what does this indicate?

    A   Contribution will fall by $356.92 if one less unit of the resource is available.

    B   Only 356.92 units of the resource are available.

    C   356.92 units of the resource are included in the optimal solution.

    D   A resource cannot have a worth.

8   It is assumed when using the simplex method of linear programming that there is interdependence between the demand for the different products/services. *True or false?*

9   When using Excel's analysis tool Solver, what is in the target cell?

    A   Objective function

    B   Resources

    C   Constraints

    D   Variables

Answers to Quick Quiz

1   any number of

2   five slack variables
total of nine variables
six rows
ten columns
five variables with a value greater than 0

3   False. It represents the amount unused.

4   B. Slack variables should always have zero coefficients.

5   increased
does not show the optimal solution

6   D. Here the minus sign indicates a fall for X.

7   A. Remember the worth column shows the shadow price of resources.

8   False. It is assumed there is no interdependence.

9   A. The target cell is the cell containing the objective function on the original Excel spreadsheet.

Now try the question below from the Exam Question Bank

Number	Level	Marks	Time
Q9	Examination	25	45 mins

BPP
LEARNING MEDIA

Pricing decisions

Introduction

Historically price was the single most important decision made by the sales department, but in **modern marketing philosophy price**, while important, is **not necessarily the predominant factor**. Modern businesses seek to interpret and **satisfy consumer wants and needs** by **modifying existing products** or **introducing new products** to the range. This contrasts with earlier production-oriented times when the typical reaction was to cut prices in order to sell more of an organisation's product.

Notwithstanding this change in emphasis, **pricing is very important**. Proper pricing of an organisation's products or services is essential to its **profitability** and hence its **survival**, and price has an important role to play as a **competitive tool** which can be used to differentiate a product and an organisation and thus exploit market opportunities.

We begin this chapter by looking at the **factors which influence the pricing decision.** We then consider **pricing to maximise profits**. Although theoretically sound, there are many problems of applying such an approach in practice. In the next chapter we will therefore be looking at alternative approaches to pricing. This chapter and the one which follows are two of the most important chapters in the text, packed full of highly-examinable material, so work through them both very carefully indeed. The topic has been tested regularly in Section A and longer questions.

Topic list	Learning outcomes	Syllabus references	Ability required
1 Demand	A(ii)	A(4)	Comprehension
2 Other issues that influence pricing decisions	A(ii)	A(4)	Comprehension
3 Profit maximisation in imperfect markets	A(iii)	A(3)	Application/evaluation
4 Deriving the demand curve	A(iii)	A(3)	Application/evaluation
5 The profit-maximising price/output level	A(iii)	A(3)	Application/evaluation

1 Demand

In the first sections of this chapter you will be learning about the many issues that need to be considered in decisions about the price which can be charged for a product or service. The first issues relate to demand.

1.1 Issue 1: the relationship between price and demand

Demand is normally **elastic** because demand will increase as prices are lowered.

There are two extremes in the relationship between price and demand. A supplier can either **sell a certain quantity, Q, at any price** (as in graph (a)). Demand is totally unresponsive to changes in price and is said to be **completely inelastic**. Alternatively, **demand might be limitless at a certain price** P (as in graph (b)), but there would be no demand above price P and there would be little point in dropping the price below P. In such circumstances demand is said to be **completely elastic**.

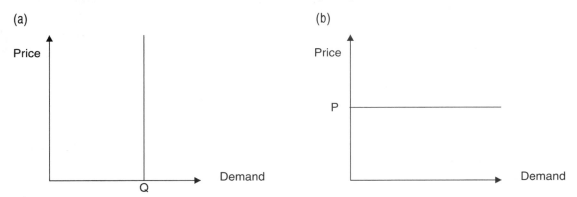

A more **normal situation** is shown below. The **downward-sloping** demand curve shows the inverse relationship between unit selling price and sales volume. As one rises, the other falls. Demand is **elastic** because demand will increase as prices are lowered.

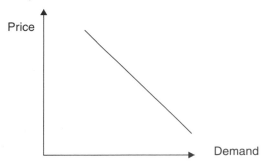

1.1.1 Price elasticity of demand (η)

Price elasticity of demand is a measure of the extent of change in market demand for a good in response to a change in its price.

Key term

> **Price elasticity of demand** (η), which is a measure of the extent of change in market demand for a good in response to a change in its price, is measured as:
>
> $$\frac{\text{The change in quantity demanded, as a \% of demand}}{\text{The change in price, as a \% of the price}}$$

Since the demand goes up when the price falls, and goes down when the price rises, the elasticity has a negative value, but it is usual to ignore the minus sign.

1.1.2 Example: price elasticity of demand

The price of a good is $1.20 per unit and annual demand is 800,000 units. Market research indicates that an increase in price of 10 pence per unit will result in a fall in annual demand of 75,000 units. What is the price elasticity of demand?

Solution

Annual demand at $1.20 per unit is 800,000 units.
Annual demand at $1.30 per unit is 725,000 units.

% change in demand = $(75{,}000/800{,}000) \times 100\% = 9.375\%$
% change in price = $(10p/120p) \times 100\% = 8.333\%$
Price elasticity of demand = $(-9.375/8.333) = -1.125$
Ignoring the minus sign, price elasticity is 1.125.

The demand for this good, at a price of $1.20 per unit, would be referred to as **elastic** because the **price elasticity of demand is greater than 1**.

1.1.3 Elastic and inelastic demand

The value of demand elasticity may be anything from zero to infinity.

ey term

> Demand is referred to as **inelastic** if the absolute value is less than 1 and **elastic** if the absolute value is greater than 1.

ttention!

> Think about what this means.
>
> (a) Where demand is inelastic, the quantity demanded falls by a smaller percentage than the percentage increase in price.
>
> (b) Where demand is elastic, demand falls by a larger percentage than the percentage rise in price.

AST FORWARD

> If **demand** is **elastic**, a reduction in price would lead to a rise in total sales revenue. If **demand** is **inelastic**, a reduction in price would lead to a fall in total sales revenue.

1.1.4 Price elasticity and the slope of the demand curve

Generally, **demand curves slope downwards**. Consumers are willing to buy more at lower prices than at higher prices. In general, **elasticity** will **vary** in value **along the length of a demand curve**.

(a) If a downward sloping demand curve becomes **steeper** over a particular range of quantity, then demand is becoming **more inelastic**.

(b) A **shallower** demand curve over a particular range indicates **more elastic** demand.

The ranges of price elasticity at different points on a downward sloping straight line demand curve are illustrated in the diagram below.

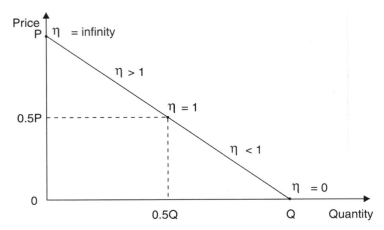

(a)   At **higher prices** on a straight line demand curve (the **top** of the demand curve), **small percentage price reductions** can bring **large percentage increases in quantity** demanded. This means that **demand is elastic** over these ranges, and **price reductions** bring **increases in total expenditure** by consumers on the commodity in question.

(b)   At **lower prices** on a straight line demand curve (the **bottom** of the demand curve), **large percentage price reductions** can bring **small percentage increases in quantity**. This means that **demand is inelastic** over these price ranges, and **price increases** result in **increases in total expenditure**.

1.1.5 Two special values of price elasticity

(a)   **Demand is perfectly inelastic ($\eta = 0$).** There is **no change in quantity** demanded, **regardless of the change in price**. The demand curve is **a vertical straight line** (as in graph (a) in Section 1.1).

(b)   **Perfectly elastic demand ($\eta = \infty$).** Consumers will want to **buy an infinite amount**, but **only up to a particular price level**. Any price increase above this level will reduce demand to zero. The demand curve is a **horizontal straight line** (as in graph (b) in Section 1.1).

1.1.6 Elasticity and the pricing decision

In practice, organisations will have only a rough idea of the shape of their demand curve: there will only be a limited amount of data about quantities sold at certain prices over a period of time *and,* of course, factors other than price might affect demand. Because any conclusions drawn from such data can only give an indication of likely future behaviour, management skill and expertise are also needed. Despite this limitation, an **awareness of the concept of elasticity can assist management with pricing decisions**.

(a)   (i)   With **inelastic demand, increase prices** because revenues will increase and total costs will reduce (because quantities sold will reduce).

(ii)   With **elastic demand**, increases in prices will bring decreases in revenue and decreases in price will bring increases in revenue. Management therefore have to **decide** whether the **increase/decrease in costs will be less than/greater than the increases/decreases in revenue**.

(b)   In situations of **very elastic demand**, overpricing can lead to massive drops in quantity sold and hence profits, whereas underpricing can lead to costly inventory outs and, again, a significant drop in profits. **Elasticity must therefore be reduced by creating a customer preference which is unrelated to price** (through advertising and promotion).

(c)   In situations of **very inelastic demand**, customers are **not sensitive to price. Quality, service, product mix and location** are therefore **more important** to a firm's pricing strategy.

(d) In practice, the **prices** of many products, such as consumer durables, need to **fall** over time if demand is to rise. **Costs** must therefore **fall by the same percentage to maintain margins**.

1.1.7 Determining factors

Factors that determine the degree of elasticity	Detail
The price of the good	
The price of other goods	For two types of good the market demand is interconnected. (a) **Substitutes**, so that an increase in demand for one version of a good is likely to cause a decrease in demand for others. Examples include rival brands of the same commodity (like *Coca-Cola* and *Pepsi-Cola*). (b) **Complements**, so that an increase in demand for one is likely to cause an increase in demand for the other (eg cups and saucers).
Income	A rise in income gives households more to spend and they will want to buy more goods. However this phenomenon does not affect all goods in the same way. (a) Normal goods are those for which a rise in income increases the demand. (b) Inferior goods are those for which demand falls as income rises, such as cheap wine. (c) For some goods demand rises up to a certain point and then remains unchanged, because there is a limit to which consumers can or want to consume. Examples are basic foodstuffs such as salt and bread.
Tastes and fashions	A change in fashion will alter the demand for a good, or a particular variety of a good. Changes in taste may stem from psychological, social or economic causes. There is an argument that tastes and fashions are created by the producers of products and services. There is undeniably some truth in this, but the modern focus on responding to customers' needs and wants suggests otherwise.
Expectations	Where consumers believe that prices will rise or that shortages will occur they will attempt to inventory up on the product, thereby creating excess demand in the short term.
Obsolescence	Many products and services have to be replaced periodically. (a) Physical goods are literally 'consumed'. Carpets become threadbare, glasses get broken, foodstuffs get eaten, children grow out of clothes. (b) Technological developments render some goods obsolete. Manual office equipment has been largely replaced by electronic equipment, because it does a better job, more quickly, quietly, efficiently and effectively.
Size of the market	The larger the market, the more inelastic the demand for the product in broad terms. For example, the demand for bread is relatively inelastic, whereas that for speciality bread such as olive ciabatta may be more elastic.
Necessities	Demand for basic items such as milk, toilet rolls and bread is, on the whole, price inelastic.

1.2 Issue 2: demand and the market

Economic theory suggests that the volume of **demand** for a good in **the market as a whole** is influenced by a variety of variables.

- The price of the good
- The price of other goods
- Expectations

- Obsolescence
- Tastes and fashion
- The perceived quality of the product
- The size and distribution of household income

1.3 Issue 3: demand and the individual firm

FAST FORWARD

The **volume of demand for one organisation's goods rather than another's** is influenced by three principal factors: product life cycle, quality and marketing.

1.3.1 Product life cycle

Key term

Product life cycle is 'The period which begins with the initial product specification, and ends with the withdrawal from the market of both the product and its support. It is characterised by defined stages including research, development, introduction, maturity, decline and abandonment.'

(CIMA *Official Terminology*)

Most products pass through the following phases.

Phase	Description
Introduction	The product is introduced to the market. Heavy capital expenditure will be incurred on product development and perhaps also on the purchase of new non-current assets and building up inventory for sale. On its introduction to the market, the product will begin to earn some revenue, but initially demand is likely to be small. Potential customers will be unaware of the product or service, and the organisation may have to spend further on advertising to bring the product or service to the attention of the market.
Growth	The product gains a bigger market as demand builds up. Sales revenues increase and the product begins to make a profit. The initial costs of the investment in the new product are gradually recovered.
Maturity	Eventually, the growth in demand for the product will slow down and it will enter a period of relative maturity. It will continue to be profitable. The product may be modified or improved, as a means of sustaining its demand.
Saturation and decline	At some stage, the market will have bought enough of the product and it will therefore reach 'saturation point'. Demand will start to fall. For a while, the product will still be profitable in spite of declining sales, but eventually it will become a loss-maker and this is the time when the organisation should decide to stop selling the product or service, and so the product's life cycle should reach its end.

 Case Study

During 2001, low cost PC maker Dell had to discount prices heavily to show continual growth despite market saturation.

The life expectancy of a product will influence the pricing decision. **Short-life products** must be quite **highly priced** so as to give the manufacturer a chance to **recover his investment** and **make a worthwhile** return. This is why fashion goods and new high technology goods, for example, tend to have high prices.

The current tendency is towards shorter product life cycles. Notwithstanding this observation, the **life cycles** of different products may **vary in terms of length of phases, overall length and shape**.

(a) Fashion products have a very short life and so do high technology products because they become rapidly out-dated by new technological developments.

(b) **Different versions of the same product may have different life cycles**, and consumers are often aware of this. For example, the prospective buyer of a new car is more likely to purchase a recently introduced Ford than a Vauxhall that has been on the market for several years, even if there is nothing to choose in terms of quality and price.

Exam focus point

Candidates in the May 2005 exam were asked to consider the relevance of the product life cycle to various pricing policies.

This topic was examined in the November 2006 exam as a Section B question where cash flow calculations had to be prepared and comments made on costs and prices over the life cycle.

1.3.2 Quality

One firm's product may be perceived to be better quality than another's, and may in some cases actually be so, if it uses sturdier materials, goes faster or does whatever it is meant to do in a 'better' way. Other things being equal, **the better quality good will be more in demand** than other versions.

1.3.3 Marketing

You may be familiar with the 'four Ps' of the marketing mix, all of which influence demand for a firm's goods.

Ps	Details
Price	
Product	
Place	This refers to the place where a good can be, or is likely to be, purchased. • If a good is difficult to obtain, potential buyers will turn to substitutes. • Some goods have no more than local appeal.
Promotion	This refers to the various means by which firms draw attention to their products and services. • A good brand name is a strong influence on demand. • Demand can be stimulated by a variety of promotional tools, such as free gifts, money off, shop displays, direct mail and media advertising.

In recent years, **emphasis** has been placed, especially in marketing, on the importance of **non-price factors in demand**. Thus the roles of product quality, promotion, personal selling and distribution and, in overall terms, brands, have grown. While it can be relatively easy for a competitor to copy a price cut, at least in the short term, it is much **more difficult to copy a successful brand image**.

Some larger organisations go to considerable effort to estimate the demand for their products or services at differing price levels; in other words, they produce estimated demand curves. A **knowledge of demand curves can be very useful**: for example, a large transport company such as *Stagecoach* might be considering an increase in bus fares or underground fares. The effect on total revenues and profit of the fares increase could be estimated from a knowledge of the demand for transport services at different price levels. If an increase in the price per ticket caused a large fall in demand (that is, if demand were price-elastic) total revenues and profits would fall; whereas a fares increase when demand is price-inelastic would boost total revenue and since a transport authority's costs are largely fixed, would probably boost total profits too.

2 Other issues that influence pricing decisions

FAST FORWARD

> As well as demand, a **range of other issues influence pricing decisions** including the market in which an organisation operates, competition, quality and price sensitivity.

2.1 Issue 4: markets

The price that an organisation can charge for its products will be determined to a greater or lesser degree by the market in which it operates. Here are some familiar terms that might feature as background for a question or that you might want to use in a written answer.

Key terms

> (a) **Perfect competition**: many buyers and many sellers all dealing in an identical product. Neither producer nor user has any market power and both must accept the prevailing market price.
>
> (b) **Monopoly**: one seller who dominates many buyers. The monopolist can use his market power to set a profit-maximising price.
>
> (c) **Monopolistic competition**: a large number of suppliers offer similar, but not identical, products. The similarities ensure elastic demand whereas the slight differences give some monopolistic power to the supplier.
>
> (d) **Oligopoly**: where relatively few competitive companies dominate the market. Whilst each large firm has the ability to influence market prices the unpredictable reaction from the other giants makes the final industry price indeterminate. **Cartels** are often formed.

Question

Markets

Learning outcome: A(ii)

A cartel is often formed in which type of market?

A   It can be formed easily in any market.   B   Perfect competition
C   Monopoly   D   Oligopoly

Answer

The correct answer is D.

2.2 Issue 5: competition

In established industries dominated by a few major firms, it is generally accepted that a price initiative by one firm will be countered by a price reaction by competitors. In these circumstances, prices tend to be fairly **stable**, unless pushed upwards by inflation or strong growth in demand.

If a rival cuts its prices in the expectation of increasing its market share, a firm has several options.

(a)   It will **maintain its existing prices** if the expectation is that only a small market share would be lost, so that it is more profitable to keep prices at their existing level. Eventually, the rival firm may drop out of the market or be forced to raise its prices.

(b)   It may **maintain its prices but respond with a non-price counter-attack**. This is a more positive response, because the firm will be securing or justifying its current prices with a product change, advertising, or better back-up services.

(c)   It may **reduce its prices**. This should protect the firm's market share so that the main beneficiary from the price reduction will be the consumer.

(d)   It may **raise its prices and respond with a non-price counter-attack**. The extra revenue from the higher prices might be used to finance an advertising campaign or product design changes. A price increase would be based on a campaign to emphasise the quality difference between the firm's own product and the rival's product.

2.2.1 Fighting a price war

Peter Bartram (*Financial Management,* March 2001) suggested a number of ways to fight a price war.

(a)   **Sell on value, not price,** where value is made up of service, response, variety, knowledge, quality, guarantee and price.

(b)   **Target service, not product market niches,** to build in the six non-price factors in (a) above.

 Case Study

The Marriott hotel chain has chosen to compete in the premium market on service. When guests arrive, instead of queuing at a busy reception, they are met at the front door by a host who gives them their room key.

(c)   **Use 'package pricing' to attract customers**

 Case Study

Computer retailers such as Time and PC World have beaten discounters by offering peripherals, discounted software and extended warranties as part of their more expensive packages.

(d)   **Make price comparisons difficult.** Terrestrial and mobile phone companies offer a bewildering variety of rates and discount offers which disguise the core price and make comparisons almost impossible.

(e)   **Build up key accounts**, as it is cheaper to get more business from an existing customer than to find a new one. Customer profitability analysis, covered in Chapter 18, is important here.

(f)   **Explore new pricing models.** E-business provides opportunities to use new pricing models.

(i)   On-line auctions for a wide range of products are carried out on certain websites.

(ii)   Other websites use a 'community shopping' pricing model, where the price of an item falls as more people buy it.

(iii) Marginal cost pricing is used on certain websites to get rid of inventory such as unsold theatre tickets and holidays.

 Case Study

Budget airlines such as EasyJet vary the price of a ticket depending on how early the traveller books. Coca Cola is experimenting with a vending machine that varies the cost of a can of coke in line with changes in temperature: the hotter the weather, the higher the price.

2.3 Other issues

Issue	Explanation/example
Price sensitivity	This will vary amongst purchasers. Those that can pass on the cost of purchases will be the least sensitive and will therefore respond more to other elements of perceived value. For example, the business traveller will be more concerned about the level of service and quality of food in looking for an hotel than price, provided that it fits the corporate budget. In contrast, the family on holiday are likely to be very price sensitive when choosing an overnight stay.
Price perception	This is the way customers react to prices. For example, customers may react to a price increase by buying more. This could be because they expect further price increases to follow (they are 'stocking up').
Compatibility with other products	A typical example is operating systems on computers, for which a user would like to have a wide range of compatible software available. For these types of product there is usually a **cumulative effect on demand**. The more people who buy one of the formats, the more choice there is likely to be of software for that format. This in turn is likely to influence future purchasers. The owner of the rights to the preferred format will eventually find little competition and will be able to charge a premium price for the product.
Competitors	An organisation, in setting prices, sends out signals. Competitors are likely to react to these signals in some way. In some industries (such as petrol retailing) pricing moves in unison; in others, price changes by one supplier may initiate a price war, with each supplier undercutting the others. Competition is discussed in more detail below.
Competition from substitute products	These are products which could be transformed for the same use or which might become desirable to customers at particular price levels. For example, train travel comes under competition as the quality, speed and comfort of coach travel rises. Similarly, if the price of train travel rises it comes under competition from cheaper coach travel and more expensive air travel.
Suppliers	If an organisation's suppliers notice a price rise for the organisation's products, they may seek a rise in the price for their supplies to the organisation on the grounds that it is now able to pay a higher price.

Issue	Explanation/example
Inflation	In periods of inflation the organisation may need to change prices to reflect increases in the prices of supplies and so on. Such changes may be needed to keep relative (real) prices unchanged.
Quality	In the absence of other information, customers tend to judge quality by price. Thus a price change may send signals to customers concerning the quality of the product. A price rise may indicate improvements in quality, a price reduction may signal reduced quality, for example through the use of inferior components.
Incomes	In times of rising incomes, price may become a less important marketing variable compared with product quality and convenience of access (distribution). When income levels are falling and/or unemployment levels rising, price will become a much more important marketing variable.
Ethics	Ethical considerations are a further factor, for example whether or not to exploit short-term shortages through higher prices.

3 Profit maximisation in imperfect markets

AST FORWARD

In imperfect markets there will be an **optimum price/output level** at which profits are maximised.

Some businesses enjoy a **monopoly** position in their market or something akin to a monopoly position, even in a competitive market. This is because they develop a unique marketing mix, for example a unique combination of price and quality, or a monopoly in a localised area.

The significance of a monopoly situation is as follows.

(a) The business has choice and flexibility in the prices it sets.

(b) Because the business has this freedom of choice in pricing, it will find that at **higher prices** demand for its products or services will be **less**. Conversely, at **lower prices**, demand for its products or services will be **higher**.

(c) There will be an **optimum** price/output level at which profits will be maximised.

(Note. Imperfect markets are markets in which price is affected by the amount supplied to the market and/or there is limited demand.)

 Case Study

A large public transport organisation might be considering an increase in bus fares or underground fares. The effect on total revenues and profit of the fares increase could be estimated from a knowledge of the demand for transport services at different price levels. If an increase in the price per ticket caused a large fall in demand (that is, if demand were price-elastic) total revenues and profits would fall; whereas a fares increase when demand is price-inelastic would boost total revenue and since a transport organisation's costs are largely fixed, would probably boost total profits too.

4 Deriving the demand curve

The demand curve shows the relationship between the price charged for a product and the subsequent demand for that product.

When demand is linear the **equation for the demand curve is P = a − bQ/ΔQ**

where P = the price
Q = the quantity demanded
a = the price at which demand would be nil
b = the amount by which the price falls for each stepped change in demand
ΔQ = the stepped change in demand

The constant a is calculated as follows.

$$a = \$ \text{ current price} + \left(\frac{\text{Current quantity at current price}}{\text{Change in quantity when price is changed by } \$b} \times \$b \right)$$

You need to learn these formulae.

This looks rather complicated in words, but it is very easy once the numbers are substituted. **Note that you are not given these formulae in the exam.**

4.1 Example: deriving the demand curve

The current price of a product is $12. At this price the company sells 60 items a month. One month the company decides to raise the price to $14, but only 45 items are sold at this price. Determine the demand equation.

Solution

Step 1 **Find the price at which demand would be nil**
Assuming demand is linear, each increase of $2 in the price would result in a fall in demand of 15 units. For demand to be nil, the price needs to rise from its current level by as many times as there are 15 units in 60 units (60/15 = 4) ie to $12 + (4 × $2) = $20.

Using the formula above, this can be shown as a = $12 + ((60/15) × $2)= $20

Step 2 **Extract figures from the question**
The **demand equation** can now be determined as P = a − bQ/ΔQ = 20 − 2Q/15

Step 3 **Check your equation**
We can check this by substituting $12 and $14 for P.

12 = 20 − (2 × 60/15) = 20 − 8 = 12
14 = 20 − (2 × 45/15) = 20 − 6 = 14

Formula to learn

The equation can also be re-arranged as $Q = \dfrac{(a \times \Delta Q) - (\Delta Q \times P)}{b}$

Question

Demand curve

Learning outcome: A(iii)

The current price of a product is $30 and the producers sell 100 items a week at this price. One week the price is dropped by $3 as a special offer and the producers sell 150 items.

Required

Fill in the blank in the sentence below.

An expression for the demand curve is ....

Answer

The correct answer is P = 36 – 3Q/50 or Q = (1,800 – 50P)/3.

a	=	$30 + (100/50 × $3)	= $36
P	=	36 – 3Q/50 or Q	= (1,800 – 50P)/3

Check

27	= 36 – 3Q/50	150	= (1,800 – 50P)/3
3Q/50	= 9	50P	= 1,800 – 450
Q	= 150	P	= 27

4.2 Example: profit maximisation and the demand curve

Maximum demand for JL's product is 10,000 units per annum. Demand will reduce by 100 units for every $1 increase in the selling price. JL has calculated that the profit-maximising level of sales for the coming year will be 8,000 units.

Required

Calculate the price at which these units will be sold.

Solution

a	=	(10,000/100 × $1) = $100
b	=	$1
ΔQ	=	100
∴ P	=	100 – Q/100
Now Q	=	8,000
∴ P	=	100 – 8,000/100 = $20

Alternative approach without using the demand curve formula

When P = 0, demand (Q) = 10,000
When P = 1, demand (Q) = 9,900
∴ Demand (Q) = 10,000 – 100 P, where P is the selling price in $
(because demand will drop by 100 for every increase (from $0) of $1 in the selling price)
∴ If Q = 8,000, P = (10,000 – 8,000)/100 = $20

Question

Profit maximisation

Learning outcome: A(iii)

Maximum demand for AL's product is 8,000 units per annum. Demand will reduce by 50 units for every $1 increase in the selling price.

AL has calculated that the profit-maximising selling price for the coming year will be $10.

The profit-maximising level of sales is 8,000 units. *True or false?*

Answer

Learning outcome: A(iii)

The correct answer is 7,500 and so the statement is false.

a	= (8,000/50) × \$1 = 160
b	= \$1
ΔQ	= 50
∴ P	= 160 – Q/50 and so Q = (160 × 50) – 50P = 8,000 – 50P
∴ If P	= \$10, Q = 8,000 – 500 = 7,500 units

Exam focus point

Objective testing questions could easily be asked on this topic.

5 The profit-maximising price/output level

5.1 Microeconomic theory and profit maximisation

Microeconomic theory suggests that **as output increases**, the marginal cost per unit might rise (due to the law of diminishing returns) and whenever the firm is faced with a downward sloping demand curve, the **marginal revenue per unit will decline.**

Eventually, a level of output will be reached where the **extra cost** of making one extra unit of output is greater than the **extra revenue** obtained from its sale. It would then be unprofitable to make and sell that extra unit.

Profits will continue to be maximised only up to the output level where marginal cost has risen to be exactly equal to the marginal revenue.

FAST FORWARD

Profits are maximised using marginalist theory when **marginal cost (MC) = marginal revenue (MR).**

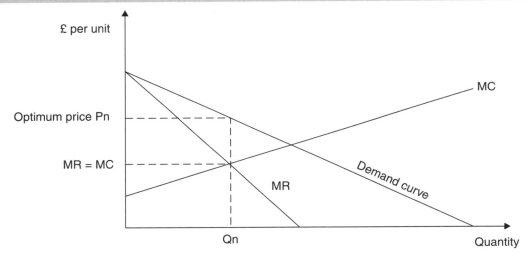

Profits are **maximised** at the point where **MC = MR**, ie at a volume of Qn units. If we add a demand curve to the graph, we can see that at an output level of Qn, the sales price per unit would be Pn.

It is important to make a clear **distinction** in your mind between the **sales price** and **marginal revenue**. In this example, the optimum price is Pn, but the marginal revenue is much less. This is because the 'additional' sales **unit** to reach output Qn has only been achieved by reducing the unit sales **price** from an amount higher than Pn for **all** the units to be sold, not just the marginal extra one. The increase in sales volume is therefore partly offset by a reduction in unit price; hence MR is lower than Pn.

5.2 Determining the profit-maximising selling price: using equations

FAST FORWARD

> The **optimal selling price** can be determined using equations (ie when MC = MR).

You could be **provided with equations for marginal cost and marginal revenue** and/or have to **devise them from information** in the question. By **equating the two equations** you can determine the optimal price. Remember, **marginal cost** is the **extra cost of producing one extra unit**, **marginal revenue** is the **extra revenue from producing one extra unit**. **Marginal revenue may not be the same as** the **price** charged for all units up to that demand level, as to increase volumes the price may have to be reduced. The following example provides an illustration.

5.2.1 Example: MC = MR

MOC makes and sells a copyrighted, executive game for two distinct markets, in which it has a monopoly. The fixed costs of production per month are $20,000 and variable costs per unit produced, and sold, are $40. (The monthly sales can be thought of as X, where $X = X_1 + X_2$, with X_1 and X_2 denoting monthly sales in their respective markets.) Detailed market research has revealed the demand functions in the markets to be as follows, with prices shown as P_1, P_2.

Market 1: $\qquad P_1 = 55 - 0.05X_1$
Market 2: $\qquad P_2 = 200 - 0.2X_2$

(Note. These formulae are simply **linear equations**. They show how the price (P) can be determined for a given level of demand (X). So in market 1, at a level of demand of 100, the price (P) will be $55 - (0.05 \times 100) = 50$.)

From these, the management accountant has derived that the marginal revenue functions in the two markets are as follows.

Market 1: $\qquad MR_1 = 55 - 0.1X_1$
Market 2: $\qquad MR_2 = 200 - 0.4X_2$

(Note. In market 1, the marginal revenue if 100 units are sold is $55 - (0.1 \times 100) = 45$.)

The management accountant believes there should be price discrimination; the price is currently $50 per game in either market.

Required

Analyse the information for the executive game and, given the management accountant's belief, do the following.

(a) Calculate the price to charge in each market, and the quantity to produce (and sell) each month, to maximise profit.

(b) Determine the revenue function for each market and the maximum monthly profit in total.

(c) Calculate and comment on the change in total profitability and prices.

Solution

(a)   In both markets, **marginal cost = variable cost per unit = $40**

Profit is maximised when **marginal revenue = marginal cost**.

Market 1

$$55 - 0.1X_1 = 40$$
$$0.1X_1 = 15$$
$$X_1 = 15/0.1 = 150$$

and price $P_1 = 55 - (0.05 \times 150) = \$47.5$.

Hence the price in market 1 should be $47.50 per unit and 150 units should be produced.

Market 2

$$200 - 0.4X_2 = 40$$
$$0.4X_2 = 160$$
$$X_2 = 160/0.4 = 400$$

and price $P_2 = 200 - (0.2 \times 400) = \$120$.

Hence the price in market 2 should be $120 per unit and 400 units should be produced.

Total number of items to be produced per month is 550.

(b)   **Revenue = unit price × number of units sold**

Market 1

Revenue $= P_1X_1 = 55X_1 - 0.05X_1^2$

Market 2

Revenue $= P_2X_2 = 200X_2 - 0.2X_2^2$

From (a), profit is maximised when

$X_1 = 150$ and $X_2 = 400$
$P_1 = 47.5$ and $P_2 = 120$

At maximum profit:

Total revenue $= (47.5 \times 150) + (120 \times 400) = \$55,125$

Total costs $= 20,000 + (40 \times 550) = \$42,000$

Total maximum monthly profit $= \$13,125$

(c)   Currently the price is $50 in both markets.

Market 1 $50 = 55 - 0.05X_1$
$0.05X_1 = 55 - 50 = 5$
$X_1 = 5/0.05 = 100$

Market 2 $50 = 200 - 0.2X_2$
$0.2X_2 = 200 - 50 = 150$
$X_2 = 150/0.2 = 750$

Therefore the **total number of units** $= 100 + 750 = 850$.

Total revenue $= \$50 \times 850 = \$42,500$.
Total cost $= 20,000 + (40 \times 850) = \$54,000$.

So the game **currently makes a loss** of $11,500.

Hence, if the prices are changed to $47.50 in market 1 and $120 in market 2, the company can expect to turn a monthly loss of $11,500 into a profit of $13,125.

Formulae for MC and MR are often derived using a mathematical technique known as differential calculus. This is well outside the scope of the syllabus, and so you will be provided with equations representing MC and MR if they are needed. Note, however, that if a question states that the extra cost of producing one extra item is $20, say, you will be expected to realise that the MC is $20. Likewise, if you are told that **100 units are sold for $10 each**, but **101 can only be sold for $9.99**, the **MR of the 101st item is (101 × $9.99) – (100 × $10) = $8.99**.

Question   Deriving a MR equation from the demand curve

Learning outcome: A(iii)

AB has used market research to determine that if a price of $250 is charged for product G, demand will be 12,000 units. It has also been established that demand will rise or fall by 5 units for every $1 fall/rise in the selling price. The marginal cost of product G is $80.

Required

If marginal revenue = a −2bx when the selling price (P) = a − bx, calculate the profit-maximising selling price for product G.

Answer

b = $1
a = $250 + ((12,000/5) × $1) = $2,650
MR = 2,650 − (2 × 1)x = 2,650 − 2x

Profits are maximised when MC = MR, ie when 80 = 2,650 − 2x
Profit-maximising demand = 1,285
∴ Profit-maximising price = $(2,650 − 1,285)
                             = $1,365

5.3 Determining the profit-maximising selling price: visual inspection of a tabulation of data

FAST FORWARD

The **optimum selling price** can also be determined using tabulation, graphs and gradients.

To determine the profit-maximising selling price:

(a)   Work out the **demand curve** and hence the **price** and the **total revenue** (PQ) at various levels of demand.

(b)   Calculate **total cost** and hence **marginal cost** at each level of demand.

(c)   Finally calculate **profit** at each level of demand, thereby determining the price and level of demand at which profits are maximised.

Question   Tabulation approach to find profit-maximising price

Learning outcome: A(iii)

An organisation operates in a market where there is imperfect competition, so that to sell more units of output, it must reduce the sales price of all the units it sells. The following data is available for prices and costs.

Total output Units	Sales price per unit (AR) $	Average cost of output (AC) $ per unit
0	–	–
1	504	720
2	471	402
3	439	288
4	407	231
5	377	201
6	346	189
7	317	182
8	288	180
9	259	186
10	232	198

The total cost of zero output is $600.

Required

Complete the table below to determine the output level and price at which the organisation would maximise its profits, assuming that fractions of units cannot be made.

Units	Price $	Total revenue $	Marginal revenue $	Total cost $	Marginal cost $	Profit $
0						
1						
2						
3						
4						
5						
6						
7						
8						
9						
10						

Answer

The correct answer is that profit is maximised at seven units of output and a price of $317, when MR is most nearly equal to MC.

Units	Price	Total revenue	Marginal revenue	Total cost	Marginal cost	Profit
	$	$	$	$	$	$
0	0	0	0	600	-	(600)
1	504	504	504	720	120	(216)
2	471	942	438	804	84	138
3	439	1,317	375	864	60	453
4	407	1,628	311	924	60	704
5	377	1,885	257	1,005	81	880
6	346	2,076	191	1,134	129	942
7	317	2,219	143	1,274	140	945
8	288	2,304	85	1,440	166	864
9	259	2,331	27	1,674	234	657
10	232	2,320	(11)	1,980	306	340

5.4 Determining the profit-maximising selling price: graphical approach

The diagrams below show that **profits are maximised** at the point where the **vertical distance** between the total revenue curve and the total costs curve is at a **maximum** (which is fairly obvious if you think about it since profits are maximised when the difference between cost and revenue is maximised). This profit-maximising demand level also **corresponds** to the point at which the **MC and MR curves intersect**, as we would expect. Notice how the profit-maximising price can be read off from the demand curve.

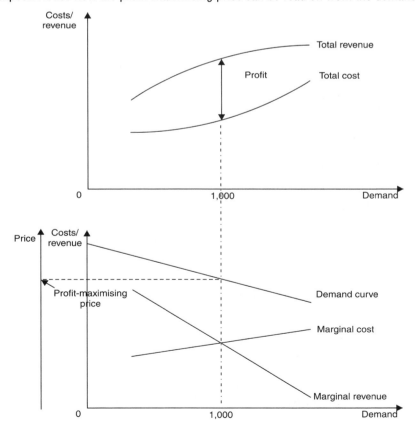

5.5 Determining the profit-maximising selling price: using gradients

Suppose we were to draw **tangents** to the total revenue and total cost curves at the **points at which profit is maximised**. As you can see, the gradients of these tangents **are the same**.

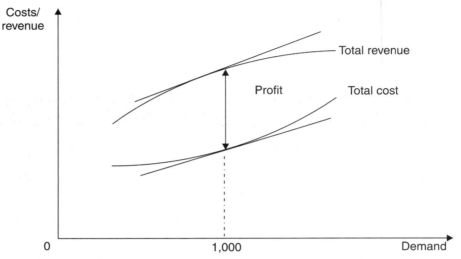

The **gradient of the total cost curve** is the **rate at which total cost changes with changes in volume,** which is simply **marginal cost**. Likewise, the **gradient of the total revenue curve** is the **rate at which total revenue changes with changes in volume,** which is the **marginal revenue**. At the **point of profit maximisation**, the two gradients are **equal** and hence, once again, **MC = MR.**

5.6 Optimum pricing in practice

There are problems with applying the approach described above in practice for the following reasons.

(a) It assumes that the demand curve and total costs can be **identified with certainty**. This is unlikely to be so.

(b) It ignores the **market research costs** of acquiring knowledge of demand.

(c) It assumes the firm has **no production constraint** which could mean that the equilibrium point between supply and demand cannot be reached.

(d) It assumes the objective is **to maximise profits**. There may be other objectives.

 Case Study

Microsoft dominates the market for many types of computer software, but this domination was not achieved by setting short-term profit-maximising selling prices for the MS-DOS and Windows operating systems. By offering cheap licences to PC manufacturers for use of these operating systems, Microsoft word processing, spreadsheet, graphics and database packages have become almost industry-standard.

(e) It assumes that **price is the only influence** on quantity demanded. We saw in Sections 1 and 2 that this is far from the case.

(f) It is **complicated by** the issue of **price discrimination** (the practice of charging different unit selling prices for the same product). We look at price discrimination in the next chapter.

(g) Although there are arguments for the **applicability** of the concept of the profit-maximising unit selling price in **traditional markets** where **homogenous, mass-produced** products are in continuous supply (such as public transport), the **modern trend** is towards **short product life cycles** and a **high degree of product differentiation**.

5.7 Further reading

Read the article that appeared in *Financial Management* in May 2006.

This article takes a humorous approach to the application of optimum pricing but could well form the basis of a question in the exam.

Chapter Roundup

- **Demand** is normally **elastic** because demand will increase as prices are lowered.

- **Price elasticity of demand** is a measure of the extent of change in market demand for a good in response to a change in its price.

- If **demand** is **elastic** a reduction in price would lead to a rise in total sales revenue. If **demand** is **inelastic**, a reduction in price would lead to a fall in total sales revenue.

- The **volume of demand for one organisation's goods rather than another's** is influenced by three principal factors: product life cycle, quality and marketing.

- As well as demand, a **range of other issues influence pricing decisions** including the market in which an organisation operates, competition, quality and price sensitivity.

- In imperfect markets there will be an **optimum price/output level** at which profits are maximised.

- When demand is linear the **equation for the demand curve** is $\mathbf{P = a - bQ/\Delta Q}$

   where P   = the price
             Q   = the quantity demanded
             a   = the price at which demand would be nil
             b   = the amount by which the price falls for each stepped change in demand
             ΔQ = the stepped change in demand

   The constant a is calculated as follows.

   $$a = \$ \text{ current price} + \left(\frac{\text{Current quantity at current price}}{\text{Change in quantity when price is changed by } \$b} \times \$b \right)$$

   You need to learn these formulae.

- **Profits are maximised** using marginalist theory when **marginal cost (MC) = marginal revenue (MR)**.

- The **optimal selling price** can be determined using equations (ie when MC = MR).

- The **optimum selling price** can also be determined using tabulation, graphs and gradients.

Quick Quiz

1   *Choose the correct words from those highlighted.*

The price elasticity of demand for a particular good at the current price is 1.2. Demand for this good at this price is (1) **elastic/inelastic**. If the price of the good is reduced, total sales revenue will (2) **rise/fall/stay the same.**

2   What are the four stages of the product life cycle?

A   Appearance, growth, maturity, saturation
B   Birth, growth, adolescence, old age
C   Introduction, expansion, maturity, death
D   Introduction, growth, maturity, saturation and decline

3   A company knows that demand for its new product will be highly elastic. The most appropriate pricing strategy for the new product will be market skimming pricing. *True or false?*

4   *Label the graph with the terms provided.*

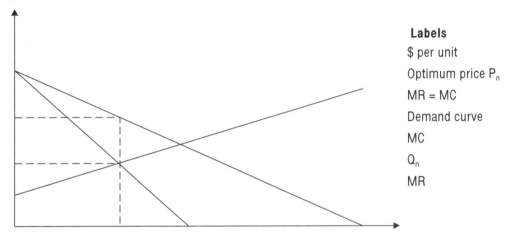

Labels
$ per unit
Optimum price P_n
MR = MC
Demand curve
MC
Q_n
MR

5   *Fill in the blanks.*

When demand is linear, the equation for the demand curve is $P = a - bQ/\Delta Q$

where

P = ...

Q = ...

a = ...

b = ...

ΔQ = ...

The constant a is calculated as $ .... $+ \left(\dfrac{........................}{........................} \times £b \right)$

6   At the point of profit maximisation, the gradients of the total cost curve and total revenue curve are the same in absolute terms, but one is positive, one is negative. *True or false?*

Answers to Quick Quiz

1   (1) elastic, (2) rise

2   D. Learn them!

3   False. Market penetration pricing would be more appropriate.

4

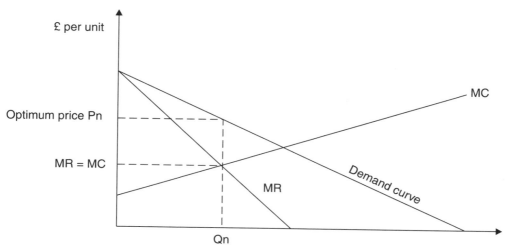

5   P =   price

     Q =   quantity demanded

     a =   price at which demand will be nil

     b =   amount by which the price falls for each stepped change in demand

     ΔQ =   the stepped change in demand

     The constant a is calculated as $ current price + $\left(\dfrac{\text{Current quantity at current price}}{\text{Change in quantity when price is changed by \$b}} \times \$b \right)$

6   False. The gradients are exactly the same.

Number	Level	Marks	Time
Q10	Examination	10	18 mins
Q11	Examination	10	18 mins

Pricing approaches and strategies

Introduction

In Chapter 8 we looked at pricing to maximise profits. Although theoretically sound, there are many problems of applying such an approach in practice. Because of this most organisations adopt **cost-based approaches** to pricing (**Sections 1 and 2**). Despite their popularity these also have significant shortcomings, however.

Sections 4 to 7 look at the pricing strategies to adopt in particular circumstances, such as when a new product is launched.

Pricing is likely to be examined on a fairly regular basis and has been a requirement of parts of longer questions in many recent papers, so this chapter needs your full attention.

Topic list	Learning outcomes	Syllabus references	Ability required
1 Full cost-plus pricing	A(ii)	A(4)	Comprehension
2 Marginal cost-plus or mark-up pricing	A(ii)	A(4)	Comprehension
3 Economists' versus accountants' views on pricing decisions	A(ii)	A(4)	Comprehension
4 Pricing based on mark-up per unit of limiting factor	A(ii)	A(4)	Comprehension
5 Pricing strategies for special orders	A(iii)	A(4)	Application/evaluation
6 Pricing strategies for new products	A(iii)	A(4)	Application/evaluation
7 Other pricing strategies	A(iii)	A(4)	Application/evaluation

1 Full cost-plus pricing

In **full cost-plus pricing** the sales price is determined by calculating the full cost of the product and then adding a percentage mark-up for profit. The most important criticism of full cost-plus pricing is that it fails to recognise that since sales demand may be determined by the sales price, there will be a profit-maximising combination of price and demand.

1.1 Reasons for its popularity

In practice cost is one of the most important influences on price. Many firms base price on simple **cost-plus rules** (costs are estimated and then a mark-up is added in order to set the price). A study by *Lanzilotti* gave a number of **reasons** for the **predominance of this method**.

    (a)   Planning and use of scarce capital resources are easier.

    (b)   Assessment of divisional performance is easier.

    (c)   It emulates the practice of successful large companies.

    (d)   Organisations fear government action against 'excessive' profits.

    (e)   There is a tradition of production rather than of marketing in many organisations.

    (f)   There is sometimes tacit collusion in industry to avoid competition.

    (g)   Adequate profits for shareholders are already made, giving no incentive to maximise profits by seeking an 'optimum' selling price.

    (h)   Cost-based pricing strategies based on internal data are easier to administer.

    (i)   Over time, cost-based pricing produces stability of pricing, production and employment.

Key term

> **Full cost-plus pricing** is a method of determining the sales price by calculating the full cost of the product and adding a percentage mark-up for profit.

1.2 Setting full-cost plus prices

The 'full cost' may be a fully absorbed production cost only, or it may include some absorbed administration, selling and distribution overhead.

A business might have an idea of the percentage profit margin it would like to earn, and so might **decide on an average profit mark-up** as a general guideline for pricing decisions. This would be particularly **useful for** businesses that carry out a large amount of **contract work or jobbing work**, for which individual job or contract prices must be quoted regularly to prospective customers. However, the percentage profit **mark-up does not have to be rigid and fixed**, but can be varied to suit the circumstances. In particular, the percentage mark-up can be varied to suit demand conditions in the market.

Question

Cost-plus pricing

Learning outcome: A(ii)

A product's full cost is $4.75 and it is sold at full cost plus 70%. A competitor has just launched a similar product selling for $7.99.

Required

Fill in the gap in the sentence below.

The cost-plus percentage will need to be reduced by...... %.

Answer

The correct answer is that the cost-plus percentage will need to be reduced by 2%.

Profits = $(7.99 – 4.75) = $3.24
Mark-up = ($3.24/$4.75) × 100% = 68%
∴ % needs to be reduced by (70 – 68)% = 2%

1.3 Example: full cost-plus pricing

Markup has begun to produce a new product, Product X, for which the following cost estimates have been made.

	$
Direct materials	27
Direct labour: 4 hrs at $5 per hour	20
Variable production overheads: machining, ½ hr at $6 per hour	3
	50

Production fixed overheads are budgeted at $300,000 per month and, because of the shortage of available machining capacity, the company will be restricted to 10,000 hours of machine time per month. The absorption rate will be a direct labour rate, however, and budgeted direct labour hours are 25,000 per month. It is estimated that the company could obtain a minimum contribution of $10 per machine hour on producing items other than product X.

The direct cost estimates are not certain as to material usage rates and direct labour productivity, and it is recognised that the estimates of direct materials and direct labour costs may be subject to an error of ± 15%. Machine time estimates are similarly subject to an error of ± 10%.

The company wishes to make a profit of 20% on full production cost from product X.

Required

Ascertain the full cost-plus based price.

Solution

Even for a relatively 'simple' cost-plus pricing estimate, some problems can arise, and certain assumptions must be made and stated. In this example, we can identify two problems.

(a)   Should the opportunity cost of machine time be included in cost or not?
(b)   What allowance, if any, should be made for the possible errors in cost estimates?

Different assumptions could be made.

(a)   **Exclude machine time opportunity costs: ignore possible costing errors**

	$
Direct materials	27.00
Direct labour (4 hours)	20.00
Variable production overheads	3.00
Fixed production overheads (at $\frac{£300,000}{25,000}$ = $12 per direct labour hour)	48.00
Full production cost	98.00
Profit mark-up (20%)	19.60
Selling price per unit of product X	117.60

(b)   **Include machine time opportunity costs: ignore possible costing errors**

	$
Full production cost as in (a)	98.00
Opportunity cost of machine time: contribution forgone (½ hr × $10)	5.00
Adjusted full cost	103.00
Profit mark-up (20%)	20.60
Selling price per unit of product X	123.60

(c)   **Exclude machine time opportunity costs but make full allowance for possible under-estimates of cost**

	$	$
Direct materials	27.00	
Direct labour	20.00	
	47.00	
Possible error (15%)	7.05	
		54.05
Variable production overheads	3.00	
Possible error (10%)	0.30	
		3.30
Fixed production overheads (4 hrs × $12)	48.00	
Possible error (labour time) (15%)	7.20	
		55.20
Potential full production cost		112.55
Profit mark-up (20%)		22.51
Selling price per unit of product X		135.06

(d)   **Include machine time opportunity costs and make a full allowance for possible under-estimates of cost**

	$
Potential full production cost as in (c)	112.55
Opportunity cost of machine time:	
potential contribution forgone (½ hr × $10 × 110%)	5.50
Adjusted potential full cost	118.05
Profit mark-up (20%)	23.61
Selling price per unit of product X	141.66

Using different assumptions, we could arrive at any of four different unit prices in the range $117.60 to $141.66.

1.4 Problems with and advantages of full cost-plus pricing

There are several serious **problems** with relying on a full cost approach to pricing.

(a) It **fails to recognise** that since demand may be determining price, **there will be a profit-maximising combination of price and demand**.

(b) There may be a need to **adjust prices to market and demand conditions**.

(c) **Budgeted output volume** needs to be established. Output volume is a key factor in the overhead absorption rate.

(d) A **suitable basis for overhead absorption** must be selected, especially where a business produces more than one product.

However, it is a **quick, simple and cheap** method of pricing which can be delegated to junior managers (which is particularly important with jobbing work where many prices must be decided and quoted each day) and, since the size of the profit margin can be varied, a decision based on a price in excess of full cost should ensure that a company working at normal capacity will **cover all of its fixed costs and make a profit**.

1.5 Example: full cost-plus versus profit-maximising prices

Tiger has budgeted to make 50,000 units of its product, timm. The variable cost of a timm is $5 and annual fixed costs are expected to be $150,000.

The financial director of Tiger has suggested that a mark-up of 25% on full cost should be charged for every product sold. The marketing director has challenged the wisdom of this suggestion, and has produced the following estimates of sales demand for timms.

Price per unit ($)	9	10	11	12	13
Demand (units)	42,000	38,000	35,000	32,000	27,000

Required

(a) Calculate the profit for the year if a full cost-plus price is charged.
(b) Calculate the profit for the year if a profit-maximising price is charged.

Assume in both (a) and (b) that 50,000 units of timm are produced regardless of sales volume.

Solution

The full cost per unit comprises $5 of variable costs plus $3 of fixed costs ($8 in total). A 25% mark-up on this cost gives a selling price of $10 per unit so that sales demand would be 38,000 units. (Production is given as 50,000 units.) **Profit using absorption costing** would be as follows.

	$	$
Sales		380,000
Costs of production (50,000 units)		
Variable (50,000 × $5)	250,000	
Fixed (50,000 × $3)	150,000	
	400,000	
Less increase in inventory (12,000 units × 8)	(96,000)	
Cost of sales		304,000
Profit		76,000

Profit using marginal costing instead of absorption costing, so that fixed overhead costs are written off in the period they occur, would be as follows. (The 38,000 unit demand level is chosen for comparison.)

	$
Contribution (38,000 × $(10 – 5))	190,000
Fixed costs	150,000
Profit	40,000

Since the company cannot go on indefinitely producing an output volume in excess of sales volume, this profit figure is more indicative of the profitability of timms in the longer term.

A **profit-maximising price** is one which gives the greatest net (relevant) cash flow, which in this case is the **contribution-maximising price**.

Price	Unit contribution	Demand	Total contribution
$	$	Units	$
9	4	42,000	168,000
10	5	38,000	190,000
11	6	35,000	210,000
12	7	32,000	224,000
13	8	27,000	216,000

The profit maximising price is $12, with annual sales demand of 32,000 units.

This example shows that a **cost-plus based price is unlikely to be the profit-maximising price**, and that a **marginal costing approach**, calculating the total contribution at a variety of different selling prices, will be **more helpful** for establishing what the profit-maximising price ought to be.

2 Marginal cost-plus pricing or mark-up pricing

FAST FORWARD

Marginal cost-plus pricing involves adding a profit margin to the marginal cost of production/sales. A marginal costing approach is more likely to help with identifying a profit-maximising price.

Whereas a full cost-plus approach to pricing draws attention to net profit and the net profit margin, a variable cost-plus approach to pricing **draws attention to gross profit** and the **gross profit margin**, or **contribution**.

Key term

Marginal cost-plus pricing/mark-up pricing is a method of determining the sales price by adding a profit margin on to either marginal cost of production or marginal cost of sales.

Exam focus point

Marginal cost pricing and full cost pricing were examined in November 2005 in a Section B question. The examiner remarked that many answers failed to address the requirements of the question which were to explain **absorption and marginal cost approaches to pricing** and instead mentioned cost and then went no further.

The examiner revisited the comparison between marginal cost pricing and full cost pricing in November 2006 as part of a longer Section C question.

Question | Marginal cost pricing

Learning outcome: A(ii)

A product has the following costs.

	$
Direct materials	5
Direct labour	3
Variable overheads	7

Fixed overheads are $10,000 per month. Budgeted sales per month are 400 units to allow the product to break even.

Required

Fill in the blank in the sentence below.

The mark-up which needs to be added to *marginal* cost to allow the product to break even is ...... %.

Answer

The correct answer is 166$\frac{2}{3}$%.

Breakeven point is when total contribution equals fixed costs.

At breakeven point, $10,000 = 400 (price − $15)
∴ $25 = price − $15
∴ $40 = price
∴ Mark-up = ((40 − 15) /15) × 100% = 166$\frac{2}{3}$%

2.1 The advantages and disadvantages of a marginal cost-plus approach to pricing

Here are the **advantages**.

(a) It is a **simple and easy** method to use.

(b) The **mark-up percentage can be varied**, and so mark-up pricing can be adjusted to reflect demand conditions.

(c) It **draws management attention to contribution**, and the effects of higher or lower sales volumes on profit. In this way, it helps to create a better awareness of the concepts and implications of marginal costing and cost-volume-profit analysis. For example, if a product costs $10 per unit and a mark-up of 150% is added to reach a price of $25 per unit, management should be clearly aware that every additional $1 of sales revenue would add 60 pence to contribution and profit.

(d) In practice, mark-up pricing is **used** in businesses **where there is a readily-identifiable basic variable cost**. Retail industries are the most obvious example, and it is quite common for the prices of goods in shops to be fixed by adding a mark-up (20% or 33.3%, say) to the purchase cost.

There are, of course, **drawbacks** to marginal cost-plus pricing.

(a) Although the **size** of the mark-up can be varied in accordance with demand conditions, it **does not ensure that sufficient attention is paid to demand conditions, competitors' prices and profit maximisation**.

(b) It **ignores fixed overheads** in the pricing decision, but the sales price must be sufficiently high to ensure that a profit is made after covering fixed costs.

Attention!

> In our study of decision making to date we have adopted a marginal cost approach in that we have considered the effects on contribution and have classed (most) fixed overheads as irrelevant. In pricing decisions, however, there is a conflict with such an approach because of the need for full recovery of all costs incurred.

3 Economists' versus accountants' views on pricing decisions

FAST FORWARD

> **Economic theory** claims that **profit is maximised** by setting a price so that **marginal cost equals marginal revenue**. But because most cost accounting systems are set up to provide information for financial reporting purposes, it can be **difficult to identify short-run or long-run marginal cost**, even if ABC is used.

Mike Lucas (*Management Accounting*, June 1999) looked at this topic. What follows is a summary of his article.

Research **by accountants** has suggested that **full costs** play an important role in many pricing and output decisions. The use of full cost is at odds with the **economists' view** that prices should be set at a level which **equates marginal cost and marginal revenue,** however.

3.1 Economic research findings

Economic research by Hall and Hitch in 1939 found that most organisations tended to **set prices by adding a fairly constant mark-up** to full cost for three principal **reasons**.

(a) **Organisations have no knowledge of their demand curves** because of a lack of information about customers' preferences and/or competitor reaction to price changes.

(b) **Price stickiness**

As illustrated in the diagram below (a **kinked demand curve**), an organisation may feel that if prices are increased above the current price P1, competitors will not match the increase, demand being very elastic. The increase in profit per unit will not compensate for the profit lost from the reduction in quantity sold, and so total profit will fall.

If price is reduced below the current price P1, competitors will match the price decrease, demand being inelastic. The small increase in the quantity sold will not compensate for the drop in profit per unit, and so total profit will fall.

The organisation would therefore be reluctant to increase or decrease the price from the current level if there are minor changes in costs or market conditions, giving rise to apparent price stickiness.

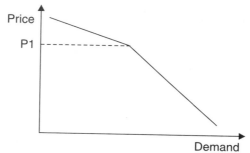

(c) The frequent price changes which are likely to occur if **profit-maximising prices** are set (as prices are changed whenever there is a change in demand or costs) can be **administratively expensive** to bring in, and can **inconvenience** sales staff, distributors and customers.

Economists countered the suggested predominance of cost-based approaches, however, with arguments of **'implicit marginalism'**, whereby **organisations act as though they are setting prices on the basis of equating MC and MR**, even if this approach is **not consciously adopted**. Evidence for this includes:

(a) Discounting prices when market circumstances change and/or accepting a lower profit margin when competition increases. This is similar to using a marginal revenue function.

(b) Reducing the overhead charged to products to reflect the short-term nature of some fixed costs. This is similar to using a marginal cost function.

3.2 Reconciling full cost pricing and marginalist, profit-maximising principles

Some economists have tried to show that full cost pricing is compatible with marginalist principles. One argument (by Koutsoylannis) is that:

Price (P) = average variable cost (AVC) + costing margin

where the costing margin = average fixed cost (AFC) + normal profit mark-up.

Taking AVC to be the best available approximation of long-run marginal cost, any adjustments made to the costing margin because of competitive forces can be viewed as the organisation attempting to establish its demand curve, and so – by implication – its marginal revenue function.

3.3 Accounting research

Problems with the methods used for accounting research may not have picked up on the fact that **organisations are constantly making adjustments to prices in order to meet market situations**, and while many organisations might believe they set prices on a cost plus basis, these prices are the actual prices charged in just a few situations.

3.4 ABC and long-run marginal cost

As you will know from your Certificate level studies, **ABC costs** should be **long-run avoidable (marginal) costs** and so in theory **organisations using ABC** costs are **following economists' views of pricing**. The **treatment of 'indivisibilities' means that this is not necessarily the case**, however.

'Indivisibilities' occur when a **reduction in the level of activity does not lead to a proportionate reduction in resource inputs**. For example, a process may be duplicated so that output can be doubled but it may not necessarily be possible to halve the process if demand drops by 50%.

The **cost of indivisible resources** should therefore **not be attributed to individual products** as, to the extent that they are indivisible, they will be incurred regardless of the activity level and so are unavoidable in relation to a particular product.

3.5 Conclusion

Economic theory claims that profit is maximised by setting a price so that marginal cost equals marginal revenue. But because most cost accounting systems are set up to provide information for financial reporting purposes, it can be **difficult to identify short-run or long-run marginal cost, even if ABC is used**.

It is difficult to know whether organisations are carrying out the analysis necessary to determine marginal cost or whether the full cost provided by the accounting system is used for pricing decisions.

The **debate** over the theory of pricing therefore **continues**.

4 Pricing based on mark-up per unit of limiting factor

Another approach to pricing might be taken when a **business is working at full capacity, and is restricted by a shortage of resources** from expanding its output further. By deciding what target profit it would like to earn, it could **establish a mark-up per unit of limiting factor**.

4.1 Example: mark-up per unit of limiting factor

Suppose that a company provides a window cleaning service to offices and factories. Business is brisk, but the company is restricted from expanding its activities further by a shortage of window cleaners. The workforce consists of 12 window cleaners, each of whom works a 35 hour week. They are paid $4 per hour. Variable expenses are $0.50 per hour. Fixed costs are $5,000 per week. The company wishes to make a contribution of at least $15 per hour.

The minimum charge per hour for window cleaning would then be as follows.

	$ per hour
Direct wages	4.00
Variable expenses	0.50
Contribution	15.00
Charge per hour	19.50

The company has a total workforce capacity of (12 × 35) 420 hours per week, and so total revenue would be $8,190 per week, contribution would be (420 × $15) $6,300, leaving a profit after fixed costs of $1,300 per week.

5 Pricing strategies for special orders

The basic approach to pricing **special orders** is **minimum pricing**.

5.1 What is a special order?

A special order is a **one-off** revenue-earning opportunity. These may arise in the following situations.

(a) When a business has a regular source of income but also has some **spare capacity** allowing it to take on extra work if demanded. For example a brewery might have a capacity of 500,000 barrels per month but only be producing and selling 300,000 barrels per month. It could therefore consider special orders to use up some of its spare capacity.

(b) When a business has **no regular source of income** and relies exclusively on its ability to respond to demand. A building firm is a typical example as are many types of sub-contractors. In the service sector consultants often work on this basis.

The reason for making the distinction is that in the case of **(a)**, a firm would normally attempt to cover its longer-term running costs in its prices for its regular product. Pricing for special orders need therefore **take no account of unavoidable fixed costs**. This is clearly not the case for a firm in (b)'s position, where special orders are the only source of income for the foreseeable future.

5.2 Minimum pricing

The minimum price is the **price at which the organisation would break even** if it undertook the work. It would have to cover the incremental costs of producing and selling the item and the opportunity costs of the resources consumed.

Question	Pricing special orders

Learning outcome: A(iii)

DDD has decided to price its jobs as follows.

(a)   It calculates the minimum price for the job using relevant costs.
(b)   It adds $5,000 to cover fixed costs.
(c)   It adds a 10% profit margin to the total cost.

A customer who has work to be performed in May says he will award the contract to DDD if its bid is reduced by $5,000.

The contract should be accepted. *True or false?*

Answer

The correct answer is true or false. (Sorry, this is a bit of a trick question and you wouldn't encounter anything so ambiguous in the exam.)

Yes, the contract should be accepted if there is no other work available, because DDD will at least earn a contribution towards fixed costs of 10% of the minimum cost. But no, if by accepting this reduced price it would send a signal to other prospective customers that they too could negotiate such a large reduction.

tention!

> The exercise above illustrates the difficulties faced by firms with high overheads. Ideally some means should be found of identifying the causes of such costs. Activity based analysis might reveal ways of attributing overheads to specific jobs or perhaps of avoiding them altogether.

In today's competitive markets it is very much the **modern trend to tailor products or services to customer demand** rather than producing for inventory. This suggests that **'special' orders may become the norm** for most businesses.

6 Pricing strategies for new products

ST FORWARD

Two pricing strategies for **new** products are **market penetration pricing** and **market skimming pricing**.

6.1 Tabulation

Suppose that Novo is about to launch a new product with a variable cost of $10 per unit. The company has carried out market research (at a cost of $15,000) to determine the potential demand for the product at various selling prices.

Selling price	Demand
$	Units
30	20,000
25	30,000
20	40,000

Its current capacity is for 20,000 units but additional capacity can be made available by using the resources of another product line. If this is done the lost contribution from the other product will be $35,000 for each additional 10,000 units of capacity.

How could we **analyse this information** for senior management in a way that helps them to **decide on the product's launch price**?

Tabulation is the approach to use with a problem of this type.

Selling price $	Demand Units ('000)	Variable costs $'000	Opportunity costs $'000	Total costs $'000	Sales revenue $'000	Contribution $'000
30	20	200	–	200	600	400
25	30	300	35	335	750	415
20	40	400	70	470	800	330

The **optimum price to maximise short-term profits is $25**. However, it is quite possible that the aim will **not** be to maximise short-term profits, and a number of other strategies may be adopted, as discussed below.

The main **objections** to the approach described above are that it only **considers a limited range of prices** (what about charging $27.50?) and it **takes no account of the uncertainty of forecast demand**. However, allowance could be made for both situations by collecting more information.

Question   Pricing new products

Learning outcome: A(iii)

JPM is just about to launch a new product.

Production capacity means that a maximum of 120 units can be manufactured each week and manufacture must be in batches of ten. The marketing department estimates that at a price of $120 no units will be sold but, for each $3 reduction in prices, ten additional units per week will be sold.

Fixed costs associated with manufacturing the product are expected to be $6,000 per week. Variable costs are expected to be $40 per unit for the first eight batches, but after that the unit variable cost of the products in the batch will be $2 more than those in the preceding batch.

Which is the most profitable level of output per week?

A   80 units
B   90 units
C   100 units
D   110 units

Answer

The correct answer is C.

Note that we cannot use the profit maximisation model because of the non-linear relationships involved.

Units		Total variable costs $	Selling price per unit $	Total sales revenue $	Total contribution $
80	(× $40)	3,200	96*	7,680	4,480
90	(× $42)	3,780	93	8,370	4,590
100	(× $44)	4,400	90	9,000	4,600
110	(× $46)	5,060	87	9,570	4,510
120	(× $48)	5,760	84	10,080	4,320

*$120 − (8 × $3)

6.2 First on the market?

A new product pricing strategy will depend largely on whether a company's product or service is the first of its kind on the market.

(a) If the **product is the first of its kind**, there will be **no competition** yet, and the company, for a time at least, will be a **monopolist**. Monopolists have more influence over price and are able to set a price at which they think they can maximise their profits. A monopolist's price is likely to be higher, and its profits bigger, than those of a company operating in a competitive market.

(b) If the new product being launched by a company is **following a competitor's product** onto the market, the pricing strategy will be **constrained by what the competitor** is already doing. The new product could be given a higher price if its quality is better, or it could be given a price which matches the competition. Undercutting the competitor's price might result in a price war and a fall of the general price level in the market.

6.2.1 Market penetration pricing

term

> **Market penetration pricing** is a policy of low prices when the product is first launched in order to obtain sufficient penetration into the market.

Circumstances in which a penetration policy may be appropriate

(a) If the firm wishes to **discourage new entrants** into the market

(b) If the firm wishes to **shorten the initial period of the product's life cycle** in order to enter the growth and maturity stages as quickly as possible

(c) If there are **significant economies of scale** to be achieved **from a high volume of output**, so that quick penetration into the market is desirable in order to gain unit cost reductions

(d) If **demand is highly elastic** and so would respond well to low prices.

Penetration prices are prices which aim to **secure a substantial share in a substantial total market**. A firm might therefore **deliberately build excess production capacity** and set its prices very low. As demand builds up the spare capacity will be used up gradually and unit costs will fall; the firm might even reduce prices further as unit costs fall. In this way, early losses will enable the firm to dominate the market and have the lowest costs.

6.2.2 Market skimming pricing

Key term

> **Market skimming pricing** involves charging high prices when a product is first launched and spending heavily on advertising and sales promotion to obtain sales.

As the product moves into the later stages of its life cycle, **progressively lower prices will be charged** and so the profitable 'cream' is skimmed off in stages until sales can only be sustained at lower prices.

The aim of market skimming is to **gain high unit profits early in the product's life**. High unit prices make it **more likely that competitors will enter the market** than if lower prices were to be charged.

Circumstances in which such a policy may be appropriate

(a)　Where the product is **new and different**, so that customers are prepared to pay high prices so as to be one up on other people who do not own it.

(b)　Where the **strength** of demand and the **sensitivity of demand** to price are **unknown**. It is better from the point of view of marketing to start by charging high prices and then reduce them if the demand for the product turns out to be price elastic than to start by charging low prices and then attempt to raise them substantially if demand appears to be insensitive to higher prices.

(c)　Where **high prices** in the early stages of a product's life might **generate high initial cash flows**. A firm with liquidity problems may prefer market-skimming for this reason.

(d)　Where the firm **can identify different market segments** for the product, each prepared to pay progressively lower prices. If **product differentiation** can be introduced, it may be possible to continue to sell at higher prices to some market segments when lower prices are charged in others. This is discussed further below.

(e)　Where products may have a **short life cycle**, and so need to recover their development costs and make a profit relatively quickly.

7 Other pricing strategies

FAST FORWARD

Product differentiation may be used to make products appear to be different. **Price discrimination** is then possible.

7.1 Product differentiation and price discrimination

Key term

> **Price discrimination** is the practice of charging different prices for the same product to different groups of buyers when these prices are not reflective of cost differences.

In certain circumstances the **same product** can be sold at different prices to **different customers**. There are a number of bases on which such discriminating prices can be set.

Basis	Detail
By market segment	A cross-channel ferry company would market its services at different prices in England and France, for example. Services such as cinemas and hairdressers are often available at lower prices to old age pensioners and/or juveniles.
By product version	Many car models have **optional extras** which enable one brand to appeal to a wider cross-section of customers. The final price need not reflect the cost price of the optional extras directly: usually the top of the range model would carry a price much in excess of the cost of provision of the extras, as a prestige appeal.
By place	Theatre seats are usually sold according to their location so that patrons pay different prices for the same performance according to the seat type they occupy.
By time	This is perhaps the most popular type of price discrimination. Off-peak travel bargains, hotel prices and telephone charges are all attempts to increase sales revenue by covering variable but not necessarily average cost of provision. Railway companies are successful price discriminators, charging more to rush hour rail commuters whose demand is inelastic at certain times of the day.

Price discrimination can only be effective if a number of **conditions** hold.

(a)   The market must be **segmentable** in price terms, and different sectors must show different intensities of demand. Each of the sectors must be identifiable, distinct and separate from the others, and be accessible to the firm's marketing communications.

(b)   There must be little or **no** chance of a **black market** developing (this would allow those in the lower priced segment to resell to those in the higher priced segment).

(c)   There must be little or **no** chance that **competitors** can and will undercut the firm's prices in the higher priced (and/or most profitable) market segments.

(d)   The cost of segmenting and **administering** the arrangements should not exceed the extra revenue derived from the price discrimination strategy.

7.1.1 'Own label' pricing: a form of price discrimination

Many supermarkets and multiple retail stores sell their 'own label' products, often at a lower price than established branded products. The supermarkets or multiple retailers do this by entering into arrangements with manufacturers, to supply their goods under the 'own brand' label.

7.2 Premium pricing

This involves making a product **appear 'different'** through **product differentiation** so as **to justify a premium price**. The product may be different in terms of, for example, quality, reliability, durability, after sales service or extended warranties. Heavy advertising can establish brand loyalty which can help to sustain a premium and premium prices will always be paid by those customers who blindly equate high price with high quality.

7.3 Product bundling

Product bundling is a variation on price discrimination which involves **selling a number of products or services as a package at a price lower than the aggregate of their individual prices**. For example a hotel might offer a package that includes the room, meals, use of leisure facilities and entertainment at a combined price that is lower than the total price of the individual components. This might encourage customers to buy services that they might otherwise not have purchased.

The **success** of a bundling strategy depends on the expected **increase in sales volume** and **changes in margin.** Other cost changes, such as in product handling, packaging and invoicing costs, are possible. **Longer-term issues** such as competitors' reactions must also be considered.

7.4 Pricing with optional extras

The decision here is very similar to that for product bundling. It rests on whether the **increase in sales revenue from the increased price that can be charged** is **greater** than the **increase in costs** required to incorporate extra features. Not all customers will be willing to pay a higher price for additional features if they do not want or need those features.

7.5 Psychological pricing

Psychological pricing strategies include **pricing a product at \$19.99 instead of \$20** and withdrawing an unsuccessful product from the market and then relaunching it at a higher price, the customer having equated the lower price with lower quality (which was not the seller's intention).

7.6 Multiple products and loss leaders

Most organisations sell a range of products. The management of the pricing function is likely to focus on the profit from the whole range rather than the profit on each single product. Take, for example, the use of **loss leaders:** a very low price for one product is intended to make consumers buy additional products in the range which carry higher profit margins.

 Case Study

Razor handles are sold at very low prices while razor blades are sold at a higher profit margin. People will buy many of the high profit items but only one of the low profit items – yet they are 'locked in' to the former by the latter.

7.7 Using discounts

Reasons for using discounts to adjust prices

- To get rid of perishable goods that have reached the end of their shelf life
- To sell off seconds
- Normal practice (eg antique trade)
- To increase sales volumes during a poor sales period without dropping prices permanently
- To differentiate between types of customer (wholesale, retail and so on)
- To get cash in quickly

7.8 Controlled prices

Many **previously nationalised industries** now operate within the private sector and are **overseen by an industry regulator** (such as OFCOM for telecommunications).

Regulators tend to concentrate on **price** so that these near monopolies cannot exploit their position (although the regulators are also concerned with quality of service/product).

If a **price is regulated**, the **elasticity of demand is zero**: 'small' customers pay less than they otherwise would, whereas 'large' customers pay more than in a competitive environment.

Prices have become **more flexible in recent years**, however.

(a)   Introduction of discounted price for very large customers
(b)   Entry of other companies into the market

> A requirement (for 15 marks) of one of the pilot paper Section C questions was to discuss various pricing strategies.

Question

Pricing strategies

Learning outcomes: A(ii),(iii)

As management accountant to a group of companies manufacturing footwear, you have been asked to consider the following two subjects that are to be discussed at the next group pricing committee meeting.

(a)   The possibility of differential pricing for different sizes of shoes

(b)   The levels of prices at which contracts with a large multiple retailer for 'own label' shoes might be negotiated

Required

Describe briefly the major topics under each of the above headings that you would include in the agenda for discussion.

Answer

(a)   **Differential pricing for different sizes of shoes**

    (i)   **Cost differences**
    If the differential pricing is to allow for differences in cost, are these cost differences sufficient to justify significant price differentials?

    (ii)   **Administration costs**
    Consideration should be given to the increased cost of administering a differential price structure.

    (iii)   **Custom and practice**
    If it is accepted practice to charge differential prices for shoes, the company may be missing an opportunity to increase profits.

    (iv)   **Reaction of retailers**
    Retailers may not react favourably because their own pricing policy will become more complicated and time consuming.

    (v)   **Effect on demand**
    If higher prices are to be charged for larger shoes, what effect will this have on demand and profits?

    (vi)   **Competitors' actions**
    If competitors are not already practising differential pricing, will they follow our lead? If not, what will be the effect on demand and profits?

    (vii)   **Differential pricing for marketing purposes**
    If, instead of pricing according to cost, the company wishes to offer lower prices for the more popular sizes, will the extra demand justify the reduction in price?

(b)   **Prices for own-label shoes**

(i)   **Capacity available**

The available capacity will dictate whether or not marginal pricing can be used. It would not be advisable to use marginal pricing if this displaces full-price work.

(ii)   **The effect on other business**

Will the sales of own-label shoes affect the demand for our other ranges? If lower prices are offered to the multiple retailer, will other customers start to demand similar reductions?

(iii)   **The terms of the negotiated contract**

The company must ensure that they will have the flexibility to change prices if costs fluctuate.

(iv)   **The cost of increased working capital**

An expansion in output will result in increased working capital. Will the retailers expect us to hold inventories for them and how much credit will they require? These facts must be evaluated and taken into account in the pricing policy.

(v)   **Exclusive designs**

Will the retailer require exclusive designs, or can cost savings be achieved by using the same designs for our own range of footwear?

Attention!

If asked to **compare** two **pricing strategies** and to determine which is the **better**, you basically need to consider which produces the **higher cash inflows**.

When asked to assess the **financial viability** of the better strategy, however, you need to perform a **DCF appraisal** on the resulting cash flows.

Chapter Roundup

- In **full cost-plus pricing** the sales price is determined by calculating the full cost of the product and then adding a percentage mark-up for profit. The most important criticism of full cost-plus pricing is that it fails to recognise that since sales demand may be determined by the sales price, there will be a profit-maximising combination of price and demand.

- **Marginal cost-plus pricing** involves adding a profit margin to the marginal cost of production/sales. A marginal costing approach is more likely to help with identifying a profit-maximising price.

- **Economic theory** claims that **profit is maximised** by setting a price so that **marginal cost equals marginal revenue**. But because most cost accounting systems are set up to provide information for financial reporting purposes, it can be **difficult to identify short-run or long-run marginal cost**, even if ABC is used.

- Another approach to pricing might be taken when a **business is working at full capacity, and is restricted by a shortage of resources** from expanding its output further. By deciding what target profit it would like to earn, it could **establish a mark-up per unit of limiting factor**.

- The basic approach to pricing **special orders** is **minimum pricing**.

- Two pricing strategies for **new** products are **market penetration pricing** and **market skimming pricing**.

- **Product differentiation** may be used to make products appear to be different. **Price discrimination** is then possible.

Quick Quiz

1   *Fill in the blanks.*

(a)   One of the problems with relying on a full cost-plus approach to pricing is that it fails to recognise that since price may be determining demand, there will be a .... combination of .... and ....

(b)   An advantage of the full cost-plus approach is that, because the size of the profit margin can be varied, a decision based on a price in excess of full cost should ensure that a company working at .... capacity will cover .... and make a ....

2   A theatre offers a special deal whereby two show tickets and pre-theatre dinner can be purchased as a package for a reduced price. This pricing strategy is usually referred to as

A   Loss leader pricing
B   Optional extras
C   Product bundling
D   Price discrimination

3   Pricing based on mark-up per unit of limiting factor is particularly useful if an organisation is not working to full capacity. *True or false?*

4   *Fill in the blank.*

The .... price is the price at which an organisation will break even if it undertakes particular work.

5   *Choose the correct word from those highlighted.*

Market **skimming/penetration** pricing should be used if an organisation wishes to discourage new entrants into a market.

6   'Own label' pricing is a form of psychological pricing. *True or false?*

7   If a price is regulated, the elasticity of demand is:

A   −1
B   0
C   1
D   Infinity

Answers to Quick Quiz

1   (a)   profit-maximising combination of price and demand
    (b)   working at normal capacity will cover all of its fixed costs and make a profit

2   C   Product bundling involves selling a number of products or services as a package at a price lower than the aggregate of their individual prices.

3   False. It is useful if the organisation is working at full capacity.

4   Minimum

5   Market penetration

6   False. It is a form of price discrimination.

7   B. The elasticity of demand is zero.

Now try the questions below from the Exam Question Bank

Number	Level	Marks	Time
Q12	Examination	10	18 mins
Q13	Examination	10	18 mins

Part C
Financial information for long-term decision making

Investment decision making

Introduction

In the next four chapters we will be examining the appraisal of **projects** which involve the **outlay of capital**.

Capital expenditure differs from day to day revenue expenditure for two reasons.

- **Capital expenditure** often involves a **bigger outlay of money**.

- The **benefits** from capital expenditure are likely to **accrue over a long period of time**, usually well over one year and often much longer. In such circumstances the benefits cannot all be set against costs in the current year's income statement.

For these reasons any proposed capital expenditure project should be **properly appraised**, and found to be worthwhile, before the decision is taken to go ahead with the expenditure.

We begin the chapter with an overview of the **investment decision-making process** in **Sections 1 and 2** before moving on to examine two capital investment appraisal techniques, the straightforward **payback method** (**Section 3**) and the slightly more involved **accounting rate of return method** (**Section 4**).

In Chapter 11 we look at methods of investment appraisal based on discounted cash flow techniques.

The examiner has included both objective test and longer questions on aspects of investment decision making in every exam under the new syllabus. So this is a key area and you will need to cover the next four chapters in some depth.

Topic list	Learning outcomes	Syllabus references	Ability required
1 The process of investment decision making	B(i)	B(1)	Comprehension
2 Post audit	B(i)	B(1)	Comprehension
3 The payback method	B(vi), (vii)	B(4), (5)	Analysis/Evaluation
4 The accounting rate of return method	B(vi), (vii)	B(4), (5)	Analysis/Evaluation

1 The process of investment decision making

1.1 Creation of capital budgets

The capital budget will normally be **prepared to cover a longer period than sales, production and resource budgets**, say from three to five years, although it should be **broken down** into periods matching those of other budgets. It should indicate the expenditure required to cover **capital projects already underway** and those it is **anticipated will start** in the three to five year period (say) of the capital budget.

The budget should therefore be **based on** the **current production budget, future expected levels of production** and the **long-term development of the organisation, and industry**, as a whole.

Organisations may have **defined time periods during which proposals are considered** so as to allow for an indication of expected capital expenditure in the forthcoming budget period. Alternatively proposals may be **accepted on a regular basis**, allowing greater scope for investment in unanticipated opportunities. **Projects which emerge during a budget period** may be **disadvantaged** compared with those anticipated when the budget was set, however, as specific funds will not be set aside for them in the budget. If funds are limited, such projects may undergo more rigorous analysis than an anticipated project to justify the allocation of funds.

Budget limits or constraints might be imposed internally or externally.

(a)   The imposition of **internal constraints**, which are often imposed when managerial resources are limited, is known as **soft capital rationing**.

(b)   **Hard capital rationing** occurs when **external limits** are set, perhaps because of scarcity of financing, high financing costs or restrictions on the amount of external financing an organisation can seek.

Projects can be **classified** in the budget into those that generally arise from top management policy decisions or from sources such as mandatory government regulations (health, safety and welfare capital expenditure) and those that tend to be appraised using the techniques covered in this chapter and the next.

(a)   Cost reduction and replacement expenditure
(b)   Expenditure on the expansion of existing product lines
(c)   New product expenditure

The **administration of** the capital budget is usually separate from that of the other budgets. Overall responsibility for **authorisation and monitoring** of capital expenditure is, in most large organisations, the **responsibility of a committee**. For example:

(a)   Expenditure up to $75,000 may be approved by individual divisional managers.
(b)   Expenditure between $75,000 and $150,000 may be approved by divisional management.
(c)   Expenditure over $150,000 may be approved by the board of directors.

1.2 The investment decision-making process

We have seen in the introduction to this chapter that capital expenditure often involves the outlay of **large sums of money**, and that any expected **benefits may take a number of years to accrue**. For these reasons it is vital that capital expenditure is subject to a rigorous process of appraisal and control.

A typical **model for investment decision making** has a number of distinct stages.

- Origination of proposals
- Project screening
- Analysis and acceptance
- Monitoring and review

We will look at these stages in more detail below.

1.3 Origination of proposals

Investment opportunities **do not just appear** out of thin air. They **must be created**. McIntyre and Coulthurst (*Capital Budgeting Practices in Medium-Sized Businesses – A Survey*, CIMA, 1986) note:

'If they do present themselves it is more likely to be a reaction to a problem (and a belated one at that), rather than the awareness of an opportunity. Even then there is no guarantee that problems will be recognised; many situations may be allowed to continue because they are never questioned. On the contrary, top management should develop systematic means of searching for investment projects, both to identify opportunities and to anticipate problems.'

An organisation must therefore set up a **mechanism that scans the environment for potential opportunities and gives an early warning of future problems**. A technological change that might result in a drop in sales might be picked up by this scanning process, and steps should be taken immediately to respond to such a threat.

Ideas for investment might come from those working in technical positions. A factory manager, for example, could be well placed to identify ways in which expanded capacity or new machinery could increase output or the efficiency of the manufacturing process. Innovative ideas, such as new product lines, are more likely to come from those in higher levels of management, given their strategic view of the organisation's direction and their knowledge of the competitive environment.

It has been suggested that the good ideas for investment are most likely to occur in environments in which staff feel free to present and develop ideas, however. For example, a two-step approach to encouraging investment ideas, in which undeveloped ideas are proposed and funds for further exploration and refinement are committed to promising projects only, could be used.

The overriding feature of any **proposal** is that it should be **consistent with the organisation's overall strategy to achieve its objectives**. For example, an organisation's strategy could be to increase revenue by introducing new products, or targeting new customers or markets. Employees from across the organisation can be involved in the evaluation of alternative technologies, machines and project specifications. Some alternatives will be rejected early on. Others will be more thoroughly evaluated.

1.4 Project screening

Each proposal must be subject to detailed screening. So that a **qualitative evaluation** of a proposal can be made, a number of key questions such as those below might be asked before any financial analysis is undertaken. Only if the project passes this initial screening will more detailed financial analysis begin.

(a) What is the purpose of the project?
(b) Does it 'fit' with the organisation's long-term objectives?
(c) Is it a mandatory investment, for example to conform with safety legislation?
(d) What resources are required and are they available, eg money, capacity, labour?
(e) Do we have the necessary management expertise to guide the project to completion?
(f) Does the project expose the organisation to unnecessary risk?
(g) How long will the project last and what factors are key to its success?
(h) Have all possible alternatives been considered?

1.5 Analysis and acceptance

The analysis stage can be broken down into a number of steps.

Step 1   Complete and submit standard format financial information as a formal investment proposal.

Step 2   Classify the project by type (to separate projects into those that require more or less rigorous financial appraisal, and those that must achieve a greater or lesser rate of return in order to be deemed acceptable).

Step 3   Carry out financial analysis of the project. We look at this in more detail in Section 1.5.1.

Step 4   Compare the outcome of the financial analysis to predetermined acceptance criteria.

Step 5   Consider the project in the light of the capital budget for the current and future operating periods.

Step 6   Make the **decision (go/no go)**. This is considered in more detail below.

Step 7   Monitor the progress of the project (covered below).

1.5.1 Financial analysis

The financial analysis will involve the **application of the organisation's preferred investment appraisal techniques**. We will be studying these techniques in detail in this chapter and the next. In many projects some of the financial implications will be extremely difficult to quantify, but every effort must be made to do so, in order to have a formal basis for planning and controlling the project.

Here are examples of the type of question that will be addressed at this stage.

    (a)   What cash flows/profits will arise from the project and when?

    (b)   Has inflation been considered in the determination of the cash flows?

    (c)   What are the results of the financial appraisal?

    (d)   Has any allowance been made for risk, and if so, what was the outcome?

Some types of project, for example a marketing investment decision, may give rise to cash inflows and **returns which are so intangible and difficult to quantify that a full financial appraisal may not be possible**. In this case more weight may be given to a consideration of the qualitative issues.

1.5.2 Qualitative issues

Financial analysis of capital projects is obviously vital because of the amount of money involved and the length of time for which it is tied up. A consideration of qualitative issues is also relevant to the decision, however (ie factors which are difficult or impossible to quantify). We have already seen that qualitative issues would be considered in the **initial screening stage**, for example in reviewing the project's 'fit' with the organisation's overall objectives and whether it is a mandatory investment. There is a very wide range of other qualitative issues that may be relevant to a particular project.

    (a)   What are the implications of not undertaking the investment, eg adverse effect on staff morale, loss of market share?

    (b)   Will acceptance of this project lead to the need for further investment activity in future?

    (c)   What will be the effect on the company's image?

    (d)   Will the organisation be more flexible as a result of the investment, and better able to respond to market and technology changes?

1.5.3 Go/no go decision

Go/no go decisions on projects may be **made at different levels within the organisational hierarchy**, depending on three factors.

(a) The type of investment
(b) Its perceived riskiness
(c) The amount of expenditure required

For example, a divisional manager may be authorised to make decisions up to $25,000, an area manager up to $150,000 and a group manager up to $300,000, with board approval for greater amounts.

Once the go/no go (or **accept/reject**) decision has been made, the organisation is committed to the project, and the decision maker must accept that the project's success or failure reflects on his or her ability to make sound decisions.

1.6 Monitoring the progress of the project

FAST FORWARD

During the project's progress, **project controls** should be applied to ensure the following.

- Capital spending does not exceed the amount authorised.
- The implementation of the project is not delayed.
- The anticipated benefits are eventually obtained.

The first two items are probably easier to control than the third, because the controls can normally be applied soon after the capital expenditure has been authorised, whereas monitoring the benefits will span a longer period of time.

1.6.1 Controls over excess spending

There are a number of controls which organisations can implement to ensure that capital spending does not exceed the amount authorised.

(a) The **authority to make capital expenditure decisions** must be **formally assigned**. For example, all spending over $250,000, say, must be authorised by, for example, the holding company's board of directors, spending over $100,000 and up to $250,000, say, must be authorised by, for example, the subsidiary company's board of directors, while spending over $10,000 and up to $100,000, say, could be authorised by heads of departments.

(b) Capital expenditure decisions should be **documented** and approval of the project should specify the **manager authorised** to carry out the expenditure (and hence responsible for the successful implementation of the project), the **amount of expenditure** authorised and the **period of time** in which the expenditure should take place.

(c) **Some overspending** above the amount authorised – say 5% or 10% – **might be allowed**. If the required expenditure exceeds the amount authorised by more than this amount, a fresh submission for reauthorisation of the project should be required. It would be bad management to approve spending of $1 million, and then to allow an overspending to $1.5 million to go by unchecked and without comment!

(d) There should be a total capital budget, and the authorisation of any **capital expenditure which would take total spending above the budget should be referred** to, for example, board level for approval.

1.6.2 Control over delays

If there is a delay in carrying out the project and the capital expenditure has not taken place before the stated deadline is reached, the project should be **resubmitted for fresh authorisation**, and the proposer should be asked to **explain the reasons for the delay**.

1.6.3 Control over the anticipated benefits

Further control can be exercised over capital projects by ensuring that the anticipated benefits do actually materialise, the benefits are as big as anticipated and running costs do not exceed expectation.

A **difficulty** with control measurements of capital projects is that most **projects are 'unique' with no standard or yardstick to judge them against** other than their own appraisal data. Therefore if actual costs were to exceed the estimated costs, it might be impossible to tell just how much of the variance is due to bad estimating and how much is due to inefficiencies and poor cost control.

In the same way, if benefits are below expectation, is this because the original estimates were optimistic, or because management has been inefficient and failed to get the benefits they should have done?

Many capital projects such as the purchase of replacement assets and marketing investment decisions **do not have clearly identifiable costs and benefits**. The incremental benefits and costs of such schemes can be estimated, but it would need a very sophisticated management accounting system to be able to identify and measure the actual benefits and many of the costs. Even so, some degree of monitoring and control can still be exercised by means of a **post-completion appraisal** or audit review.

2 Post audit

A **post audit** cannot reverse the decision to incur the capital expenditure, because the expenditure has already taken place, but it does have a certain control value.

Key term

A **post-completion audit (PCA)** is 'An objective independent assessment of the success of a capital project in relation to plan. Covers the whole life of the project and provides feedback to managers to aid the implementation and control of future projects.' (CIMA *Official Terminology*)

The PCA is therefore is therefore a **forward-looking** rather than a backward-looking technique. It seeks to **identify general lessons** to be learned from a project.

2.1 Why perform a post-completion appraisal (PCA) or audit?

(a) The **threat** of the PCA will **motivate managers** to work to achieve the promised benefits from the project.

(b) If the audit takes place before the project life ends, and if it finds that the benefits have been less than expected because of management inefficiency, steps can be taken to **improve efficiency**. Alternatively, it will **highlight those projects which should be discontinued**.

(c) It can help to **identify** managers who have been **good performers** and those who have been poor performers.

(d) It might identify weaknesses in the forecasting and estimating techniques used to evaluate projects, and so should help to **improve** the discipline and quality of **forecasting** for future investment decisions.

(e) Areas where improvements can be made in methods which should help to achieve **better results in general from capital investments** might be revealed.

(f)   The **original estimates may be more realistic** if managers are aware that they will be monitored, but post-completion audits **should not be unfairly critical**.

Research by Neale and Homes (1990) found that managers see the following **advantages** to PCAs.

(a)   They improve the quality of decision making.
(b)   They improve organisational performance.
(c)   They improve control and guidance.
(d)   They encourage a more realistic approach to new investment project decision making.
(e)   They help to identify critical success factors.
(f)   They enable changes to be made more quickly to projects that are not doing very well.
(g)   They encourage (when relevant) project termination.

2.2 Which projects should be audited?

It may be too expensive to audit all capital expenditure projects, and so managers may need to select **a sample** for a post-completion audit. The selection will depend on the probability that the audit of any particular project will produce benefits, which is obviously difficult to determine.

Generally size is likely to be the best guide as to which projects should be audited. However, **managers should perceive that every capital expenditure project has a chance of being the subject of a detailed post-completion audit**.

A reasonable **guideline** might be to **audit all projects above a certain size, and a random selection of smaller projects**.

A PCA does not need to focus on all aspects of an investment, but should **concentrate on those aspects which have been identified as particularly sensitive or critical to the success of a project**. The most important thing to remember is that post-completion audits are time-consuming and costly and so **careful consideration should be given to the cost-benefit trade-off** arising from the post-completion audit results.

2.3 When should projects be audited?

If the audit is carried out too soon, the information may not be complete. On the other hand, if the audit is too late then management action will be delayed and the usefulness of the information is greatly reduced.

There is no correct answer to the question of when to audit, although research suggests that in practice most companies perform the PCA **approximately one year after the completion of the project**.

2.4 Who performs a PCA?

Because it can be very difficult to evaluate an investment decision completely objectively, it is generally appropriate to **separate responsibility** for the **investment decision** from that for the **PCA**. Line management involved in the investment decision should therefore not carry out the PCA. To avoid conflicts of interest, **outside experts** could even be used.

2.5 Problems with PCA

(a)   There are many **uncontrollable factors** which are outside management control in long-term investments, such as environmental changes.

(b)   It **may not be possible** to **identify separately the costs and benefits** of any particular project.

(c)   PCA can be a **costly** and **time-consuming** exercise, although 'contrary to what is often thought, conducting a PCA does not appear to be an expensive business' reported Brantjes, von Eije, Eusman and Prins in *Management Accounting* ('Post-completion auditing with Heineken) in April 1999.

(d)   Applied punitively, post-completion audit exercises may lead to **managers becoming over cautious** and unnecessarily **risk averse**.

(e)   The **strategic effects** of a capital investment project **may take years** to materialise and it may in fact **never be possible** to identify or quantify them effectively.

Despite the growth in popularity of post-completion audits, you should bear in mind the possible **alternative** control processes.

(a)   **Teams** could manage a project from beginning to end, control being used **before** the project is started and **during** its life, rather than at the end of its life.

(b)   **More time could be spent choosing projects** rather than checking completed projects.

Now that we have discussed all the stages involved in the capital budgeting process, we will return to study in detail the stage that many managers consider to be the most important: the financial appraisal. We will begin with what is probably the most straightforward appraisal technique: the payback method.

 Case Study

A 1999 *Management Accounting* article looked at post completion auditing at Heineken and how it was applied to a project to replace a 20-year old bottling line. The following table shows the planned objectives of the investment and the actual situation at the time a PCA was carried out on the investment. This should give you an idea of the type of objectives that can be monitored with a PCA.

Objectives	Plan	Actual
Efficiency	Increase from 65% to 80%	No increase yet
Staff savings	From 13 to 7 per shift	Achieved
Forklift savings	1 vehicle less	1 and possibly 2 vehicles less
Savings on overhaul of old bottling line	1.3 million guilders of savings	Savings achieved, but as a result of reusing part of the old bottling line another 1.8 million guilders was spent in additional overhaul costs
Savings on maintenance	Savings of 0.4 million guilders annually	Savings estimated at 0.3 million guilders annually
Quality	50% reduction in damage	Achieved
Working conditions	Level of noise Accessibility Safety Attainability	All much improved, but not quantified

3 The payback method

The **payback method** looks at how long it takes for a project's net cash inflows to equal the initial investment.

Key term

Payback is 'The time required for the cash inflows from a capital investment project to equal the cash outflows'.

(CIMA *Official Terminology*)

When **deciding between two or more competing projects**, the usual decision is to **accept the one with the shortest payback**.

Payback is often used as a **'first screening method'**. By this, we mean that when a capital investment project is being subjected to financial appraisal, the first question to ask is: 'How long will it take to pay back its cost?' The organisation might have a target payback, and so it would reject a capital project unless its payback period were less than a certain number of years.

However, a project should not be evaluated on the basis of payback alone. Payback should be a *first* screening process, and if a project gets through the payback test, it ought **then to be evaluated with a more sophisticated project appraisal technique**.

You should note that when payback is calculated, we take **profits before depreciation**, because we are trying to estimate the *cash* returns from a project and profit before depreciation is likely to be a **rough approximation of cash flows**.

Exam focus point

The May 2006 and November 2006 exams have both tested simple calculations of the payback method in Section A questions. Make sure you can calculate payback as this could mean an easy couple of marks and the difference between a pass and a fail.

3.1 Why is payback alone an inadequate project appraisal technique?

Look at the figures below for two mutually exclusive projects (this means that only one of them can be undertaken).

	Project P	Project Q
Capital cost of asset	$60,000	$60,000
Profits before depreciation		
Year 1	$20,000	$50,000
Year 2	$30,000	$20,000
Year 3	$40,000	$5,000
Year 4	$50,000	$5,000
Year 5	$60,000	$5,000

Project P pays back in year 3 (about one quarter of the way through year 3). Project Q pays back half way through year 2. **Using payback alone** to judge projects, **project Q would be preferred. But the returns from project P over its life are much higher than the returns from project Q**. Project P will earn total profits before depreciation of $200,000 on an investment of $60,000, whereas Project Q will earn total profits before depreciation of only $85,000 on an investment of $60,000.

Question

Payback

Learning outcome: B(vi)

An asset costing $120,000 is to be depreciated over ten years to a nil residual value. Profits after depreciation for the first five years are as follows.

Year	$
1	12,000
2	17,000
3	28,000
4	37,000
5	8,000

How long is the payback period to the nearest month?

A   3 years 7 months

B   3 years 6 months

C   3 years

D   The project does not payback in five years

Answer

The correct answer is A.

Profits before depreciation should be used.

Year	Profit after depreciation $'000	Depreciation $'000	Profit before depreciation $'000	Cumulative profit $'000
1	12	12	24	24
2	17	12	29	53
3	28	12	40	93
4	37	12	49	142
5	8	12	20	

$$\therefore \text{Payback period} = 3 \text{ years} + \left(\frac{(120-93)}{(142-93)} \times 12 \text{ months} \right)$$

$$= 3 \text{ years 7 months}$$

3.2 Disadvantages of the payback method

There are a number of serious drawbacks to the payback method.

(a)   It **ignores the timing of cash flows** within the payback period, the cash flows after the end of the payback period and therefore the total project return.

(b)   It **ignores the time value of money** (a concept incorporated into more sophisticated appraisal methods). This means that it does not take account of the fact that $1 today is worth more than $1 in one year's time. An investor who has $1 today can either consume it immediately or alternatively can invest it at the prevailing interest rate, say 10%, to get a return of $1.10 in a year's time.

There are also other disadvantages.

(a)   The method is **unable to distinguish between projects with the same payback period**.

(b)   The **choice of any cut-off payback period** by an organisation is **arbitrary**.

(c)   It may lead to excessive **investment in short-term projects**.

(d)   It takes account of the risk of the timing of cash flows but **does not take account of the variability of those cash flows**.

3.3 Advantages of the payback method

The use of the payback method does have advantages, especially as an initial screening device.

- (a) Long payback means **capital is tied up**
- (b) Focus on early payback can **enhance liquidity**
- (c) **Investment risk is increased** if payback is longer
- (d) **Shorter-term forecasts** are likely to be **more reliable**
- (e) The calculation is **quick** and **simple**
- (f) Payback is an **easily understood** concept

4 The accounting rate of return method

FAST FORWARD

Like the payback method, the **accounting rate of return method** is popular despite its limitations.

Key term

The **accounting rate of return (ARR) method** (also called **the return on capital employed (ROCE) method** or the **return on investment (ROI) method**) of appraising a project is to estimate the accounting rate of return that the project should yield. If it exceeds a target rate of return, the project will be undertaken.

The CIMA *Official Terminology* definition is $\dfrac{\text{Average annual profit from investment} \times 100}{\text{Average investment}}$

Unfortunately there are several different definitions of ARR.

$$\text{ARR} = \frac{\text{Estimated total profits}}{\text{Estimated initial investment}} \times 100\%$$

$$\text{ARR} = \frac{\text{Estimated average profits}}{\text{Estimated initial investment}} \times 100\%$$

Attention!

There are arguments in favour of each of these definitions. The most important point is, however, that the **method selected should be used consistently**. For **examination** purposes we recommend the **first definition** unless the question clearly indicates that some other one is to be used.

Note that this is the only appraisal method that we will be studying that **uses profit** instead of cash flow. If you are not provided with a figure for profit, **assume that net cash inflow minus depreciation equals profit**.

4.1 Example: the accounting rate of return

A company has a target accounting rate of return of 20% (using the CIMA definition above), and is now considering the following project.

Capital cost of asset	$80,000
Estimated life	4 years
Estimated profit before depreciation	
Year 1	$20,000
Year 2	$25,000
Year 3	$35,000
Year 4	$25,000

The capital asset would be depreciated by 25% of its cost each year, and will have no residual value.

Required

Assess whether the project should be undertaken.

Solution

The annual profits after depreciation, and the mid-year net book value of the asset, would be as follows.

Year	Profit after depreciation $	Mid-year net book value $	ARR in the year %
1	0	70,000	0
2	5,000	50,000	10
3	15,000	30,000	50
4	5,000	10,000	50

As the table shows, the ARR is low in the early stages of the project, partly because of low profits in Year 1 but mainly because the NBV of the asset is much higher early on in its life. The project does not achieve the target ARR of 20% in its first two years, but exceeds it in years 3 and 4. Should it be undertaken?

When the **ARR from a project varies from year to year**, it makes sense to **take an overall or 'average' view of the project's return**. In this case, we should look at the return over the four-year period.

	$
Total profit before depreciation over four years	105,000
Total profit after depreciation over four years	25,000
Average annual profit after depreciation	6,250
Original cost of investment	80,000
Average net book value over the four year period ((80,000 + 0)/2)	40,000

The project would not be undertaken because its ARR is 6,250/40,000 = 15.625% and so it would fail to yield the target return of 20%.

4.2 The ARR and the comparison of mutually exclusive projects

The ARR method of capital investment appraisal can also be used to compare two or more projects which are mutually exclusive. The project with the highest ARR would be selected (provided that the expected ARR is higher than the company's target ARR).

Question	The ARR and mutually exclusive projects

Learning outcome: B(vi)

Arrow wants to buy a new item of equipment. Two models of equipment are available, one with a slightly higher capacity and greater reliability than the other. The expected costs and profits of each item are as follows.

	Equipment item X	Equipment item Y
Capital cost	$80,000	$150,000
Life	5 years	5 years
Profits before depreciation	$	$
Year 1	50,000	50,000
Year 2	50,000	50,000
Year 3	30,000	60,000
Year 4	20,000	60,000
Year 5	10,000	60,000
Disposal value	0	0

ARR is measured as the average annual profit after depreciation, divided by the average net book value of the asset.

Equipment item Y should be selected if the company's target ARR is 30%. *True or false?*

Answer

The correct answer is that X should be selected and so the statement is false.

	Item X $	Item Y $
Total profit over life of equipment		
Before depreciation	160,000	280,000
After depreciation	80,000	130,000
Average annual profit after depreciation	16,000	26,000
Average investment = (capital cost + disposal value)/2	40,000	75,000
ARR	40%	34.7%

Both projects would earn a return in excess of 30%, but since **item X would earn a bigger ARR, it would be preferred to item Y**, even though the profits from Y would be higher by an average of $10,000 a year.

4.3 The drawbacks and advantages to the ARR method of project appraisal

The ARR method has the serious **drawback** that it **does not take account of the timing of the profits from a project**. Whenever capital is invested in a project, money is tied up until the project begins to earn profits which pay back the investment. Money tied up in one project cannot be invested anywhere else until the profits come in. Management should be aware of the benefits of early repayments from an investment, which will provide the money for other investments.

There are a number of other disadvantages.

(a) It is **based on accounting profits** which are **subject to a number of different accounting treatments**

(b) It is a **relative measure** rather than an absolute measure and hence **takes no account of the size of the investment**

(c) **It takes no account of the length of the project**

(d) Like the payback method, it **ignores the time value of money**

There are, however, **advantages** to the ARR method.

(a) It is quick and **simple** to calculate

(b) It involves a **familiar concept** of a percentage return

(c) Accounting profits can be **easily calculated from financial statements**

(d) It **looks at the entire project life**

(e) Managers and investors are accustomed to thinking in terms of profit, and so an appraisal method which **employs profit** may therefore be more **easily understood**

Question

Learning outcomes: B(vi), (vii)

A company is considering two capital expenditure proposals. Both proposals are for similar products and both are expected to operate for four years. Only one proposal can be accepted.

The following information is available.

	Profit/(loss) after depreciation	
	Proposal A	Proposal B
	$	$
Initial investment	46,000	46,000
Year 1	6,500	4,500
Year 2	3,500	2,500
Year 3	13,500	4,500
Year 4	(1,500)	14,500
Estimated scrap value at the end of year 4	4,000	4,000

Depreciation is charged on the straight line basis.

Required

(a)   Calculate the following for both proposals.

  (i)   The payback period to one decimal place
  (ii)   The return on capital employed on initial investment, to one decimal place

(b)   Give two advantages for each of the methods of appraisal used in (a) above.

Answer

(a)   Depreciation must first be **added back** to the **annual profit figures**, to arrive at the annual cash flows.

$$\text{Depreciation} = \frac{\text{Initial investment } £46,000 - \text{scrap value } £4,000}{4 \text{ years}}$$

   = $10,500 pa

Adding $10,500 per annum to the profit figures produces the cash flows for each proposal.

	Proposal A		Proposal B	
	Annual	Cumulative	Annual	Cumulative
Year	cash flow	cash flow	cash flow	cash flow
	$	$	$	$
0	(46,000)	(46,000)	(46,000)	(46,000)
1	17,000	(29,000)	15,000	(31,000)
2	14,000	(15,000)	13,000	(18,000)
3	24,000	9,000	15,000	(3,000)
4	9,000	18,000	25,000	22,000
4	4,000	22,000	4,000	26,000

(i)   *Proposal A*

  Payback period =

$$2 + \left(\frac{15,000}{24,000} \times 1 \text{ year} \right)$$

  = 2.6 years

  Proposal B

  Payback period =

$$3 + \left(\frac{3,000}{25,000} \times 1 \text{ year} \right)$$

  = 3.1 years

(ii) The return on capital employed (ROCE) is calculated using the accounting profits given in the question.

Proposal A   Average profit   = $(6,500 + 3,500 + 13,500 − 1,500)/4

= $22,000/4 = $5,500

ROCE   = $\dfrac{£5,500}{£46,000} \times 100\% = 12.0\%$

Proposal B   Average profit   = $(4,500 + 2,500 + 4,500 + 14,500)/4

= $26,000/4 = $6,500

ROCE   = $\dfrac{£6,500}{£46,000} \times 100\% = 14.1\%$

(b) Two advantages of each of the methods of appraisal can be selected from the following.

Payback period

(i)   It is simple to calculate.
(ii) It preserves liquidity by preferring early cash flows.
(iii) It uses cash flows instead of more arbitrary accounting profits.
(iv) It reduces risk by preferring early cash flows.

Return on capital employed

(i)   It uses readily available **accounting profits**.
(ii) It is **understood** by **non-financial managers**.
(iii) It is a measure used by **external analysts** which should be monitored by the company.

Chapter Roundup

- A typical **model for investment decision making** has a number of distinct stages.

    – Origination of proposals
    – Project screening
    – Analysis and acceptance
    – Monitoring and review

- During the project's progress, **project controls** should be applied to ensure the following.

    – Capital spending does not exceed the amount authorised.
    – The implementation of the project is not delayed.
    – The anticipated benefits are eventually obtained.

- A **post audit** cannot reverse the decision to incur the capital expenditure, because the expenditure has already taken place, but it does have a certain control value.

- The **payback method** looks at how long it takes for a project's net cash inflows to equal the initial investment.

- Like the payback method, the **accounting rate of return method** is popular despite its limitations.

Quick Quiz

1 Fill in the blanks in these statements about the advantages of the payback method.

   (a) Focus on early payback can enhance ....

   (b) Investment risk is .... if payback is longer.

   (c) .... –term forecasts are likely to be more reliable.

2 The accounting rate of return method of investment appraisal uses accounting profits before depreciation charges. *True or false?*

3 Which of the following statements about post-completion audit is correct?

   A Size should not be used as a guide as to which projects should be audited.

   B Managers should perceive that every capital expenditure project has a chance of being the subject of a detailed audit.

   C All capital expenditure projects should be audited.

   D In general, projects should be audited approximately one week after completion.

4 *Choose the correct words from those highlighted.*

   (a) The imposition of internal capital budget constraints is known as **hard/soft** capital rationing

   (b) **Hard/soft** capital rationing occurs when external capital budget limits are set.

5 *Fill in the blank.*

   The average net book value of an asset is calculated as ....

6 Applied punitively, PCA exercises may lead to managers becoming risk seekers. *True or false?*

7 *Fill in the blanks.*

   The recommended definition of ARR is: $\dfrac{\text{.........................}}{\text{.........................}} \times 100\%$

Answers to Quick Quiz

1 (a) liquidity   (b) increased   (c) shorter

2 False

3 B. This should improve the overall capital expenditure decision-making process.

4 (a) soft   (b) hard

5 (Capital cost + disposal value)/2

6 False. They are likely to become unnecessarily risk averse.

7 $\dfrac{\text{Average annual profit from investment}}{\text{Average investment}} \times 100\%$

Now try the questions below from the Exam Question Bank

Number	Level	Marks	Time
Q14	Examination	10	18 mins
Q15	Examination	10	18 mins

DCF techniques of investment appraisal

Introduction

Having considered two relatively straightforward investment appraisal techniques in Chapter 10, we are now going to turn our attention to methods based on discounted cashflow (DCF) techniques.

You will have encountered discounting at an introductory level in your earlier studies but we go over the basics again to begin with.

Sections 1, 2 and 4 look at the calculations required when using the DCF techniques of net present value (NPV), internal rate of return (IRR) and discounted payback. **Sections 3 and 5** cover issues that could be examined in discursive questions.

This chapter is where you learn the groundwork for more sophisticated analysis. This is therefore one of the **key chapters** in this Text. The topics in this chapter have been examined in every sitting so far and in all sections of the paper.

In Chapters 12 and 13 we look at further aspects of investment appraisal and in particular sensitivity analysis and accounting for inflation and taxation.

Topic list	Learning outcomes	Syllabus references	Ability required
1 The net present value method	B(vi),(vii)	B(4), (5)	Analysis/Evaluation
2 The internal rate of return method	B(vi),(vii)	B(4), (5)	Analysis/Evaluation
3 NPV and IRR compared	B(vii)	B(5)	Analysis/Evaluation
4 Discounted payback	B(vi),(vii)	B(4), (5)	Analysis/Evaluation
5 DCF: additional points	B(ii),(v)	B(5)	Comprehension/ Application

1 The net present value method

1.1 Discounting

Suppose that a company has $10,000 to invest, and wants to earn a return of 10% (compound interest) on its investments. This means that if the $10,000 could be invested at 10%, the value of the investment with interest would build up as follows.

(a)   After 1 year $10,000 × (1.10)   = $11,000
(b)   After 2 years $10,000 × (1.10)^2   = $12,100
(c)   After 3 years $10,000 × (1.10)^3   = $13,310

and so on.

This is **compounding**. The formula for the future value of an investment plus accumulated interest after n time periods is $V = X(1 + r)^n$

where V is the future value of the investment with interest

X is the initial or 'present' value of the investment

r is the compound rate of return per time period, expressed as a proportion (so 10% = 0.10, 5% = 0.05 and so on)

n is the number of time periods.

FAST FORWARD

Discounting starts with the future value (a sum of money receivable or payable at a future date), and converts the future value to a **present value**, which is the cash equivalent now of the future value.

For example, if a company expects to earn a (compound) rate of return of 10% on its investments, how much would it need to invest now to have the following investments?

(a) $11,000 after 1 year
(b) $12,100 after 2 years
(c) $13,310 after 3 years

The answer is $10,000 in each case, and we can calculate it by discounting.

FAST FORWARD

The **discounting formula** to calculate the present value (X) of a future sum of money (V) at the end of n time periods is $X = V/(1+r)^n$.

(a)   After 1 year, $11,000 × 1/1.10 = $10,000
(b)   After 2 years, $12,100 × 1/1.10^2 = $10,000
(c)   After 3 years, $13,310 × 1/1.10^3 = $10,000

Key term

> **Present value** is 'The cash equivalent now of a sum of money receivable or payable at a future date'.
>
> (CIMA *Official Terminology*)

The **timing of cash flows is taken into account by discounting them**. The effect of discounting is to **give a bigger value per $1 for cash flows that occur earlier**: $1 earned after one year will be worth more than $1 earned after two years, which in turn will be worth more than $1 earned after five years, and so on.

BPP
LEARNING MEDIA

Question

Learning outcome: B(vi)

Spender expects the cash inflow from an investment to be $40,000 after 2 years and another $30,000 after 3 years. Its target rate of return is 12%.

Required

Fill in the blank in the sentence below.

The present value of these future returns is $.................. .

Answer

The correct answer is $53,240.

Year	Cash flow $	Discount factor 12%	Present value $
2	40,000	$\dfrac{1}{(1.12)^2}=0.797$	31,880
3	30,000	$\dfrac{1}{(1.12)^3}=0.712$	21,360
		Total PV	53,240

Question

Learning outcome: B(vi)

Look back at the detail of the question above and then fill in the gaps in the paragraph below.

The present value of the future returns, discounted at ......, is .... This means that if Spender can invest now to earn a return of .... on its investments, it would have to invest .... now to earn .... after 2 years plus .... after 3 years.

Answer

The correct answer is: The present value of the future returns, discounted at **12%**, is **$53,240**. This means that if Spender can invest now to earn a return of **12%** on its investments, it would have to invest **$53,240** now to earn **$40,000** after 2 years plus **$30,000** after 3 years.

---

y term

Discounted cash flow is 'The discounting of the projected net cash flows of a capital project to ascertain its present value. The methods commonly used are:

- yield, or internal rate of return (IRR), in which the calculation determines the return in the form of a percentage;

- net present value (NPV), in which the discount rate is chosen and the present value is expressed as a sum of money;

- discounted payback, in which the discount rate is chosen, and the payback is the number of years required to repay the original investment.'

(CIMA *Official Terminology*)

We will be looking at these methods in the remainder of this chapter.

Attention!

DCF looks at the **cash flows** of a project, **not the accounting profits**. Like the payback technique of investment appraisal, DCF is concerned with liquidity, not profitability. Cash flows are considered because they show the costs and benefit of a project when they actually occur. For example, the capital cost of a project will be the original cash outlay, and not the notional cost of depreciation which is used to spread the capital cost over the asset's life in the financial accounts.

1.2 The net present value method

FAST FORWARD

The **NPV method of project appraisal** is to accept projects with a positive NPV.

Key term

Net present value (NPV) is 'The difference between the sum of the projected discounted cash inflows and outflows attributable to a capital investment or other long-term project'.   (CIMA *Official Terminology*)

The NPV method therefore **compares the present value of all the cash inflows** from a project **with the present value of all the cash outflows** from a project. The **NPV** is thus calculated as the **PV of cash inflows minus the PV of cash outflows**.

(a)   If the **NPV is positive**, it means that the cash inflows from a project will yield a return in excess of the cost of capital, and so the **project should be undertaken** if the cost of capital is the organisation's target rate of return.

(b)   If the **NPV is negative**, it means that the cash inflows from a project will yield a return below the cost of capital, and so the **project should not be undertaken** if the cost of capital is the organisation's target rate of return.

(c)   If the **NPV is exactly zero**, the cash inflows from a project will yield a return which is exactly the same as the cost of capital, and so if the cost of capital is the organisation's target rate of return, the **project will be only just worth undertaking**.

1.3 Example: NPV

Slogger has a cost of capital of 15% and is considering a capital investment project, where the estimated cash flows are as follows.

Year	Cash flow
	$
0 (ie now)	(100,000)
1	60,000
2	80,000
3	40,000
4	30,000

Required

Calculate the NPV of the project, and assess whether it should be undertaken.

Solution

Year	Cash flow $	Discount factor 15%	Present value $
0	(100,000)	1.000	(100,000)
1	60,000	1/(1.15)= 0.870	52,200
2	80,000	$1/1.15^2 = 0.756$	60,480
3	40,000	$1/1.15^3 = 0.658$	26,320
4	30,000	$1/1.15^4 = 0.572$	17,160
		NPV =	56,160

(*Note.* The **discount factor for any cash flow 'now' (time 0) is always 1**, whatever the cost of capital.)

The **PV of cash inflows exceeds the PV of cash outflows** by $56,160, which means that the project will earn a DCF yield in excess of 15%. It should therefore be **undertaken**.

1.4 Timing of cash flows: conventions used in DCF

Discounting reduces the value of future cash flows to a present value equivalent and so is clearly concerned with the timing of the cash flows. As a general rule, the following guidelines may be applied.

(a) A **cash outlay to be incurred at the beginning of an investment project ('now') occurs in time 0**. The **present value of $1 now, in time 0, is $1** regardless of the value of the discount rate r. This is common sense.

(b) A **cash flow** which occurs **during the course of a time period** is **assumed to occur** all at once at the **end of the time period** (at the end of the year). Receipts of $10,000 during time period 1 are therefore taken to occur at the end of time period 1.

(c) A **cash flow** which occurs **at the beginning of a time period** is **taken to occur at the end of the previous time period**. Therefore a cash outlay of $5,000 at the beginning of time period 2 is taken to occur at the end of time period 1.

1.5 Discount tables for the PV of $1

The discount factor that we use in discounting is $1/(1+r)^n = (1+r)^{-n}$. Instead of having to calculate this factor every time we can use **tables**. Discount tables for the present value of $1, for different **integer** values of r and n, are **shown in the Appendix at the back of this Study Text** and **will be provided in the exam**. Use these tables to work out your own solution to the following question.

Question

NPV

Learning outcome: B(vi)

LCH manufactures product X which it sells for $5 per unit. Variable costs of production are currently $3 per unit, and fixed costs 50p per unit. A new machine is available which would cost $90,000 but which could be used to make product X for a variable cost of only $2.50 per unit. Fixed costs, however, would increase by $7,500 per annum as a direct result of purchasing the machine. The machine would have an expected life of four years and a resale value after that time of $10,000. Sales of product X are estimated to be 75,000 units per annum. LCH expects to earn at least 12% per annum from its investments.

Required

Choose the appropriate words in the sentence below from those highlighted.

LCH **should purchase/should not purchase** the machine.

Answer

The correct answer is that **LCH should purchase the machine**.

Savings are 75,000 × ($3 − $2.50) = $37,500 per annum.

Additional costs are $7,500 per annum.

Net cash savings are therefore $30,000 per annum. (Remember, depreciation is not a cash flow and must be ignored as a 'cost'.)

The first step in calculating an NPV is to establish the **relevant costs** year by year. All future cash flows arising as a direct consequence of the decision should be taken into account.

It is **assumed** that the machine will be sold for $10,000 at the end of year 4.

Year	Cash flow $	PV factor 12%	PV of cash flow $
0	(90,000)	1.000	(90,000)
1	30,000	0.893	26,790
2	30,000	0.797	23,910
3	30,000	0.712	21,360
4	40,000	0.636	25,440
		NPV =	+7,500

The **NPV is positive** and so the project is expected to **earn more than 12%** per annum and is therefore **acceptable**.

Attention!

Discount tables are provided in the exam, but they cover only integer values of r. If you need to use a discount rate of, say, 10.5%, you would need to use the discounting formula.

1.6 Annuities

FAST FORWARD

An **annuity** is a constant cash flow for a number of years.

In the previous exercise, the calculations could have been simplified for years 1–3 as follows.

$$
\begin{array}{rl}
 & 30,000 \times 0.893 \\
+ & 30,000 \times 0.797 \\
+ & 30,000 \times 0.712 \\
= & 30,000 \times 2.402
\end{array}
$$

Key term

An **annuity** is a constant cash flow from year to year.

Where there is a **constant cash flow from year to year** (in this case $30,000 per annum for years 1–3) it is quicker to calculate the present value by adding together the discount factors for the individual years. These total factors could be described as 'same cash flow per annum' factors, **'cumulative present value' factors** or **'annuity' factors**. They are **shown in the table for cumulative PV of $1 factors which is shown in the Appendix at the back of this Study Text** (2.402, for example, is in the column for 12% per annum and the row for year 3). If you have not used them before, check that you can understand annuity tables by trying this question.

BPP
LEARNING MEDIA

Question

Learning outcome: B(vi)

What is the present value of $2,000 costs incurred each year from years 3–6 when the cost of capital is 5%?

A $6,300
B $6,434
C $6,000
D $4,706

Answer

The correct answer is B.

The PV of $2,000 in costs each year from years 3–6 when the cost of capital is 5% per annum is calculated as follows.

$$£2,000 \times \begin{bmatrix} \text{PV of £1per annum for years1 - 6 at 5%} = 5.076 \\ \text{Less PV of £1per annum for years1 - 2 at 5%} = \underline{1.859} \\ \text{PV of £1per annum for years3 - 6} \qquad = \underline{\underline{3.217}} \end{bmatrix}$$

PV   = $2,000 × 3.217 = $6,434

If you chose **Option A**, you performed the calculation $2,000 x 105% x 3 years. You need to use a discount factor.

If you chose **Option C,** you simply took the sum of $2,000 paid annually for three years.

If you chose **Option D**, you deducted the cumulative discount factor for years 1 to 3 instead of the factor for years 1 and 2 from that for years 1 to 6.

tention!

As well as incorporating the use of annuity tables, the example which follows includes **working capital requirements**. Take note of how this is dealt with as such a feature could well be a complicating factor in an exam question.

1.6.1 Example: NPV including use of annuity tables

Elsie is considering the manufacture of a new product which would involve the use of both a new machine (costing $150,000) and an existing machine, which cost $80,000 two years ago and has a current net book value of $60,000. There is sufficient capacity on this machine, which has so far been under-utilised. Annual sales of the product would be 5,000 units, selling at $32 per unit. Unit costs would be as follows.

	$
Direct labour (4 hours at $2 per hour)	8
Direct materials	7
Fixed costs including depreciation	9
	24

The project would have a five-year life, after which the new machine would have a net residual value of $10,000. Because direct labour is continually in short supply, labour resources would have to be diverted from other work which currently earns a contribution of $1.50 per direct labour hour. The fixed overhead absorption rate would be $2.25 per hour ($9 per unit) but actual expenditure on fixed overhead would not alter. Working capital requirements would be $10,000 in the first year, rising to $15,000 in the second year and remaining at this level until the end of the project, when it will all be recovered.

Required

Assess whether the project is worthwhile, given that the company's cost of capital is 20%. Ignore taxation.

Solution

The relevant cash flows are as follows.

Year 0	Purchase of new machine	$150,000

		$
Years 1–5	Contribution from new product (5,000 units × $(32 – 15))	85,000
	Less contribution forgone (5,000 × (4 × $1.50))	30,000
		55,000

The project requires $10,000 of working capital at the start of year 1 and a further $5,000 at the start of year 2. Increases in working capital reduce the net cash flow for the period to which they relate. When the working capital tied up in the project is 'recovered' at the end of the project, it will provide an extra cash inflow (for example customers will eventually pay up).

All other costs, which are past costs, notional accounting costs or costs which would be incurred anyway without the project, are not relevant to the investment decision.

The NPV is calculated as follows.

Year	Equipment $	Working capital $	Contribution $	Net cash flow $	Discount factor 20%	PV of net cash flow $
0	(150,000)	(10,000)		(160,000)	1.000	(160,000)
1		(5,000)		(5,000)	0.833	(4,165)
1–5			55,000	55,000	2.991	164,505
5	10,000	15,000		25,000	0.402	10,050
					NPV =	10,390

The NPV is positive and the project is worthwhile, although there is not much margin for error. Some risk analysis of the project is recommended.

1.7 Annual cash flows in perpetuity

FAST FORWARD A **perpetuity** is a constant cash flow forever.

It can sometimes be useful to calculate the **cumulative present value of $1 per annum** for every year in perpetuity (that is, **forever**).

Key term

A **perpetuity** is an annuity that lasts forever.

When the cost of capital is r, the cumulative PV of $1 per annum in perpetuity is **$1/r**. For example, the PV of $1 per annum in perpetuity at a discount rate of 10% would be $1/0.10 = $10.

Similarly, the PV of $1 per annum in perpetuity at a discount rate of 15% would be $1/0.15 = $6.67 and at a discount rate of 20% it would be $1/0.20 = $5.

Question

Perpetuities

Learning outcome: B(vi)

An organisation with a cost of capital of 14% is considering investing in a project costing $500,000 that would yield cash inflows of $100,000 pa in perpetuity.

Required

Choose the appropriate words from those highlighted in the sentence below.

The project **should be/should not be** undertaken.

Answer

The correct answer is: The project should be undertaken.

Year	Cash flow $	Discount factor 14%	Present value $
0	(500,000)	1.00	(500,000)
1 – ∞	100,000	1/0.14 = 7.14	714,000
		Net present value	214,000

The NPV is positive and so the project should be undertaken.

You might well wonder what is the use of cash flows in perpetuity. This surely is an impractical and nonsensical notion? **Cash flows in perpetuity** do actually have **two practical uses**.

(a)   They are **used in the calculation of a company's cost of capital.**

(b)   They **indicate the maximum value of the cumulative present value factor of $1 per annum.** For example, we can say that the maximum present value of $1 pa for any period of time at a discount rate of 10% is $1/0.1 = $10. The longer the period of time under review, and the more years that are in the project period, the closer the cumulative PV factor of $1 pa will get to $10 at a 10% discount rate.

(i)   The PV factor of $1 pa at 10% for years 1 to 15 is $7.606
(ii)   The PV factor of $1 pa at 10% for years 1 to 20 is $8.514
(iii)   The PV factor of $1 pa at 10% for years 1 to 30 is $9.427
(iv)   The PV factor of $1 pa at 10% for years 1 to 50 is $9.915

As you can see, the cumulative PV gets closer to the limit of $10 as time progresses and the limit has almost been reached by year 50, and even by year 30. Knowing what the limit is might help with project analysis when capital projects extend over a long period of time and certainly it can provide a very useful yardstick and 'ready-reckoner' for managers who must carry out DCF evaluations as a regular part of their job.

In the next chapter we will see a practical example of the application of the present value of an annuity.

1.8 Net terminal value

> **Net terminal value (NTV)** is the cash surplus remaining at the end of a project after taking account of interest and capital repayments.

The NTV discounted at the cost of capital will give the NPV of the project.

1.8.1 Example: the net terminal value

A project has the following cash flows.

Year	$
0	(5,000)
1	3,000
2	2,600
3	6,200

The project has an NPV of $4,531 at the company's cost of capital of 10% (workings not shown).

Required

Calculate the net terminal value of the project.

Solution

The net terminal value can be determined directly from the NPV, or by calculating the cash surplus at the end of the project.

Assume that the $5,000 for the project is borrowed at an interest rate of 10% and that cash flows from the project are used to repay the loan.

	$
Loan balance outstanding at beginning of project	5,000
Interest in year 1 at 10%	500
Repaid at end of year 1	(3,000)
Balance outstanding at end of year 1	2,500
Interest year 2	250
Repaid year 2	(2,600)
Balance outstanding year 2	150
Interest year 3	15
Repaid year 3	(6,200)
Cash surplus at end of project	6,035

The net terminal value is $6,035.

Check

NPV = $6,035 × 0.751 (discount factor for year 3) = $4,532

Allowing for the rounding errors caused by three-figure discount tables, this is the correct figure for the NPV.

1.9 Assumptions in the NPV model

(a) Forecasts are assumed to be certain.

(b) Information is assumed to be freely available and costless.

(c) The discount rate is a measure of the opportunity cost of funds which ensures wealth maximisation for *all* individuals and companies.

Question

Learning outcome: B(vi)

A project has the following forecast cash flows.

Year	$
0	(280,000)
1	149,000
2	128,000
3	84,000
4	70,000

Using two decimal places in all discount factors, what is the net present value of the project at a cost of capital of 16.5%?

A $27,906   B $29,270   C $32,195   D $33,580

Answer

The correct answer is D.

There are no present value tables for 16.5%, therefore you need to calculate your own discount factors, using discount factor = $1/(1 + r)^n$ where r = cost of capital and n = number of years.

Year		16.5% factor	Cash flow $	Present value $
0		1.00	(280,000)	(280,000)
1	$\dfrac{1}{(1 + 0.165)}$	0.86	149,000	128,140
2	$\dfrac{1}{(1 + 0.165)^2}$	0.74	128,000	94,720
3	$\dfrac{1}{(1 + 0.165)^3}$	0.63	84,000	52,920
4	$\dfrac{1}{(1 + 0.165)^4}$	0.54	70,000	37,800
			Net present value	33,580

2 The internal rate of return method

The **IRR method of project appraisal** is to accept projects which have an IRR (the rate at which the NPV is zero) that exceeds a target rate of return. The IRR can be estimated either from a graph or using interpolation.

The **IRR method** of project appraisal is to **calculate the exact DCF rate of return which the project is expected to achieve**, in other words the **rate at which the NPV is zero**.

If the expected rate of return (the IRR yield or DCF yield) exceeds a target rate of return, the project would be worth undertaking (ignoring risk and uncertainty factors).

The **internal rate of return (IRR)** is 'The annual percentage return achieved by a project, at which the sum of the discounted cash inflows over the life of the project is equal to the sum of the discounted cash outflows'.

(CIMA *Official Terminology*)

Without a computer or calculator program, an estimate of the internal rate of return is made using either a graph or using a hit-and-miss technique known as the interpolation method.

2.1 Graphical approach

The easiest way to estimate the IRR of a project is to **find the project's NPV at a number of costs of capital** and **sketch a graph of NPV against discount rate**. You can then use the sketch to estimate the **discount rate at which the NPV is equal to zero (the point where the curve cuts the axis)**.

2.1.1 Example: graphical approach

A project might have the following NPVs at the following discount rates.

Discount rate %	NPV $
5	5,300
10	2,900
15	(1,700)
20	(3,200)

This could be sketched on a graph as follows.

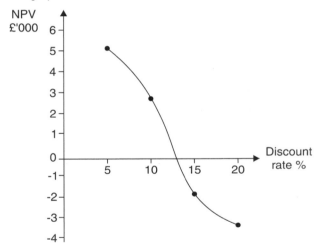

The IRR can be **estimated as 13%.** The NPV should then be **recalculated using this interest rate**. The resulting NPV **should be equal to, or very near, zero. If it is not, additional NPVs at different discount rates should be calculated, the graph resketched and a more accurate IRR determined.**

2.2 Interpolation method

If we were to draw a graph of a 'typical' capital project, with a negative cash flow at the start of the project, and positive net cash flows afterwards up to the end of the project, we could draw a graph of the project's NPV at different costs of capital. It would look like this.

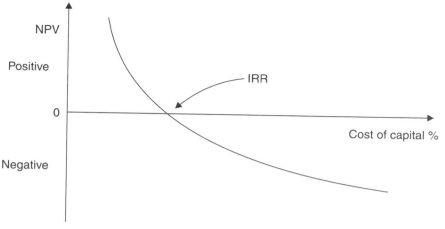

If we determine **a cost of capital where the NPV is slightly positive, and another cost of capital where it is slightly negative**, we can **estimate the IRR – where the NPV is zero – by drawing a straight line between the two points** on the graph that we have calculated.

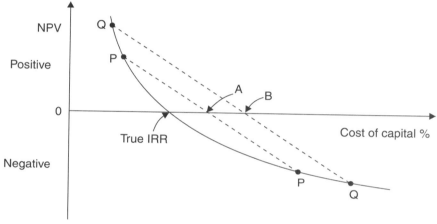

- If we **establish the NPVs at the two points P**, we would estimate the **IRR** to be at **point A**.
- If we **establish the NPVs at the two points Q**, we would estimate the **IRR** to be at **point B**.

The **closer our NPVs are to zero, the closer our estimate will be to the true IRR**.

The **interpolation method assumes that the NPV rises in linear fashion between the two NPVs close to 0**. The real rate of return is therefore assumed to be on a straight line between the two points at which the NPV is calculated.

AST FORWARD

The **IRR interpolation formula** to apply is:

$$IRR = A + \left[\frac{P}{P+N} \times (B-A) \right]\%$$

where A is the (lower) rate of return with a positive NPV
B is the (higher) rate of return with a negative NPV
P is the amount of the positive NPV
N is the absolute value of the negative NPV

Where both NPVs are positive, use a modified version of the formula:

$$IRR = A + \left[\frac{P}{P-N} \times (B-A) \right]\%$$

2.2.1 Example: the IRR method and interpolation

A company is trying to decide whether to buy a machine for $80,000 which will save costs of $20,000 per annum for 5 years and which will have a resale value of $10,000 at the end of year 5.

Required

If it is the company's policy to undertake projects only if they are expected to yield a DCF return of 10% or more, ascertain using the IRR method whether this project should be undertaken.

Solution

The first step is to calculate two net present values, both as close as possible to zero, using rates for the cost of capital which are whole numbers. One NPV should be positive and the other negative.

Choosing rates for the cost of capital which will give an NPV close to zero (that is, rates which are close to the actual rate of return) is a hit-and-miss exercise, and several attempts may be needed to find satisfactory rates. **As a rough guide**, try starting at a **return figure which is about two thirds or three quarters of the ARR**.

Annual depreciation would be $(80,000 − 10,000)/5 = $14,000.

The **ARR** would be (20,000 − depreciation of 14,000)/(½ of (80,000 + 10,000)) = 6,000/45,000 = 13.3%

Two thirds of this is 8.9% and so we can start by trying 9%.

Try 9%.	Year	Cash flow	PV factor	PV of cash flow
		$	9%	$
	0	(80,000)	1.000	(80,000)
	1–5	20,000	3.890	77,800
	5	10,000	0.650	6,500
			NPV	4,300

This is **fairly close to zero**. It is also **positive**, which means that the **real rate of return** is **more than 9%**. We can use 9% as one of our two NPVs close to zero, although for greater accuracy, we should try 10% or even 11% to find an NPV even closer to zero if we can. As a guess, it might be worth trying 12% next, to see what the NPV is.

Try 12%.	Year	Cash flow	PV factor	PV of cash flow
		$	12%	$
	0	(80,000)	1.000	(80,000)
	1–5	20,000	3.605	72,100
	5	10,000	0.567	5,670
			NPV	(2,230)

This is **fairly close to zero** and **negative**. The **real rate of return** is therefore **greater than 9%** (positive NPV of $4,300) but **less than 12%** (negative NPV of $2,230).

Note. **If the first NPV is positive, choose a higher rate for the next calculation to get a negative NPV. If the first NPV is negative, choose a lower rate for the next calculation**.

So $IRR = 9 + \left[\dfrac{4,300}{4,300 + 2,230} \times (12 - 9) \right]\% = 10.98\%$, say 11%

If it is company policy to undertake investments which are expected to yield 10% or more, this project would be undertaken.

Exam focus
point

There have been objective test questions in most of the exams so far which required candidates to calculate the IRR of a project. The questions typically give one PV at a discount rate and the other PV would need to be calculated using another discount rate. The technique was also tested for three marks as part of a longer Section C question in November 2006. A gift of a question *if* you knew the formula!

Question

IRR

Learning outcome: B(vi)

The project shown below should be accepted if the company requires a minimum return of 17%. *True or false?*

Time		$
0	Investment	(4,000)
1	Receipts	1,200
2	Receipts	1,410
3	Receipts	1,875
4	Receipts	1,150

Answer

The correct answer is that the IRR is 15% and so the statement is false.

The **total receipts** are $5,635 giving a **total profit** of $1,635 and **average profits** of $409. The **average investment** is $2,000. The **ARR** is $409 ÷ $2,000 = 20%. **Two thirds of the ARR** is approximately 14%. The **initial estimate of the IRR** that we shall try is therefore **14%**.

		Try 14%		Try 16%	
Time	Cash flow	Discount factor	PV	Discount factor	PV
	$	14%	$	16%	$
0	(4,000)	1.000	(4,000)	1.000	(4,000)
1	1,200	0.877	1,052	0.862	1,034
2	1,410	0.769	1,084	0.743	1,048
3	1,875	0.675	1,266	0.641	1,202
4	1,150	0.592	681	0.552	635
		NPV	83	NPV	(81)

The **IRR must be less than 16%, but higher than 14%.** The NPVs at these two costs of capital will be used to estimate the IRR.

Using the **interpolation formula**

$$IRR = 14\% + \left[\frac{83}{83 + 81} \times (16\% - 14\%) \right] = 15.01\%$$

The IRR is, in fact, exactly 15%.

The project should be **rejected** as the **IRR is less than the minimum return demanded**.

2.3 The IRR of an annuity

Suppose an investment now of $100,000 will produce inflows of $30,000 each year over the next four years. We know that the IRR is the discount rate which produces an NPV of zero. **At the IRR (rate r) the PV of inflows must therefore equal the PV of outflows**.

∴ $100,000 = PV of $30,000 for years 1 to 4 at rate r
∴ $100,000 = (cumulative PV factor for years 1 to 4 at rate r) × $30,000
∴ $100,000/$30,000 = cumulative PV factor for years 1 to 4 at rate r
∴ 3.333 = cumulative PV factor for years 1 to 4 at rate r

We can now **look in cumulative PV tables along the line for year 4 to find a discount factor which corresponds to 3.333. The corresponding rate is the IRR**. The nearest figure is 3.312 and so the IRR of the project is approximately 8%.

2.4 The IRR of a perpetuity

Suppose an investment of $25,000 will produce annual cash flows in perpetuity of $2,000. Using the **same reasoning** as in Section 2.3:

$25,000 = PV of $2,000 in perpetuity

∴ $25,000 = $2,000/r (where r = IRR)

$$\therefore r = \frac{£2,000}{£25,000} = 0.08 = 8\%$$

| | | Question | | NPV and IRR |

Learning outcome: B(vi)

The VWXYZ Company produces a variety of high-quality garden furniture and associated items, mostly in wood and wrought iron.

There is potential to expand the business. The directors have identified three main options for a four-year plan.

(a)   Expand its flourishing retail outlet to include all products.
(b)   Branch out into mail order.
(c)   Produce greenhouses and conservatories.

These options would require initial expenditure of (a) $75,000, (b) $120,000 or (c) $200,000. The best information on year-end cash flows is as follows.

	Year 1	Year 2	Year 3	Year 4
	$'000	$'000	$'000	$'000
(a)	40	50	50	50
(b)	50	60	80	100
(c)	50	100	150	150

Required

(a)   Using the data on expansion plans, evaluate the three investment options using the net present value (NPV) technique, assuming the cost of capital to be 10%, and recommend, with reasons, one option.

(b)   Find the approximate internal rate of return (IRR) of your choice in (a) above.

Answer

(a)   **Option A – Expand retail outlet**

Year	Cash flow	Discount factor	NPV
	$'000	10%	$'000
0	(75)	1.000	(75.00)
1	40	0.909	36.36
2	50	0.826	41.30
3	50	0.751	37.55
4	50	0.683	34.15
			74.36

Option B – Mail order

Year	Cash flow	Discount factor	NPV
	$'000	10%	$'000
0	(120)	1.000	(120.00)
1	50	0.909	45.45
2	60	0.826	49.56
3	80	0.751	60.08
4	100	0.683	68.30
			103.39

Option C – Greenhouses and conservatories

Year	Cash flow	Discount factor	NPV
	$'000	10%	$'000
0	(200)	1.000	(200.00)
1	50	0.909	45.45
2	100	0.826	82.60
3	150	0.751	112.65
4	150	0.683	102.45
			143.15

Option C gives the highest net present value and therefore this should be chosen.

(b)   The NPV for option C is quite high relative to the initial investment and the IRR is therefore probably considerably higher than 10%.

Try 30%

Year	Cash flow	Discount factor	NPV
	$'000	30%	$'000
0	(200)	1.000	(200.00)
1	50	0.769	38.45
2	100	0.592	59.20
3	150	0.455	68.25
4	150	0.350	52.50
			18.40

Try 40%

Year	Cash flow $'000	Discount factor 40%	NPV $'000
0	(200)	1.000	(200.0)
1	50	0.714	35.7
2	100	0.510	51.0
3	150	0.364	54.6
4	150	0.260	39.0
			(19.7)

$$\text{IRR} = 30\% + \left[\frac{18.4}{18.4 + 19.7} \times 10 \right]\% = 34.83\%$$

3 NPV and IRR compared

FAST FORWARD

When compared with the NPV method, the **IRR method** has a number of **disadvantages**.

– It ignores the relative size of investments.

– There are problems with its use when a project has non-conventional cashflows or when deciding between mutually exclusive projects.

– Discount rates which differ over the life of a project cannot be incorporated into IRR calculations.

3.1 Advantages of IRR method

(a) The main advantage is that the information it provides is more **easily understood** by managers, especially non-financial managers. 'The project will be expected to have an initial capital outlay of $100,000, and to earn a yield of 25%. This is in excess of the target yield of 15% for investments' is easier to understand than 'The project will cost $100,000 and have an NPV of $30,000 when discounted at the minimum required rate of 15%'.

(b) A **discount rate does not have to be specified** before the IRR can be calculated. A hurdle discount rate is simply required to which the IRR can be compared.

3.2 Disadvantages of IRR method

(a) If managers were given information about both **ROCE (or ROI) and IRR**, it might be easy to get their relative **meaning and significance mixed up**.

(b) It **ignores the relative size of investments**. Both projects below have an IRR of 18%.

	Project A $	Project B $
Cost, year 0	350,000	35,000
Annual savings, years 1–6	100,000	10,000

Clearly, project A is bigger (ten times as big) and so more 'profitable' but if the only information on which the projects were judged were to be their IRR of 18%, project B would be made to seem just as beneficial as project A, which is not the case.

(c) **When discount rates are expected to differ over the life of the project, such variations can be incorporated easily into NPV calculations, but not into IRR calculations**. And an **adjustment** can be made to the **discount rate** used in NPV calculations to include an allowance for project **risk**.

(d)   There are **problems** with using the IRR **when the project has non-conventional cash flows** (see Section 3.3) or when **deciding between mutually exclusive projects** (see Section 3.4).

'In spite of all the efforts to convince managers that the net present value (NPV) is the 'correct' method of investment appraisal to use, recent research shows that they continue to prefer the internal rate of return (IRR). And, although a number of modified versions of the IRR have been developed, they too have been condemned by some academics even though such modifications are an improvement on the conventional IRR. No single investment appraisal technique will give the right answer in all investment situations, however, and the NPV is no exception. This is reflected again in recent research which shows that companies now use a greater number of financial appraisal techniques than in the past, but with no consensus on the actual combination. This increase in usage has been attributed to the increase in computer software that is now readily available to perform the basic calculations of the various financial appraisal techniques such as payback (PB), accounting rate of return (ARR), IRR, and NPV.'

'The NPV profile – a creative way of looking at the NPV', Frank Lefley and Malcolm Morgan, *Management Accounting,* June 1999

3.3 Non-conventional cash flows

The projects we have considered so far have had **conventional cash flows (an initial cash outflow followed by a series of inflows)** and in such circumstances the NPV and IRR methods give the same accept or reject decision. When flows vary from this they are termed non-conventional. The following project has non-conventional cash flows.

Year	Project X
	$'000
0	(1,900)
1	4,590
2	(2,735)

Project X above has two IRRs as shown by the diagram which follows.

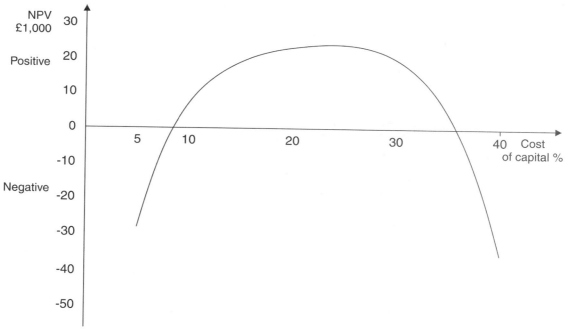

Suppose that the required rate of return on project X is 10% but that the IRR of 7% is used to decide whether to accept or reject the project. The project would be rejected since it appears that it can only yield 7%. The diagram shows, however, that **between rates of 7% and 35% the project should be accepted**. Using the IRR of 35% would produce the correct decision to accept the project. **Lack of knowledge of**

multiple IRRs could therefore lead to serious **errors in the decision** of whether to accept or reject a project.

In general, if the sign of the net cash flow changes in successive periods (inflow to outflow or vice versa), it is possible for the calculations to produce **as many IRRs as there are sign changes**.

The use of the **IRR** is therefore **not recommended** in circumstances in which there are **non-conventional cash flow patterns** (unless the decision maker is aware of the existence of multiple IRRs). The NPV method, on the other hand, gives clear, unambiguous results whatever the cash flow pattern.

3.4 Mutually exclusive projects

The IRR and NPV methods give conflicting rankings as to which project should be given priority. Let us suppose that a company with a cost of capital of 16% is considering two mutually exclusive options, option A and option B. The cash flows for each are as follows.

Year		Option A $	Option B $
0	Capital outlay	(10,200)	(35,250)
1	Net cash inflow	6,000	18,000
2	Net cash inflow	5,000	15,000
3	Net cash inflow	3,000	15,000

The NPV of each project is calculated below.

		Option A		Option B	
Year	Discount factor	Cash flow $	Present value $	Cash flow $	Present value $
0	1.000	(10,200)	(10,200)	(35,250)	(35,250)
1	0.862	6,000	5,172	18,000	15,516
2	0.743	5,000	3,715	15,000	11,145
3	0.641	3,000	1,923	15,000	9,615
			NPV = +610		NPV = +1,026

The **DCF yield (IRR) of option A is 20%, while the yield of option B is only 18%** (workings not shown.)

On a **comparison of NPVs, option B would be preferred**, but on a **comparison of IRRs, option A would be preferred**.

The **preference should go to option B**. This is because the **differences in the cash flows** between the two options, when discounted at the cost of capital of 16%, shows that the present value of the incremental benefits from option B compared with option A exceed the PV of the incremental costs. This can be re-stated in the following ways.

(a)   The **NPV of the differential cash flows (option B cash flows minus option A cash flows) is positive**, and so it is worth spending the extra capital to get the extra benefits.

(b)   The **IRR of the differential cash flows exceeds the cost of capital 16%,** and so it is worth spending the extra capital to get the extra benefits.

Year	Option A cash flow $	Option B cash flow $	Difference $	Discount factor 16%	Present value of difference $
0	(10,200)	(35,250)	(25,050)	1.000	(25,050)
1	6,000	18,000	12,000	0.862	10,344
2	5,000	15,000	10,000	0.743	7,430
3	3,000	15,000	12,000	0.641	7,692
				NPV of difference	416

The **NPV of the difference**, not surprisingly, **is also the difference between the NPV of option A ($610) and the NPV of option B ($1,026).**

The **IRR of the differential cash flows** (workings not shown) **is approximately 18%.**

It must be stressed that the investment represented by (B – A) is a notional one, but the inflows from this notional project would be enjoyed by the company if project B were accepted and would be lost if project A were accepted.

Mutually exclusive investments do not have to be considered over equal time periods. For example, suppose an organisation has two investment options, one lasting two years and one lasting four years. The two options can be compared and the one with the highest NPV chosen. If, however, the investment is an asset which is required for four years, the organisation will have to re-invest if it chooses the two-year option. In such circumstances the investment options should be compared over a similar period of time. We will be looking at how to do this in the next chapter.

3.5 Reinvestment assumption

An assumption underlying the NPV method is that any net cash inflows generated during the life of the project will be reinvested elsewhere at the cost of capital (that is, the discount rate). The IRR method, on the other hand, assumes these cash flows can be reinvested elsewhere to earn a return equal to the IRR of the original project. In the example in Paragraph 3.4, the NPV method assumes that the cash inflows of $6,000, $5,000 and $3,000 for option A will be reinvested at the cost of capital of 16% whereas the IRR method assumes they will be reinvested at 20%. If the IRR is considerably higher than the cost of capital this is an unlikely assumption. In theory, a firm will have accepted all projects which provide a return in excess of the cost of capital and any other funds which become available can only be reinvested at the cost of capital. (This is the assumption implied in the NPV rule.) If the assumption is not valid the IRR method overestimates the real return.

3.6 Modified internal rate of return (MIRR)

The MIRR **overcomes the problem of the reinvestment assumption** and the fact that **changes in the cost of capital over the life of the project cannot be incorporated in the IRR method.**

Consider a project requiring an initial investment of $8,000, with cash inflows of $5,000 in years 1 and 2 and cash inflows of $900 in years 3 and 4. The cost of capital is 10%.

The table below shows the **values of the inflows if they were immediately reinvested at 10%.** For example the $5,000 received at the end of year 1 could be reinvested for three years at 10% pa (multiply by $1.1 \times 1.1 \times 1.1 = 1.331$).

Year	Cash inflows $	Interest rate multiplier	Amount when reinvested $
1	5,000	1.331	6,655
2	5,000	1.21	6,050
3	900	1.1	990
4	900	1.0	900
			14,595

The **total cash outflow in year 0 ($8,000)** is **compared with the possible inflow at year 4**, and the **resulting figure** of $8,000/$14,595 = 0.548 is the **discount factor in year 4**. By **looking along the year 4 row** in present value tables you will see that this gives a **return of about 16%**. This means that the $14,595 received in year 4 is equivalent to $8,000 if the discount rate is 16%.

Despite its ability to overcome the reinvestment assumption problem associated with the traditional IRR method, the MIRR is a **fairly recent development** and it is not yet clear whether it will become widely used in practice.

4 Discounted payback

FAST FORWARD

Payback can be combined with DCF and a **discounted payback period** calculated.

Key term

The **discounted payback period (DPP)** is the time it will take before a project's cumulative NPV turns from being negative to being positive.

Exam focus point

A short three-mark question appeared in the May 2006 exam requiring a simple calculation of a discounted payback period.

For example if we have a cost of capital of 10% and a project with the cash flows shown below, we can calculate a discounted payback period.

Year	Cash flow	Discount factor	Present value	Cumulative NPV
	$	10%	$	$
0	(100,000)	1.000	(100,000)	(100,000)
1	30,000	0.909	27,270	(72,730)
2	50,000	0.826	41,300	(31,430)
3	40,000	0.751	30,040	(1,390)
4	30,000	0.683	20,490	19,100
5	20,000	0.621	12,420	31,520
			NPV = 31,520	

The DPP is early in year 4.

A company can set a target DPP, and choose not to undertake any projects with a DPP in excess of a certain number of years, say five years.

4.1 Advantages and disadvantages of discounted payback period

The approach has **all the perceived advantages of the payback period** method of investment appraisal: it is easy to understand and calculate, and it provides a focus on liquidity where this is relevant. In addition, however, it **also takes into account the time value of money**. It therefore bridges the gap between the theoretically superior NPV method and the regular payback period method.

However, it does differ to NPV in that the discount rate used is the **unadjusted cost of capital** whereas NPV often uses an **adjusted rate to reflect project risk and uncertainty**.

Because the DPP approach takes the time value of money into consideration, it **produces a longer payback period** than the non-discounted payback approach, and **takes into account more of the project's cash flows**.

Another advantage it has over traditional payback is that it has a **clear accept-or-reject criterion**. Using payback, acceptance of a project depends on an arbitrarily determined cut-off time. Using DPP, a project is acceptable if it pays back within its lifetime.

DPP still shares one disadvantage with the payback period method: **cashflows which occur after the payback period are ignored** (although as the DPP is longer than the payback period, fewer of these are ignored).

4.2 Discounted payback index (DPBI) or profitability index

This is a measure of the number of times a project recovers the initial funds invested, something that is particularly important if funds are scarce.

$$DPBI = \frac{\text{Present value of net cash inflows}}{\text{Initial cash outlay}}$$

The higher the figure, the greater the returns. A DPBI less than 1 indicates that the present value of the net cash inflows is less than the initial cash outlay.

Alternatively the index might be shown as:

$$\frac{\text{NPV of project}}{\text{Initial outlay}}$$

This form of the index is known as the **profitability index** and shows the NPV per $1 invested in a project. As we will see in a later chapter, it is particularly useful if investment funds are limited and choices have to be made between different investment options.

4.3 NPV profile

It has been suggested that instead of just relying on the NPV as an absolute figure, a **wider profile** of the capital investment should be provided. This profile should include not only the **NPV**, but **DPB**, **DPBI** and a **marginal growth rate (MGR).** (The MGR is a measure of the project's rate of net profitability.) This enables management to take into consideration any liquidity restrictions that an organisation may have and allows them to be more flexible in their general approach to capital investment appraisal as they can place different emphasis on different parts of the profile to suit particular situations.

5 DCF: additional points

> One of the principal advantages of the DCF appraisal method is that it takes account of the **time value of money**.

5.1 The time value of money

DCF is a project appraisal technique that is based on the concept of the time value of money, that $1 earned or spent sooner is worth more than $1 earned or spent later. Various reasons could be suggested as to **why a present $1 is worth more than a future $1**.

(a) **Uncertainty.** The business world is full of risk and uncertainty, and although there might be the promise of money to come in the future, it can never be certain that the money will be received until it has actually been paid. This is an important argument, and risk and uncertainty must always be considered in investment appraisal. But this argument does not explain why the discounted cash flow technique should be used to reflect the time value of money.

(b) **Inflation.** Because of inflation it is common sense that $1 now is worth more than $1 in the future. It is important, however, that the problem of inflation should not confuse the meaning of DCF, and the following points should be noted.

    (i) If there were no inflation at all, discounted cash flow techniques would still be used for investment appraisal.

    (ii) Inflation, for the moment, has been completely ignored.

    (iii) It is obviously necessary to allow for inflation.

(c) **An individual attaches more weight to current pleasures than to future ones, and would rather have $1 to spend now than $1 in a year's time**. Individuals have the choice of consuming or investing their wealth and so the return from projects must be sufficient to persuade individuals to prefer to invest now. Discounting is a measure of this time preference.

(d)   Money is invested now to make profits (more money or wealth) in the future. **Discounted cash flow techniques** can therefore be used to **measure** either of two things.

   (i)   **What alternative uses of the money would earn (NPV method)** (assuming that money can be invested elsewhere at the cost of capital)

   (ii)   **What the money is expected to earn (IRR method)**

5.2 Advantages of DCF methods of appraisal

Taking account of the time value of money (by discounting) is one of the principal advantages of the DCF appraisal method. Other advantages include:

(a)   The method uses all cash flows relating to the project.
(b)   It allows for the timing of the cash flows.
(c)   There are universally accepted methods of calculating the NPV and IRR.

5.3 A comparison of the ARR and NPV methods

Managers are often judged on the return on investment (ROI) of their division or business unit. They will only want to **invest in projects that increase divisional ROI** but on occasion such a strategy **may not correspond** with the **decision** that would be arrived at if **NPV** were used to appraise the investment.

For example, suppose that Division M is considering an investment of $200,000 which will provide a net cash inflow (before depreciation) of $78,000 each year for the four years of its life. It is group policy that investments must show a minimum return of 15%.

As the working below shows, using net book value at the start of each year and depreciating on a straight line basis to a nil residual value, in year 1 the ROI would be below the target rate of return of 15%. If management were to take a **short-term view** of the situation, the **investment would be rejected if** the **ROI** measure were to be **used**, despite the fact that the investment's **NPV is positive** and that in **years 2 to 4** the **ROI** is **greater** than the **target** rate of return.

	Years			
	1	*2*	*3*	*4*
	$	$	$	$
NBV of investment at start of year	200,000	150,000	100,000	50,000
Cash flow (before depreciation)	78,000	78,000	78,000	78,000
Less depreciation	(50,000)	(50,000)	(50,000)	(50,000)
Net profit	28,000	28,000	28,000	28,000
ROI	14.00%	18.67%	28.00%	56.00%

Net present value = –$200,000 + ($78,000 × 2.855) = $22,690.

5.4 Future cash flows: relevant costs

The principles of relevant cash flow analysis covered in Chapter 2 can also be applied to long-term projects.

The **cash flows to be considered** in investment appraisal are those which arise as a consequence of the investment decision under evaluation. When comparing two decision options, they are the expected future cash flows that differ between the alternatives.

It therefore follows that any costs incurred in the past, or any committed costs which will be incurred regardless of whether or not an investment is undertaken, are not relevant cash flows. They have occurred, or will occur, whatever investment decision is taken.

To a management accountant, it might be apparent that the annual profits from a project can be calculated as the incremental contribution earned minus any incremental fixed costs which are cash items of expenditure (that is, ignoring depreciation and so on).

There are, however, other cash flows to consider. These might include the following.

(a) The extra **taxation** that will be payable on extra profits, or the reductions in tax arising from capital allowances or operating losses in any year. We cover this topic in a later chapter.

(b) The **residual value or disposal value of equipment at the end of its life, or its disposal cost**.

(c) **Working capital**. If a company invests $20,000 in working capital and earns cash profits of $50,000, the net cash receipts will be $30,000. Working capital will be released again at the end of a project's life, and so there will be a cash inflow arising out of the eventual realisation into cash of the project's inventory and receivables in the final year of the project.

Finance-related cash flows, on the other hand, are normally **excluded** from DCF project appraisal exercises because the discounting process takes account of the time value of money, that is the opportunity cost of investing the money in the project. The cash inflow from, say, a loan could be included but then the cash outflows of the interest payments and the loan repayment would also have to be included. These flows would all be discounted at the cost of capital (which we assume is the same as the cost of the loan) and they would reduce to a zero net present value. They would therefore have had no effect on the NPV and are thus deemed irrelevant to the appraisal.

Finance-related cash flows are **only relevant if they incur a different rate of interest from that which is being used as the discount rate**. For example, a company may be offered a loan at a preferential rate below that which it uses for its discount rate and so the inclusion and discounting of the loan's cash flows produces a differential NPV.

5.5 The discount rate

Throughout our study of DCF techniques we have been using the same discount rate across all years of the project under consideration, on the assumption that the cost of capital will remain the same over the life of the project. There are a range of factors that influence the cost of capital, however, including inflation and interest rates, and these can fluctuate widely over fairly short periods of time. An organisation may therefore wish to **use different discount rates at different points over the life of a project** to reflect this. This is **possible if NPV and discounted payback methods of appraisal are being used**, but IRR and ARR methods are based on a single rate.

Another problem is **deciding on the correct rate in the first place**. This is difficult enough in year one of a project's life, but even more problematic five years later, say, because of economic changes and so on.

xam focus
ɔint

So far in the last two sittings and the pilot paper there have been five Section A questions, four Section B questions and three Section C questions examining aspects of DCF investment appraisal.

Particularly in Section B and C, this will not be straightforward and you will need to consider risk, inflation, tax and other 'twists' such as sensitivity analysis.

Nonetheless, if you know the basic techniques you are already on the way to answering the question well.

5.6 Further reading

You are probably aware of the regular articles included in Financial Management. In March 2006, an article appeared on decision making techniques which it is worth reading as this covers both decision techniques and their application in long-term projects.

Chapter Roundup

- **Discounting** starts with a future value (a sum of money receivable or payable at a future date), and converts the future value to a **present value**, which is the cash equivalent now of the future value.

- The **discounting formula** to calculate the present value (X) of a future sum of money (V) at the end of n time periods is $X = V/(1 + r)^n$.

- The **NPV method of project appraisal** is to accept projects with a positive NPV.

- An **annuity** is a constant cash flow for a number of years.

- A **perpetuity** is a constant cash flow forever.

- The **IRR method of project appraisal** is to accept projects which have an IRR (the rate at which the NPV is zero) that exceeds a target rate of return. The IRR can be estimated either from a graph or using interpolation.

- The **IRR interpolation formula** is:

$$IRR = A + \left[\frac{P}{P + N} \times (B - A) \right] \%$$

  where   A is the (lower) rate of return with a positive NPV
             B is the (higher) rate of return with a negative NPV
             P is the amount of the positive NPV
             N is the absolute value of the negative NPV

  Where both NPVs are positive, use a modified version of the formula:

$$IRR = A + \left[\frac{P}{P - N} \times (B - A) \right] \%$$

- When compared with the NPV method, the **IRR method** has a number of **disadvantages**.

  - It ignores the relative size of investments.

  - There are problems with its use when a project has non-conventional cashflows or when deciding between mutually exclusive projects.

  - Discount rates which differ over the life of a project cannot be incorporated into IRR calculations.

- Payback can be combined with DCF and a **discounted payback period** calculated.

- One of the principal advantages of the DCF appraisal method is that it takes account of the **time value of money**.

- The **cash flows to be considered** in investment appraisal are those which arise as a consequence of the investment decision under evaluation. When comparing two decision options, they are the expected future cash flows that differ between the alternatives.

Quick Quiz

1   In a discounted cash flow exercise, what is the discount factor (to 3 decimal places) for year 4 when the cost of capital is 11.5%?

    A 0.647   B 0.115   C 3.587   D 1.546   E 0.721

2   What is the present value of a cash inflow of $3,000 each year from years 1 – 5, when the required return on investment is 12%?

    A $15,000   B $16,800   C $13,393   D $9,111   E $10,815

3   With a cost of capital of 13%, what is the present value of $2,500 received every year in perpetuity?

    A $2,825   B $17,563   C $2,212   D $28,736   E None of these options

4   For a certain project, the net present value at a discount rate of 15% is $3,670, and at a rate of 18% the net present value is negative at ($1,390). What is the internal rate of return of the project?

    A 15.7%   B 16.5%   C 16.6%   D 17.2%   E None of these options

5   *Tick the correct box to indicate whether or not the following items are included in the cash flows when determining the net present value of a project.*

                                              Included   *Not included*

    (a)   The disposal value of equipment at the end of its life

    (b)   Depreciation charges for the equipment

    (c)   Research costs incurred prior to the appraisal

    (d)   Interest payments on the loan to finance the investment

6   *At what point on the graph below is the project's IRR?*

    A   Point A   B   Point B   C   Point C   D   Point D

7   *Choose the correct word from those highlighted.*

When there are non-conventional cashflow patterns, the **IRR/NPV** method is not recommended.

8   *Fill in the blanks.*

$$DPBI = \frac{\cdots\cdots\cdots\cdots\cdots\cdots\cdots}{\cdots\cdots\cdots\cdots\cdots\cdots\cdots}$$

9   *Fill in the blank in the sentence below.*

The present value of $1,000 in contribution earned each year from years 1–10, when the required return on investment is 11%, is $............... .

Answers to Quick Quiz

1   A $1/(1 + 0.115)^4 = 0.647$

2   E $\$3,000 \times 3.605 = \$10,815$

3   E $\$2,500/0.13 = \$19,231$

4   D $15\% + \{(3,670/[3,670 + 1,390]) \times 3\%\} = 17.2\%$

5   (a)   Included

    (b)   Not included (non-cash)

    (c)   Not included (past cost)

    (d)   Not usually included, unless the loan incurs a different rate of interest from that which is being used as the discount rate

6   B. The IRR is the rate (cost of capital) at which the NPV is zero.

7   IRR

8    $DPBI = \dfrac{\text{Sum of net discounted cash inflows}}{\text{Initial cash outlay}}$

9   The PV of $1,000 earned each year from year 1–10 when the required earning rate of money is 11% is calculated as follows.

    $\$1,000 \times 5.889 = \$5,889$

Now try the questions below from the Exam Question Bank

Number	Level	Marks	Time
Q16	Examination	10	18 mins
Q17	Examination	10	18 mins

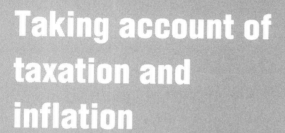

Taking account of taxation and inflation

Introduction

So far, in considering how to appraise projects, we have ignored inflation and taxation, but in this chapter we look at how to **incorporate their effects into investment appraisal**.

It is complexities such as sensitivity analysis (covered in Chapter 13), inflation and taxation which are likely to be included in Paper 2 investment appraisal questions and have appeared in most sittings to date. You are unlikely to get a straightforward NPV calculation at this stage of your studies.

Topic list	Learning outcomes	Syllabus references	Ability required
1 Allowing for inflation	B(iii)	B(2)	Application
2 Allowing for taxation	B(iii)	B(2)	Application

1 Allowing for inflation

Inflation is a feature of all economies, and it must be accommodated in investment appraisal.

As the **inflation rate increases so will the minimum return required by an investor**. For example, you might be happy with a return of 5% in an inflation-free world, but if inflation was running at 15% you would expect a considerably greater yield.

1.1 Example: inflation (1)

An organisation is considering investing in a project with the following cash flows.

Time	Actual cash flows
	$
0	(15,000)
1	9,000
2	8,000
3	7,000

The organisation requires a minimum return of 20% under the present and anticipated conditions. Inflation is currently running at 10% a year, and this rate of inflation is expected to continue indefinitely. Should the organisation go ahead with the project?

Let us first look at the organisation's required rate of return. Suppose that it invested $1,000 for one year on 1 January, then on 31 December it would require a minimum return of $200. With the initial investment of $1,000, the total value of the investment by 31 December must therefore increase to $1,200. During the course of the year the purchasing value of the pound would fall due to inflation. We can restate the **amount received on 31 December in terms of the purchasing power of the pound at 1 January** as follows.

Amount received on 31 December in terms of the value of the pound at 1 January = $\dfrac{£1,200}{(1.10)^1}$ = $1,091

In terms of the value of the pound at 1 January, the organisation would make a profit of $91 which represents a rate of return of 9.1% in **'today's money' terms**. This is known as the **real rate of return**. The required rate of 20% is a **money rate of return** (sometimes called a **nominal rate of return**).

(a) The **money rate** measures the **return in terms of the pound** which is, of course, **falling in value**.

(b) The **real rate** measures the return in **constant price level** terms.

The two rates of return and the inflation rate are linked by an equation.

(1+ money rate of return) = (1 + real rate of return) × (1 + rate of inflation)

Formula to learn

(1 + money rate) = (1 + real rate) × (1 + inflation rate)

where all the rates are expressed as proportions.

In our example, (1 + 0.20) = (1 + 0.091) × (1 + 0.10) = 1.20

Money cash flows should be discounted at a money discount rate.

Real cash flows (ie adjusted for inflation) should be discounted at a real discount rate.

We must decide **which rate** to use for discounting, the **money rate** or the **real rate**. The rule is as follows.

(a)   If the cash flows are expressed in terms of the **actual number of pounds** that will be received or paid on the various future dates, we **use the money rate for discounting**.

(b)   If the cash flows are expressed in terms of the **value of the pound at time 0 (that is, in constant price level terms), we use the real rate**.

The **cash flows** given in Section 1.1 are expressed **in terms of the actual number of pounds** that will be received or paid at the relevant dates. We should, therefore, **discount** them using the **money rate of return**.

Time	Cash flow $	Discount factor 20%	PV $
0	(15,000)	1.000	(15,000)
1	9,000	0.833	7,497
2	8,000	0.694	5,552
3	7,000	0.579	4,053
			2,102

The project has a positive net present value of $2,102.

The future **cash flows** can be **re-expressed** in terms of the **value of the pound at time 0** as follows, given inflation at 10% a year.

Time	Actual cash flow $	Cash flow at time 0 price level		$
0	(15,000)			(15,000)
1	9,000	$9,000 \times \dfrac{1}{1.10}$	=	8,182
2	8,000	$8,000 \times \dfrac{1}{(1.10)^2}$	=	6,612
3	7,000	$7,000 \times \dfrac{1}{(1.10)^3}$	=	5,259

The cash flows expressed in terms of the value of the pound at time 0 can now be **discounted using the real rate** of 9.1%.

Time	Cash flow $	Discount factor 9.1%	PV $
0	(15,000)	1.00	(15,000)
1	8,182	$\dfrac{1}{1.091}$	7,500
2	6,612	$\dfrac{1}{(1.091)^2}$	5,555
3	5,259	$\dfrac{1}{(1.091)^3}$	4,050
		NPV	2,105

The NPV is the same as before (and the present value of the cash flow in each year is the same as before) apart from rounding errors with a net total of $3.

1.2 The advantages and misuses of real values and a real rate of return

Although it is recommended that **companies should discount money values at the money cost of capital**, there are some advantages of using real values discounted at a real cost of capital.

(a)   **When all costs and benefits rise at the same rate of price inflation, real values are the same as current day values**, so that no further adjustments need be made to cash flows before discounting. In contrast, when money values are discounted at the money cost of capital, the prices in future years must be calculated before discounting can begin.

(b)   The government or nationalised industries might prefer to set a real return as a target for investments, as being more suitable to their particular situation than a commercial money rate of return.

1.3 Costs and benefits which inflate at different rates

Not all costs and benefits will rise in line with the general level of inflation. In such cases, we can **apply the money rate** to inflated values to determine a project's NPV.

1.3.1 Example: inflation (2)

RR is considering a project which would cost $5,000 now. The annual benefits, for four years, would be a fixed income of $2,500 a year, plus other savings of $500 a year in year 1, rising by 5% each year because of inflation. Running costs will be $1,000 in the first year, but would increase at 10% each year because of inflating labour costs. The general rate of inflation is expected to be 7½% and the organisation's required money rate of return is 16%. Is the project worthwhile? Ignore taxation.

Solution

The cash flows at inflated values are as follows.

Year	Fixed income	Other savings	Running costs	Net cash flow
	$	$	$	$
1	2,500	500	1,000	2,000
2	2,500	525	1,100	1,925
3	2,500	551	1,210	1,841
4	2,500	579	1,331	1,748

The NPV of the project is as follows.

Year	Cash flow	Discount factor	PV
	$	16%	$
0	(5,000)	1.000	(5,000)
1	2,000	0.862	1,724
2	1,925	0.743	1,430
3	1,841	0.641	1,180
4	1,748	0.552	965
			+ 299

The NPV is positive and the project would seem therefore to be worthwhile.

Question

Investment appraisal and inflation

Learning outcome: B(iii)

An investment requires an immediate cash outflow of $120,000. It will have zero residual value at the end of four years. The annual cost inflow will be $40,000. The cost of capital is 10% and the annual inflation rate is 3%.

What is the maximum monetary cost of capital for this project to remain viable (to the nearest %)?

A   16%
B   13%
C   10%
D   7%

Answer

The correct answer is A.

The rate required is the IRR (the rate at which the project breaks even).

Let the rate = r

∴ $120,000 = PV of $40,000 for years 1 to 4 at rate r

∴ $120,000 = (cumulate PV factor for years 1 to 4 at rate r) × $40,000

∴ $120,000/$40,000 = cumulative PV factor for years 1 to 4 at rate r

∴ 3.000 = cumulative PV factor for years 1 to 4 at rate r

In cumulative PV tables this corresponds to a rate of approximately 12.5% over 4 years.

∴ The real cost of capital to give an NPV of zero = 12.5%

Substituting in the formula, with X = monetary cost of capital:

$$\frac{(1+X)}{1.03} - 1 = 0.125$$

∴ X = 15.875%

Option B is the real cost of capital. **Option C** is the current cost of capital. **Option D** is the difference between the current cost of capital and the rate of inflation.

**am focus
Int**

A ten mark question in the November 2005 paper required candidates to inflate cash flows and discount back to NPV. This technique and how it was tackled is detailed in the following chapter in Section 1 as the lowest common multiple method.

2 Allowing for taxation

ST FORWARD

Taxation is a major practical consideration for businesses. It is vital to take it into account in making decisions.

Payments of tax, or reductions in the capital of tax that has to be paid, are **relevant cash flows** and so the amounts connected with a project ought to be included in the DCF appraisal.

2.1 Introduction to the calculation of taxation in capital projects

The calculation of taxation in relation to capital projects may seem daunting at first. However, there is a method using simple steps which you could follow. This breaks the calculation down into manageable elements. The method is also summarised at the end of the chapter as an aide memoire.

(a)   Calculate the **total** cost of any new asset.

(b)   Calculate WDA for each year and multiply by the tax rate to give the tax saving.

(c)   Half of tax saving is a benefit in the year in question, half in the following year.

(d)   Calculate a balancing allowance or charge on the sale of the asset

     (i)   If sales price > reducing balance ⇒ balancing charge (increases taxable profit)
     (ii)   If sales price < reducing balance ⇒ balancing allowance (reduces taxable profit)

(e)   Effect of the balancing charge / allowance (which is calculated as amount × tax rate) is felt half in year in which the asset is sold and half in the following year.

(f)   Include in the appraisal: tax on WDAs and balancing allowance/charge, net cash inflows due to project (ie taxable profits) and tax on these net cash inflows.

2.2 Corporation tax

FAST FORWARD

Under the UK system, corporation tax is **payable** by large companies **quarterly**.

- In the **seventh and tenth months** of the year in which the profit is earned
- In the **first and fourth months** of the following year

This simply means that **half the tax is payable in the year in which the profits are earned** and **half in the following year.**

2.2.1 Example: payment of corporation tax

If a project increases taxable profits by $10,000 in year 2, there will be tax payments of $10,000 × 30% × 50% = $1,500 in both year 2 and in year 3 (assuming a tax rate of 30%). It is these tax payments (that are a direct result of the project) that need to be included in a DCF analysis.

Attention!

Note that **net cash flows from a project** should be considered as the **taxable profits** arising from the project (unless an indication is given to the contrary).

2.3 Capital allowances/writing down allowances (WDAs)

FAST FORWARD

Capital allowances/WDAs reduce taxable profits and hence tax payable.

Just as depreciation is a way of charging the cost of plant and machinery against financial accounting profits over a number of periods (thereby reducing profits), WDAs or capital allowances are a way of charging the cost of plant and machinery against taxable profits over a number of periods, thereby **reducing taxable profits and hence the tax payable.**

The **reduction in tax payable** (to be included in the DCF analysis) = **amount of WDA × tax rate.**

As half the tax on profit is paid in the year to which the profits relate, and half in the following year, the **benefit of the WDA** is also felt **half in the year to which it relates** and **half in the following year.**

Attention!

The rate at which the allowance is given will always be provided in the question, although it is more than likely to be 25% on a reducing balance basis.

2.3.1 Example: WDAs

Suppose an organisation purchases plant costing $80,000. The rate of corporation tax is 30% and WDAs are given on a 25% reducing balance basis. Here are the WDAs and reductions in tax payable for years 1 to 4.

	Reducing balance	Tax saved	Benefit received			
			Yr 1	Yr 2	Yr 3	Yr 4
	$	$	$	$	$	$
Purchase price	80,000					
Yr 1 WDA (25%)	(20,000)	6,000	3,000	3,000		
Value at start year 2	60,000					
Yr 2 WDA (25%)	(15,000)	4,500		2,250	2,250	
Value at start year 3	45,000					
Yr 3 WDA (25%)	(11,250)	3,375			1,687	1,688
Value at start year 4	33,750					
Yr 4 WDA (25%)	(8,438)	2,531				1,266
Value at start year 5	25,312					

Points to note

(a) The tax saved is 30% of the WDA.

(b) Half of the tax saved is a benefit in the year in question, half in the following year.

> You should always make the following assumptions unless told otherwise.
>
> - The organisation in question generates enough profit from other projects to absorb any tax benefits in the year to which they relate.
>
> - Assume the organisation has elected to use **'short life' asset treatment**. This means that the asset is kept separate from the general pool of the organisation's assets provided it is sold within five years of purchase.

You also need to be sure that you **start off with the correct balance** on which to calculate the capital allowances. For example, in addition to the original capital costs of a machine, it may be possible to claim capital allowances on the costs of installation, such as the labour and overhead costs of removing an old machine, levelling the area for the new machine and/or altering part of a building to accommodate the new machine. Remember to **state** your **assumptions** concerning this type of item.

> Assumptions about capital allowances could be simplified in an exam question. For example, you might be told that capital allowances can be claimed at the rate of 25% of cost on a straight line basis (that is, over four years), or a question might refer to 'tax allowable depreciation', so that the capital allowances equal the depreciation charge.

2.4 Balancing allowances and balancing charges

Suppose an organisation sells an item of plant in year 3 at a price which differs from the reducing balance amount **before year 3 WDAs** are included.

(a) If the **selling price is greater than the reducing balance amount**, the difference between the two is treated as a **taxable profit (balancing charge)**.

(b) If the **selling price is less than the reducing balance amount**, the difference between the two is treated as a **reduction in tax payable (balancing allowance)**.

'Short-life' asset treatment means any balancing allowance/charge should be dealt with in the year of sale.

2.4.1 Example: balancing allowances/charges

If, in the example above, the plant is sold during year 4 for $20,000, there will be a balancing allowance of $(33,750 – 20,000) = $13,750, being the difference between the reducing balance amount at the end of year 3 / beginning of year 4 and the selling price.

This allowance results in a reduction in tax paid of $13,750 × 30% = $4,125, the benefits of which are received in years 4 and 5.

Here is the full calculation.

	Reducing balance $	Tax saved $	Yr 1 $	Yr 2 $	Yr 3 $	Yr 4 $	Yr 5 $
					Benefits received		
Purchase price	80,000						
Yr 1 WDA (25%)	(20,000)	6,000	3,000	3,000			
	60,000						
Yr 2 WDA (25%)	(15,000)	4,500		2,250	2,250		
	45,000						
Yr 3 WDA (25%)	(11,250)	3,375			1,687	1,688	
	33,750						
Yr 4 sales price	20,000						
Balancing allowance	13,750	4,125				2,062	2,063

If the asset had been sold for $40,000, however, there would be a **balancing charge** of $(40,000 – 33,750) = $6,250, being the difference between the reducing balance amount at the end of year 3 / beginning of year 4 and the selling price.

This charge has to be included in year 4 taxable profits, resulting in an **increase in tax paid** of $6,250 × 30% = $1,875, which must be paid half in year 4 and half in year 5.

Let's now look at how to integrate all of this into a DCF appraisal.

2.5 Example: taxation

An organisation is considering whether or not to purchase an item of machinery costing $40,000. It would have a life of four years, after which it would be sold for $5,000. The machinery would create annual cost savings of $14,000.

The machinery would attract writing down allowances of 25% on the reducing balance basis. A balancing allowance or charge would arise on disposal. The rate of corporation tax is 30%. Tax is payable quarterly in the seventh and tenth months of the year in which the profit is earned and in the first and fourth months of the following year. The after-tax cost of capital is 8%.

Should the machinery be purchased?

Solution

Step 1

WDAs and balancing charges/allowances

We begin by calculating the WDAs and balancing charge / allowance.

Year		Reducing balance $
0	Purchase	40,000
1	WDA	10,000
	Value at start of year 2	30,000
2	WDA	7,500
	Value at start of year 3	22,500
3	WDA	5,625
	Value at start of year 4	16,875
4	Sale	5,000
	Balancing allowance	11,875

Step 2

Calculate tax savings/payments

Having calculated the allowances each year, the **tax savings** can be computed. The tax savings affect two years, the year for which the allowance is claimed and the following year.

Year of claim	Allowance $	Tax saved $	Tax saving				
			Yr 1 $	Yr 2 $	Yr 3 $	Yr 4 $	Yr 5 $
1	10,000	3,000	1,500	1,500			
2	7,500	2,250		1,125	1,125		
3	5,625	1,688			844	844	
4	11,875	3,562	–	–	–	1,781	1,781
	35,000 *		1,500	2,625	1,969	2,625	1,781

* Net cost $(40,000 – 5,000) = $35,000

These tax savings relate to capital allowances. We must also take the **tax effects of the annual savings** of $14,000 into account.

The savings increase taxable profit (costs are lower) and so extra tax must be paid. Each saving of $14,000 will lead to extra tax of $14,000 × 30% × 50% = $2,100 in the year in question and the same amount in the following year.

Step 3

Calculate NPV

The **net cash flows and the NPV** are now calculated as follows.

Year	Equipment $	Savings $	Tax on savings $	Tax saved on capital allowances $	Net cash flow $	Discount factor 8%	Present value of cash flow $
0	(40,000)				(40,000)	1.000	(40,000)
1		14,000	(2,100)	1,500	13,400	0.926	12,408
2		14,000	(4,200)	2,625	12,425	0.857	10,648
3		14,000	(4,200)	1,969	11,769	0.794	9,345
4	5,000	14,000	(4,200)	2,625	17,425	0.735	12,807
5			(2,100)	1,781	(319)	0.681	(217)
							4,991

The NPV is positive and so the purchase appears to be worthwhile.

2.6 An alternative and quicker method of calculating tax payments or savings

In the above example, the tax computations could have been combined, as follows.

Year	1	2	3	4	5
	$	$	$	$	$
Cost savings	14,000	14,000	14,000	14,000	
Capital allowance	10,000	7,500	5,625	11,875	
Taxable profits	4,000	6,500	8,375	2,125	
Tax (paid)/received at 30%	(1,200)	(1,950)	(2,512)	(638)	
Yr of (payment)/saving	(600)	(600)			
		(975)	(975)		
			(1,256)	(1,256)	
				(319)	(319)
(Payment)/saving	(600)	(1,575)	(2,231)	(1,575)	(319)

The net cash flows would then be as follows.

Year	Equipment	Savings	Tax	Net cash flow
	$	$	$	$
0	(40,000)			(40,000)
1		14,000	(600)	13,400
2		14,000	(1,575)	12,425
3		14,000	(2,231)	11,769
4	5,000	14,000	(1,575)	17,425
5			(319)	(319)

The net cash flows are exactly the same as calculated previously in Step 3 above.

2.7 Taxation and DCF

FAST FORWARD

If **taxation is ignored** in the project cash flows, the discount rate should be the **pre-tax** cost of capital. When **taxation is included** in the cash flows, the **after tax** cost of capital should be used.

The effect of taxation on capital budgeting is theoretically quite simple. Organisations must pay tax, and the effect of undertaking a project will be to increase or decrease tax payments each year. These **incremental tax cash flows should be included in the cash flows** of the project for discounting to arrive at the project's NPV.

When **taxation is ignored** in the DCF calculations, the **discount rate** will reflect the **pre-tax rate of return** required on capital investments. When **taxation is included** in the cash flows, a **post-tax required rate** of return should be used.

Question

Taxation

Learning outcome: B(iii)

An organisation is considering the purchase of an item of equipment, which would earn profits before tax of $25,000 a year. Depreciation charges would be $20,000 a year for six years. Capital allowances would be $30,000 a year for the first four years. Corporation tax is at 30%.

Assume that tax payments occur half in the same year as the profits giving rise to them, half in the following year, and there is no balancing charge or allowance when the machine is scrapped at the end of the sixth year.

Required

Fill in the blanks below.

The net cash inflows of the project after tax in the first six years are:

Year 1 ....

Year 2 ....

Year 3 ....

Year 4 ....

Year 5 ....

Year 6 ....

Answer

The correct answer is:

Year 1 $42,750

Year 2 $40,500

Year 3 $40,500

Year 4 $40,500

Year 5 $36,000

Year 6 $31,500

(a)

	Years 1–4	Years 5–6
	$	$
Profit before tax	25,000	25,000
Add back depreciation	20,000	20,000
Net cash inflow before tax	45,000	45,000
Less capital allowance	30,000	0
	15,000	45,000
Tax at 30%	4,500	13,500

	Yr 1	Yr 2	Yr 3	Yr 4	Yr 5	Yr 6	Yr 7
	$	$	$	$	$	$	$
Tax on yr 1 profit	2,250	2,250					
Tax on yr 2 profit		2,250	2,250				
Tax on yr 3 profit			2,250	2,250			
Tax on yr 4 profit				2,250	2,250		
Tax on yr 5 profit					6,750	6,750	
Tax on yr 6 profit						6,750	6,750
	2,250	4,500	4,500	4,500	9,000	13,500	
Net cash inflow before tax	45,000	45,000	45,000	45,000	45,000	45,000	
Net cash inflow after tax	42,750	40,500	40,500	40,500	36,000	31,500	

Question

Taxation and cash flow

Learning outcome: B(iii)

An organisation is considering the purchase of a machine for $150,000. It would be sold after four years for an estimated realisable value of $50,000. By this time capital allowances of $120,000 would have been claimed. The rate of corporation tax is 30%.

The cash flow arising as a result of the tax implications of the sale of the machine at the end of the four years is

A $6,000 inflow
B $6,000 outflow
C $15,000 outflow
D $20,000 outflow

Answer

The correct answer is B.

There will be a balancing charge on the sale of the machine of $(50,000 – (150,000 – 120,000)) = $20,000. This will give rise to a tax payment of 30% × $20,000 = $6,000.

If you chose A you got the calculations correct but the direction of the cash flow was wrong.

Option C is 30% taxation on the estimated sales value. The revenue from the actual sale is not taxed directly, but any remaining balancing charge will be taxable.

If you chose option D you forgot to calculate the 30% corporation tax on the balancing charge of $20,000.

2.8 Sensitivity analysis and taxation

FAST FORWARD ▶▶

To carry out **sensitivity analysis** when taxation is relevant, **use after-tax cashflows**.

Exam focus point

Questions in both the pilot paper and the May 2005 paper included sensitivity analysis on variables within a DCF analysis which incorporated taxation. Make sure that you attempt the questions when you come to work through the Practice and Revision Kit for Paper P2 as it is obviously a key examination technique.

Look back at the example in Section 2.5. Suppose you were required to calculate the sensitivity of the project to changes in the annual cost savings.

To do this you have to calculate (as before) (**NPV of project/PV of annual cost savings**) × 100% but both figures must be **after-tax figures**.

We therefore need to calculate the PV of the savings.

Year	Savings	Tax on savings	Net cash flow	Discount factor	Present value
	$	$	$	8%	$
1	14,000	(2,100)	11,900	0.926	11,019
2	14,000	(4,200)	9,800	0.857	8,399
3	14,000	(4,200)	9,800	0.794	7,781
4	14,000	(4,200)	9,800	0.735	7,203
		(2,100)	(2,100)	0.681	(1,430)
					32,972

The overall NPV of the project is $4,991 and so the sensitivity is therefore (4,991/32,972) × 100% = 15.14%.

Don't forget that when carrying out sensitivity analysis we need to **consider the cashflows affected by the variables under consideration**. So if you were asked to examine the **sensitivity of a project to price** you would need to calculate the **post-tax PV of revenue** (as a change in selling price affects revenue and hence revenue is the cashflow affected), whereas **sensitivity to volume** would require the calculation of **post-tax contribution** (as a change in volume affects revenue and variable costs and hence contribution can be used as the cashflow affected).

2.9 Summary

(a) Calculate the **total** cost of any new asset.

(b) Calculate WDA for each year and multiply by the tax rate to give the tax saving. **See example in 2.3.1.**

(c) Half of tax saving is a benefit in the year in question, half in the following year. **See example in 2.3.1.**

(d) Calculate a balancing allowance or charge on the sale of the asset. **See 2.4.1.**

  (i) If sales price > reducing balance $\Rightarrow$ balancing charge (increases taxable profit)
  (ii) If sales price < reducing balance $\Rightarrow$ balancing allowance (reduces taxable profit)

(e) Effect of the balancing charge / allowance (which is calculated as amount $\times$ tax rate) is felt half in year in which the asset is sold and half in the following year. **See 2.4.1**

(f) Include in the appraisal: tax on WDAs and balancing allowance / charge, net cash inflows due to project (ie taxable profits) and tax on these net cash inflows. **See 2.5 and 2.6.**

Question   Tax effects

Learning outcome: B(iii)

Describe the potential major effects of taxation on capital investment decisions.

Answer

Taxation can affect investment decisions in various ways.

(a) The existence of taxation will **reduce the returns** and **mitigate the costs** of projects.

(b) The arrangements for paying tax will determine by how much tax payments are **discounted** in the investment appraisal. It will be significant whether tax is payable in the year profits are earned or in the following year.

(c) Tax is payable on **taxable profits that relate to the investment**, which are not necessarily the same as the **cash flows**. There may be **timing differences between expenditure being accrued** for accounting and tax purposes, and payment being made.

(d) Taxation arrangements are complicated by the availability of **capital allowances**, which allow businesses to write off the costs of non-current assets against taxable profit. Businesses need to consider for what types of asset claims can be made and the **timing** of allowances, as this will again affect by how much allowances are discounted. This may determine when an asset is purchased; it may be advantageous to purchase an asset just before the end of a tax year, and thus claim capital allowances a year earlier than would be the case if the asset was purchased early in the new tax year.

(e) If the effects of taxation are included in the investment appraisal, a **post-tax rate of return** should be used.

**m focus
nt**

Ten-mark questions in the pilot paper, the May 2005 exam and the November 2005 exam were on taxation and DCF, while Section C questions in the pilot paper, the May 2005 exam, the November 2005 exam and the November 2006 exam incorporated taxation and inflation. The ability to incorporate the effects of taxation into DCF analysis is therefore a key exam technique. See if you can reproduce the summary above as a check on whether you have taken in the contents of this section.

Chapter Roundup

- **Inflation** is a feature of all economies, and it must be accommodated in investment appraisal.

- (1+ money rate of return) = (1 + real rate of return) × (1 + rate of inflation)

- **Money cash flows** should be discounted at a money discount rate.

- **Real cash flows** (ie adjusted for inflation) should be discounted at a real discount rate.

- **Taxation** is a major practical consideration for businesses. It is vital to take it into account in making decisions.

- Under the UK system, corporation tax is **payable** by large companies **quarterly**.
  - In the seventh and tenth months of the year in which the profit is earned
  - In the first and fourth months of the following year

- **Capital allowances/WDAs** reduce taxable profits and hence tax payable.

- If **taxation is ignored** in the project cash flows, the discount rate should be the **pre-tax** cost of capital. When **taxation is included** in the cash flows, the **after tax** cost of capital should be used.

- To carry out **sensitivity analysis** when taxation is relevant, **use after-tax cashflows**.

Quick Quiz

1   *Fill in the gaps.*

    The relationship between the money rate of return, the real rate of return and the rate of inflation is (1 + ... rate) = (1 + ... rate) x (1 + ... rate).

2   The money cost of capital is 11%. The expected annual rate of inflation is 5%. What is the real cost of capital?

    A 16.6%   B 6.0%   C 16.0%   D None of these options

3   A company wants a minimum real return of 3% a year on its investments. Inflation is expected to be 8% a year. What is the company's minimum money cost of capital?

    A 4.9%   B 11.24%   C 5%   D 11%

4   A company is appraising an investment that will save electricity costs. Electricity prices are expected to rise at a rate of 15% per annum in future, although the general inflation rate will be 10% per annum. The money cost of capital for the company is 20%. What is the appropriate discount rate to apply to the forecast actual money cash flows for electricity?

    A 20.0%   B 22.0%   C 26.5%   D 32.0%

5   *Choose the correct words from those highlighted.*

    Capital allowances are used to (1) **increase/reduce** taxable profits, and the consequent reduction in a tax payment should be treated as a (2) **cash saving/cash payment** arising from the acceptance of a project.

    Writing down allowances are generally allowed on the cost of (3) **materials and labour/plant and machinery** at the rate of (4) **25%/30%** on a (5) **straight line/reducing balance** basis.

    When the plant is eventually sold, the difference between the sales price and the reducing balance amount will be treated as a (6) **taxable profit/tax allowable loss** if the sales price exceeds the reducing balance, and as a (7) **taxable profit/tax allowable loss** if the reducing balance exceeds the sales price.

BPP
LEARNING MEDIA

The cash saving on the capital allowances (or the cash payment for a charge) is calculated by (8) **multiplying/dividing** the allowances (or charge) by (9) the **reducing balance rate/corporation tax rate**.

6   *Fill in the blanks.*

The sensitivity of a project's NPV to changes in volume can be determined using:

(.........................../.........................) × 100%

Answers to Quick Quiz

1   (1 + money rate) = (1 + real rate) × (1 + inflation rate)

2   D   1.11/1.05 = 1.057. The real cost of capital is 5.7%.

3   B   1.03 × 1.08 = 1.1124. The money cost of capital is 11.24%.

4   A   The money rate of 20% is applied to the money cash flows.

5   (1)   reduce   (4)   25%   (7)   tax allowable loss
     (2)   cash saving   (5)   reducing balance   (8)   multiplying
     (3)   plant and machinery   (6)   taxable profit   (9)   corporation tax rate

6   (Overall project NPV/PV of contribution) × 100%

Now try the question below from the Exam Question Bank

Number	Level	Marks	Time
Q18	Examination	25	45 mins

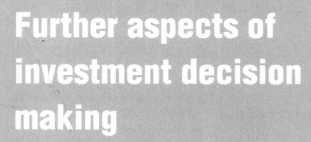

Further aspects of investment decision making

Introduction

This chapter builds on the knowledge gained in Chapter 11 and looks at a number of related project appraisal topics.

In **Section 1** of this chapter we will be looking at **how to choose between mutually exclusive projects with unequal lives**. In the DCF examples we have considered to date, the choice has been between projects with lives of equal length.

In **Section 2** we see how to decide when, and how frequently, an asset should be replaced. This contrasts with the simple 'invest/do not invest' decisions we looked at in Chapter 12. **Section 3** considers decisions about project abandonment.

We have seen that the general rule when appraising projects using DCF techniques is to accept all projects with a positive NPV. In **Section 4** we will be looking at the approach to take if there are **insufficient funds** to accept all such projects.

Because project appraisal involves estimating, and taking into account, future cash flows, projects will always be (to varying degrees) **risky** simply because the future is risky. **Sensitivity analysis** (covered in **Section 5**) is one method of assessing the risk associated with a project.

In **Section 6** we look at probability analysis, which will be explained in detail in Chapter 14, but here we consider long-term decision making only.

In **Section 7** we look at some of the non-financial considerations to incorporate into decision support information for management.

Once again, this is a key chapter. Techniques covered in Sections 1, 2, 4, 5 and 6 have all been examined in recent sittings.

This is the last of the four chapters in this part of the text.

Topic list	Learning outcomes	Syllabus references	Ability required
1 Mutually exclusive projects with unequal lives	B(viii)	B(7)	Evaluation
2 Asset replacement	B(viii)	B(7)	Evaluation
3 Project abandonment	B(vi)	B(4)	Evaluation
4 Capital rationing	A(vii),(viii),B(viii)	A(8),B(7)	Application/Analysis/ Evaluation
5 Sensitivity analysis	B(ix),C(i),(ii)	B(6),C(2)	Evaluation/Application
6 Probability analysis and long-term decisions	C(iii), (iv)	C(3), (4), (5)	Application/ Analysis
7 Non-financial considerations in long-term decisions	B(x)	B(1)	Analysis

1 Mutually exclusive projects with unequal lives

All of the discounted cash flow examples that we have seen so far have involved a choice between projects with equal lives. However if managers are **deciding between projects with different time spans** a direct **comparison of the NPV generated by each project would not be valid**.

For example if an organisation decides to invest in a project with a shorter life it may then have the opportunity to invest in a new project in the future sooner than if a longer term project is accepted. This should be taken into account in the analysis in order to be able to make direct comparisons between projects with unequal lives.

FAST FORWARD

Annualised equivalents are used to enable a comparison to be made between the net present values of projects with different durations. **However, this method cannot be used when inflation is a factor**. Another method, the **lowest common multiple method, is used** instead. In the next section there is an example of this method for you to follow and work through.

1.1 Example: annualised equivalents

An organisation has the opportunity to invest in either project G or project H. The forecast cash flows from the projects are as follows.

	Project G	Project H
	$'000	$'000
Capital cost	(200)	(143)
Cash inflows: year 1	90	100
year 2	120	80
year 3	50	–

The company's cost of capital is 12%. Which project should be accepted?

Solution

Project G

Year	Cash flow	PV factor	PV of cash flow
	$	12%	$
0	(200,000)	1.000	(200,000)
1	90,000	0.893	80,370
2	120,000	0.797	95,640
3	50,000	0.712	35,600
			NPV = 11,610

Project H

Year	Cash flow	PV factor	PV of cash flow
	$	12%	$
0	(143,000)	1.000	(143,000)
1	100,000	0.893	89,300
2	80,000	0.797	63,760
			NPV = 10,060

These NPVs **cannot be compared directly** because they each relate to a different number of years. In order to make a comparison we must convert each NPV to an **annualised equivalent cost**. In other words, we convert the project's NPV into an equivalent annual annuity over its expected life. We do this by using **cumulative discount factors** that you met in the last chapter.

	Project G	Project H
	Project G	Project H
NPV at 12%	$11,610	$10,060
Cumulative 12% discount factor	÷ 2.402	÷ 1.69
Annualised equivalent	$4,833	$5,953

Project H is offering an equivalent annual annuity of $5,953 which is higher than that offered by project G, therefore project H is preferable.

am focus
int

The lowest common multiple (LCM) method appeared in the November 2005 exam as a full 10 mark question. *When inflation is a factor, LCM must be used rather than annualised equivalents.*

Work through this example carefully bearing in mind the differences between the use of annualised equivalents and LCM.

1.2 Example: lowest common multiple (LCM)

Where asset replacement includes inflation you would not be able to use annualised equivalent costs. The correct method, lowest common multiple, is illustrated in a question based on that which appeared in the November 2005 exam. The key points when using the lowest common multiple method are:

(a)   Calculate cash flows including inflated values for both alternatives

(b)   Use a lowest common multiple to establish a common time period and base asset lives on that

Fred is considering the replacement of a caravan he lets out for hire. He is planning to retire in six years' time and is therefore only concerned with that period of time, but cannot decide whether it is better to replace the caravan every two years or every three years.

The following data have been estimated (all values at today's price levels):

Purchase cost and trade-in values

		$
Cost of a new caravan		20,000
Trade-in value of caravan:	after two years	10,000
	after three years	5,000

Annual costs and revenues

	Per year
	$
Caravan running cost	10,000
Lettings charged to customers, that is revenue for Fred	20,000

Caravan servicing and repair costs

Caravan servicing and repair costs depend on the age of the caravan. In the following table, year 1 represents the cost in the first year of the caravan ownership; year 2 represents the cost in the second year of ownership, and so on:

	$
Year 1	500
Year 2	2,500
Year 3	4,000

Inflation

New caravan costs and trade in-values are expected to increase by 5% per year. Caravan running costs and lettings are expected to increase by 7% per year. Caravan servicing and repair costs are expected to increase by 10% per year.

Required

Advise Fred on the optimum replacement cycle for his caravan and state the net present value of the opportunity cost of making the wrong decision. Use a discount rate of 12% per year. All workings and assumptions should be shown. Ignore taxation.

Solution

In this example you need to consider a six-year time horizon, six being the lowest common multiple of two and three.

Projected cash flows – 2 year trade in

	Year 0 $	Year 1 $	Year 2 $	Year 3 $	Year 4 $	Year 5 $	Year 6 $
Caravan cost (+ 5% pa)	(20,000)		(22,050)		(24,310)		
Trade in value (+ 5% pa)			11,025		12,155		13,401
Annual costs and revenues (net of costs) (+ 7% pa)		10,700	11,449	12,250	13,108	14,026	15,007
Servicing and repair (+ 10% pa)	–	(550)	(3,025)	(666)	(3,660)	(805)	(4,429)
Net cash flow	(20,000)	10,150	(2,601)	11,584	(2,707)	13,221	23,979
Discount at 12%	× 1.000	× 0.893	× 0.797	× 0.712	× 0.636	× 0.567	× 0.507
PV of cash flow	(20,000)	9,064	(2,073)	8,248	(1,722)	7,496	12,157

NPV of cash flow = $13,170

Projected cash flows – 3 year trade in

	Year 0 $	Year 1 $	Year 2 $	Year 3 $	Year 4 $	Year 5 $	Year 6 $
Caravan cost (+ 5% pa)	(20,000)			(23,153)			
Trade in value (+ 5% pa)				5,788			6,700
Annual costs and revenues (net) (+ 7% pa)		10,700	11,449	12,250	13,108	14,026	15,007
Servicing and repair (+ 10% pa)	–	(550)	(3,025)	(5,324)	(732)	(4,026)	(7,086)
Net cash flow	(20,000)	10,150	8,424	(10,439)	12,376	10,000	14,621
Discount at 12%	× 1.000	× 0.893	× 0.797	× 0.712	× 0.636	× 0.567	× 0.507
PV of cash flow	(20,000)	9,064	6,714	(7,433)	7,871	5,670	7,413

NPV of cash flow = $9,299

Assumptions: inflation applies from year 0 to all costs and revenues, which are stated at their values in year 0 in the question.

Based on the NPVs of the two alternative replacement cycles, that with the higher positive NPV is the two-year replacement cycle and so this should be chosen as the optimum replacement cycle.

A word of warning!

Not all mutually exclusive investments need to be considered over the same level of time. It very much depends on what the organisation intends to do once the shorter-life **project ends**. If the organisation has to **invest in similar assets** again at that point, the **projects should be compared over equal time periods**. Investment in manufacturing equipment for a product that will be made for more years than the life of an asset is an example.

If the organisation does **not have to invest in similar assets when the asset's life ends**, however, the approach we have described is not needed. If the investments are alternative advertising campaigns for a short-life product such as a commemorative item, the investments will be one-offs and so can be **compared over different lives**.

2 Asset replacement

As well as assisting with decisions between particular assets, DCF techniques combined with annualised equivalents can be used to assess **when** and **how frequently an asset should be replaced**.

2.1 Identical replacement

AST FORWARD

When an asset is **being replaced** with an **identical asset**, the **equivalent annual cost method** can be used.

When an asset is to be replaced by an **'identical' asset**, the problem is to decide the optimum interval between replacements. As the asset gets older, it may cost more to maintain and operate, its residual value will decrease, and it may lose some productivity/operating capability.

2.1.1 Example: replacement of an identical asset

James operates a machine which costs $25,000 to buy and has the following costs and resale values over its four-year life.

	Year 1 $	Year 2 $	Year 3 $	Year 4 $
Running costs (cash expenses)	7,500	10,000	12,500	15,000
Resale value (end of year)	15,000	10,000	7,500	2,500

The organisation's cost of capital is 10%.

Required

Assess how frequently the asset should be replaced.

Solution

To begin, it is necessary to **calculate the present value of costs for each replacement cycle, but over one cycle only**.

	Replace every year		Replace every 2 years		Replace every 3 years		Replace every 4 years	
Year	Cash flow $	PV at 10% $	Cash flow $	PV at 10% $	Cash flow $	PV at 10% $	Cash flow $	PV at 10% $
0	(25,000)	(25,000)	(25,000)	(25,000)	(25,000)	(25,000)	(25,000)	(25,000)
1	7,500	6,818	(7,500)	(6,818)	(7,500)	(6,818)	(7,500)	(6,818)
2			0	0	(10,000)	(8,260)	(10,000)	(8,260)
3					(5,000)	(3,755)	(12,500)	(9,388)
4							(12,500)	(8,538)
PV of cost over one replacement cycle	(18,182)		(31,818)		(43,833)		(58,004)	

ints to
te

- The zeros in the 'Replace every 2 years' column arise from the fact that the running costs in year 2 are $10,000, but if the machine is sold at the end of year 2 James will get $10,000, so the net effect in year 2 is zero.

- In general, in the year in which the machine is replaced, the cash flow is the difference between the running costs in that year and the resale value. In the years leading up to replacement, the cash flow is the running costs for that year.

These **costs are not comparable, because they refer to different time periods, whereas replacement is continuous**. We need to convert each of them to an equivalent annual cost.

Given a discount rate of 10%, the equivalent annual cost is calculated as follows.

	Replace every year	Replace every 2 years	Replace every 3 years	Replace every 4 years
PV of cost over one replacement cycle	$18,182	$31,818	$43,833	$58,004
Cumulative PV factor	÷ 0.909	÷ 1.736	÷ 2.487	÷ 3.170
Annualised equivalent cost	$20,002	$18,328	$17,625	$18,298

The **optimum replacement policy** is the one with the **lowest equivalent annual cost**, every three years.

Question

Learning outcome: B(viii)

An organisation is deciding whether to replace company cars after a three, four or five year cycle. The relevant cash flows are as follows.

	Year	Three-year cycle $	Four-year cycle $	Five-year cycle $
Capital cost	0	(6,000)	(6,000)	(6,000)
Running costs	1	(280)	(280)	(280)
Running costs	2	(1,090)	(1,090)	(1,090)
Running costs	3	(1,120)	(1,120)	(1,120)
Trade in value	3	1,000	–	–
Running costs	4		(1,590)	(1,590)
Trade in value	4		700	–
Running costs	5			(1,260)
Trade in value	5			300
NPV at 15% *		(7,146.6)	(8,313.68)	(9,191.2)

* The workings are not shown, but as an exercise you could check the NPV calculations yourself.

Required

Fill in the blank in the sentence below.

The optimum replacement policy for company cars is every ………… years.

Answer

The correct answer is five years.

	Three-year cycle	Four-year cycle	Five-year cycle
NPV at 15%	$(7,146.6)	$(8,313.68)	$(9,191.2)
Cumulative 15% discount factor	÷ 2.283	÷ 2.855	÷ 3.352
Annualised equivalent cost	$3,130	$2,912	$2,742

The **lowest annualised equivalent cost** results from a five year cycle, therefore the company should replace its cars every five years.

Exam focus point

There was a 10-mark question in the pilot paper requiring this technique.

2.2 Non-identical replacement

When a machine is to be replaced by a machine of a different type, there is a different replacement problem.

ST FORWARD

When an asset is being **replaced with a non-identical asset**, the decision is when to replace the asset rather than how frequently. The **present value of an annuity in perpetuity** must be calculated.

2.2.1 Example: non-identical replacement

Suppose that James's machine (in our example in Section 2.1.1) is a new machine, and will be introduced to replace a non-identical existing machine which is nearing the end of its life and has a maximum remaining life of only three years. James wishes to decide when is the best time to replace the old machine, and estimates of relevant costs have been drawn up as follows.

Year	Resale value of current machine	Extra expenditure and opportunity costs of keeping the existing machine in operation during the year
	$	$
0	8,500	n/a
1	5,000	9,000
2	2,500	12,000
3	0	15,000

Required

Calculate the best time to replace the existing machine.

Solution

The costs of the new machine will be those given in Section 2.1.1, so that the optimum replacement cycle for the new machine will already have been calculated as three years, with an equivalent annual cost of $17,625 (Solution in Section 2.1.1).

The best time to replace the existing machine will be the option which gives the lowest NPV of cost in perpetuity, for both the existing machine and the machine which eventually replaces it.

We saw in the last chapter that the present value of an annuity, $a per annum, in perpetuity is a/r, where r is the cost of capital.

This formula may be used to calculate the PV of cost in perpetuity of the new machine. In our example, PV of cost = $17,625/0.1 = $176,250.

The new machine will have a PV of cost in perpetuity of $176,250 from the start of the year when it is eventually purchased.

The present value relates to the beginning of the year when the first annual cash flow occurs, so that if replacement occurs now, the first annuity is in year 1, and the PV of cost relates to year 0 values. If replacement occurs at the end of year 1 the first annuity is in year 2, and the PV of cost relates to year 1, and so on.

The total cash flows of the replacement decision may now be presented as follows. These cash flows show the **PV of cost in perpetuity of the new machine**, the **running costs of the existing machine**, and the **resale value of the existing machine**, at the **end of year 0, 1, 2 or 3 as appropriate**.

Year	Replace now $	Replace in 1 year $	Replace in 2 years $	Replace in 3 years $
0	(176,250) 8,500	–	–	–
1	–	(176,250) (9,000) 5,000	(9,000)	(9,000)
2	–	–	(176,250) (12,000) 2,500	(12,000)
3	–	–	–	(176,250) (15,000)

The PVs of each replacement option are as follows.

	Year	Cash flow $	Discount factor 10%	Present value $
Replace now	0	(176,250) 8,500		
		(167,750)	1.000	(167,750)
Replace in one year	1	(176,250) (9,000) 5,000		
		(180,250)	0.909	(163,847)
Replace in two years	1	(9,000)	0.909	(8,181)
	2	(185,750)	0.826	(153,430)
				(161,611)
Replace in three years	1	(9,000)	0.909	(8,181)
	2	(12,000)	0.826	(9,912)
	3	(191,250)	0.751	(143,629)
				(161,722)

The marginally **optimum policy** would be to replace the existing machine in two years' time, because this has the **lowest total PV of cost in perpetuity**.

3 Project abandonment

A decision on whether or not a project should be **abandoned** should be made by selecting the option (continue or abandon) with the higher NPV.

Initial project appraisals are based on forecasts of cash inflows and outflows and a decision is made on the basis of these forecasts. These forecasts are subject to uncertainty, however, and the assumptions upon which the original estimates were based become invalid: demand may not be at the level anticipated, costs may have increased due to labour or material shortages and so on.

As part of the **post-completion audit** discussed in Chapter 10, the following factors should therefore be considered at each stage of a project's life.

(a)   The NPV of the cash flows associated with abandoning the project. Many cash flows could be relevant.

   (i)   Redundancy payments
   (ii)   Sale of machinery
   (iii) **Opportunity cost** of tying up funds if there is a more profitable use for them.

(b)   The option with the highest NPV (continue or abandon) should be selected.

3.1 Possible abandonment scenarios

3.1.1 Scenario 1

Suppose project B has expected cash flows as shown in the table below.

Year	Expected cash flow $	Discount factor 12%	Present value $
0	(21,000)	1.000	(21,000)
1	9,500	0.893	8,484
2	9,500	0.797	7,572
3	9,500	0.712	6,764
NPV			1,820

The initial investment is in a machine built specifically for the organisation in question, and so it has a low resale value of only $5,000 after it has been purchased. Once the machine is **purchased**, the **expected value of abandoning the project** of $5,000 × 1.000 = $5,000 must therefore be **compared with the expected value of continuing** ($(8,484 + 7,572 + 6,764) = $22,820). The expected benefits from continuing with the project are therefore far greater than those from abandoning it immediately and so the project should continue.

3.1.2 Scenario 2

A decision to abandon a project will usually be made because of revised estimates of costs and revenues likely to be received over the remaining life of the project. These revised estimates might be consistent with the data used to make the initial decision, or they might alter initial estimates.

If the revised estimates are consistent with the original data, project abandonment would have been one of the possible outcomes of the project from the outset.

Suppose the cash flows in the table in scenario 1 were based on the probabilities shown below.

Year 0 $	Year 1 p	Year 1 $	Year 2 p	Year 2 $	Year 3 p	Year 3 $
(21,000)	0.33˙(note)	15,000	0.33˙	15,000	0.33˙	15,000
	0.33˙	9,000	0.33˙	9,000	0.33˙	9,000
	0.33˙	4,500	0.33˙	4,500	0.33˙	4,500
EV		9,500		9,500		9,500

Note. These probabilities are each 1/3 which is expressed as 0.33˙ ie recurring. When you calculate the EV, you need to use 1/3 rather than 0.33 to get the correct answer.

At time 0, the expected net present value of the cash inflows from the project in each of years 1-3 is $9,500. The actual outcome in any of the three years is unknown, however, and there is an equal chance of any of the three possible outcomes occurring each year.

It could be that the **outcome in year 1 will determine the outcomes in years 2 and 3**. For example, an outcome of $9,000 in year 1 could mean that the outcomes in years 2 and 3 will definitely be $9,000 as well. Alternatively outcomes of $15,000 or $4,500 in year 1 may result in the same cash flows in years 2 and 3. In such circumstances, future cash flows are therefore known with certainty at the end of year 1.

If the cash flow in year 1 (and hence in years 2 and 3) is $15,000 or $9,000, the actual overall NPV of the project will be positive. If it is $4,500, however, the actual NPV will be –$10,191.

Should the project be abandoned? The **information on which to base the decision is now certain** and should be **based on using a risk-free interest rate** rather than the 12% cost of capital. If the risk-free rate were 6%, say, the present value of continuing at the end of year 1 would be:

Year	Cashflow	Discount rate	PV
	$	6%	$
1	4,500	0.943	4,244
2	4,500	0.890	4,005
			8,249

If the cash inflow is $4,500 (in all three years) the project should therefore **not** be abandoned (as the present value of abandonment is $5,000).

3.1.3 Scenario 3

Now let's suppose that the original sale agreement included a **buy-back clause** which meant that the supplier had to buy back the machine for $13,000 on demand at any time up to and including one year after the sale.

Suppose the cash inflow in year 1 was $4,500, which made the inflows in years 2 and 3 $4,500 as well. At the end of year 1 the value of abandonment will therefore be $13,000, the value of continuing with the project $8,249 ($4,500 × 1.833, where 1.833 = discount factors at 6% for years 1 and 2). The project should therefore be abandoned at the end of year 1 if the actual outcome in that year is $4,500. (If the cash flow were $15,000 or $9,000 it would not be abandoned.)

If the **buy-back option is included in the analysis from the outset**, however, the possible **outcomes change** as follows.

Year 0		Year 1		Year 2		Year 3	
$	p	$	p	$	p	$	
(21,000)	0.33*	15,000	0.33*	15,000	0.33*	15,000	
	0.33*	9,000	0.33*	9,000	0.33*	9,000	
	0.33*	4,500	0.33*	0	0.33*	0	
		13,000					
EV		13,833		8,000		8,000	

Note that because we would abandon if cashflows per annum were $4,500, we do not include these flows in years 2 and 3. Also remember that 0.33* is 1/3 rather than 0.33.

Including the abandonment option in the analysis increases the NPV by $(3,425 − 1,820) = $1,605.

Year	Expected cash flow	Discount factor	Present value
	$	12%	$
0	(21,000)	1.000	(21,000)
1	13,833	0.893	12,353
2	8,000	0.797	6,376
3	8,000	0.712	5,696
NPV			3,425

The analysis could also be presented in a **decision tree**.

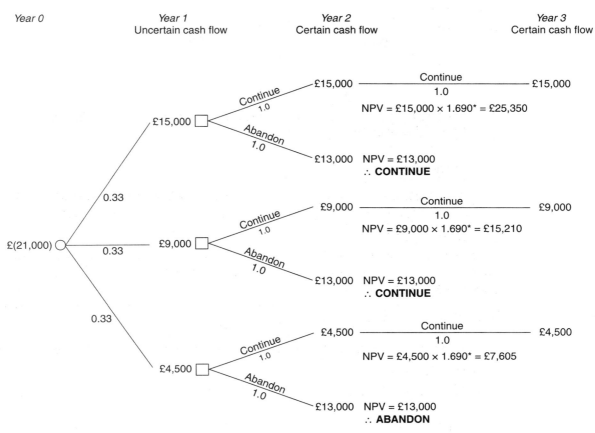

* 1.690 = discount factor at 12% for two years.

Unless the cash flows in years 2 and 3 are **totally independent** of those that occur in year 1, you **can use this approach** as the information gained in year 1 will enable you to refine the forecast for years 2 and 3 to some degree. You can then compare the present value of continuing with the present value of abandonment.

3.1.4 Scenario 4

During the life of a project, **events** may occur that were **not expected when the decision** was **originally taken** and which have an impact on predicted future cash flows.

For example, a new tax introduced during year 1 may reduce the cash inflows from the project by 40%, which would have the following result on expected cash flows.

Year 0		Year 1		Year 2		Year 3
$	p	$	p	$	p	$
(21,000)	0.33	15,000	0.33	9,000	0.33	9,000
	0.33	9,000	0.33	5,400	0.33	5,400
	0.33	4,500	0.33	2,700	0.33	2,700
EV		9,500		5,700		5,700

The introduction of the new tax means that a cash inflow of $9,500 will be followed by inflows of only $5,700 in years 2 and 3. Given that an inflow of $9,000 in years 2 and 3 compared with a buy back figure of $13,000 results in a marginal decision to continue (see decision tree above), inflows of $5,700 would result in the project being abandoned in year 1.

3.2 Example: abandoning projects

When EFG carried out the initial appraisal for project P, it contained the following forecast cash flows.

Year	0	1	2	3	4	5
Cash flow ($'000)	(1,000)	(700)	(400)	900	1,500	1,600

It is now the end of year 0 and the investment is about to be made for year 1. The actual cash outflow for year 0 amounted to $1,300,000 and it seems likely that the required investment in year 1 will be $1,000,000. The estimates of the projected cash flows for years 2 to 5 have not altered.

Another company has offered to take over the project from EFG immediately for a consideration of $1,400,000. If EFG did abandon the project they would be obliged to make redundancy payments of $100,000.

EFG's cost of capital is 12%

Should project P be abandoned?

Solution

The $1,300,000 already spent in year 0 is a sunk cost that is not relevant to the abandonment decision (although the post-completion audit process should investigate the reasons for the overspending, to prevent such an occurrence in future.)

The NPV of the future cash flows associated with continuing the project should be calculated, starting again with a 'new' year 0.

Year X	Cash flow $'000	Discount factor 12%	Present value $'000
0	(1,000)	1.000	(1,000)
1	(400)	0.893	(357)
2	900	0.797	717
3	1,500	0.712	1,068
4	1,600	0.636	1,018
Net present value of the decision to continue			1,446

The present value of abandoning the project   = $1,400,000 – $1,000,000
                                         = $1,300,000

This is lower than the net present value of the cash flows to be generated by continuing, therefore the project should not be abandoned.

The decision to continue with the project in this example relied heavily on management predictions that the forecast cash flows for the remainder of the project were still reliable. In view of the errors in their forecasts for the original years 0 and 1 this may seem rather doubtful.

It may be difficult for managers who are heavily involved with a project to admit that early problems are likely to continue. For this reason it is important that abandonment reviews are carried out objectively, preferably overseen by a manager who was not involved in the initial appraisal.

If the reasons for abandonment are caused by external events, however (as in scenario 4 above), resistance to project termination is likely to be low.

3.3 The role of the PCA in project abandonment

If there are problems implementing a project, those involved may try to resolve the situation by changing the original plans and/or incurring additional expenditure to meet the original objective(s).

The appropriateness of these actions will depend on the circumstances, but **all major changes to plans** should be **documented** and formally **approved** by more senior management. **Expected cost overruns**

should come to light during routine expenditure monitoring by finance staff, and these should be **formally approved** after a **detailed justification** is provided.

Such controls should ensure that **all major changes** to the character of a project have **senior management approval**, but they do not **ensure** that **project abandonment** is automatically **considered** (although it is unlikely that senior management would not consider this option).

An audit can be carried out on all projects that require **additional funding**, and the funding request can then be viewed in conjunction with the **audit report**, which will focus on costs and revenues and – most importantly – the **future**. This puts the audit team in an ideal position to advise senior management on the **value of continuing** with the project.

4 Capital rationing

> **Capital rationing**: a situation in which a company has a limited amount of capital to invest in potential projects, such that the different possible investments need to be compared with one another in order to allocate the capital available most effectively.
>
> **Soft capital rationing** is brought about by internal factors; **hard capital rationing** is brought about by external factors.

If an organisation is in a **capital rationing** situation it will **not be able to enter into all projects with positive NPVs because there is not enough capital for all of the investments**.

4.1 Soft and hard capital rationing

Soft capital rationing may arise for one of the following reasons.

(a)   Management may be **reluctant** to **issue additional share capital** because of concern that this may lead to **outsiders gaining control** of the business.

(b)   Management may be **unwilling** to **issue additional share capital** if it will lead to a **dilution of earnings** per share.

(c)   Management may **not want to raise additional debt capital** because they do not wish to be committed to **large fixed interest payments**.

(d)   Management may wish to **limit investment** to a level that can be **financed solely from retained earnings**.

(e)   **Capital expenditure budgets** may restrict spending.

Hard capital rationing may arise for one of the following reasons.

(a)   Raising money through the inventory market may not be possible if **share prices** are **depressed**.
(b)   There may be **restrictions** on **bank lending** due to government control.
(c)   Lenders may consider an organisation to be **too risky** to be granted further loan facilities.
(d)   The **costs** associated with making small **issues** of capital may be too great.

4.2 Capital rationing and DCF

To make a decision in a capital rationing situation we need to make a number of **assumptions**.

(a)   Capital rationing occurs in a single period, and capital is freely available at all other times.

(b)   If a project is not accepted and undertaken during the period of capital rationing, the opportunity to undertake it is lost. It cannot be postponed until a subsequent period when no capital rationing exists.

(c)   There is complete certainty about the outcome of each project, so that the choice between projects is not affected by considerations of risk.

(d)   Projects are divisible, so that it is possible to undertake, say, half of Project X in order to earn half of the net present value (NPV) of the whole project.

4.2.1 Basic approach

FAST FORWARD

> When an organisation has a limited amount of capital to invest in potential projects (**capital rationing**) in a single period, projects should be ranked in terms of the **profitability index**.

Rank all investment opportunities so that the NPVs can be maximised from the use of the available funds.

Note that ranking **in terms of NPVs** will normally give **incorrect** results since this method leads to the selection of large projects, each of which has a high individual NPV but which have, in total, a lower NPV than a large number of smaller projects with lower individual NPVs.

Ranking is therefore in terms of what is called the **profitability index,** which can be defined as the **ratio of the present value of the project's future cash flows (not including the capital investment) divided by the PV of the total capital outlays**.

This ratio measures the PV of future cash flows per $1 of investment, and so indicates which investments make the best use of the limited resources available.

Suppose that HT is considering four projects, W, X, Y and Z. Relevant details are as follows.

Project	Investment required $	Present value of cash inflows $	NPV $	Profitability index (PI)	Ranking as per NPV	Ranking as per PI
W	(10,000)	11,240	1,240	1.12	3	1
X	(20,000)	20,991	991	1.05	4	4
Y	(30,000)	32,230	2,230	1.07	2	3
Z	(40,000)	43,801	3,801	1.10	1	2

Without capital rationing all four projects would be viable investments. Suppose, however, that only $60,000 was available for capital investment.

Resulting NPV if we select projects in the order of ranking per NPV

Project	Priority	Outlay $	NPV $	
Z	1st	40,000	3,801	
Y (balance)*	2nd	20,000	1,487	(²/₃ of $2,230)
		60,000	5,288	

* Projects are divisible. By spending the balancing $20,000 on project Y, two thirds of the full investment would be made to earn two thirds of the NPV.

Profitability index approach

Project	Priority	Outlay $	NPV $	
W	1st	10,000	1,240	
Z	2nd	40,000	3,801	
Y (balance)	3rd	10,000	743	(¹/₃ of $2,230)
		60,000	5,784	

By choosing projects according to the PI, the resulting NPV if only $60,000 is available is increased by $496.

As we mentioned when discussing the discounted payback index in Chapter 11, the profitability index can be stated as (NPV of project/initial outlay).

Exam focus point

There is a two-mark OT question on the November 2005 paper requiring ranking using the profitability index.

4.2.2 Problems with the profitability index method

(a) The approach can **only be used if projects are divisible**. If the projects are not divisible a decision has to be made by examining the absolute NPVs of all possible combinations of complete projects that can be undertaken within the constraints of the capital available. The combination of projects which remains at or under the limit of available capital without any of them being divided, and which maximises the total NPV, should be chosen. We look at this in Section 4.3.

(b) The selection criterion is fairly simplistic, **taking no account** of the possible **strategic value** of individual investments in the context of the overall objectives of the organisation.

(c) The method is of **limited use** when projects have **differing cash flow patterns**. These patterns may be important to the company since they will affect the timing and availability of funds. With multi-period capital rationing, it is possible that the project with the highest profitability index is the slowest in generating returns.

(d) The profitability index **ignores the absolute size** of individual projects. A project with a high index might be very small and therefore only generate a small NPV.

Question

Capital rationing

Learning outcome: B(viii)

Bleak House is experiencing capital rationing in year 0, when only $60,000 of investment finance will be available. No capital rationing is expected in future periods, but none of the three projects under consideration can be postponed. The expected cash flows of the three projects are as follows.

Project	Year 0 $	Year 1 $	Year 2 $	Year 3 $	Year 4 $
A	(50,000)	(20,000)	20,000	40,000	40,000
B	(28,000)	(50,000)	40,000	40,000	20,000
C	(30,000)	(30,000)	30,000	40,000	10,000

The cost of capital is 10%.

Projects A and B only should be undertaken in year 0, in view of the capital rationing, given that projects are divisible. *True or false?*

Answer

The correct answer is that all of projects C and B should be undertaken and part of project A, and so the statement is false.

The ratio of NPV at 10% to outlay in year 0 (the year of capital rationing) is as follows.

Project	Outlay in Year 0 $	PV $	NPV $	Ratio	Ranking
A	50,000	55,700	5,700	1.114	3rd
B	28,000	31,290	3,290	1.118	2nd
C	30,000	34,380	4,380	1.146	1st

The optimal investment policy is as follows.

Ranking	Project	Year 0 outlay $	NPV $
1st	C	30,000	4,380
2nd	B	28,000	3,290
3rd	A (balance)	2,000 (4% of 5,700)	228
NPV from total investment			7,898

Attention!

> This is the approach to adopt if capital is rationed in a single period. If it is restricted in a number of years, linear programming is needed. We look at that in Section 4.4.

4.3 Indivisible projects and single period capital rationing

Suppose AB has $100,000 to invest and is considering the following indivisible projects.

Project	Initial outlay $'000	Return pa to perpetuity $'000
V	20	4
W	45	7
X	15	3
Y	30	5
Z	50	9

AB's cost of capital is 10%.

Let's look at how to select the best mix of projects.

Step 1 **Calculate the NPV of the projects**

Project	Initial outlay $'000	PV of cash flows* $'000	NPV $'000
V	20	40	20
W	45	70	25
X	15	30	15
Y	30	50	20
Z	50	90	40

*PV of a perpetuity = annual cashflow/r

Step 2 **Consider all possible combinations of projects under the investment limit of $100,000.**

The optimum selection of projects is as follows.

Project	Initial outlay $'000	NPV $'000
V	20	20
Y	30	20
Z	50	40
	100	80
Unused funds	-	
Funds available	100	

The **maximum NPV** available is therefore $80,000.

4.4 Solution by linear programming

When capital rationing occurs in a **number of periods and two products are under consideration,** the **graphical approach to linear programming** is used to arrive at an NPV-maximising mix of products. If there are **three or more projects** the **simplex method** should be applied.

We have already covered the **graphical approach to linear programming** in Chapter 6 and so you will be aware that the technique can only be used if there are two variables. The variables in this instance are the **individual investment projects.** This method is therefore confined to dealing with those scenarios concerned with a choice between just two investment projects. As you have covered graphical linear programming you should be able to attempt the following question.

Question

Graphical linear programming approach

Learning outcomes: A(vii), (viii), B(viii)

Finch has the chance to invest in two projects, A and B, details of which are set out below.

Investment project	Present value of outlay in period 1 $'000	Present value of outlay In period 2 $'000	Present value of outlay in period 3 $'000	Net present value of investment at time 0 $'000
A	30	10	10	56
B	20	4	2	8

Capital investment limits, as set by Finch's parent company, are as follows.

	$'000
Period 1	36
Period 2	8
Period 3	6

It is assumed that the capital investment limits are absolute and cannot be expanded by project generated cash inflows. Projects are divisible but cannot be repeated more than once.

Required

Formulate and solve the linear programming model which will maximise net present value.

Answer

Step 1   **Define variables**

Let x = the proportion of project A accepted.
Let y = the proportion of project B accepted.

Step 2   **Establish constraints**

$30x + 20y \le 36$ (period 1 investment)
$10x + 4y \le 8$ (period 2 investment)
$10x + 2y \le 6$ (period 3 investment)
$x, y \le 1$ (proportion must be less than or equal to 1)
$x, y \ge 0$ (proportion must be greater than or equal to 0)

The last two constraints ensure that a project cannot be undertaken more than once but allows for a project to be partially accepted.

Step 3 **Establish objective function**
The objective is to maximise the NPV from the total investment in periods 1, 2 and 3.

Maximise $56x + 8y$.

Step 4 **Graph the model**

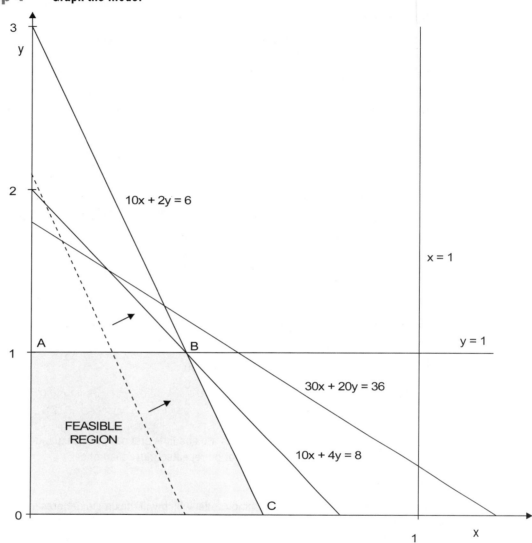

The feasible region is represented by OABC.

Step 5 **Find the best solution**
Using the 'iso-NPV line' plotted on the graph, the optimal solution can be established as at point C (0.6, 0). The optimal solution is therefore to invest in 0.6 of project A and to make no investment in project B.

The total NPV available is therefore $0.6 \times \$56,000 = \$33,600$.

4.4.1 More than two investments under consideration

When there are more than two investments under consideration the **simplex method**, covered in Chapter 7, should be applied.

BPP
LEARNING MEDIA

4.4.2 Limitations of the linear programming approach to capital rationing

When two decision variables apply, the graphical approach to linear programming may be a useful method of selecting projects but there are a number of assumptions and limitations which must be kept in mind if the use of the technique is to be considered.

(a) It assumes that variables are **linearly related**.

(b) It assumes that projects are **divisible** or that scalar multiples of projects are possible.

(c) It assumes that the **returns** of the projects are in **proportion** to the amount invested in each project.

(d) **Uncertainty** is **ignored**. It assumes that all future cash flows and available resources are known with certainty.

(e) It assumes that all projects and constraints are independent.

(f) It is possible that **other investment opportunities** not included in the linear programming model could realise a higher NPV.

(g) Linear programming cannot be used when projects are **mutually exclusive** in multi-period capital rationing situations. Instead integer programming (not part of your syllabus) has to be used.

(h) No account of **risk** attached to the projects or the company's attitude to risk is taken.

5 Sensitivity analysis

5.1 Risk

In general risky projects are those whose future cash flows, and hence the project returns, are likely to be variable – the greater the variability, the greater the risk. The problem of **risk is more acute with capital investment decisions** than other decisions because estimates of costs and benefits might be for up to 20 years ahead, and such long-term estimates can at best be approximations.

5.1.1 Why are projects risky?

A decision about whether or not to go ahead with a project is based on expectations about the future. Forecasts of cash flows (whether they be inflows or outflows) that are likely to arise following a particular course of action are made. These forecasts are made, however, on the basis of what is expected to happen given the present state of knowledge and the future is, by definition, uncertain. Actual cash flows are almost certain to differ from prior expectations. It is this **uncertainty about a project's future income and costs that gives rise to risk in business generally and investment activity in particular**.

5.2 Using sensitivity analysis

AST FORWARD

Sensitivity analysis is one method of analysing the risk surrounding a capital expenditure project and enables an assessment to be made of how responsive the project's NPV is to changes in the variables that are used to calculate that NPV.

The NPV could depend on a number of uncertain independent variables.

- Estimated selling price
- Estimated sales volume
- Estimated cost of capital
- Estimated initial cost

- Estimated operating costs
- Estimated benefits
- Estimated length of project

5.3 The margin of error approach to sensitivity analysis

FAST FORWARD

The **margin of error approach to sensitivity analysis** assesses how responsive the project's NPV (or payback period or ARR) is to changes in the variables used to calculate that NPV (or payback period or ARR).

This basic approach involves **calculating the project's NPV under alternative assumptions to determine how sensitive it is to changing conditions, thereby indicating those variables to which the NPV is most sensitive (critical variables)** and the **extent to which those variables may change before the investment decision would change** (ie a **positive NPV becoming a negative NPV**).

Once these critical variables have been identified, management should review them to assess whether or not there is a strong possibility of events occurring which will lead to a change in the investment decision. Management should also pay particular attention to controlling those variables to which the NPV is particularly sensitive, once the decision has been taken to accept the investment.

Attention!

The sensitivity of an NPV computation to changes in a variable that affects the cashflows is

$$\frac{\text{NPV of project}}{\text{PV of cashflow affected}} \times 100\%$$

5.3.1 Example: sensitivity analysis

KE, which has a cost of capital of 8%, is considering a project. The 'most likely' cash flows associated with the project are as follows.

Year	0	1	2
	$'000	$'000	$'000
Initial investment	(7,000)		
Variable costs		(2,000)	(2,000)
Cash inflows (650,000 units at $10 per unit)		6,500	6,500
Net cashflows	(7,000)	4,500	4,500

Required

Measure the sensitivity of the project to changes in variables.

Solution

The PVs of the cash flow are as follows.

Year	Discount factor 8%	PV of initial investment $'000	PV of variable costs $'000	PV of cash inflows $'000	PV of net cash flow $'000
0	1.000	(7,000)			(7,000)
1	0.926		(1,852)	6,019	4,167
2	0.857		(1,714)	5,571	3,857
		(7,000)	(3,566)	11,590	1,024

The project has a positive NPV and would appear to be worthwhile. The **changes in cash flows which would need to occur for the project to only just break even (and hence be on the point of being unacceptable) are as follows**.

(a) **Initial investment**. The initial investment can rise by $1,024,000 before the investment breaks even. The initial investment may therefore increase by (1,024/7,000) × 100% = 14.6%.

(b) **Sales volume**. Sales volume affects the level of variable costs and the level of cash inflows. We know that the PV of cash inflows less the PV of variable costs (ie PV of contribution) will have to fall to $7,000,000 for the NPV to be zero. The PV of contribution can therefore fall by ((1,024/(11,590 − 3,566)) × 100%) = 12.8% before the project breaks even.

(c) **Selling price**. The PV of cash inflows can fall by $1,024,000 before the investment breaks even. On the assumption that sales volumes remain the same, the selling price can therefore fall by ((1,024/11,590) × 100%) = 8.8% before the project just breaks even.

(d) **Variable costs**. The PV of variable costs can rise by $1,024,000 before the investment breaks even. Variable costs may therefore increase by (1,024/3,566) × 100%) = 28.7%.

(e) **Cost of capital/IRR**. We need to calculate the IRR of the project. Let us try discount rates of 15% and 20%.

Year	Net cash flow $'000	Discount factor 15%	PV $'000	Discount factor 20%	PV $'000
0	(7,000)	1.000	(7,000)	1.000	(7,000)
1	4,500	0.870	3,915	0.833	3,749
2	4,500	0.756	3,402	0.694	3,123
		NPV =	317	NPV =	(128)

IRR = 0.15 +[(317/(317 + 128)) × (0.20 − 0.15)] = 18.56%

The **cost of capital** can therefore increase by 132% before the NPV becomes negative.

Alternatively the **IRR** can fall by (18.56% − 8%)/18.56% = 59% before the project would be rejected on the basis of IRR.

The elements to which the NPV appears to be **most sensitive** are the **selling price** followed by the **sales volume**, and it is therefore important for management to pay particular attention to these factors so that they can be carefully monitored.

Given this information, it might be possible to **re-engineer** the project in some way so as to **alter its risk/return profile**. For example, customers might be prepared to contract for a $9.75 fixed selling price, but guarantee to buy the 650,000 units. Obviously the NPV would drop but a major source of uncertainty affecting project viability would be eliminated.

am focus
int

There were five marks available in one of the 25-mark pilot paper questions for a straightforward sensitivity analysis calculation. Ten marks could be earned in the May 2005 exam for a more complicated analysis. There were also ten marks available in the May 2006 exam in a Section B question on this topic.

Question

Sensitivity analysis

Learning outcome: B(ix)

NU has a cost of capital of 8% and is considering a project with the following 'most-likely' cash flows.

Year	Purchase of plant $	Running costs $	Savings $
0	(7,000)		
1		2,000	6,000
2		2,500	7,000

Required

Fill in the blanks in the sentences below about the sensitivity of the project to changes in the levels of expected costs and savings.

(a) Plant costs would need to .... by a PV of $........ or ....% for the project to break even.

(b) Running costs would need to .... by a PV of $.......... or ....% for the project to break even.

(c) Savings would need to .... by a PV of $..........or............ % for the project to break even.

Answer

The correct answer is:

(a) Plant costs would need to **increase** by a PV of **$560**, that is by (560/7,000) × 100% = **8%** for the project to break even.

(b) Running costs would need to **increase** by a PV of **$560**, that is by (560/3,995) × 100% = **14%** for the project to break even.

(c) Savings would need to **fall** by a PV of **$560**, that is by (560/11,555) × 100% = **4.8%** for the project to break even.

The PVs of the cash flows are as follows.

Year	Discount factor 8%	PV of plant cost $	PV of running costs $	PV of savings $	PV of net cash flow $
0	1.000	(7,000)			(7,000)
1	0.926		(1,852)	5,556	3,704
2	0.857		(2,143)	5,999	3,856
		(7,000)	(3,995)	11,555	560

Alternatively you can **change each variable** affecting the NPV of a project in turn **by a certain percentage** and **recalculate the NPV** to determine whether the project is more vulnerable to changes in some key variables than it is to changes in others.

5.3.2 Sensitivity analysis and payback

This would involve determining by how much profit could change in particular years before the decision to accept/not accept was no longer valid.

For example, suppose project B requires initial capital expenditure of $250,000 and that profits before depreciation from the project are likely to be $80,000 in year one, $100,000 in year 2 and $140,000 in year 3. The payback period is therefore two and a half years. If the target payback is three years project B would be accepted. For project B to be rejected:

(a) The initial expenditure would have to increase by at least $70,000 (or 28%).
(b) The profits in year 1 would need to fall by at least $70,000 (or 87.5%).
(c) The profits in year 2 would need to fall by at least $70,000 (or 70%).
(d) The profits in year 3 would need to fall by at least $70,000 (or 50%).

The project is therefore most sensitive to changes in the initial capital expenditure and year 3 profits.

5.3.3 Sensitivity analysis and ARR

Suppose CC has a target ARR of 20% and is considering project D.

	$
Total profit before depreciation over five years	120,000
Total profit after depreciation over five years	40,000
Average annual profit after depreciation	8,000
Original cost of investment	64,000
Residual value of investment	nil
Average net book value over the five-year period	32,000

The project's ARR is ($8,000/$32,000) × 100% = 25% and so it would be acceptable.

For project D to be rejected:

(a) Average annual profit after depreciation would need to fall by at least $1,600 to $6,400 (a fall of 20%).

(b) The original cost of the investment would need to increase by at least $16,000 to $80,000 (an increase of 25%).

(c) The residual value of the investment would need to increase by at least $16,000 to $16,000 (an infinite rise from the original $0).

The project is therefore most sensitive to changes in average annual profit.

5.3.4 Weaknesses of the margin of error approach to sensitivity analysis

(a) The method requires that changes in each key variable are isolated but management is more interested in the combination of the effects of changes in two or more key variables. Looking at factors in isolation is unrealistic since they are often interdependent.

(b) Sensitivity analysis does not examine the probability that any particular variation in costs or revenues might occur.

5.4 Diagrammatic approach to sensitivity analysis

We can use a **graph** either to **show how sensitive a project is to changes in a key variable** or to **compare the sensitivities of two or more projects to changes in a key variable**.

Suppose that an organisation wishes to compare two machines (A and B), both of which produce product X. The machines' initial costs, annual fixed running costs and variable cost of producing one unit of product X are different. Annual demand for product X varies unpredictably between 0 and 10,000 units. The selling price of product X is regulated by government and so is fixed at a certain level, whatever the demand.

The NPV of investments in machines A and B at the highest and lowest demand levels are as follows.

	NPVs	
Demand pa	*Machine A*	*Machine B*
Units	$'000	$'000
0	(1)	(4)
10,000	8	11

If we plot these four points we can **see how the NPV changes as demand for product X changes**. Note that the NPV does not change in a linear fashion with changes in other variables but **we can plot straight lines to approximate to the curvilinear behaviour** that would be evident if we calculated the NPV at more demand levels.

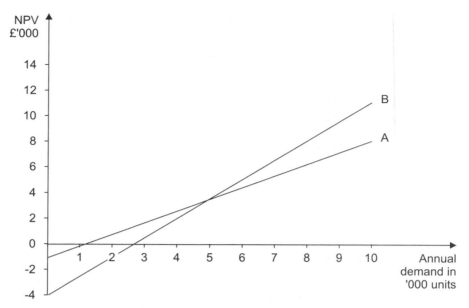

(a)   The two lines cross at demand of 5,000 units so **machine B returns a higher NPV in 50% of the possible outcomes that could arise**.

(b)   On the other hand, machine A crosses the horizontal axis at around 1,100 units. This means that in **approximately 89% of the possible outcomes, machine A would produce a positive NPV**. Contrast this with machine B, where only about 73% of outcomes result in a positive NPV.

(c)   The point at which the **two lines cross** is the point at which the **two machines are equally viable**.

5.5 Sensitivity to changes in discount rate

In all our examples we have assumed, for simplicity, a constant rate of interest. Changes in interest rates can be easily accommodated in NPV and discounted payback calculations but they are not so easily incorporated into IRR or ARR calculations since an IRR or ARR or reflects an average rate of return over a project's life. In **periods of great discount rate volatility** the **NPV method should** therefore **be used**.

In situations of **non-conventional cash flows** a graph can help show the sensitivity of projects to changes in discount rates. Take the following two projects with non-conventional cash flows.

Time	Project Y	Project Z
	$'000	$'000
0	1,920	1,700
1	(4,800)	(4,800)
2	3,000	3,300
NPV @ 10%	$34,800	$62,600

If the projects were **mutually exclusive Project Z would be chosen. If interest rates were not likely to be stable, however, the graph below would illustrate the relative sensitivity of the projects**. (This kind of graph can be sketched by calculating the NPV of the projects at various discount rates but the calculations have not been shown here.)

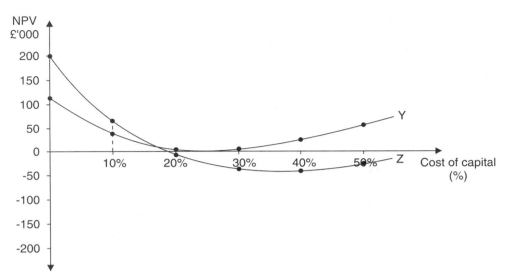

The graph shows that project **Y will remain profitable at any interest rate**, but project **Z would not be worthwhile if interest rates increased beyond about 18%** (unless they then increased to something over 50%). Therefore if one wished to avoid all risk, project Y would be favourable.

5.6 Limitation of sensitivity analysis

One of the **assumptions** commonly made by decision makers in conditions of uncertainty is that the **probability distribution of possible project outcomes is grouped symmetrically around a mean** and **most likely outcome**, outcomes close to this mean being more likely than ones far from it. And many business projects do exhibit this tendency.

The **problem with sensitivity analysis**, however, is that it tends to **focus on ranges** of possible outcomes **without considering the probabilities of different results within those ranges**. It is possible that outcomes at one end of the range are far more likely to occur than outcomes around the central point.

In the scenario illustrated in the graph in Section 5.4, if low levels of demand were more likely than demand in excess of 5,000 units, machine A would be preferred.

6 Probability analysis and long-term decisions

T FORWARD

Probability distributions of variables in NPV calculations can be drawn up and an **EV of the NPV** calculated.

ention!

Before you study this section you might find it useful to read through Section 2 of Chapter 14. Refer to the knowledge brought forward boxes and the simple example in Section 2.2.1.

In the example in Section 5.3.1 attention was drawn to the selling price, which only needed to fall by 8.8% before the project's NPV became negative. A fuller understanding of the impact of the selling price on the attractiveness of the project may therefore be required.

The original NPV was calculated using the 'most likely' selling price, no probability of occurrence having been assigned to this figure. If a **full probability distribution** of selling price were to be drawn up, however, it would indicate the level of confidence that management could have in the original estimate and the probability of other selling prices occurring.

Obviously, it is far more demanding to draw up a full probability distribution than to provide a 'most likely' figure to which no probability has to be attached.

A probability distribution for the selling price could be as follows.

Probability (p)	Price (P)	pP
	£	
0.2	9	1.80
0.5	10	5.00
0.2	11	2.20
0.1	12	1.20
	EV of selling price =	10.20

The **NPV could be recalculated using the EV of the selling price** (£10.20) **or** alternatively the **NPV could be calculated using each price and then the expected value of the NPVs calculated** (using the probabilities 0.2, 0.5, 0.2 and 0.1).

Such additional information gives management a much greater **awareness** of the financial consequences to the project if **the 'most likely' price proves not to be the actual price**. They are then in a much better position to decide whether or not to proceed with the project. (Don't forget that the outcome of the project depends on the performance of all of the variables, however, not just (for example) the selling price.)

Exam focus point

A 25-mark question in the November 2005 exam paper included the application of expected values to NPV calculations.

Question

Probability analysis and long-term decisions

Learning outcomes: C(i),(iii),(iv)

A company is considering a project involving the outlay of £300,000 which it estimates will generate cash inflows over its two year life at the probabilities shown in the following table.

Cash flows for project

Year 1

Cash flow	Probability
£	
100,000	0.25
200,000	0.50
300,000	0.25
	1.00

Year 2

If cash flow in Year 1 is:	there is a probability of:	that the cash flow in Year 2 will be:
£		£
100,000	0.25	Nil
	0.50	100,000
	0.25	200,000
	1.00	
200,000	0.25	100,000
	0.50	200,000
	0.25	300,000
	1.00	
300,000	0.25	200,000
	0.50	300,000
	0.25	350,000
	1.00	

The company's investment criterion for this type of project is 10% DCF.

Required

Calculate the expected value (EV) of the project's NPV and the probability that the NPV will be negative.

Answer

Step 1   **Calculate expected value of the NPV.**
First we need to draw up a probability distribution of the expected cash flows. We begin by calculating the present values of the cash flows.

Year	Cash flow £'000	Discount factor 10%	Present value £'000
1	100	0.909	90.9
1	200	0.909	181.8
1	300	0.909	272.7
2	100	0.826	82.6
2	200	0.826	165.2
2	300	0.826	247.8
2	350	0.826	289.1

Year 1 PV of cash flow £'000 (a)	Probability (b)	Year 2 PV of cash flow £'000 (c)	Probability (d)	Joint probability (b) × (d)	Total PV of cash inflows £'000 (a) + (c)	EV of PV of cash inflows £'000
90.9	0.25	0.0	0.25	0.0625	90.9	5.681
90.9	0.25	82.6	0.50	0.1250	173.5	21.688
90.9	0.25	165.2	0.25	0.0625	256.1	16.006
181.8	0.50	82.6	0.25	0.1250	264.4	33.050
181.8	0.50	165.2	0.50	0.2500	347.0	86.750
181.8	0.50	247.8	0.25	0.1250	429.6	53.700
272.7	0.25	165.2	0.25	0.0625	437.9	27.369
272.7	0.25	247.8	0.50	0.1250	520.5	65.063
272.7	0.25	289.1	0.25	0.0625	561.8	35.113
						344.420

	£
EV of PV of cash inflows	344,420
Less project cost	300,000
EV of NPV	44,420

Step 2   **Measure risk.**
Since the EV of the NPV is positive, the project should go ahead unless the risk is unacceptably high. The probability that the project will have a negative NPV is the probability that the total PV of cash inflows is less than £300,000. From the column headed 'Total PV of cash inflows', we can establish that this probability is 0.0625 + 0.125 + 0.0625 + 0.125 = 0.375 or 37.5%. This might be considered an unacceptably high risk.

6.1 The standard deviation of the NPV

The disadvantage of using the EV of NPV approach to assess the risk of the project is that the **construction of the probability distribution** can become **very complicated**. If we were considering a project over 4 years, each year having five different forecasted cash flows, there would be 625 (5^4) NPVs to calculate. To avoid all of these calculations, an indication of the risk may be obtained by calculating the **standard deviation** of the NPV. We will look at this technique in Chapter 14.

6.2 The expected value of a payback period

An EV of a payback period can be determined using EVs of cashflows for each year of a project.

In the previous question, for example, the EV of the year 1 cashflow is £((100,000 × 0.25) + (200,000 × 0.50) + (300,000 × 0.25)) = £200,000.

The EV of the year 2 cashflows requires the use of the joint probabilities calculated in the answer to the question.

Year 1 cashflow	Prob	Year 2 cashflow	Prob	Joint prob	EV of Year 2 cashflow*
£					
100,000	0.25	Nil	0.25	0.0625	-
100,000	0.25	100,000	0.50	0.1250	12,500
100,000	0.25	200,000	0.25	0.0625	12,500
200,000	0.50	100,000	0.25	0.1250	12,500
200,000	0.50	200,000	0.50	0.2500	50,000
200,000	0.50	300,000	0.25	0.1250	37,500
300,000	0.25	200,000	0.25	0.0625	12,500
300,000	0.25	300,000	0.50	0.1250	37,500
300,000	0.25	350,000	0.25	0.0625	21,875
					196,875

* Year 2 cashflow × joint probability

We can now calculate the EV of the payback period.

	EV of cashflow	EV of cumulative cashflow
	£	£
Year 0	(300,000)	(300,000)
Year 1	200,000	(100,000)
Year 2	196,875	96,875

∴ EV of payback period = 1 year and ((100,000/196,875) × 12) months
= 1 year 6.1 months

6.3 Problems with expected values and investment decisions

There are the following problems with using expected values in making investment decisions.

- An investment may be **one-off**, and 'expected' NPV may never actually occur.
- **Assigning probabilities** to events is highly **subjective**.
- Expected values **do not evaluate the range** of possible NPV outcomes.

6.4 Use of different cost of money rates

A fairly straightforward way in which organisations can attempt to take account of risk is to use a **higher cost of money rate for higher-risk projects** and a lower rate for lower-risk projects. Higher-risk projects would therefore have to generate larger positive cash flows to be accepted.

Alternatively, **riskier projects can be assessed over a shorter length of time**, so that they have to generate larger positive cashflows than those deemed less risky.

The obvious **disadvantage** of such approaches is that they are **subjective**, because someone must decide what is high risk and what is low risk.

7 Non-financial considerations in long-term decisions

As well as financial considerations, any decision support information provided to management should also incorporate **non-financial considerations**.

Here are some examples.

(a) **Impact on employee morale**. Most investments affect employees' prospects, sometimes for the better, sometimes for the worse. A new cafeteria for employees would have a favourable impact, for example.

(b) **Impact on the community**. This is a particularly important consideration if the investment results in loss of jobs, more jobs or elimination of small businesses.

(c) **Impact on the environment**. The opening of a new mine, the development of products which create environmentally-harmful waste and so on all have an impact on the environment. This can affect an organisation's image and reputation and hence its long-term growth and survival prospects. Some of these environmental effects can also impact directly on project cash flows because organisations have to pay fines, incur legal costs, incur disposal and cleanup costs and so on.

(d) **Ethical issues**. Some investments might be legal but might not be in line with the ethics and code of conduct demanded by various stakeholder groups.

(e) **Learning**. Many investments, particularly those which advance an organisation's technology, provide opportunities for learning. For example, investment in new computerised equipment to revolutionise a production process would enable an organisation to better use highly-technical production methods.

Chapter Roundup

- **Annualised equivalents** are used to enable a comparison to be made between the net present values of projects with different durations. However the method cannot be used when inflation is a factor. Another method, the **lowest common multiple** method is used instead. In the next section there is an example of this method for you to follow and work through.

- When an asset is **being replaced** with an **identical asset**, the **equivalent annual cost method** can be used.

- When an asset is being **replaced with a non-identical asset**, the decision is when to replace the asset rather than how frequently. The **present value of an annuity in perpetuity** must be calculated.

- A decision on whether or not a project should be **abandoned** should be made by selecting the option (continue or abandon) with the higher NPV.

- When an organisation has a limited amount of capital to invest in potential projects (**capital rationing**) in a single period, projects should be ranked in terms of the **profitability index**.

- When capital rationing occurs in a **number of periods and two products are under consideration,** the **graphical approach to linear programming** is used to arrive at an NPV-maximising mix of products. If there are **three or more projects** the **simplex method** should be applied.

- **Sensitivity analysis** is one method of analysing the risk surrounding a capital expenditure project and enables an assessment to be made of how responsive the project's NPV is to changes in the variables that are used to calculate that NPV.

- The **margin of error approach to sensitivity analysis** assesses how responsive the project's NPV (or payback period or ARR) is to changes in the variables used to calculate that NPV (or payback period or ARR).

- Probability distributions of variables in NPV calculations can be drawn up and an **EV of the NPV** calculated.

- As well as financial considerations, any decision support information provided to management should also incorporate **non-financial considerations**.

Quick Quiz

1   The net present value of the costs of operating a machine for the next three years is $10,724 at a cost of capital of 15%. What is the equivalent annual cost of operating the machine?

   A $4,697   B $3,575   C $4,111   D $3,109

2   What is the cost of operating the machine detailed in question 1 in perpetuity?

   A $31,313   B $71,493   C $23,831   D $12,333

3   Sensitivity analysis allows for uncertainty in project appraisal by assessing the probability of changes in the decision variables. *True or false*?

4   *Fill in the blanks.*

   The profitability index used to rank projects in situations where capital is limited is calculated as

   .... ÷ ....

5   An organisation's cost of capital is 12%. The IRR of project X is 19.7% and the NPV is $7,900. By how much can the cost of capital increase before the NPV becomes negative?

   A   7.7%
   B   39.1%
   C   19.7%
   D   64.2%

6   *Fill in the blanks.*

   The sensitivity of a project appraised using DCF to changes in a variable is calculated as:

   (................../..................) × 100%.

7   An organisation is deciding whether to replace specialised machinery after a three, four or five year cycle. The NPVs for each cycle are as follows.

	Three-year cycle $	Four-year cycle $	Five-year cycle $
NPV at 10%	(7,150)	(8,300)	(9,190)

   Required

   Calculate the optimum replacement policy (in years) for the machinery.

Answers to Quick Quiz

1   A $10,724/2.283 = $4,697

2   A $4,697/0.15 = $31,313

3   False

4   The profitability index used to rank projects in situations where capital is limited is calculated as **the present value of the project's future cash flows** (not including the capital investment) ÷ **the present value of the total capital outlay**.

5   D   ((19.7 − 12)/12) × 100% = 64.2%

6   (NPV of project/PV of cashflow affected) × 100%

7   The optimum replacement policy is five years.

	Three-year cycle	Four-year cycle	Five-year cycle
NPV at 10%	$(7,150)	$(8,300)	$(9,190)
Cumulative 10% discount factor	÷ 2.487	÷ 3.170	÷ 3.791
Annualised equivalent cost	$2,875	$2,618	$2,424

The **lowest annualised equivalent cost** results from a five year cycle, therefore the company should replace its machinery every five years.

Now try the question below from the Exam Question Bank

Number	Level	Marks	Time
Q19	Examination	25	45 mins

Part D
The treatment of uncertainty in decision making

Risk and uncertainty in decision making

14

Introduction

In this chapter we will be looking at a number of **techniques** that can be used to **take account of risk or uncertainty** surrounding decisions.

Decision making involves making decisions now about what will happen in the future. Ideally, the decision maker would know with certainty what the future consequences would be for each choice facing him. But, in reality, decisions must be made in the knowledge that their **consequences**, although perhaps probable, are **rarely 100% certain**. In this chapter we look at methods of assessing risk and uncertainty for short-term decision making. In Chapter 13, we looked at probability analysis and long-term decision making.

Data tables have also been examined in recent exams including as part of a longer question in the November sitting. Expected values are a favourite topic both in shorter and longer questions and were tested in both May and November 2006 exams in Section C. Finally, minimax regret appeared as a four mark Objective Test question in the November 2005 sitting.

We begin this chapter with a general discussion of risk and uncertainty (**Section 1**). Various methods of analysing **uncertainty and risk using probability** will be described in **Sections 2 to 6** of this chapter. Some methods may seem more sensible or practical than others, but you should judge each method on its merits, and be able to apply and discuss it in an examination.

The uncertainty about the future outcome from taking a decision can sometimes be reduced by obtaining more information first about what is likely to happen. In **Section 7** we look at how to **value** that **information** to see if it is worth obtaining it.

Section 8 looks in general at a topic we have considered at a number of points throughout this text – **sensitivity analysis**. **Simulation models**, the topic of **Section 9**, can be used to deal with decision problems involving a number of uncertain variables.

Topic list	Learning outcomes	Syllabus references	Ability required
1 Risk and uncertainty in decision making	C(i)	C(1)	Evaluation
2 Probability analysis and expected values	C(iii),(iv)	C(3),(4),(5)	Application, Analysis
3 Data tables	C(iii)	C(3)	Analysis
4 The maximin, maximax and minimax regret bases for decision making	C(iii)	C(3),(4)	Analysis
5 Using the standard deviation to measure risk	C(iii)	C(3),(4)	Analysis
6 Decision trees	C(v)	C(6)	Application
7 The value of information	C(iv)	C(5)	Application
8 Sensitivity analysis	C(ii)	C(2)	Application
9 Simulation models	C(i)	C(3),(4)	Evaluation

1 Risk and uncertainty in decision making

1.1 What are risk and uncertainty?

Key terms

Risk involves situations or events which may or may not occur, but whose probability of occurrence can be calculated statistically and the frequency of their occurrence predicted from past records. Thus insurance deals with risk.

Uncertain events are those whose outcome cannot be predicted with statistical confidence.

FAST FORWARD

An example of a **risky situation** is one in which we can say that there is a 70% probability that returns from a project will be in excess of $100,000 but a 30% probability that returns will be less than $100,000. If no information can be provided on the returns from the project, we are faced with an **uncertain** situation.

1.2 Risk and capital investment decisions

In general, **risky projects** are those which have **future cash flows**, and hence project returns, that are likely to be **variable**. The **greater the variability**, the **greater the risk**.

The problem of **risk is more acute with capital investment decisions** for the following reasons.

(a) **Estimates** of capital expenditure might be for **several years ahead,** such as those for major construction projects. Actual costs may well escalate well above budget as the work progresses.

(b) Estimates of benefits will be for several years ahead, sometimes 10, 15 or 20 years ahead or even longer, and such long-term estimates can at best be approximations.

Exam focus point

In everyday usage the terms risk and uncertainty are not clearly distinguished. If you are asked for a definition, do not make the **mistake of believing that the latter** is a more **extreme version of the former**. It is not a question of degree, it is a question of whether or **not sufficient information is available to allow the lack of certainty to be quantified**. As a rule, however, the terms are used interchangeably.

1.3 Risk preference

FAST FORWARD

People may be **risk seekers**, **risk neutral** or **risk averse**.

Key terms

- A **risk seeker** is a decision maker who is interested in the best outcomes no matter how small the chance that they may occur.

- A decision maker is **risk neutral** if he is concerned with what will be the most likely outcome.

- A **risk averse** decision maker acts on the assumption that the worst outcome might occur.

This has clear implications for managers and organisations. A **risk seeking manager** working for an **organisation** that is characteristically **risk averse** is likely to make decisions that are **not congruent with the goals of the organisation**. There may be a role for the management accountant here, who could be instructed to present decision-making information in such a way as to ensure that the manager considers *all* the possibilities, including the worst.

What is an acceptable amount of risk will vary from organisation to organisation. For large public companies it is largely a question of what is acceptable to the shareholders. A 'safe' investment will attract investors who are to some extent risk averse, and the company will thus be obliged to follow relatively 'safe' policies. A company that is recognised as being an innovator or a 'growth' inventory in a relatively new market, like *Yahoo!*, will attract investors who are looking for high performance and are prepared to accept some risk in return. Such companies will be expected to make 'bolder' (more risky) decisions.

The risk of an individual strategy should also be considered in the context of the overall 'portfolio' of investment strategies adopted by the company.

(a) If a **strategy is risky**, but its outcome is **not related to the outcome of other strategies**, then adopting that strategy will help the company to **spread its risks**.

(b) If a **strategy is risky**, but is **inversely related** to other adopted strategies, so that if strategy A does well, other adopted strategies will do badly and vice versa, then adopting strategy A would actually **reduce the overall risk of the company's investment portfolio**.

2 Probability analysis and expected values

2.1 Histograms and probability distributions

2.1.1 Frequency distributions

A **frequency distribution** (or **table**) records the number of times each value of a variable occurs.

2.1.2 Histograms

A frequency distribution can be represented pictorially by means of a **histogram**. As you should remember from your earlier studies, a histogram is a chart that looks like a bar chart except that the bars are joined together. On a histogram, frequencies are represented by the area covered by the bars (not the height of the bars).

2.1.3 Probability distributions

If we convert the frequencies in the following frequency distribution table into proportions, we get a **probability distribution**.

Marks out of 10 (statistics test)	Number of students (Frequency distribution)	Proportion or probability (Probability distribution)
0	0	0.00
1	0	0.00
2	1	0.02 (1/50)
3	2	0.04
4	4	0.08
5	10	0.20
6	15	0.30
7	10	0.20
8	6	0.12
9	2	0.04
10	0	0.00
	50	1.00

Key term

> A **probability distribution** is an analysis of the proportion of times each particular value occurs in a set of items.

A **graph of the probability distribution** would be the same as the graph of the frequency distribution (histogram), but with the **vertical axis marked in proportions** rather than in numbers.

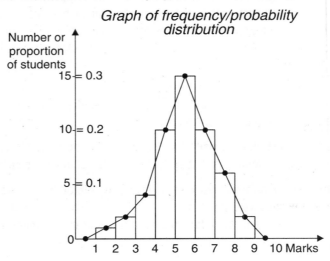

Graph of frequency/probability distribution

(a)   The area under the curve in the frequency distribution represents the total number of students whose marks have been recorded, 50 people.

(b)   **The area under the curve in a probability distribution is 100%, or 1** (the total of all the probabilities).

2.2 Expected values

> Knowledge brought forward from earlier studies

Probability

- **Mutually exclusive outcomes** are outcomes where the occurrence of one of the outcomes excludes the possibility of any of the others happening.

- **Independent events** are events where the outcome of one event in no way affects the outcome of the other events.

- **Dependent** or **conditional** events are events where the outcome of one event depends on the outcome of the others.

- The **addition laws** for two events, A and B, are as follows.

  P(A or B) = P(A) + P(B) when A and B have mutually exclusive outcomes.
  P(A or B) = P(A) + P(B) − P(A and B) when A and B are independent events.

- The **multiplication laws** for two events, A and B, are as follows.

  P(A and B) = 0 when A and B have mutually exclusive outcomes.
  P(A and B) = P(A) P(B) when A and B are independent events.
  P(A and B) = P(A) P(B/A) = P(B) P(A/B) when A and B are dependent/conditional events.

Although the outcome of a decision may not be certain, there is some likelihood that probabilities could be assigned to the various possible outcomes from an analysis of previous experience.

Where probabilities are assigned to different outcomes, it is common to evaluate the worth of a decision as the expected value, or weighted average, of these outcomes.

y term

> **Expected value** is 'The financial forecast of the outcome of a course of action multiplied by the probability of achieving that outcome. The probability is expressed as a value ranging from 0 to 1.'
>
> (CIMA *Official Terminology*)

rmula to arn

> The **expected value** of an opportunity is equal to the sum of the probabilities of an outcome occurring multiplied by the return expected if it does occur:
>
> $$EV = \Sigma\ px$$
>
> where p is the probability of an outcome occurring and x is the value (profit or cost) of that outcome.

ST FORWARD

If a decision maker is faced with a number of alternative decisions, each with a range of possible outcomes, the optimum decision will be the one which gives the highest **expected value** (EV = Σpx). This is **Bayes' strategy**.

y term

> The choice of the option with the highest EV is known as **Bayes' strategy**.

2.2.1 Example: Bayes' strategy

Suppose a manager has to choose between mutually exclusive options A and B, and the probability distributions of the profits of both options are as follows.

	Option A		Option B	
	Probability	Profit	Probability	Profit
		$		$
	0.8	5,000	0.1	(2,000)
	0.2	6,000	0.2	5,000
			0.6	7,000
			0.1	8,000

The expected value (EV) of profit of each option would be measured as follows.

Probability		Option A Profit		EV of Profit	Probability		Option B Profit		EV of Profit
		$		$			$		$
0.8	×	5,000	=	4,000	0.1	×	(2,000)	=	(200)
0.2	×	6,000	=	1,200	0.2	×	5,000	=	1,000
		EV	=	5,200	0.6	×	7,000	=	4,200
					0.1	×	8,000	=	800
							EV	=	5,800

In this example, since it offers a higher EV of expected profit, option B would be selected in preference to A, unless further risk analysis is carried out.

| Question | EV calculations |

Learning outcome: C(iii)

A manager has to choose between mutually exclusive options A, B, C and D and the probable outcomes of each option are as follows.

Option A		Option B		Option C		Option D	
Probability	Cost	Probability	Cost	Probability	Cost	Probability	Cost
	$		$		$		$
0.1	30,000	0.5	21,000	0.29	15,000	0.03	14,000
0.1	60,000	0.5	20,000	0.54	20,000	0.30	17,000
0.1	80,000			0.17	30,000	0.35	21,000
0.7	5,500					0.32	24,000

All options will produce an income of $30,000.

Which option should be chosen?

A   Option A
B   Option B
C   Option C
D   Option D

Answer

The correct answer is C.

A: EV of cost = $20,850
     EV of profit = $9,150

B: EV of cost = $20,500
     EV of profit = $9,500

C: EV of cost = $20,250
     EV of profit = $9,750

D: EV of cost = $20,550
     EV of profit = $9,450

C has the highest EV of profit.

Exam focus point

There have been simple objective test questions requiring an EV calculation in recent exam papers and the pilot paper.

2.2.2 Limitations of expected values

Referring back to the example in 2.2.1, the preference for B over A on the basis of expected value is marred by the fact that A's **worst possible outcome is a profit of $5,000**, whereas **B might incur a loss of $2,000** (although there is a 70% chance that profits would be $7,000 or more, which would be more than the best profits from option A).

Since the **decision must be made once only** between A and B, the expected value of profit (which is merely a weighted average of all possible outcomes) has severe limitations as a decision rule by which to judge preference as it ignores the range of outcomes and their probabilities. We consider the concept of **utility** later in this section, which can help overcome this problem.

Expected values are more **valuable** as a guide to decision making where they refer to **outcomes which will occur many times over**.

- The probability that so many customers per day will buy a tin of peaches
- The probability that a call centre will receive so many phone calls per hour

2.3 EVs and elementary risk analysis

Where some analysis of risk is required when probabilities have been assigned to various outcomes, an elementary, but extremely useful, form of risk analysis is a form of the worst possible/most likely/best possible analysis.

2.3.1 Example: elementary risk analysis

Skiver has budgeted the following results for the coming year.

Sales Units	Probability	EV of Sales Units
30,000	0.3	9,000
40,000	0.4	16,000
50,000	0.3	15,000
		40,000

The budgeted sales price is $10 per unit, and the expected cost of materials is as follows.

Cost per unit of output $	Probability	EV $
4	0.2	0.8
6	0.6	3.6
8	0.2	1.6
		6.0

Materials are the only variable cost. All other costs are fixed and are budgeted at $100,000.

The **expected value of profit** is $60,000.

	$
Sales (EV 40,000 units) at $10 each	400,000
Variable costs (40,000 × $6)	240,000
Contribution	160,000
Fixed costs	100,000
Profit	60,000

The worst possible outcome would be sales of 30,000 units and material costs of $8 per unit.

If sales are only 30,000 units, the total contribution would be:

- (a) $180,000 at a material cost of $4 (contribution $6 per unit)
- (b) $120,000 at a material cost of $6 (contribution $4 per unit)
- (c) $60,000 at a material cost of $8 (contribution $2 per unit).

Since there is a 20% chance that materials will cost $8, there is a **20% chance of making a loss,** given fixed costs of $100,000. This applies only if **sales are 30,000 units**.

If materials cost $8 per unit, there would be a **loss** at sales volumes of both 30,000 and 40,000 units. The **chance** that one or other of these events will occur is **14%**, as calculated below.

Sales	Probability	Material cost	Probability	Joint probabilities
30,000 units	0.3	$8	0.2	0.06
40,000 units	0.4	$8	0.2	0.08
		Combined probabilities		0.14

However there is also a chance that sales will be 50,000 units and material will cost $4, so that contribution would be $300,000 in total and profits $200,000. This is the **best possible outcome** and it has a $0.3 \times 0.2 = 0.06$ or 6% probability of occurring.

A **risk averse** decision maker might feel that a 14% chance of making a loss was unacceptable, whereas a **risk seeker** would be attracted by the 6% chance of making $200,000 profit. The **risk neutral** decision maker would need to consider the EV of profit of $60,000.

2.4 EVs and more complex risk analysis

FAST FORWARD

The calculation of **joint probabilities** and **cumulative probabilities** adds to the information for risk analysis.

As we have seen, EVs can be used to compare two or more mutually exclusive alternatives: the alternative with the most favourable EV of profit or cost would normally be preferred. However, **alternatives can also be compared** by looking at the **spread of possible outcomes**, and the **probabilities** that they will occur. The technique of drawing up **cumulative probability tables** might be helpful, as the following example shows.

2.4.1 Example: mutually exclusive options and cumulative probability

QRS is reviewing the price that it charges for a major product line. Over the past three years the product has had sales averaging 48,000 units per year at a standard selling price of $5.25. Costs have been rising steadily over the past year and the company is considering raising this price to $5.75 or $6.25. The sales manager has produced the following schedule to assist with the decision.

Price	$5.75	$6.25
Estimates of demand (units)		
Pessimistic estimate (probability 0.25)	35,000	10,000
Most likely estimate (probability 0.60)	40,000	20,000
Optimistic estimate (probability 0.15)	50,000	40,000

Currently the unit cost is estimated at $5.00, analysed as follows.

	$
Direct material	2.50
Direct labour	1.00
Variable overhead	1.00
Fixed overhead	0.50
	5.00

The cost accountant considers that the most likely value for unit variable cost over the next year is $4.90 (probability 0.75) but that it could be as high as $5.20 (probability 0.15) and it might even be as low as $4.75 (probability 0.10). Total fixed costs are currently $24,000 p.a. but it is estimated that the corresponding total for the ensuing year will be $25,000 with a probability of 0.2, $27,000 with a probability of 0.6, $30,000 with a probability of 0.2. (Demand quantities, unit costs and fixed costs can be assumed to be statistically independent.)

Required

Analyse the foregoing information in a way which you consider will assist management with the problem, give your views on the situation and advise on the new selling price. Calculate the expected level of profit that would follow from the selling price that you recommend.

Discussion and solution

In this example, there are two mutually exclusive options, a price of $5.75 and a price of $6.25. Sales demand is uncertain, but would vary with price. Unit contribution and total contribution depend on sales price and sales volume, but total fixed costs are common to both options. Clearly, it makes sense to begin looking at EVs of contribution and then to think about fixed costs and profits later.

(a)   A probability table can be set out for each alternative, and an EV calculated, as follows.

Price $5.75

Sales Demand Units	Probability (a)	Variable cost per unit $	Probability (b)	Unit cont'n $	Total cont'n $'000	Joint proba- bility * (a × b)	EV of cont'n $'000
35,000	0.25	5.20	0.15	0.55	19.25	0.0375	0.722
		4.90	0.75	0.85	29.75	0.1875	5.578
		4.75	0.10	1.00	35.00	0.0250	0.875
40,000	0.60	5.20	0.15	0.55	22.00	0.0900	1.980
		4.90	0.75	0.85	34.00	0.4500	15.300
		4.75	0.10	1.00	40.00	0.0600	2.400
50,000	0.15	5.20	0.15	0.55	27.50	0.0225	0.619
		4.90	0.75	0.85	42.50	0.1125	4.781
		4.75	0.10	1.00	50.00	0.0150	0.750
						EV of contribution	33.005

The EV of contribution at a price of $5.75 is $33,005.

* Remember to check that the joint probabilities sum to 1.

Alternative approach

An alternative method of calculating the EV of contribution is as follows.

EV of contribution   =   EV of sales revenue − EV of variable costs

EV of sales revenue =   EV of sales units × selling price
                      = $((35,000 \times 0.25) + (40,000 \times 0.60) + (50,000 \times 0.15)) \times \$5.75$
                      =   40,250 × $5.75 = $231,437.50

EV of variable costs =   EV of sales units × EV of unit variable costs
                      = $40,250 \times ((\$5.20 \times 0.15) + (\$4.90 \times 0.75) + (\$4.75 \times 0.10)) = 40,250$
                           × $4.93 = $198,432.50

∴ EV of contribution = $(231,437.50 − 198,432.50) = $33,005

This method is quicker and simpler, but an extended table of probabilities will help the risk analysis when the two alternative selling prices are compared.

Price $6.25

Sales demand Units	Probability (a)	Variable cost per unit $	Probability (b)	Unit cont'n $	Total cont'n $'000	Joint proba- bility (a × b)	EV of cont'n $'000
10,000	0.25	5.20	0.15	1.05	10.50	0.0375	0.394
		4.90	0.75	1.35	13.50	0.1875	2.531
		4.75	0.10	1.50	15.00	0.0250	0.375
20,000	0.60	5.20	0.15	1.05	21.00	0.0900	1.890
		4.90	0.75	1.35	27.00	0.4500	12.150
		4.75	0.10	1.50	30.00	0.0600	1.800
40,000	0.15	5.20	0.15	1.05	42.00	0.0225	0.945
		4.90	0.75	1.35	54.00	0.1125	6.075
		4.75	0.10	1.50	60.00	0.0150	0.900
						EV of contribution	27.060

The EV of contribution at a price of $6.25 is $27,060.

Exam focus point

Question

More complex EV analysis

Learning outcome: C(iii), (iv)

Calculate the EV of contribution at a selling price of $6.25 using the alternative approach set out above.

(b)   The EV of **fixed costs** is $27,200.

Fixed costs	Probability	EV
$		$
25,000	0.2	5,000
27,000	0.6	16,200
30,000	0.2	6,000
		27,200

(c)   **Conclusion**

On the basis of EVs alone, a price of $5.75 is preferable to a price of $6.25, since it offers an EV of contribution of $33,005 and so an EV of profit of $5,805; whereas a price of $6.25 offers an EV of contribution of only $27,060 and so an EV of loss of $140.

Additional information

A comparison of cumulative probabilities would add to the information for risk analysis. The cumulative probabilities can be used to compare the **likelihood of earning a total contribution of a certain size with each selling price**.

Refer back to the two probability tables above. You should be able to read the probabilities and related total contributions straight from each table.

The table below shows that no matter whether fixed costs are $25,000, $27,000 or $30,000, the **probability of at least breaking even** is much higher with a price of $5.75 than with a price of $6.25. The only reason for favouring a price of $6.25 is that there is a better **probability of earning bigger profits** (a contribution of $50,000 or more), and so although a risk-averse decision maker would choose a price of $5.75, a risk-seeking decision maker might gamble on a price of $6.25.

Probability of total contribution of at least $	Price $5.75 Probability	Workings	Price $6.25 Probability	Workings
15,000	1.0000		0.7750	(1 – 0.0375 – 0.1875)
20,000	0.9625	(1 – 0.0375)	0.7500	(0.775 – 0.025)
25,000	0.8725	(0.9625 – 0.09)	0.6600	etc
27,000	0.8725		0.6600	
30,000	0.6625	(0.8725 – 0.1875 – 0.0225)	0.2100	
35,000	0.2125	etc	0.1500	
40,000	0.1875		0.1500	
50,000	0.0150		0.1275	
60,000	0.0000		0.0150	

2.5 The advantages and disadvantages of point estimate probabilities

A **point estimate probability** means an estimate of the **probability of particular outcomes occurring**. In the previous example, there were point estimate probabilities for **variable costs** ($5.20 or $4.90 or $4.75) but in **reality**, the **actual** variable cost per unit **might be any amount**, from below $4.75 to above $5.20. Similarly, point estimate probabilities were given for period fixed costs ($25,000 or $27,000 or $30,000) but in reality, actual fixed costs might be any amount between about $25,000 and $30,000.

This is a disadvantage of using point estimate probabilities: they can be **unrealistic**, and can only be an **approximation** of the risk and uncertainty in estimates of costs or sales demand.

In spite of their possible disadvantages, point estimate probabilities can be very helpful for a decision maker.

(a) They provide some estimate of risk, which is probably **better than nothing**.

(b) **If there are enough point estimates** they are likely to be a **reasonably good approximation of** a continuous probability distribution.

(c) Alternatively, it can be **assumed** that point estimate probabilities **represent a range** of values, so that if we had the probabilities for variable cost per unit, say, of $5.20, $4.90, and $4.75 we could assume that those actually represent probabilities for the ranges, say, $5.05 to $5.30, and $4.82 to $5.04 and $4.70 to $4.81.

2.6 Utility theory

Earlier in this section we explained that there are limitations to using EV as a basis for making one-off decisions because only one outcome will occur, and the possible 'worst' result could matter to a greater or lesser extent to different people.

It was Bernoulli who first suggested that: 'The decision of an individual on whether or not to accept a particular gamble depends on the utility which he attaches to the sums of money involved not just on the sums themselves.'

Bernoulli therefore suggested that sums of money be converted into their utility values (utility being measured in units called **utiles**) using a diminishing marginal utility curve, an example of which is shown below. Let's say it represents the utility investor X attaches to certain sums of money.

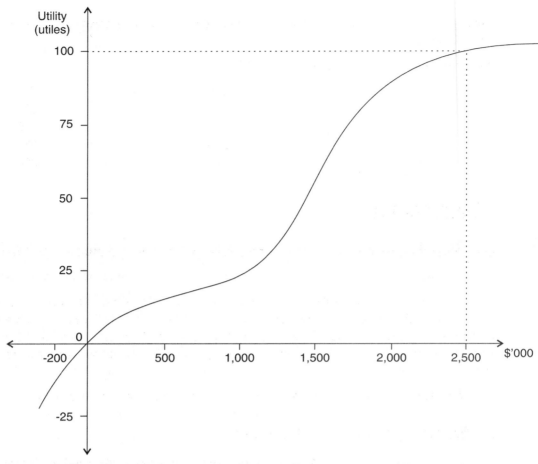

So, by reading from the curve we see that for investor X the monetary value of $500,000 is equal to 15 utiles, while $1,000,000 is equal to 23 utiles.

Now suppose that investor X has to choose between three possible projects, A, B or C. Details of possible cash benefits from the projects with associated probabilities are shown below.

Investment A		Investment B		Investment C	
Cash benefit	Prob	Cash benefit	Prob	Cash benefit	Prob
$'000		$'000		$'000	
(100)	0.50	(130)	0.35	(150)	0.60
200	0.40	200	0.40	350	0.05
900	0.05	2,000	0.25	800	0.10
1,200	0.05			2,500	0.25

Just as we calculate an EV using cash flows and probabilities, we can determine expected utility values (EUV) by multiplying probabilities and utilities of monetary values (read from the graph).

Investment A			Investment B			Investment C		
Utility	Prob	EUV	Utility	Prob	EUV	Utility	Prob	EUV
(5)	0.50	(2.5)	(8)	0.35	(2.8)	(10)	0.60	(6.0)
9	0.40	3.6	9	0.40	3.6	13	0.05	0.7
20	0.05	1.0	89	0.25	22.3	19	0.10	1.9
30	0.05	1.5			23.1	100	0.25	25.0
		3.6						21.6

Based on the measure of EUV, investment B should be selected. Any project with a negative EUV should never be chosen.

This is not the decision we would get if we used EV, however.

Investment	EUV	EV
	Utiles	$'000
A	3.6	135
B	23.1	535
C	21.6	633

3 Data tables

FAST FORWARD

Data tables are often produced using spreadsheet packages and show the effect of changing the values of variables.

A **one-way or one-input data table shows the effect of a range of values of one variable**. For example it might show the effect on profit of a range of selling prices. A **two-way or two-input data table shows the results of combinations of different values of two key variables.** The effect on contribution of combinations of various levels of demand and different selling prices would be shown in a two-way data table.

Any combination of variable values can therefore be changed and the **effects monitored.**

3.1 Example: a one-way data table

Suppose a company has production costs which it would expect to be in the region of $5m were it not for the effects of inflation. Economic forecasts for the inflation rate in the coming year range from 2% to 10%. Profit before inflation is taken into account is expected to be $475,000.

By using a spreadsheet package and with three or four clicks of the mouse, the data table below is produced. This shows the effects of different levels of inflation on production costs and profit.

		Production costs	Profit
		$'000	$'000
	2%	5,100	375
	3%	5,150	325
Inflation rate	4%	5,200	275
	5%	5,250	225
	6%	5,300	175
	7%	5,350	125
	8%	5,400	75
	9%	5,450	25
	10%	5,500	(25)

So if inflation were to be 7%, the company could expect production costs to be in the region of $5,350,000 and profit to be about $125,000 ($(475,000 − (7% × $5m)).

3.2 Example: two-way data table

Suppose now that the company mentioned in the example above is not sure that its production costs will be $5m. They could alternatively be only $4.5m or else they could be up to $5.5m.

We therefore need to examine the effects of both a range of rates of inflation and three different production costs on profit, and so we need a two-way data table as shown below.

Two-way data table showing profit for a range of rates of inflation and production costs

		Production costs		
		$4,500,000	*$5,000,000*	*$5,500,000*
		$'000	$'000	$'000
	2%	385	375	365
	3%	340	325	310
Inflation rate	4%	295	275	255
	5%	250	225	200
	6%	205	175	145
	7%	160	125	90
	8%	115	75	35
	9%	70	25	(20)
	10%	25	(25)	(75)

So if production costs were $5,500,000 and the rate of inflation was 4%, the profit should be $255,000 ($(475,000 − (4% × $5,500,000)).

Exam focus point

Simple two-way data tables had to be analysed in Section C questions in the pilot paper, the May 2005 exam and the November 2006 exam.

3.3 Data tables and probability

If a probability distribution can be applied to either or both of the variables in a data table, a revised table can be prepared to provide improved management information.

3.3.1 Example: data tables and probability

Estimates of levels of demand and unit variable costs, with associated probabilities, for product B are shown below. Unit selling price is fixed at $100.

Levels of demand

Pessimistic	Probability of 0.4	10,000 units
Most likely	Probability of 0.5	12,500 units
Optimistic	Probability of 0.1	13,000 units

Unit variable costs

Pessimistic	Probability of 0.3	$20
Most likely	Probability of 0.4	$30
Optimistic	Probability of 0.3	$35

Required

Produce a two-way data table showing levels of contribution that incorporates information about both the variables and the associated probabilities.

Solution

Table of total contributions

The shaded area on this table shows the possible total contributions and the associated joint probabilities.

Demand Probability			10,000 0.4	12,500 0.5	13,000 0.1
Unit variable cost	Probability	Unit contribution			
$20	0.3	$80	$800,000 0.12	$1,000,000 0.15	$1,040,000 0.03
$30	0.4	$70	$700,000 0.16	$875,000 0.20	$910,000 0.04
$35	0.3	$65	$650,000 0.12	$812,500 0.15	$845,000 0.03

4 The maximin, maximax and minimax regret bases for decision making

The **assumption** made so far in this chapter has been that when there is a decision to make, and probabilities of the various outcomes have been estimated, the decision maker should **prefer the option with the highest EV of profit**.

For **once-only decisions**, this choice of option with the best EV does not necessarily make sense. It provides one rational basis for decision making, but it is not the only rational basis. There are **several other ways of making a choice**, including the following.

(a) **Playing safe**, and **choosing the option with the least damaging results if events were to turn out badly**.

(b) Looking for the **best outcome**, no matter how small the chance that it might occur.

(c) Looking at the opportunity loss when we choose an option but come to regret it.

(d) **Balancing the EV of profit against the risk**, measured as the **standard deviation of variations in possible profit around the EV**. We cover this in Section 5.

FAST FORWARD

The 'play it safe' basis for decision making is referred to as the **maximin basis**. This is short for '**maximise the minimum achievable profit**'. (It might also be called '**minimax**' which is short for '**minimise the maximum potential cost or loss**'). Maximin decisions are taken by **risk-averse** decision makers.

A basis for making decisions by looking for the best outcome is known as the **maximax basis**, short for '**maximise the maximum achievable profit**'. (It can also be called the **minimin cost rule** – minimise the minimum costs or losses.) Maximax decisions are taken by **risk-seeking** decision makers.

The 'opportunity loss' basis for decision making is known as **minimax regret**.

Exam focus point

There was a four-mark question covering minimax regret in the November 2005 exam. This emphasises how any of this section could easily appear as a question in a future exam. Ensure that you are clear about the techniques by following the three examples included here in the text.

4.1 Example: maximin decision basis

Suppose that a manager is trying to decide which of three mutually exclusive projects to undertake. Each of the projects could lead to varying net profits which are classified as outcomes I, II and III. The manager has constructed the following **pay-off table or matrix** (a **conditional profit table**).

	Net profit if outcome turns out to be		
Project	*I*	*II*	*III*
A	$50,000	$65,000	$80,000
B	$70,000	$60,000	$75,000
C	$90,000	$80,000	$55,000
Probability	0.2	0.6	0.2

Required

Decide which project should be undertaken.

Solution

If the project with the **highest EV of profit** were chosen, this would be project C.

Outcome	*Probability*	*Project A* EV $	*Project B* EV $	*Project C* EV $
I	0.2	10,000	14,000	18,000
II	0.6	39,000	36,000	48,000
III	0.2	16,000	15,000	11,000
		65,000	65,000	77,000

However, if the **maximin criterion** were applied the assessment would be as follows.

Project selected	*The worst outcome that could happen*	*Profit* $
A	I	50,000
B	II	60,000
C	III	55,000

By **choosing B**, we are **'guaranteed' a profit of at least $60,000**, which is more than we would get from projects A or C if the worst outcome were to occur for them.

The decision would therefore be to **choose project B**.

The main **weakness** of the maximin basis for decision making is that it **ignores the probabilities** that **various different outcomes might occur**, and so in this respect, it is not as good as the EV basis for decision making.

4.2 Example: maximax

Here is a payoff table showing the profits that will be achieved depending upon the action taken (D, E or F) and the circumstances prevailing (I, II or III).

		Profits Actions		
		D	E	F
	I	100	80	60
Circumstances	II	90	120	85
	III	(20)	10	85
Maximum profit		100	120	85

Action E would be chosen if the maximax rule is followed.

Criticisms of this approach would again be that it ignores probabilities and that it is over-optimistic.

4.3 Minimax regret

Minimax regret considers the extent to which we might come to regret an action we had chosen.

Regret for any combination of action and circumstances	=	Payoff for **best** action in those circumstances	−	Payoff of the action **actually taken** in those circumstances

An alternative term for regret is **opportunity loss**. We may apply the rule by considering the maximum opportunity loss associated with each course of action and choosing the course which offers the smallest maximum. If we choose an action which turns out not to be the best in the actual circumstances, we have lost an opportunity to make the extra profit we could have made by choosing the best action.

Here are payoff tables for two separate decisions.

		Profits Actions		
		A	B	C
Circumstances	I	100	80	60
	II	90	120	85
	III	−20	10	40
Max profit		100	120	85
Difference between best and worst circumstances		120	110	45

		Costs Actions		
		D	E	F
Circumstances	IV	40	50	60
	V	70	80	25
	VI	20	30	30
Min cost		20	30	25
		50	50	35

(i)   For the first decision, action B (payoff 120) would be chosen using maximax, or C using maximin (payoff 40) and using minimax regret.

(ii) For the second decision, action D would be chosen using maximax, F using maximin and using minimax regret.

Look at the example below. Follow through the solution and make sure you understand how the maximum regret is arrived at.

4.3.1 Example: minimax regret

A manager is trying to decide which of three mutually exclusive projects to undertake. Each of the projects could lead to varying net costs which the manager calls outcomes I, II and III. The following payoff table or matrix has been constructed.

		Outcomes (Net profit)		
		I (Worst)	II (Most likely)	III (Best)
Project	A	50	85	130
	B	70	75	140
	C	90	100	110

Which project should be undertaken?

Solution

A table of regrets can be compiled, as follows, showing the amount of profit that might be forgone for each project, depending on whether the outcome is I, II or III.

	Outcome			Maximum
	I	*II*	*III*	
Project A	40 *	15 ***	10	40
Project B	20 **	25	0	25
Project C	0	0	30	30

* 90 – 50   ** 90 – 70   *** 100 – 85   etc

The **maximum regret** is 40 with project A, 25 with B and 30 with C. The lowest of these three maximum regrets is 25 with B, and so project B would be selected if the minimax regret rule is used.

5 Using the standard deviation to measure risk

FAST FORWARD

Risk can be measured by the possible variations of outcomes around the expected value. One useful measure of such variations is the **standard deviation of the expected value**.

Formula to learn

The standard deviation is $s = \sqrt{\Sigma p(x - \bar{x})^2} = \sqrt{\text{variance}}$

where $\bar{x}$ is the EV of profit
   x represents each possible profit
   p represents the probability of each possible profit

The decision maker can then **weigh up the EV of each option against the risk** (the standard deviation) that is **associated with it**.

5.1 Example: measuring risk

The management of RC is considering which of two mutually exclusive projects to select. Details of each project are as follows.

Project S		Project T	
Probability	*Profit*	*Probability*	*Profit*
	$'000		*$'000*
0.3	150	0.2	(400)
0.3	200	0.6	300
0.4	250	0.1	400
		0.1	800

Required

Determine which project seems preferable, S or T.

Solution

On the basis of EVs alone, **T is marginally preferable** to S, by $15,000.

	Project S				Project T	
Probability	*Profit*	*EV*		*Probability*	*Profit*	*EV*
	$'000	*$'000*			*$'000*	*$'000*
0.3	150	45		0.2	(400)	(80)
0.3	200	60		0.6	300	180
0.4	250	100		0.1	400	40
				0.1	800	80
	EV of profit	205			EV of profit	220

Project T is more risky, however, offering the prospect of a profit as high as $800,000 but also the possibility of a loss of $400,000.

One measure of this risk is the standard deviation of the EV of profit.

(a) **Project S**

Probability	Profit		
p	x	$x - \bar{x}$	$p(x - \bar{x})^2$
	$\$'000$		
0.3	150	−55	907.5*
0.3	200	−5	7.5
0.4	250	45	810.0
		Variance	1,725.0

* $0.3 \times (-55)^2$

Standard deviation = $\sqrt{1,725}$ = 41.533 = $41,533

(b) **Project T**

Probability	Profit		
p	x	$x - \bar{x}$	$p(x - \bar{x})^2$
	$\$'000$		
0.2	(400)	−620	76,880
0.6	300	80	3,840
0.1	400	180	3,240
0.1	800	580	33,640
		Variance	117,600

Standard deviation = $\sqrt{117,600}$ = 342.929 = $342,929

If the management are **risk averse**, they might therefore **prefer project S** because, although it has a smaller EV of profit, the possible profits are subject to less variation.

The **risk associated with project T can be compared with the risk associated with project S** if we calculate the **coefficient of variation** for each project: the **ratio of the standard deviation of each project to its EV**.

	Project S	Project T
Standard deviation	$41,533	$342,929
EV of profit	$205,000	$220,000
Coefficient of variation (standard deviation/EV of profit)	0.20	1.56

Question — Using the standard deviation to measure risk

Learning outcome: C(iii)

Fill in the blank in the sentence below.

On the basis of the information below a 'risk averse' decision maker would choose project ....

Project A		Project B	
Estimated net cash flow	Probability	Estimated net cash flow	Probability
$		$	
		1,000	0.2
2,000	0.3	2,000	0.2
3,000	0.4	3,000	0.2
4,000	0.3	4,000	0.2
		5,000	0.2

Answer

The correct answer is project A.

The projects have the same EV of net cash flow ($3,000); therefore a risk averse manager would choose the project with the smaller standard deviation of expected profit.

Project A

Cash flow	Probability	EV of cash flow	Cash flow minus EV of cash flow $(x - \bar{x})$	$p(x - \bar{x})^2$
$		$	$	$
2,000	0.3	600	−1,000	300,000
3,000	0.4	1,200	0	0
4,000	0.3	1,200	+1,000	300,000
		EV = 3,000		Variance = 600,000

Standard deviation = $\sqrt{600{,}000}$ = $775

Project B

Cash flow	Probability	EV of cash flow	Cash flow minus EV of cash flow $(x - \bar{x})$	$p(x - \bar{x})^2$
$		$	$	$
1,000	0.2	200	−2,000	800,000
2,000	0.2	400	−1,000	200,000
3,000	0.2	600	0	0
4,000	0.2	800	+1,000	200,000
5,000	0.2	1,000	+2,000	800,000
		EV = 3,000		Variance = 2,000,000

Standard deviation = $\sqrt{2{,}000{,}000}$ = $1,414

 Question   **Standard deviation of the net present value**

Learning outcome: C(iii)

Frame is considering which of two mutually exclusive projects, A or B, to undertake. There is some uncertainty about the running costs with each project, and a probability distribution of the NPV for each project has been estimated, as follows.

	Project A		Project B	
NPV	Probability		NPV	Probability
$'000			$'000	
− 20	0.15		+ 5	0.2
+ 10	0.20		+ 15	0.3
+ 20	0.35		+ 20	0.4
+ 40	0.30		+ 25	0.1

Required

Choose the correct words from those highlighted in the sentence below.

The organisation should choose **project A/project B** if management are risk averse.

Answer

The correct answer is project B.

We can begin by calculating the EV of the NPV for each project.

	Project A				Project B	
NPV	*Prob*	*EV*		*NPV*	*Prob*	*EV*
$'000		*$'000*		*$'000*		*$'000*
− 20	0.15	(3.0)		5	0.2	1.0
10	0.20	2.0		15	0.3	4.5
20	0.35	7.0		20	0.4	8.0
40	0.30	12.0		25	0.1	2.5
		18.0				16.0

Project A has a higher EV of NPV, but what about the risk of variation in the NPV above or below the EV? This can be measured by the standard deviation of the NPV.

The standard deviation of a project's NPV can be calculated as $\sqrt{\Sigma p(x - \bar{x})^2}$, where $\bar{x}$ is the EV of the NPV.

	Project A, $\bar{x}$ = 18				Project B, $\bar{x}$ = 16		
x	*p*	$x - \bar{x}$	$p(x - \bar{x})^2$	*x*	*p*	$x - \bar{x}$	$p(x - \bar{x})^2$
$'000		*$'000*		*$'000*		*$'000*	
− 20	0.15	− 38	216.6	5	0.2	− 11	24.2
10	0.20	− 8	12.8	15	0.3	− 1	0.3
20	0.35	+ 2	1.4	20	0.4	+ 4	6.4
40	0.30	+ 22	145.2	25	0.1	+ 9	8.1
			376.0				39.0

	Project A			Project B
Standard deviation	=	√376	Standard deviation =	√39.0
	=	19.391	=	6.245
	=	$19,391	=	$6,245

Although **Project A has a higher EV of NPV**, it also has a **higher standard deviation of NPV**, and so has **greater risk** associated with it.

Which project should be selected? Clearly it depends on the attitude of the company's management to risk. If management are **risk-averse**, they will opt for the **less risky project B**.

(If management were prepared **to take the risk of a low NPV in the hope of a high NPV** they will opt for **project A**.)

6 Decision trees

ST FORWARD **Decision trees** are diagrams which illustrate the choices and possible outcomes of a decision.

term A **decision tree** is 'A pictorial method of showing a sequence of interrelated decisions and their expected outcomes. Decision trees can incorporate both the probabilities of, and values of, expected outcomes, and are used in decision-making.' (CIMA *Official Terminology*)

A probability problem such as 'what is the probability of throwing a six with one throw of a die?' is fairly straightforward and can be solved using the basic principles of probability.

More complex probability questions, although solvable using the basic principles, require a clear logical approach to ensure that all possible choices and outcomes of a decision are taken into consideration. **Decision trees** are a useful means of interpreting such probability problems.

Exactly how does the use of a decision tree permit a clear and logical approach?

- All the possible **choices** that can be made are shown as **branches** on the tree.
- All the possible **outcomes** of each choice are shown as **subsidiary branches** on the tree.

6.1 Constructing a decision tree

There are two stages in preparing a decision tree.

- Drawing the tree itself to show all the choices and outcomes
- Putting in the numbers (the probabilities, outcome values and EVs)

Every **decision tree starts** from a **decision point** with the **decision options** that are currently being considered.

(a)   It helps to identify the **decision point**, and any subsequent decision points in the tree, with a symbol. Here, we shall use a **square shape**.

(b)   There should be a **line**, or **branch**, for each **option** or **alternative**.

It is conventional to draw decision trees from left to right, and so a decision tree will start as follows.

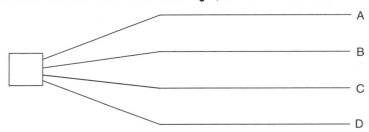

The **square** is the **decision point**, and A, B, C and D represent **four alternatives** from which a choice must be made (such as buy a new machine with cash, hire a machine, continue to use existing machine, raise a loan to buy a machine).

If the outcome from any choice is certain, the branch of the decision tree for that alternative is complete.

If the outcome of a particular choice is uncertain, the various possible outcomes must be shown.

We show the various possible outcomes on a decision tree by inserting an **outcome point** on the **branch** of the tree. Each possible outcome is then shown as a **subsidiary branch**, coming out from the outcome point. The probability of each outcome occurring should be written on to the branch of the tree which represents that outcome.

To distinguish decision points from outcome points, **a circle will be used as the symbol for an outcome point**.

In the example above, there are two choices facing the decision-maker, A and B. The outcome if A is chosen is known with certainty, but if B is chosen, there are two possible outcomes, high sales (0.6 probability) or low sales (0.4 probability).

When several outcomes are possible, it is usually simpler to show two or more stages of outcome points on the decision tree.

6.2 Example: several possible outcomes

A company can choose to launch a new product XYZ or not. If the product is launched, expected sales and expected unit costs might be as follows.

	Sales		Unit costs
Units	Probability	$	Probability
10,000	0.8	6	0.7
15,000	0.2	8	0.3

(a)   The decision tree could be drawn as follows.

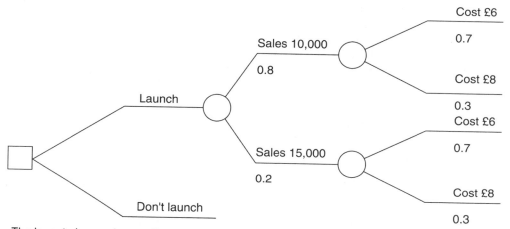

(b)   The layout shown above will usually be easier to use than the alternative way of drawing the tree, which is as follows.

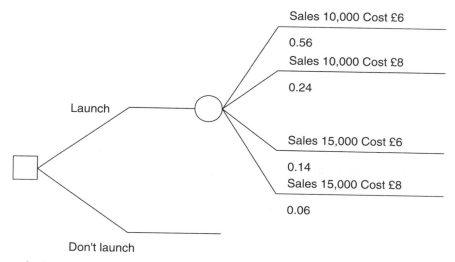

Sometimes, a **decision taken now** will lead to **other decisions to be taken in the future**. When this situation arises, the decision tree can be drawn as a **two-stage tree**, as follows.

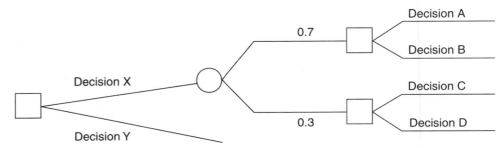

In this tree, either a choice between A and B or else a choice between C and D will be made, depending on the outcome which occurs after choosing X.

The decision tree should be in **chronological order** from **left to right**. When there are two-stage decision trees, the first decision in time should be drawn on the left.

6.3 Example: a decision tree

Beethoven has a new wonder product, the vylin, of which it expects great things. At the moment the company has two courses of action open to it, to test market the product or abandon it.

If the company test markets it, the cost will be $100,000 and the market response could be positive or negative with probabilities of 0.60 and 0.40.

If the response is positive the company could either abandon the product or market it full scale.

If it markets the vylin full scale, the outcome might be low, medium or high demand, and the respective net gains/(losses) would be (200), 200 or 1,000 in units of $1,000 (the result could range from a net loss of $200,000 to a gain of $1,000,000). These outcomes have probabilities of 0.20, 0.50 and 0.30 respectively.

If the result of the test marketing is negative and the company goes ahead and markets the product, estimated losses would be $600,000.

If, at any point, the company abandons the product, there would be a net gain of $50,000 from the sale of scrap. All the financial values have been discounted to the present.

Required

(a)   Draw a decision tree.
(b)   Include figures for cost, loss or profit on the appropriate branches of the tree.

Solution

The starting point for the tree is to **establish what decision has to be made now**. What are the options?

(a)   To test market
(b)   To abandon

The outcome of the 'abandon' option is known with certainty. There are two possible outcomes of the option to test market, positive response and negative response.

Depending on the outcome of the test marketing, another decision will then be made, to abandon the product or to go ahead.

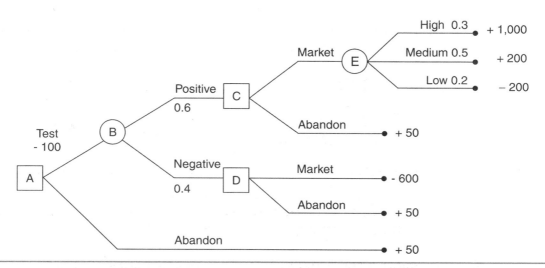

:ention!

In an examination, remember to draw decision trees (and *all* diagrams) neatly, using a sharp pencil and ruler. Remember also to label decision points and branches as clearly as possible.

6.4 Evaluating the decision with a decision tree

ST FORWARD ⟩

Rollback analysis evaluates the EV of each decision option. You have to work from right to left and calculate EVs at each outcome point.

The EV of each decision option can be evaluated, using the decision tree to help with keeping the logic properly sorted out. The basic rules are as follows.

(a)   We start on the **right hand side** of the tree and **work back** towards the left hand side and the current decision under consideration. This is sometimes known as the **'rollback' technique** or '**rollback analysis**'.

(b)   Working from **right to left**, we calculate the **EV of revenue, cost, contribution or profit** at each outcome point on the tree.

In the above example, the right-hand-most outcome point is point E, and the EV is as follows.

	Profit	Probability		
	x	*p*		*px*
	$'000			$'000
High	1,000	0.3		300
Medium	200	0.5		100
Low	(200)	0.2		(40)
			EV	360

This is the EV of the decision to market the product if the test shows positive response. It may help you to write the EV on the decision tree itself, at the appropriate outcome point (point E).

(a)   **At decision point C**, the **choice** is as follows.

(i)   Market, EV = + 360 (the EV at point E)
(ii)   Abandon, value = + 50

The choice would be to market the product, and so the EV at decision point C is +360.

(b)   **At decision point D**, the **choice** is as follows.

(i)   Market, value = − 600
(ii)   Abandon, value = +50

The choice would be to abandon, and so the EV at decision point D is +50.

411

The second stage decisions have therefore been made. If the original decision is to test market, the company will market the product if the test shows positive customer response, and will abandon the product if the test results are negative.

The evaluation of the decision tree is completed as follows.

(a)   **Calculate the EV at outcome point B.**

$$
\begin{array}{ll}
0.6 \times 360 & \text{(EV at C)} \\
+\quad 0.4 \times 50 & \text{(EV at D)} \\
=\quad 216 + 20 = 236.
\end{array}
$$

(b)   **Compare the options at point A**, which are as follows.

(i)   Test: EV = EV at B minus test marketing cost = 236 – 100 = 136
(ii)   Abandon: Value = 50

The choice would be to test market the product, because it has a **higher EV of profit**.

| Question | Simple decision tree |

Learning outcome: C(v)

Consider the following diagram.

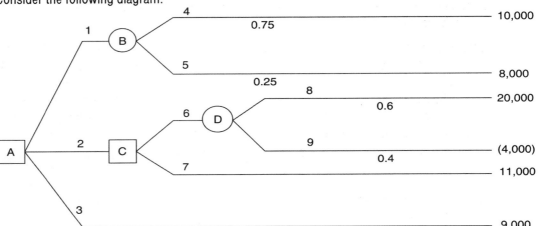

If a decision maker wished to maximise the value of the outcome, which options should be selected?

A   Option 2 and option 7
B   Option 3
C   Option 1 and option 4
D   Option 2, option 6 and option 8

Answer

The correct answer is A.

The various outcomes must be evaluated using expected values.

EV at point B: (0.75 × 10,000) + (0.25 × 8,000) = 9,500

EV at point D: (0.6 × 20,000) + (0.4 × (4,000)) = 10,400

EV at point C: Choice between 10,400 and 11,000

EV at point A: Choice between B (9,500), C (10,400 or 11,000) and choice 3 (9,000).

If we are trying to maximise the figure, option 2 and then option 7 are chosen to give 11,000.

Evaluating decisions by using **decision trees has a number of limitations**.

(a)   The time value of money may not be taken into account.

(b)   Decision trees are not very suitable for use in complex situations.

(c)   The outcome with the highest EV may have the greatest risks attached to it. Managers may be reluctant to take risks which may lead to losses.

(d)   The probabilities associated with different branches of the 'tree' are likely to be estimates, and possibly unreliable or inaccurate.

exam focus point

The May 2006 exam included a longer Section C question where candidates were asked to **prepare** a decision tree to illustrate an investment decision. The tree must show the decisions to be made and the correct symbols for decisions and outcomes. Practise this question (Health clinic) from your revision kit.

Question
More complex decision tree

Learning outcome: C(v)

A software company has just won a contract worth $80,000 if it delivers a successful product on time, but only $40,000 if it is late. It faces the problem now of whether to produce the work in-house or to sub-contract it. To sub-contract the work would cost $50,000, but the local sub-contractor is so fast and reliable as to make it certain that successful software is produced on time.

If the work is produced in-house the cost would be only $20,000 but, based on past experience, would have only a 90% chance of being successful. In the event of the software *not* being successful, there would be insufficient time to rewrite the whole package internally, but there would still be the options of either a 'late rejection' of the contract (at a further cost of $10,000) or of 'late sub-contracting' the work on the same terms as before. With this late start the local sub-contractor is estimated to have only a 50/50 chance of producing the work on time or of producing it late. In this case the sub-contractor still has to be paid $50,000, regardless of whether he meets the deadline or not.

Required

(a)   Draw a decision tree for the software company, using squares for decision points and circles for outcome (chance) points, including all relevant data on the diagram.

(b)   Calculate expected values as appropriate and recommend a course of action to the software company with reasons.

Answer

(a)   All values in $'000

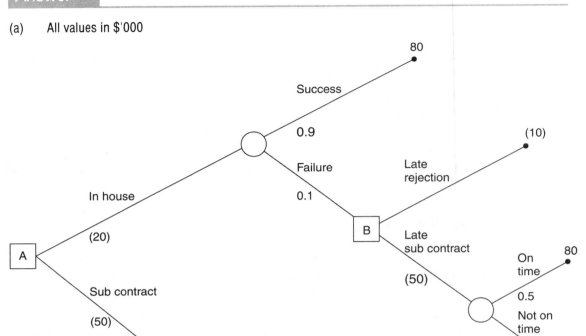

(b)   **At decision point B**

EV of late rejection = –10
EV of late sub-contract = (80 × 0.5) + (40 × 0.5) – 50 = 10
The optimum strategy at B is therefore to subcontract with EV = 10.

At decision point A
EV of sub-contract = 80 – 50 = 30
EV of in-house = (80 × 0.9) + (10* × 0.1) – 20 = 53
The optimum strategy at A is therefore to produce in-house with EV = 53.
*This is the optimum EV at decision point B.

Conclusions

The decisions which will maximise expected profits are to attempt initially to produce in-house and if this fails to sub-contract. The expected profit is $53,000.

Assuming that the probabilities have been correctly estimated, the company has a 90% chance of making a profit of $60,000, a 5% chance of making $10,000 and a 5% chance of making a $30,000 loss. If the company is not willing to risk making a loss, the initial option of subcontracting should be taken since this offers a guaranteed profit of $30,000.

6.5 Sensitivity analysis and decision trees

Look again at **Question: more complex decision tree**. By how much can the probability of success fall before the optimal EV decision changes?

Suppose the probability of success = p (and so the probability of failure = 1 – p). At decision **point A** we want to find the point where **EV (sub-contract) = EV (in-house)**.

$$30 = (80 \times p) + (10 \times (1 - p)) - 20$$
$$30 = 80p + 10 - 10p - 20$$
$$40 = 70p$$
$$p = 0.57$$

Since the probability of success can drop to 57% from 90% before we change our decision, we would probably consider the decision insensitive to this factor.

6.6 Further reading

Two articles appeared in *Financial Management* in November 2006, and December/January 2007. The articles explain how decision trees and expected values could be used to solve a problem faced by a company where quality and cost were major factors. The articles were in a series so they must be read together.

7 The value of information

Perfect information is guaranteed to predict the future with 100% accuracy. **Imperfect information** is better than no information at all but could be wrong in its prediction of the future.

Perfect information removes all doubt and uncertainty from a decision, and enables managers to make decisions with complete confidence that they have selected the optimum course of action.

7.1 The value of perfect information

The **value of perfect information** is the difference between the EV of profit with perfect information and the EV of profit without perfect information.

Step 1 If we **do not have perfect information** and we must choose between two or more decision options, we would **select** the decision option which offers the **highest EV** of profit. This option will not be the best decision under all circumstances. There will be some probability that what was really the best option will not have been selected, given the way actual events turn out.

Step 2 With **perfect information**, the **best decision option will always be selected**. Just what the profits from the decision will be must depend on the future circumstances which are predicted by the information; nevertheless, the EV of profit with perfect information should be higher than the EV of profit without the information.

Step 3 The **value of perfect information** is **the difference between these two EVs**.

7.1.1 Example: the value of perfect information

The management of Ivor Ore must choose whether to go ahead with either of two mutually exclusive projects, A and B. The expected profits are as follows.

	Profit if there is strong demand	Profit/(loss) if there is weak demand
Option A	$4,000	$(1,000)
Option B	$1,500	$500
Probability of demand	0.3	0.7

Required

(a) Ascertain what the decision would be, based on expected values, if no information about demand were available.

(b) Calculate the value of perfect information about demand.

Solution

Step 1   If there were **no information** to help with the decision, the project with the higher EV of profit would be selected.

Probability	Project A		Project B	
	Profit	EV	Profit	EV
	$	$	$	$
0.3	4,000	1,200	1,500	450
0.7	(1,000)	(700)	500	350
		500		800

Project B would be selected.

This is clearly the better option if demand turns out to be weak. However, if demand were to turn out to be strong, project A would be more profitable. There is a 30% chance that this could happen.

Step 2   **Perfect information** will indicate for certain whether demand will be weak or strong. If demand is forecast 'weak' project B would be selected. If demand is forecast as 'strong', project A would be selected, and perfect information would improve the profit from $1,500, which would have been earned by selecting B, to $4,000.

Forecast demand	Probability	Project chosen	Profit	EV of profit
			$	$
Weak	0.7	B	500	350
Strong	0.3	A	4,000	1,200
EV of profit with perfect information				1,550

Step 3

	$
EV of profit without perfect information (that is, if project B is always chosen)	800
EV of profit with perfect information	1,550
Value of perfect information	750

Provided that the information does not cost more than $750 to collect, it would be worth having.

 Question   **Decision based on EV of profit**

Learning outcome: C(iv)

Watt Lovell must decide at what level to market a new product, the urk. The urk can be sold nationally, within a single sales region (where demand is likely to be relatively strong) or within a single area. The decision is complicated by uncertainty about the general strength of consumer demand for the product, and the following conditional profit table has been constructed.

		Weak	Demand Moderate	Strong
		$	$	$
Market	nationally (A)	(4,000)	2,000	10,000
	in one region (B)	0	3,500	4,000
	in one area (C)	1,000	1,500	2,000
Probability		0.3	0.5	0.2

Option B should be selected, based on EVs of profit. *True or false?*

Answer

The correct answer is option B and so the statement is true.

Without perfect information, the option with the highest EV of profit will be chosen.

Probability	Option A (National) Profit $	EV $	Option B (Regional) Profit $	EV $	Option C (Area) Profit $	EV $
0.3	(4,000)	(1,200)	0	0	1,000	300
0.5	2,000	1,000	3,500	1,750	1,500	750
0.2	10,000	2,000	4,000	800	2,000	400
		1,800		2,550		1,450

Marketing regionally (option B) has the highest EV of profit, and would be selected.

Question   **Perfect information**

Learning outcome: C(iv)

Using the information in your answer to the question above (Decision based on EV of profit), fill in the blank in the sentence below.

The value of information about the state of demand is $.......... .

Answer

The correct answer is $1,500.

If perfect information about the state of consumer demand were available, option A would be preferred if the forecast demand is strong and option C would be preferred if the forecast demand is weak.

Demand	Probability	Choice	Profit $	EV of profit $
Weak	0.3	C	1,000	300
Moderate	0.5	B	3,500	1,750
Strong	0.2	A	10,000	2,000
EV of profit with perfect information				4,050
EV of profit, selecting option B				2,550
Value of perfect information				1,500

m focus
nt

> The November 2006 exam asked candidates to calculate the maximum price that should be paid for perfect information. This features in a longer 25 mark Section C question.

7.2 Perfect information and decision trees

When the option exists to obtain information, the decision can be shown, like any other decision, in the form of a decision tree, as follows. We will suppose, for illustration, that the cost of obtaining perfect information is $400.

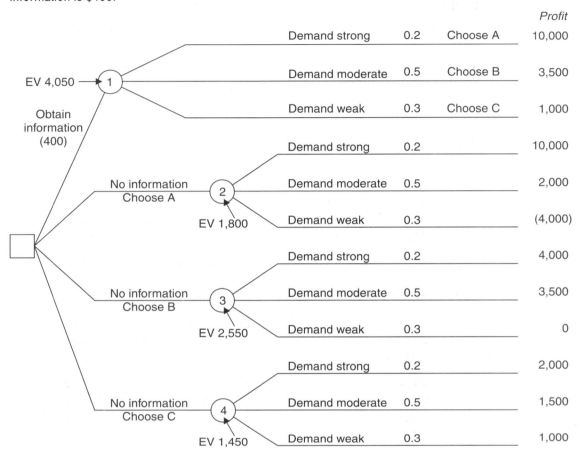

The decision would be to obtain perfect information, since the EV of profit is $4,050 – $400 = $3,650.

Attention!

> You should check carefully that you understand the logic of this decision tree and that you can identify how the EVs at outcome boxes 1, 2, 3 and 4 have been calculated.

7.3 The value of imperfect information

There is one serious drawback to the technique we have just looked at: in practice **useful information is never perfect** unless the person providing it is the sole source of the uncertainty. Market research findings or information from pilot tests and so on are likely to be reasonably accurate, but they can still be wrong: they provide imperfect information. It is possible, however, to arrive at an assessment of **how much it would be worth paying for such imperfect information, given that we have a rough indication of how right or wrong it is likely to be**.

Suppose we are considering the sex and hair colour of people in a given group or population consisting of 70% men and 30% women. We have established the probabilities of hair colourings as follows.

	Men	Women
Brown	0.60	0.35
Blonde	0.35	0.55
Red	0.05	0.10

This shows, for example, that 5% of men in such a sample have red hair. These probabilities of sex and hair colouring might be referred to as **prior probabilities**.

Posterior probabilities consider the situation in reverse or retrospect, so that we can ask the question: 'Given that a person taken at random from the population is brown-haired what is the probability that the person is male (or female)?'

The information can be presented in a table. Let's suppose that the population consists of 1,000 people.

	Male	Female	Total
Brown	420 (W3)	105 (W4)	525 (W5)
Blonde	245	165	410
Red	35	30	65
	700 (W1)	300 (W2)	1,000

Workings

1    $1,000 \times 70\%$
2    $1,000 - 700$
3    $700 \times 60\%$ (the other two values in the column being calculated in a similar way)
4    $300 \times 35\%$ (the other two values in the column being calculated in a similar way)
5    $420 + 105$ (the other two values in the column being calculated in a similar way)

$\therefore$ P(Person selected is a male, given that that person is brown-haired) = $420/525 = 0.8$

7.3.1 Example: the value of imperfect information

Suppose that the Small Oil Company (SOC) is trying to decide whether or not to drill on a particular site. The chief engineer has assessed the probability that there will be oil, based on past experience, as 20%, and the probability that there won't be oil as 80%.

It is possible for SOC to hire a firm of international consultants to carry out a complete survey of the site. SOC has used the firm many times before and has estimated that if there really is oil, there is a 95% chance that the report will be favourable, but if there is no oil, there is only a 10% chance that the report will indicate that there is oil.

Required

Determine whether drilling should occur.

Solution

Read the information given carefully. We are given *three* sets of probabilities.

(a)   The probability that there will be oil (0.2) or there will not be (0.8). These outcomes are mutually exclusive.

(b)   The probability that, if there is oil, the report will say there is oil (0.95) or say there is no oil (0.05).

(c)   The probability that, if there is no oil, the report will say there *is* oil (0.1) or say there is no oil (0.9).

Both (b) and (c) describe conditional events, since the existence of oil or otherwise influences the chances of the survey report being correct.

SOC, meanwhile faces a number of choices which we can show as a decision tree.

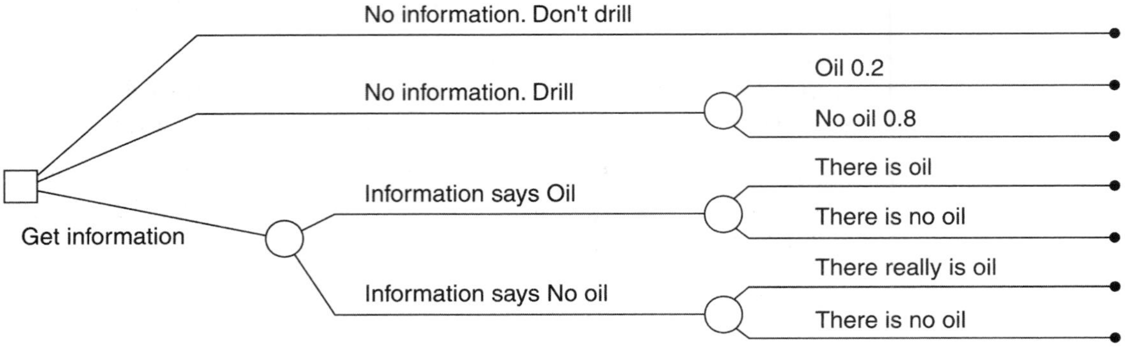

We must now calculate the probabilities of the following outcomes.

- The information will say 'oil' or 'no oil'
- The information will be right or wrong if it says 'oil'
- The information will be right or wrong if it says 'no oil'

If you check the information given in the problem, you will find that these probabilities are not given.

(a) We are told that the engineer has assessed that there is a 20% chance of oil and an 80% chance of no oil (ignoring information entirely). These are the **prior probabilities** of future possible outcomes.

(b) The **probabilities that there will be oil or no oil once the information has been obtained are posterior probabilities**.

Step 1 We can tabulate the various probabilities as percentages.

		Actual outcome					
		Oil		*No oil*		*Total*	
Survey	oil	19	(W2)	8	(W3)	27	(W4)
result:	no oil	1		72		73	
Total		20	(W1)	80		100	

Workings

1 The engineer estimates 20% probability of oil and 80% of no oil.

2 If there is oil, ie in 20 cases out of 100, the survey will say so in 95% of these cases, ie in 20 × 0.95 = 19 cases. The 1 below the 19 is obtained by subtraction.

3 In the 80 per 100 cases where there is in fact no oil, the survey will wrongly say that there is oil 10% of the time; ie 80 × 0.10 = 8 cases. The 72 below the 8 is obtained by subtraction.

4 The horizontal totals are given by addition.

Step 2 We can now provide all the probabilities needed to complete the tree.

P (survey will say there is oil) = 27/100 = 0.27

P (survey will say there is no oil) = 73/100 = 0.73

If survey says oil	P (there is oil)	= 19/27 = 0.704
	P (there is no oil)	= 8/27 = 0.296 (or 1–0.704)
If survey says no oil	P (there is oil)	= 1/73 = 0.014
	P (there is no oil)	= 72/73 = 0.986 (or 1–0.014)

Step 3   We can now go on to complete the decision tree. Let us make the following assumptions. (In an exam question such information would have been given to you from the start.)

- The cost of drilling is $10m.
- The value of the benefits if oil is found is $70m, giving a net 'profit' of $60m.
- The cost of obtaining information from the consultants would be $3m.

An assumption is made that the decision maker will take whichever decision the information indicates is the best. If the information says 'oil', the company will drill, and if the information says 'no oil' it will not drill.

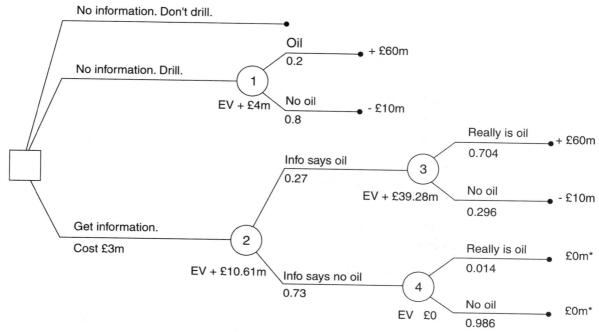

* The information is 'no oil', so the company won't drill, regardless of whether there really is oil or not.

Step 4   We can now perform rollback analysis.

		$m
EV at point 3 =	0.704 × $60m	42.24
	0.296 × ($10m)	(2.96)
		+ 39.28

		$m
EV at point 2 =	0.27 × $39.28m	10.61
	0.73 × $0	0.00
		+ 10.61

Step 5   There are three choices.

		EV
(a)	Do not obtain information and do not drill	$0
(b)	Do not obtain information and drill	+$4 million
(c)	Obtain information first, decide about drilling later ($(10.61m − 3m))	
		+$7.61 million

The decision should be to obtain the information from a survey first.

Step 6   The value of the imperfect information is the difference between (b) and (c), $3.61 million.

am focus
int

If the examiner asks you to calculate the maximum amount that should be paid for a forecast, you need to calculate 'the value of imperfect information' using the approach we have explained.

8 Sensitivity analysis

We will encounter sensitivity analysis in relation to a number of techniques throughout this text. Here we look at it in more general terms.

Key term

Sensitivity analysis is 'A modelling and risk assessment procedure in which changes are made to significant variables in order to determine the effect of these changes on the planned outcome. Particular attention is thereafter paid to variables identified as being of special significance.'

(CIMA *Official Terminology*)

FAST FORWARD

Two useful approaches to sensitivity analysis

(a) Estimate by how much costs and revenues would need to differ from their estimated values before the decision would change

(b) Estimate whether a decision would change if estimated costs were x% higher than estimated, or estimated revenues y% lower than estimated.

The essence of the approach is therefore to **carry out the calculations with one set of values for the variables** and then **substitute other possible values** for the variables to see **how this affects the overall outcome**.

8.1 Example: sensitivity analysis

SS has estimated the following sales and profits for a new product which it may launch on to the market.

		$	$
Sales	(2,000 units)		4,000
Variable costs:	materials	2,000	
	labour	1,000	
			3,000
Contribution			1,000
Less incremental fixed costs			800
Profit			200

Required

Analyse the sensitivity of the project.

Solution

The **margin of safety** = ((budgeted sales − breakeven sales)/budgeted sales) × 100%

The breakeven point = fixed costs/contribution per unit
$\qquad\qquad$ = $800/($1,000/2,000 units) = 1,600 units

∴ Margin of safety = ((2,000 − 1,600)/2,000) × 100% = 20%

If any of the **costs increase by more than $200**, the profit will disappear and there will be a **loss**.

Changes in variables which would result in a loss

- More than ((200/800) × 100%) 25% increase in incremental **fixed costs**
- More than ((200/2,000) × 100%) 10% increase in unit cost of **materials**
- More than ((200/1,000) × 100%) 20% increase in **unit labour costs**
- More than ((200/4,000) × 100%) 5% drop in **unit selling price**

Management would now be able to judge more clearly whether the product is likely to be profitable. The **items to which profitability is most sensitive** in this example are the **selling price** (5%) and **material costs** (10%). Sensitivity analysis can help to **concentrate management attention on the most important forecasts**.

8.2 'What if' analysis

'What if' analysis looks at the results of varying a model's key variables, parameters or estimates.

Sensitivity analysis is a 'what if' technique that examines how a result will change if the original predicted values are not achieved or if an underlying assumption changes.

In its **simplest form** 'what if' analysis can be carried out using a **hand-held calculator** (which is the case for the sensitivity analysis questions we have considered throughout this Text). As you have seen in Chapter 4, **spreadsheet packages** can be used for more complex scenarios, with answers to 'what if' questions obtained quickly and simply. **Commercial software packages** are now available for the most complex tasks, such as sensitivity analysis on the financial statements found in a master budget. These packages do the calculations for financial planning models, which are mathematical representations of the relationships across operating activities, financial activities and financial statements.

8.2.1 Example

Estimate by how much a variable would need to differ before a decision maker was indifferent between two options.

Option 2 is £10,000 more expensive than option 1 and involves taking a discount of 10% from a supplier from whom you purchase £50,000 of goods (before discount) pa for 4 years. Ignore the time value of money. Discount needs to be £10,000 (difference) + £20,000 (current discount) if option 2 is as good as option 1.

$\therefore (4 \times £50,000) \times X\% = £30,000$
$\therefore X = 15\%$ (rate at which you are indifferent between the two options)

9 Simulation models

One of the chief problems encountered in decision making is the uncertainty of the future. Where only a few factors are involved, probability analysis and expected value calculations can be used to find the most likely outcome of a decision. Often, however, in real life, there are so **many uncertain variables** that this approach does not give a true impression of possible variations in outcome. To get an idea of what will happen in real life one possibility is to use a **simulation model** in which the **values and the variables are selected at random**. Obviously this is a situation **ideally suited to a computer** (large volume of data, random number generation).

9.1 The Monte Carlo method

The **Monte Carlo method of simulation** makes use of random numbers.

The term 'simulation' model is often used more specifically to refer to modelling which **makes use of random numbers**. This is the 'Monte Carlo' method of simulation. In the business environment it can, for example, be used to examine inventory, queuing, scheduling and forecasting problems.

9.1.1 Example: inventory system

In an inventory system, it may be decided to examine inventory levels at the end of each day or each week.

Suppose that a computer has been programmed to generate the weekly demand for an item of inventory to be, in units, 15, 22, 12, 17, 10, 5, 14, and 20 over a period of eight weeks. If the simulation model also assumes that 50 units of inventory are ordered at the end of any week when the balance of units in inventory falls below 20, and that the delivery takes one week, a simulation model might produce the following report of inventory levels at the end of each week.

Week	Event	End of week inventory level
0		50
1	Demand 15 units	35
2	Demand 22 units	13
	Order 50 units	
3	Demand 12 units	1
	50 units delivered	51
4	Demand 17 units	34
5	Demand 10 units	24
6	Demand 5 units	19
	Order 50 units	
7	Demand 14 units	5
	50 units delivered	55
8	Demand 20 units	35

The simulation model **shows how inventory levels might vary**, and **what average inventory and inventory costs might be**. It would also be possible to **test whether the reorder level should be altered** to a different amount by changing the parameter that the reorder level should be '20 or less at the end of the week'. A reorder level of, say '15 or less' could be tested, re-running the model over a simulated period of time to determine the balance in inventory or the number of inventory-outs each week, and the expected **cost of inventory holding, re-ordering and inventory-outs could then be estimated**.

Exam focus point

> The November 2005 exam, Section C part of a question, asked for an explanation of how probabilities can be used in a simulation model to evaluate risk. This part of the question was not well answered but the examiner's own answer required only five lines explaining how a Monte Carlo simulation would be applied to generate estimated values. Alternatively, you could have applied your own simulation to the probabilities calculated in the question to give an example. If you refer to the Revision Kit Question 9 (2007 edition) this gives an example of the method applied.

9.2 Designing a simulation model

9.2.1 Probability distributions and random numbers

In the preceding example, it was implied that a computer could be used to generate the demand per week from defined probability distributions of weekly demand. When designing a simulation model, the modeller will need to specify the probability distribution that reflects the real system most accurately. When the simulation model is used, the **values of the variables** (in our example, demand each week) **will be selected at random, but in such a way as to preserve the properties of the chosen probability distribution**. This is achieved for any variable **by allocating to each possible value (or range of values) a group of numbers**. The **size** of the group of numbers for each value will be **directly proportional to the probability that the value will occur 'in real life'**. The actual value chosen at a particular point in the simulation will then be determined by selecting a number at random. The example below will make this clear if you are a bit confused.

Constructing and using a simulation model therefore hinges upon the following.

(a) **Identifying probability distributions for variables with a changeable value**

(b) **Allocating a range of numbers to each possible value based on the probability distribution**

(c) When the model is used, **generating random numbers to derive 'actual' values for the variable**

Random numbers can be generated by computer or, alternatively, a string of numbers can be selected manually from an arbitrary place in a printed random number table.

Random numbers are allocated to each possible value of the uncertain variable in proportion to the probabilities, so that a probability of 0.1 gets 10% of the total numbers to be assigned. These random numbers are used to assign values to the variables.

9.2.2 Example: simulation and spreadsheets

A supermarket sells a product for which the daily demand varies. An analysis of daily demand over a period of about a year shows the following probability distribution.

Demand per day Units	Probability
35	0.10
36	0.20
37	0.25
38	0.30
39	0.08
40	0.07
	1.00

To develop a simulation model in which one of the variables is daily demand, we would **assign a group of numbers to each value for daily demand**. The **probabilities are stated** to two decimal places, and so there must be **100 random numbers in total**, 00 – 99 (we use 00-99 rather than 1-100 so that we can use **two-digit random numbers.) Random numbers are assigned in proportion to the probabilities**, so that a probability of 0.1 gets 10% of the total numbers to be assigned, that is 10 numbers: 0, 1, 2, 3, 4, 5, 6, 7, 8 and 9.

The assignments would therefore be as follows.

Demand per day Units	Probability	Numbers assigned
35	0.10	00 – 09
36	0.20	10 – 29
37	0.25	30 – 54
38	0.30	55 – 84
39	0.08	85 – 92
40	0.07	93 – 99

When the simulation model is run, random numbers will be generated to derive values for daily demand. For example, if the model is used to simulate demand over a ten day period, the **random numbers generated** might be as follows.

19007174604721296802

The model would then **assign values to the demand per** day as follows.

Day	Random number	Demand Units
1	19	36
2	00	35
3	71	38
4	74	38
5	60	38
6	47	37
7	21	36
8	29	36
9	68	38
10	02	35

You might notice that on none of the ten days is the demand 39 or 40 units, because the random numbers generated did not include any value in the range 85 – 99. When a simulation model is used, there must be a long enough run to give a good representation of the system and all its potential variations.

Question

Simulation

Learning outcome: C(i)

Gleamy Windows is a company that provides a window cleaning service to offices and shops in a local area. The work force consists of ten workers, but there is a problem with absenteeism and the probability distribution of daily attendance is as follows.

Number at work	Probability
10	0.6
9	0.3
8	0.1

An analysis of past performance has shown that the number of windows that each worker can do in a day is as follows.

Number of windows per worker per day	Probability
120	0.15
125	0.24
130	0.27
135	0.19
140	0.15

The price charged for each window is 50p.

There are two variables, numbers at work and windows cleaned per worker per day.

Required

Complete the table below to show the allocation of groups of numbers to each value for each variable.

Number at work	Probability	Numbers allocated	Windows per worker per day	Probability	Numbers allocated
10	0.6		120	0.15	
9	0.3		125	0.24	
8	0.1		130	0.27	
			135	0.19	
			140	0.15	

Answer

Number at work	Probability	Numbers allocated	Windows per worker per day	Probability	Numbers allocated
10	0.6	0 – 5	120	0.15	00 – 14
9	0.3	6 – 8	125	0.24	15 – 38
8	0.1	9	130	0.27	39 – 65
			135	0.19	66 – 84
			140	0.15	85 – 99

Note how the numbers are allocated in the above exercise.

(a)   The **probabilities** for the numbers at work each day are **given to just one decimal place**, and so we can use **numbers in the range 0 – 9** rather than 00 – 99.

(b)   You might find it easiest to allocate number ranges by dealing with the lowest numbers in each range first. In the case of windows per worker per day, the lowest number range starts with 00. We can then add 15, 24, 27 and 19 respectively to get the lowest numbers in the higher ranges.

If we were to run the simulation model in the above exercise over a six-day period to estimate the daily revenue over this period, the **random numbers generated** might be as follows.

- For the number at work, 971088.
- For the windows per worker per day,   230998429964.

The **results** from the model would then be as follows.

Day	Random number	Number at work	Random number	Windows per worker per day	Total windows cleaned	Total revenue, at $0.50 per window $
1	9	8	23	125	1,000	500
2	7	9	09	120	1,080	540
3	1	10	98	140	1,400	700
4	0	10	42	130	1,300	650
5	8	9	99	140	1,260	630
6	8	9	64	130	1,170	585

If you have not already done so, **check to see how the figures in the number at work column and windows per worker per day column are derived** and perform the calculations for yourself.

The technique is often used to estimate **queues in shops**, banks, post offices and building societies. The length of waiting time predicted will enable estimates of staff requirements to be made. There are **two uncertainties** in such a scenario, however, as customers do not arrive at a constant rate and some customers require more or less time than the average service time. Two probability distributions and two allocations of random numbers would therefore be required.

9.3 Simulation models and project appraisal

Imagine trying to construct a decision tree of a simple project stretching over three years, the net cash flow each year being forecast at five different levels. It would have 125 different outcomes. In practice, it may be necessary to produce separate probabilities for alternative sales revenue outcomes, different items of costs and different possible life spans. A decision tree could therefore have thousands of different branches. In addition, cash flows may be correlated over time. A new project which is successful in early years is also likely to be successful in later years. Simulation will overcome these problems.

9.3.1 Example: simulation model

The following probability estimates have been prepared for a proposed project.

	Year	Probability	$
Cost of equipment	0	1.00	(40,000)
Revenue each year	1–5	0.15	40,000
		0.40	50,000
		0.30	55,000
		0.15	60,000
Running costs each year	1–5	0.10	25,000
		0.25	30,000
		0.35	35,000
		0.30	40,000

The cost of capital is 12%.

Required

Assess how a simulation model might be used to assess the project's NPV.

Solution

We construct a simulation model by **assigning a range of random number digits to each possible value for each of the uncertain variables**.

The **random numbers must exactly match their respective probabilities**. This is achieved by working upwards cumulatively from the lowest to the highest cash flow values and assigning numbers that will correspond to probability groupings as follows.

	Revenue					Running costs		
$	Prob	Random numbers			$	Prob	Random numbers
40,000	0.15	00 – 14	*		25,000	0.10	00 – 09
50,000	0.40	15 – 54	**		30,000	0.25	10 – 34
55,000	0.30	55 – 84	***		35,000	0.35	35 – 69
60,000	0.15	85 – 99			40,000	0.30	70 – 99

*   Probability is 0.15 (15%). Random numbers are 15% of range 00 – 99.
**   Probability is 0.40 (40%). Random numbers are 40% of range 00 – 99 but starting at 15.
***   Probability is 0.30 (30%). Random numbers are 30% of range 00 – 99 but starting at 55.

For revenue, the selection of a random number in the range 00 and 14 has a probability of 0.15. This probability represents revenue of $40,000. Numbers have been assigned to cash flows so that when numbers are selected at random, the cash flows have exactly the same probability of being selected as is indicated in their respective probability distribution.

Random numbers would be generated, for example by a computer program, and these would be used to assign values to each of the uncertain variables. For example, if random numbers 378420015689 were generated, the values assigned to the variables would be as follows.

Calculation	Revenue		Costs	
	Random number	Value $	Random number	Value $
1	37	50,000	84	40,000
2	20	50,000	01	25,000
3	56	55,000	89	40,000

A computer would calculate the NPV many times over using the values established in this way with more random numbers, and the results would be analysed to provide an expected NPV for the project and a statistical distribution pattern for the possible variation in the NPV above or below this average. The decision whether to go ahead with the project would then be made on the basis of expected return and risk.

Chapter Roundup

- An example of a **risky situation** is one in which we can say that there is a 70% probability that returns from a project will be in excess of $100,000 but a 30% probability that returns will be less than $100,000. If no information can be provided on the returns from the project, we are faced with an **uncertain** situation.

- People may be **risk seekers**, **risk neutral** or **risk averse**.

- If a decision maker is faced with a number of alternative decisions, each with a range of possible outcomes, the optimum decision will be the one which gives the highest **expected value** (EV = Σpx). This is **Bayes' strategy**.

- The calculation of **joint probabilities** and **cumulative probabilities** adds to the information for risk analysis.

- **Data tables** are often produced using spreadsheet packages and show the effect of changing the values of variables.

- The 'play it safe' basis for decision making is referred to as the **maximin basis**. This is short for '**maximise the minimum achievable profit**'. (It might also be called '**minimax**' which is short for '**minimise the maximum potential cost or loss**'). Maximin decisions are taken by **risk-averse** decision makers.

- A basis for making decisions by looking for the best outcome is known as the **maximax basis**, short for '**maximise the maximum achievable profit**'. (It can also be called the **minimin cost rule** – minimise the minimum costs or losses.) Maximax decisions are taken by **risk-seeking** decision makers.

- The 'opportunity loss' basis for decision making is known as **minimax regret**.

- Risk can be measured by the possible variations of outcomes around the expected value. One useful measure of such variations is the **standard deviation of the expected value**.

- **Decision trees** are diagrams which illustrate the choices and possible outcomes of a decision.

- **Rollback analysis** evaluates the EV of each decision option. You have to work from right to left and calculate EVs at each outcome point.

- **Perfect information** is guaranteed to predict the future with 100% accuracy. **Imperfect information** is better than no information at all but could be wrong in its prediction of the future.

- The **value of perfect information** is the difference between the EV of profit with perfect information and the EV of profit without perfect information.

- **Two useful approaches to sensitivity analysis**

    – Estimate by how much costs and revenues would need to differ from their estimated values before the decision would change.

    – Estimate whether a decision would change if estimated costs/revenues were x%/y% higher/lower than estimated.

- The **Monte Carlo method of simulation** makes use of random numbers.

- **Random numbers** are allocated to each possible value of the uncertain variable in proportion to the probabilities, so that a probability of 0.1 gets 10% of the total numbers to be assigned. These random numbers are used to assign values to the variables.

Quick Quiz

1   A particular decision maker is concerned with what will be the most likely outcome of a decision. He would be described as

    A   a risk seeker   C   risk neutral

    B   risk averse   D   a risk reducer

2   A probability can be expressed as any value from –1 to +1. *True or false?*

3   A manager is trying to decide which of three mutually exclusive projects to undertake. Each of the projects could lead to varying net costs which the manager calls outcomes I, II and III. The following payoff table or matrix has been constructed.

		I (Worst)	Outcomes (Net profit) *II (Most likely)*	*III (Best)*
	A	60	70	120
Project	B	85	75	140
	C	100	120	135

Using the minimax regret decision rule, decide which project should be undertaken?

4   *Choose the correct words from those highlighted.*

In a particular class of CIMA students, 65% are female and 80% have brown eyes. Given that a student selected at random from this class has brown eyes, to determine the probability that the student is male would require a consideration of **prior probabilities/posterior probabilities**.

5   If the decision maker is trying to maximise the figure, what figure would the decision maker choose at point B in the diagram below?

    A   40,000   C   13,900

    B   11,800   D   22,000

6   Given the probability distribution shown below, ranges of numbers to reach value in order to run a simulation model.

Probability	Numbers assigned	Probability	Numbers assigned
0.132	....	0.083	....
0.410	....	0.060	....
0.315	....		

7   *Fill in the blanks*

Standard deviation, $s = \sqrt{\rule{1cm}{0pt}}$

where $\bar{x}$ is ...., x represents ...., p represents ....

8   The following data relates to both of the following questions

AB can choose from five mutually exclusive projects. The projects will each last for one year only and their net cash inflows will be determined by the prevailing market conditions. The forecast net cash inflows and their associated probabilities are shown below.

Market conditions	Poor	Good	Excellent
Probability	0.20	0.40	0.40
	$'000	$'000	$'000
Project L	550	480	580
Project M	450	500	570
Project N	420	450	480
Project O	370	410	430

Market conditions	Poor	Good	Excellent
Project P	590	580	430

i   Based on the expected value of the net cash inflows, which project should be undertaken?

ii   The value of perfect information about the state of the market is calculated as:

Answers to Quick Quiz

1   C. Risk reducer is not a term we have covered!

2   False. Should be 0 to 1.

3   A table of regrets can be compiled, as follows, showing the amount of profit that might be forgone for each project, depending on whether the outcome is I, II or III.

	Outcome			Maximum
	I	*II*	*III*	
Project A	40 *	50	20	50
Project B	15 **	45	0	45
Project C	0	0	5	5

* 100 – 60   ** 100 – 85 etc

The **maximum regret** is 50 with project A, 45 with B and 5 with C. The lowest of these three maximum regrets is 5 with C, and so project C would be selected if the minimax regret rule is used.

4   posterior probabilities

5   D   Choice between $((0.2 \times 33,000) + (0.8 \times 14,000)) = 17,800$ at C, 22,000, and $((0.1 \times 40,000) + (0.9 \times 11,000)) = 13,900$ at D.

6

Probability	Numbers assigned	Probability	Numbers assigned
0.132	000-131	0.083	857-939
0.410	132-541	0.060	940-999
0.315	542-856		

7   Standard deviation, $s = \sqrt{\Sigma p(x - \bar{x})^2}$

where $\bar{x}$ is the EV of profit, x represents each possible profit, p represents the probability of each possible profit

8   (i)

		EV $'000
Project L	(550 x 0.20+480 x 0.40+580 x 0.40)	534
Project M	(450 x 0.20+500 x 0.40+570 x 0.40)	518
Project N	(420 x 0.20+450 x 0.40+480 x 0.40)	456
Project O	(370 x 0.20+410 x 0.40+430 x 0.40)	410
Project P	(590 x 0.20+580 x 0.40+430 x 0.40)	522

Project L has the highest EV of expected cash inflows and should therefore be undertaken.

(ii)

Market condition	Probability	Project chosen	Net cash inflow	EV of net cash inflow $'000
Poor	0.20	P	590	118
Good	0.40	P	580	232
Excellent	0.40	L	580	232
EV of net cash inflows with perfect information				582
EV of net cash inflows without perfect information				534
Value of perfect information				48

Now try the question below from the Exam Question Bank

Number	Level	Marks	Time
Q20	Examination	25	45 mins

Part E
Cost planning and analysis for competitive advantage

Forecasting and managing future costs

Introduction

This chapter looks at both recently-developed and more established techniques for forecasting times and costs for new products and services and managing the level at which costs for new products and services are likely to be incurred.

Learning curve theory (Section 1) is concerned with the reduction in unit labour times (and hence cost) with the repetition of complex, labour intensive activities. Clearly this has an impact on forecasting future costs of products and services.

Life cycle costing (Section 2) is a technique for reviewing and hence managing the costs of a product (or service or customer) for its entire life, not just during the production stage.

Target costing (Section 3) aims to control and manage costs of production at the product design stage, rather than when production starts.

Value analysis (Section 4) looks at how a product can be produced (or a service delivered) more economically without reducing its value to the customer or user.

Functional analysis (Section 5) uses the functions of a product as the basis for cost management purposes.

The examiner has included short Section A questions on learning curves in nearly every paper so far under the new syllabus.

He has also begun to test other topics in this part of the syllabus including target costing, value analysis and functional analysis all in May 2006. Life cycle costing was examined in a ten-mark question in November 2006.

Topic list	Learning outcomes	Syllabus references	Ability required
1 The learning curve	D(iv)	D(4)	Comprehension/ Application
2 Life cycle costing	D(vii)	D(7)	Comprehension
3 Target costing	D(vi)	D(6)	Comprehension
4 Value analysis	D(i)	D(1)	Analysis
5 Functional analysis	D(i)	D(1)	Analysis

1 The learning curve

Whenever an individual starts a job which is **fairly repetitive** in nature, and provided that the speed of working is not dictated by the speed of machinery (for example a production line), the worker is likely to become **more confident and knowledgeable** about the work as experience is gained, to become **more efficient**, and **to do the work more quickly. Eventually**, however, when the worker has acquired enough experience, there will be nothing more to learn, and so the **learning process will stop**.

FAST FORWARD

Learning curve theory is used to measure how, in some industries and some situations, the incremental cost per unit of output continues to fall for each extra unit produced.

1.1 When does learning curve theory apply?

Labour time should be expected to get shorter, with experience, in the production of items which exhibit any or all of the following features.

(a) **Made largely by labour effort** rather than by a highly mechanised process

(b) **Brand new** or relatively **short-lived** product (the learning process does not continue indefinitely)

(c) **Complex** and **made in small quantities for special orders**

1.2 The learning curve theory

FAST FORWARD

The theory is that the **cumulative average time per unit produced is assumed to fall by a constant percentage every time total output of the product doubles**. Cumulative average time is the average time per unit for all units produced so far, back to and including the first unit made.

Key term

The **learning curve** is 'The mathematical expression of the commonly observed effect that, as complex and labour-intensive procedures are repeated, unit labour times tend to decrease.' The learning curve models mathematically this reduction in unit production time.'   (CIMA *Official Terminology*)

More specifically, the learning curve theory states that the **cumulative average time per unit** produced is assumed to **decrease by a constant percentage every time total output of the product doubles**.

For instance, where an **80% learning effect or rate** occurs, the **cumulative average time required per unit of output is reduced to 80% of the previous cumulative average time when output is doubled**.

Attention!

By cumulative average time, we mean the average time per unit for all units produced so far, back to and including the first unit made.

The **doubling of output** is an **important feature** of the learning curve measurement. With a 70% learning curve, the cumulative average time per unit of output will fall to 70% of what it was before, every time output is doubled.

1.2.1 Example: an 80% learning curve

If the first unit of output requires 100 hours and an 80% learning curve applies, the production times would be as follows.

Cumulative number of units produced		Cumulative average time per unit		Total time required	Incremental time taken		
		Hours		Hours	Total hours		Hours per unit
1		100.0	(× 1)	100.0			
2*	(80%)	80.0	(× 2)	160.0	60.0	÷ 1	60.0
4*	(80%)	64.0	(× 4)	256.0	96.0	÷ 2	48.0
8*	(80%)	51.2	(× 8)	409.6	153.6	÷ 4	38.4

* Output is being doubled each time.

Notice that the incremental time per unit at each output level is much lower than the average time per unit.

1.3 Graph of the learning curve

This learning effect can be shown on a **graph** as a learning curve, either for **unit times (graph (a))** or for **cumulative total times or costs (graph (b))**.

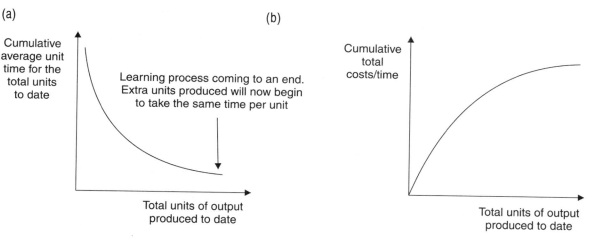

(a)

Cumulative average unit time for the total units to date

Learning process coming to an end. Extra units produced will now begin to take the same time per unit

Total units of output produced to date

(b)

Cumulative total costs/time

Total units of output produced to date

The curve on graph (a) becomes horizontal once a sufficient number of units have been produced. At this point the learning effect is lost and production time should become a constant standard, to which a standard efficiency rate may be applied.

1.4 Example: the learning curve effect

Captain Kitts has designed a new type of sailing boat, for which the cost and sales price of the first boat to be produced has been estimated as follows.

	£
Materials	5,000
Labour (800 hrs × £5 per hr)	4,000
Overhead (150% of labour cost)	6,000
	15,000
Profit mark-up (20%)	3,000
Sales price	18,000

It is planned to sell all the yachts at full cost plus 20%. An 80% learning curve is expected to apply to the production work. Only one customer has expressed interest in buying the yacht so far, but he thinks £18,000 is too high a price to pay. He might want to buy two, or even four of the yachts during the next six months.

He has asked the following questions.

(a)   If he paid £18,000 for the first yacht, what price would he have to pay later for a second yacht?

(b)   Could Captain Kitts quote the same unit price for two yachts, if the customer ordered two at the same time?

(c)   If the customer bought two yachts now at one price, what would be the price per unit for a third and fourth yacht, if he ordered them both together later on?

(d)   Could Captain Kitts quote a single unit price for the following numbers of yachts if they were all ordered now?

    (i)   Four yachts
    (ii)   Eight yachts

Assuming there are no other prospective customers for the yacht, how would the questions be answered?

Solution

Number of yachts		Cumulative average time per yacht		Total time for all yachts to date		Incremental time for additional yachts
		Hours		Hours		Hours
1		800.0		800.0		
2	(× 80%)	640.0	(× 2)	1,280.0	(1,280 − 800)	480.0
4	(× 80%)	512.0	(× 4)	2,048.0	(2,048 − 1,280)	768.0
8	(× 80%)	409.6	(× 8)	3,276.8	(3,276.8 − 2,048)	1,228.8

(a)   *Separate price for a second yacht*

	£
Materials	5,000
Labour (480 hrs × £5)	2,400
Overhead (150% of labour cost)	3,600
Total cost	11,000
Profit (20%)	2,200
Sales price	13,200

(b)   *A single price for the first two yachts*

	£
Materials cost for two yachts	10,000
Labour (1,280 hrs × £5)	6,400
Overhead (150% of labour cost)	9,600
Total cost for two yachts	26,000
Profit (20%)	5,200
Total sales price for two yachts	31,200
Price per yacht (÷ 2)	15,600

(c)   *A price for the third and fourth yachts*

	£
Materials cost for two yachts	10,000
Labour (768 hours × £5)	3,840
Overhead (150% of labour cost)	5,760
Total cost	19,600
Profit (20%)	3,920
Total sales price for two yachts	23,520
Price per yacht (÷ 2)	11,760

(d)   A price for the first four yachts together and for the first eight yachts together

		First four yachts £		First eight yachts £
Materials		20,000		40,000
Labour	(2,048 hrs)	10,240	(3,276.8 hrs)	16,384
Overhead	(150% of labour cost)	15,360	(150% of labour cost)	24,576
Total cost		45,600		80,960
Profit (20%)		9,120		16,192
Total sales price		54,720		97,152
Price per yacht	(÷ 4)	13,680	(÷ 8)	12,144

Question

Learning outcome: D(iv)

A 90 per cent learning curve applies to the manufacture of product X. If the time taken for the first unit is three hours, what will be the average time per unit for units 5 to 8?

A 1.944 hours   B 2.187 hours   C 7.776 hours   D 17.496 hours

Answer

The correct answer is A.

You should have been able to eliminate options C and D because they are longer times than the three hours taken for the first unit. In fact they are the total time for units 5 to 8 and for units 1 to 8 respectively. Option B is incorrect because it is the average time for units 1 to 8.

Cumulative number of units produced		Cumulative average time per unit Hours	Total time Hours
1		3	
2	(90%)	2.7	
4	(90%)	2.43	9.720
8	(90%)	2.187	17.496

Time taken for units 5 to 8   7.776

Average time per unit (÷ 4)   1.944 hours

1.5 A formula for the learning curve

ST FORWARD

The formula for the learning curve is **$Y_x = aX^b$**, where b, the learning coefficient or learning index, is defined as (log of the learning rate/log of 2).

rmula to
rn

The formula for the learning curve shown in Section 1.3(a) is **$Y_x = aX^b$**

where Y =	cumulative average time per unit to produce X units	a	= the time required to produce the first unit of output
X =	the cumulative number of units	b	= the learning coefficient or the index of learning/learning index

By calculating the value of b, using logarithms or a calculator, you can calculate expected labour times for certain work.

1.5.1 Logarithms

We need to take a look at logarithms because they appear in the definition of b, the learning coefficient.

Key term

> The **logarithm** of a number is the power to which ten has to be raised to produce that number.

If you have never learnt how to use logarithms, here is a brief explanation.

The logarithm of a number, x, is the value of x expressed in terms of '10 to the power of'.

$10 = 10^1$ The logarithm of 10 is 1.0
$100 = 10^2$ The logarithm of 100 is 2.0
$1,000 = 10^3$ The logarithm of 1,000 is 3.0

Your **calculator** will provide you with the logarithm of any number, probably using the **button marked log 10^x**. For example, the log of 566 is, using a calculator, 2.7528, which means that $10^{2.7528} = 566$.

Logarithms are useful to us for two principal reasons.

(a)   The logarithm of the product of two numbers is the sum of their logarithms: **log (c × d) = log c + log d**.

(b)   The logarithm of one number (say, f) to the power of another number (say, g), is the second number multiplied by the logarithm of the first: **log (f^g) = g log f.**

Logarithms can therefore be used to derive non-linear functions of the form **y = ax^n**.

If y = ax^n, the logarithm of y and the logarithm of ax^n must be the same and so **log y = log a + nlog x. This gives us a linear function similar to y = a + nx**, the only difference being that in place of y we have to use the logarithm of y and in place of x we must use the logarithm of x. **Using simultaneous equations, we can get a value for n and a value for log a**, which we can convert back into a 'normal' figure using antilogarithms (the button probably marked 10^x on your calculator).

For example, suppose the relationship between x and y can be described by the function y = ax^n, and suppose we know that if x = 1,000, y = 80,000 and if x = 750, y = 63,750.

Substitute these value into log y = log a + n log x.

log 80,000 = log a + n log 1,000
4.9031 = log a + 3n
∴ 4.9031 − 3n = log a   (1)

log 63,750 = log a + n log 750
4.8045 = log a + 2.8751n   (2)

Sub (1) into (2).

4.8045 = 4.9031 − 3n + 2.8751n
∴ 0.1249n = 0.0986
∴ n = 0.7894

Sub value of n into (1)

4.9031 − (3 × 0.7894) = log a
2.5349 = log a
∴ 342.69 = a

∴ Our function is **y = 342.69x $^{0.7894}$**

This technique will be useful when we come to look at the derivation of the learning rate in Section 1.5.4.

1.5.2 Logarithms and the value of b

When $Y_x = aX^b$ in learning curve theory, the value of **b = log of the learning rate/log of 2**. The learning rate is expressed as a proportion, so that for an 80% learning curve, the learning rate is 0.8, and for a 90% learning curve it is 0.9, and so on.

For an 80% learning curve, b = log 0.8/log 2.

Using the button on your calculator marked log 10^x

$$n = \frac{-0.0969}{0.3010} = -0.322$$

Question

Learning curve formula

Learning outcome: D(iv)

The value of b when a 90% learning curve applies is −0.0458. *True or false?*

Answer

The correct answer is −0.152 and so the statement is false.

b = log 0.9/log 2 = −0.0458/0.3010 = −0.152

You might also be expected to use the formula to calculate expected labour times for some work.

1.5.3 Example: using the formula

Suppose, for example, that an 80% learning curve applies to production of item ABC. To date (the end of June) 230 units of ABC have been produced. Budgeted production for July is 55 units.

The time taken to produce the very first unit of ABC, in January, was 120 hours.

Required

Calculate the budgeted total labour time for July.

Solution

To solve this problem, we need to calculate three things.

(a)   The cumulative total labour time needed so far to produce 230 units of ABC

(b)   The cumulative total labour time needed to produce 285 units of ABC, that is adding on the extra 55 units for July

(c)   The extra time needed to produce 55 units of ABC in July, as the difference between (b) and (a)

Calculation (a)

$Y_x = aX^b$ and we know that for 230 cumulative units, a = 120 hours (time for first unit), X = 230 (cumulative units) and b = −0.322 (80% learning curve) and so Y = (120) × ($230^{-0.322}$) = 20.83.

So when X = 230 units, the cumulative average time per unit is 20.83 hours.

Calculation (b)

Now we do the same sort of calculation for X = 285.

If X = 285, Y = 120 × ($285^{-0.322}$) = 19.44

So when X = 285 units, the cumulative average time per unit is 19.44 hours.

Calculation (c)

Cumulative units	Average time per unit	Total time
	Hours	Hours
230	20.83	4,791
285	19.44	5,540
Incremental time for 55 units		749

Average time per unit, between 230 and 285 units = 749/55 = 13.6 hours per unit approx

Instead of the formula you can use the **graphical methodology** (Section 1.3) to determine cumulative average time per unit but you will need considerable drawing skill to obtain an accurate result.

1.5.4 Derivation of the learning rate

The approach to derive the learning rate very much depends on the information given in the question. If you are provided with **details about cumulative production levels of 1, 2, 4, 8 or 16 (etc) units** you can use the **first approach** shown below. If details are given about other levels, however, you need to use the second approach, which involves the use of logarithms.

Question

Calculation of the percentage learning effect

Learning outcome: D(iv)

BL is planning to produce product A. Development tests suggest that 60% of the variable manufacturing cost of product A will be affected by a learning and experience curve. This learning effect will apply to each unit produced and continue at a constant rate of learning until cumulative production reaches 4,000 units, when learning will stop. The unit variable manufacturing cost of the first unit is estimated to be £1,200 (of which 60% will be subject to the effect of learning), while the average unit variable manufacturing cost of four units will be £405.

Required

Calculate the rate of learning that is expected to apply.

Answer

Let the rate of learning be r.

Cumulative production	Cumulative average cost
	£
1	720*
2	720 × r
4	720 × r^2

$$\therefore \quad £720r^2 \quad = \quad £405$$
$$r^2 \quad = \quad £405/£720 = 0.5625$$
$$r \quad = \quad 0.75$$

∴ The rate of learning is 75%.

* £1,200 × 60%

Question

Calculation of percentage learning effect using logs

Learning outcome: D(iv)

XX is aware that there is a learning effect for the production of one of its new products, but is unsure about the degree of learning. The following data relate to this product.

Time taken to produce the first unit   28 direct labour hours
Production to date   15 units
Cumulative time taken to date   104 direct labour hours

What is the percentage learning effect?

A 70%   B 75%   C 80%   D 90%

Answer

The correct answer is A.

You could answer this by hit and miss, trying all the learning rates given. But it is quicker to use the learning curve formula in reverse.

Average time taken per unit to date = $(104 \div 15) = 6.933$ hours

Since

$$Y_x = aX^b$$
$$6.933 = 28(15)^b$$
$$15^b = 6.933 \div 28 = 0.2476$$

Taking logs $b \log 15 = \log 0.2476$

Since $\log 15 = 1.1761$ (using log 10^x on your calculator)

And $\log 0.2476 = -0.6062$

$$b = \frac{\log 0.2476}{\log 15} = \frac{-0.6062}{1.1761} = -0.515$$

$$b = \frac{\log \text{ of learning rate}}{\log 2}$$

$$-0.515 = \frac{\log \text{ of learning rate}}{0.3010}$$

Log of learning rate $= -0.515 \times 0.3010 = -0.155$

Using the button on your calculator probably marked 10^x, -0.155 converts back to a 'normal' figure of 0.70. Thus the learning rate is 70%.

---

am focus
nt

There were straightforward objective test questions in nearly all of the exams under this syllabus requiring the calculation of the time taken to produce a particular product given that the learning effect applies. This is likely to be a frequently-examined topic. The May 2005 and the November 2005 questions were worth three marks and the May 2006 question had four marks available – all of which can easily turn a fail into a pass. So you really do need to know how to apply learning curve theory. Learning curve theory also appeared in one of the optional Section C questions in both the May 2005 and May 2006 exams.

Question

Learning outcome: D(iv)

Sciento Products manufactures complex electronic measuring instruments for which highly skilled labour is required.

Analysis of production times has shown that there is a learning curve effect on the labour time required to manufacture each unit and it has been decided to allow for this in establishing future forecast times and costs. Records have been kept of the production times for one particular instrument, the V8, an extract of which follows.

Cumulative production	Cumulative time	Average time per unit
Units	Hours	Hours
1	200	200.0
2	360	180.0
4	648	162.0
8	1,166	145.8

The labour time analyses have shown that the learning curve follows the general form $Y = aX^b$

where Y = average labour hours per unit X = cumulative number of units
         a = number of labour hours for first unit b = the learning index

Sciento Products is planning to produce a new version of the V8, the V8II, and believes that the same learning effect will apply to its production.

The company wishes to forecast the cost per V8II in a future period, to which the following data applies.

Estimated cumulative production at start of period	528 units
Estimated production in period	86 units
Estimated overheads	£150,903
Estimated labour cost	£10 per hour
Estimated material cost per unit	£250

Required

(a)   Calculate an estimated cost for the V8II in the period in question.

(b)   Discuss the usefulness of allowing for the learning effect in forecasting future labour costs and times.

Answer

You need to start with a working that provides you with an **average time per unit for the units actually produced within the period**. This means that you need to determine **the number of hours worked in the period**. By calculating the average time per unit for the units produced up to the beginning of the period, you can work out the number of hours worked in total before the beginning of the period by multiplying the average time by the total output. The same calculations can then be performed but for the output produced by the end of the period. The difference between the two total times is the number of hours worked in the period, from which the period average can be calculated.

It might be tempting to take the **average time as an average of the two averages you calculate** ((77.124 + 75.375)/2 = 76.25 hours per unit). This would be **wrong**, however, since this average would include the time taken for the first unit (200 hours) and the second, third, fourth and so on, whereas we should really be wanting a 'standard' time for the units currently being produced. Our average of 65 hours per unit is the average time needed for the 529th to the 614th units, which is much less than 76.25 hours per unit.

Workings for solution

A 90% learning curve applies because the cumulative average time per unit is 90% of what it was previously each time that cumulative total output doubles.

$Y = aX^b$, where b = log of the learning rate (as a proportion)/log of 2

With a 90% learning curve, b = log 0.9/log 2 = −0.152

(1) X = 528,

The average labour hours per unit = $aX^{-0.152}$ = $(200)(528)^{-0.152}$ = 77.124

(2) X = (528 + 86) = 614

The average labour hours per unit = $aX^{-0.152}$ = $(200)(614)^{-0.152}$ = 75.375

Total output	Average time	Total time per unit
Units	Hours	Hours
614	75.375	46,280
528	77.124	40,721
86		5,559

The average time per unit for the 86 units produced in the period should be 5,559/86 = 64.64 hours, say 65 hours per unit.

Suggested solution

(a) The standard overhead rate per hour = £150,903/(86 × 65 hrs) = £27

	Estimated cost per V8II £
Material cost	250
Labour cost (65 hours × £10 per hour)	650
Overheads (65 hours × £27 per hour)	1,755
Estimated cost per unit	2,655

(b) **Usefulness**

(i) Where there is a learning effect, it would be inaccurate and unrealistic to estimate labour times and labour costs without taking this effect into account.

(ii) It is particularly important where the learning effect applies to labour which makes up a large proportion of total costs of production and sales.

(iii) Accurate estimates of labour times are needed for efficient capacity scheduling and competitive pricing, if prices are set on a cost plus basis.

Limitations

(i) An accurate estimate of labour times depends on reliable estimates of:

(1) the learning rate; and
(2) estimated output in the period.

There will almost certainly be some margin of error in the estimated times.

(ii) The learning effect does not apply in all situations. When a product is long-established, the learning effect will have worn off, and standard times per unit will be constant. The learning effect will not be significant in capital intensive operations.

1.6 Incremental time model

The model described so far is the cumulative average time model and is the one most commonly encountered. An alternative is the incremental (**or marginal or direct**) model. This model uses the same formula as the cumulative average time model but Y represents the time required to produce the final unit.

Exam focus point

> When learning curve theory is incorporated in an examination question, you can assume that the cumulative average time model is applicable unless explicit instructions are given to the contrary.

1.7 The practical application of learning curve theory

What costs are affected by the learning curve?

    (a)   Direct labour time and costs

    (b)   Variable overhead costs, if they vary with direct labour hours worked

    (c)   **Materials costs** are usually **unaffected** by learning among the workforce, although it is conceivable that materials handling might improve, and so wastage costs be reduced.

    (d)   **Fixed overhead expenditure** should be **unaffected** by the learning curve (although in an organisation that uses absorption costing, if fewer hours are worked in producing a unit of output, and the factory operates at full capacity, the **fixed overheads recovered or absorbed per unit** in the cost of the output **will decline** as more and more units are made).

1.8 The relevance of learning curve effects in management accounting

1.8.1 Situations in which learning curve theory can be used

    (a)   To **calculate the marginal (incremental) cost of making extra units** of a product.

    (b)   To **quote selling prices for products/services**, where prices are calculated at cost plus a percentage mark-up for profit. An awareness of the learning curve can make all the difference between winning contracts and losing them, or between making profits and selling at a loss-making price.

    (c)   To **prepare realistic production budgets** and more **efficient production schedules**.

    (d)   To **prepare realistic standard costs** for cost control purposes.

1.8.2 Further considerations

Further considerations that should be borne in mind	Detail
Sales projections, advertising expenditure and delivery date commitments	Identifying a learning curve effect should allow an organisation to plan its advertising and delivery schedules to coincide with expected production schedules. Production capacity obviously affects sales capacity and sales projections.
Budgeting with standard costs	Companies that use standard costing for much of their production output cannot apply standard times to output where a learning effect is taking place. This problem can be overcome in practice by establishing standard times for output once the learning effect has worn off or become insignificant and introducing a 'launch cost' budget for the product for the duration of the learning period. Alternatively, a standard average time per unit can be estimated for a budgeted volume of output, which makes allowance for the expected learning rate.

Further considerations that should be borne in mind	Detail
Cash budgets	Since the learning effect reduces unit variable costs as more units are produced, it should be allowed for in cash flow projections.
Work scheduling and overtime decisions	To take full advantage of the learning effect, idle production time should be avoided and work scheduling/overtime decisions should take account of the expected learning effect.
Pay	Where the workforce is paid a productivity bonus, the time needed to learn a new production process should be allowed for in calculating the bonus for a period.
Recruiting new labour	When a company plans to take on new labour to help with increasing production, the learning curve assumption will have to be reviewed.
Market share	The significance of the learning curve is that by increasing its share of the market, a company can benefit from shop-floor, managerial and technological 'learning' to achieve economies of scale.

1.9 Experience curves

A 'learning curve' is a term usually applied to the time taken by the skilled labour element in shop floor production.

An **experience curve** is a term applied to the 'corporate embodiment' of the shop floor, managerial and technological learning effects within an organisation and it expresses the way in which the average cost per unit of production changes over time due to technological and organisational changes as well as changes to factory size, product design, materials used and so on, not just 'learning' by skilled workers.

Experience curves therefore cover **all costs** and yet they are very similar in percentage terms to learning curves. All costs reduce with experience to a certain extent.

(a) Material costs will decrease slightly due to quantity discounts.

(b) Variable overheads often follow the pattern of direct labour.

(c) As volumes increase, fixed overheads per unit will fall.

The experience curve is best exploited by growth and achieving a sizeable market share, so that an organisation can benefit from mass production techniques.

1.10 Problems with applying learning curve theory

(a) The learning curve phenomenon is **not always present**.

(b) It **assumes stable conditions at work** which will enable learning to take place. This is not always practicable (for example because of labour turnover).

(c) It must also **assume a certain degree of motivation** amongst employees.

(d) **Breaks** between repeating production of an item must not be too long, or **workers will 'forget'** and the learning process would have to begin all over again.

(e) It might be difficult to **obtain enough accurate data** to determine the learning rate.

(f) **Workers might not agree** to a gradual reduction in production times per unit.

(g) **Production techniques might change**, or product design alterations might be made, so that it **takes a long time for a 'standard' production method to emerge**, to which a learning effect will apply.

2 Life cycle costing

FAST FORWARD

Life cycle costing involves a number of techniques that assist in the planning and control of a product's life cycle costs by monitoring spending and commitment to spend during a product's life cycle. Its aim is to minimise cost and maximise sales revenue over the life of the product.

Exam focus point

Life cycle costing was examined in a ten-mark question in November 2006. The question asked for simple calculations of costs and selling prices over the life cycle of a product.

It then asked for an explanation of the reasons why costs and prices changed over the life cycle.

2.1 What are life cycle costs?

Product life cycle costs are incurred **from the design stage through development to market launch, production and sales, and their eventual withdrawal from the market**.

Component elements of a product's cost over its life cycle

(a) **Research & development costs**

   (i)   Design
   (ii)   Testing
   (iii) Production process and equipment

(b) **Technical data cost**. Cost of purchasing any technical data required.

(c) **Training costs** including initial operator training and skills updating.

(d) **Production costs**

(e) **Distribution costs**. Transportation and handling costs.

(f) **Marketing costs**

   (i)   Customer service
   (ii)   Field maintenance
   (iii) Brand promotion

(g) **Inventory costs**. Holding spare parts, warehousing and so on.

(h) **Retirement and disposal costs**. Costs occurring at the end of the product's life.

Life cycle costs can **apply** to **services** as well as to physical **products**, and to **customers** and **projects**.

Traditional management accounting systems are based on the financial accounting year and tend to dissect the product's life cycle into a series of annual sections. This means that management accounting systems do not accumulate costs over the entire life cycle. They **do not**, therefore, **assess a product's profitability over its entire life** but rather on a periodic basis.

Life cycle costing, on the other hand, **tracks and accumulates actual costs and revenues** attributable to each product **over the entire product life cycle.** Hence the total profitability of any given product can be determined.

Key term

Life cycle costing is 'the profiling of cost over a product's life, including the pre-production stage'.

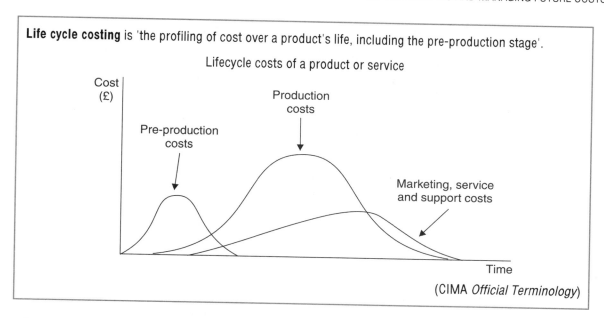

Lifecycle costs of a product or service

(CIMA *Official Terminology*)

2.2 The product life cycle

Every product goes through a life cycle (a concept we considered in Chapter 8), the curve of which resembles the generic curve in the following diagram.

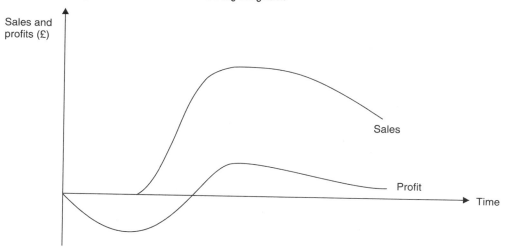

The product represented in the diagram above had a research and development stage prior to production.

The horizontal axis measures the duration of the **life cycle**, which **can last** from, say, **18 months to several hundred years**. Children's crazes or fad products have very short lives while some products, such as binoculars (invented in the eighteenth century) can last a very long time.

It is important to know **where the product is in its life cycle**, as this will **affect the returns** that are expected.

Performance measure	Stage in the life cycle			
	Introduction	Growth	Maturity	Decline
Cash	Net user	Net user	Generator	Generator
Return on capital	Not important	Not important	Important	Important
Growth	Vital	Vital	Grow with new uses	Negative growth
Profit	Not expected	Important	Important	Very important

If a product is in the **introductory or growth stages** it **cannot be expected to be a net generator of cash** as all the cash it generates will be used in expansion through increased sales and so on. As the product moves from **maturity towards decline**, it is of **prime importance** that the product still **generates a profit and cash** and that its **return on capital** is **acceptable**.

2.3 Problems with traditional accounting systems

Traditional accounting systems **do not tend to relate research and development costs to the products that caused them**. Instead they **write off** these costs on an **annual basis against the revenue generated by existing products**. This makes the **existing products seem less profitable** than they really are and there is a danger that they might be **scrapped** too quickly. If research and development costs are not related to the causal product the true profitability of that product cannot be assessed.

Traditional management accounting systems usually **total all non-production costs** and record them as a **period expense**. With **life cycle costing** these costs are **traced to individual products** over complete life cycles.

(a) The total of these costs for each individual product can therefore be reported and compared with revenues generated in the future.

(b) The visibility of such costs is increased.

(c) **Individual product profitability can be more fully understood** by attributing *all* costs to products.

(d) As a consequence, **more accurate feedback information** is available on the organisation's success or failure in developing new products. In today's competitive environment, where the ability to produce new and updated versions of products is paramount to the survival of an organisation, this information is vital.

(e) When an entire product life is analysed, cost reduction, cost minimisation and revenue expansion opportunities are more likely to appear than if management attempt to maximise profit on a year by year basis.

2.4 Maximising the return over the product life cycle

2.4.1 Design costs out of products

Between 70% to 90% of a product's life cycle costs are determined by decisions made early in the life cycle, at the design or development stage. Careful design of the product and manufacturing and other processes will keep cost to a minimum over the life cycle.

2.4.2 Minimise the time to market

This is the time from the conception of the product to its launch. More products come onto the market nowadays and development times have been reduced over the years. Competitors watch each other very carefully to determine what types of product their rivals are developing. If an organisation is launching a new product it is vital to get it to the market place as soon as possible. This will give the product as long a period as possible without a rival in the market place and should mean increased market share in the long run. Furthermore, the life span may not proportionally lengthen if the product's launch is delayed and so sales may be permanently lost. It is not unusual for the product's overall profitability to fall by 25% if the launch is delayed by six months. This means that it is usually worthwhile incurring extra costs to keep the launch on schedule or to speed up the launch.

2.4.3 Minimise breakeven time (BET)

A short BET is very important in keeping an organisation liquid. The sooner the product is launched the quicker the research and development costs will be repaid, providing the organisation with funds to develop further products.

2.4.4 Maximise the length of the life span

Product life cycles are not predetermined; they are set by the actions of management and competitors. Once developed, some products lend themselves to a number of different uses; this is especially true of materials, such as plastic, PVC, nylon and other synthetic materials. The life cycle of the material is then a series of individual product curves nesting on top of each other as shown below.

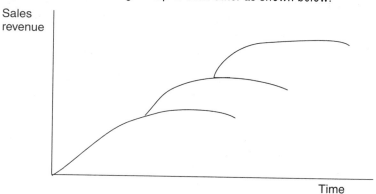

By entering different national or regional markets one after another an organisation may be able to maximise revenue. This allows resources to be better applied, and sales in each market to be maximised. On the other hand, in today's fast moving world, an organisation could lose out to a competitor if it failed to establish an early presence in a particular market.

2.4.5 Minimise product proliferation

If products are updated or superseded too quickly, the life cycle is cut short and the product may just cover its R and D costs before its successor is launched.

2.4.6 Manage the product's cashflows

Hewlett-Packard developed a **return map** to manage the lifecycle of their products. Here is an example.

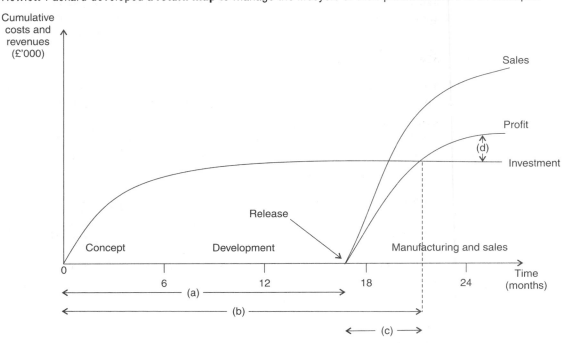

Key time periods are measured by the map:

(a) Time to market
(b) Breakeven time
(c) Breakeven time after product launch
(d) Return factor (the excess of profit over the investment)

Changes to planned time periods can be incorporated into the map (for example, if the development plan takes longer than expected) and the resulting changes to the return factor at set points after release highlighted.

Question   Pricing strategies

Learning outcome: D(vii)

Fill in the blank in the sentence below.

The pricing strategy discussed in the chapter on pricing that could be used to prolong a product's life and to maximise the revenue over it is ....

Answer

The correct answer is market skimming pricing.

2.5 Service and project life cycles

A service organisation will have services that have life cycles. The only difference is that the **R & D stages will not exist in the same way** and will **not have the same impact on subsequent costs**. The **different processes that go to form the complete service** are important, however, and **consideration should be given in advance as to how to carry them out and arrange them so as to minimise cost.**

Products that **take years to produce** or **come to fruition** are usually called **projects**, and **discounted cash flow calculations** are invariably used to **cost them over their life cycle in advance**. The projects need to be **monitored** very carefully **over their life** to make sure that they **remain on schedule and that cost overruns are not being incurred**.

2.6 Customer life cycles

Customers also have life cycles, and an organisation will wish to **maximise the return from a customer over their life cycle**. The aim is to **extend the life cycle of a particular customer** or decrease the 'churn' rate, as the Americans say. This means **encouraging customer loyalty**. For example, some supermarkets and other retail outlets issue **loyalty cards** that offer discounts to loyal customers who return to the shop and spend a certain amount with the organisation. As existing customers tend to be more profitable than new ones they should be retained wherever possible.

Customers become more profitable over their life cycle. The profit can go on increasing for a period of between approximately four and 20 years. For example, if you open a bank account, take out insurance or invest in a pension, the company involved has to set up the account, run checks and so on. The initial cost is high and the company will be keen to retain your business so that it can recoup this cost. Once customers get used to their supplier they tend to use them more frequently, and so there is a double benefit in holding on to customers. For example, you may use the bank to purchase shares on your behalf, or you may take out a second insurance policy with the same company.

The projected cash flows over the full lives of customers or customer segments can be analysed to highlight the worth of customers and the importance of customer retention. It may take a year or more to **recoup the initial costs of winning a customer**, and this could be referred to as the **payback period** of the investment in the customer. The investment in the customer and the consequent returns can be analysed in the same way as an investment in a capital project, a topic that we looked at in Part B.

2.7 Life cycle costs and marketing strategies

As a product progresses through its life cycle, it faces different challenges and opportunities which require changes in the marketing mix (covered in Chapter 8) and alternative marketing strategies.

2.7.1 Introduction stage

(a)   The principal aim during this stage is to establish a market and build demand.

(b)   Some organisations may market a product before it is actually introduced, but this will alert competitors and remove any element of surprise.

(c)   Advertising costs are usually high so as to increase customer awareness of the product and to target early adopters.

(d)   Costs associated with the initial distribution of the product are likely to be incurred.

(e)   **Implications for the marketing mix**

    (i)   **Product.** There are one or two, relatively undifferentiated products.

    (ii)   **Price.** Prices are generally high, on the assumption that a market skimming strategy is adopted in order to earn a high profit margin from early adopters and recoup development costs quickly. If a penetration pricing policy is adopted, introductory prices will be low to gain market share.

    (iii)   **Distribution.** This will be selective and scattered.

    (iv)   **Promotion.** This is aimed at building brand awareness. Early adopters may be offered samples or trial incentives.

2.7.2 Growth stage

(a)   The aim during this stage is to gain consumer preference and increase sales.

(b)   Revenue grows rapidly.

(c)   More customers become aware of the product and additional market segments are targeted.

(d)   As customers begin asking for the product, more retailers will want to carry it.

(e)   Expansion of distribution channels may be required at this point.

(f)   As competitors enter the market, promotional costs may increase (to convince consumers of the superiority of the organisation's version of the product) or price competition may occur.

(g)   **Implications for the marketing mix**

   (i)   **Product.** There will be improvements in the quality of the product, new product features may be introduced and alternative packaging options may be considered.

   (ii)   **Price.** Prices will be high if demand is high, but will be reduced if demand needs stimulating.

   (iii)   **Distribution.** This becomes more intensive.

   (iv)   **Promotion.** In order to build a preference for the brand, there may be increased advertising.

2.7.3 Maturity stage

(a)   The aim during this, the most profitable stage, is to maintain market share and extend the product's life cycle.

(b)   The rate of increase in sales slows down.

(c)   Advertising expenditure is reduced as brand awareness should be strong.

(d)   Market share and/or prices may fall as competition increases.

(e)   Product differentiation will become increasingly difficult given the similarity of competitors' offerings.

(f)   Marketing efforts are focused on finding new customers, encouraging customers to switch from competitors and increasing volumes of purchases per customer.

(g)   Sales promotions may be used to encourage retailers to give the product more shelf space than competitors' products.

(h)   **Implications for the marketing mix**

   (i)   **Product.** To differentiate the product from those of competitors, modifications are made and features are added.

   (ii)   **Price.** In the face of competition and to avoid a price war, prices may be cut.

   (iii)   **Distribution.** New distribution channels may be sought. Incentives may be given to maintain shelf space.

   (iv)   **Promotion.** The product will need to be differentiated from those of competitors. Brand loyalty should be built. Incentives can be given to entice competitors' customers to switch.

2.7.4 Decline stage

An organisation usually has three options.

(a) Keep the product on the market in the hope that competitors will remove theirs. Reduce costs and find new uses for the product.

(b) Reduce marketing support and let the product continue until profits dry up.

(c) Discontinue the product when profits dry up or a replacement product is available.

Implications for the marketing mix

(a) **Product.** The number of products in a product line may need to be reduced. Remaining products could be rejuvenated.

(b) **Price.** Prices of products to be discontinued may need to be reduced to get rid of remaining inventory.

(c) **Distribution.** Unprofitable channels are no longer used.

(d) **Promotion.** Expenditure is reduced and focuses on reinforcing the brand image of remaining products.

2.7.5 Advantages and disadvantages of the product life cycle concept for marketing strategies

The life cycle curves of different products vary immensely and so the concept is not always an accurate tool for sales forecasting purposes.

And it has been suggested that the product life cycle may become self fulfilling: if it is thought that a product is in the decline stage and the advertising budget is cut, the product will decline further.

The product life cycle does offer a framework within which alternative marketing strategies can be planned, however, which will address the various challenges products are likely to face.

It also offers a means for comparing performance with products with similar life cycles.

3 Target costing

AST FORWARD

Target costing is a pro-active cost control system. The target cost is calculated by deducting the target profit from a predetermined selling price based on customers' views. Functional analysis, value engineering and value analysis are used to change production methods and/or reduce expected costs so that the target cost is met.

am focus int

Target costing appeared in a May 2006 Section C question as part of an examination of costs and pricing in general. There were four marks available for an explanation of the differences between standard costing and target costing.

3.1 The importance of product design

In order to compete effectively in today's competitive market, organisations need to **redesign continually their products** with the result that **product life cycles** have become much **shorter**. The **planning, design and development stages of a product's cycle** are therefore **critical to an organisation's cost management process**. Cost reduction at this stage of a product's life cycle, rather than during the production process, is one of the most important ways of reducing product cost.

 Case Study

General Motors estimate that 70% of the cost of manufacturing truck transmissions is determined in the design stage. Estimates for other companies and products often exceed 80%.

3.1.1 Factors that build in costs at the design stage

(a) **The number of different components**. Production time increases as the number increases.

(b) **Whether the components are standard or not**. Standard components are reliable and reduce inventory and handling costs.

(c) **The number of extra features** (included as a standard or paid for separately)

(d) **Type of packaging**. The aim is to protect the product and minimise handling costs by not breaking pallets or cases during distribution.

3.2 What is target costing?

Japanese companies developed **target costing** as a response to the problem of managing **costs over the product life cycle**.

Key term

> '**Target costing** is an activity which is aimed at reducing the life-cycle costs of new products, while ensuring quality, reliability, and other consumer requirements, by examining all possible ideas for cost reduction at the product planning, research and development, and the prototyping phases of production. But it is not just a cost reduction technique; it is part of a comprehensive strategic profit management system.'
>
> (Kato, 1993)

'Target cost management has been defined as a system that is effective in managing costs in new-product design and development stages. It has also been viewed as allowing the production cost of a proposed product to be identified so that when sold it generates the desired profit level. ... Target cost management has also been viewed as playing a useful role in enabling an enterprise to set and support the attainment of cost levels to effectively reflect its planned financial performance. ...What appears to be evident is that there are almost as **many conceptions of target costing** as there are companies deploying the approach and there are probably many **companies engaging in various aspects of target cost management without referring to the term**.

Target cost management has been posited to assist in the pursuit of product development time reduction, as well as the quality definition for a new product and cost containment generally. It has therefore been perceived as a managerial tool simultaneously to **address time, quality and cost issues**.'

(A Bhimani and H Okano, 'Targeting excellence: target cost management at Toyota in the UK', *Management Accounting*, June 1995 (with BPP's emphasis))

 Case Study

'When Toyota developed the Lexus to compete with BMW, Mercedes and Jaguar, it employed two basic concepts: reverse engineering and target costing. In essence, it sought to produce a car with BMW 7-series attributes at a BMW 5-series price. Cost was the dominant design parameter that shaped the development of the Lexus, as it was later with Nissan's Infiniti.

 BPP LEARNING MEDIA

The response from Mercedes Benz, one of the competitors who lost market share through this strategy, was to acknowledge that its cars were over-engineered and too expensive and to change its product-development process to determine target product costs from competitive market prices.

(B Nixon, J Innes and J Rabinowitz, Management Accounting for Design, *Management Accounting*, September 1997)

Target costing requires managers to think differently about the relationship between cost, price and profit.

(a) The **traditional approach** is to **develop a product, determine the expected standard production cost** of that product and **then set a selling price** (probably based on cost) with a resulting profit or loss. Costs are controlled through monthly variance analysis.

(b) The **target costing approach** is to develop a **product concept** and the primary specifications for performance and design and then to **determine the price customers would be willing to pay** for that concept. The **desired profit margin is deducted from the price leaving a figure that represents total cost.** This is the target cost and the product must be capable of being produced for this amount otherwise the product will not be manufactured. **During the product's life the target cost will constantly be reduced** so that the **price can fall. Continuous cost reduction techniques** must therefore be employed.

ey term

> **Target cost** is 'A product cost estimate derived by subtracting a desired profit margin from a competitive market price.'
>
> (CIMA *Official Terminology*)

Because it **encourages cost consciousness** and **focuses on profit margins**, target costing is a **useful tool for strengthening an organisation's competitive position.**

3.3 Setting the target price

Products that are **varieties of existing products** or **new brands of existing products** enter an already established market and therefore a competitive **price should be fairly easy to set**. There is no existing market price for **new products**, however and so **market research** will probably be used to assist in price setting. Many Japanese companies use **functional analysis** and **pricing by function** in such circumstances. We cover functional analysis in Section 5 of this chapter.

Selling price will also be **affected by factors such as the stage in the product life cycle, expected sales volume and the price charged by rivals** in the market.

3.4 Setting the target profit requirement

This should **not be simply a standard mark-up** but instead should be **based on strategic profit plans**. Procedures used to derive the target profit must be agreed by all staff responsible for achieving it and it must be seen as something more than just an expectation. In this way **staff will both accept responsibility for achieving it** and **be committed to achieving it**.

3.5 The target costing process

Step 1   **Analyse the external environment** to ascertain what customers require and what competitors are producing. Determine the **product concept**, the **price** customers will be willing to pay and thus the **target cost**.

Step 2   **Split the total target cost into broad cost categories** such as development, marketing, manufacturing and so on. **Then split up the manufacturing target cost per unit across the different functional areas of the product. Design the product so that each functional product**

area can be made within the target cost. If a functional product area cannot be made within the target cost, the targets for the other areas must be reduced, or the product redesigned or scrapped. The product should be developed in an atmosphere of **continuous improvement** using **value engineering techniques** and **close collaboration with suppliers**, to enhance the product (in terms of service, quality, durability and so on) and reduce costs. We cover value engineering in Section 4 of this chapter.

Step 3   Once it is decided that it is feasible to meet the total target cost, **detailed cost sheets** will be prepared and **processes formalised**.

It is possible that management may decide to go ahead and manufacture a product whose target cost is well below the currently attainable cost, determined by current technology and processes. If this is the case management will **set benchmarks for improvement** towards the target costs, by specified dates.

Options available to reduce costs

> (a)   **Training** staff in more efficient techniques
> (b)   Using **cheaper staff**
> (c)   Acquiring new, more **efficient technology**
> (d)   Cutting out **non-value-added activities**

Even if the product can be produced within the target cost the story does not end there. **Once the product goes into production target costs will gradually be reduced**. These reductions will be incorporated into the budgeting process. This means that cost savings must be actively sought and made continuously. Value analysis will be used to reduce costs if and when targets are missed. Value analysis is covered in Section 4 of this chapter.

3.5.1 Cost tables

Cost tables are useful value engineering tools. They are **high volume, computerised databases of detailed cost information based on various manufacturing variables**. They are a source of information about the effect on product costs of using different resources, production methods, designs and so on.

 Case Study

> (a)   The following comments appeared in an article in the *Financial Times* in January 1993. (Emphasis is BPP's.)
>
> 'Mercedes-Benz, one of the world's most prestigious and tradition-laden carmakers, has taken its time to wake up to the daunting dimensions of the challenges it faces in the **rapidly-changing world car market** of the 1990s.
>
> The company has accepted that radical changes in the world car market mean that Mercedes-Benz will no longer be able to demand premium prices for its products based on an image of effortless superiority and a content of the ultimate in automotive engineering.
>
> Instead of developing the ultimate car and then charging a correspondingly sky-high price as in the past, Mercedes-Benz is taking the dramatic and radical step of moving to '**target pricing'. It will decide what the customer is willing to pay** in a particular product category – priced against its competitors – it will **add its profit margin** and then the real work will begin to **cost every part and component to bring in the vehicle at the target price.'**

The following extracts are from an article which appeared three months later.

> 'The marketing motto for the Mercedes-Benz compact C-class is that it offers customers more car for their money.

It is the first practical example of the group's new pricing policy. The range embodies a principle new to Mercedes which states that **before any work starts a new product will be priced according to what the market will bear and what the company considers an acceptable profit. Then each component and manufacturing process will be costed to ensure the final product is delivered at the target price**.

Under the old system of building the car, adding up the costs and then fixing a price, the C-class would have been **between 15 per cent and 20 per cent dearer** than the 10-year-old outgoing 190 series, Mr Vöhringer said.

Explaining the practical workings of the new system, he explained that project groups for each component and construction process were instructed without exception to increase productivity by between 15 and 25 per cent. And they had to reach their targets in record time.

One result was that development time on the new models was cut to 40 months, about a third less than usual. But the most important effect, according to Mr Vöhringer, has been to **reduce** the **company's cost disadvantages** *vis-à-vis* **Japanese competitors in this class from 35 per cent to only 15 per cent**.'

(b) The following extracts from Bhimani's and Okano's article (with BPP's emphasis) illustrate the way in which the Japanese target cost management approach has been introduced at Toyota in the UK.

'…the target cost for the model essentially reflects the difference between the target price and the target profit. The **target** price is **established** primarily by TMC [Toyota Motor Corporation in Japan] which first obtains input on **expected European sales** from TMME [Toyota Motor Europe Marketing and Engineering]. The **target profit** is a **function of Toyota's long-term strategy for the European market** as well as commercial viability considerations concerning TMUK [Toyota Motor Manufacturing UK Ltd].

It is in fact the Department of Purchasing which is more directly engaged in pursuing target costs. … One role of this department is to identify European **producers** of sub-components who are **able to meet TMUK's stringent product specification criteria**. From a total of 2,000 potential suppliers approached in the period 1989-91, approximately 160 will ultimately become the core base of parts manufacturers. It is these model parts which provide the focus of target cost management activities at TMUK. Suppliers' prototypes are assessed in the UK and in Japan for approval as a starting point, **but suppliers are expected to generate ideas for cost reduction and operational improvements**. An important part of the target cost management exercise is to undertake **inspection visits** by members of the Purchasing Department's staff and the Technical Support segment's 'Supplier Parts Tracking Team'. These periodic visits are carried out to check plant and facilities layout of suppliers with a **view to pinpointing cost reduction and quality enhancement possibilities**.'

3.6 Target costing support systems

Target costing cannot operate in isolation. **Information** to enable it to operate successfully is needed from a wide range of support systems.

(a) **Sales pricing support systems**, which can, for example, break down product functions into sub-functions and provide information on that basis, and can convert the value placed on each function into a price

(b) **Target profit computation support systems**, which can, for example, calculate the optimal product mix in the future (product portfolio planning system)

(c) **Research and development support systems**, which include computer-aided design and computer-aided engineering

(d) Support systems for **infusing target costs** into products, which include **value engineering** and **variety reduction**

(e) **Human resource management systems**, which are particularly important when an organisation uses target costing for the first time

3.7 Target costing versus standard costing

	Standard costing	Target costing
How costs are controlled	Costs must be kept within predetermined standard costs. Variances are calculated to check that this has happened.	There is no cost slashing but continual pressure to ensure costs are kept to a minimum.
Relationship between product concept, cost and price	Predetermined product design ↓ Cost ↓ Price	Product design concept ↓ Selling price ↓ Target cost ↑ Profit margin
Link with strategic plans	None. The approach is short-term cost control through variance analysis.	The product concept and target profit margin take into account medium-term strategic plans.
Time frame for cost control	Standards are usually revised annually.	Continual cost reduction. Target costs are revised monthly.

3.8 Possible adverse effects of target costing

(a) Longer product development times because of numerous changes to designs and costings

(b) Employee demotivation because of pressure to meet targets

(c) Organisational conflict between designers who try to reduce costs and marketing staff who give away promotional items costing even more

Question
Standard costing v target costing

Learning outcome: D(vi)

Fill in the blank spaces ((a) to (d)) in the table below to show how standard costing and target costing differ.

Stage in product lifecycle	Standard costing approach	Target costing approach
Product concept stage	No action	(a)
Design stage	(b)	Keep costs to a minimum
Production stage	Costs are controlled using variance analysis	(c)
Remainder of life	(d)	Target cost reduced, perhaps monthly

Answer

(a)   Set the selling price and required profit and determine the resulting target cost
(b)   Set standard cost and a resulting standard price
(c)   Constant cost reduction
(d)   Standards usually revised annually

ention!

Bhimani and Okano's article provides a useful summary of this important technique.

'... target cost management has been seen as an activity which is aimed at reducing lifecycle costs of new products, while ensuring speedy quality, reliability and other customer requirements, by examining all ideas for cost reduction at the product planning, research and development process.'

4 Value analysis

m focus
nt

The May 2006 exam devoted a ten-mark Section B question to the topic of value analysis. The question asked for an explanation and how the method would be implemented . Candidates were also asked to contrast this method with functional analysis.

One approach to cost reduction, which embraces many of the techniques already mentioned, is value analysis (VA).

ST FORWARD

Value analysis is a planned, scientific approach to cost reduction which reviews the material composition of a product and production design so that modifications and improvements can be made which do not reduce the value of the product to the customer or to the user.

y term

Value analysis is 'A systematic inter-disciplinary examination of factors affecting the cost of a product or service, in order to devise means of achieving the specified purpose most economically at the required standard of quality and reliability'.   (CIMA *Official Terminology*)

The **value of the product must therefore be kept the same or else improved, at a reduced cost.**

ST FORWARD

Value engineering is the application of value analysis techniques to new products.

y term

Value engineering is 'Redesign of an activity, product or service so that value to the customer is enhanced while costs are reduced (or at least increase by less than the resulting price increase).
(CIMA *Official Terminology*)

Another definition, from G Scullion and A Galway (*Management Accounting,* March 1984) is as follows.

'Value analysis is a method of ensuring worth, whereby the value of each product is critically analysed, part by part, with the objective of achieving the required function with reduced cost. The design stage of a product is the most advantageous time at which to minimise costs. However, during the production period the costs will be subject to change owing to prevailing environmental conditions. These costs need to be examined and reduced using value analysis.'

The distinction between value engineering and value analysis is not clear cut but, in general, **value engineering is cost avoidance or cost prevention before production** whereas **value analysis is cost reduction during production**.

4.1 What is different about value analysis?

There are two features of value analysis that distinguish it from other approaches to cost reduction.

(a)   It encourages innovation and a more radical outlook for ways of reducing costs because ideas for cost reduction are not constrained by the existing product design.

(b)   It recognises the various types of value which a product or service provides, analyses this value, and then seeks ways of improving or maintaining aspects of this value but at a lower cost.

Conventional cost reduction techniques try to achieve the lowest production costs for a specific product design whereas value analysis tries to find the least-cost method of making a product that achieves its desired function, not the least-cost method of accomplishing a product design to a mandatory and detailed specification.

4.2 Value

FAST FORWARD   Four aspects of value should be considered in value analysis (**cost value, exchange value, use value, esteem value**).

Key term

- **Cost value** is the cost of producing and selling an item.
- **Exchange value** is the market value of the product or service.
- **Use value** is what the article does, the purposes it fulfils.
- **Esteem value** is the prestige the customer attaches to the product.

(a)   Value analysis seeks to reduce unit costs, and so cost value is the one aspect of value to be reduced.

(b)   Value analysis attempts to provide the same (or a better) use value at the lowest cost. Use value therefore involves considerations of the performance and reliability of the product or service.

(c)   Value analysis attempts to maintain or enhance the esteem value of a product at the lowest cost.

Question

Value

Learning outcome: D(i)

Below are three features of a product.

(a)   The product can be sold for £27.50.
(b)   The product is available in six colours to suit customers' tastes.
(c)   The product will last for at least ten years.

What are the correct classifications of the features using the types of value in the key terms box above?

A   (a) Exchange value (b) Esteem value (c) Use value
B   (a) Esteem value (b) Use value (c) Exchange value
C   (a) Cost value (b) Esteem value (c) Use value
D   (a) Exchange value (b) Use value (c) Esteem value

Answer

The correct answer is A.

Value analysis involves the systematic investigation of every source of cost and technique of production with the aim of getting rid of all unnecessary costs. An unnecessary cost is an additional cost incurred without adding use, exchange or esteem value to a product.

Of course, value analysis is not quite as simple as this, and in practice there might be a conflict between reducing costs and maintaining the aesthetic value (esteem value) of a product. Where cost cutting and aesthetics are incompatible, there should be a clear direction from senior management about which is more important.

4.3 The scope of value analysis

Any commercial organisation should be continually seeking lower costs, better products and higher profits. These can be achieved in any of the following ways.

  (a) Cost elimination or cost prevention
  (b) Cost reduction
  (c) Improving product quality and so selling greater quantities at the same price as before
  (d) Improving product quality and so being able to increase the sales price

Value analysis can achieve all four of these objectives.

Question   Benefits of a VA programme

Learning outcome: D(i)

In addition to the above, what other benefits of a VA programme can you think of?

Answer

  (a) Improved product performance and product reliability

  (b) Improved product quality

  (c) An increased product life, in terms of both the marketable life of the product (for the company) and the usable life of each product unit (for the customer)

  (d) Possibly, shorter delivery 'lead times' to customers because of a shorter production cycle

  (e) The increased use of standard parts and components which contribute to lower costs for the customer

  (f) A more economic use of scarce resources

  (g) Encouraging employees to show innovation and creative ideas

Three areas of special importance are as follows.

Area	Method
Product design	At the design stage value analysis is called value engineering. The designer should be cost conscious and avoid unnecessary complications. Simple product design can avoid production and quality control problems, thereby resulting in lower costs.
Components and material costs	The purchasing department should beware of lapsing into habit with routine buying decisions. It has a crucial role to play in reducing costs and improving value by procuring the desired quality materials at the lowest possible price.
Production methods	These ought to be reviewed continually, on a product-by-product basis, especially with changing technology.

4.4 Carrying out a value analysis

4.4.1 Typical considerations in value analysis

(a) **Can a cheaper substitute material be found** which is as good, if not better, than the material currently used?

(b) **Can unnecessary weight or embellishments be removed** without reducing the product's attractions or desirability?

(c) **Is it possible to use standardised components** (or to make components to a particular standard) thereby reducing the variety of units used and produced? Variety reduction through standardisation facilitates longer production runs at lower unit costs.

(d) **Is it possible to reduce the number of components,** for example could a product be assembled safely with a smaller number of screws?

The origins of value analysis were in the engineering industry, but it **can be applied to services, or aspects of office work, or to management information systems** (for example the value of information, reports and so on).

4.4.2 The steps in value analysis

A value analysis study should be carried out by a team of experts, preferably with varying backgrounds, which blends experience, skill and imagination.

Step 1 **Selecting a product or service for study**. The product selected should be one which accounts for a high proportion of the organisation's costs, since the greatest cost savings should be obtainable from high cost areas. The choice should also take into account the stage of its 'life cycle' that it has reached. A product reaching the end of its marketable life is unlikely to offer scope for substantial savings.

Step 2 **Obtaining and recording information**. The questions to be asked include: what is the product or service supposed to do? Does it succeed? Are there alternative ways of making or providing it? What do these alternatives cost?

Step 3 **Analysing the information and evaluating the product**. Each aspect of the product or service should now be analysed. Any cost reductions must be achieved without the loss of use or esteem value. (Or at least, cost savings must exceed any loss in value suffered, and customers would then have to be compensated for the loss in use or esteem value in the form of a lower selling price.) The type of questions to be asked and answered in the analysis stage are as follows.

(a) Are all the parts necessary?
(b) Can the parts be obtained or made at a lower cost?
(c) Can standardised parts be used?
(d) Does the value provided by each feature justify its cost?

Step 4 **Considering alternatives**. From the analysis, a variety of options can be devised. This is the 'new ideas' stage of the study, and alternative options would mix ideas for eliminating unnecessary parts or features or standardising certain components or features.

Step 5 **Selection of the least cost alternative**. The costs (and other aspects of value) of each alternative should be compared.

Step 6 **Recommendation**. The preferred alternative should then be recommended to the decision makers for approval.

Step 7 **Implementation and follow-up**. Once a value analysis proposal is approved and accepted, its implementation must be properly planned and co-ordinated. The VA team should review the implementation and, where appropriate, improve the new product or method in the light of practical experience.

To be successful, **value analysis programmes must have the full backing of senior management**.

 Case Study

The following case study was taken from the website of the Department of Trade and Industry (www.dti.gov.uk) in June 2004. The emphasis is BPPs.

'With 10 staff, IBD Ltd is at the leading edge in the design, development, manufacture and marketing of a variety of products for specialist users, mainly in the electronic instrumentation field – electrostatic fieldmeters being a key interest. IBD makes extensive use of value engineering in product design for clients that include British Steel, European Space Agency, BT, ICI and central and local government. "Innovation is our life-blood," says IBD managing director Emlyn Jones. "And value engineering is central to this."

IBD Ltd is a wholly owned subsidiary of the University of Wales, Bangor, that won a SMART (Small Firms Merit Award for Research and Technology) award to develop an instrument to measure artificial biomembranes only two molecules thick. **"Our strength lies in our ability to design to our customer's exact specification and value engineering is important in determining how to meet customer needs in a highly competitive market**," says Emlyn. "**It applies from the inception of the design right through to manufacture**."

IBD's close connection with Bangor's School of Electronic Engineering Science helps IBD maintain best value engineering practice. The School's MEng programme, established at Bangor at the suggestion of HRH Prince of Wales, gives emphasis to value engineering as a key design methodology. But Value Management is also seen as applying to the wider organisation of enterprises as well as to technology, extending into functions such as sales and administration.

"Students are taught how to apply the value engineering job plan to secure innovation in design," says lecturer Peter Hughes who is responsible for value engineering. "**Value engineering is vital to good innovation and design**," he says. "The key lies in maintaining a hard-nosed practical approach. Small to medium enterprises in particular should find that **value engineering will give them a distinct market advantage**." '

5 Functional analysis

am focus
int

In the May 2006 exam, four marks could be earned for an explanation of functional analysis and a comparison with value analysis.

Functional analysis is a cost management technique which has similarities with value analysis. In basic terms, it is a group activity, most commonly applied during the development of new products, which uses the functions of a product or service (such as 'to make a mark' for a pen) as the **basis for cost management**.

ST FORWARD

Functional analysis is concerned with improving profits by attempting to reduce costs and/or by improving products by adding new features in a cost-effective way that are so attractive to customers that profits actually increase.

The basics of the technique were developed in the West and used by Western companies such as General Electric and Chrysler.

> **Functional analysis** is 'An analysis of the relationships between product functions, their perceived value to the customer and their cost of provision'.
>
> (CIMA *Official Terminology*)

5.1 Basic steps

The technique involves the following nine steps, some of which are similar to those required in value analysis.

Step 1   **Choose the object of analysis (such as product, service or overhead area)**. If it is not a new product, **a high volume** product with a complex design and relatively large production costs is often an ideal candidate. Other reasons for selecting a particular product might include apparently high cost, low yield rates, manufacturing problems, market demand (such as remodelling required) or a need for a more compact design. The product selected will determine the precise objective of the analysis exercise (reduce weight by 25%, reduce cost by 30% while maintaining the existing level of quality).

Step 2   **Select members for the functional analysis team**. The team will usually consist of six to eight members from a number of different departments (such as accounting, production, purchasing, engineering, design and marketing).

Step 3   **Gather information**. This will include information both from inside the organisation (detailed design, manufacturing and marketing information, for example) and from outside the organisation (such as information about new technologies).

Step 4   **Define the functions of the object**. The various functions of the product should be defined in terms of a verb and a noun. 'The major function of a propelling ball-point pen can be described as 'make a mark', but supporting functions are also required, such as 'put colour', 'guide tip' and 'prevent loss'. These, in turn, may also require their own supporting functions.' (*Contemporary Cost Management*, Tanaka, Yoshikawa, Innes and Mitchell). Functions should be classified as basic or secondary in terms of the importance of that particular function for the product.

Step 5   **Draw a functional family tree**. The functions identified in step 4 should be arranged in a logical order in a family-tree diagram. A table illustrating the relationship between the functions and the parts of the product, as well as relevant existing costs, should also be drawn up. An extract for a propelling ball point pen is shown below.

| | | Function | | |
Part number	Name of part	Verb	Noun	Cost
5	ink	put	colour	£0.03
9	clip	prevent	loss	£0.02

Step 6   **Evaluate the functions**. The relative value of each function to a total target cost from the customers' point of view has to be estimated (either using market research or by each member of the team placing values and a consensus being reached for each function). This relative value provides a target cost for each function. Those functions where the actual cost is greater than the assigned target cost should be highlighted as potential problem functions (although the absolute amount of money involved should also be taken into consideration).

Step 7   **Suggest alternatives and compare these with the target cost**. Alternatives might include the use of new materials or parts, a different method of manufacturing the product, suggestions for completely new products or new product functions, modifications to the functions of the product, the combination of different functions or even the elimination of certain functions.

Step 8   **Choose the alternatives for manufacturing**. The alternatives must be assessed and a final choice made of those to implement.

Step 9   **Review the actual results**. An audit or review of the changes implemented should be conducted promptly and the findings reported to senior management. This will prevent over-optimistic assessments of the functional analysis exercise and provide feedback so that future functional analysis can be improved.

5.2 Advantages

(a)   Competitive advantage resulting from improved, cost-effective design or redesign of products

(b)   Probably of most benefit during the planning and design stages of new products (because up to 90% of the costs of many products are committed by the end of the design stage)

(c)   Flexible application (has been applied to services, particular overhead areas, organisational restructuring and corporate strategy) because it views objects in abstract (service potential) terms rather than in physical (parts and people) terms

(d)   Information about product functions and about the views of customers is integrated into the formal reporting system

5.3 Functional analysis and ABC

An activity based costing (ABC) system will provide useful information about what drives specific overheads in the organisation. These **cost drivers** can then be used to **link overhead costs to individual functions or groups of functions** so that when a **function is changed**, a basis for ascertaining the **effect (if any) on the overheads** is available. ABC is explained in detail in the next chapter.

Chapter Roundup

- **Learning curve theory** is used to measure how, in some industries and some situations, the incremental cost per unit of output continues to fall for each extra unit produced.

- The theory is that the **cumulative average time per unit produced is assumed to fall by a constant percentage every time total output of the product doubles**. Cumulative average time is the average time per unit for all units produced so far, back to and including the first unit made.

- The formula for the learning curve is $Y_x = aX^b$, where b, the learning coefficient or learning index, is defined as (log of the learning rate/log of 2).

- **Life cycle costing** involves a number of techniques that assist in the planning and control of a product's life cycle costs by monitoring spending and commitment to spend during a product's life cycle. Its aim is to minimise cost and maximise sales revenue over the life of the product.

- **Target costing** is a pro-active cost control system. The target cost is calculated by deducting the target profit from a predetermined selling price based on customers' views. Functional analysis, value engineering and value analysis are used to change production methods and/or reduce expected costs so that the target cost is met.

- **Value analysis** is a planned, scientific approach to cost reduction which reviews the material composition of a product and production design so that modifications and improvements can be made which do not reduce the value of the product to the customer or to the user.

- **Value engineering** is the application of value analysis techniques to new products.

- Four aspects of value should be considered in value analysis (**cost value, exchange value, use value, esteem value**).

- **Functional analysis** is concerned with improving profits by attempting to reduce costs and/or by improving products by adding new features in a cost-effective way that are so attractive to customers that profits actually increase.

Quick Quiz

1   In the formula for the learning curve, $Y_x = aX^b$, how is the value of b calculated?

    A   Log of the learning rate/log of 2
    B   Log of 2/learning rate
    C   Learning rate × log of 2
    D   Log of learning rate/2

2   Life cycle costing is the profiling of cost over a product's production life. *True or false?*

3   *Put the three terms below in the correct order to represent (a) the target costing process and (b) traditional costing process.*

- Selling price
- Cost
- Profit

4   *Choose the correct words from those highlighted.*

Value **engineering/analysis** is cost avoidance or cost prevention before production whereas value **engineering/analysis** is cost reduction during production.

5   Match the terms to the correct definitions.

Terms

Cost value
Exchange value
Use value
Esteem value

Definitions

(a)   The prestige the customer attaches to the product
(b)   The market value of the product
(c)   What the product does
(d)   The cost of producing and selling the product

6   Fill in the action to take at each step in a value analysis.

Step 1 --
Step 2 --
Step 3 --
Step 4 --
Step 5 --
Step 6 --
Step 7 --

7   Fill in the blanks.

Functional analysis is an analysis of the relationships between ...., their .... and their ....

8   Draw a curve of a typical product life cycle.

Answers to Quick Quiz

1   A. Make sure you can use the log function on your calculator.

2   False. It includes development costs and so on prior to production and any costs such as dismantling costs when production has ceased.

3   (a)   Selling price, profit, cost
    (b)   Cost, selling price, profit

4   First term should be value engineering, the second term value analysis.

5   Cost value   (d)
    Exchange value   (b)
    Use value   (c)
    Esteem value   (a)

6   **Step 1**   Select a product or service for study

          Step 2   Obtain and record information

          Step 3   Analyse the information and evaluate the product

          Step 4   Consider alternatives

          Step 5   Select the least cost alternative

          Step 6   Make a recommendation

          Step 7   Implement and follow up

7   Functional analysis is an analysis of the relationships between product functions, their perceived value to the customer and their cost of provision.

8

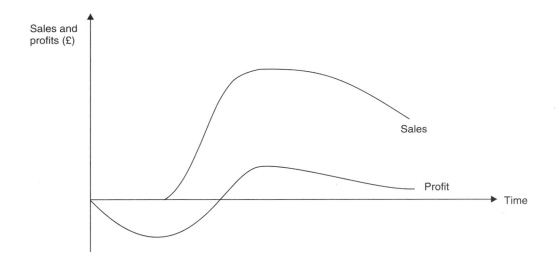

Now try the questions below from the Exam Question Bank			
Number	**Level**	**Marks**	**Time**
Q21	Examination	10	18 mins
Q22	Examination	25	45 mins
Q23	Examination	10	18 mins

Activity based management

Introduction

This chapter continues the theme of cost management begun in Chapter 15 and considers activity based management (ABM) and related topics.

Section 1 sets the scene, while **Section 2** looks at **activity based costing (ABC)**, a topic you may have encountered in your earlier studies.

ABM (covered in **Section 3**) is basically the cost management application of ABC.

One particular aspect of ABM is **business process re-engineering (BPR)**, the topic of **Section 4**. BPR can be used to eliminate non-value-adding activities and reduce activity costs.

Further aspects of ABC and its interaction with other techniques are considered in the final chapter where ABC is used to determine the profitability of customers and distribution channels.

The examiner set a 25-mark question in the November 2005 exam which required an in-depth awareness and application of ABC and ABM. It is worth spending some time on this chapter to understand the ideas behind ABC/ABM and practising questions.

The November 2006 exam included a calculation of full product cost using ABC and an explanation of how ABC could provide useful information to management.

Topic list	Learning outcomes	Syllabus references	Ability required
1 The nature of costs	D(v)	D5	Application
2 Activity based costing (ABC)	B(iv), D(v)	B3, D5	Application
3 Activity based management (ABM)	D(v)	D5	Application
4 Business process re-engineering (BPR)	D(v)	D5	Comprehension

1 The nature of costs

FAST FORWARD

In the **modern business environment**, most costs can be analysed into **short-term variable costs** (that vary with the volume of production) and **long-term variable costs** (that are fixed in the short term and vary not with volume of production but with a different measure of activity).

1.1 The problem of accounting for overheads in the modern business environment

1.1.1 Problem 1

Traditionally, **virtually all costs** with the **exception of material and labour** were classified as **indirect** expenses, meaning that they were not caused by cost objects such as products.

In the **modern business environment**, however, their absorption into products on the **basis of direct labour hours does not recognise the causal factors** of overheads.

1.1.2 Problem 2

Overheads or indirect costs accounted for a **very small proportion of total cost** in the **past.** Their **absorption** into products using **misleading bases** such as in line with direct labour hours **did not therefore produce errors** in product costs that were **too significant**.

Such costs have become a **greater proportion of total production costs**, however, and the **direct labour cost proportion has declined**, in some cases to less than ten per cent of the total cost. This has resulted in a large volume of costs being spread on the basis of the behaviour of a small volume of costs, thereby producing **misleading** and **even inaccurate cost information**.

1.1.3 Problem 3

Nowadays **most costs are fixed in the short term** rather than variable, and so **marginal costing is not a particularly appropriate** costing convention to use. Some method of absorption costing is preferred by the majority of companies – hence the development of ABC and the other systems described in this chapter.

1.2 Cost analysis in the modern business environment

Most costs can be analysed between the following.

(a)   **Short-term variable costs**, that vary with the volume of production

(b)   **Long-term variable costs**, that are fixed in the short-term and do *not* vary with the volume of production, but that do **vary with a different measure of activity**

It has been suggested that **long-term variable costs** are **related** to the **complexity** and **diversity of production** rather than to simple volume of output. For example, costs for support services such as set-ups, handling of inventory, expediting (progress chasing) and scheduling do not increase with the volume of output. They are fixed in the shorter term but they vary in the longer term according to the range and complexity of product items manufactured. If **another product** or product variation is added to the range, the **support activities** will become more **complex**. If a **single product** is made **some support activities**, such as production scheduling, will **not exist**.

The problem of producing a **small number of products in volume** against producing a **large variety of products in small runs** is known as **volume versus variety** and can be expressed graphically.

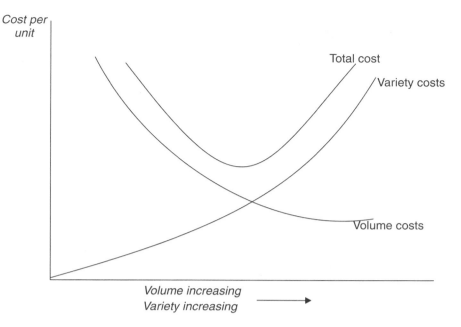

Long production runs (volume) reduce some costs, **short production runs (variety) increase some costs**. Research has shown that when volume doubles, the average cost per unit decreases by 15% to 25% (the experience curve effect). Stalk & Hout (1990) found that when the variety of products manufactured doubles the average unit costs rise by 20% to 35%.

When a company adopts the **modern philosophy** and **manufactures in variety, costs of support activities** therefore **increase** and **emphasis is inevitably put on controlling these costs**, such as minimising production scheduling and set-up costs. In **order to control costs some attempt must be made to relate these costs to products via their causal factors in as accurate a way as possible**.

2 Activity based costing (ABC)

FAST FORWARD

ABC has been developed as an alternative costing system to traditional overhead absorption costing.

    (a)   More **accurate product costs** can be obtained.
    (b)   **Cost of serving individual or different categories of customers** can be **determined**.
    (c)   **Better long-term decisions** will be made.

Key term

Activity based costing (ABC) is 'An approach to the costing and monitoring of activities which involves tracing resource consumption and costing final outputs. Resources are assigned to activities and activities to cost objects based on consumption estimates. The latter use **cost drivers** to attach activity costs to outputs.'

(CIMA *Official Terminology*)

Exam focus point

A 25 mark question in the November 2005 exam required candidates to use an ABC approach to attribute costs to client groups and then compare the results with a more traditional costing system.

In the November 2006 exam, fifteen marks were available as part of a longer Section C question for calculating costs using ABC. The question also asked for an explanation of the relevance of information provided by ABC.

FAST FORWARD

The ABC approach is to relate costs to the factors that cause or 'drive' them to be incurred in the first place and to change subsequently. These factors are called '**cost drivers**'.

2.1 Cost drivers and cost pools

Key term

> A **cost driver** is 'factor influencing the level of cost. Often used in the context of ABC to denote the factor which links activity resource consumption to product outputs, for example, the number of purchase orders would be a cost driver for procurement cost.'
>
> (CIMA *Official Terminology*)

2.1.1 Examples of cost drivers

Support department costs	Possible cost driver
Set-up costs	Number of production runs
Production scheduling	Number of production runs
Material handling	Number of production runs
Inspection costs	Number of inspections or inspection hours
Raw materials inventory handling etc	Number of purchase orders delivered
Despatch costs	Number of customer orders delivered

All of the costs associated with a particular cost driver (for example production runs) would be grouped into **cost pools**.

Miller and Vollman ('The Hidden Factory', *Harvard Business Review*, 1985) provided a useful system for analysing the activities (transactions) which cause costs to be incurred.

Types of transaction	Detail
Logistical transactions	Those activities concerned with organising the flow of resources throughout the manufacturing process.
Balancing transactions	Those activities which ensure that demand for and supply of resources are matched.
Quality transactions	Those activities which relate to ensuring that production is at the required level of quality.
Change transactions	Those activities associated with ensuring that customers' requirements (delivery date, changed design and so on) are met.

Professor Kaplan commented ('Relevance regained', *Management Accounting,* September 1988) as follows (with BPP's emphasis).

'Our task is to **dissect these activities**, find out how much is being spent on them and **come up with a quantity measure that can be related to a finished product**. These measures will be things like how many items are being inspected, how many purchase orders are being produced, how many engineering changes are being processed, how much material is being moved, how many set-up hours are being delivered, how many customer calls are being made.

Remarkably, the old traditional methods of cost accounting never had quantity measures related to overhead. We had quantity measures for labour, we had quantity measures for direct material, but **overhead was always a big glob of money to be allocated**. That's exactly the wrong way to think about it. The **goal is to think about what are the quantities of overhead that are being delivered**.'

In order to understand how ABC operates in detail we need to look at two types of cost driver.

A **resource cost driver** is a measure of the quantity of resources consumed by an activity. It is used to assign the cost of a resource to an activity or cost pool.

An **activity cost driver** is a measure of the frequency and intensity of demand placed on activities by cost objects. It is used to assign activity costs to cost objects.

ABC relates overhead/resource costs to the activities that cause or drive them. This is done using **resource cost drivers**. The costs of activities are related to cost units using **activity cost drivers**.

An **example** of a resource cost driver is **area**, which can be used to assign office occupancy costs to purchasing, the accounts department and so on.

An **example** of an **activity cost driver** is **number of customer orders,** the number of orders measuring the consumption of order entry activities by each customer.

In **traditional absorption costing** overheads are first related to **cost centres** and then to **cost objects** (products). In **ABC** overheads are first related to **activities** or grouped into **cost pools** (depending on the terminology preferred) and then related to the **cost objects**. (Unlike traditional absorption costing, ABC has other cost objects such as customers. This will be discussed later). **The two processes** are therefore **very similar**, but the first stage is different as ABC uses activities instead of cost centres (functional departments).

Proponents of **ABC** therefore claim that it gives a **more realistic picture of cost behaviour.**

(a)   Costs collected into cost pools tend to behave in the same way (they have the same cost driver).

(b)   Costs related to cost centres might behave in different ways.

Like traditional absorption costing rates, **ABC rates** are **calculated in advance,** usually for **a year ahead**.

2.2 Stages in ABC calculations

Step 1   **Identify the different activities**. The number of activities may range from, say, 20 to 150. There is an **accuracy/cost trade-off**. In 'The Design of Costing Systems' (1998) Cooper & Kaplan expressed it this way (with BPP emphasis): 'The goal is **not to have the most accurate cost system**...(it) should be to **have the best cost system**, one that **balances the cost of errors** made from inaccurate estimates **with the cost of measurement**'. This effect is demonstrated in the following graph.

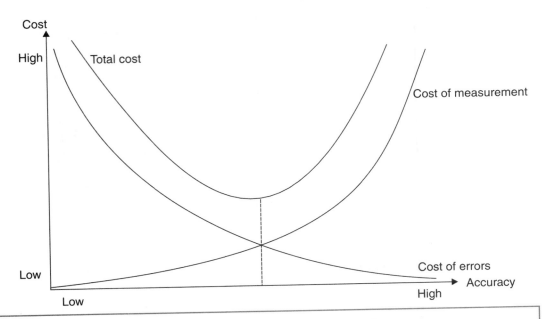

Key term	**Primary activities** are those performed directly for products, services or customers. **Support activities** create the environment that enables the primary activities to be performed, eg the activities of the human resources department.

Step 2   **Relate overheads** (such as heat and light) **to the activities**, both primary and support (such as purchasing), that caused them. This creates **cost pools**. This will be done using **resource cost drivers** (such as volume).

Step 3   **Spread the support activities across the primary activities** based on some suitable cost driver, which reflects the use of the support activity.

Step 4   **Determine the activity cost drivers** that will be used to relate the overheads collected in the cost pools to the cost objects. This is done by selecting the **factor that drives the consumption of the activity**.

Step 5   **Calculate activity cost driver rates.**

$$\text{Activity cost driver rate} = \frac{\text{Total cost of activity}}{\text{Activity driver}}$$

The **activity driver rate** can be used to **cost products**, as in traditional absorption costing, but it can also cost **other cost objects** such as **customers** or groups of customers. The possibility of **costing objects other than products** is part of the **benefit of ABC**. The activity cost driver rates will be multiplied by the different amounts of each activity that each cost object consumes.

2.3 Example: ABC

The following example illustrates how traditional cost accounting techniques could result in a misleading and inequitable division of costs between low-volume and high-volume products, and demonstrates that ABC may provide a more meaningful allocation of costs.

Suppose that Cooplan manufactures four products, W, X, Y and Z. The direct labour cost per hour is $5. Other output and cost data for the period just ended are as follows.

	Output units	Number of production runs in the period	Material cost per unit	Direct labour hours per unit	Machine hours per unit
			$		
W	10	2	20	1	1
X	10	2	80	3	3
Y	100	5	20	1	1
Z	100	5	80	3	3
		14			

Overhead costs

Short run variable costs	$3,080	Expediting and scheduling costs	$9,100
Set-up costs	$10,920	Materials handling costs	$7,700

Required

Prepare unit costs for each product using traditional costing and ABC.

Solution

Using a **conventional absorption costing approach** and an absorption rate for overheads based on either direct labour hours or machine hours, the product costs would be as follows.

	W	X	Y	Z	Total
	$	$	$	$	$
Direct material	200	800	2,000	8,000	
Direct labour	50	150	500	1,500	
Overheads *	700	2,100	7,000	21,000	
	950	3,050	9,500	30,500	44,000
Units produced	10	10	100	100	
Cost per unit	$95	$305	$95	$305	

* $30,800 ÷ 440 hours = $70 per direct labour or machine hour.

Using **activity based costing** and assuming that the number of production runs is the cost driver for set-up costs, expediting and scheduling costs and materials handling costs and that machine hours are the cost driver for short-run variable costs, unit costs would be as follows.

	W	X	Y	Z	Total
	$	$	$	$	$
Direct material	200	800	2,000	8,000	
Direct labour	50	150	500	1,500	
Short-run variable overheads (W1)	70	210	700	2,100	
Set-up costs (W2)	1,560	1,560	3,900	3,900	
Expediting, scheduling costs (W3)	1,300	1,300	3,250	3,250	
Materials handling costs (W4)	1,100	1,100	2,750	2,750	
	4,280	5,120	13,100	21,500	44,000
Units produced	10	10	100	100	
Cost per unit	$428	$512	$131	$215	

Workings

1	$3,080 ÷ 440 machine hours =		$7 per machine hour
2	$10,920 ÷ 14 production runs =		$780 per run
3	$9,100 ÷ 14 production runs =		$650 per run
4	$7,700 ÷ 14 production runs =		$550 per run

Summary

Product	Traditional costing Unit cost $	ABC Unit cost $	Difference per unit $	Difference in total $
W	95	428	+ 333	+3,330
X	305	512	+ 207	+2,070
Y	95	131	+ 36	+3,600
Z	305	215	− 90	−9,000

The figures suggest that the traditional volume-based absorption costing system is flawed.

(a)   It **under-allocates overhead costs to low-volume products** (here, W and X) and **over-allocates overheads to higher-volume products** (here Z in particular).

(b)   It **under-allocates overhead costs to smaller-sized products** (here W and Y with just one hour of work needed per unit) and **over-allocates overheads to larger products** (here X and particularly Z).

ABC traces the appropriate amount of input to each product. However, it is **important** to realise that although **ABC should be** a **more accurate** way of relating overheads to products **it is not a perfect system** and **product costs** could still be **inaccurate** as ABC is based on a number of assumptions.

2.4 The merits and criticisms of activity based costing

FAST FORWARD

There are both **merits and criticisms** of ABC.

2.4.1 Merits

As the above example illustrates, there is nothing difficult about ABC. Once the necessary information has been obtained it is similar to traditional absorption costing. This **simplicity** is part of its appeal. Further merits of ABC are as follows.

(a)   The **complexity** of many businesses has **increased**, with wider product ranges, shorter product life cycles, the greater importance of quality and more complex production processes. ABC **recognises this complexity** with its **multiple cost drivers**, many of which are transaction-based rather than volume-based.

(b)   In modern manufacturing systems, overhead functions include a lot of non-factory-floor activities such as product design, quality control, production planning, sales order planning and customer service. ABC is **concerned with all overhead costs**, including the costs of these functions, and so it takes cost accounting beyond its 'traditional' factory floor boundaries.

(c)   Many companies sell products at a loss, subsidising their customers because they do not understand the true cost of the product. In today's **competitive** environment, companies must be able to **assess product profitability realistically**. To do this, they must have a good understanding of what drives overhead costs. ABC gives a meaningful analysis of costs which should provide a suitable basis for decisions about pricing, product mix, design and production.

(d)   ABC helps with **cost reduction** because it provides an insight into causal activities and allows organisations to consider the possibility of **outsourcing particular activities**, or even of **moving to different areas in the industry value chain**. This is discussed later in the chapter under activity based management.

(e)   Many **costs are driven by customers** (delivery costs, discounts, after-sales service and so on), but traditional cost accounting does not account for this. Companies may be trading with certain customers at a loss but may not realise it because costs are not analysed in a way that would reveal the true situation. ABC can be **used in conjunction with customer profitability analysis (CPA)**, discussed in a later chapter, to determine more accurately the profit earned by serving particular customers.

(f) ABC can be used by **service and retail organisations**. This will be discussed later in the chapter. Many service and retail businesses have characteristics very similar to those required for the successful application of ABC in modern manufacturing industry.

 (i) A highly **competitive** market

 (ii) **Diversity** of products, processes and customers

 (iii) **Significant overhead costs** which are not easily assigned to individual products

 (iv) **Demands placed on overhead resources** by individual products and customers, which are **not proportional to volume**.

 If ABC were to be used in a hotel, for example, attempts could be made to identify the activities required to support each guest by category and the cost drivers of those activities. The cost of a one-night stay midweek by a businessman could then be distinguished from the cost of a one-night stay by a teenager at the weekend. Such information may prove invaluable for customer profitability analysis.

2.4.2 Criticisms

Activity based costing has some serious flaws and concern is now growing that ABC is seen by many as a panacea for management accounting ills, despite the fact that its suitability for all environments remains unproven.

(a) The **cost** of obtaining and interpreting the new information may be considerable. **ABC should not be introduced unless it can provide additional information** for management to use in planning or control decisions.

(b) Some arbitrary **cost apportionment** may still be required at the cost pooling stage for items like rent, rates and building depreciation. If an ABC system has many cost pools the amount of apportionment needed may be greater than ever.

(c) Many **overheads relate neither to volume nor to complexity**. The ability of a **single cost driver** to fully explain the cost behaviour of all items in its associated pool is **questionable**.

(d) There will have to be a **trade off between accuracy, the number of cost drivers and complexity**.

(e) ABC tends to **burden low-volume (new) products** with a punitive level of overhead costs and hence threatens opportunities for successful innovation if it is used without due care.

(f) Some people have questioned the fundamental assumption that activities cause cost, they suggest **that decisions cause cost or the passage of time causes cost** – or that there may be **no clear cause of cost.**

2.5 Wider uses of ABC

FORWARD

The **information** provided by **analysing activities** can support the management functions of **planning, control and decision making**, provided it is used carefully and with full appreciation of its implications.

2.5.1 Planning

Before an ABC system can be implemented, management must **analyse** the **organisation's activities**, determine the **extent of their occurrence**, and establish the **relationship between activities, products/services and their cost**. This can be used as a basis for **forward planning and budgeting**.

2.5.2 Control

Knowledge of activities also provides an **insight into the way in which costs are structured and incurred in service and support departments**. Traditionally it has been difficult to control the costs of such departments because of the lack of relationship between departmental output levels and departmental cost. With ABC, however, it is possible to **control or manage the costs by managing the activities which underlie them** using a number of key performance measures which must be monitored if costs and the business generally are to be controlled.

2.5.3 Decision making

Many of **ABC's supporters** claim that it can **assist with decision making** because it provides accurate and reliable cost information. This is a **contentious issue** among accountants. Many 'purists' consider that **marginal costing** alone provides the correct information on which to **make short-term decisions such as the following.**

  (a)   Pricing
  (b)   Make or buy decisions
  (c)   Promoting or discontinuing products or parts of the business
  (d)   Developing and designing changed products

ABC establishes a long-run product cost and because it provides data which can be used to evaluate different business possibilities and opportunities it is particularly suited for the types of decision listed above. Those decisions have long-term strategic implications and **average cost** is probably **more important** than **marginal cost** in many circumstances. **An ABC cost is an average cost**, but it is **not always a true cost** because some costs such as depreciation are usually arbitrarily allocated to products. An ABC cost is therefore **not a relevant cost for all decisions**.

Raiborn *et al* explain how a product cost is determined using an ABC approach.

'Traditionally, accounting has assumed that if costs did not vary with changes in production at the unit level, those costs were fixed rather than variable. Such an assumption is not true. Batch level, product level, and organisational level costs are all variable, but these types of costs vary for reasons other than changes in production volume. For this reason, to determine an accurate estimate of product or service cost, costs should be accumulated at each successively higher level of costs. Because unit, batch and product level costs are all related to units of products (merely at different levels), these costs can be gathered together at the product level to match with the revenues generated by product sales. Organisational level costs, however, are not product related and, thus, should only be subtracted in total from net product revenues.'

2.5.4 ABC and long-term decisions

ABC is **particularly suited for long-term and strategic decisions** (such as long-run pricing, capacity management and product mix decisions) for a number of reasons.

  (a)   It assumes all costs are variable in relation to product choice or production level decisions.

  (b)   It has strategic relevance because it allows for a full understanding of activities and their resource consumption.

  (c)   Short-run changes in consumption do not translate into changes in spending (as real cash savings or expenditure are not made/incurred in the short run).

Question

Learning outcome: D(v)

(a) List the features of organisations that would find ABC particularly useful for product costing.

(b) Briefly explain the reasons why ABC is particularly suitable in a modern business environment and describe any situations where it is not appropriate.

Answer

(a) Here are our suggestions.

    (i) Production overheads are a high proportion of total production costs.

    (ii) The product range is wide and diverse.

    (iii) The amounts of overhead resources used by products varies.

    (iv) Volume is not the primary driver of overhead resource consumption.

(b) **Reasons for suitability**

    (i) Most modern organisations tend to have a high level of overhead costs, especially relating to support services such as maintenance and data processing. ABC, by the use of carefully chosen cost drivers, traces these overheads to product lines in a more logical and less arbitrary manner than traditional absorption costing.

    (ii) The determination and use of cost drivers helps to measure and improve the efficiency and effectiveness of support departments.

    (iii) Many costs included in general overheads can actually be traced to specific product lines using ABC. This improves product costing and cost management because the costs are made the responsibility of the line manager.

    (iv) ABC forces the organisation to ask such searching questions as 'What causes the demand for the activity?', 'What does the department achieve?', 'Does it add value?' and so on.

    (v) ABC systems may encourage reductions in throughput time and inventory and improvements in quality.

Unsuitable situations

    (i) A number of businesses have recently been split into several small autonomous sections. In this situation there may be no need for a sophisticated costing system such as ABC because staff should be aware of cost behaviour.

    (ii) ABC can work against modern manufacturing methods such as just-in-time (JIT). JIT seeks to reduce set-up time so that very small batches can be made economically.

    (iii) The aim of set-up time reduction is to allow more set-ups, not just to reduce set-up costs. The use of a cost driver based on the number of set-ups will therefore work against JIT principles as it will tend to encourage larger batches.

2.6 Pricing and ABC

The implication for **pricing if ABC is used** is that the full cost on which prices are based may be radically different from a price based on full cost determined using traditional absorption costing.

2.6.1 Example: activity based costing and pricing

ABP makes two products, X and Y, with the following cost patterns.

	Product X	Product Y
	$	$
Direct materials	27	24
Direct labour at $5 per hour	20	25
Variable production overheads at $6 per hour	3	6
	50	55

Production fixed overheads total $300,000 per month and these are absorbed on the basis of direct labour hours. Budgeted direct labour hours are 25,000 per month. However, the company has carried out an analysis of its production support activities and found that its 'fixed costs' actually vary in accordance with non volume-related factors.

Activity	Cost driver	Product X	Product Y	Total cost
				$
Set-ups	Production runs	30	20	40,000
Materials handling	Production runs	30	20	150,000
Inspection	Inspections	880	3,520	110,000
				300,000

Budgeted production is 1,250 units of product X and 4,000 units of product Y.

Required

Given that the company wishes to make a profit of 20% on full production costs calculate the prices that should be charged for products X and Y using the following.

(a)   Full cost pricing
(b)   Activity based cost pricing

Solution

(a)   The **full cost and mark-up** will be calculated as follows.

	Product X	Product Y
	$	$
Variable costs	50.00	55.00
Fixed prod o/hds ($300,000/25,000 = $12 per direct labour hr)	48.00	60.00
	98.00	115.00
Profit mark-up (20%)	19.60	23.00
Selling price	117.60	138.00

(b)   Using **activity based costing**, overheads will be allocated on the basis of cost drivers.

	X	Y	Total
	$	$	$
Set ups (30:20)	24,000	16,000	40,000
Materials handling (30:20)	90,000	60,000	150,000
Inspections (880:3,520)	22,000	88,000	110,000
	136,000	164,000	300,000
Budgeted units	1,250	4,000	
Overheads per unit	$108.80	$41.00	

The price is then calculated as before.

	Product X $	Product Y $
Variable costs	50.00	55.00
Production overheads	108.80	41.00
	158.80	96.00
Profit mark-up (20%)	31.76	19.20
	190.56	115.20

(c)   **Commentary**

The results in (b) are radically different from those in (a). On this basis it appears that the company has **previously been making a huge loss** on every unit of product X sold for $117.60. If the market will not accept a price increase, it may be worth considering ceasing production of product X entirely. It also appears that there is scope for a reduction in the price of product Y, and this would certainly be worthwhile if demand for the product is elastic.

2.6.2 The pricing implications of activity based costing

Consider a business that produces a **large volume** standard product and a number of **variants** which are more refined versions of the basic product and sell in low volumes at a higher price. Such companies are common in practice in the modern business environment. In practice, also, such companies absorb fixed overheads on a conventional basis such as direct labour hours, and price their products by adding a mark up to full cost.

In the situation described, the **majority of the overheads** would be allocated to the **standard** range, and only a small percentage to the up-market products. The result would be that the profit margin achieved on the standard range would be much lower than that on the up-market range.

Thus the traditional costing and pricing system indicates that the firm might be wise to concentrate on its high margin, up-market products and drop its standard range. This is **absurd**, however. Much of the overhead cost incurred in such an organisation is the cost of support activities like production scheduling: the more different **varieties** of product there are, the higher the level of such activities will become. The cost of marketing and distribution also increase disproportionately to the volume of products being made.

The bulk of the overheads in such an organisation are actually the 'costs of complexity'. Their arbitrary allocation on the basis of labour hours gives an entirely **distorted** view of production line profitability; many products that appear to be highly profitable actually make a loss if costs are allocated on the basis of what activities cause them.

The problem arises with **marginal cost-plus** approaches as well as with absorption cost based approaches, particularly in a modern manufacturing environment, where a relatively small proportion of the total cost is variable. The implication in both cases is that conventional costing should be abandoned in favour of ABC.

2.7 Using ABC in service and retail organisations

ABC was **first introduced in manufacturing organisations** but it can equally well be used in **other types of organisation**. For example, the management of the Post Office in the USA recently introduced ABC. They analysed the activities associated with cash processing as follows.

Activities	Examples	Possible cost driver
Unit level	Accept cash	Number of transactions
	Processing of cash by bank	Number of transactions
Batch level	'Close out' and supervisor review of clerk	Number of 'close outs'
	Deposits	Number of deposits
	Review and transfer of funds	Number of accounts
Product level	Maintenance charges for bank accounts	Number of accounts
	Reconciling bank accounts	Number of accounts

Retail organisations are considered in more detail in the context of direct product profitability later in this text, but they too **can use ABC**.

Question · ABC and retail organisations

Learning outcome: D(v)

Complete the following table to show activities and drivers that might be used in a retail organisation.

Activities	Possible cost driver

Answer

Activities	Possible cost driver
Procure goods	Number of orders
Receive goods	Number of orders or pallets
Store goods	Volume of goods
Pick goods	Number of packs
Handle returnables/recyclables	Volume of goods

3 Activity based management (ABM)

Recently the emphasis has switched away from using activity based approaches for product costing to using it to improve cost management.

> **FAST FORWARD**
>
> The terms **activity based management (ABM)** and **activity-based cost management (ABCM)** are used to describe the cost management applications of ABC.

3.1 What is ABM?

There are a great many different **definitions** of activity based management.

3.1.1 Definition 1

Here is Drury's (from *Management and Cost Accounting*), with BPP's emphasis.

'ABM views the business as a set of linked activities that ultimately add value to the customer. It focuses on managing the business on the basis of the activities that make up the organisation. ABM is based on the premise that activities consume costs. Therefore **by managing activities costs will be managed in the long term**. The **goal of ABM is to enable customer needs to be satisfied while making fewer demands on organisation resources**. The measurement of activities is a key role of the management accounting function. In particular, activity cost information is useful for prioritising those activities that need to be studied closely so that they can be eliminated or improved.

In recent years ABM information has been used for a variety of business applications. They include cost reduction, activity-based budgeting, performance measurement, benchmarking and business process re-engineering.'

3.1.2 Definition 2

Horngren, Foster and Datar in *Cost Accounting: A Managerial Emphasis* define it broadly to '**include pricing and product-mix decisions**, **cost reduction** and **process improvement decisions**, and **product design decisions**'.

3.1.3 Definition 3

In *Managerial Accounting*, Raiborn, Barfield and Kinney include **activity analysis**, **cost driver analysis**, **continuous improvement**, **operational control and performance evaluation** as the concepts covered by activity based management. 'These concepts help companies to produce more efficiently, determine costs more accurately, and control and evaluate performance more effectively.'

3.1.4 Definition 4

Clark and Baxter (*Management Accounting*, June 1992) provide a description which appears to include every management accounting buzzword. The emphasis is BPP's.

'The aim of activity-based management (ABM) is to provide management with a method of introducing and **managing 'process and organisational change'**.

It focuses on activities within a process, decision-making and planning relative to those activities and the need for continuous improvement of all organisational activity. Management and staff must determine which activities are critical to success and decide how these are to be clearly defined across all functions.

Everyone must co-operate in defining:

(a)   cost pools
(b)   cost drivers
(c)   key performance indicators

They must be trained and **empowered** to act; all must be fairly treated and success recognised.

Clearly, ABM and employee empowerment take a critical step forward beyond ABC by recognising the contribution that people make as the key resource in any organisation's success.

(a)   It nurtures good communication and team work
(b)   It develops quality decision-making
(c)   It leads to quality control and continuous improvement

Some accountants do not appear to understand that ABM provides an essential link to total quality management (**TQM**) and its concepts of 'continuous improvement'.

ABM helps deliver:

(b)   improved quality
(b)   increased customer satisfaction
(c)   lower costs
(d)   increased profitability

It provides accountants and other technical managers with a meaningful path into the business management team.'

3.1.5 Definition 5

Perhaps the clearest and most concise definition is offered by Kaplan *et al* in *Management Accounting*.

Activity based management (ABM) is '...the management processes that use the information provided by an activity-based cost analysis to improve organisational profitability. Activity-based management (ABM) includes performing activities more efficiently, eliminating the need to perform certain activities that do not add value for customers, improving the design of products, and developing better relationships with customers and suppliers. The goal of ABM is to enable customer needs to be satisfied while making fewer demands on organisational resources.'

Key term

Activity-based management (ABM) is: **operational ABM.** Actions based on activity driver analysis, that increase efficiency, lower costs and improve asset utilisation.

Strategic ABM Actions based on activity-based cost analysis, that aim to change the demand for activities so as to improve profitability.   *(CIMA Official Terminology)*

In the following paragraphs we examine some of the aspects of ABM mentioned in the definitions above.

3.2 Cost reduction and process improvement

Traditional cost analysis analyses costs by types of expense for each responsibility centre. ABM, on the other hand, analyses costs on the basis of cross-departmental activities and therefore provides management information on why costs are incurred and on the output of the activity in terms of cost drivers. **By controlling or reducing the incidence of the cost driver, the associated cost can be controlled or reduced**.

This difference is illustrated in the example below of a customer order processing activity.

Traditional analysis

	$
Salaries	5,700
Stationery	350
Travel	1,290
Telephone	980
Equipment depreciation	680
	9,000

ABC analysis

	$
Preparation of quotations	4,200
Receipt of customer orders	900
Assessment of customer creditworthiness	1,100
Expedition of orders	1,300
Resolution of customer problems	1,500
	9,000

Suppose that the analysis above showed that it cost $250 to process a customer's order. This would indicate to sales staff that it may not be worthwhile chasing orders with a low sales value. By eliminating lots of small orders and focusing on those with a larger value, demand for the activities associated with customer order processing should fall, with spending decreasing as a consequence.

3.2.1 Problems associated with cost reduction and ABM

(a) The extent to which activity based approaches can be applied is very dependent on an organisation's ability to identify its main activities and their associated cost drivers.

(b) If a system of 'conventional' responsibility centres has been carefully designed, this may already be a reflection of the key organisational activities.

(c) In some circumstances, the 'pooling' of activity based costs and the identification of a single cost driver for every cost pool may even hamper effective control if the cost driver is not completely applicable to every cost within that cost pool.

3.3 Activity analysis

The activity based analysis above provides information not available from a traditional cost analysis. Why was $1,500 spent on resolving customer orders, for example. An **activity analysis** usually **surprises managers** who had not realised the amount being spent on certain activities. This leads to **questions** about the **necessity for particular activities** and, if an activity is required, whether it can be carried out more effectively and efficiently.

Such questions can be answered by classifying activities as value added or non-value added (or as core/primary, support or diversionary/discretionary).

3.3.1 Value-added and non-value-added activities

 term

An activity may increase the worth of a product or service to the customer; in this case the customer is willing to pay for that activity and it is considered **value-added.** Some activities, though, simply increase the time spent on a product or service but do not increase its worth to the customer; these activities are **non-value-added.**   (Rayborn, Barfield and Kinney, *Managerial Accounting*)

As an example, **getting luggage on the proper flight is a value-added activity** for airlines, **dealing with the complaints from customers whose luggage gets lost is not**.

The **time** spent on **non-value-added activities** creates additional costs that are unnecessary. If such activities were **eliminated**, **costs** would **decrease without affecting the market value or quality of the product or service**.

ST FORWARD ▶▶

Two questions can be used to **assess whether an activity adds value**.

- Would an external customer encourage the organisation to do more of the activity?
- Would the organisation be more likely to achieve its goals by performing the activity?

If both answers are yes, the activity adds value.

Case Study

'In a competitive environment, an organization should waste as few resources on non-value-added activities as possible because competitors are continuously striving to create more customer value at lower cost. For example, many banks recently eliminated most levels of approval for consumer and commercial loans because the multiple approval layers almost never affected the decision of granting the loans. The multiple approvals merely used scarce resources and delayed final approval, and the delays greatly annoyed customers. Those loan approval levels represented non-value-added activities because neither customers nor the bank realised value from them. By substituting information technology for multiple levels of manual assessments of loan applications, some banks now are able to advertise nearly instant loan decisions. These businesses seek to attract customers from less effective banks by offering more value through faster loan decisions at lower cost because their process needs fewer approval levels.'

(Hilton, Maher and Selto, *Cost Management: Strategies for Business Decisions*)

The processing **time** of an organisation is made up of four types.

(a) **Production** or **performance time** is the actual time that it takes to perform the functions necessary to manufacture the product or perform the service.

(b) Performing quality control results in **inspection time.**

(c) Moving products or components from one place to another is **transfer time**.

(d) Storage time and time spent waiting at the production operation for processing are **idle time**.

Production time is value added. The other three are not. The time from receipt of an order to completion of a product or performance of a service equals production time plus non-value-added time.

JIT would of course eliminate a significant proportion of the idle time occurring from storage and wait processes but it is important to realise that **very few organisations can completely eliminate all quality control functions and all transfer time**. If managers understand the non-value-added nature of these functions, however, they should be able to **minimise** such activities as much as possible.

Sometimes **non-value added activities** arise because of inadequacies in existing processes and so they **cannot be eliminated unless these inadequacies are addressed**.

(a) The National Health Service (NHS) is a classic example of this. Some heart patients on the NHS wait up to four months for critical heart surgery. During this time they are likely to be severely ill on a number of occasions and have to be taken to hospital where they spend the day receiving treatment that will temporarily relieve the problem. This non-value-added activity is totally unnecessary and is dependent on an inadequate process: that of providing operations when required.

(b) Customer complaints services can be viewed in the same way: eliminate the source of complaints and the need for the department greatly reduces.

(c) Setting up machinery for a new production run is a non-value-added cost. If the number of components per product can be reduced the number of different components made will reduce and therefore set-up time will also reduce.

One of the **costliest** things an organisation can do is to **invest in equipment and people to make non-value-added activities more efficient**. The objective is to eliminate them altogether or subject them to a major overhaul, not make them more efficient. For example, if a supplier of raw materials makes a commitment to supply high-quality materials, inspection is no longer required, and buying testing equipment and hiring more staff to inspect incoming raw material would waste time and money. **Non-value-added activities are not necessary for an organisation to stay in business.**

3.3.2 Core/primary, support and diversionary/discretionary activities

This is an alternative classification of activities.

Key terms

> A **core** or **primary activity** is one that adds value to a product, for example cutting and drilling materials and assembling them.
>
> A **support** or **secondary activity** is one that supports a core activity, but does not add value in itself. For example setting up a machine so that it drills holes of a certain size is a secondary activity.
>
> **Diversionary** or **discretionary activities** do not add value and are symptoms of failure within an organisation. For instance repairing faulty production work is such an activity because the production should not have been faulty in the first place.

The aim of ABM is to try to eliminate as far as possible the diversionary activities but, as with non-value-added activities, experience has shown that it is usually impossible to eliminate them all, although the time and cost associated with them can be greatly reduced.

3.4 Cost management of activities

Costs are assigned using cost driver rates (calculated on the basis of available resource) to cost objects on the basis of the objects' demand for an activity or consumption of a resource.

But the amount of resource available in a period is not necessarily the same as the amount of resource consumed by cost objects.

If the staff of a purchasing department are **fully occupied**, **all costs** of the department will be **assigned**, via a cost driver rate based on, say, number of orders, to cost objects. Unlike inventories of material, however, **unused capacity** in the purchasing department **cannot be stored** for the future. Management must therefore **control the provision of activities and the associated resources if costs are to be kept to a minimum**.

A **change in the level of demand for an activity does not necessarily lead to a change in the level of provision of that activity**, however.

(a)   If the demand for orders increases, the existing purchasing department staff may be able to meet this extra demand with overtime working, but in the medium to long term additional staff would be required. It is not usually possible to take on and get rid of staff at short notice, however, and so there is usually a delay between changes in demand for activity and change in the availability of resource for that activity.

(b)   If the demand for orders decreases, the purchasing department staff are not likely to bring to management attention the fact that they now have slack in their working hours. A traditional absorption costing system would not highlight this situation for management attention, either. If ABC is used, however, the drop in demand for the resource/activity will be obvious as the cost driver rate will be applied to fewer orders/units of output.

The application of **ABC** therefore offers the possibility of **turning costs that were deemed to be fixed into variable costs**: variability is a function of managers' decisions about levels of expenditure and the speed at which the supply of resources should be changed as requirements change.

Whereas **absorption costing aims to recover costs, ABC aims to highlight inefficiencies**, and so cost drivers should be based on the possible level of activity rather than the expected level of activity. If the cost driver rate is $100 per order and 50 orders are handled in a month, the cost assigned is $5,000. If budgeted expenditure is $6,000, the cost of unused capacity is $1,000.

ABC therefore enables management to **identify resources that are not being fully utilised.**

3.5 Design decisions

In many organisations today, roughly 80% of a product's costs are committed at the product design stage, well before production begins. By **providing product designers with cost driver information** they can be encouraged to **design low cost products that still meet customer requirements.**

The identification of appropriate cost drivers and tracing costs to products on the basis of these cost drivers has the potential to **influence behaviour to support the cost management strategies of the organisation.**

For example, suppose product costs depend on the number and type of components. A product which is designed so that it uses fewer components will be cheaper to produce. A product using standard components will also be cheaper to produce. Management can influence the action of designers through overhead absorption rates if overheads are related to products on the basis of the number of component parts they contain. Hitachi's refrigeration plant uses this method to influence the behaviour of their product designers and ultimately the cost of manufacture.

3.6 Cost driver analysis

Exam focus point

> Part of a 25-mark question in the November 2005 exam asked candidates to discuss activities classified according to the manufacturing cost hierarchy. This was not well answered so it is important that you learn the four classification levels as well as understand applications to specific organisations.

FAST FORWARD

> The **manufacturing cost hierarchy** categorises costs and activities as unit level, batch level, product/ process level and organisational/facility level.

To reflect today's more **complex business environment**, recognition must be given to the fact that **costs are created and incurred because their cost drivers occur at different levels. Cost driver analysis investigates, quantifies and explains the relationships between cost drivers and their related costs.**

Activities and their related costs fall into four different categories, known as the **manufacturing cost hierarchy**. The **categories determine the type of activity cost driver required**.

Classification level	Cause of cost	Types of cost	Necessity of cost
Unit level activities and costs	Production/acquisition of a single unit of product or delivery of single unit of service	Direct materials Direct labour	Once for each unit produced
Batch level activities and costs	A group of things being made, handled or processed	Purchase orders Set-ups Inspection	Once for each batch produced
Product/process level activities and costs	Development, production or acquisition of different items	Equipment maintenance Product development	Supports a product type or a process

Classification level	Cause of cost	Types of cost	Necessity of cost
Organisational/ facility level activities and costs	Some costs cannot be related to a particular product line, instead they are related to maintaining the buildings and facilities. These costs cannot be related to cost objects with any degree of accuracy and are often excluded from ABC calculations for this reason.	Building depreciation	Supports the overall production or service process

(Adapted from Raiborn *et al*)

Traditionally it has been assumed that if costs did not vary with changes in production at the unit level, they were fixed rather than variable. The analysis above shows this assumption to be false, and that costs vary for reasons other than production volume. To determine an accurate estimate of product or service cost, **costs should be accumulated at each successively higher level of costs.**

Unit level costs are allocated over number of units produced, batch level costs over the number of units in the batch, product level costs over the number of units produced by the product line. These costs are all related to units of product (merely at different levels) and so can be gathered together at the product level to match with revenue. Organisational level costs are not product related, however, and so should simply be deducted from net revenue.

Such an approach gives a far greater insight into product profitability.

Question

Classification of activities

Learning outcome: D(v)

A food processing company operates an ABC system. Which of the following would be classified as a facility-sustaining activity?

(i) General staff administration
(ii) Plant management
(iii) Technical support for individual products and services
(iv) Updating of product specification database
(v) Property management

A (i) and (ii) only
B (i), (ii) and (v)
C (ii), (iii) and (iv)
D (ii), (iii), (iv) and (v)

Answer

The correct answer is B.

Options (iii) and (iv) would be product level activities. The level of **internal** support cost would be driven by the degree of **variety** between different products, not by production volume. If item (iii) refers to **external** technical support, this cost would most probably be driven by the fact that the product is too complicated for its market or the instructions provided (product packaging) are inadequate.

3.7 Continuous improvement

As we will see in Chapter 17, continuous improvement **recognises the concept of eliminating non-value-added activities** to reduce lead time, make products or perform services with zero defects, reduce product costs on an ongoing basis and simplify products and processes. It focuses on including employees in the process as they are often the best source of ideas.

3.8 Operational control

'**To control costs, managers must understand where costs are being incurred and for what purpose**. Some of this understanding will come from differentiating between value-added and non-value-added activities. Some will come from the better information generated by more appropriate tracing of overhead costs to products and services. Some will come from viewing fixed costs as long-term variable overheads and recognising that certain activities will cause those costs to change. Understanding costs allows managers to visualise what needs to be done to controls those costs, to implement cost reduction activities, and to plan resource utilisation.

......By better understanding the underlying cost of making a product or performing a service, managers obtain **new insight into product or service profitability**. Such insight could **result in management decisions** about expanding or contracting product variety, raising or reducing prices, and entering or leaving a market. For example, managers may decide to raise selling prices or discontinue production of low-volume speciality output, since that output consumes more resources than does high-volume output. Managers may decide to discontinue manufacturing products that require complex operations. Or, managers may reap the benefits from low-volume or complex production through implementing high-technology processes.'

(Raiborn *et al*, with BPP emphasis)

Innes and Mitchell ('*Activity Based Costing*') report (with BPP emphasis) that in some organisations:

'ABCM has also been used in **make-or-buy decisions** and has led to the sub-contracting of certain activities. In another engineering company the ABCM information on purchasing **concentrated** managers' **attention** on problems such as **late deliveries, short deliveries and poor-quality raw materials**. This information enabled this engineering company to identify twenty problem suppliers and take the necessary corrective action, which varied from changing suppliers to working with others to overcome the existing problems.'

3.9 Performance evaluation

ABM encourages and rewards employees for developing new skills, accepting greater responsibilities, and making suggestions for improvements in plant layout, product design, and staff utilisation. Each of these improvements reduces non-value-added time and cost. In addition, by focusing on activities and costs, ABM is better able to provide more appropriate measures of performance than are found in more traditional systems.

FAST FORWARD

To monitor the effectiveness and efficiency of activities using **ABM**, **performance measures** relating to **volume**, **time**, **quality** and **costs** are needed.

(a)   Activity **volume** measures provide an indication of the throughput and capacity utilisation of activities. For example reporting the number of times an activity such as setting-up is undertaken focuses attention on the need to investigate ways of reducing the volume of the activity and hence future costs.

(b)   To increase customer satisfaction, organisations must provide a speedy response to customer requests and reduce the time taken to develop and bring a new product to the market. Organisations must therefore focus on the **time** taken to complete an activity or sequence of activities. This time can be reduced by eliminating (as far as is possible) the time spent on non-value-added activities.

(c)   A focus on value chain analysis is a means of enhancing customer satisfaction. The value chain is the linked set of activities from basic raw material acquisition all the way through to the end-use product or service delivered to the customer. By viewing each of the activities in the value chain as a supplier-customer relationship, the opinions of the customers can be used to provide useful feedback on the **quality** of the service provided by the supplying activity. For example the quality of the service provided by the processing of purchase orders activity can be evaluated by users of the activity in terms of the speed of processing orders and the quality of the service provided by the supplier chosen by the purchasing activity. Such qualitative evaluations can be supported by quantitative measures such as percentage of deliveries that are late.

(d)   **Cost** driver rates (such as cost per set-up) can be communicated in a format that is easily understood by all staff and can be used to motivate managers to reduce the cost of performing activities (given that cost driver rate × activity level = cost of activity). Their use as a measure of performance can induce dysfunctional behaviour, however. By splitting production runs and therefore having more set-ups, the cost per set-up can be reduced. Workload will be increased, however, and so in the long run costs could increase.

3.10 Benchmarking

Traditionally, control involves the comparison of actual results with an internal standard or target. The practice of **setting targets using external information** is known as benchmarking.

> **Benchmarking**. 'The establishment, through data gathering, of targets and comparators, that permit relative levels of performance (and particularly areas of underperformance) to be identified. Adoption of identified best practices should improve performance. Types of benchmarking include the following.
>
> - **Internal benchmarking**. Comparing one operating unit or function with another within the same industry.
>
> - **Functional benchmarking**. Comparing internal functions with those of the best external practitioners, regardless of their industry (also known as operational benchmarking or generic benchmarking).
>
> - **Competitive benchmarking**. Information is gathered about direct competitors, through techniques such as reverse engineering.
>
> - **Strategic benchmarking**. A type of competitive benchmarking aimed at strategic action and organisational change.
>
> (CIMA *Official Terminology*)

Benchmarking can be divided into stages.

Step 1	**Set objectives** and determine the areas to benchmark
Step 2	Establish **key performance measures**
Step 3	**Select organisations** to study
Step 4	**Measure** own and others' performance
Step 5	**Compare** performances
Step 6	Design and implement **improvement programme**
Step 7	**Monitor** improvements

There are three levels of benchmarking.

Level of benchmarking	Through	Examples of measures
Resources	Resource audit	Quantity of resources • Revenue/employee • Capital intensity Quality of resources • Qualifications of employees • Age of machinery • Uniqueness (eg patents)
Competences in separate activities	Analysing activities	Sales calls per salesperson Output per employee Materials wastage
Competences in linked activities	Analysing overall performances	Market share Profitability Productivity

When selecting an appropriate benchmark basis, companies should ask themselves the following questions.

(a)   Is it possible and easy to obtain **reliable competitor** information?

(b)   Is there any wide **discrepancy** between different **internal divisions**?

(c)   Can **similar processes** be identified in **non-competing environments** and are these non-competing companies willing to co-operate?

(d)   Is best practice operating in a similar environmental setting?

(e)   Is there time to complete the study?

(f)   Is it possible to benchmark companies with similar objectives and strategies?

3.10.1 Advantages of benchmarking

(a)   **Position audit**. Benchmarking can assess a firm's existing position, and provide a basis for establishing standards of performance.

(b)   The comparisons are **carried out by the managers who have to live with any changes implemented** as a result of the exercise.

(c)   Benchmarking **focuses** on **improvement in key areas** and sets **targets** which are **challenging but evidently 'achievable'.**

(d)   The sharing of information can be a **spur to innovation**.

3.10.2 Dangers of benchmarking

(a)   It implies there is **one best way** of doing business – arguably this boils down to the difference between efficiency and effectiveness. A process can be efficient but its output may not be useful. Other measures (such as amending the value chain) may be a better way of securing competitive advantage.

(b)   The benchmark may be **yesterday's solution to tomorrow's problem**. For example, a cross-channel ferry company might benchmark its activities (eg speed of turnround at Dover and

Calais, cleanliness on ship) against another ferry company, whereas the real competitor is the Channel Tunnel.

(c)   It is a **catching-up exercise** rather than the development of anything distinctive. After the benchmarking exercise, the competitor might improve performance in a different way.

(d)   It depends on **accurate** information about comparator companies.

 Case Study

Below are extracts from a report on benchmarking in *The Times* in 2003.

British police are to be compared with overseas forces under Home Office plans. Within three years, 43 forces including the Metropolitan Police will be measured on international league tables covering murder rates, burglaries, street crime and arrests.

Scotland Yard's operations will also be tested against the crime-solving records of a group of 'world cities', including Tokyo, Sydney, Paris, Frankfurt and New York.

The [Home Office standards] unit has already created a series of measurements for groups of similar forces and chief constables can now check their officers' performance against regional and national figures each month.

Dr Bond [head of the unit] told MPs: 'We are working up some benchmarking data internationally. The wider question once you have looked at UK police performance is, "How does that compare internationally?" We don't know at the moment.'

He said that international comparisons could include the number of crimes in different categories, detection rates and underlying patterns of crime. The comparisons would also take into account the infrastructure of countries and cities such as transport systems.

Dr Bond said that officers in a small country station can already check national databanks for the record of a comparable station on the other side of the country and look at new ideas for improving crime reduction.

The international comparison will include a similar databank where British police can look at the work of other forces and learn new techniques.

3.11 Other issues

Business process re-engineering is covered in the next section, customer profitability analysis in Chapter 18.

3.12 Implementing ABM

In an article in *Financial Management* in 2001 ('Tool of the trade'), Stephanie Gourdie provided the following 'Tips for ABM'.

(a)   Get the support of senior management

(b)   Recognise that ABM requires a major investment in time and resources

(c)   Know what ABM can achieve and what information you want from the system

(d)   Decide which model to use

(e)   Choose the model approach that emphasises the operational understanding of all activities in the business

(f)   Involve people in the field

(g)   Transfer ownership of cost management from the accounts department to the departments and processes where costs are incurred

(h)   Don't underestimate the need to manage the change process

(i)   Link ABM to corporate objectives in the form of increased product profitability and added value for customers'

In 'Voyage of discovery' (*Financial Manager*, May 2002), Selvan Naidoo describes the key decisions to be made and the major pitfalls to be avoided when implementing ABM.

(a)   Decide on whether results are to be used at a strategic level or for cost management, as this will affect the level of analysis of activities required.

(b)   Establish if implementation will be in certain areas only, such as head office, or across the organisation.

(c)   Agree the acceptable level of accuracy.

(d)   Decide on the products and services to be costed. [*BPP note*. Pareto analysis could be applied. See Chapter 18.]

(e)   Involve operational staff from the start of the project.

(f)   Gain full support from senior management.

(g)   Manage expectations. ABC will not solve all of an organisation's problems.

(h)   Implement effective project management.

(i)   Provide regular progress reports for management.

(j)   Do not underestimate the effort needed to obtain the information required in the correct format.

(k)   Consider using a pilot implementation if ABC is being implemented across a number of sites.

(l)   Be wary of running ABC and another project with similar deadlines and demands on resources in a business unit.

3.13 Problems with ABM

ABM is not a panacea, however.

(a)   The **amount of work** in setting up the system and in data collection must be considered.

(b)   **Organisational and behavioural consequences**. Selected activity cost pools may not correspond to the formal structure of cost responsibilities within the organisation (the purchasing activity may spread across purchasing, production, stores, administrative and finance departments) and so determining 'ownership' of the activity and its costs may be problematic. We have already mentioned the behavioural impact of some performance measures.

4 Business process re-engineering (BPR)

T FORWARD

Business process re-engineering involves focusing attention inwards to consider how business processes can be redesigned or re-engineered to improve efficiency.

It *can* lead to fundamental changes in the way an organisation functions. In particular, it has been realised that processes which were developed in a paper-intensive processing environment may not be suitable for an environment that is underpinned by IT.

The main writing on the subject is Hammer and Champy's *Reengineering the Corporation* (1993), from which the following definition is taken.

term

Business Process Re-engineering (BPR) is the fundamental rethinking and radical redesign of business processes to achieve dramatic improvements in critical contemporary measures of performance, such as cost, quality, service and speed.

The key words here are **fundamental, radical, dramatic** and **process**.

(a) **Fundamental** and **radical** indicate that BPR is somewhat akin to zero base budgeting: it starts by asking basic questions such as 'why do we do what we do', without making any assumptions or looking back to what has always been done in the past.

(b) **Dramatic** means that BPR should achieve 'quantum leaps in performance', not just marginal, incremental improvements.

(c) **Process**. BPR recognises that there is a need to change functional hierarchies: 'existing hierarchies have evolved into functional departments that encourage functional excellence but which do not work well together in meeting customers' requirements' (Rupert Booth, *Management Accounting*, 1994).

term

A **process** is a collection of activities that takes one or more kinds of input and creates an output.

For example, order fulfilment is a process that takes an order as its input and results in the delivery of the ordered goods. Part of this process is the manufacture of the goods, but under **BPR** the **aim** of **manufacturing** is **not merely to make** the goods. Manufacturing should aim to **deliver the goods that were ordered,** and any aspect of the manufacturing process that hinders this aim should be re-engineered. The first question to ask might be 'Do they need to be manufactured at all?'

A **re-engineered process** has certain **characteristics**.

(a) Often several jobs are **combined** into one.
(b) Workers often **make decisions.**
(c) The **steps** in the process are performed in **a logical order.**
(d) **Work** is performed where it **makes most sense.**
(e) Checks and controls may be reduced, and **quality 'built-in'.**
(f) One manager provides a **single point of contact.**
(g) The advantages of **centralised and decentralised** operations are combined.

 Case Study

Based on a problem at a *major car manufacturer*.

A company employs 25 staff to perform the standard accounting task of matching goods received notes with orders and then with invoices. About 80% of their time is spent trying to find out why 20% of the set of three documents do not agree.

One way of improving the situation would have been to computerise the existing process to facilitate matching. This would have helped, but BPR went further: why accept any incorrect orders at all? What if all the orders are entered onto a computerised database? When goods arrive at the goods inwards department they either agree to goods that have been ordered or they don't. It's as simple as that. Goods that agree to an order are accepted and paid for. Goods that are not agreed are sent back to the supplier. There are no files of unmatched items and time is not wasted trying to sort out these files.

The re-engineering of the process resulted in gains for the company: less staff time wasted, quicker payment for suppliers, lower inventory and lower investment in working capital.

4.1 Principles of BPR

Seven principles for BPR (Hammer)

(a) Processes should be designed to achieve a desired **outcome rather than** focusing on existing **tasks.**

(b) **Personnel who use** the **output** from a process should **perform the process**. For example, a company could set up a database of approved suppliers; this would allow personnel who actually require supplies to order them themselves, perhaps using on-line technology, thereby eliminating the need for a separate purchasing function.

(c) **Information processing** should be **included in the work which produces the information**. This eliminates the differentiation between information gathering and information processing.

(d) **Geographically dispersed resources** should be **treated** as if they are **centralised.** This allows the benefits of centralisation to be obtained, for example, economies of scale through central negotiation of supply contracts, without losing the benefits of decentralisation, such as flexibility and responsiveness.

(e) **Parallel activities** should be **linked rather than integrated.** This would involve, for example, co-ordination between teams working on different aspects of a single process.

(f) **'Doers'** should be allowed to be **self-managing.** The traditional **distinction** between **workers** and **managers** can be **abolished**: decision aids such as expert systems can be provided where they are required.

(g) **Information** should be **captured once** at **source.** Electronic distribution of information makes this possible.

 Case Study

The case of **Taco Bell** is one of the examples quoted in Hammer and Champy's book. The emphasis is BPP's.

In the 1980s, the company was entrenched in a command and control hierarchy that claimed to understand what customers wanted, but did not ask directly. But major re-engineering efforts – automating, changing the organisational structure and management system, reducing kitchen space, and increasing customer space – focusing on what customers really wanted, greatly simplified their processes.

These changes have had a huge impact on the company. It went from a failing regional Mexican-American fast food chain with $500 million in sales in 1982, to a $3 billion national company 10 years later, with a goal to expand further to $20 billion.

One BPR initiative was the **K-Minus program, or kitchenless restaurant**. Based on the belief that they were a service company, not a manufacturer, a large majority of the restaurants' food preparation now occurs at central commissaries rather than in the restaurant, **pushing 15 hours of work a day out of the restaurant**, **improving quality control and employee morale**, **reducing employee accidents and injuries**, and resulting in **substantial savings on utilities**. The K-Minus program saves Taco Bell about $7 million a year.

4.2 Examples of business process re-engineering

(a)   A move from a traditional functional plant layout to a JIT cellular product layout is a simple example.

(b)   **Elimination of non-value-added activities.** Consider a materials handling process which incorporates scheduling production, storing materials, processing purchase orders, inspecting materials and paying suppliers.

This process could be re-engineered by sending the production schedule direct to nominated suppliers with whom contracts are set up to ensure that materials are delivered in accordance with the production schedule and that their quality is guaranteed (by supplier inspection before delivery).

Such re-engineering should result in the elimination or permanent reduction of the non-value-added activities of storing, purchasing and inspection.

Chapter Roundup

- In the **modern business environment**, most costs can be analysed into **short-term variable costs** (that vary with the volume of production) and **long-term variable costs** (that are fixed in the short term and vary not with volume of production but with a different measure of activity).

- **ABC** has been developed as an alternative costing system to traditional overhead absorption costing.

- The ABC approach is to relate costs to the factors that cause or 'drive' them to be incurred in the first place and to change subsequently. These factors are called '**cost drivers**'.

- ABC relates overhead/resource costs to the activities that cause or drive them. This is done using **resource cost drivers**. The costs of activities are related to cost units using **activity cost drivers**.

- There are both **merits and criticisms** of ABC.

- The **information** provided by **analysing activities** can support the management functions of **planning, control and decision making**, provided it is used carefully and with full appreciation of its implications.

- The implication for **pricing if ABC is used** is that the full cost on which prices are based may be radically different from a price based on full cost determined using traditional absorption costing.

- The terms **activity based management (ABM)** and **activity-based cost management (ABCM)** are used to describe the cost management applications of ABC.

- **Activity based management (ABM)** is '…the management processes that use the information provided by an activity-based cost analysis to improve organisational profitability. Activity-based management (ABM) includes performing activities more efficiently, eliminating the need to perform certain activities that do not add value for customers, improving the design of products, and developing better relationships with customers and suppliers. The goal of ABM is to enable customer needs to be satisfied while making fewer demands on organisational resources.'

- Two questions can be used to **assess whether an activity adds value**.

    - Would an external customer encourage the organisation to do more of the activity?
    - Would the organisation be more likely to achieve its goals by performing the activity?

    If both answers are yes, the activity adds value.

- The **manufacturing cost hierarchy** categorises costs and activities as unit level, batch level, product/process level and organisational/facility level.

- To monitor the effectiveness and efficiency of activities using **ABM**, **performance measures** relating to **volume**, **time**, **quality** and **costs** are needed.

- **Business process re-engineering** involves focusing attention inwards to consider how business processes can be redesigned or re-engineered to improve efficiency.

Quick Quiz

1   The cost driver for quality inspection is likely to be batch size. *True or false?*

2   ABC is not a system that is suitable for use by service organisations. *True or false*?

3   Which of the following is incorrect as a description of part of the ABC process?

    A   Transactions undertaken by support department personnel are appropriate cost drivers for long-term variable overheads.

    B   Longer-term production overhead costs are partly driven by volume of output.

    C   Longer-term production overhead costs are partly driven by the complexity and diversity of production work.

    D   Short-term variable overhead costs should normally be traced to products using volume-related cost drivers.

4   As volume increases, variety costs increase. *True or false?*

5   The processing time of an organisation is made up of four types. Classify the types as either value-added or non-value-added.

6   *Choose the correct word from those highlighted.*

The aim of ABM is to try to eliminate as far as possible the **core/primary/secondary/diversionary/ discretionary** activities.

7   *Put the following seven stages of benchmarking into the correct order.*

Select organisations to study
Monitor improvements
Set objectives and determine the areas to benchmark
Compare performances
Establish key performance measures
Measure own and others' performance
Design and implement improvement programme

8   BPR can be likened to continuous budgeting. *True or false?*

Answers to Quick Quiz

1   True, assuming that the first item in each batch is inspected.

2   False. It is highly suitable.

3   B.   Short-term variable overhead costs are driven by volume of output but longer-term costs, such as set-up costs, design and so on, are driven by the number of different products (diversity).

4   False

5   **Value-added**   **Non-value-added**
    Production/performance time   Inspection time
                                        Transfer time
                                        Idle time

6   diversionary or discretionary activities

7   Set objectives and determine the areas to benchmark
    Establish key performance measures
    Select organisations to study
    Measure own and others' performance
    Compare performances
    Design and implement improvement programme
    Monitor improvements

8   False. It is somewhat akin to ZBB.

Now try the questions below from the Exam Question Bank

Number	Level	Marks	Time
Q24	Examination	10	18 mins
Q25	Examination	10	18 mins

Contemporary techniques

Introduction

'Traditional' methods of inventory control, purchasing, production planning and scheduling, product mix decision making, quality control and management are simply not suitable for the **new manufacturing environment** (which we cover in **Section 1**).

More in keeping are contemporary techniques such as **just-in-time (Section 2)**, **theory of constraints (Section 4)** and **total quality management (Section 8)** which are a stark contrast to 'traditional' methods, but can have a major impact on efficiency, inventory and cost within this new environment.

Throughput accounting (Section 5) is a system of cost and management accounting which can be used with just-in-time, as can **backflush costing (Section 3)**, while **Kaizen costing (Section 6)** and **continuous improvement (Section 7)** are central to total quality management.

These contemporary methods are popular with the examiner who has set longer 10- and 25-mark questions in most sittings under the new syllabus. Questions so far have covered JIT, throughput accounting and costs of quality but the whole of this area of the syllabus is, of course, potentially examinable.

Topic list	Learning outcomes	Syllabus references	Ability required
1 Costing systems and manufacturing philosophy	D(ii)	D(2)	Evaluation
2 Just-in-time (JIT)	D(ii)	D(2)	Evaluation
3 Backflush costing	D(ii)	D(2)	Evaluation
4 Theory of constraints (TOC)	D(ii)	D(2)	Evaluation
5 Throughput accounting (TA)	D(ii)	D(2)	Evaluation
6 Kaizen costing	D(iii)	D(3)	Comprehension
7 Continuous improvement	D(iii)	D(3)	Comprehension
8 Total quality management (TQM)	D(ii)	D(2)	Evaluation
9 Costs of quality and cost of quality reports	D(iii)	D(3)	Comprehension

1 Costing systems and manufacturing philosophy

Costing systems have evolved to reflect a **manufacturing philosophy** that is based on the need to achieve **competitive advantage**.

- Flexibility and the ability to respond quickly to customer demands are vital.
- Product life cycles are shorter and products must be brought to the market quickly.
- New technology has been introduced.

1.1 Costing systems

(a) Designed to **compliment** the organisation's **operations flow**

(b) Should **reflect management philosophy** and **style**

(c) Provide **information** which management can use to **plan and control** operations on a daily, monthly and longer-term basis

(d) **Changes in manufacturing philosophy and new technology** (CAM (computer aided manufacturing) and FMS (flexible manufacturing system)) require **changes in information and cost reporting systems**

    (i) Collecting information in a different way
    (ii) Rethinking what data needs to be collected
    (iii) Rethinking what information should be reported

(e) **New systems**

    (i) Unit quantities (rather than monthly monetary values) reported to production employees

    (ii) Performance measures based on output (rather than hours worked) reported to management

(f) **Activities important to the organisation's success** should **determine the information required**. These might include:

    (i) Accurate product costing
    (ii) Knowledge of customer costs
    (iii) Information to control costs
    (iv) Cost reduction

1.2 Traditional manufacturing philosophy

(a) Labour and manufacturing equipment are so valuable they should not be left idle.

(b) Resulting inventory not needed should be stored (thus hiding inefficient and uneven production methods).

(c) To increase efficiency and reduce production cost per unit, batch sizes and production runs should be as large as possible.

(d) Concerned with balancing production run costs and inventory holding costs.

Question

Learning outcome: D(ii)

The production manager of AB has advocated long production runs in an attempt to reduce manufacturing costs per unit. The accountant has hit back with the fact that stockholding costs per unit will increase.

Required

List five manufacturing costs per unit that will reduce if production runs are longer, and four stockholding costs per unit that will increase.

Answer

If production runs become longer:

Manufacturing costs per unit that will fall:	Stockholding costs per unit that will rise:
Production scheduling costs	Space costs
Set-up costs	Labour costs
Waiting time/costs	Insurance costs
Purchasing costs	Interest charges
Labour costs	

1.3 Modern manufacturing philosophy

(a) **Smooth, steady** production flow (**throughput**)

(b) **Flexibility**, providing the customer with exactly what is wanted, exactly when it is wanted (making the organisation a more complex affair to manage), so as to achieve **competitive advantage**.

(c) **Volume versus variety** (see Section 1 of Chapter 16)

(d) **JIT**

2 Just-in-time (JIT)

2.1 The traditional approach

There are a number of **'traditional' responses to the problems of improving manufacturing capacity and reducing unit costs of production**.

(a) Longer production runs
(b) Economic batch quantities
(c) Fewer products in the product range
(d) More overtime
(e) Reduced time on preventative maintenance, to keep production flowing

In general terms, longer production runs and large batch sizes should mean less disruption, better capacity utilisation and lower unit costs.

T FORWARD

Just-in-time systems challenge 'traditional' views of manufacturing.

2.2 Overview of JIT

Just-in-time is an approach to operations planning and control based on the idea that **goods and services should be produced only when they are needed**, and neither too early (so that inventories build up) nor too late (so that the customer has to wait).

In **traditional** manufacturing, where there is a production process with several stages, management seek to **insulate each stage** in the process from disruption by another stage, by means of **producing for**, and **holding, inventory**.

For example, suppose a manufacturing process consists of four consecutive stages. In a traditional manufacturing system, there would be inventories of raw materials and finished goods, and also inventories of part-finished items between stage 1 and stage 2, between stage 2 and stage 3 and between stage 3 and stage 4. If there is disruption to production at, say, stage 2, the other stages would not be immediately affected. Stages 3 and 4 would continue to operate, using the inventories of part-finished items from stages 2 and 3. Stage 1 would also continue to operate, producing inventory for stage 2. The responsibility for resolving the disruption would fall mainly on the managers of the stage affected, which in this example would be the management of stage 2.

In contrast, in its extreme form, a JIT system seeks to hold zero inventories. In the same four-stage process described above, a disruption at any stage would immediately have an impact on all the other stages. For example, if a disruption occurs at stage 2, stages 3 and 4 will have to stop working because they have no output from stage 2. Stage 1 will also have to stop working, because it will only produce when stage 2 is ready to receive and use its output.

With JIT, a **disruption at any point in the system becomes a problem for the whole operation to resolve**. Supporters of JIT management argue that this will improve the likelihood of the problem being resolved, because it is in the interests of everyone to resolve it. They also argue that inventories help to hide problems within the system, so that problems go unnoticed for too long.

2.3 Definitions of JIT

(a)   'JIT aims to meet demand instantaneously, with perfect quality and no waste.' (Bicheno, *Implementing Just-in-time*)

(b)   'Just-in-time is a disciplined approach to improving overall productivity and eliminating waste. It provides for the cost-effective production and delivery of only the necessary quantity of parts at the right quality, at the right time and place, while using a minimum amount of facilities, equipment, materials and human resources. JIT is dependent on the balance between the supplier's flexibility and the user's flexibility. It is accomplished through the application of elements which require total employee involvement and teamwork. A key philosophy of JIT is simplification.' (Voss, *Just-in-Time Manufacture*).

JIT consists of **JIT purchasing** and **JIT production**.

terms

> **Just-in-time (JIT)** is a system whose objective is to produce or to procure products or components as they are required (by a customer or for use) rather than for inventory. A just-in-time system is a 'pull' system, which responds to demand, in contrast to a 'push' system, in which inventories act as buffers between the different elements of the system, such as purchasing, production and sales.
>
> **Just-in-time production** is a production system which is driven by demand for finished products whereby each component on a production line is produced only when needed for the next stage.
>
> **Just-in-time purchasing** is a purchasing system in which material purchases are contracted so that the receipt and usage of material, to the maximum extent possible, coincide.
>
> (CIMA *Official Terminology*)

2.4 Operational requirements of JIT

(a) **High quality**. Disruption in production due to errors in quality will reduce throughput and reduce the dependability of internal supply.

(b) **Speed**. Throughput in the operation must be fast, so that customer orders can be met by production rather than out of inventory.

(c) **Reliability**. Production must be reliable and not subject to hold-ups.

(d) **Flexibility**. To respond immediately to customer orders, production must be flexible, and in small batch sizes.

(e) **Lower cost**. As a consequence of high quality production, and with a faster throughput and the elimination of errors, costs will be reduced.

A consequence of JIT is that if there is **no immediate demand for output**, the operation **should not produce goods for inventory**. Average capacity utilisation could therefore be low (lower than in a traditional manufacturing operation). With a traditional manufacturing system, however, a higher capacity utilisation would only be achieved by producing for inventory at different stages of the production process. Supporters of JIT argue that there is no value in producing for inventory, and, as suggested above, it could damage the overall efficiency of an operation. So whereas **traditional manufacturing systems** are **'push'** systems (a delivery from a supplier pushes products through production), **JIT systems** are **'pull'** systems (demand from a customer pulls products through production).

'Push' systems	**'Pull' systems**
Supplier → Production → Customer	Supplier ← Production ← Customer

2.5 The JIT philosophy

JIT can be regarded as an approach to management that encompasses a **commitment to continuous improvement** and the **search for excellence** in the **design and operation of the production management system**. Its aim is to streamline the flow of products through the production process and into the hands of customers.

The JIT philosophy originated in Japan in the 1970s, with companies such as the car manufacturer Toyota. At its most basic, the philosophy is:

(a) To do things well, and gradually do them better (**continuous improvement**)
(b) To **squeeze waste out** of the system

A criticism of JIT, in its extreme form, is that having no inventory between any stages in the production process ignores the fact that some stages, by their very nature, could be less reliable than others, and more prone to disruption. It could therefore be argued that some inventory should be held at these stages to provide a degree of extra protection to the rest of the operation.

2.5.1 Three key elements in the JIT philosophy

Elimination of waste, **involvement of all staff** and **continuous improvement** are the three key elements in the JIT philosophy.

Elimination of waste	**Waste** is defined as **any activity that does not add value**. Examples of waste identified by Toyota were: • **Overproduction** (producing more than immediately needed by the next stage in the process). All parts of the production process should be operated at a speed which matches the rate at which the final product is demanded by the customer. **Production runs** will therefore be **shorter** and there will be **smaller inventories of finished goods** because output is being matched more closely with demand (and so **storage costs will be reduced**). • **Waiting time**. Waiting time can be measured by labour efficiency and machine efficiency. • **Transport**. Moving items around a plant does not add value. Waste can be reduced by **changing the layout of the factory floor so as to minimise the movement of materials**. • **Waste in the process itself**. Some activities might be carried out only **because there are design defects** in the product, or **because of poor maintenance work**. • **Inventory**. The target should be to eliminate all inventory by tackling the things that cause it to build up. • **Unnecessary work**. An employee does not necessarily add value by working. Simplifying work is an important way of getting rid of waste in the system because it eliminates unnecessary actions. • **Defective goods**
The involvement of all staff in the operation	JIT is a cultural issue, and its philosophy has to be embraced by everyone involved in the operation if it is to be applied successfully. Critics of JIT argue that management efforts to involve all staff can be patronising.
Continuous improvement	The ideal target is to meet demand immediately with perfect quality and no waste. In practice, this ideal is never achieved. The JIT philosophy is that an organisation should **work towards the ideal**, however.

2.6 JIT techniques

2.6.1 Management techniques

JIT is not just a philosophy, it is also a **collection of management techniques**. Some of these techniques relate to basic working practices.

(a) **Work standards**. Work standards should be established and followed by everyone at all times.

(b) **Flexibility in responsibilities**. The organisation should provide for the possibility of expanding the responsibilities of any individual to the extent of his or her capabilities, regardless of the individual's position in the organisation. Grading structures and restrictive working practices should be abolished.

(c) **Equality of all people working in the organisation**. Equality should exist and be visible. For example, there should be a single staff canteen for everyone, without a special executive dining area; and all staff including managers might be required to wear the same uniform. An example of where such practices occur is the car manufacturer Honda.

(d) **Autonomy**. Authority should be delegated to the individuals directly responsible for the activities of the operation. Management should support people on the shop floor, not direct them. For example, if a quality problem arises, an operative on the production line should have the authority to bring the line to a halt. Gathering data about performance should be delegated to the shop floor and the individuals who use it. Shop floor staff should also be given the first opportunity to solve problems affecting their work, and expert help should only be sought if it is needed.

(e) **Development of personnel**. Individual workers should be developed and trained.

(f) **Quality of working life**. The quality of working life should be improved, through better work area facilities, job security, involvement of everyone in job-related decision making, and so on.

(g) **Creativity**. Employees should be encouraged to be creative in devising improvements to the way their work is done.

2.6.2 Other JIT techniques and methodologies

(a) **Design for manufacture**. In many industries, the way that a product is designed determines a large proportion of its eventual production costs. Production costs can therefore be significantly reduced at the design stage, for example by reducing the number of different components and sub-assemblies required in the product.

(b) **Use several small, simple machines**, rather than a single large and more complex machine. Small machines can be moved around more easily, and so offer greater flexibility in shop floor layout. The risk of making a bad and costly investment decision is reduced, because relatively simple small machines usually cost much less than sophisticated large machines.

(c) **Work floor layout and work flow**. Work can be laid out to promote the smooth flow of operations. Work flow is an important element in JIT, because the work needs to flow without interruption in order to avoid a build-up of inventory or unnecessary down-times. Machines or workers should be grouped by product or component instead of by type of work performed. The non-value-added activity of materials movement between operations is therefore minimised by eliminating space between work stations. Products can flow from machine to machine without having to wait for the next stage of processing or return to stores. Lead times and work in progress are thus reduced.

(d) **Total productive maintenance (TPM).** Total productive maintenance seeks to eliminate unplanned breakdowns and the damage they cause to production and work flow. Staff working on the production line are brought into the search for improvements in maintenance, and are encouraged to take ownership of their machines and carry out simple repairs on them. This frees up maintenance specialists to use their expertise to look for higher-level ways to improve maintenance systems, instead of spending their time on fire fighting repairs and maintenance jobs.

(e) **Set-up reductions**. Set-up is the collection of activities carried out between completing work on one job or batch of production and preparing the process or machine to take the next batch. Set-up time is non-productive time. An aim in JIT is to reduce set-up times, for example by pre-preparing set-up tasks that can be done in advance. Alternatively, set-up time can be reduced by undertaking some tasks previously not done until the machines had stopped whilst the machines are running.

(f) **Total people involvement**. Staff are encouraged to take on more responsibility for using their abilities for the benefit of the organisation. They are trusted and given authority for tasks such as:

    (i) Monitoring and measuring their own performance

    (ii) Reviewing the work they have done each day

    (iii) Dealing directly with suppliers about quality issues and to find out about materials delivery times

    (iv) Dealing with customer problems and queries

    (v) Selecting new staff to work with them

(g) **Visibility**. The work place and the operations taking place in it are made more visible, through open plan work space, visual control systems (such as kanbans, described later), information displays showing performance achievements, and signal lights to show where a stoppage has occurred.

(h) **JIT purchasing**. With JIT purchasing, an organisation establishes a close, long-term relationship with trusted suppliers, and develops an arrangement with the supplier for being able to purchase materials only when they are needed for production. The supplier is required to have a flexible production system capable of responding immediately to purchase orders from the organisation. Responsibility for the quality of goods lies with the supplier. If an organisation has confidence that suppliers will deliver material of 100% quality, on time, so that there will be no rejects, returns and hence no production delays, usage of materials can be matched exactly with delivery of materials and inventories can be kept at near zero levels.

2.7 Elimination of non-value added costs

 JIT aims to **eliminate all non-value-added costs**.

As you know from the previous chapter, value is only added while a product is actually being processed. Whilst it is being inspected for quality, moving from one part of the factory to another, waiting for further processing and held in store, value is not being added. **Non-value added activities** (or diversionary activities) **should therefore be eliminated**.

 Question   Non-value-added activities

Learning outcome: D(ii)

Solo produces one product, the P. Parts for the product are quality inspected on arrival and stored in a warehouse until needed. They are then moved from the warehouse to the machine room where they are machined to the product specification. This work is then inspected and, if satisfactory, the machined parts are moved to the assembly area. Once this processing is complete, the finished product is inspected and tested. This is then passed to the despatch department, where employees pack it in an attractive box with a printed instruction sheet. Finished goods are stored back in the warehouse until despatched to customers.

Required

Eliminate the non-value-added activities from Solo's current activities listed below to produce the set of activities that would take place under a JIT approach. Comment upon your answer.

Parts received
Parts quality inspected
Parts stored in warehouse
Parts moved to machine room
Parts machined
Machined parts inspected
Machined parts moved to assembly area

Machined parts assembled
Finished product inspected and tested
Finished goods passed to despatch department
Finished goods packaged
Packed goods moved back to warehouse
Packed goods stored
Packed goods despatched to customer

Answer

The correct answer is:

Parts received
~~Parts quality inspected~~
~~Parts stored in warehouse~~
~~Parts moved to machine room~~
Parts machined
~~Machined parts inspected~~
~~Machined parts moved to assembly area~~

Machined parts assembled
~~Finished product inspected and tested~~
~~Finished goods passed to despatch department~~
Finished goods packaged
~~Packed goods moved back to warehouse~~
~~Packed goods stored~~
Packed goods despatched to customer

Comment

The JIT approach has five value-added activities, compared with 14 activities under the traditional approach – nine non-value-added activities have been eliminated.

Receipt of parts, their machining, assembly, packaging and despatch to the customer are essential activities that increase the saleability of the product.

Solo needs to negotiate with its suppliers to guarantee the delivery of high quality parts to eliminate the need for quality inspection on arrival.

Storage and movement of parts, work in progress and finished goods do not add value; rather they introduce unnecessary delays. The machining, assembly and packaging areas should be in close proximity to avoid excessive movement, and ordering and processing should be scheduled so that there is no need to store parts before they go into production. Similarly, production should be scheduled to finish goods just as they are needed for despatch to avoid storage of finished goods.

Proper maintenance of machinery and good staff training in quality production procedures should ensure finished goods of a consistently high quality, removing the need for inspection and testing.

Thus the JIT approach eliminates all wastage of time in the storage of goods, unnecessary movement of goods and all quality checks, resulting in one continuous string of value-added activities.

Question

Value-added activity

Learning outcome: D(ii)

Which of the following is a value-added activity?

A   Setting up a machine so that it drills holes of a certain size
B   Repairing faulty production work
C   Painting a car, if the organisation manufactures cars
D   Storing materials

Answer

The correct answer is C.

The other activities are non-value-adding activities.

Case Study

The following extract from an article in the *Financial Times* illustrates how 'just-in-time' some manufacturing processes can be. The emphasis is BPP's.

'Just-in-time manufacturing is down to a fine art at *Nissan Motor Manufacturing (UK)*. **Stockholding of some components is just ten minutes** – and the holding of all parts bought in Europe is less than a day.

Nissan has moved beyond just-in-time to **synchronous supply** for some components, which means manufacturers deliver these components directly to the production line minutes before they are needed.

These manufacturers do not even receive an order to make a component until the car for which it is intended has started along the final assembly line. Seat manufacturer *Ikeda Hoover*, for example, has about 45 minutes to build seats to specification and deliver them to the assembly line a mile away. It delivers 12 sets of seats every 20 minutes and they are mounted in the right order on an overhead conveyor ready for fitting to the right car.

Nissan has **close relationships with this dozen or so suppliers** and deals exclusively with them in their component areas. It involves them and even their own suppliers in discussions about future needs and other issues. These companies have generally established their own manufacturing units close to the Nissan plant.

Other parts from further afield are collected from manufacturers by *Nissan* several times a month at fixed times. This is more efficient than having each supplier making individual haulage arrangements.'

2.8 JIT planning and control with Kanban

Holding inventories is one source of waste in production. Not having materials or parts when they are needed is another. In other words, both having inventory when it is not needed and not having it when it is needed is wasteful practice.

Kanban is the Japanese word for card or signal. A **kanban control system** is a system for **controlling the flow of materials between one stage in a process and the next**. In its simple form, a card is used by an 'internal customer' as a signal to an 'internal supplier' that the customer now requires more parts or materials. The card will contain details of the parts or materials required.

Kanbans are the only means of authorising a flow of materials or parts. The receipt of a card from an internal customer sets in motion the movement or production or supply of one unit of an item, or one standard container of the item. The receipt of two cards will trigger the movement, production or supply of two units or two standard containers, and so on.

There are variants on the basic kanban system. For example, a production system might use **kanban squares**. A space is marked out on the work shop floor. When the space is empty, it acts as a signal for production to start at the previous stage. When it is full, it acts as a signal that production at the previous stage should be halted.

2.9 JIT in service operations

The JIT philosophy can be applied to service operations as well as to manufacturing operations. Whereas JIT in manufacturing seeks to eliminate inventories, JIT in service operations **seeks to remove queues of customers**.

Queues of customers are wasteful because:

(a) They **waste customers' time**.

(b) Queues require **space for customers to wait in**, and this **space is not adding value**.

(c) **Queuing lowers the customer's perception of the quality of the service**.

The application of JIT to a service operation calls for the **removal of specialisation of tasks**, so that the work force can be **used more flexibly and moved from one type of work to another**, in response to demand and work flow requirements.

Case Study

A postal delivery service allocates postmen or postwomen to their own routes. There may be scenarios where, say, Route A is overloaded whilst Route B has a very light load of post, however.

Rather than have letters for Route A piling up at the sorting office, the person responsible for Route B might help out on Route A when he or she has finished his or her route.

Teamwork and flexibility are difficult to introduce into an organisation because people might be more comfortable with clearly delineated boundaries in terms of their responsibilities. The customer is usually not interested in the company organisation structure, however, because he or she is more interested in receiving a timely service.

In practice, service organisations are likely to use a **buffer operation** to minimise customer queuing times. For example, a hairdresser will get an assistant to give the client a shampoo to reduce the impact of waiting for the stylist.

Question   JIT

Learning outcome: D(ii)

Japanese car manufacturer Toyota was the first company to develop JIT, and JIT was originally called the Toyota Production System. After the end of the world war in 1945, Toyota recognised that it had much to do to catch up with the US automobile manufacturing industry. The company was making losses. In Japan, however, consumer demand for cars was weak, and consumers were very resistant to price increases. Japan also had a bad record for industrial disputes. Toyota itself suffered from major strike action in 1950.

The individual credited with devising JIT in Toyota from the 1940s was Taiichi Ohno, and JIT techniques were developed gradually over time. The kanban system for example, was devised by Toyota in the early 1950s, but was only finally fully implemented throughout the Japanese manufacturing operation in 1962.

Ohno identified seven wastes.

(a) Overproduction

(b) Waste caused by transportation

(c) Waiting

(d) Waste caused by physical movement of items

(e) Over processing

(f) Waste caused by inventory

(g) Defects/corrections

He worked to eliminate them from operations in Toyota. Measures that were taken by the company included the following.

(a)   The aim of reducing costs was of paramount importance in the late 1940s.

(b)   The company aimed to level the flow of production and eliminate unevenness in the work flow.

(c)   The factory layout was changed. Previously all machines, such as presses, were located in the same area of the factory. Under the new system, different types of machines were clustered together in production cells.

(d)   Machine operators were re-trained.

(e)   Employee involvement in the changes was seen as being particularly important. Team work was promoted.

(f)   The kanban system was eventually introduced, but a major problem with its introduction was the elimination of defects in production.

Required

Explain how each of the changes described above came to be regarded as essential by Toyota's management.

Answer

(a)   **Cost reduction**. Toyota was losing money, and market demand was weak, preventing price rises. The only way to move from losses into profits was to cut costs, and cost reduction was probably essential for the survival of the company.

(b)   **Production levelling**. Production levelling should help to minimise idle time whilst at the same time allowing the company to achieve its objective of minimum inventories.

(c)   The **change in factory layout** was to improve the work flow and eliminate the waste of moving items around the work floor from one set of machines to another. Each cell contained all the machines required to complete production, thus eliminating unnecessary materials movements.

(d)   With having **cells of different machines**, workers in each work cell would have to be trained to use each different machine, whereas previously they would have specialised in just one type of machine.

(e)   A **change of culture** was needed to overcome the industrial problems of the company. Employee involvement would have been an element in this change. Teamwork would have helped with the elimination of waste: mistakes or delays by one member of a team would be corrected or dealt with by others in the team. The work force moved from a sense of individual responsibility/blame to collective responsibility.

(f)   The **kanban system** is a 'pull' system of production scheduling. Items are only produced when they are needed. If a part is faulty when it is produced, the production line will be held up until the fault is corrected. For a kanban system to work properly, defects must therefore be eliminated.

Exam focus point

> JIT was the subject of ten-mark questions in both the pilot paper and the May 2005 exam. The pilot paper question required a comparison of traditional inventory control and JIT and consideration of its use in conjunction with quality control. The May 2005 exam question asked how its use might affect profitability.

BPP
LEARNING MEDIA

2.10 Problems associated with JIT

JIT should not be seen as a panacea for all the endemic problems associated with Western manufacturing. It might not even be appropriate in all circumstances.

(a)   It is **not always easy to predict patterns of demand**.

(b)   JIT makes the organisation **far more vulnerable to disruptions in the supply chain**.

(c)   JIT was designed at a time when all of Toyota's manufacturing was done within a 50 km radius of its headquarters. Wide geographical spread, however, makes this difficult.

 Case Studies

(a)   'Just-in-time works well during normal business times. Companies that once kept months of safety inventory now get by with days, or even hours of materials .... . But how about when your industry [high-tech] suddenly undergoes a tremendous boom, and demand far exceeds projections for parts? ... Just look at cell phones. The worldwide boom in cellular phone sales wasn't exactly a surprise – sales of these units have been on a fast climb for years. Yet one distributor reports a wait of 18 months to obtain high-frequency transistors for hand held devices.'

('Just in time, or just too late?', Doug Bartholomew, *Industry Week,* August 2000)

(b)   The Kobe earthquake in Japan in 1995 severely disrupted industry in areas unaffected by the actual catastrophe. Plants that had not been hit by the earthquake were still forced to shut down production lines less than 24 hours after the earthquake struck because they held no buffer inventories which they could use to cover the shortfall caused by non delivery by the Kobe area suppliers.

(c)   In October 1991 the workforce at the French state-owned car maker *Renault's* gear-box production plant at Cléon went on strike. The day afterwards a British plant had to cease production. Within two weeks *Renault* was losing 60% of its usual daily output. The weaknesses were due to the following.

(i)   Sourcing components from one plant only
(ii)   Heavy dependence on in-house components
(iii)   Low inventory
(iv)   The fact '...that Japanese-style management techniques depend on stability in labour relations, something in short supply in the French public sector'.

(*Financial Times*, 31 October 1991)

 Question   JIT manufacturing environment

Learning outcome: D(ii)

Batch sizes within a JIT manufacturing environment may well be smaller than those associated with traditional manufacturing systems.

What costs might be associated with this feature of JIT?

1   Increased set-up costs

2   Opportunity cost of lost production capacity as machinery and the workforce reorganise for a different product

3   Additional materials handling costs

4   Increased administrative costs

A None of the above
B 1, 2, 3 and 4
C 1 only
D 2 and 3 only

Answer

The correct answer is B.

2.11 Modern versus traditional inventory control systems

There is no reason for the newer approaches to supersede the old entirely. A restaurant, for example, might find it preferable to use the traditional economic order quantity approach for staple non-perishable food, but adopt JIT for perishable and 'exotic' items. In a hospital, a lack of inventory could, quite literally, be fatal, and JIT would be quite unsuitable.

2.12 Manufacturing cycle efficiency

2.12.1 Customer response time (CRT)

As product life cycles shorten and customers demand quick response to orders, organisations are seeking to improve **CRT** (the length of time between an order being placed and delivery of goods/services to the customer) and **on-time delivery rate**.

CRT is a measure of an organisation's ability to respond to a customer's request and is in general determined by internal factors (delay between order and work starting, length of time the order spends in the production process), both of which are linked to the length of the manufacturing cycle.

2.12.2 Manufacturing cycle time (MCT)

MCT is the length of time between starting and finishing the production of an order and is typically made up of:

(a) Processing time
(b) Waiting time
(c) Moving time
(d) Inspection time

Manufacturing cycle efficiency (MCE) shows (in ratio form) the proportion of time during which value is being added during the production process, and is calculated as:

Processing time/(processing time + waiting time + moving time + inspection time)

The closer the ratio is to 1, the **more efficient the production operation**. As the **ratio increases**:

(a) **WIP investment will fall** (with all the associated benefits). For example, if an organisation has an annual cost of goods sold of $5,000,000 and the MCT reduces from 20 days to 15 days, the average value of WIP will fall by $((20 - 15)/365) \times \$5,000,000 = \$68,493$.

(b) An organisation's ability to act **flexibly** and **respond to rush orders** or sudden market changes is improved.

(c) **Production throughput** can be **increased** without increasing plant capacity. The need for overtime may fall or additional production may be possible without increasing fixed production costs.

Reducing MCT links well with Total Quality Management (see Section 8) because of the need to reduce reworking and inspection.

Improving MCE will increase costs, however. A reduction in cycle times may require the manufacturing process to be redesigned or investment in new machinery. The net benefits will very much depend on the circumstances under consideration. Will the investment required be justified by the increase in volumes or reduction in costs? Relevant costing can be used: the proportion of, say, stockholding costs which would be avoidable can be determined, perhaps by using activity based costing. If the reduction in cycle time produces X extra additional saleable units, the opportunity cost of a cycle hour can be calculated and used to assist in the decision of whether or not to invest in reducing cycle time.

2.12.3 MCT and JIT

(a)   The reduction in MCT is a key phase in the introduction of JIT.

(b)   JIT has advantages in certain manufacturing environments, but the benefits of increasing MCE apply to all organisations, irrespective of whether they also use JIT.

(c)   Just as JIT can be applied to the supply chain, so too can the concept of MCE. For example, by requiring a guaranteed level of quality from suppliers, inspection time can be reduced. We look at supply chain analysis in Chapter 18.

3 Backflush costing

ST FORWARD

Backflush costing is suitable for use in a JIT environment. Costs are attached to output only, thereby simplifying the costing system.

Backflush accounting is the name given to the method of keeping cost accounts employed if **backflush costing** is used. The two terms are almost interchangeable.

3.1 Traditional costing systems v backflush costing

Traditional costing systems use **sequential tracking** (also known as **synchronous tracking**) to track costs sequentially as products pass from raw materials to work in progress, to finished goods and finally to sales. In other words, material costs are charged to WIP when materials are issued to production, direct labour and overhead costs are charged in a similar way as the cost is incurred or very soon after.

If a production system such as **JIT** is used, sequentially tracking means that **all entries are made at almost the same moment** and so a different accounting system can be used. In **backflush costing/accounting, costs are calculated and charged when the product is sold, or when it is transferred to the finished goods store**.

term

> **Backflush costing** is 'A method of costing, associated with a JIT production system, which applies cost to the output of a process. Costs do not mirror the flow of products through the production process, but are attached to the output produced (finished goods inventory and cost of sales), on the assumption that such backflushed costs are a realistic measure of the actual costs incurred.'   (CIMA *Official Terminology*)

3.2 Backflush costing and standard costs

The CIMA definition above omits the fact that **budgeted or standard costs are used to work backwards to 'flush' out manufacturing costs** for the units produced. (Hence the rather unattractive name for the system!) The application of **standard costs** to finished goods units, or to units sold, is used in order to **calculate cost of goods sold**, thereby **simplifying** the costing system and creating **savings in administrative effort**. **In a true backflush accounting system, records of materials used and work in progress are not required** as material cost can be calculated from either finished goods or goods sold.

3.3 Backflush costing and SSAP 9

Backflush costing runs **counter to the principle enshrined in SSAP 9**, and the staple of cost accounting for decades, that inventory and WIP should be accounted for by calculating cost and net realisable value of 'each item of inventory separately'. The substantial **reduction in inventories that is a feature of JIT** means that **inventory valuation is less relevant,** however, and therefore the **costing system** can be **simplified** to a considerable extent. In the 1980s, Johnson & Kaplan in fact wrote that **management rarely requires a value to be placed on inventory for internal management purposes**, the **value only being required for external reporting.**

3.4 When backflush costing is appropriate

Backflush costing is therefore **appropriate** for organisations trying to keep **inventories to the very minimum**. In such circumstances, the **recording** of every little increase in inventory value, as each nut and bolt is added, is simply an expensive and **non-value-added activity** that should be **eliminated**.

3.5 Example: Working backwards from output

To take a **very simplified example**, if backflush costing is used, the management accountant might extract the following information from the monthly accounting transaction records and production records.

Orders completed and despatched in July	196 units
Orders prepared in advance 1 July	3 units
Orders prepared in advance 31 July	2 units
Scrapped items	5 units
Conversion costs in the month	$250,000
Material costs in the month	$475,000

This is enough to place a value on inventories and production as follows.

	Units		$
B/f	(3)	Conversion costs	250,000
Despatched	196	Material costs	475,000
Scrapped	5	Total costs	725,000
C/f	2		
Units produced	200		

Cost per unit is $725,000 divided by 200 units = $3,625

In this case a single process account could be drawn up as follows.

	Dr ($)	Cr ($)
Inventory b/fwd (3 × $3,625)	10,875	
Materials	475,000	
Conversion costs	250,000	
To finished goods (196 × $3,625)		710,500
Losses etc written off to P& L (5 × $3,625)		18,125
Inventory c/fwd (2 × $3,625)		7,250
	735,875	735,875

3.5.1 Arguments of traditional management accountants

(a) The figure for **losses** here is **inaccurate**. They would say that in reality the faulty goods would have been scrapped when only partially complete and it is wrong to value them at the same cost as a fully finished good unit.

(b) Using this approach, the figure for inventories b/fwd and c/fwd will not tie up with the accounts for last month and next month, because the material and conversion costs may be different.

3.5.2 Reply of modern management accountants

(a) **Losses** represent only about 2% of total cost and are **not material**. In any case putting a value to them is less **important** than **improving the quality of production procedures** (on the basis of **TQM** practices and non-financial production information) to ensure that they do not occur again.

(b) **Finished good inventories represent between 1% and 2% of total cost and are immaterial**. Slight discrepancies in valuation methods of b/fwds and c/fwds will amount to a **fraction** of a percentage, and can be written off in the month as a small **variance**.

(c) Even with computers the **cost of tracing units** every step of the way through production – with 'normal' and 'abnormal' losses, equivalent units and numerous process accounts – **is simply not worth it, in terms of the benefit derived** from the information it provides.

3.6 Variants of backflush costing

(a) **Trigger points determine when the entries are made in the accounting system**. There will be either one or two trigger points that trigger entries in the accounts.

   (i)   When materials are purchased/received
   (ii) When goods are completed or when they are sold

   In a **true JIT system** where no inventories are held the **first trigger**, when raw materials are purchased, is **unnecessary**.

(b) **Actual conversion costs are recorded as incurred**, just as in conventional recording systems. **Conversion costs are applied to products at the second trigger point based on a standard cost**. It is assumed that any conversion costs not applied to products are carried forward and disposed of at the period end.

(c) **Direct labour** is included as an **indirect cost in conversion cost with overheads**. (Production is only required when there is demand for it in a JIT system, and so production labour will be paid regardless of the level of activity.)

(d) All **indirect costs** are treated as a **fixed period expense**.

3.6.1 Example: Accounting entries at different trigger points

The transactions for period 8 20X1 for CW are as follows.

Purchase of raw materials	$24,990
Conversion costs incurred	$20,220
Finished goods produced (used in methods 2 & 3 only)	4,900 units
Sales	4,850 units

There are no opening inventories of raw materials, WIP or finished goods. The standard cost per unit is made up of $5.10 for materials and $4.20 for conversion costs.

Solution for 1 trigger point – when goods are sold (method 1)

This is the simplest method of backflush costing. There is only one **trigger point** and that is **when the entry to the cost of goods sold account is required** when the goods are sold. (This method assumes that units are sold as soon as they are produced.)

			$	$
(a)	DEBIT	Conversion costs control	20,220	
	CREDIT	Expense payables		20,220
	Being the actual conversion costs incurred		

			$	$
(b)	DEBIT	Cost of goods sold (4,850 × $9.30)	45,105	
	CREDIT	Payables (4,850 × $5.10)		24,735
	CREDIT	Conversion costs allocated (4,850 × $4.20)		20,370
	Being the standard cost of goods sold		

			$	$
(c)	DEBIT	Conversion costs allocated	20,370	
	CREDIT	Cost of goods sold		150
	CREDIT	Conversion costs control		20,220
	Being the under or over allocation of conversion costs		

Solution for 1 trigger point – when goods are completed (method 2)

This is very similar to the solution above but in this instance the **trigger** is the completion of a unit and its **movement into finished goods store**. The accounting entries are as follows.

			$	$
(a)	DEBIT	Conversion costs control	20,220	
	CREDIT	Expense payables		20,220
	Being the actual conversion costs incurred		

			$	$
(b)	DEBIT	Finished goods inventory (4,900 × $9.30)	45,570	
	CREDIT	Payables (4,900 × $5.10)		24,990
	CREDIT	Conversion costs allocated (4,900 × $4.20)		20,580
	Being the standard cost of goods produced		

			$	$
(c)	DEBIT	Cost of goods sold (4,850 × $9.30)	45,105	
	CREDIT	Finished goods inventory		45,105
	Being the standard cost of goods sold		

			$	$
(d)	DEBIT	Conversion costs allocated	20,580	
	CREDIT	Cost of goods sold		360
	CREDIT	Conversion costs control		20,220
	Being the under or over allocation of conversion costs		

The end of period finished goods inventory balance is $465 (50 × $9.30).

Solution for 2 trigger points – (method 3)

There are two trigger points, the first when materials and components are received and the other at the point of transfer to finished goods.

			$	$
(a)	DEBIT	Raw materials	24,990	
	CREDIT	Payables		24,990
	Being the purchase of raw materials on credit		

			$	$
(b)	DEBIT	Conversion costs control	20,220	
	CREDIT	Payables		20,220
	Being the actual conversion costs incurred		

			$	$
(c)	DEBIT	Finished goods inventory (4,900 × $9.30)	45,570	
	CREDIT	Raw materials		24,990
	CREDIT	Conversion costs allocated		20,580

Being the standard cost of goods produced

			$	$
(d)	DEBIT	Cost of goods sold (4,850 × $9.30)	45,105	
	CREDIT	Finished goods inventory		45,105

Being the standard cost of goods sold

			$	$
(e)	DEBIT	Conversion costs allocated	20,580	
	CREDIT	Cost of goods sold		360
	CREDIT	Conversion costs control		20,220

Being the under or over allocation of conversion costs

3.7 Points to note

Note that the **WIP account is eliminated** using all methods. In a JIT system the vast majority of manufacturing costs will form part of the cost of sales and will not be deferred in closing inventory values. In such a situation the amount of work involved in tracking costs through WIP, cost of sales and finished goods is unlikely to be justified. This considerably **reduces the volume of transactions recorded** in the internal accounting system.

The successful operation of backflush costing rests upon **predictable levels of efficiency** and **stable material prices and usage**. In other words there should be **insignificant cost variances**.

3.8 Possible problems with backflush costing

(a) **It is only appropriate for JIT operations** where production and sales volumes are approximately equal.

(b) Some people claim that it **should not be used for external reporting** purposes. If, however, **inventories are low** or are practically **unchanged** from one accounting period to the next, operating income and inventory valuations derived from backflush accounting will **not be materially different from the results using conventional systems**. Hence, in such circumstances, backflush accounting is acceptable for external financial reporting.

(c) It is **vital** that adequate production controls exist so that **cost control during the production process is maintained**.

3.9 Advantages of backflush costing

(a) It is much **simpler**, as there is no separate accounting for WIP.

(b) Even the **finished goods** account is **unnecessary**, as shown in the first example above.

(c) The number of **accounting entries should be greatly reduced**, as are the supporting vouchers, documents and so on.

(d) The system should **discourage** managers from **producing simply for inventory** since working on material does not add value until the final product is completed or sold.

4 Theory of constraints (TOC)

Theory of constraints (TOC) is a set of concepts which aim to identify the binding constraints in a production system and which strive for evenness of production flow so that the organisation works as effectively as possible. No inventory should be held, except prior to the binding constraint.

The use of a JIT operating system, whether in a manufacturing or service organisation, requires a particular type of costing system. **Throughput accounting** is a technique that has been developed to deal with this. The name was first coined in the late 1980s when *Galloway and Waldron* developed the system in the UK. Throughput accounting is based on the concept of the **theory of constraints** (TOC) which was formulated by Goldratt and Cox in the U.S.A. in 1986. Its key financial concept is to **turn materials into sales as quickly as possible**, thereby maximising throughput and the net cash generated from sales. This is to be achieved by striving for **balance in production processes**, and so **evenness of production flow** is an important aim.

Key terms

Theory of constraints (TOC) is 'Procedure based on identifying bottleneck (constraints), maximising their use, subordinating other facilities to the demands of the bottleneck facilities, alleviating bottlenecks and re-evaluating the whole system.'

Bottleneck is 'facility that has lower capacity than preceding or subsequent activities, and restricts output based on current capacity'.

(CIMA *Official Terminology*)

One process will inevitably act as a bottleneck (or limiting factor) and constrain throughput – this is known as the **binding constraint** in TOC terminology. The important concept behind TOC is that the production rate of the entire factory is set at the pace of the bottleneck. (Goldratt advocates a **drum – buffer – rope system**, with the bottleneck as the drum.) Steps should therefore be taken to remove this bottleneck.

(a)   Buy more equipment
(b)   Provide additional training for slow workers
(c)   Change a product design to reduce the processing time on a bottleneck activity
(d)   Eliminate idle time at the bottleneck (eg machine set-up time)

But ultimately there will always be a binding constraint, unless capacity is far greater than sales demand or all processes are totally in balance, which is unlikely even if it is a goal to be aimed for.

Output through the binding constraint should never be delayed or held up otherwise sales will be lost. To avoid this happening **a buffer inventory should be built up immediately prior to the bottleneck** or binding constraint. **This is the only inventory that the business should hold,** with the exception of possibly a very small amount of finished goods inventory and raw materials that are consistent with the JIT approach. (This is Goldratt's **buffer** in the drum – buffer – rope system.)

Operations prior to the binding constraint should operate at the same speed as the binding constraint, otherwise work in progress (other than the buffer inventory) will be built up. (Here the **rope** links all upstream operations to the pace of the bottleneck.) According to TOC, **inventory costs money** in terms of storage space and interest costs and so inventory is **not desirable**. In a **traditional** production system an **organisation will often pay staff a bonus to produce as many units as possible. TOC** views this as **inefficient** since the organisation is paying extra to build up inventory which then costs money to store until it is required.

4.1 Simple example

Machine X can process 1,000 kg of raw material per hour, machine Y 800 kg. Of an input of 900 kg, 100 kg of processed material must wait on the bottleneck machine (machine Y) at the end of an hour of processing.

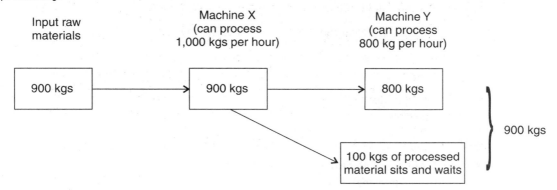

The **traditional view** is that **machines should be working, not sitting idle**. So if the desired output from the above process were 8,100 kgs, **machine X would be kept in continual use** and all 8,100 kgs would be processed through the machine in nine hours. There would be a **backlog** of 900 kgs [8,100 − (9 hrs × 800)] of processed material in front of machine Y, however. All this material **would require handling** and **storage space** and **create the additional costs related to these non-value added activities**. Its **processing would not increase throughput contribution**.

4.2 Key measures

To apply TOC ideas, Goldratt and Cox recommend the use of three key measures.

terms

> **Throughput contribution (the rate at which profit is generated through sales) = sales revenue − direct material cost**
>
> **Conversion costs (other operational expenses) = all operating costs except direct material cost**
>
> **Investments (inventory) = inventories + research and development costs + costs of equipment and buildings**

The **aim is to maximise throughput contribution while keeping inventory and operational expenses to a minimum**. If a strategy for increasing throughput contribution is being considered it will therefore only be accepted if operational expenses and inventory increase by a lower amount than contribution. TOC considers the short term and assumes operating expenses to be fixed costs.

4.3 Bottlenecks and quality control

Quality control points should be placed before bottlenecks: 'Make sure the bottleneck works only on good parts by weeding out the ones that are defective. If you scrap a part before it reaches the bottleneck, all you have lost is a scrapped part. But if you scrap the part after it's passed through the bottleneck, you have lost time that cannot be recovered.' (Goldratt and Cox, *The Goal*)

ention!

> It is important to realise that TOC is not an accounting system but a production system.

The following extracts are taken from the web-based version of the June 2004 edition of *Bandolier*, an independent journal about healthcare. They illustrate that TOC is not just applicable in manfuacturing organisations, but can be applied successfully in the service sector too. The emphasis is BPP's.

'Using the "Theory of Constraints" methodology to improve services to patients.

Why was the initiative launched?

The Radcliffe Infirmary, in common with many other organisations, was seeking innovative ways to tackle a long standing problem: how to reduce waiting lists in ways that did not sacrifice the quality of care provided to patients.

Problems

A series of meetings were held with clinical team and managers to explore the optimum operating theatre capacity [in opthalmology]. The discussions quickly confirmed that even working to absolute capacity it would not be possible to meet target levels of activity. **Using the TOC approach surgical time was identified as the constraint** within the system: a bottleneck that had to be eliminated.

Solutions

A number of ideas for extending theatre time were considered and the team chose to organise a trial to test twilight operating. There was some initial concern about how the idea would be received by patients. In the event it soon became evident that for some patients these sessions were much more convenient. It was easier for working members of families to escort patients to and from hospital, for instance. It also provided a calmer environment than the normal busy hubbub of hospital activity.

Phasing the workload throughout the day and evening was **using theatre time more effectively** and in ways that **suited patients**. This approach to increasing workload **used ward staff more evenly** during the working day. Progress was being made but the team was keen to explore other ways to ensure that sessions were used effectively.

Session start times and intervals between patients seemed to offer promising ways to speed the process. Other obstacles had already been removed. Patients no longer changed their clothing for surgery and where possible they walked from the clinic to the theatre. Traditionally the hospital had provided a chair to transport patients to theatre but it was clear that for most patients this was not needed. This change of policy **released a good deal of porter time**.

Ringing the changes

The team's discussions with staff suggested that further improvement might be possible if a **buffer system** was set up to ensure that **surgeons would not have any wasted time between patients**. Instead of calling patients one at a time it was suggested that two patients were called to ensure that a surgeon never waits for a patient to be brought. A small room close to the theatre was provided as a waiting area. Over time the practice fell out of use, yet productivity remained high. It was felt that the heightened appreciation of the issue of surgeons waiting for patients to be brought created by focusing on efficiency negated the need for such a buffer. Creation of a buffer follows a basic TOC principle that constraints should not be starved.

Is it working?

The work started in earnest in the summer of 1998 and within a matter of months good progress was being made. **Between March 1998 and March 1999 the waiting list was reduced by about 10% with an increase in activity overall of about 900 cases**. Activity increased overall by about 24%. **Over eighteen months**:

(a)   **Throughput was up by 20%**

(b)   **Waiting list performance was significantly improved**

(c)   **Average waiting time is down to ten weeks and has been consistent for over a year**

(d)   **No additional resources were required**

There has been similar success with work in neurosurgery with reductions in elective cancellations and increased throughput. Taken together these projects have enabled staff in the Trust to make real progress in exploring how TOC can help them improve efficiency and the quality of care to patients. The **need for flexibility** is evident. Overcoming the main constraint in the system by supporting it and using buffer management often means the creation of others – that will require attention in the **continuous quality cycle**. The Trust has now set in hand a further programme to extend the approach into other specialities.

Tips for success

(a)   Remember TOC is a thinking process and not a list of possible solutions.

(b)   Success is more likely if the methodology is embraced by a core group of senior people in the organisation.

(c)   Involve all staff levels in finding solutions.

(d)   Watch the use of language because the jargon of TOC is not necessary for everyone.

(e)   Don't think of TOC as yet another expensive management tool. It is a relatively simple set of basic principles that are accessible to all.

(f)   Don't allow historical tradition, "we've always done it this way", to inhibit innovation.'

4.4 TOC and linear programming

Given that TOC aims to maximise throughput contribution subject to production capacity and production demand, linear programming could be used to make decisions about bottlenecks.

5 Throughput accounting (TA)

> **ST FORWARD**
>
> The concept of **throughput accounting (TA)** has been developed from TOC as an alternative system of cost and management accounting in a JIT environment.

term

'**Throughput accounting (TA)** is an approach to accounting which is largely in sympathy with the JIT philosophy. In essence, TA assumes that a manager has a given set of resources available. These comprise existing buildings, capital equipment and labour force. Using these resources, purchased materials and parts must be processed to generate sales revenue. Given this scenario the most appropriate financial objective to set for doing this is the maximisation of throughput (Goldratt and Cox, 1984) which is defined as: sales revenue *less* direct material cost.'

(Tanaka, Yoshikawa, Innes and Mitchell, *Contemporary Cost Management*)

TA is different from all other management accounting systems because of what it **emphasises**.

(a)   Firstly **throughput**

(b)   Secondly minimisation of inventory

(c)   Thirdly **cost control**

5.1 TA concepts

TA is based on **three concepts**.

- In the short run, most costs in the factory (with the exception of materials costs) are fixed.
- The ideal inventory level is zero.
- Profitability is determined by the rate at which sales are made.

5.1.1 Concept 1

Because TA differentiates between fixed and variable costs it is often compared with marginal costing and **some people argue that there is no difference between marginal costing and throughput accounting.** In marginal costing direct labour costs are usually assumed to be variable costs. Years ago this assumption was true, but employees are not usually paid piece rate today and they are not laid off for part of the year when there is no work, and so labour cost is not truly variable. If this is accepted the two techniques are identical in some respects, but **marginal costing is generally thought of as being purely a short-term decision-making technique** while **TA, or at least TOC, was conceived with the aim of changing manufacturing strategy to achieve evenness of flow. It is therefore much more than a short-term decision technique.**

Because **TA combines all conversion costs** together and does not attempt to examine them in detail it is particularly **suited to use with ABC**, which examines the behaviour of these costs and assumes them to be variable in the long-run.

5.1.2 Concept 2

In a JIT environment, all inventory is a 'bad thing' and the **ideal inventory level is zero**. Products should not be made unless there is a customer waiting for them. This means **unavoidable idle capacity must be accepted in some operations,** but not for the operation that is the bottleneck of the moment. There is one exception to the zero inventory policy, being that a buffer inventory should be held prior to the bottleneck process.

5.1.3 Concept 3

Profitability is determined by the rate at which 'money comes in at the door' (that is, sales are made) and, in a JIT environment, this depends on how quickly goods can be produced to satisfy customer orders. Since the goal of a profit-orientated organisation is to make money, inventory must be sold for that goal to be achieved.

The buffer inventory and any other work in progress or finished goods inventory should be **valued at material cost only** until the output is eventually sold, so that **no value will be added and no profit earned until the sale takes place.** Producing output just to add to work in progress or finished goods inventory creates no profit, and so should not be encouraged.

Question

TA v conventional cost accounting

Learning outcome: D(ii)

How are these concepts a direct contrast to the fundamental principles of conventional cost accounting?

Answer

Conventional cost accounting	Throughput accounting
Inventory is an asset.	Inventory is *not* an asset. It is a result of unsynchronised manufacturing and is a barrier to making profit.
Costs can be classified either as direct or indirect.	Such classifications are no longer useful.
Product profitability can be determined by deducting a product cost from selling price.	Profitability is determined by the rate at which money is earned.
Profit is a function of costs.	Profit is a function of throughput as well as costs.

5.2 Bottleneck resources

FAST FORWARD

The TA philosophy entails the identification and elimination of **bottleneck resources**.

The aim of **modern manufacturing** approaches is to match production resources with the demand for them. This implies that there are **no constraints, termed bottleneck resources** in TA, within an organisation. The throughput philosophy entails the **identification** and **elimination** of these bottleneck resources. Where they **cannot be eliminated production must be limited to the capacity of the bottleneck resource in order to avoid the build-up of work in progress.** If a rearrangement of existing resources (such as moving a machine) or buying-in resources does not alleviate the bottleneck, investment in new equipment may be necessary. The **elimination of one bottleneck is likely to lead to the creation of another** at a previously satisfactory location, however. The **management of bottlenecks** therefore becomes a **primary concern** of the manager seeking to increase throughput.

(a) There is nothing to be gained by measuring and encouraging the efficiency of machines that do not govern the overall flow of work.

(b) Likewise, there is little point in measuring the efficiency of production staff working on non-bottleneck processes.

(c) Bonuses paid to encourage faster working on non-bottleneck processes are wasted and could lead to increased storage costs and more faulty goods.

Other factors that might limit throughput other than a lack of production resources (bottlenecks)

(a) The existence of a non-competitive selling price

(b) The need to deliver on time to particular customers, which may disrupt normal production flow

(c) The lack of product quality and reliability, which may cause large amounts of rework or an unnecessary increase in production volume

(d) Unreliable material suppliers, which will lead to poor quality products that require rework

5.3 Throughput measures

FAST FORWARD

Throughput measures include **return per time period, return per time period on the bottleneck resource** and the **TA ratio**.

5.3.1 Return per time period

In a throughput accounting environment, the overall **focus of attention** is the **rate at which the organisation can generate profits**. To monitor this, the return on the throughput **through the bottleneck resource** is monitored using:

$$\textbf{Return per time period} = \frac{\text{sales revenue} - \text{material costs}}{\text{time period}}$$

This measure shows the **value added** by an organisation during a particular time period. Time plays a crucial role in the measure, so **managers** are strongly **encouraged to remove bottlenecks that might cause production delays**.

5.3.2 Return per time period on bottleneck resource

In throughput accounting, the limiting factor is the bottleneck. The return per time period measure can be adapted and used for **ranking products to optimise production** in the **short term**.

$$\textbf{Product return per minute} = \frac{\text{sales price} - \text{material costs}}{\text{minutes on key/bottleneck resource}}$$

Ranking products on the basis of throughput contribution per minute (or hour) on the bottleneck resource is **similar in concept to maximising contribution per unit of limiting factor**. Such product rankings are for **short-term production scheduling only**. In throughput accounting, bottlenecks should be eliminated and so rankings may change quickly. Customer demand can, of course, cause the bottleneck to change at short notice too.

Rankings by TA product return and by contribution per unit of limiting factor may be different. Which one leads to profit maximisation? The correct approach depends on the variability or otherwise of labour and variable overheads, which in turn depends on the time horizon of the decision. Both are short-term profit maximisation techniques and given that labour is nowadays likely to be fixed in the short term, it could be argued that TA provides the more correct solution. An analysis of variable overheads would be needed to determine their variability.

Exam focus point

> In the November 2005 exam, there were six marks available out of 25 for stating the principles of throughput accounting and the effects of using it for short-term decision making. The examiner wanted a written response here. However he also expected candidates to prepare calculations of costs using the throughput method to answer later parts of the question. An objective test question in the pilot paper required application of this measure in order to rank products.

Attention!

> Bear in mind that the huge majority of organisations cannot produce and market products based on short-term profit considerations alone. Strategic-level issues such as market developments, product developments and stage reached in the product life cycle must also be taken into account.

5.3.3 TA ratio

Products can also be ranked according to the **throughput accounting ratio (TA ratio).**

$$\text{TA ratio} = \frac{\text{throughput contribution or value added per time period}}{\text{conversion cost per time period}}$$

$$= \frac{(\text{sales} - \text{material costs}) \text{ per time period}}{(\text{labour} + \text{overhead}) \text{ per time period}}$$

This measure has the **advantage** of **including the costs involved in running the factory. The higher the ratio, the more profitable the company**.

Here's an example.

	Product A	Product B
	$ per hour	$ per hour
Sales price	100	150
Material cost	(40)	(50)
Conversion cost	(50)	(50)
Profit	10	50
TA ratio	$\frac{60}{50} = 1.2$	$\frac{100}{50} = 2.0$

Profit will be maximised by manufacturing as much of product B as possible.

ention!

> If conversion cost cannot be directly allocated to products (because it is not a unit-level manufacturing cost), the TA ratio cannot be calculated and products have to be ranked in terms of throughput contribution per hour or minute of bottleneck resource.

5.3.4 Effectiveness measures and cost control

Traditional efficiency measures such as standard costing variances and labour ratios are **unsuitable** in a TA environment because traditional efficiency should not be encouraged (as the **labour force should not produce just for inventory**).

Effectiveness is a **more important** issue. The **current effectiveness ratio** compares current levels of effectiveness with the standard and is calculated as:

$$\frac{standard\,minutes\,of\,throughput\,achieved}{minutes\,available}$$

Generally adverse variances are not considered to be a good thing. In a TA environment, however, if overtime is worked at the bottleneck to increase throughput, an adverse labour rate variance would arise. Provided the increase in value added was greater than the extra labour cost, this would be a good thing, however.

5.4 TA and non-value-added activities

Like JIT, TA aims to minimise production time. In order that **process time approaches lead time**, **all non-value-added activities need to be minimised or eliminated**. Set-up time, waiting time, inspection time and so on should therefore be minimised or eliminated.

5.5 Is it good or bad?

TA is seen by some as **too short term**, as all costs other than direct material are regarded as fixed. This is not true. But it does **concentrate on direct material costs** and does nothing for the control of other costs. These characteristics make throughput accounting a **good complement for ABC**, as ABC focuses on labour and overhead costs.

TA attempts to maximise throughput whereas traditional systems attempt to maximise profit. By attempting to maximise throughput an organisation could be producing in excess of the profit-maximising output.

Where TA helps direct attention

    (a)   Bottlenecks
    (b)   Key elements in making profits
    (c)   Inventory reduction

(d)   Reducing the response time to customer demand

(e)   Evenness of production flow

(f)   Overall effectiveness and efficiency

A **global measure of throughput** at factory level can produce an insight into the effectiveness of factory management, especially in a multi-product, multi-process organisation in which product demand is unpredictable and prices are set by negotiation between supplier and buyer. With a given level of resources (employees, machines, buildings and so on), an increase period by period in the level of throughput would indicate an improvement in the flow of products through the factory to the customer. If bottleneck resources are highlighted, management can focus their attention on removing factors limiting the profitability of the factory as a whole (as opposed to subunits or product lines).

 Case Studies

(a)   An article in *Management Accounting* in April 1992 describes a case study of *Garrett Automotive* that adopted TA with the particular aim of managing and alleviating bottlenecks in the production process and moving towards 'evenness of flow'. When the project started one particular manufacturing area had three machines with the following outputs:

Machine A   30 units per hour
Machine B   18 units per hour
Machine C   80 units per hour

The production system was certainly not in balance.

As a result of the initial analysis, machine D was moved to assist B and this increased capacity at this point to 21 units per hour. Then machine E was purchased very cheaply and this increased output at B to 26 units per hour. (Machine E paid for itself in just five weeks.) Machine C was due for replacement shortly afterwards and it was replaced with a new and cheaper machine that produced just 26 units per hour. These three changes raised output from 2,025 units to 2,700 units per week and greatly increased profit.

Changing the production process brought considerable financial benefits and changed the reporting emphasis to the critical need to adhere to production schedules and to 'first-time capability' (getting it right first time). The monthly management report was reduced from more than forty pages to five pages and it was made available if requested to all employees. It forced management accounting staff to get back to understanding what is actually happening on the shop floor and to be inventive about performance measures.

(b)   An article in the *Harvard Business Review* September-October 1996 cites the instance of *Pratt & Whitney* the jet engine manufacturer, which had ten computer controlled grinding machines that were used to shape cast blades. The machines cost $80m and were technical marvels, grinding a blade in just three minutes. They were fed and unloaded by robots but it took eight hours to change the machines so that they could grind a different sort of blade. In addition each blade had to be encased in a special metal alloy to prevent it fracturing during grinding and this was difficult to remove after the process. Twenty two members of staff were required to maintain the complicated computerised control system. As a result of all this, each blade took ten days to pass through the grinding department.

After studies, eight simple grinding machines that did not require the blades to be encased in metal were purchased to replace the computer controlled machines. The time it took to change from grinding one type of blade to the next took just 100 seconds with these machines and it only took the labour of one full-time and one part-time member of staff to feed and control the machines. Processing time increased from three minutes to 75 minutes, however, but this was not a major disadvantage. The factory space required was halved and the time for a blade to pass through the grinding department fell from ten days to 75 minutes.

5.6 Example: throughput accounting

Corrie produces three products, X, Y and Z. The capacity of Corrie's plant is restricted by process alpha. Process alpha is expected to be operational for eight hours per day and can produce 1,200 units of X per hour, 1,500 units of Y per hour, and 600 units of Z per hour.

Selling prices and material costs for each product are as follows.

Product	Selling price $ per unit	Material cost $ per unit	Throughput contribution $ per unit
X	150	70	80
Y	120	40	80
Z	300	100	200

Conversion costs are $720,000 per day.

Requirements

(a) Calculate the profit per day if daily output achieved is 6,000 units of X, 4,500 units of Y and 1,200 units of Z.

(b) Calculate the TA ratio for each product.

(c) In the absence of demand restrictions for the three products, advise Corrie's management on the optimal production plan.

Solution

(a) Profit per day = throughput contribution − conversion cost

= [($80 × 6,000) + ($80 × 4,500) + ($200 × 1,200)] − $720,000

= $360,000

(b) TA ratio = throughput contribution per factory hour/conversion cost per factory hour

Conversion cost per factory hour = $720,000/8 = $90,000

Product	Throughput contribution per factory hour	Cost per factory hour	TA ratio
X	$80 × (60 ÷ 0.05 mins) = $96,000	$90,000	1.07
Y	$80 × (60 ÷ 0.04 mins) = $120,000	$90,000	1.33
Z	$200 × (60 ÷ 0.10 mins) = $120,000	$90,000	1.33

(c) An attempt should be made to remove the restriction on output caused by process alpha's capacity. This will probably result in another bottleneck emerging elsewhere. The extra capacity required to remove the restriction could be obtained by working overtime, making process improvements or product specification changes. Until the volume of throughput can be increased, output should be concentrated upon products Y and Z (greatest TA ratios), unless there are good marketing reasons for continuing the current production mix.

Now try a question for yourself.

Question | **Performance measurement in throughput accounting**

Growler manufactures computer components. Health and safety regulations mean that one of its processes can only be operated 8 hours a day. The hourly capacity of this process is 500 units per hour. The selling price of each component is $100 and the unit material cost is $40. The daily total of all factory costs (conversion costs) is $144,000, excluding materials. Expected production is 3,600 units per day.

Required

Calculate

(a) Total profit per day
(b) Return per factory hour
(c) Throughput accounting ratio

Answer

(a) Total profit per day = Throughput contribution – Conversion costs

= $(3,600 \times (100 - 40) - 144,000)$

= $72,000

(b) Return per factory hour = $\dfrac{\text{Sales} - \text{direct material costs}}{\text{Usage of bottleneck resource in hours (factory hours)}}$

= $\dfrac{100 - 40}{1/500}$

= $30,000

(c) Throughput accounting ratio = $\dfrac{\text{Return per factory hour}}{\text{Total conversion cost per factory hour}}$

= $\dfrac{30,000}{144,000/8}$

= 1.67

Case Study

In 'Accounting for Throughput' (*Management Accounting,* May 1996), Dugdale and Jones discuss the consequences of introducing throughput ideas into the accounting, production and marketing functions of a particular company. The emphasis is BPP's.

(a) 'Measures of efficiency and overhead recovery were no longer considered useful ... The danger of traditional measures causing sub-optimal behaviour was now recognised and the **key measure became 'schedule adherence'** ... The use of schedule adherence was later accompanied by the introduction of a **throughput income statement** ... [which was] extremely simple.

	$
Sales revenue	X
Less: Materials	(X)
Materials price and exchange variances	X
Throughput	X
Less: Expense	(X)
Net profit	X

Gradually other measures were added to cell managers' monthly accounting packages – **days' inventory on-hand, manufacturing cycle time, cost of quality, customer due-date performance.**'

(b)   '... most [cell managers] thought that schedule adherence was a good measure but its credibility depended on the creation of **realistic schedules** ... Without such [financially-based] measures [of departmental performance], many managers considered that they were operating in a measurement vacuum in which they had insufficient information ... It may be that this [creating new local performance measures] is an intractable problem in accounting for throughput.'

(c)   'Whilst there was some disagreement about the use of throughput measures in production there were no such reservations in **marketing**... the move towards marginal cost pricing [throughput accounting being a form of marginal costing, only material costs being treated as variable] and away from absorbed costs and gross margin targets was an unmitigated success.'

5.7 Throughput accounting in service and retail industries

Sales staff have always preferred to use a marginal costing approach so that they can use their discretion on discounts, and **retail organisations** have traditionally thought in terms of sales revenue less the bought in price of goods. The throughput accounting approach is therefore **nothing new** to them.

Throughput accounting can be used very effectively in **support departments and service industries** to **highlight and remove bottlenecks**. For example, if there is a delay in processing a potential customer's application, business can be lost or the potential customer may decide not to proceed. Sometimes credit rating checks are too detailed, slowing the whole procedure unnecessarily and delaying acceptance from say 24 hours to eight days.

A similar problem could occur in hospitals where work that could be done by nurses has to be carried out by doctors. Not only does this increase the cost of the work but it may well cause a bottleneck by tying up a doctor's time unnecessarily.

Question

Product costing v TA

Learning outcome: D(ii)

Here are some statements about traditional product costing. Provide the equivalent statements about throughput accounting.

Statement 1: Inventory is valued in the financial statements at full production cost.

Statement 2: Labour, material and variable overheads are treated as variable costs.

Statement 3: A process is deemed efficient if labour and machine time are fully utilised.

Statement 4: Value is added when a unit of product is produced.

Answer

1   Inventory is valued at material cost only (ie variable cost).

2   Only direct material is treated as a variable cost.

3   Effectiveness is measured in terms of schedule adherence and meeting delivery dates.

4   Value is added when an item is sold.

6 Kaizen costing

Key term

Kaizen costing focuses on obtaining small incremental cost reductions during the production stage of the product life cycle.

Kaizen costing has been used by some Japanese firms for over twenty years and is now widely used in the electronics and automobile industries, for example. 'Kaizen' translates as **continuous improvement**.

FAST FORWARD

The aim of **Kaizen costing** is to reduce current costs by using various tools such as value analysis and functional analysis.

6.1 The kaizen costing process

Functional analysis is applied at the design stage of a new product, and a **target cost for each function** is set. The functional target costs are added together and the total becomes the **product target cost**. Once the product has been in production for a year, the **actual cost of the first year becomes the starting point for further cost reduction**. It is this **process of continuous improvement, encouraging constant reductions by tightening the 'standards'**, that is known as kaizen costing.

The following Kaizen costing chart is based on one used at Daihatsu, the Japanese car manufacturer owned in part by Toyota, and reported in Monden and Lee's 'How a Japanese Auto Maker Reduced Costs' *(Management Accounting* (US Version), 2002).

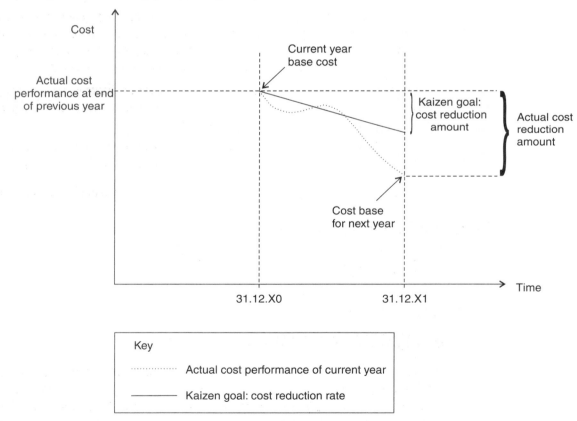

The previous year's actual production cost serves as the cost base for the current year's production cost. A reduction rate and reduction amount are set (**Kaizen cost goals**). **Actual performance** is **compared** to the **Kaizen goals** throughout the year and **variances are monitored**. At the end of the current year, the current actual cost becomes the cost base for the next year. New (lower) Kaizen goals are set and the whole process starts again.

6.2 Kaizen costing v standard costing

Standard costing is used in conjunction with management by exception (management's attention is directed towards situations where actual results differ from expected results). The expected results are based on standards which have been derived from the capability of current organisational processes. **Standard costing** therefore **reflects current levels of performance** and **fails to provide any motivation to improve**.

The following table sets out the **principal differences between Kaizen costing and standard costing techniques**.

	Standard costing	Kaizen costing
Concepts	It is used for cost control.	It is used for cost reduction.
	It is assumed that current manufacturing conditions remain unchanged.	It assumes continuous improvement.
	The cost focus is on standard costs based on static conditions.	The cost focus is on actual costs assuming dynamic conditions.
	The aim is to meet cost performance standards.	The aim is to achieve cost reduction targets.
Techniques	Standards are set every six or twelve months.	Cost reduction targets are set and applied monthly.
	Costs are controlled using variance analysis based on standard and actual costs.	Costs are reduced by implementing continuous improvement (kaizen) to attain the target profit or to reduce the gap between target and estimated profit.
	Management should investigate and respond when standards are not met.	Management should investigate and respond when target kaizen amounts are not attained.
Employees	They are often viewed as the cause of problems.	They are viewed as the source of, and are empowered to find, the solutions.

(Adapted from Monden and Lee)

6.3 How are Kaizen goals met?

(a) Reduction of non-value added activities and costs
(b) Elimination of waste
(c) Improvements in production cycle time

7 Continuous improvement

In today's highly competitive environment, performance against static historical standards is no longer appropriate and successful organisations must be **open to change** if they are to **maintain their business advantage**. Being **forward looking** and **receptive to new ideas** are **essential elements of continuous improvement**. The concept was popularised in Japan, where it is known as kaizen, and many of Japan's economic advances over the past 20 years have been attributed to it.

Key term

> **Continuous improvement** is an 'ongoing process that involves a continuous search to reduce costs, eliminate waste, and improve the quality and performance of activities that increase customer value or satisfaction'.
>
> Drury, *Management and Cost Accounting*

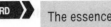 **FAST FORWARD**

> The essence of **continuous improvement** is the use of an organisation's human resources to produce a constant stream of improvements in all aspects of customer value, including quality, functional design, and timely delivery, while lowering cost at the same time.

The implementation of continuous improvement does not necessarily call for significant investment, but it does require a great deal of **commitment and continuous effort**.

Continuous improvement is often associated with **incremental changes** in the day-to-day process of work **suggested by employees** themselves. This is not to say that continuous improvement organisations do not engage in radical change. **Quantum leaps in performance** can occur when cumulative improvements synergise, the sum of a number of small improvements causing a profound net effect greater than the sum of all the small improvements.

Continuous means **ongoing**. The process must never stop and sustained success is more likely in organisations which regularly review their business methods and processes in the drive for improvement.

 ## Case Study

The following extracts are taken from the website of Pilgrim's Pride, an American food production company with $5 billion revenue, employing 40,000 people. The emphasis is BPP's.

'Continuous Improvement [CI] is our guiding management philosophy – it is the way we choose to do business. Through CI, our **Partners** [employees] are **empowered to identify, quantify and eliminate waste by examining each and every one of their processes on a daily basis**.

Through the practice of CI, the company **creates leaders who are customer focused** and can understand and manage variation within their processes for maximum customer satisfaction. In addition, CI helps leaders understand and communicate to others not only the "big picture" but also how each process and every Partner fits into Pilgrim's as a whole. One of the most important goals of the CI process is to create an **empowering environment** where all Partners can excel.

Continuous Improvement is based on three basic concepts or Cornerstones: Quality, Process Improvement and Teamwork.

Cornerstones of Continuous Improvement

Quality – is **defined by the needs of our customers (both internal and external)**. Quality alone does not make us a "World Class Food Company."

Process Improvements – our lack of complacency in our process helps us succeed in becoming a "World Class Food Company." We strive for Process Improvements through **technology** and the **innovative ideas** of our Partners.

Teamwork – among departments and locations is essential in providing the best possible solutions to our challenges. **Through Teamwork we differentiate ourselves from our competition**, we become more than our machines.

All three Cornerstones must be present for Continuous Improvement to work. If one is left out we lose the battle to become "Better than the Best." Quality without Teamwork leaves us competing against ourselves. Teamwork without Process Improvements leaves us vulnerable to our competition. Process Improvements without Quality leaves us without customers.'

7.1 Essential factors for continuous improvement

(a)   Total **commitment from senior management**

(b)   The **opportunity for all employees to contribute** to the continuous improvement process. Tactical and operational level staff, rather than senior management, usually have the information required. The most successful continuous improvement programs are the ones that have the highest staff involvement.

(c)   Good, objective **information about the organisation's environment** so that its outcomes (what it does) and its processes (how it does it) can be evaluated

(d)   **Employees' awareness of their role** in the achievement of the organisation's strategy

(e)   **Management of the performance and contribution of employees**

(f)   **Good communications** throughout the organisation

(g)   Implementation of **recognised quality management systems and standards**

(h)   **Measurement and evaluation of progress against key performance indicators and benchmarks**. Some organisations have found that simply displaying productivity and quality data every day or week raises production and quality because staff can tell when they are doing things right, and so find themselves in a personal continuous improvement cycle.

It is claimed that if these areas are **regularly reviewed**, change can be managed effectively and **continuous improvement becomes a natural part of the organisational processes**. It should create steady growth and development by keeping the organisation focused on its aims, priorities and performance.

Case Study

Pilgrim's Pride (see earlier case study) have ten Basic Beliefs of Continuous Improvement.

1   **The customer's needs are critical** – The customer should be the focus of all our activities.

2   **Anything can be improved** – All processes, products, and services can be made better. Only a consistent concern for Continuous Improvement can ensure high quality and good service.

3   **Quality is everyone's job** – Quality products and services are the result of quality processes and quality work. To leave any Partner out of the process is to miss an opportunity to improve.

4   **The person doing the job knows it best** – Nobody else knows how to do your job like you do. You are the expert of your process.

5   **People deserve respect** – Everyone wants to be treated as a valued and important member of the team. People do their best when they feel good about themselves and their contributions.

6   **Teamwork works** – People working together accomplish more than they would working alone.

7   **There is value in difference** – We all have unique backgrounds, skills and experiences. Without differences, there would be no new ideas.

8   **Involvement builds commitment** – People are more motivated to act when they have had a say in deciding what actions to take. People desire and deserve a stake in the decisions that affect their lives and their customers.

9   **Support builds success** – Sometimes people will succeed without their Partners' support, but people rarely fail when they have their Partners' support.

10   **YOU make the difference** – An organization is only as good as its people. Everyone affects quality, cost, productivity and customer satisfaction.'

The Pilgrim's Pride website goes on to explain that:

'Pilgrim's Pride Partners believe in and follow the 14 Points of Continuous Improvement. These 14 Points of CI are our guiding principles and all Partners are encouraged to put them into practice every day. By following the 14 Points of CI we will achieve our Vision: "To be a World Class Food Company... Better than the Best," and our Mission: "Our Job is Outstanding Customer Satisfaction... Every Day."

1   **Constancy of purpose** – We should all work towards the same goal of achieving our Vision and Mission.

2   **Adopt a new style of management** – Management must be responsive to the needs of all Partners. Managers should provide leadership by example, coaching and empowerment.

3   **Cease dependence on inspection** – Quality cannot be "inspected into" a product. We must build quality into the process or product from the start.

4   **Avoid doing business on price tag alone** – We must consider quality of product and services as well as the cost. Cheaper is not always better if it does not meet our needs.

5   **Continuous Improvement of processes** – We must constantly look for ways to eliminate waste and improve our processes. All work should be "value-added."

6   **Training and re-training** – Our customers' needs and the technology required to meet those needs is constantly changing. Ongoing training and re-training on processes and equipment will help us meet those needs.

7   **Continuous Improvement of leadership** – Management must practise "servant leadership" and help their Partners develop. Also, we must provide management with the skills they need to be successful leaders, such as communications, teamwork, and coaching.

8   **Drive out fear** – Management should not intimidate or instil fear in their Partners. We must also overcome the fear of change.

9   **Departments must work together** – This must occur not just at each site, but also across locations. We are all working towards the same goal and we have to communicate our needs, problems and successes in order to get there.

10   **Continuous Improvement provides its own motivation** – Success motivates us to further improve our processes.

11   **Work standards and quotas shall not limit our performance** – Quotas and standards tend to "cap" our abilities to make improvements.

12   **Remove barriers that rob Partners of their right to pride in workmanship** – Management must help remove obstacles that prevent Partners from doing their best.

13   **Institute education and self-improvement** – Management must support the Company's practice of investing in our Partners and encouraging their development.

14   **Do it** – Everyone must accept responsibility for Continuous Improvement.'

7.1.1 Quality circles

A quality circle consists of a **group of employees**, often from different areas of the organisation, who meet regularly to **discuss problems of quality and quality control** in their area of work, and perhaps to suggest **ways of improving quality**. It is also a way to **encourage innovation**. The aim of quality circles is to **improve employee development and morale** so as to create a **sense of ownership of the quality** of products and services.

Teamwork, in the form of quality circles and **group problem-solving activities**, is the cornerstone of continuous improvement.

7.2 Benefits of continuous improvement

(a)   Better performance, which produces increased profits

(b)   Improvements in customer satisfaction

(c)   Increases in staff morale

(d)   Improvement on a continual, step-by-step basis is more prudent than changing things all at once

(e)   Better communication within the organisation

(f)   Improvements in relations with suppliers

(g)   Better use of resources

(h)   More efficient planning

 Case Studies

The continuous improvement process has been shown to bring significant benefits to all types of organisation in a variety of sectors, as illustrated by the following case studies. The emphasis is BPPs.

(a)   The following is taken from the Volex Group plc's website and is fairly typical of the way in which organisations are keen to demonstrate their commitment to continuous improvement.

'Volex is committed to a program of Continuous Improvement across all its operations. All improvement projects have a **specific customer focus** and are based on **measured progress against firm targets or industry benchmarks**. We also encourage the **active involvement of our employees**. Many sites operate Kaizen schemes with cross-functional project teams applying working-level improvement actions on many topics including environmental, health and safety programs.

At Volex, Continuous Improvement is considered a **crucial process to achieve competitive advantage for our customers and ourselves**. We accord high management priority to key product and service-level improvement projects. Programs that integrate the results using international models of performance improvement are then used to set senior management performance targets for subsequent years.

The process of improvement links closely with personal development. Volex is strongly committed to the training and development of its employees worldwide. Through our knowledge, skills and experience, we help ensure the success of our customers' projects around the world every day.'

(b)   The Charter Mark is a well-established government award scheme promoting and recognising public sector excellence in customer service. **Continuous improvement** is a **key principle** of the **Charter Mark award**. The principle requires that organisations continually look for ways to improve their services and the facilities they offer. They do this by:

(i)   Promoting innovation, creativity and striving for excellence.
(ii)   Recognising that, no matter how good, service can always improve.
(iii)   Adopting the latest technologies to change the way business is done.

(c)   One of the aims of North Somerset Council is 'ensuring continuous improvement.....

(i)   ensure that the customer is at the heart of the Council's thinking through a One Council approach to service delivery

(ii) implement the Human Resources strategy and work towards achieving Investors in People award

(iii) improve communications

(iv) improve business and resource planning, financial and performance monitoring.'

(d) Chrysler's Five Star Dealer Incentive Program is designed for 'improving or creating processes to quickly find what creates customer dissatisfaction and find ways to fix these issues'. The first step for dealers is to contact their customers to get feedback on their sales or service experience. The use of this feedback is mandatory, as getting information and not using it is seen to lower trust, increase frustration and cost money. Dealers are required to put in place processes that not only resolve customer problems but also allow them to learn from them. This is a **hallmark of continuous improvement: collecting information at every opportunity and putting it to use**. Dealers are also required to provide training for staff who deal with customers, as efforts to make change are seen to be constrained unless all staff understand not only that they can have an effect, but that they are expected to have an effect.

8 Total quality management (TQM)

The modern business environment is remarkably different from the business environment of a decade or so ago. One change has been the **switch in emphasis away from quantity towards quality**. Consumers and **customers** have become **more sophisticated and discerning** in their requirements. They are no longer satisfied with accepting the late delivery of the same old unreliable products from an organisation which does not appear to care for its customers. They want new products, superior on-time delivery performance and an immediate response to their requests. Many organisations are therefore turning to quality to help them to survive the competitive modern business environment. **By developing new products quickly and supplying them on time at a consistently high level of quality such organisations are likely to become the success stories of the early part of the twenty first century.**

8.1 Management of quality

Quality means 'the **degree of excellence of a thing**' – how well made it is, or how well performed if it is a service, how well it serves its purpose, and how it measures up against its rivals. These criteria imply two things.

(a) That quality is something that **requires care on the part of the provider**.
(b) That quality is largely **subjective** – it is in the eye of the beholder, the **customer**.

The **management** of quality is the process of:

(a) Establishing **standards of quality** for a product or service

(b) Establishing **procedures or production methods** which ought to ensure that these required standards of quality are met in a suitably high proportion of cases

(c) **Monitoring** actual quality

(d) Taking **control action** when actual quality falls below standard

Take the postal service as an example. The postal service might establish a standard that 90% of first class letters will be delivered on the day after they are posted, and 99% will be delivered within two days of posting.

(a) Procedures would have to be established for ensuring that these standards could be met (attending to such matters as frequency of collections, automated letter sorting, frequency of deliveries and number of staff employed).

(b) Actual performance could be monitored, perhaps by taking samples from time to time of letters that are posted and delivered.

(c) If the quality standard is not being achieved, management should take control action (employ more postmen or advertise the use of postcodes again).

8.2 Total quality management

Quality management becomes **total (Total Quality Management (TQM)) when it is applied to everything a business does**.

---

term

Total quality management (TQM) is 'an integrated and comprehensive system of planning and controlling all business functions so that products or services are produced which meet or exceed customer expectations. TQM is a philosophy of business behaviour, embracing principles such as employee involvement, continuous improvement at all levels and customer focus, as well as being a collection of related techniques aimed at improving quality such as full documentation of activities, clear goal setting and performance measurement from the customer perspective.' (CIMA *Official Terminology*)

The **main focus of TQM** is **100% satisfaction of both internal and external customers** through the **improvement of all activities and processes**.

FORWARD

In the context of **total quality management**, 'quality' means getting it right first time, and improving continuously.

8.2.1 Get it right, first time

One of the basic principles of TQM is that the **cost of preventing mistakes is less than the cost of correcting them** once they occur. The aim should therefore be **to get things right first time**. Every mistake, delay and misunderstanding, directly costs an organisation money through **wasted time and effort**, including time taken in pacifying customers. The **lost potential for future sales because of poor customer service must also be taken into account.**

8.2.2 Continuous improvement

A second basic principle of TQM is dissatisfaction with the *status quo*: the belief that it is **always possible to improve** and so the aim should be to **'get it more right next time'**. TQM should foster a consistent, systematic approach to continuous improvement that involves every aspect of the organisation.

8.3 Key elements of TQM

FORWARD

Key elements of TQM include preventing the cause of defects in the first place (rather than relying on inspecting to a predefined level of quality) and aiming towards an environment of zero defects at minimum cost.

There are nine key elements of TQM.

(a) Acceptance that the only thing that matters is the **customer**.

(b) Recognition of the all-pervasive nature of the **customer-supplier relationship**, including internal customers: passing sub-standard material to another division is not satisfactory or acceptable.

(c)   A move from relying on inspecting to a predefined level of quality to **preventing the cause** of the defect in the first place.

(d)   Personal responsibility for each operative or group of operatives for defect-free production or service in their domain. TQM requires an awareness by **all personnel** of the quality requirements compatible with supplying the customer with products of the agreed design specification.

(e)   A move away from 'acceptable' quality levels. **Any** level of defects is **unacceptable**. TQM aims towards an environment of **zero defects** at minimum cost.

(f)   An aim to **eliminate waste**, where waste is defined as anything other than the minimum essential amount of equipment, materials, space and workers' time.

(g)   Obsessive attempts by **all departments** to get things right first time: this applies to misdirected telephone calls and typing errors as much as to production.

(h)   Introduction of **quality certification** programmes.

(i)   Emphasis on the **cost of poor quality**: good quality generates savings.

8.4 Quality assurance procedures

Because TQM embraces every activity of a business, quality assurance procedures **cannot be confined to the production process** but must also cover the work of sales, distribution and administration departments, the efforts of external suppliers, and the reaction of external customers.

8.4.1 Quality assurance of goods inwards

The quality of output depends on the quality of input materials, and so quality control should include **procedures for acceptance and inspection of goods inwards and measurement of rejects**. Each supplier can be given a 'rating' for the quality of the goods they tend to supply, and preference with purchase orders can be given to well-rated suppliers. This method is referred to as 'vendor rating'.

Where a **quality assurance scheme** is in place the supplier guarantees the quality of goods supplied and allows the customers' inspectors access while the items are being manufactured. The **onus is on the supplier to carry out the necessary quality checks**, or face cancellation of the contract.

Suppliers' quality assurance schemes are being used increasingly, particularly where extensive sub-contracting work is carried out, for example in the motor industries. One such scheme is **BS EN ISO 9000** certification. A company that gains registration has a certificate testifying that it is operating to a structure of written policies and procedures which are designed to ensure that it can consistently deliver a product or service to meet customer requirements.

8.4.2 Inspection of output

This will take place at various key stages in the production process and will provide a continual check that the production process is under control. The aim of inspection is *not* really to sort out the bad products from the good ones after the work has been done. The **aim is to satisfy management that quality control in production is being maintained**.

The **inspection of samples** rather than 100% testing of all items will keep inspection costs down, and smaller samples will be less costly to inspect than larger samples. The greater the confidence in the reliability of production methods and process control, the smaller the samples will be.

8.4.3 Monitoring customer reaction

Some sub-standard items will inevitably be produced. Checks during production will identify some bad output, but other items will reach the customer who is the ultimate judge of quality. **Complaints ought to be monitored** in the form of letters of complaint, returned goods, penalty discounts, claims under guarantee, or requests for visits by service engineers. Some companies actually survey customers on a regular basis.

8.5 Internal customers and internal suppliers

T FORWARD TQM promotes the concept of the **internal customer** and **internal supplier**.

The work done by an internal supplier for an internal customer will eventually affect the quality of the product or service to the external customer. In order to satisfy the expectations of the external customer, it is therefore also necessary to satisfy the expectations of the internal customer at each stage of the overall operation. Internal customers are therefore linked in **quality chains**. Internal customer A can satisfy internal customer B who can satisfy internal customer C who in turn can satisfy the external customer.

The management of each 'micro operation' within an overall operation has the responsibility for managing its internal supplier and internal customer relationships. They should do this by specifying the requirements of their internal customers, for example in terms of quality, speed, dependability and flexibility, and the requirements for the operation itself (for example, in terms of cost).

The **concept of internal supplier-customer relationships in a series of micro-operations** helps to **focus attention on the 'up-stream' activities in an operation**, several stages removed from the external customer. Failure at an early stage of the operation, for example in new product design, has an adverse impact on all the supplier-customer relationships down the line to the external customer. The **cost of rectifying an error** becomes **more expensive the further it goes down the 'supply chain'** without rectification.

Some organisations **formalise the internal supplier-internal customer concept** by requiring each internal supplier to make a **service level agreement** with its internal customer. A service level agreement is a statement of the standard of service and supply that will be provided to the internal customer and will cover issues such as the range of services supplied, response times, dependability and so on. Boundaries of responsibility and performance standards might also be included in the agreement.

Service level agreements have been criticised, however, for over-formalising the relationship between the internal supplier and internal customer, and so creating barriers to the development of a constructive relationship and genuine co-operation between them.

8.6 Employees and quality

Employees often have a poor attitude towards quality, as a system imposed 'from outside' by non-operational staff and as an implication of lack of trust in workers to maintain quality standards or to apply a control system with objectivity themselves.

Attitudes to quality control and the management of it have, however, been **undergoing changes**.

(a)   As the pace of change in the environment has increased so attention to quality and a commitment to quality standards has become a **vital factor for organisational adaptation and survival**.

(b)   It is being recognised that **workers can be motivated by a positive approach to quality**: producing quality work is a tangible and worthwhile objective. Where responsibility for quality checking has been given to the worker himself (encouraging self-supervision), **job**

satisfaction may be increased: it is a kind of job enrichment, and also a sign of trust and respect, because imposed controls have been removed.

(c)   **Non-aversive ways of implementing quality control** have been devised. **Cultural orientation** (the deep 'belief' in quality, filtered down to all operatives) can be enlisted. **Inter-group competition** to meet and beat quality standards, for example, might be encouraged. **Quality circles** may be set up, perhaps with responsibility for implementing improvements which they identify.

Problems can therefore be overcome by **changing people's attitudes** rather than teaching them new tricks. The key issue is to instil **understanding of, and commitment to, working practices that lead to quality**.

 Case Study

As part of its TQM programme *BICC Cables* reorganised its factory from its traditional process-based operation into a dedicated product layout. It then launched two separate but related training and development activities, teamwork training and JIT training.

'To implement (JIT) working it was decided to use a firm of consultants in the first manufacturing cell to ensure a comprehensively structured introduction, with our own people working alongside them, and then to implement JIT in the other three cells ourselves.

We decided to create a **game** to convey JIT principles, and all employees in the first cell participated in it. This was followed by a series of **training/information sessions**, during which the importance of bottleneck management and inventory control was emphasised.

Employees rapidly gained an understanding of JIT and learnt the basic lessons that lots of work in progress was not necessary for the factory to be productive and that people did not always have to be busy to be effective. As in the game, we installed **'Kanbans'** on the shopfloor to limit and control the flow of inventory. When the Kanban is full, it acts as a signal to the previous process not to transfer any more work and, if required, to stop the previous process.

This was a difficult idea to take on. In effect we went **against traditional practice** by asking people to stop processes even though there was work to be done and to make themselves available for other work. This focuses attention on where effort needs to be applied to get products dispatched.

This cycle of training and implementation was repeated in the remaining three cells until the complete factory unit was operating along the JIT lines. The use of Kanbans has significantly reduced work in progress, and space has been released which has been used to accommodate new machines.'

FAST FORWARD

Workers themselves are frequently the best source of information about how (or how not) to improve **quality**.

Empowerment has two key aspects.

(a)   Allowing workers to have the **freedom to decide how to do** the necessary work, using the skills they possess and acquiring new skills as necessary to be an effective team member.

(b)   Making workers **responsible** for achieving production targets and for quality control.

It is important to **question the value of these developments**, however.

'Do employees and management really find 'empowerment' to be liberating? Empirical studies suggest that 'empowerment' often amounts to the delegation of additional duties to employees. Limits have to be placed on what employees can do, so empowerment is often associated with rules, bureaucracy and form-filling. That apart, many employees find most satisfaction from outside work activities and are quite happy to confine themselves to doing what they are told while at work. The proponents of TQM are often very work-centred people themselves and tend to judge others by their own standards.

Do teams contribute to organisational effectiveness? Just calling a group of people who work in the same office 'a team' does not make it a team. A team requires a high level of co-operation and consensus. Many competitive and motivated people find working in a team environment to be uncongenial. It means that every time you want to do anything you have to communicate with and seek approval from fellow team members. In practice, this is likely to involve bureaucracy and form-filling.

… it can be argued that TQM merely moves empowerment from management to employees. It has been argued that the latter cannot be expected to succeed where the former have failed.'

'Quality Streak', Bob Scarlett, *CIMA Insider,* September 2001

8.7 Design for quality

A TQM environment aims to get it right first time, and this means that **quality, not faults, must be designed into the organisation's products and operations from the outset**.

Quality control happens at various stages in the process of designing a product or service.

   (a)   At the **product design stage**, quality control means trying to design a product or service so that its specifications provide a suitable balance between price and quality (of sales and delivery, as well as manufacture) which will make the product or service competitive. Modern manufacturing businesses use **Computer Aided Design (CAD)** to identify or rectify design features. This might involve:

        (i)   Reducing the **number of parts** in a product overall. The fewer the number of parts, the less parts there are to go wrong.

        (ii)   Using parts or materials that are **already used** (or could be used) by other products. The more common parts overall, the less chance there is of a product failing to meet quality standards due to a rogue supplier of just one of many components. For example if a car with electric windows can be designed to use the same glass as a cheaper model with manually-wound windows, there will only be one glass supplier to keep a check on.

        (iii)   Improving **physical characteristics** such as shape, size or positioning of controls and so on to make the product more user-friendly.

   (b)   **Production engineering** is the **process of designing the methods for making a product** (or service) **to the design specification**. It sets out to make production methods as efficient as possible, and to avoid the manufacture of sub-standard items.

   (c)   **Information systems** should be designed to get the required information to the right person at the right time; **distribution systems** should be designed to get the right item to the right person at the right time; and so on.

8.8 Quality control and inspection

A distinction should be made between **quality control** and **inspection**.

   (a)   **Quality control** involves setting controls for the process of manufacture or service delivery. It is aimed at **preventing the manufacture of defective items** or the provision of defective services.

   (b)   **Inspection** is a technique of **identifying when defective items are being produced at an unacceptable level.** Inspection is usually carried out at three main points.

(i)   Receiving inspection – for raw materials and purchased components
(ii)   Floor or process inspection for WIP
(iii) Final inspection or testing for finished goods

Question

Learning outcome: D(ii)

Read the following extract from an article in the *Financial Times*, and then list the features and methods of a quality information system that *Lloyds Bank* might have devised to collect information on the impact of the 'service challenge' described here.

'If you telephone a branch of *Lloyds Bank* and it rings five times before there is a reply; if the person who answers does not introduce him or herself by name during the conversation; if you are standing in a queue with more people in it than the number of tills, then something is wrong.'

'If any of these things happen then the branch is breaching standards of customer service set by the bank since last July ... the "service challenge" was launched in the bank's 1,888 branches last summer after being tested in 55 branches ...'

'*Lloyds* already has evidence of the impact. Customers were more satisfied with pilot branches in 1991 than with others.'

Answer

A wide variety of answers is possible. The article goes on to explain how the bank is actually going about monitoring the impact of the initiative.

(a)   It has devised a 100 point scale showing average satisfaction with branch service.

(b)   It conducts a 'first impressions' survey of all new customers.

(c)   There is also a general survey carried out every six months which seeks the views of a weighted sample of 350 customers per branch.

(d)   A survey company telephones each branch anonymously twice a month to test how staff respond to enquiries about products.

(e)   A quarter of each branch's staff answer a monthly questionnaire about the bank's products to test their knowledge.

(f)   Groups of employees working in teams in branches are allowed to set their own additional standards. This is to encourage participation.

(g)   Branches that underperform are more closely watched by 24 managers who monitor the initiative.

8.9 Benefits of TQM

(a)   Elimination of waste
(b)   Elimination of non-value-adding activities and processes
(c)   Reduced costs
(d)   Increased profitability
(e)   Greater competitive advantage
(f)   Reduction in the variability in processes and outputs to ensure customer satisfaction
(g)   Increased staff morale, leading to greater productivity and efficiency
(h)   Increased customer loyalty and hence more repeat purchases

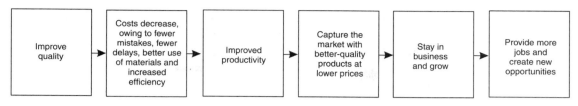

Source: W Edwards Deming

8.10 Summary

A useful conclusion to this section is offered by Bob Scarlett *(CIMA Insider,* September 2001).

'The main features of a TQM oriented organisation include:

(a) Top priority is given to satisfying customers and the organisation is structured in a way that ensures interest convergence of owners, employees, suppliers and management in achieving this. Managers should act as facilitators rather than controllers.

(b) People are considered to be the key internal guarantors of success. Decision-making processes are participative. Management is both visible and accessible.

(c) Constant change is considered a way of life and the organisation is structured in a manner that readily embraces change. The organisation structure is flat, requiring employees to use initiative and communicate directly with customers and suppliers.

(d) The organisation pursues continuous improvement and not static optimisation. The concept of 'an optimum defects level' ... is entirely alien to TQM. Performance is measured against an external benchmark and not against an internal standard.

(e) The emphasis is on prevention of problems and faults rather than detection. Employees have a wide span of activity but a short span on control.'

9 Costs of quality and cost of quality reports

FAST FORWARD

Quality costs can be analysed into **prevention**, **appraisal**, **internal failure** and **external failure** costs and should be detailed in a **cost of quality report**.

Exam focus point

The examiner set a ten-mark question testing quality costs in the May 2006 exam. Candidates were asked to write a report discussing quality costs and their importance in the organisation, giving examples.

When we talk about quality-related costs you should remember that a concern for **good quality saves money**; it is **poor quality that costs money**.

Cost of quality reports highlight the total cost to an organisation of producing products or services that do not conform with quality requirements. Four categories of cost should be reported: prevention costs, appraisal costs, internal failure costs and external failure costs.

Key terms

The **cost of quality** is 'The difference between the actual cost of producing, selling and supporting products or services and the equivalent costs if there were no failures during production or usage'. The cost of quality can be analysed into the following.

- **Cost of prevention** – 'the costs incurred prior to or during production in order to prevent substandard or defective products or services from being produced'

- **Cost of appraisal** – 'costs incurred in order to ensure that outputs produced meet required quality standards'

- **Cost of internal failure** – 'the costs arising from inadequate quality which are identified before the transfer of ownership from supplier to purchaser'

- **Cost of external failure** – 'the cost arising from inadequate quality discovered after the transfer of ownership from supplier to purchaser'

(CIMA *Official Terminology*)

External failure costs are the **costs of failing to deliver a quality product externally**. The **sum of internal failure costs, prevention and appraisal costs** is the **cost of failing to deliver a quality product internally**.

Quality-related cost	Example
Prevention costs	Quality engineering
	Design/development of quality control/inspection equipment
	Maintenance of quality control/inspection equipment
	Administration of quality control
	Training in quality control
Appraisal costs	Acceptance testing
	Inspection of goods inwards
	Inspection costs of in-house processing
	Performance testing
Internal failure costs	Failure analysis
	Re-inspection costs
	Losses from failure of purchased items
	Losses due to lower selling prices for sub-quality goods
	Costs of reviewing product specifications after failures
External failure costs	Administration of customer complaints section
	Costs of customer service section
	Product liability costs
	Cost of repairing products returned from customers
	Cost of replacing items due to sub-standard products/marketing errors

9.1 Views on quality costs

9.1.1 View one

Key terms

Cost of conformance is 'The cost of achieving specified quality standards'.

Cost of non-conformance is 'The cost of failure to deliver the required standard of quality'.

(CIMA *Official Terminology*)

The **cost of conformance** is a **discretionary** cost which is incurred with the intention of **eliminating the costs of internal and external failure**. The **cost of non-conformance**, on the other hand, can **only be reduced by increasing the cost of conformance**. The **optimal investment in conformance costs** is when **total costs of quality reach a minimum** (which may be below 100% quality conformance). This is illustrated in the following diagram.

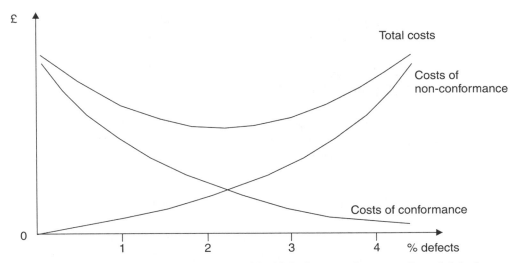

To achieve **0% defects, costs of conformance must be high**. As a **greater proportion of defects are accepted**, however, these costs can be **reduced**. At a level of **0% defects, costs of non-conformance** should be **nil** but these will **increase** as the **accepted level of defects rises**. There should therefore be an **acceptable level of defects** at which the **total costs of quality are at a minimum**.

9.1.2 View two

A 'traditional' approach to quality management (view one) is that there is an **optimal level of quality effort, that minimises total quality costs**, and there is a point beyond which spending more on quality yields a benefit that is less than the additional cost incurred. Diminishing returns set in beyond the optimal quality level.

The **TQM philosophy** is different.

(a) Failure and poor quality are unacceptable. It is **inappropriate to think of an optimal level of quality** at which some failures will occur, and the **inevitability of errors is not something that an organisation should accept**. The target should be zero defects.

(b) Quality costs are difficult to measure, and failure costs in particular are often seriously under estimated. The **real costs of failure include** not just the cost of scrapped items and re-working faulty items, but also the **management time spent sorting out problems** and the **loss of confidence** between different parts of the organisation whenever faults occur.

(c) A TQM approach does not accept that the prevention costs of achieving zero defects becomes unacceptably high as the quality standard improves and goes above a certain level. In other words, **diminishing returns do not necessarily set in**. If everyone in the organisation is involved in improving quality, the cost of continuous improvement need not be high.

(d) If an organisation **accepts an optimal quality level** that it believes will minimise total quality costs, there will be **no further challenge** to management to improve quality further.

The **TQM quality cost model** is based on the view that:

(a) **Prevention costs and appraisal costs** are **subject to management influence** or control. It is **better to spend money on prevention**, before failures occur, than on inspection to detect failures after they have happened.

(b) **Internal failure costs and external failure costs** are the **consequences of the efforts spent on prevention and appraisal**. Extra effort on prevention will reduce internal failure costs and this in turn will have a knock-on effect, reducing external failure costs as well.

In other words, **higher spending on prevention will eventually lead to lower total quality costs**, because appraisal costs, internal failure costs and external failure costs will all be reduced. The emphasis should be on 'getting things right first time' and 'designing in quality' to the product or service.

9.2 Cost of quality reports

Shown below is a typical cost of quality report. **Some figures** in the report, such as the contribution forgone due to sales lost because of poor quality, may have to be **estimated,** but it is better to include an estimate rather than omit the category from the report.

The report has the following **uses**.

(a) By expressing each cost category as a percentage of sales revenue, **comparisons** can be made with previous periods, divisions within the group or other organisations, thereby highlighting problem areas. A comparison of the proportion of external failure costs to sales revenue with the figures for other organisations, for example, can provide some idea of the level of customer satisfaction.

(b) It can be used to make senior management aware of **how much is being spent** on quality-related costs.

(c) It can provide an indication of **how total quality costs could be reduced by a more sensible division of costs between the four categories.** For example, an increase in spending on prevention costs should reduce the costs of internal and external failure and hence reduce total spending.

COST OF QUALITY REPORT
YEAR ENDING 31 DECEMBER 20X0

	$'000	$'000	Cost as % of annual revenue ($10 million)
Prevention costs			
Design of quality control equipment	80		
Quality control training	80		
		160	1.6
Appraisal costs			
Inspection of goods inwards	90		
Inspection of WIP	100		
		190	1.9
Internal failure costs			
Scrap	150		
Rework	200		
		350	3.5
External failure costs			
Returns	500		
Contribution forgone on lost sales	400		
Handling customer complaints	100		
		1,000	10.0
		1,700	17.0

Although cost of quality reports provide a useful summary of the costs, effort and progress of quality, **non-financial quality measures** may be more appropriate for **lower levels of management**. Here are some examples of such measures.

(a) Number of customer complaints
(b) Number of warranty claims
(c) Number of defective units delivered to customers as a percentage of total units delivered

Learning outcome: D(iii)

LL designs and makes a single product, the X4, used in the telecommunications industry. The organisation has a goods received store which employs staff who carry out random checks to ensure materials are of the correct specification. In addition to the random checks, a standard allowance is made for failures due to faulty materials at the completion stage and the normal practice is to charge the cost of any remedial work required to the cost of production for the month. Once delivered to the customer, any faults discovered in the X4 during its warranty period become an expense of the customer support department.

At the end of each month, management reports are prepared for the Board of Directors. These identify the cost of running the stores and the number of issues, the cost of production and the number of units manufactured, and the cost of customer support.

Required

(a)   Briefly discuss why the current accounting system fails to highlight the cost of quality.

(b)   Identify four general categories (or classifications) of LL's activities where expenditure making up the explicit cost of quality will be found and provide an example of a cost found within each category.

(c)   Give one example of a cost of quality not normally identified by the accounting system.

Answer

(a)   **Failure of the current accounting system to highlight the cost of quality**

Traditionally, the costs of scrapped units, wasted materials and reworking have been **subsumed within the costs of production** by assigning the costs of an expected level of loss (a normal loss) to the costs of good production, while accounting for **other costs of poor quality** within **production or marketing overheads**. Such costs are therefore not only considered as **inevitable** but are not **highlighted** for management attention. Moreover, traditional accounting reports tend to **ignore the hidden but real costs of excessive inventory levels** (held to enable faulty material to be replaced without hindering production) and the facilities necessary for storing that **inventory**.

(b)   **Explicit costs of quality**

There are four recognised categories of cost identifiable within an accounting system which make up the cost of quality.

(1)   **Prevention costs** are the costs of any action taken to investigate, prevent or reduce the production of faulty output. Included within this category are the costs of training in quality control and the cost of the design/development and maintenance of quality control and inspection equipment.

(2)   **Appraisal costs** are the costs of assessing the actual quality achieved. Examples include the cost of the inspection of goods delivered and the cost of inspecting production during the manufacturing process.

(3)   **Internal failure costs** are the costs incurred by the organisation when production fails to meet the level of quality required. Such costs include losses due to lower selling prices for sub-quality goods, the costs of reviewing product specifications after failures and losses arising from the failure of purchased items.

(4)   **External failure costs** are the costs which arise outside the organisation (after the customer has received the product) due to failure to achieve the required level of quality. Included within this category are the costs of repairing products returned from customers, the cost of providing replacement items due to sub-standard products or marketing errors and the costs of a customer service department.

(c)   **Quality costs not identified by the accounting system**

Quality costs which are not identified by the accounting system tend to be of two forms.

(1)   Opportunity costs such as the loss of future sales to a customer dissatisfied with faulty goods.

(2)   Costs which tend to be subsumed within other account headings such as those costs which result from the disruption caused by stockouts due to faulty purchases.

 Case Study

The following extracts are taken from 'Total Quality Management and effective leadership' on the Department of Trade and Industry's website. The emphasis is BPP's.

'A German customer seeking to buy a power tool will often shake it in the shop. If it rattles, he may well reject it out of hand, and buy another one that seems to be more solidly made. The rattle may have no significance at all in terms of the drill's functionality – but it has great significance for the customer, and even greater significance for the maker of the drill, who will have lost a sale.

Robin Mair, Director of Manufacturing for Black & Decker UK, tells that story as an illustration of his dictum: "Customer perception is the only reality."

"Packaging, presentation, aesthetics, ergonomics, after-sales service, even whether a switch goes click or clunk can affect the customer's perception of the product," he says. "Of course, the tool must do the job it's meant to do efficiently and reliably, but that's not enough in itself. **Customers are more and more demanding** – and they have the choice.

You must form a relationship with the customer, and **understand his requirements and expectations**."

This is the essential difference between Black & Decker's approach to quality today, and its approach at the beginning of the '80s. Then, the definition of quality was "conformance to specification".

"We say that's too narrow," says Robin Mair. "It limits quality to design and manufacture. It's a negative approach, measuring quality only by the level of rejects. We have to integrate the functions of the business, and get manufacturing's perception of quality in line with the customer's perceptions.

We decided we had to change the culture of the organisation, so we took up an initiative called Total Customer Service."

In trying to establish exactly what the customer did require and expect, Black & Decker discovered what Robin Mair calls a gold mine of information – its own service stations, 38 of them, all near major centres of population. They interfaced with two million people in the UK every year. Using the service station records, the company was able to categorise failure modes, and analyse them.

Retailers, of course, are customers of Black & Decker, as well as the final link with the ultimate individual customers. To ensure that their requirements from manufacturing are perfectly clear, they are now **encouraged to visit the factory to exchange information** of benefit to both parties in pursuit of total customer service.

The work force is then kept in touch by regular weekly briefings from the area supervisors. Because the **operatives** have little direct contact with the end customer, they **focus their efforts on supplying the**

needs and expectations of their internal customers – the next people in the plant to receive the products of their work.

The introduction of Statistical Process Control has enhanced the **self-management** by giving the operators themselves direct control over quality, stimulating their interest in process capability and the pursuit of continuous conformance to specification.

Problems are tackled by self-managing project groups, which have largely superseded the quality circles which flourished for some years. Project groups are formed to tackle specific problems, bringing together interested parties, with expert help where necessary. They have even 'colonised' other companies by making contact with their opposite numbers in the supplier's factory to solve problems in bought-in components, thus short-circuiting the usual ponderous reference up one chain of command, and down the other.

One project group had the task of reducing the noise made by drills, which had been identified as a customer requirement. ...

... **the cost of new machines [for overcoming the problem] ... would put 7p on the unit cost of manufacture**.

Fortunately, Black & Decker has had a **quality costs system in place** since the mid '80s, and the project group was able to discover the **unit cost of scrap, rework and other inefficiencies arising from the noisy gear problem. It proved to be no less than 50p!**

Robin Mair did not need much persuading to back the investment in the new machines.

The success of this kind of self-management has led to the **removal of several layers of old-style, hierarchical management**. The number of supervisors has been reduced from 68 to 20, whose jobs are now redefined as business managers, with responsibility for skills and employee relations, capital assets and customer services.

The **reductions in costs have been significant**, but Robin Mair does not emphasise this aspect.

"I use cost as the broad indicator that we are going in the right direction," he says, "but I don't want people to get the idea that it is the sole motivation. Quality as perceived by the customer is what we are aiming at."

In a competitive consumer market already saturated with product (who does not have a drill and accessories?) there is a need for constant innovation, which Black & Decker sees as an inevitable part of total customer service. Hundreds of new ideas are reduced every year to a handful of front-runners. Many of them fall by the wayside; some – like the hot air paint-stripper – turn into an unexpected bonanza.'

Chapter Roundup

- **Costing systems** have evolved to reflect a **manufacturing philosophy** that is based on the need to achieve **competitive advantage**.
  - Flexibility and the ability to respond quickly to customer demands are vital.
  - Product life cycles are shorter and products must be brought to the market quickly.
  - New technology has been introduced.

- **Just-in-time systems** challenge 'traditional' views of manufacturing.

- **Just-in-time** is an approach to operations planning and control based on the idea that **goods and services should be produced only when they are needed**, and neither too early (so that inventories build up) nor too late (so that the customer has to wait).

- **JIT** consists of **JIT purchasing** and **JIT production.**

- **Elimination of waste, involvement of all staff** and **continuous improvement** are the three key elements in the JIT philosophy.

- **JIT** aims to **eliminate all non-value-added costs**.

- **Backflush costing** is suitable for use in a JIT environment. Costs are attached to output only, thereby simplifying the costing system.

- **Theory of constraints (TOC)** is a set of concepts which aim to identify the binding constraints in a production system and which strive for evenness of production flow so that the organisation works as effectively as possible. No inventory should be held, except prior to the binding constraint.

- The concept of **throughput accounting (TA)** has been developed from TOC as an alternative system of cost and management accounting in a JIT environment.

- **TA is based on three concepts**.
  - In the short run, most costs in the factory (with the exception of materials costs) are fixed.
  - The ideal inventory level is zero.
  - Profitability is determined by the rate at which sales are made.

- The TA philosophy entails the identification and elimination of **bottleneck resources**.

- Throughput measures include **return per time period, return per time period on the bottleneck resource** and the **TA ratio**.

- The aim of **Kaizen costing** is to reduce current costs by using various tools such as value analysis and functional analysis.

- The essence of **continuous improvement** is the use of an organisation's human resources to produce a constant stream of improvements in all aspects of customer value, including quality, functional design, and timely delivery, while lowering cost at the same time.

- In the context of **total quality management**, 'quality' means getting it right first time, and improving continuously.

- **Key elements of TQM** include preventing the cause of defects in the first place (rather than relying on inspecting to a predefined level of quality) and aiming towards an environment of zero defects at minimum cost.

- TQM promotes the concept of the **internal customer** and **internal supplier**.

- **Workers** themselves are frequently the best source of information about how (or how not) to improve **quality**.

- **Quality costs** can be analysed into **prevention, appraisal, internal failure** and **external failure** costs and should be detailed in a **cost of quality report**.

Quick Quiz

1   What four key words/phrases describe modern manufacturing philosophy?

(a)   ....

(b)   ....

(c)   ....

(d)   ....

2   The cost of inspecting a product for quality is a value-added cost. *True or false?*

3   Which of the following is/are correct?

(a)   Cost of conformance = cost of prevention + cost of internal failure
(b)   Cost of conformance = cost of internal failure + cost of external failure
(c)   Cost of non-conformance = cost of internal failure + cost of external failure
(d)   Cost of conformance = cost of appraisal + cost of prevention
(e)   Cost of non-conformance = cost of prevention + cost of appraisal
(f)   Cost of non-conformance = cost of appraisal + cost of external failure

4   *Match the cost to the correct cost category.*

Costs

(a)   Administration of quality control
(b)   Product liability costs
(c)   Acceptance testing
(d)   Losses due to lower selling prices for sub-quality goods

Cost categories

•   Prevention costs
•   Appraisal costs
•   Internal failure costs
•   External failure costs

5   *Choose the appropriate words from those highlighted.*

JIT purchasing requires **small, frequent/large, infrequent** deliveries **well in advance of/as near as possible to** the time the raw materials and parts are needed.

In a JIT environment, the responsibility for the quality of goods lies with the **supplier/purchaser.**

6   *Fill in the blanks in the statements below, using the words in the box. Some words may be used twice.*

(a)   The theory of constraints is an approach to production management which aims to maximise (1)............. less (2)......... . It focuses on factors such as (3)................ which act as (4).....................

(b)   Throughput contribution = (5)............. minus (6) ....

(c)   TA ratio = (7) .... per factory hour ÷ (8) ....per factory hour

•   bottlenecks
•   material costs
•   sales revenue
•   throughput contribution
•   constraints
•   conversion cost

7   Put a tick in the boxes of those statements that relate to Kaizen costing, and a cross for statements about standard costing.

☐ Employees are often viewed as the cause of problems.

☐ Costs are reduced by implementing continuous improvement.

☐ The aim is to meet cost performance targets.

☐ The aim is to achieve cost reduction targets.

☐ It is assumed that current manufacturing conditions remain unchanged.

8   Continuous improvement organisations never engage in radical change. *True or false?*

9   *Fill in the right hand side of the table below, which looks at the differences between throughput accounting and traditional product costing.*

Traditional product costing	Throughput accounting
Labour costs and 'traditional' variable overheads are treated as variable costs.	
Inventory is valued in the income statement and balance sheet at total production cost.	
Variance analysis is employed to determine whether standards were achieved.	
Efficiency is based on labour and machines working to full capacity.	
Value is added when an item is produced.	

10 Try the following question that tests your knowledge of backflush costing. The transactions for period 1 20X7 for AB are as follows.

Purchase of raw materials	$32,000
Conversion costs incurred	$18,500
Sales	5,100 units

There are no opening inventories of raw materials, WIP or finished goods. The standard cost per unit is made up of $3.20 for materials and $3.80 for conversion costs. Show the journals required if the trigger point is when the goods are sold.

Answers to Quick Quiz

1   (a)   Smooth, steady production flow (throughput)
    (b)   Flexibility
    (c)   Volume versus variety
    (d)   JIT

2   False

3   (c) and (d) are correct.

4   (a)   Prevention costs
    (b)   External failure costs
    (c)   Appraisal costs
    (d)   Internal failure costs

5   small, frequent
    as near as possible to
    supplier

6   1   sales revenue
     2   material costs
     3   bottlenecks
     4   constraints
     5   sales revenue
     6   material costs
     7   throughput contribution
     8   conversion cost

7   ☒   Employees are often viewed as the cause of problems.

     ☑   Costs are reduced by implementing continuous improvement.

     ☒   The aim is to meet cost performance targets.

     ☑   The aim is to achieve cost reduction targets.

     ☒   It is assumed that current manufacturing conditions remain unchanged.

8   False. Quantum leaps in performance can occur.

9

Traditional product costing	Throughput accounting
Labour costs and 'traditional' variable overheads are treated as variable costs.	They are not normally treated as variable costs.
Inventory is valued in the income statement and balance sheet at total production cost.	It is valued at material cost only.
Variance analysis is employed to determine whether standards were achieved.	It is used to determine why the planned product mix was not produced.
Efficiency is based on labour and machines working to full capacity.	Efficiency requires schedule adherence and meeting delivery dates.
Value is added when an item is produced.	It is added when an item is sold.

10   This is the simplest method of backflush costing. This method assumes that units are sold as soon as they are produced.

			$	$
(a)	DEBIT	Conversion costs control	18,500	
	CREDIT	Payables		18,500

Being the actual conversion costs incurred

			$	$
(b)	DEBIT	Cost of goods sold (5,100 × $7.00)	35,700	
	CREDIT	Payables (5,100 × $3.20)		16,320
	CREDIT	Conversion costs allocated (5,100 × $3.80)		19,380

Being the standard cost of goods sold

			$	$
(c)	DEBIT	Conversion costs allocated	19,380	
	CREDIT	Cost of goods sold		880
	CREDIT	Conversion costs control		18,500

Being the under allocation of conversion costs

Now try the question below from the Exam Question Bank

Number	Level	Marks	Time
Q26	Examination	25	45 mins

Externally-orientated management accounting techniques

Introduction

In this final chapter of the Text we look at some **externally-orientated** management accounting techniques and how they can be **used to derive competitive advantage**.

Sections 1 to 4 consider how the organisation interacts with suppliers and customers. **Sections 5 to 8** look at how ABC can be used to determine the profitability of customers and distribution channels, while **Section 9** covers Pareto analysis, which can be used to present the results of some of the analyses covered in the chapter.

The examiner set a question on the value chain in November 2006.

And then that's it! You've finished! Congratulations. You now need to move on to the revision and practice stage of your studies.

Topic list	Learning outcomes	Syllabus references	Ability required
1 The value chain	D(viii)	D(8)	Comprehension/Analysis
2 Supply chain management	D(viii)	D(8)	Comprehension/Analysis
3 Outsourcing	D(viii)	D(8)	Comprehension/Analysis
4 Partnering, incentives and gain-sharing arrangements	D(ix)	D(9)	Analysis
5 Direct product profitability (DPP)	D(x)	D(10)	Application
6 Customer profitability analysis (CPA)	D(x)	D(10)	Application
7 Distribution channel profitability	D(x)	D(10)	Application
8 Activity-based profitability analysis	D(x)	D(10)	Application
9 Pareto analysis	D(xi)	D(11)	Application

1 The value chain

Exam focus
point

> The value chain was examined in the November 2006 exam in a ten-mark question. The question was a bit tricky as it asked for an explanation of the **extended** value chain.

FAST FORWARD

> The **value chain model**, developed by Michael Porter, offers a bird's eye view of an organisation, of what it does and the way in which its business activities are organised.

According to Porter, the **activities of any organisation** can be divided into nine types and **analysed into a value chain**. This is a model of the activities (which procure inputs, process them and add value to them in some way, to generate outputs for customers) and the relationships between them.

Key term

> The **value chain** is 'The sequence of business activities by which, from the perspective of the end user, value is added to the products and services produced by an entry.' (CIMA *Official Terminology*)

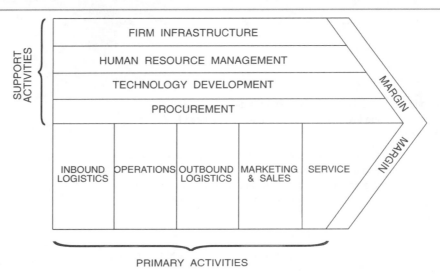

1.1 Activities

Key term

> **Activities** are the means by which an organisation creates value in its products.

It is important to realise that **business activities are not the same as business functions**.

(a) Functions are the familiar departments of an organisation (production, finance and so on). They reflect the formal organisation structure and the distribution of labour.

(b) Activities are what actually goes on, and the work that is done. A single activity can be performed by a number of functions in sequence. Activities are the means by which an organisation creates value in its products. (They are sometimes referred to as value activities). Activities incur costs and, in combination with other activities, provide a product or service that earns revenue.

For example, most organisations need to secure resources from the environment. This activity can be called procurement. Procurement will involve more departments than purchasing, however; the accounts department will certainly be involved and possibly production and quality assurance.

FAST FORWARD

> **Activities** or **value activities** can be categorised as **primary** or **support**.

1.1.1 Primary activities

Primary activities are directly related to production, sales, marketing, delivery and service.

	Comment
Inbound logistics	Receiving, handling and storing inputs to the production system (warehousing, transport, inventory control and so on)
Operations	Converting resource inputs into a final product. Resource inputs are not only materials. 'People' are a 'resource' especially in service industries.
Outbound logistics	Storing the product and its distribution to customers (packaging, warehousing, testing and so on)
Marketing and sales	Informing customers about the product, persuading them to buy it, and enabling them to do so (advertising, promotion and so on)
After sales service	Installing products, repairing them, upgrading them, providing spare parts and so on

1.1.2 Support activities

Support activities provide purchased inputs, human resources, technology and infrastructural functions to support the primary activities.

Activity	Comment
Procurement	Acquiring the resource inputs to the primary activities (such as purchase of materials, subcomponents equipment)
Technology development	Designing products, improving processes and/or resource utilisation
Human resource management	Recruiting, training, developing and rewarding people
Firm infrastructure	Planning, finance, quality control (Porter believes they are crucially important to an organisation's strategic capability in all primary activities.)

1.2 Creating value

FAST FORWARD

The ultimate **value** an organisation creates is measured by the amount customers are willing to pay for its products and services above the cost of carrying out value activities.

An organisation is profitable if the realised value to customers exceeds the collective cost of performing the activities.

(a) **Customers 'purchase' value**, which they measure by comparing an organisation's products and services with similar offerings by competitors.

(b) **An organisation 'creates' value** by carrying out its activities either more efficiently than other organisations, or by combining them in such a way as to provide a unique product or service. We return to this point below.

Question | Creating value

Learning outcome: D(viii)

Outline different ways in which a restaurant can 'create' value.

Answer

Here are some ideas. Each of these options is a way of organising the activities of buying, cooking and serving food in a way that customers will value.

(a) It can become more efficient, by automating the production of food, as in a fast food chain.

(b) The chef can develop commercial relationships with growers, so he or she can obtain the best quality fresh produce.

(c) The chef can specialise in a particular type of cuisine (such as French or Thai).

(d) The restaurant can be sumptuously decorated for those customers who value 'atmosphere' and a sense of occasion, in addition to a restaurant's purely gastronomic pleasures.

(e) The restaurant can serve a particular type of customer (such as celebrities).

1.3 The focus of the value chain

FAST FORWARD

The **focus of the value chain** is **external to the organisation**, each organisation being viewed in the context of the overall chain of value-creating activities of which it is only a part, from basic raw materials to end-use consumers.

This contrasts with **traditional management accounting**, which takes a value-added perspective, which has a focus largely **internal** to the organisation, each organisation being viewed in relation to its purchases, its processes, its functions, its products, its customers.

1.4 Value system

Activities that add value do not stop at the organisation's boundaries. For example, when a restaurant serves a meal, the quality of the ingredients – although they are chosen by the cook – is determined by the grower. The grower has added value, and the grower's success in growing produce of good quality is as important to the customer's ultimate satisfaction as the skills of the chef. An **organisation's value chain** is **connected** to what Porter calls a **value system**.

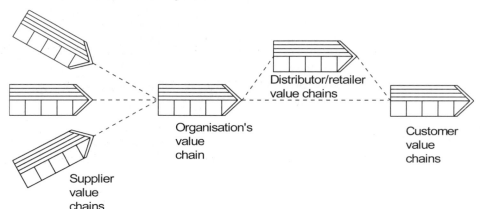

1.5 Linkages

Linkages **connect the activities of the value chain**. Linkages might be with suppliers or with customers, or within the organisation itself.

(a) Activities in the value chain affect one another.

    (i) More costly product design or better quality production might reduce the need for after-sales service and post-purchase costs for customers. Designing a product to reduce post-purchase costs can be a major weapon in **capturing competitive advantage**.

    (ii) JIT requires close partnerships with suppliers. Its introduction might save an organisation storage costs, say, but production schedule instability for suppliers might cause them to raise their prices.

(b) Linkages require **co-ordination**. Unlike the value-added concept, value chain analysis explicitly recognises the fact that various activities within an organisation are **interdependent**. There is little point in a fast-food chain running a promotional campaign (one value activity) if there is insufficient capacity within 'production' (another value activity) to cope with the increased demand. These linked activities must be coordinated if the full effect of the promotion is to be realised.

Beneficial linkages are linkages with customers or suppliers that are managed in such a way that all parties benefit.

Case Study

'…the container industry. Some container producers have constructed manufacturing facilities near beer breweries and deliver the containers through overhead conveyers directly onto the customers' assembly line. This practice results in significant cost reductions for both the container producers and their customers by expediting the transport of empty containers, which are bulky and heavy.'

Shank and Govindarajan ('Strategic Cost Management and the Value Chain',
Journal of Cost Management, 1992)

1.6 The value chain and competitive advantage

According to Porter, an organisation can develop sustainable competitive advantage by following one of two strategies.

(a) **Low-cost strategy.** Essentially this is a strategy of cost leadership, which involves achieving a lower cost than competitors via, for example, economies of scale and tight cost control. Hyundai (in cars) and Timex (wrist watches) are examples of organisations that have followed such a strategy.

(b) **Differentiation strategy.** This involves creating something that customers perceive as being unique via brand loyalty, superior customer service, product design and features, technology and so on. Mercedes Benz (in cars) and Rolex (wrist watches) are examples of organisations that have followed such a strategy.

ST FORWARD

An organisation's ability to develop and sustain **cost leadership** or **product differentiation**, and hence **gain competitive advantage**, depends on how well it manages its own value chain relative to competitors.

As **competitive advantage** is gained either from providing **better customer value for equivalent cost** or **equivalent customer value for lower cost**, value chain analysis is essential to determine **where in an organisation's value chain costs can be lowered or value enhanced**.

1.6.1 Strategic cost management and the value chain

Shank and Govindarajan explained how an organisation's value chain can be used with a view to lowering costs and enhancing value: '.. the value chain framework is a method for breaking down the chain – from basic raw materials to end-use customers – into strategically relevant activities to understand the behaviour of costs and the sources of differentiation'.

They suggest a three-step approach.

Step 1   **Build up the industry's value chain to determine the various activities in the value chain** and to allocate operating costs, revenues and assets to individual value activities. (It is vital to understand the entire value chain, not just the portion of the chain in which the organisation participates. Suppliers and distribution channels have profit margins that impact on an organisation's cost or differentiation positioning, because the final customer has to pay for all the profit margins throughout the value chain.)

Step 2   Establish the cost drivers of the costs of each value activity, which are one of two types.

    (a)   **Structural cost drivers.** These are derived from an organisation's decisions about its underlying economic structure and include:

        (i)   Scale of operations (giving rise to economies or diseconomies of scale)
        (ii)   Scope (degree of vertical integration)
        (iii)   Experience (has the organisation climbed the learning curve?)
        (iv)   Technology used in the value chain
        (v)   Complexity (number of products/services being sold)

    (b)   **Executional cost drivers.** These relate to an organisation's ability to deliver the product/service successfully to the customer. According to Shank and Govindarajan, the 'more' of these cost drivers there is, the better. Basic examples include:

        (i)   Employee participation
        (ii)   TQM
        (iii)   Capacity utilisation
        (iv)   Plant layout efficiency
        (v)   Product configuration
        (vi)   Linkages with suppliers or customers

Step 3   **Develop sustainable competitive advantage, by controlling these drivers better than competitors or by configuring the value chain.** For each value activity, **sustainable competitive advantage can be developed by reducing costs whilst maintaining value (sales) and/or increasing value (sales) whilst maintaining costs**.

    (a)   **Cost reduction.** Compare the value chain of the organisation with the value chain of one or two major competitors, then identify the action required to manage the organisation's value chain better than competitors manage theirs.

    (b)   **Increasing value.** Identify where in the value chain payoffs could be significant.

1.6.2 Example: using the value chain in competitive strategy

The examples below are based on two supermarket chains, **one concentrating on low prices**, the **other differentiated on quality and service**. See if you can tell which is which.

(a)

	INBOUND LOGISTICS	OPERATIONS	OUTBOUND LOGISTICS	MARKETING & SALES	SERVICE
Firm infrastructure	Minimum corporate HQ				
Human resource management		De-skilled store operatives	Dismissal for checkout error		
Technology development	Computerised warehousing		Checkouts simple		
Procurement	Branded only purchases Big discounts	Low cost sites			Use of concessions
	Bulk warehousing	1,000 lines only Price points Basic store design		Low price promotion Local focus	Nil

(b)

	INBOUND LOGISTICS	OPERATIONS	OUTBOUND LOGISTICS	MARKETING & SALES	SERVICE
Firm infrastructure	Central control of operations and credit control				
Human resource management	Recruitment of mature staff	Client care training	Flexible staff to help with packing		
Technology development		Recipe research	Electronic point of sale	Consumer research and tests	Itemised bills
Procurement	Own label products	Prime retail positions		Adverts in quality magazines	
	Dedicated refrigerated transport	In store food halls Modern store design Open front refrigerators Tight control of sell-by dates	Collect by car service	No price discounts on food past sell-by dates	No quibble refunds

The two supermarkets represented are based on the following.

(a) The value chain in (a) is similar to that of Lidl, a 'discount' supermarket chain which sells on price. This can be seen in the limited product range and its low-cost sites.

(b) The value chain in (b) is based on Marks and Spencer, which seeks to differentiate on quality and service. Hence the 'no quibble' refunds, the use of prime retail sites, and customer care training.

Case Study

'By comparing two organisations from the computer retail sector we can observe the strategic choices that organisations make. Dell chooses to use the Internet and telesales as the main channels for its marketing and sales activity, and uses distributors to fulfil its outbound logistics. PC World uses shops as well as the Internet. Both firms employ sales staff, but PC World, consistent with its decision to use retail outlets, has identified that its target customers value the personal touch, so it has chosen to employ trained staff (HR management activity) who can deal with them face to face. Its TV advertising (marketing and sales activity) emphasises this expert personal service as a benefit (differentiating factor) of shopping at PC World.

Compare this approach with that of a retailer such as Ikea, which believes that its target customers do not place a high value on personal customer service and has therefore decided against employing large numbers of sales staff. This allows it to keep employment costs down, supporting its low-cost strategy and its position in the market. Note that competitive advantage and what the customer values are the factors that have driven the decision.'

Graham Pitcher, 'The Missing Link', CIMA *Insider*, April 2004

1.7 Summary

The value chain is a technique with an **external emphasis** not only in relation to competitors but also back to suppliers and forward to customers. It provides the following insights.

(a)   No two organisations compete in exactly the same set of value activities, and so it provides understanding of how an organisation is positioned within the industry.

(b)   Strategic decisions such as make or buy become clearer when viewed within the framework of the overall chain and from the perspective of the organisation's place within it.

(c)   It helps identify ways to exploit linkages with suppliers and customers.

(d)   Achievement of low costs and differentiation requires a detailed understanding of the drivers of costs, revenues and assets of each value activity, and the interdependencies between them.

Question   Value chain analysis v conventional management accounting

Learning outcome: D(viii)

Compare and contrast value chain analysis with conventional management accounting by completing the table below.

	Traditional management accounting	Value chain analysis
Focus		
Perspective		
Cost driver concept		
Cost containment philosophy		
Insights for strategic decisions		

Answer

	Traditional management accounting	Value chain analysis
Focus	Internal	External
Perspective	Value-added	Entire set of linked activities from suppliers to final-use customers
Cost driver concept	Single driver (volume) Applied at organisational level	Multiple cost drivers (structural and executional) Unique cost drivers for each value activity
Cost containment philosophy	'Across the board' cost reductions	By regulating cost drivers Exploit linkages with customers and suppliers Spend to save
Insights for strategic decisions	None readily apparent	Develop cost/differentiation advantage by controlling drivers better than competitors or by reconfiguring the value chain For each value activity, consider make versus buy, forwards/backwards integration and so on Exploit linkages with customers and suppliers

Adapted from Shank and Govindarajan

2 Supply chain management

2.1 The supply chain

ST FORWARD

A **supply chain** is the network of suppliers, manufacturers and distributors that is involved in the process of moving goods for a customer order from the raw materials stage through the production and distribution stages to the customer. Every organisation operates somewhere within a supply chain.

term

A **supply chain** is a network of facilities and distribution options that performs the functions of procurement of materials, transformation of these materials into intermediate and finished products and the distribution of these finished products to customers.

(Ganeshan and Harrison, *Supply Chain Management*).

Within a supply chain, many processes might take place between the origination of raw materials to the eventual delivery of the finished product or service to the end customer. For each organisation inside a supply chain, some of the processes are carried out by the organisation itself, and others are carried out by suppliers or by other organisations further down the supply chain.

Case Study

For example, a company manufacturing motor vehicles might have a plant where the vehicles are assembled and finished. It might manufacture some parts itself and produce the car body work, but most sub-assemblies and the tyres will be purchased from outside suppliers. The suppliers of sub-assemblies might make some components themselves, but will also purchase many of their components from other suppliers. The manufacturer, suppliers and sub-suppliers might all purchase raw materials, such as steel, from other suppliers. The manufacturer will also purchase capital equipment from equipment suppliers, who are another part of the supply chain. The finished cars will not be sold directly to the end customer, but to distributors, and the distributors will sell to the end customer.

2.2 The concept of supply chain management

FAST FORWARD ▶

A **commonly-held view** by management is that **to improve profitability** it is necessary to **get the lowest prices from suppliers** and to **obtain the best prices from the customers** next in line down the supply chain.

If there is a **given amount of profit** in a particular market for a finished product, this profit will be **shared out between all the organisations involved in the supply chain**. In this sense, suppliers and their customers **compete** with each other for **a bigger share of the available profit**. This 'traditional' **adversarial arms' length** attitude is evident in negotiations between an organisation and its suppliers, and efforts by the organisation to get the best terms possible and the lowest prices in their purchasing negotiations.

This view of the supply chain is **challenged by** the concept of **supply chain management**.

FAST FORWARD ▶

Supply chain management looks at the supply chain as a whole, and starts with the view that all organisations in the supply chain collaborate to produce something of value for the end customer.

This has two advantages.

(a) By **adding value** within the supply chain, **customer satisfaction** will be **improved** and **customers** will **pay more** for what they buy.

(b) **Organisations can also benefit collectively by reducing waste and inefficiency**. A lot of **wasteful activity** (activity that does not add any value to the final product) **occurs at the interface between organisations within the supply chain**. For example, a supplier might spend money on checking outwards supplies for quality, and the same goods will be checked by the organisation buying them when they are delivered. Inspection costs could be reduced by closer collaboration between the organisations, both to improve quality and to reduce inspection activities.

By looking at the supply chain as a collaborative effort, managers can look for ways of enhancing the profitability of the supply chain as a whole, so that everyone, including the end customer, benefits.

2.2.1 Developing relationships

Developing strong relationships is not an easy task, however. The arms' length supplier-purchaser relationship has been based on both sides winning as much short-term gain as possible, and so sharing sensitive information and developing long-term ties is often difficult.

There are a number of practices which can be used to foster improved relationships with key suppliers.

(a) **Power balancing** occurs if the proportion of a supplier's total output that is sold to a customer roughly equals the proportion of total purchases acquired by the customer from that supplier. Maintaining relative dependence between suppliers and buyers increases the likelihood that both parties will have a vested interest in the success of the other.

(b) **Codependency.** When a supplier commits substantial specialised resources to meeting the demands of a purchaser and the purchaser chooses to single-source from that supplier, both parties have a vested interest in the success of the purchaser.

(c) **Target costing.** Suppliers can be rewarded when targets are reached.

(d) **Personal ties.** The establishment of teams of employees from both supplier and purchaser helps foster good working relationships and develop trust.

Case Study

'To design vehicle and production systems [for the M-class], Mercedes Benz US International used *function groups* that included representatives from every area of the company.... The role of these function groups was to develop specifications and cost projections.

Mercedes included suppliers early in the design stage of the vehicle. By including suppliers as members of the function groups, Mercedes was able to take advantage of their expertise and advice on matters such as supplier capability, cost and quality. The synergy generated by these cross-function groups also allowed the groups to solve larger design issues, such as how to more efficiently and economically switch from manufacturing left-side-drive vehicles to right-side-vehicles. Significant time savings were recognised because of the design improvements implemented by the function groups. Because supplier personnel were at the Mercedes plant on a full-time basis during the launch, other issues (such as quality problems or slight modifications to the product) could be addressed in a more timely fashion.'

(Albright and Davis, 'The Elements of Supply Chain Management', *International Journal of Strategic Cost Management*, Autumn 1999)

term

> **Supply chain management** (or **pipeline management** or **value stream management**) views all the buyers and sellers in this chain as part of a continuum, and the aim should be to look at the supply chain as a whole and seek to optimise the functioning of the entire chain. In other words, a company should look beyond its immediate suppliers and its immediate customers to add value, for example by improving efficiency and eliminating waste.

2.2.2 Adding value

The overall supply chain can be thought of as a **sequence of operations, each of which should add value**. An activity has value if it gives the customer something that the customer considers worth having (ie values), but an activity only adds value if the amount of value added exceeds the cost of creating it. Value is therefore added by making something worth more (in terms of the price the customer will pay, or the quality the customer perceives) or by reducing the cost of the operation (without sacrificing quality).

2.3 Elements of supply chain management

To apply the concept of supply chain management fully, there has to be **close collaboration** between organisations within the supply chain. A company must be able to work constructively with its suppliers. At the same time, it should continually **look for ways of improving the supply chain structure**, and this could involve switching to **different suppliers**, or selling **output through new channels**. The **Internet** has opened up new possibilities for identifying new suppliers worldwide and for **selling direct to customers** instead of through distributors.

There is no single model for the ideal supply chain, and supply chain management can involve:

(a)   Decisions about improving collaboration with suppliers by sharing information and through the joint development of new products

(b)   Switching to new suppliers by purchasing on-line

(c)   Outsourcing some activities that were previously performed in-house

2.4 Issues facing supply chain managers

FAST FORWARD

> Supply chain managers need to consider **production, supply, inventory, location, transportation and information.**

2.4.1 Production

The customer often wants suppliers to respond to their particular requirements, and to customise orders to their specific needs. A supply chain that can **respond quickly to individual customer requirements** is known as an **'agile' supply chain**.

Issues for management include deciding **what** products or components to make, and **where** to make them. Should the production of components, sub-assemblies or even the final product be done in-house or by external suppliers?

Management **focus** is on **capacity**, **quality** and **order volume**. Production has to be scheduled so as to provide a sufficient workload for the production resources, and to achieve work load balance (so as to avoid both production bottlenecks and under-utilisation of resources). Quality control is an issue, because producing poor-quality output has implications for both cost and customer dissatisfaction.

The **challenge** is to **meet customer orders immediately**, **without** having to invest heavily in **inventories** of finished goods, which are wasteful and expensive.

2.4.2 Supply

Most manufacturing companies cannot make everything themselves and still keep the quality of their output high. Decisions have to be made about how much should be purchased from 'outside'. Some companies have chosen to **close in-house production facilities** and **switch to external suppliers**, so that they can **concentrate on their 'core competences' where they add most value**.

In choosing external suppliers, management need to consider the capabilities of the supplier, and the extent to which a close collaboration will be necessary. (Collaboration is much more important for key supplies, and much less important for low-cost general supplies that can be purchased from numerous sources.) **Distinctive competences** of supplier and the organisation should be **similar.** An organisation selling 'cheap and cheerful goods' will want suppliers who are able to supply 'cheap and cheerful' subcomponents. The management focus should be on the **speed, quality and flexibility of supply**, as well as on cost.

2.4.3 Inventory

If a firm holds large amounts of inventory, it should be able to meet many customer orders immediately out of inventory and should not suffer hold-ups due to inventory shortages. Holding inventory is expensive, however, and there is no certainty that finished goods inventories will ever find a customer, unless they have been made to satisfy specific customer orders. **Ideally, inventory levels should be minimised, but without damaging the ability of the firm to meet customer orders quickly or holding up work flow due to a stock-out of key supplies**.

In managing inventory levels, organisations need to know, with as much certainty as possible, the **lead time** for delivery of supplies and for the production of goods. Unknown lead times increase the chance of too little or too much inventory, both of which are costly for organisations.

Hewlett Packard tracks, for each supplier, on-time performance, average days or hours late, and the degree of inconsistency (the standard deviation of late measures) so that it has an idea of how much extra inventory to hold whilst minimising the probability of stockouts.

To control costs and improve the supply chain, leading organisations use **vendor-managed inventory (VMI)**. By giving over (or sharing) the responsibility of managing inventories with (or to) suppliers, buyers reduce inventory carrying costs and receive improved service from suppliers. Suppliers gain better insight into buyers' requirements and processes and have a clearer picture of future demands.

2.4.4 Location

Decisions need to be made about where to locate production facilities and warehousing facilities. Cost and tax issues might result in production facilities being constructed in **emerging market economies**.

2.4.5 Transportation

Logistics management is another aspect of supply chain management. Supplies need to be delivered to a firm's premises and finished goods delivered to customers **efficiently, reliably** and at a **low cost**.

2.4.6 Information

Information resources throughout the supply chain need to be **linked together**, for speed of information exchange and to reduce wasteful paper work. Some firms link their computer networks, or share information through the Internet.

2.4.7 Overall management

Managing the supply chain therefore calls for an **understanding of** and **knowledge about**:

    (a)   **Customer demand patterns**
    (b)   **Service level requirements** (speed of delivery expectations, quality expectations, and so on)
    (c)   **Distance considerations** (logistics)
    (d)   **Cost**

2.5 Using information and technology

T FORWARD

EDI, the **Internet** and **software applications** have had a huge impact on supply chain management.

A firm can **share** its **information** about expected customer demand and orders in the pipeline, so that the **suppliers can get ready** themselves for orders that might come to them from the firm. 'Modern' supply chain management uses the **Internet** to share information as soon as it is available. A firm might have an integrated **enterprise resource planning (ERP)** system sitting on a web site or on a server running on the internet. The ERP runs the supply chain database, holding information about a wide range of items, such as customer orders, inventory levels, pricing structures and so on.

The use of EDI, Internet technology and software applications means that **suppliers know what a customer needs before the customer asks**. A supplier that 'knows' what his customers want does not have to guess or wait until the customer places an order. It will be able to **better plan its own delivery systems**. Technology has made the concept of the **'seamless' supply chain** a reality. The development of creative links with suppliers and customers provides organisations with the chance of **competitive advantage over competitors unwilling or unable to invest the time and resources in improving their supply chains**.

A critical issue for successful supply chain management is the **speed** with which activities can be carried out and customer demands met. If a firm, helped by its suppliers and sub-suppliers in the chain, can **respond quickly and flexibly** to customer requirements, the benefits will come from **lower inventories, lower operating costs, better product availability and greater customer satisfaction**.

 Case Study

Supply chain management and customisation of orders

Personal computer production provides an interesting example of how supply chain management can be used to provide fast delivery of customised products, thereby creating a 'flexible' or 'agile' supply chain.

When customers expect fast delivery of their orders for personal computers, and at the same time want PCs produced to their individual specifications, the parts needed to deliver the item to the customer must exist somewhere within the supply chain. A PC manufacturer operating in a build-to-order market relies on suppliers keeping inventory available, so that the manufacturer can minimise its own inventories without compromising the time needed to deliver the order to the customer. In the case of Dell Computers (reported in a *Financial Times* supplement on supply chain management, 20 June 2001), Dell itself held about five days' supply and other firms in the supply chain held about ten days' inventory of supplier-owned items. Replenishment of inventories took between 12 hours and two days.

'Build-to-order involves balancing what is available with what the customers want and Dell has become expert in gently massaging both these factors. Any shortage in a particular component is immediately countered by offering other available products on promotion.... By monitoring component inventory availability in real time, Dell and its suppliers can quickly see problems with any particular part. A first step is to increase lead time, informing customers that their preferred configuration will take eight to 10 days to deliver rather than the usual five. If that does not slow up demand, then would-be customers are offered a more expensive upgrade for the same price. "Everyone wins," [says Dell's vice president in the US]. "Our customers get a better deal, the suppliers get business and we can satisfy demand."'

The efficiency of the Dell build-to-order system depends on data sharing between Dell and its suppliers, and the integrity of the information databases. All systems throughout the supply chain are integrated, with common parts numbers and automated order processing and parts management.

 Case Study

20% Savings to be had in Sausage Supply Chain

Savings of up to 20% are potentially available across the pork sausage supply chain, according to a comprehensive case study published today by the Food Chain Centre and Red Meat Industry Forum.

The team mapped the pork sausage chain from farm to checkout and uncovered tremendous scope for improvement:

(a) Waste from losses and defects in the chain (eg quality faults, part-loaded vehicles, damaged goods, theft) amounted to almost 20%

(b) Total time from farm to shelf was just over seven days, of which value-adding time was just 1.4 hours

(c) Average product availability on the shelf was less than 95%

(d) Inventory in the system from abattoir to supermarket totalled seven days

This is despite the fact that many practices in the supply chain were leading edge and highlights the scope for improvement in all food chains.

The group involving Tesco and its pork suppliers ... examined how they could improve business efficiency and quality for the consumer. Any cost savings made will be shared equitably among the group members.

As a result, key projects have been identified as priorities over the next year. They include:

(a) Improving the system of pig production through better feed rations, reducing transport times eg by linking farms and abattoirs in the same area

(b) Using new technology to assess the value of producers' animals more accurately

(c) A production line for sausage manufacture, which reduces physical handling of the product

These projects affect all parts of the sausage supply chain and will form part of the continuous improvement process that Tesco and its suppliers are embarking upon.

(Taken from the website of *The Food Chain Centre* (8 June 2004), part of a national strategy to improve the competitiveness and profitability of farming)

3 Outsourcing

A significant trend in recent years has been for organisations and government bodies to **concentrate on their core competences** – what they are really good at (or set up to achieve) – and **turn other activities over to specialist contractors.** An organisation that earns its profits from, say, manufacturing bicycles, does not also need to have expertise in, say, mass catering or office cleaning. **Facilities management companies** such as Rentokil have grown in response to this.

term

Outsourcing is 'The use of external suppliers as a source of finished products, components or services. This is also known as **contract manufacturing** or **sub-contracting.** (CIMA *Official Terminology*)

3.1 Reasons for this trend

(a)   Frequently the decision is made on the grounds that **specialist contractors** can offer **superior quality** and **efficiency**. If a contractor's main business is making a specific component it can invest in the specialist machinery and labour and knowledge skills needed to make that component. However, this component may be only one of many needed by the contractor's customer, and the complexity of components is now such that attempting to keep internal facilities up to the standard of specialists detracts from the main business of the customer. For example, Dell Computers buys the Pentium chip for its personal computers from Intel because it does not have the know-how and technology to make the chip itself.

(b)   Contracting out manufacturing **frees capital** that can then be invested in core activities such as market research, product definition, product planning, marketing and sales.

(c)   **Contractors** have the **capacity** and **flexibility** to start production very quickly to meet sudden **variations in demand**. In-house facilities may not be able to respond as quickly, because of the need to redirect resources from elsewhere.

FAST FORWARD

Some observers predict that in ten to 20 years, most organisations will have **outsourced** every part of the value chain except for the few key components that are unique and sources of **competitive advantage**.

Case Studies

(a)   '… chocolate confectionary companies in the UK will sell Easter eggs promoting their brands and products every spring. Mars, for instance, will provide chocolate eggs containing mini Mars products, or in packaging highlighting Mars products around the egg. The reason that you might be tempted to buy one of these eggs is because it has Mars products associated with it. Mars therefore doesn't have to produce the egg itself – that activity can be outsourced. After all, it would be expensive to maintain production facilities for chocolate eggs for only a couple of months a year.

However, you might buy a Cadbury's Easter egg because it is made of Cadbury's chocolate. Therefore Cadbury's needs the operational capability to produce Easter eggs. The company has focused on marketing and sales activities to develop the Cadbury's Crème Egg into a product that is sold all year round, thereby making the operation viable. The decision whether or not to outsource can often be bound strongly to an organisation's competitive strategy and focuses on how strategic the activity is to the organisation.'   (G Pitcher, 'The Missing Link', CIMA *Student*)

(b)   The Sara Lee Corporation has outsourced every part of its value chain except for the management and control of its Sara Lee brand name of pastries and other food items, its most important competitive advantage.

3.2 Internal and external services

In administrative and support functions, too, organisations are increasingly likely to use specialist companies. **Decisions** such as the following are now common.

(a)   Whether the **design and development of a new computer system** should be entrusted to in-house data processing staff or whether an external software house should be hired to do the work

(b)   Whether **maintenance and repairs** of certain items of equipment should be dealt with by in-house engineers, or whether a maintenance contract should be made with a specialist organisation

Even if you are not aware of specialist 'facilities management' companies such as Securicor, you will be familiar with the idea of office cleaning being done by contractors.

3.3 Choosing the activities to outsource

FAST FORWARD

Any activity is a candidate for outsourcing unless the organisation **must control it to maintain its competitive position** or if the organisation can **deliver it on a level comparable with the best organisations in the world**.

Within the value chain, both primary activities and support activities are candidates for outsourcing, although many can be **eliminated** from the list immediately either **because the activity cannot be contracted out or because the organisation must control it to maintain its competitive position**. Coca Cola does not outsource the manufacture of its concentrate to safeguard its formula and retain control of the product.

Of the remaining activities, an organisation **should carry out only those that it can deliver on a level comparable with the best organisations in the world**. If the organisation cannot achieve benchmarked levels of performance, the activity should be outsourced so that the organisation is **only concentrating on those core activities that enhance its competitive advantage**.

A differential cost analysis should then be carried out on outsourcing possibilities. Some argue that this analysis should be over the long term, using discounted cash flow analysis.

3.4 Advantages and disadvantages

The **advantages** of outsourcing are as follows.

(a) It **frees up time** taken by existing staff on the contracted-out activities.

(b) It allows the company to **take advantage of specialist expertise and equipment** rather than investing in these facilities itself and underutilising them. If the contractor is judiciously chosen it is likely that the service will be performed more **quickly** and to a **higher standard** than is currently the case.

(c) It **frees up time spent supporting the contracted-out services** by staff not directly involved, for example supervisory staff, personnel staff. There may also be no need to provide facilities for the service to be performed (though not in all cases: a contracted-out canteen would still usually be located on the business premises of the workers it serves).

(d) It may be **cheaper**, once time savings and opportunity costs are taken into account

(e) It is particularly **appropriate** when an organisation is **attempting to expand in a time of uncertainty**, because it allows the use of facilities on a short-term (readily-cancelled) basis which would only otherwise be available via the relatively long-term investments of a permanent employee and the training he or she requires. In other words it is a way of gaining all the benefits of extra capacity without having to find the full cost.

However there are also a number of **disadvantages**.

(a) Without monitoring there is **no guarantee** that the service will be **performed to the organisation's satisfaction**. There may be **penalty clauses** built into the contract for poor performance, but financial compensation will not necessarily undo the damage caused. However, if a contract has to be too closely monitored this weakens the argument for contracting out in the first place.

(b) There is a good chance that contracting out will be **more expensive** than providing the service in-house.

(c)   By performing services itself the organisation retains or develops **skills** that may be needed in the future and will otherwise be **lost**.

(d)   Contracting out any aspect of information-handling carries with it the possibility that **commercially sensitive data will get into the wrong hands.** The contractor will not be able to guarantee absolute security.

(e)   There may be some **ethical reservations**. For example, contract cleaning companies are notorious for exploiting staff, offering inadequate pay and poor conditions.

(f)   There will almost certainly be **opposition from employees** and their representatives if contracting out involves redundancies. Great care is needed in this area as the contracting-out organisation and the new supplier have statutory responsibilities under 'transfer of undertakings' legislation.

> **FAST FORWARD**
>
> To minimise the risks associated with outsourcing, organisations generally enter into **long-run contracts** with their suppliers that specify costs, quality and delivery schedules. They build **close partnerships** or **alliances** with a few key suppliers, collaborating with suppliers on design and manufacturing decisions, and building a culture and commitment for quality and timely delivery.

Organisations such as Ford and Sony have allowed suppliers to gain expertise and grow. These suppliers have researched and developed innovative new products, met demands for increased quantities, maintained quality and on-time delivery and lowered costs – actions that Ford and Sony would not have had the competences to achieve.

 Case Studies

(a)   **'VW takes outsourcing to the limit**

Volkswagen's bus and truck plant in Resende, Brazil, is a virtual plant. VW has completely outsourced manufacturing to a team of carefully selected supplier-partners in a radical experiment in production operations. At Resende, VW is transformed from manufacturer to general contractor, overseeing assembly operations performed by seven German, US, Brazilian and Japanese components suppliers, with no one VW employee so much as turning a screw. Only 200 of the total 1,000 Resende workers are actual VW employees.

When designing the Resende plant, VW asked suppliers to bid for the opportunity to own one of seven major modules required to build a car, such as axles and brakes, and engine and transmission. Suppliers have invested $50 million to build, equip and inventory their areas. VW's contract with suppliers is for 10- to 15-year periods with the conditions that suppliers must achieve specified cost and performance targets and maintain cutting-edge technologies.

The plant is divided into seven zones, demarcated by yellow floor stripes. Within the boundaries of its zone, each supplier assembles its component from subcomponents sourced from 400 minor suppliers. In parallel with subcomponent assembly, final assembly occurs as the chassis (the vehicle platform) passes through the zones, and each company adds its respective component-module until the finished VW rolls off the line. Following each vehicle through the line is a single VW employee – a master craftsman assigned to track the vehicle and solve problems on the spot. Suppliers are paid for each completed vehicle that passes final inspection.

Despite representing seven different companies, the suppliers operate as a highly integrated team, wearing the same uniforms and receiving the same pay. The assembly line is highly cross-functional, with representatives from each supplier meeting each morning to plan the day's production, and each evening to address issues and solve any problems. Each supplier has visibility of the entire production process, which stimulates ideas for simplification, streamlining and product and process changes.

The specialization and superior component knowledge of each supplier, combined with the close interaction among suppliers, improves quality and efficiency. Co-location of the major components and final assemblies improves production flow and compresses total assembly time. It also simplifies logistics and reduces materials-handling, production control, manufacturing engineering and co-ordination costs.

Although the plan remains in start-up mode, preliminary results look promising. Resende employs 800 manufacturing workers instead of 2,500 at a comparable older VW plant. The time to assemble a truck has been reduced from 52 hours to 35 hours. These improvements have enabled VW to quickly earn a 19% share in the Brazilian truck market and a 23% share in the bus market.'

(Horngren, Foster, Datar, *Cost Accounting: A Managerial Emphasis*)

(b) Albright and Davis ('The Elements of Supply Chain Management') describe the extreme outsourcing approach adopted by Mercedes.

Instead of contracting with suppliers for parts, Mercedes outsourced the modules making up a completed M-class to suppliers who purchase the subcomponents and assemble the modules for Mercedes.

This has led to a reduction in plant and warehouse space needed, and a dramatic reduction in the number of suppliers used (from 35 to one for the cockpit, for example).

At the beginning of the production process Mercedes maintained strict control in terms of quality and cost on both the first tier suppliers (who provide finished modules) and the second tier suppliers (from whom the first tier suppliers purchase parts). As the level of trust grew between Mercedes and the first tier suppliers, Mercedes allowed them to make their own arrangements with second tier suppliers.

Benefits of this approach for Mercedes

(i) Reduction in purchasing overhead

(ii) Reduction in labour and employee-related costs

(iii) Higher level of service from suppliers

(iv) Supplier expertise in seeking ways to improve current operations

(v) Suppliers working together to continuously improve both their own module and the integrated product

3.5 Current trends in outsourcing

FORWARD

In an effort to cut costs, many organisations are now outsourcing activities both **near shore (such as Eastern Europe)** and **offshore (such as the Far East and India).**

Improvements in technology and telecommunications and more willingness for managers to manage people they can't see have fuelled this trend.

Before taking the decision to outsource overseas, a number of points should be **considered**.

(a) **Environmental** (location, infrastructure, risk, cultural compatibility, time differences)

(b) **Labour** (experience in relevant fields, language barriers, size of labour market, level of education of the workforce)

(c) **Management** (remote management)

(d) **Bad press** associated with the perception of jobs leaving the home country

Case Study

Call centres

The inside of a call centre will look virtually the same wherever it is in the world, similar headsets, hardware and software being used, for example. With pressure to provide adequate customer service at low cost, many organisations are closing call centres in parts of Western Europe and relocating to low-cost countries and regions, such as India and South Africa.

It is claimed that savings on call centre costs range from 35% to 55% for near shore outsourcing and 50% to 75% for offshore outsourcing.

3.5.1 Outsourcing to Eastern Europe

The newly-enlarged EU is providing organisations in Western Europe with a range of outsourcing opportunities. The vast **manufacturing facilities that were used to produce for the massive Soviet market,** many of which have been re-equipped, provide the opportunity for manufacturing to be outsourced.

At the moment, **labour is relatively cheap in Eastern Europe**, and it is **closer than the Far East** – an important consideration in today's rapidly-moving environment. The fact that **English is widely taught** and the existence of a **Western culture** are added attractions.

Currently the Czech Republic, Hungary and Poland are popular, but as wage differentials with Western Europe narrow and eradicate much of the rationale for going there, countries such as the Ukraine, Bulgaria and Romania become alternative options. Romania, for instance, has a 97% literacy rate and high school graduates must be fluent in two other languages. And in less than five years the economic, political and telecom infrastructures of these countries should have improved to the point where they can sustain servicing Western European call centres, for example.

There are problems associated with outsourcing to Eastern Europe, however. Operations in many countries are bound by an **excess of red tape**, for example, and **current political and market uncertainty in Russia** could constrain growth there for some time.

 Case Study

In September 2003, DHL, the logistics firm, announced it was shifting its data centre in Britain and parts of its IT operations in Switzerland to a state-of-the-art services centre in Prague that will oversee all of the organisation's European IT operations.

3.5.2 Outsourcing to India

Moving **back-office functions 'offshore'** began in earnest in the early 1990s when organisations such as American Express, British Airways, General Electric and Swissair set up their own 'captive' outsourcing operations in India.

Indian IT organisations got their big breaks as subcontractors to overloaded Western firms **during the Y2K software crisis** and are now powerful players in the market for offshore IT services. And **big Western outsourcing organisations** such as Accenture are now **developing their own facilities abroad** in order to move more of their outsourcing business, currently performed in the West, to offshore destinations.

The **low labour cost** in India has always made the outsourcing option attractive. But not only is it cheap, it is **highly skilled**. India has one of the most developed education systems in the world. One third of college graduates speak more than two languages fluently and of the two million graduates per annum, 80% speak English. These language skills, along with **improved telecomms capabilities**, make it an ideal choice for **call centres**. GE, Accenture and IBM have all set up call centres in India.

The existence of **large, English-speaking scientific specialist computer institutions** mean that India has **attracted huge chunks of the outsourced IT market**. It has more software companies with ISO 9000 accreditation than any other country in the world (G M Noceti, 'Why it makes sense to outsource'. *Strategic Publishing Partners*, June 2004).

'A report by HSBC says that the cost of a one-minute telephone call from India to America and Britain has fallen by more than 80% since January 2001. With high-grade jobs, the saving on wages is not as high as with lower-grade ones. NASSCOM, India's National Association of Software and Service Companies, reckons that an IT professional with three to five years' programming experience earns $96,000 in Britain, $75,000 in America and $26,000 in India. At the other end of the scale, low-grade call-centre jobs that in Britain earn a salary of $20,000 earn less than one-tenth of that in India.' ('Relocating the back office', *The Economist,* December 2003)

The vast majority of service jobs being outsourced offshore are **paper-based back office ones** that can be **digitalised and telecommunicated anywhere around the world**, and **routine telephone enquiries** that can be bundled together into call centres.

3.5.3 Reasons for the popularity of India for outsourcing

(a)   Infrastructure improvements

(b)   Rapid access to the high-quality, numerous and readily-available IT professionals

(c)   Lower costs, not just labour costs (such as falling telecommunications costs)

(d)   The Internet

(e)   Time differences (India is four hours behind the UK) can be used to extend the working day, which is particularly useful if the off-shore organisation provides support or maintenance

(f)   Tax incentives

(g)   Quality certifications (Six Sigma, ISO 9000 and so on)

 Case Studies

(a)   In October 2003, HSBC announced it was taking 4,000 jobs from Britain to India.

(b)   In December 2003, Aviva (the insurance group) said it was transferring 2,350 jobs to India.

Cost advantages of outsourcing are **being eroded**, however. Salaries in the IT sector in India have been rising in line with demand for skilled workers as firms like Infosys invest heavily in training and facilities.

3.5.4 The future

According to the *Economist* article, a study in 2002 by Forrester, a research group, claimed that 3.3 million white-collar American jobs (500,000 in IT) would shift offshore to countries like India by 2015. But there is **still a long way to go**. Offshoring accounts for just 3% to 4% of US organisations' outsourcing, and 60% of the US Fortune 1,000 companies have done nothing to investigate the potential for offshoring.

Case Study

In 'Tuning into offshore value,' (*Sunday Business Post On-line*, 5 October 2003), Fran Gleeson explained why traditional offshore locations (such as Ireland) are losing out to India and Eastern Europe.

(a)   Dell, which was considered to be Ireland's biggest exporter by the Irish Export Association, has quite a sizeable presence in India. For example, in 2001, the company set up Dell International Services in Bangalore, India, to provide technical support by phone and e-mail to its customers in the US, Europe, and the Asia-Pacific region. In less than a year and a half its staff had grown from 180 to 800.

(b)   In the last ten years, Ireland's automotive jobs have moved largely to Eastern Europe and textile facilities were largely relocated to the Far East, giving way to more high tech industries.

(c)   Education is an area where Ireland is having difficulty competing, falling short by thousands of India's annual number of PhD graduates, with Eastern European countries and parts of Latin America closing the gap in the education sector as a whole.

(d)   The uncompetitive cost of doing business in Ireland was highlighted in a recent study conducted by AT Kearney and reviewed by the World Bank, Unesco and other research houses, in which 11 countries were assessed to determine their attractiveness for outsourcing.

Ireland was the second least favourable destination in terms of cost, after Canada. The cost factor in the study was broken into the cost of labour, management and infrastructure, and tax or treasury impact. Ireland had the second highest labour costs and management and infrastructure costs after Canada and the impact of taxation here was the greatest of all 11 countries, which included India, China, Russia and the Czech Republic.

India was the most cost competitive. Labour costs in Ireland are three times those in India, according to the report. At that rate, a business moving to India would save over €40,000 on an experienced software programmer, when compared to the IDA (Watson) rate of €61,518.

4 Partnering, incentives and gain-sharing arrangements

FAST FORWARD

In some situations, normal competitive pressures do not apply in relationships between customers and contractors. This might be because of the size of the project (say in the construction or civil engineering industries), because there are a limited number of contractors or because of security issues (as in defence work). In such circumstances, **partnering**, **incentives** and **gain-sharing arrangements** are required.

4.1 Partnering

Key term

'**Partnering** involves two or more organisations working together to improve performance through agreeing mutual objectives, devising a way for resolving any disputes and committing themselves to continuous improvement, measuring progress and sharing gains.'

Egan Report '*Rethinking Construction*', 1998

Partnering is therefore a **structured management approach** to **facilitate team working across the boundaries of contracts**. It is widely used in the construction industry and within Government departments such as the Ministry of Defence.

4.1.1 Fundamental components of partnering

(a) Mutual interdependence and trust (as opposed to a blame culture)
(b) Identification of common goals for success
(c) Agreed decision-making and problem-solving procedures
(d) Commitment to continuous improvement
(e) Team working down the entire product and supply chain
(f) Gain share and pain share arrangements (incentives)
(g) Open book accounting
(h) Targets that provide continuous measurable improvements in performance

4.1.2 Claimed benefits of partnering

(a) Cost savings
(b) Improved profit margins
(c) Reduction in project times
(d) More predictability of costs and quality
(e) Increased customer satisfaction
(f) Improved quality and safety

4.1.3 When to use partnering

For partnering arrangements to be successful, they need the full and visible **support from very senior management** of each organisation. Partnering is not just a bolt on extra that delivers results through one partnering workshop. It is a **continuous process** that needs **sustained effort** by all of the parties to deliver measurable benefits. Partnering arrangements are likely to fail if efforts to contribute to their success are not sustained.

Partnering is **particularly suitable in the following circumstances**.

(a) If significant input is required from specialist contractors or subcontractors (such as in the construction of a new airport terminal)

(b) If there is a rapid expansion of a programme of construction (say, if a supermarket chain opens lots of new branches)

(c) If time is a critical factor

(d) If projects are repetitive and based upon a set of standard designs (such as the construction of McDonalds restaurants)

(e) If there is a particular construction problem which is best solved by a team of experts (such as the construction of oil rigs)

Partnering is **less suitable in the following circumstances**.

(a) If it is important that costs can be predicted with certainty

(b) If the project is a one-off, commissioned by a one-off customer (as the benefits of team building and supply chain management cannot be easily achieved on a single project)

(c) If the customer has little knowledge of the construction process (as partnering requires active involvement of a knowledgeable client)

4.1.4 Types of partnering

Two key types of partnering arrangement exist.

(a) **Strategic partnering** (longer-term partnering for agreements involving more than one project)

(b) **Project specific partnering**.

The Reading Construction Forum report "The Seven Pillars of Partnering" notes that Strategic Partnering has been known to deliver cost savings of 40% and time savings of more than 50%. In comparison, the cost savings for project specific partnering lie in the range 2% to 10%.

The **greater benefits from strategic partnering** arrangements arise because the lessons learnt from one project can be applied to further similar projects through a process of continuous improvement. Strategic partnering arrangements should be adopted in preference to project specific partnering arrangements wherever possible.

Irrespective of the type of partnering relationship that the customer enters into with a primary supplier (such as the main contractor or main consultant), significant benefits (in achieving overall value for money) can be obtained where a primary supplier has entered into strategic partnering arrangements with secondary suppliers (such as sub-contractors or sub-consultants). Supply chain relationships of this type are essential to obtain the maximum benefits from partnering.

4.1.5 Partnering contracts

A contract is required to ensure that all parties are certain of their risks and responsibilities. This encourages **openness and trust**.

An effective partnering contract must be able to deal with any problems in the project and a team-based solution found.

The **defensive attitude embodied in traditional contracts** is a major **obstacle** to the partnering process, however, and so a new form of contractual arrangement is required.

4.2 Incentivisation

Incentives should be **included** in contracts or in **partnering arrangements**, to encourage designers, constructors and/or other suppliers to **provide benefits** to the client significantly **beyond those contracted for** (by using innovation or different working practices to deliver the same or better service whilst yielding cost savings) and **rewarding them for doing so**.

Incentives should **encourage the parties to work together to eliminate wasteful activities that do not add value to the client** and to **identify and implement process improvements, alternative designs, working methods and other activities that result in added value**.

Incentives should **not be given merely for doing a good job** (in other words, meeting the contractual requirements) nor should they be made for improvements in performance that are of no value to the client (such as completing a building contract three months early when the client is still committed to paying rent, rates and other charges on the existing premises).

Here are some examples of features of project performance that can be considered for incentivisation.

(a)   Cost
(b)   Time
(c)   Quality
(d)   Operational efficiency
(e)   Productivity
(f)   Value for the customer
(g)   Safety

Savings can also be **shared amongst members of the supply chain**, **based on pre-agreed proportions**, so that profits for contractors and suppliers are increased. Alternatively, cost savings can be used by the customer to commission additional work from the partnering team, which again increases the profitability of the supply chain.

Incentive schemes can **also operate 'negatively'**, with the costs of unforeseen risks and problems being shared.

4.2.1 Examples of incentivisation

(a) **Better fee structure**

This applies if the timing and scope of payments deliver a better or lower priced contract.

Case Study

The Highways Agency sets a target completion date for major road maintenance contracts. If contractors 'beat' this date, a bonus is paid. Failure to meet the target date results in a reduction in baseline fees (subject to a maximum figure).

(b) **Enhanced performance and quality**

This applies if a contractor provides a better or faster service than would be delivered under a traditional contract.

Case Study

In a contract for facilities management at one of its sites, the Inland Revenue benchmarked the service required against similar contracts, studied the performance required, established the degree of risk and extent of the profit and savings that might accrue. Fees and costs were fixed and incentives for sharing savings were established. Open book accounting regimes were agreed. Savings were achieved and at the conclusion of each year these savings became a base line for future years. The Inland Revenue makes a 50/50 payment share of increased margin to the contractor.

(c) **Target cost incentive scheme**

This applies where a target cost is set based on a given set of parameters. If this fixed target is exceeded or undercut, the outcome is split between the contractor and the customer. These are also known as gain-sharing arrangements.

4.3 Gain sharing arrangements

In pain/gain sharing arrangements, **all cost overruns and cost savings are shared between the customer and the contractor**. A target cost is negotiated and agreed. If the actual cost is less than the target cost, the customer and contractor (and sometimes the contractor's supply chain) split any savings between them in agreed proportions. Likewise any cost overruns are shared by both parties. Sometimes the contractor's share of any cost overrun is up to a pre-arranged limit, and there may be time limits for the gain to be realised.

This does not mean that contractors or suppliers get extra for doing what they are basically contracted to do, but for exceeding those targets. Cost savings should not be seen as incentives to be shared if the scope or standard of work is simply reduced.

Cost savings might be generated from reducing the cost of raw materials, implementing new technologies or suggesting and implementing improvements in operations. The Ministry of Defence see gain sharing as 'a reward for innovative thinking by the contractor'.

Because the resulting benefits from a gain-sharing arrangement are shared, there is an incentive for both parties to look for cost-cutting opportunities.

Many contracts involving these arrangements have **emphasis on greater openness** and **shared development and improvement**.

The Ministry of Defence, for example, is committed to gain sharing as a method of improving the efficient use of the defence procurement budget.

4.3.1 What are the gains?

The gain, benefit or advantage to be shared is **not necessarily financial**, although financial benefits are likely to occur frequently. The Ministry of Defence, for example, will not necessarily take cost savings in the form of a lower contract value but might require a higher specification.

4.3.2 Where might gain-sharing opportunities exist?

Gain-sharing opportunities can exist in various areas of a contract and the associated supply chain.

(a) Reduced or increased **technical specifications or levels of performance** required, perhaps through advances in technology

(b) Revised **delivery** times may lead to reduced costs and/or improved performance

(c) Opportunities for the generation of an **income stream** from the use of the customer's assets by or for a **third party** could emerge or be developed.

(d) Opportunities may be found **within the supply chain**.

4.3.3 How are financial gains assessed?

In order to assess any financial benefit, both parties should provide each other with access to relevant cost data to determine the basis for the valuation of the benefit and the calculation and sharing of the benefit (**open book accounting**).

 Case Studies

(a) Portsmouth City Council and Clenmay Maintenance Services shared gains from a saving of $71,330 on a target cost of $1.4 million.

(b) Camden Council expanded a roofing refurbishment programme to include window replacement from savings identified by the contractor.

(c) The consortium which manages the UK arm of the Eurostar train service between London, Paris and Brussels (EUKL) is incentivised to maximise the performance of EUKL with pain-share/gain-share arrangements based on agreed annual targets for EUKL's operating cashflow.

(d) **Christchurch Junior School Replacement Project Partnering**

'This is a $2.25 million partnering contract between Dorset County Council, Alfred McAlpine Special Projects and other supply chain partners; the **school** and local community were closely involved during design and construction. The **project** incorporated the principles of a guaranteed maximum price within incentivised arrangements using a 50/50 pain/gain share arrangement. The key outcomes and benefits of this **project** are:

(i)   Savings against the guaranteed maximum price of around $0.25 million and a saving against conventional construction of 9%

(ii)   **Project** duration 7 weeks less than prediction using conventional construction

(iii)   Innovative sustainable construction benefits to reduce running costs, energy and water usage including recycling of rainwater to flush WC's.'

(From the website of the Local Government Association www.lga.gov.uk)

(e)   The Army Base Repair Organisation use target cost incentives in contracts for the maintenance of equipment. Bidders are required to quote a target cost and an additional payment is made if that target is bettered, whilst the payment is reduced if it is exceeded. Both minimum and maximum payments are capped by a predetermined percentage.

(f)   The Office of the Gas and Electricity Markets (Ofgem), which supports the Gas and Electricity Markets Authority, the regulator of the gas and electricity industries in Great Britain has a system operator incentive scheme which sets National Grid Company (NGC) a target cost for running the system efficiently and economically. If NGC outperforms this target it keeps a percentage of the savings, if it overspends it bears a percentage of the costs. In this way the incentive scheme encourages NGC to operate the transmission system efficiently and economically by providing it with an appropriate balance of risk and reward. Ofgem has proposed a target of $415m, compared to the current target of $416m. The proposals sharpen the existing incentives and should see further reductions in the costs of system operation over time to the benefit of customers, who ultimately pay these costs.

Question

Gain sharing arrangements

Learning outcome: D(ix)

The Prime Contracting Initiative marks an innovation in the approach adopted by the Defence Estates on behalf of the Ministry of Defence (MoD) in the UK for the procurement of its capital and maintenance construction work. The Defence Estates arm of the MoD spends well in excess of $1 billion a year and its portfolio ranges from simple structures to complex airfields, garrisons and naval bases.

Required

Describe briefly what you think could be the main features of Prime Contracting.

Note. You are not required to know the specifics of the initiative. You should simply set out some general principles for supply contracts between contractors and the MoD.

Answer

Here are some of the actual principles of and details about the Prime Contracting Initiative, taken from 'Prime Contracting – the UK experience and the way forward' by David M Jones, an external adviser to the Defence Estates and a member of the small working party empowered to deliver Prime Contracting. Obviously you are unlikely to have come up with this level of detail but you should have mentioned some of the basic points.

(a)   **Collaborative working**. 'The intention behind the Prime Contracting Initiative in facilitating best value to the customer is to foster a more collaborative and less adversarial relationship between the MoD and the Prime Contractor…..The Core Conditions give opportunities throughout the contract period for collaboration and discussion between the Defence Estates Project Manager (DEPM) for each contract and the Prime Contractor….. There are opportunities for continual adjustment and improvement within the relationship, not least to provide good feedback among the contract members. This will be vital to develop trust, to work on upgrading performance and to add value…… and having a common interest and willingness to co-operate to meet mutual goals'.

(b)   **Gain-sharing arrangement**. 'Of importance, the Core Conditions include a Target Cost pricing mechanism and a pain/gain sharing arrangement between the MoD and the Prime Contractor for both cost under-runs and over-runs up to a Maximum Price Target Cost (MPTC). In the most important area, therefore, there is significant sharing and incentives on both parties......This arrangement is considered to provide the strongest incentive for industry to improve performance and innovate thereby increasing value to the MoD and providing an opportunity for the Prime Contractor's level of profit to increase to reflect his improved performance.... It is expected that Prime Contractors will be entitled to a fair profit margin, bringing tangible benefits from the Prime Contracting approach, which should be passed down through the Supply Chain.'

(c)   **Open book accounting**. 'Throughout the entire contract period the Prime Contractor will be required to operate an "Open Book" accounting regime providing the MoD with access to such relevant financial information as may reasonably be required to, amongst other things:

(i)   monitor actual incurred costs against Target Cost;

(ii)   substantiate claims for payment against milestones;

(iii)   agree changes to the Target Cost to reflect additions/deletions from scope of contract;

(iv)   assess final out-turn costs and final price payable;

(v)   consider impact of innovative proposals. '

(d)   **Project teams**. 'One of the critical success factors of Prime Contracting will be the Authority's ability to become a better-informed client. To achieve this, Prime Contracts will be managed by an MoD Integrated Project Team (IPT) consisting of full time members with all the necessary skills and functions required to deliver the project supported, as appropriate, by specialist advice from industry. Any such support provided will be an integral part of the IPT. Throughout the bidding process organisations will be given the opportunity for greater access to the IPT to ensure that a full understanding of the project can be gained. There will in future be a direct MoD/Prime Contractor interface. After contract award the Prime Contractor will become a full member of the IPT along with his supply chain.'

(e)   **Innovative solutions**. 'Throughout the entire Prime Contract process ie, from advertising the requirement through selection and evaluation and ultimately to delivery of the requirement, Prime Contractors will be encouraged to think of innovative ways of delivering the requirements which demonstrate improved value for money and continuous improvement.'

(f)   **Size and length of contract**. 'Prime Contracts because of their size (they will be substantially concerned with geographical areas rather than single sites) and their duration [often five to seven years] will offer better value for money to both the MoD and to the Prime Contractor than traditional procurement contracts. They represent long term commitment and application by both participants and provide an opportunity for shared learning and development.'

4.4 Further reading

An article appeared in *Financial Management* in June 2006. This article gives a clear explanation of how gain-sharing works and includes plenty of examples.

Read the article and work through the examples yourself.

5 Direct product profitability (DPP)

FAST FORWARD

DPP is a **costing system used by retail businesses.**

5.1 A history lesson

Direct product profitability was first defined in 1963 in a McKinsey study and was further developed during the 1960s by Harvard Business School. It was not until **EPOS** (electronic point of sale) tills and **electronic scanning** were introduced in the late 1980s that the **detailed data became available to allow DPP** to be used fully. Work has been carried out by a number of industry organisations in different countries to produce **unified industry DPP models** with common standards for cost treatment. These include the Institute of Grocery Distribution in the UK and the Food Marketing Institute in the USA.

Prior to the introduction of DPP retail organisations relied on **gross margin** (sales revenue less purchase price) per product group and **sales per square metre** as profitability measures. **Gross margin includes none of the organisation's own costs** and so it provides little information for controlling and planning resources. As some product categories consume more of the organisation's resources than others (storage resource, for example), some attempt had to be made to **relate these direct costs to the products**.

Key terms

> **Direct product profitability (DPP)** is 'Used primarily within the retail sector, [and] involves the attribution of both the purchase price and other indirect costs (eg distribution, warehousing, retailing) to each product line. Thus a net profit, as opposed to a gross profit, can be identified for each product. The cost attribution process utilises a variety of measures (eg warehousing space, transport time) to reflect the resource consumption of individual products.'
> (CIMA, *Official Terminology*)
>
> **Direct product profit** is the contribution a product category makes to fixed costs and profits. It is calculated by deducting direct product costs (such as warehousing and transport) from the product's gross margin.

5.2 Calculation of direct product profit

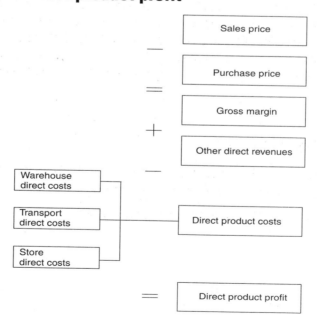

5.2.1 What are other direct revenues?

They occur occasionally, for example if the retailer receives a discount from the manufacturer for point of sale promotion.

5.2.2 What are direct product costs?

These can be **directly attributed** to the handling and storing of individual products.

Direct product cost	Examples
Warehouse direct costs	Offloading, unpacking, picking and sorting, space costs, inventory financing costs
Transport direct costs	Fuel, depreciation of vehicle, driver's salary, vehicle servicing
Store/supermarket direct costs	Receiving and inspecting, moving, shelf filling, space costs, inventory financing costs

Direct product costs may include other product specific costs such as retailer brand development costs.

In general, warehouse, transport and store costs will tend to be spread across the different goods sold in relation to volume or area occupied, as most costs increase in proportion to the volume of the good or the space it occupies.

Rather confusingly, direct product cost also contains **part of the indirect cost** that can be **apportioned** to the product, **based on one or more product characteristics**. For example, the **cost of shelf space** is apportioned by means of the **physical volume** of the product. All other costs, for example Head Office costs, are not included.

In practice each product would be charged with a number of different costs but the following example deals only with the space costs in a store.

5.3 Example: DPP

A supermarket group has estimated that its store space cost is $0.50 per cubic metre per day.

Its product range includes the following products.

(a)   Six-packs of lager – volume: 0.01 cubic metres, days in store: 5
(b)   Detergent – volume: 0.005 cubic metres, days in store: 4
(c)   Double roll of kitchen paper – volume: 0.185 cubic metres, days in store: 3.

Solution

The space costs would be allocated as follows.

Lager $0.50 × 0.01 × 5 = $0.025 per pack
Detergent $0.50 × 0.005 × 4 = $0.01 per pack
Kitchen paper $0.50 × 0.185 × 3 = $0.278 per pack

The results show the need to achieve a high turnover with bulky low price goods. Refrigerated items would carry a higher space cost due to the cost of refrigeration.

5.4 Benefits of using DPP

(a)   Detailed information is provided on the **performance** of an **individual product**.

(b)   Products can be **ranked** according to product profitability.

(c) **Diagnostic capabilities**. Why did a product under perform? Was the inventory turn acceptable?

(d) Profitable product lines can be identified and given more **prominent shelf space**.

(e) Leads to a **mutual understanding** of **product and supply chain** costs and **improves supplier/retailer relationships**

(f) **Better pricing decisions**

(g) **Improved management of store** and **warehouse space**

5.5 Comparison of DPP and gross margin

In 1990 Touche Ross Management Consultants carried out a study of detergent products which highlighted the **inadequacy of using gross margin**. The first chart below shows the gross margin per week of eight detergent products and the first subsequent chart shows the DPP per week for the same products. The difference is dramatic; decisions made on the basis of gross margin in this instance were likely to be incorrect.

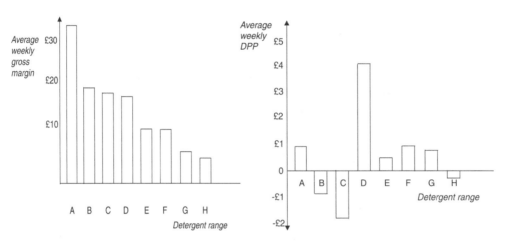

5.6 DPP and ABC

In recent years DPP has become more sophisticated and is now very similar to ABC.

5.7 DPP software systems

These allow 'what if?' analysis to be carried out. A number of key variables can be changed to analyse different scenarios.

(a) **Prices at which products are bought and sold**. The higher the selling price relative to other retailers, the slower the likely inventory movement.

(b) **Rate of selling.** This is a key variable and needs to be as high as possible to minimise warehouse and store space costs, and to ensure that interest on money tied up in inventory is not lost.

(c) **Size of stockholding.** In line with JIT principles, inventory should be kept to a minimum but stock-outs avoided.

(d) **Size of the product.** This variable requires consideration as it is one of the drivers of space cost per item.

(e) **Configuration of pallets.** The handling cost per unit falls as the number of cases on a pallet increases.

(f) **Ordering cost.** A balance has to be found because ordering only occasionally will mean ordering costs are minimised but inventory levels are higher.

(g) **Distribution routes.** The software can model whether direct delivery to the store or the use of a central warehouse offers the cheaper option. It is likely to be the latter.

6 Customer profitability analysis (CPA)

FAST FORWARD

Customer profitability analysis uses an activity based approach to relate revenues and costs to groups of customers in order to assess their relative profitability.

Traditionally, **management accounting reports** have been analysed on a **product by product** basis. In the **modern business environment**, however, in which it is vital that organisations respond promptly to the demands of customers, **analysis on the basis of customers** can provide vital management information.

6.1 Analysing customers

Profitability can vary widely between different customers because various **overhead costs** are, to some extent, **variable and customer driven**.

(a) Discounts
(b) Sales force (eg telesales are cheaper and more time-efficient than a field sales force)
(c) Quality control (some customers demand higher quality)
(d) Merchandising
(e) Distribution (full-pallet transactions are cheaper than breaking bulk)
(f) Promotions
(g) Financing costs
(h) Enquiries

Suppose a hotel offers a number of services such as a swimming pool, a gym and a nightly dinner dance.

(a) Older guests may attend the dinner dance.
(b) Families may use the swimming pool.
(c) People without children may appreciate the gym.

By charging services to the guests using them, a cost per bed night can be calculated for each guest group. **Strategies for attracting the most profitable guest group** can then be adopted.

Whether individual customers or groups of customers are costed largely depends on the number of customers.

(a) A manufacturing company supplying six companies would cost each customer separately.

(b) A supermarket or bank would cost groups of similar customers. UK banks divide their customers into categories such as single and 30ish, married with young children, older couples with spending money and so on, and give each category a colourful 'fruity' name such as plum or lemon.

Marketing departments should be aiming to **attract and retain profitable customers** but in order to do this they need to **know which customers are profitable** and **how much can be spent on retaining them**. The **costing system** should **provide the necessary answers**.

Key term

Customer profitability analysis (CPA) is 'the analysis of the revenue streams and service costs associated with specific customers or customer groups'.   (CIMA *Official Terminology*)

Customer profitability analysis (CPA) provides important information which allows an organisation to determine both **which classes of customers it should concentrate on** and the **prices it should charge for customer services**. Its use ensures that those customers **contributing sizeably to the profitability** of the organisation receive a **comparable amount of attention** from the organisation.

6.2 Customer revenues

Customer revenues are cash flows from customers. They are influenced by different factors, mainly **allowances and discounts**.

(a) Some types of customer **store and distribute goods** (eg wholesalers) or **promote** the goods in return for an **allowance**.

(b) By giving a **discount** a company may **encourage bulk orders**, which may be cheaper to provide and may result in higher sales volume. Studies on customer profitability have found large price discounting to be a key explanation for a group of customers being below expected profitability, however. Sales representatives may have given customers large price discounts unrelated to their current or potential value to the company, perhaps to meet bonuses dependent on sales volumes. Two customers may be purchasing the same volumes but the price discount given to one may make it unprofitable, while the other is profitable.

Case Study

The USA company *General Electric*, which manufactures and sells refrigerators and so on, used to give substantial discounts to customers who placed large orders. This did not result in customers buying more products. Instead GE's sales orders bunched in particular weeks of the year. In turn this led to an uneven production and distribution flow, which increased costs. The company found that, by removing the discounts while at the same time guaranteeing swift delivery, order size decreased and profits increased.

6.3 Customer costs and ABC

The creation of cost pools for activities in **ABC** systems allows organisations to arrange costs in a variety of different ways. Because different customers use different amounts of activities, it is possible to **build up costs for individual customers or groups of customers** on an activity basis so that their **relative profitability** can be assessed.

Examples of the build up of customer costs using an activity based system

Activity	Cost driver
Order taking	Number of orders taken
Sales visits	Number of sales visits
Emergency orders	Number of rushed orders
Delivery	Miles travelled
Product handling	Number of pallets or part-pallets handled
After sales service and support	Number of visits
Product repairs and service	Number of repair visits

Case Study

Drury cites the case of Kanthal, a Swedish company that sells electric heating elements. Customer-related selling costs represented 34% of total costs. In the past Kanthal had allocated these costs on the basis of sales value when customer profitability studies were carried out. The company then introduced an ABC system in order to determine the resources consumed by different customers.

An investigation identified two cost drivers for the resources used to service different customers.

(a) **Number of orders placed.** Each order had a large fixed cost, which did not vary with the number of items ordered. A customer ordering 10 items 100 times cost more to service than a customer placing a single order for 1,000 items.

(b) **Non-standard production items.** These cost more to manufacture than standard items.

A cost per order and the cost of handling standard and non-standard items were calculated and a CPA carried out on the basis of the previous year's sales. The analysis showed that only 40% of customers were profitable, and a further 10% lost 120% of the profits. In other words, 10% of customers incurred losses equal to 120% of Kanthal's total profits. Two of the most unprofitable customers were actually in the top three in terms of total sales volume but made many small orders of non-standard items.

Unprofitable customers identified by CPA should be persuaded to **alter their buying behaviour** so they become profitable customers. In the Kanthal example above, unprofitable customers should be discouraged from placing lots of small orders and/or from buying non-standard products.

The **activity based approach** also **highlights where cost reduction efforts should be focused**. Kanthal should concentrate on reducing ordering cost and the cost of handling non-standard items.

Activity-based CPA allows an organisation to adopt a more **market-orientated approach** to management accounting.

 Question   CPA

Learning outcome: D(x)

BB manufactures components for the heavy goods vehicle industry. The following annual information regarding three of its key customers is available.

	P	Q	R
Gross margin	$897,000	$1,070,000	$1,056,000
General administration costs	$35,000	$67,000	$56,000
Units sold	4,600	5,800	3,800
Orders placed	300	320	480
Sales visits	80	50	100
Invoices raised	310	390	1,050

The company uses an activity based costing system and the analysis of customer-related costs is as follows.

Sales visits	$420 per visit
Order processing	$190 per order placed
Despatch costs	$350 per order placed
Billing and collections	$97 per invoice raised

 LEARNING MEDIA

Using customer profitability analysis, the ranking of the customers would be:

	P	Q	R
A	1st	2nd	3rd
B	1st	3rd	2nd
C	2nd	1st	3rd
D	2nd	3rd	1st

Answer

The correct answer is C.

	P	Q	R
	$'000	$'000	$'000
Gross margin	897.00	1,070.00	1,056.00
Less: Customer specific costs			
Sales visits (80/50/100 × $420)	(33.60)	(21.00)	(42.00)
Order processing (300/320/480 × $190)	(57.00)	(60.80)	(91.20)
Despatch costs (300/320/480 × $350)	(105.00)	(112.00)	(168.00)
Billing and collections (310/390/1,050 × $97)	(30.07)	(37.83)	(101.85)
	671.33	838.37	652.95
Ranking	2	1	3

6.4 Customer profitability statement

There is no set format, but it would normally be similar to the one below. Note that financing costs have been included.

	$'000	$'000
Revenue at list prices		100
Less: discounts given		8
Net revenue		92
Less: cost of goods sold		50
Gross margin		42
Less: customer specific costs (such as those listed above)	28	
financing costs:		
credit period	3	
customer specific inventory	2	
		33
Net margin from customer		9

Question

Profitable customers

Learning outcome: D(x)

Seth supplies shoes to Narayan and Kipling. Each pair of shoes has a list price of $50 and costs Seth $25. As Kipling buys in bulk it receives a 10% trade discount for every order for 100 pairs of shoes or more. Narayan receives a 15% discount irrespective of order size, because that company collects the shoes, thereby saving Seth any distribution costs. The cost of administering each order is $50 and the distribution cost is $1,000 per order. Narayan makes 10 orders in the year, totalling 420 pairs of shoes, and Kipling places 5 orders for 100 pairs.

Required

Fill in the blank in the sentence below.

The most profitable customer for Seth is ....

Answer

The correct answer is Narayan.

It can be shown that Seth earns more from supplying Narayan, despite the larger discount percentage.

	Kipling	Narayan
	$	$
Revenue	25,000	21,000
Less: discount	2,500	3,150
Net revenue	22,500	17,850
Less: cost of shoes	(12,500)	(10,500)
customer transport cost	(5,000)	–
customer administration cost	(250)	(500)
Net gain	4,750	6,850

The difference on a unit basis is considerable.

Number of pair of shoes sold	500	420
Net gain per pair of shoes sold	$9.50	$16.31
Net gain per $1 of sales revenue	$0.19	$0.33

6.5 Costing customers

Not all customers cost the same to serve even if they require the same products. A customer will cost more to serve if based a long way from the factory (delivery costs increase), or places rush orders (production scheduling is interrupted, special transport is required), or requires a high level of after-sales service and technical assistance.

In order to analyse different customers it may therefore be useful to review **non-financial data**.

	Customer		
	X	Y	Z
Number of purchase orders	10	20	30
Number of sales visits	5	5	5
Number of deliveries	15	20	55
Distance per delivery	50	20	70
Number of emergency orders	1	0	4

Customer Y may be the cheapest to serve because of the number of deliveries per order, the lower distance travelled and the lack of emergency orders.

6.6 Categorising customers

It is not possible to 'cost' future dealings with customers accurately because the number and size of orders and rush orders is likely to be unpredictable. It is, however, possible to gain a broad idea of the amount of profit that can be expected from a particular category of customer. Customers can be categorised in the following grid.

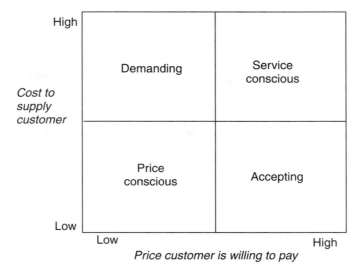

Price customer is willing to pay

The aim is to **attract as many accepting customers as possible**. Such customers will have a low 'cost to supply' perhaps because they are located close by or do not place rush orders, and are prepared to accept a high price. **Many large retail organisations fall into the demanding category** because they expect the supplier to deal with rush orders, change production methods to suit them and so on. It is undesirable for a **small supplier to be tied to a large demanding customer** who has the power to threaten the withdrawal of its custom if the supplier does not acquiesce.

Alternatively, customers can be analysed using **decision grid analysis (DGA)**, as illustrated in the following diagram.

6.7 Customers and life cycle costing

Customers can also be **costed over their expected 'life cycle'** and expected future cash flows relating to the customer may be discounted. It is rarely possible to predict accurately the life cycle of a particular customer unless contracts are awarded for a specific time period. Nevertheless the information is valuable as **the longer the customer remains with the organisation** the **more profitable** the customer becomes. This is valuable information and may show the **importance of creating and retaining loyal customers**.

Case Study

The following extracts are from 'Why Service Stinks' by Diane Brady, which appeared in the 23 October 2000 edition of *Business Week on-line*. They illustrate how organisations are using CPA to increase profitability. The emphasis is BPP's.

'Welcome to the new consumer apartheid. Those long lines and frustrating telephone trees aren't always the result of companies simply not caring about pleasing the customer anymore. Increasingly, **companies have made a deliberate decision to give some people skimpy service because that's all their business is worth**. Call it the dark side of the technology boom, where marketers can amass a mountain of data that gives them an almost Orwellian view of each buyer.

More important, **technology** is creating a radical new business model that alters the whole dynamic of customer service. For the first time, **companies can truly measure exactly what such service costs on an individual level** and assess the return on each dollar. They can know exactly how much business someone generates, what he is likely to buy, and how much it costs to answer the phone. That allows them to **deliver a level of service based on each person's potential to produce a profit** – and not a single phone call more.

A few years ago, GE Capital decided to charge $25 a year to GE Rewards MasterCard holders who didn't rack up at least that much in annual interest charges.

Charles Schwab Corp's top-rated Signature clients .... never wait longer than 15 seconds to get a call answered, while other customers can wait 10 minutes or more. At Sears, Roebuck & Co., big spenders on the company's credit card get to choose a preferred two-hour time slot for repair calls while regular patrons are given a four-hour slot. Maytag Corp provides premium service to people who buy pricey products such as its front-loading Neptune washing machines, which sell for about $1,000, twice the cost of a top-loading washer.

For top-dollar clients, all this technology **allows corporations to feign an almost small-town intimacy**. Marketers can know your name, your spending habits, and even details of your personal life. Centura Banks Inc .... now rates its 2 million customers on a profitability scale from 1 to 5. The real moneymakers get calls from service reps several times a year for what Controller Terry Earley calls ''a friendly chat'' and even an annual call from the CEO to wish them happy holidays.

Banks are especially motivated to take such steps because they have one of the widest gaps in profitability. Market Line Associates, an Atlanta financial consultancy, estimates that the **top 20% of customers at a typical commercial bank generate up to six times as much revenue as they cost, while the bottom fifth cost three to four times more than they make for the company**.

Already, innovative players are striving to **use their treasure trove of information to move customers up the value chain instead of letting them walk out the door**. Capital One Financial Corp ... is an acknowledged master of tiering, offering more than 6,000 credit cards and up to 20,000 permutations of other products, from phone cards to insurance. That range lets the company match clients with someone who has appropriate expertise. ''We look at every single customer contact as an opportunity to make an unprofitable customer profitable or make a profitable customer more profitable,'' says Marge Connelly, senior vice-president for domestic card operations.'

 Question   CPA and competitive advantage

Learning outcome: D(x)

Explain how customer profitability analysis can enhance an organisation's competitive advantage.

Answer

By **focusing on the way in which costs are allocated to customers** rather than to the products and services sold, CPA attempts to provide answers to the following types of question.

(a) What profit or contribution is the organisation making on sales to the customer, after taking account of all costs which can be specifically identified with the customer?

(b) What would be the financial consequences of losing the customer?

(c) Is the customer buying in order sizes that are unprofitable to supply?

(d) What is the return on investment on any plant that is used specifically for this customer?

(e) Is any inventory held specifically for this customer and what period of credit do they require?

(f) Are there any other specific costs involved in supplying this customer, such as technical and test facilities, R&D facilities, dedicated sales or administrative staff?

(g) What is the ratio of the customer's net contribution to the investment made on the customer's behalf?

The technique **enhances an organisation's competitive advantage** because it considers the profits generated by customers and **allows the organisation to focus its efforts on those customers who promise the highest profit**. The organisation is also in a better position to **rationalise its approach** to customers who demonstrate a low potential for generating profit.

7 Distribution channel profitability

As well as focusing on individual customers or groups of customers (in terms of revenue, number of transactions and so on), a similar analysis can be carried out on different distribution channels. A computer manufacturer, for example, might consider CPA in terms of major computer chain customers, large retail stores, independent retail chain stores, corporate accounts and direct mail accounts. The **demands placed by customers in different distribution channels will vary considerably and hence so will the profitability** of different distribution channels.

Almost every manufacturer, supplier and distributor incurs distribution costs and hence it is vital that these participants in the supply chain understand the profit implications of their choice of delivery channel for products and services.

FORWARD

Just as **ABC** can be used in conjunction with CPA, it can also be used to determine the relative **profitability of different distribution channels**.

7.1 Traditional approach to determining distribution channel profitability

Product costs are **allocated** to distribution channels **based on standard costs and the product mix** sold through the channel.

Sales, general and administrative costs are typically **allocated** to distribution channels on the **basis of sales volume or net revenue** for each channel.

This approach is shown diagrammatically below.

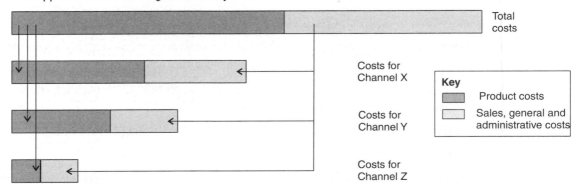

Such an approach may provide **useful information if the organisation is structured on the basis of distribution channels**, but structures tend to be based around regions, product lines or manufacturing locations, making allocation of costs to channels difficult. The approach also obviously has all the **disadvantages associated with the traditional approach to product costing**.

7.2 The ABC approach to determining distribution channel profitability

Material costs and activity costs are allocated direct to products to produce product-related costs, which are **then allocated** to distribution channels on the **basis of the mix of products sold** in each channel.

This approach, which carries with it all the **advantages of ABC** and should result in **more accurate** information, is illustrated in the diagram below.

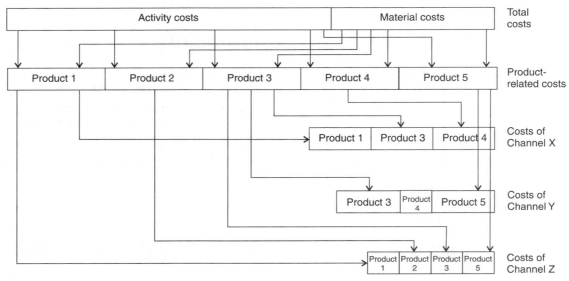

The main **disadvantage** to this approach is that the allocation is based on the **assumption** that **all costs are driven by the production of particular products** and hence must be allocated to products. For most organisations, however, the **products** they produce is just **one of a range of cost drivers**.

7.3 A refined ABC approach to determining distribution channel profitability

This approach, illustrated below, is based on the **assumption** that **costs are driven** not only by **products produced**, but by the **customers served** and the **channels through which the products are offered**. This allows managers to see the effect on the costs of channels of all three categories.

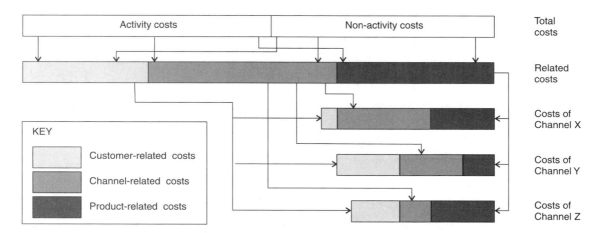

7.3.1 Developing accurate costs for distribution channels

Step 1 **Separate the organisation's costs into activity-related costs and costs not related to activities**

Step 2 **Identify all costs within the two classifications as product related, customer related or channel related**

(a) Activity costs for a manufacturing organisation might include production scheduling (product related), collection of bad debts (customer related) and advertising brand X (channel related).

(b) Costs not related to activities might include material costs (product related), customer rebates (customer related) and trade discounts (channel related).

Step 3 **Trace these costs to individual products, customers and channels**
Cost drivers can be used to trace activity-related costs. Direct allocation to the product, customer or channel that caused them should be possible for other costs.

Step 4 **Link the product-related and customer-related costs to channels**
Split total product costs across customers by analysing customer purchases on a product-by-product basis. Then split total customer costs across channels by analysing this customer data on a channel-by-channel basis.

Obviously revenue information for the same products, customers and distribution channels also needs to be captured.

7.4 Comparison of the two ABC approaches

The traditional product-related ABC approach fits in with the way in which most organisations are formed around product lines and product groups.

Nowadays customers are being served through a variety of distribution channels, however (distributors, catalogues, mega-stores, direct mail and so on). Understanding the cost and profitability of using different distribution channels will therefore become increasingly important for good business decision making.

8 Activity-based profitability analysis

FORWARD

By comparing the costs of products, customers and distribution channels with revenues, a **tier of contribution levels** can be established by applying the concept of the activity based cost hierarchy.

The hierarchical classification of activities which we covered in Chapter 16 can be extended by applying it to profitability analysis. This is illustrated in the diagram below (which is based on one in Drury adapted from an approach advocated by Kaplan ('Contribution margin analysis: no longer relevant', *Journal of Management Accounting Research (USA),* Fall, 1990)).

Unit-level product contributions

Product contributions after deducting batch-related expenses

Product contributions after deducting product-sustaining expenses

Product-line contributions after deducting product-line sustaining expenses

| Product line 1 | Product line 2 | Product line 3 |

Plant profit after deducting facility-sustaining expenses

| Plant profit |

At the point at which **product-level contribution margins for each individual product in the product line** have been calculated, there has been **no cost allocation**. **Some costs incurred at the product-line level**, such as research and development, advertising and distribution, are common to all products in the product line, however, and within this analysis they are **traced to product lines** rather than individual products within the line.

The resulting product-line contribution margin is the sum of the individual product-level contributions sold within the line and shows whether the products sold within the line earn enough contribution to cover the costs of activities required to sustain the line.

Plant profit is arrived at by deducting facility-sustaining costs from the sum of the product-line contributions.

8.1 Using this approach for customers and distribution channels

This approach should not be limited to analysing the profitability of products and product lines. Customers and distribution channels should also be considered, by **summing the product-level contribution margins of the products sold to each customer or through each distribution channel**, and **then deducting costs incurred for individual customers or distribution channels**.

8.2 Dealing with marketing and distribution costs

These costs should be **included** within such an analysis and dealt with in a similar way to production costs. The activity-based analysis therefore assigns the costs to the appropriate level in the hierarchy (depending on whether a cost is incurred in relation to an activity that supports a product, product line/customer/distribution channel) and then aggregates the costs down the hierarchy to determine contribution margins by product, product line, customer and distribution channel.

9 Pareto analysis

FAST FORWARD

Pareto analysis is used to highlight the general principle that 80% of value (inventory value, wealth, profit and so on) is concentrated in 20% of the items in a particular population.

Key term

Pareto analysis is based on the observations of the economist Vilfredo Pareto, who suggested that 80% of a nation's wealth is held by 20% of its population (and so the remaining 80% of the population holds only 20% of the nation's wealth).

Pareto analysis is the **80/20 rule** and it has been applied to many other situations.

(a)   In inventory control, where 20% of inventory items might represent 80% of the value
(b)   In product analysis, where 80% of company profit is earned by 20% of the products

9.1 Example: Pareto analysis and products

(a)   A company produces ten products which it sells in various markets. The revenue from each product is as follows.

Product	Revenue
	$'000
A	231
B	593
C	150
D	32
E	74
F	17
G	1,440
H	12
I	2
J	19
	2,570

(b)   Rearranging revenue in descending order and calculating cumulative figures and percentages gives us the following analysis.

Product	Revenue	Cumulative revenue (W1)	% (W2)
	$'000	$'000	
G	1,440	1,440	56.0
B	593	2,033	79.1
A	231	2,264	88.1
C	150	2,414	93.9
E	74	2,488	96.8
D	32	2,520	98.1
J	19	2,539	98.8
F	17	2,556	99.5
H	12	2,568	99.9
I	2	2,570	100.0
	2,570		

Workings

1   This is calculated as follows:

1,440 + 593 = 2,033
2,033 + 231 = 2,264   and so on.

2   $(1/2,570 \times 1,440 \times 100)\% = 56.0\%$
$(1/2,570 \times 2,033 \times 100)\% = 79.1\%$ and so on.

(Enter 1/2,570 into your calculator as a constant – do the calculation and then tap the multiplication button twice until 'k' appears on the screen – and then simply enter each cumulative revenue figure and press the 'equals' button to get the percentage as a decimal.)

(c)   In this case the Pareto rule applies – almost 80% of revenue is brought in by just two products, G and B. The point of Pareto analysis is to highlight the fact that the effort that is put into a company's products is often barely worth the trouble in terms of the sales revenue generated.

Attention!

You should not expect that the 80/20 rule will always apply as precisely as in the above example. It may be, that, say, 25% of products will account for 90% of revenue. **The basic principle is that a small number of products often yields a high proportion of income**.

It does not necessarily follow that the products generating the highest income are the most profitable. The costs of producing the products needs to be taken into account. It may be, for example, that products G and B both cost more to produce than the income they bring in, whereas products A, C and E cost virtually nothing. In other words **Pareto analysis can be carried out for costs and contribution as well as for sales**.

Poor performers could also be new products which are establishing themselves in the market and which have more profitable futures.

9.2 Further analysis

Suppose the figures you are given provide some additional information, and you are asked to analyse them and comment on them in a way that will be useful to management.

Product	Revenue $'000	Profit $'000
A	231	46
B	593	108
C	150	52
D	32	7
E	74	16
F	17	4
G	1,440	202
H	12	8
I	2	1
J	19	8
	2,570	452

An analysis might take the following form.

(a)   The revenue figures can be **ranked** and **expressed as percentages** and in **cumulative terms** (as before), and profit can be ranked and analysed in the same way.

The figures are pretty self-explanatory, but make sure that you understand how all of them are calculated, because you may well have to do this yourself in an exam.

Product	Revenue $'000	Rev. %	Cum. revenue $'000	Cum. %	Product	Profit $'000	Profit %	Cum. profit $'000	Cum. %
G	1,440	56.0	1,440	56.0	G	202	44.7	202	44.7
B	593	23.1	2,033	79.1	B	108	23.9	310	68.6
A	231	9.0	2,264	88.1	C	52	11.5	362	80.1
C	150	5.8	2,414	93.9	A	46	10.2	408	90.3
E	74	2.9	2,488	96.8	E	16	3.5	424	93.8
D	32	1.2	2,520	98.1	H	8	1.8	432	95.6
J	19	0.7	2,539	98.8	J	8	1.8	440	97.4
F	17	0.7	2,556	99.5	D	7	1.5	447	98.9
H	12	0.5	2,568	99.9	F	4	0.9	451	99.8
I	2	0.1	2,570	100.0	I	1	0.2	452	100.0
	2,570					452			

This shows us that, whereas the top ranking products are G, B and A in revenue terms, G, B and C are the top three in terms of profit. In **revenue terms** product C produces under 6%

of the overall total but in **profit terms** it produces over 10%. Four products each produce 10% or more of the overall **profit**, but only three products individually produce more than 9% of **revenue**.

(b)   We can also calculate the **profit margin** (the profit divided by the revenue expressed as a percentage) for individual products and overall. The figures shown below indicate that while most of the products vary slightly around the overall profit margin of 17.6%, some have much higher margins, notably products H, I and J, although these are relatively insignificant in overall revenue terms. The product that provides the greatest amount of revenue and profit, product G, actually has the lowest profit margin of all.

Product	Revenue $'000	Profit $'000	Profit margin %
A	231	46	19.9
B	593	108	18.2
C	150	52	34.7
D	32	7	21.9
E	74	16	21.6
F	17	4	23.5
G	1,440	202	14.0
H	12	8	66.7
I	2	1	50.0
J	19	8	42.1
	2,570	452	17.6

Your overall recommendations to management might be to make efforts to **save costs** to **improve the profit margin** of product G, and to put **extra marketing effort** into products C, H, I and J where the potential returns are greatest. Obviously what can be done depends on the nature of the products themselves: the smaller revenue items may be specialist add-ons that are only ever likely to be purchased by a few people.

9.3 Analysing customers

Instead of analysing products, customers can be analysed to determine their relative profitability.

When a **customer profitability analysis** is first carried out it is often found that something close to **Pareto's rule** applies. This is illustrated in the following diagram where **20 of the 100** customers generate approximately **80%** of the company's total margin. As 50 of the 100 customers generate 100% of the total margin, resources appear to be wasted serving the remaining 50 customers.

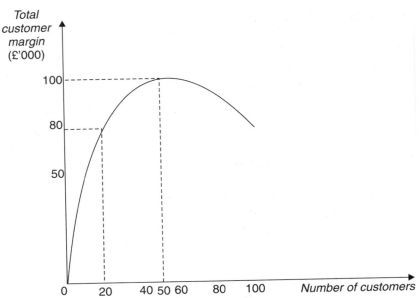

In order to produce a chart such as that above customers need to be **ranked** according to their **relative profitability** to the company. A bar chart, such as that below, produces an alternative view and may prove more useful for the marketing department.

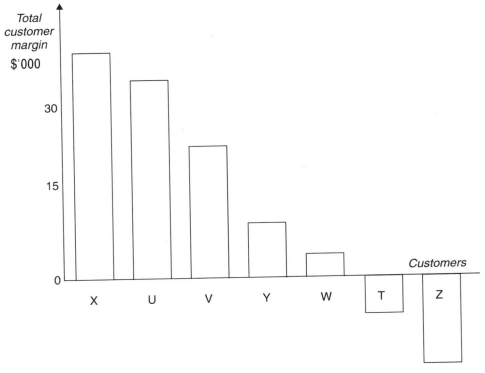

The more evenly customers contribute to profit, the better, as the position of the organisation is stabilised. If customers do not contribute evenly, the loss of two key customers could be disastrous for an organisation.

9.4 Analysing inventory

Pareto analysis can be used to improve inventory control.

(a) 15% of inventory volume might represent 80% of inventory value and so control should be concentrated on that 15%.

(b) 10% of inventory might require 75% of storage space (so that storage costs are particularly high). A just-in-time system could therefore be used for this 10%, saving money and space.

9.5 Analysing overheads

If an organisation uses activity based costing, a Pareto analysis of cost drivers or activities might show that, say, 15% of cost drivers or activities are responsible for 80% of total cost. Analysing, monitoring and controlling these cost drivers or activities will provide improved cost control and increased understanding of the way in which costs behave.

9.6 Diagrammatic representations

Pareto analysis can be presented in a variety of forms.

(a) Here is the revenue information from above presented as a Pareto curve.

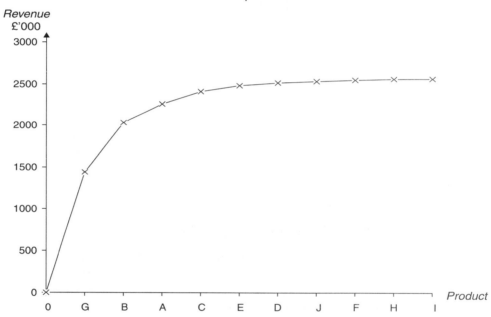

(b) Below we show both the revenue and profit figures as percentages in bar charts side by side.

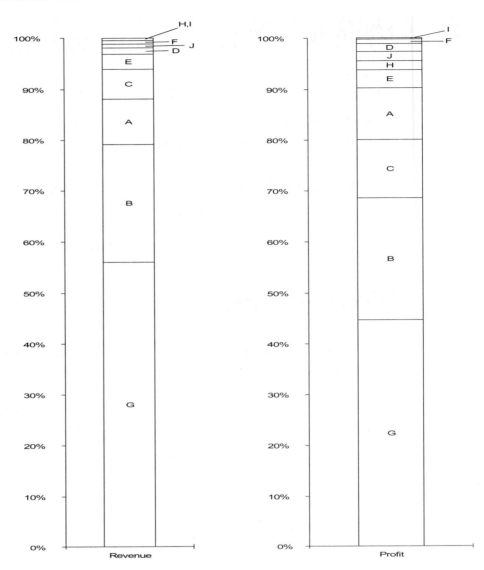

9.7 Pareto diagrams and quality

The term 'Pareto diagram' usually refers to a **histogram or frequency chart on product quality**, following research in the 1950s which showed that a **few causes of poor quality usually accounted for most of the quality problems** – hence the name Pareto. Such diagrams highlight the area or areas to which attention should be given to produce the best returns.

Chapter Roundup

- The **value chain model**, developed by Michael Porter, offers a bird's eye view of an organisation, of what it does and the way in which its business activities are organised.

- **Activities** or **value activities** can be categorised as **primary** or **support.**

- The ultimate **value** an organisation creates is measured by the amount customers are willing to pay for its products and services above the cost of carrying out value activities.

- The **focus of the value chain** is **external to the organisation**, each organisation being viewed in the context of the overall chain of value-creating activities of which it is only a part, from basic raw materials to end-use consumers.

- An organisation's ability to develop and sustain **cost leadership** or **product differentiation**, and hence **gain competitive advantage**, depends on how well it manages its own value chain relative to competitors.

- A **supply chain** is the network of suppliers, manufacturers and distributors that is involved in the process of moving goods for a customer order from the raw materials stage through the production and distribution stages to the customer. Every organisation operates somewhere within a supply chain.

- A **commonly-held view** by management is that **to improve profitability** it is necessary to **get the lowest prices from suppliers** and to **obtain the best prices from the customers** next in line down the supply chain.

- **Supply chain management** looks at the supply chain as a whole, and starts with the view that all organisations in the supply chain collaborate to produce something of value for the end customer.

- Supply chain managers need to consider **production, supply, inventory, location, transportation** and **information**.

- **EDI, the Internet** and **software applications** have had a huge impact on supply chain management.

- Some observers predict that in ten to 20 years, most organisations will have **outsourced** every part of the value chain except for the few key components that are unique and sources of **competitive advantage**.

- Any activity is a candidate for outsourcing unless the organisation must **control it to maintain its competitive position** or if the organisation can **deliver it on a level comparable with the best organisations in the world.**

- To minimise the risks associated with outsourcing, organisations generally enter into **long-run contracts** with their suppliers that specify costs, quality and delivery schedules. They build **close partnerships** or **alliances** with a few key suppliers, collaborating with suppliers on design and manufacturing decisions, and building a culture and commitment for quality and timely delivery.

- In an effort to cut costs, many organisations are now outsourcing activities both **near shore (such as Eastern Europe)** and **off shore (such as the Far East and India).**

- In some situations, normal competitive pressures do not apply in relationships between customers and contractors. This might be because of the size of the project (say in the construction or civil engineering industries), because there are a limited number of contractors or because of security issues (as in defence work). In such circumstances, **partnering, incentives** and **gain-sharing arrangements** are required.

- DPP is a **costing system used by retail businesses.**

- **Customer profitability analysis** uses an activity based approach to relate revenues and costs to groups of customers in order to assess their relative profitability.

Chapter Roundup cont'd

- Just as **ABC** can be used in conjunction with CPA, it can also be used to determine **the relative profitability of different distribution channels.**

- By comparing the costs of products, customers and distribution channels with revenues, a **tier of contribution levels** can be established by applying the concept of the activity based cost hierarchy.

- **Pareto analysis** is used to highlight the general principle that 80% of value (inventory value, wealth, profit and so on) is concentrated in 20% of the items in a particular population.

Quick Quiz

1   Complete the following diagram of the value chain.

2   *Choose the correct term from those highlighted.*

   If the proportion of a supplier's total output that is sold to a customer roughly equals the proportion of total purchases acquired by the customer from that supplier, this is known as **power balancing/ target balancing/ codependency/ power ties.**

3   Activities that are a source of competitive advantage should be outsourced. *True or false?*

4   List in the spaces below six features of project performance that can be considered for incentivisation.

   1   4   ....

   2   5   ....

   3   6   ....

5   On the axes below, sketch and label correctly a Pareto curve to demonstrate a situation where 75% of an organisation's profit is derived from 25% of its retail outlets.

6   A wholesaler has estimated that its store space cost is $1.00 per cubic metre per day.

   Its product range includes the following products.

   (a)   Six-packs of lager – volume: 0.02 cubic metres, days in store: 5
   (b)   Bleach – volume: 0.01 cubic metres, days in store: 4
   (c)   Packs of toilet rolls – volume: 0.37 cubic metres, days in store: 3.

   State how space costs would be allocated to the products using direct product profitability

7   Customers can be classified in accordance with **CPA** using a two-way grid. The grid allocates customers to one of four types based on two criteria. These criteria are the cost of supply to the customer and the price that the customer is willing to pay. Complete the four cells with customer categories.

Answers to Quick Quiz

1

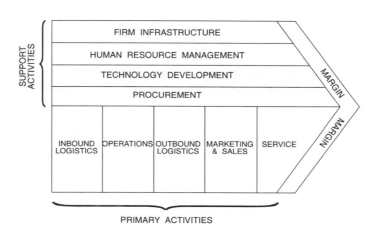

2   The correct answer is power balancing.

3   False. These are the activities an organisation should keep in-house.

4   You could have listed cost, time, quality, operational efficiency, productivity, value for the customer or safety.

5

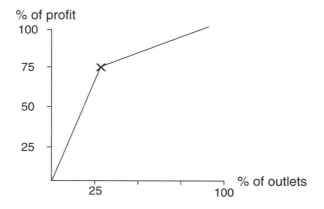

6   The space costs would be allocated as follows.

Lager $1.00 × 0.02 × 5 = $0.1 per pack
Bleach $1.00 × 0.01 × 4 = $0.04 per pack
Packs of toilet rolls $1.00 × 0.37 × 3 = $1.11 per pack

The results show the need to achieve a high turnover with bulky low price goods such as toilet paper. Refrigerated items would carry a higher space cost due to the cost of refrigeration.

7

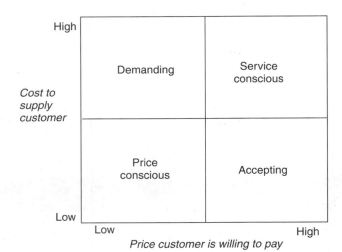

Now try the questions below from the Exam Question Bank

Number	Level	Marks	Time
Q27	Examination	10	18 mins
Q28	Examination	10	18 mins

Appendix 1
International terminology

International Accounting Terminology and Formats

Terminology

Below is a short list of the most important terms you are likely to use or come across, together with their international equivalents.

UK term	International term
Profit and loss account	Income statement
Profit and loss reserve (in balance sheet)	Retained earnings
Turnover	Revenue
Debtor account	Account receivable
Debtors (eg 'debtors have increased')	Receivables
Debtor	Customer
Creditor account	Account payable
Creditors (eg 'creditors have increased')	Payables
Creditor	Supplier
Debtors control account	Receivables control account
Creditors control account	Payables control account
Stock	Inventory
Fixed asset	Non-current asset (generally). Tangible fixed assets are also referred to as 'property, plant and equipment'.
Long-term liability	Non-current liability
Provision (eg for depreciation)	Allowance (You will sometimes see 'provision' used too.)
General ledger	Nominal ledger
VAT	Sales tax
Debentures	Loan notes
Preference shares/dividends	Preferred shares/dividends

Formats

Note that the international financial statements are generally expressed in dollars rather than pounds.

In general the format for the income statement (international) is the same as the profit and loss account (UK) except for a couple of differences in terminology. Here is a simple example, with the differences highlighted.

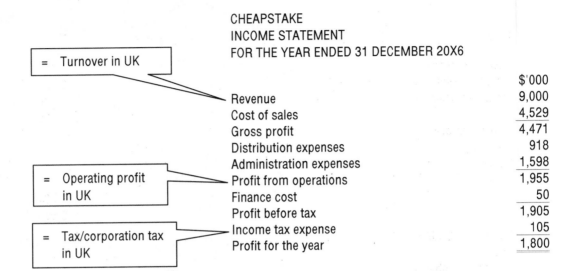

CHEAPSTAKE
INCOME STATEMENT
FOR THE YEAR ENDED 31 DECEMBER 20X6

= Turnover in UK

	$'000
Revenue	9,000
Cost of sales	4,529
Gross profit	4,471
Distribution expenses	918
Administration expenses	1,598
Profit from operations	1,955
Finance cost	50
Profit before tax	1,905
Income tax expense	105
Profit for the year	1,800

= Operating profit in UK

= Tax/corporation tax in UK

The format of the balance sheet is different from the UK. **Instead of having net assets (assets less liabilities) equal to capital and reserves, it has total assets in the top half equal to equity and liabilities in the bottom half.**

CHEAPSTAKE
BALANCE SHEET AS AT 31 DECEMBER 20X6

ASSETS	$'000	$'000
Non-current assets		
Tangible assets: property and plant		2,720
Intangible asset: goodwill		270
		2,990
Current assets		
Inventory	1,950	
Receivables	1,544	
Bank	200	
		3,694
		6,684
EQUITY AND LIABILITIES		
Equity		
$1 Ordinary shares		400
10% preferred shares		600
Revaluation reserve		350
Retained earnings		2,274
		3,624
Non-current liabilities		
5% Loan notes	1,000	
Deferred tax	120	1,120
Current liabilities		1,940
		6,684

(As you can see, assets = capital plus liabilities, rather than assets less liabilities = capital.)

Appendix 2

Mathematical tables and exam formulae

PRESENT VALUE TABLE

Present value of £1 ie $(1+r)^{-n}$ where r = interest rate, n = number of periods until payment or receipt.

Periods (n)					Interest rates (r)					
	1%	2%	3%	4%	5%	6%	7%	8%	9%	10%
1	0.990	0.980	0.971	0.962	0.952	0.943	0.935	0.926	0.917	0.909
2	0.980	0.961	0.943	0.925	0.907	0.890	0.873	0.857	0.842	0.826
3	0.971	0.942	0.915	0.889	0.864	0.840	0.816	0.794	0.772	0.751
4	0.961	0.924	0.888	0.855	0.823	0.792	0.763	0.735	0.708	0.683
5	0.951	0.906	0.863	0.822	0.784	0.747	0.713	0.681	0.650	0.621
6	0.942	0.888	0.837	0.790	0.746	0.705	0.666	0.630	0.596	0.564
7	0.933	0.871	0.813	0.760	0.711	0.665	0.623	0.583	0.547	0.513
8	0.923	0.853	0.789	0.731	0.677	0.627	0.582	0.540	0.502	0.467
9	0.914	0.837	0.766	0.703	0.645	0.592	0.544	0.500	0.460	0.424
10	0.905	0.820	0.744	0.676	0.614	0.558	0.508	0.463	0.422	0.386
11	0.896	0.804	0.722	0.650	0.585	0.527	0.475	0.429	0.388	0.350
12	0.887	0.788	0.701	0.625	0.557	0.497	0.444	0.397	0.356	0.319
13	0.879	0.773	0.681	0.601	0.530	0.469	0.415	0.368	0.326	0.290
14	0.870	0.758	0.661	0.577	0.505	0.442	0.388	0.340	0.299	0.263
15	0.861	0.743	0.642	0.555	0.481	0.417	0.362	0.315	0.275	0.239
16	0.853	0.728	0.623	0.534	0.458	0.394	0.339	0.292	0.252	0.218
17	0.844	0.714	0.605	0.513	0.436	0.371	0.317	0.270	0.231	0.198
18	0.836	0.700	0.587	0.494	0.416	0.350	0.296	0.250	0.212	0.180
19	0.828	0.686	0.570	0.475	0.396	0.331	0.277	0.232	0.194	0.164
20	0.820	0.673	0.554	0.456	0.377	0.312	0.258	0.215	0.178	0.149

Periods (n)					Interest rates (r)					
	11%	12%	13%	14%	15%	16%	17%	18%	19%	20%
1	0.901	0.893	0.885	0.877	0.870	0.862	0.855	0.847	0.840	0.833
2	0.812	0.797	0.783	0.769	0.756	0.743	0.731	0.718	0.706	0.694
3	0.731	0.712	0.693	0.675	0.658	0.641	0.624	0.609	0.593	0.579
4	0.659	0.636	0.613	0.592	0.572	0.552	0.534	0.516	0.499	0.482
5	0.593	0.567	0.543	0.519	0.497	0.476	0.456	0.437	0.419	0.402
6	0.535	0.507	0.480	0.456	0.432	0.410	0.390	0.370	0.352	0.335
7	0.482	0.452	0.425	0.400	0.376	0.354	0.333	0.314	0.296	0.279
8	0.434	0.404	0.376	0.351	0.327	0.305	0.285	0.266	0.249	0.233
9	0.391	0.361	0.333	0.308	0.284	0.263	0.243	0.225	0.209	0.194
10	0.352	0.322	0.295	0.270	0.247	0.227	0.208	0.191	0.176	0.162
11	0.317	0.287	0.261	0.237	0.215	0.195	0.178	0.162	0.148	0.135
12	0.286	0.257	0.231	0.208	0.187	0.168	0.152	0.137	0.124	0.112
13	0.258	0.229	0.204	0.182	0.163	0.145	0.130	0.116	0.104	0.093
14	0.232	0.205	0.181	0.160	0.141	0.125	0.111	0.099	0.088	0.078
15	0.209	0.183	0.160	0.140	0.123	0.108	0.095	0.084	0.074	0.065
16	0.188	0.163	0.141	0.123	0.107	0.093	0.081	0.071	0.062	0.054
17	0.170	0.146	0.125	0.108	0.093	0.080	0.069	0.060	0.052	0.045
18	0.153	0.130	0.111	0.095	0.081	0.069	0.059	0.051	0.044	0.038
19	0.138	0.116	0.098	0.083	0.070	0.060	0.051	0.043	0.037	0.031
20	0.124	0.104	0.087	0.073	0.061	0.051	0.043	0.037	0.031	0.026

CUMULATIVE PRESENT VALUE TABLE

This table shows the present value of £1 per annum, receivable or payable at the end of each year for n years $\dfrac{1-(1+r)^{-n}}{r}$.

Periods (n)	Interest rates (r)									
	1%	2%	3%	4%	5%	6%	7%	8%	9%	10%
1	0.990	0.980	0.971	0.962	0.952	0.943	0.935	0.926	0.917	0.909
2	1.970	1.942	1.913	1.886	1.859	1.833	1.808	1.783	1.759	1.736
3	2.941	2.884	2.829	2.775	2.723	2.673	2.624	2.577	2.531	2.487
4	3.902	3.808	3.717	3.630	3.546	3.465	3.387	3.312	3.240	3.170
5	4.853	4.713	4.580	4.452	4.329	4.212	4.100	3.993	3.890	3.791
6	5.795	5.601	5.417	5.242	5.076	4.917	4.767	4.623	4.486	4.355
7	6.728	6.472	6.230	6.002	5.786	5.582	5.389	5.206	5.033	4.868
8	7.652	7.325	7.020	6.733	6.463	6.210	5.971	5.747	5.535	5.335
9	8.566	8.162	7.786	7.435	7.108	6.802	6.515	6.247	5.995	5.759
10	9.471	8.983	8.530	8.111	7.722	7.360	7.024	6.710	6.418	6.145
11	10.368	9.787	9.253	8.760	8.306	7.887	7.499	7.139	6.805	6.495
12	11.255	10.575	9.954	9.385	8.863	8.384	7.943	7.536	7.161	6.814
13	12.134	11.348	10.635	9.986	9.394	8.853	8.358	7.904	7.487	7.103
14	13.004	12.106	11.296	10.563	9.899	9.295	8.745	8.244	7.786	7.367
15	13.865	12.849	11.938	11.118	10.380	9.712	9.108	8.559	8.061	7.606
16	14.718	13.578	12.561	11.652	10.838	10.106	9.447	8.851	8.313	7.824
17	15.562	14.292	13.166	12.166	11.274	10.477	9.763	9.122	8.544	8.022
18	16.398	14.992	13.754	12.659	11.690	10.828	10.059	9.372	8.756	8.201
19	17.226	15.679	14.324	13.134	12.085	11.158	10.336	9.604	8.950	8.365
20	18.046	16.351	14.878	13.590	12.462	11.470	10.594	9.818	9.129	8.514

Periods (n)	Interest rates (r)									
	11%	12%	13%	14%	15%	16%	17%	18%	19%	20%
1	0.901	0.893	0.885	0.877	0.870	0.862	0.855	0.847	0.840	0.833
2	1.713	1.690	1.668	1.647	1.626	1.605	1.585	1.566	1.547	1.528
3	2.444	2.402	2.361	2.322	2.283	2.246	2.210	2.174	2.140	2.106
4	3.102	3.037	2.974	2.914	2.855	2.798	2.743	2.690	2.639	2.589
5	3.696	3.605	3.517	3.433	3.352	3.274	3.199	3.127	3.058	2.991
6	4.231	4.111	3.998	3.889	3.784	3.685	3.589	3.498	3.410	3.326
7	4.712	4.564	4.423	4.288	4.160	4.039	3.922	3.812	3.706	3.605
8	5.146	4.968	4.799	4.639	4.487	4.344	4.207	4.078	3.954	3.837
9	5.537	5.328	5.132	4.946	4.772	4.607	4.451	4.303	4.163	4.031
10	5.889	5.650	5.426	5.216	5.019	4.833	4.659	4.494	4.339	4.192
11	6.207	5.938	5.687	5.453	5.234	5.029	4.836	4.656	4.486	4.327
12	6.492	6.194	5.918	5.660	5.421	5.197	4.988	4.793	4.611	4.439
13	6.750	6.424	6.122	5.842	5.583	5.342	5.118	4.910	4.715	4.533
14	6.982	6.628	6.302	6.002	5.724	5.468	5.229	5.008	4.802	4.611
15	7.191	6.811	6.462	6.142	5.847	5.575	5.324	5.092	4.876	4.675
16	7.379	6.974	6.604	6.265	5.954	5.668	5.405	5.162	4.938	4.730
17	7.549	7.120	6.729	6.373	6.047	5.749	5.475	5.222	4.990	4.775
18	7.702	7.250	6.840	6.467	6.128	5.818	5.534	5.273	5.033	4.812
19	7.839	7.366	6.938	6.550	6.198	5.877	5.584	5.316	5.070	4.843
20	7.963	7.469	7.025	6.623	6.259	5.929	5.628	5.353	5.101	4.870

Learning curve

$$Y_x = aX^b$$

where Y_x = the cumulative average time per unit to produce X units

a = the time required to produce the first unit of output

X = the cumulative number of units

b = the index of learning

The exponent b is defined as the log of the learning curve improvement rate divided by log 2.

Objective test
question bank

1 LL manufactures three products, the selling price and cost details of which are as follows.

	KK	DD	MM
	$ per unit	$ per unit	$ per unit
Selling price	40	54	72
Direct material ($4 per litre)	8	4	16
Direct labour ($6 per hour)	3	12	9
Variable overhead	5	20	15
Fixed overhead	4	16	12

In a period when direct materials are in short supply, the most and least profitable use of direct materials are:

	Most profitable	Least profitable
A	KK	DD
B	MM	KK
C	DD	MM
D	DD	KK

(2 marks)

2 Sid Brown runs a small engineering business and is trying to decide whether to take on an extra job for a customer (to produce 60 units of a particular component). Each component requires 6 hours of skilled labour and 9 hours of unskilled labour. There is currently sufficient skilled labour in Sid's business to do the work, but they would have to be taken off another job, which would then have to be done by unskilled labour. There is a shortage of unskilled labour and so Sid would have to recruit temporary agency staff to do any required unskilled work. Skilled workers are paid $15 per hour, unskilled workers $9 per hour, agency workers $12 per hour.

What would be the incremental labour costs for Sid Brown's business if the extra job were to be carried out?

A $4,320
B $10,260
C $6,480
D $10,800

(2 marks)

3 An organisation manufactures two products. Product X requires six minutes of labour grade A time, Product Y ten minutes. If x represents the number of product X manufactured and y represents the number of Y manufactured and in the next control period 720 hours of labour grade A time are available, how can the labour grade A constraint on production of X and Y be written as an inequality?

A $0.1x + 0.167y \geq 43,200$
B $10x + 6y \leq 720$
C $x + 1.67y \leq 720$
D $0.1x + 0.167y \leq 720$

(2 marks)

4 ABC manufactures and sells two products, Y and Z.

	Y	Z
	$ per unit	$ per unit
Selling price	57	41
Variable cost	35	20
Contribution	22	21

For every six units of Y sold, seven units of Z are sold. Annual fixed costs are $558,000.

Budgeted annual sales revenue in the standard mix is $1,446,700. What is the margin of safety as a %?

(Write your answer in the space below.)

The margin of safety is [   ]   (3 marks)

5   VC is considering investing in a printing machine for a capital cost of $900,000. The machine will have a useful life of four years. Annual running costs will amount to $828,000, including straight line depreciation of $210,000. The estimated disposal value of the machine at the end of year 4 is its net book value.

The printing capacity of the machine will be 6 million copies per annum for each of the first two years, and 5 million copies per annum for the third and fourth years. VC expects to be able to sell whatever the machine produces. Average contribution will be $180 per 1,000 copies.

The payback period for the machine, assuming all cash flows occur evenly, is [   ]
(2 marks)

Data for questions 6 and 7

Mart is launching a new product next year. Forecasts of sales are as follows.

Annual sales $'000	Probability
4,000	0.10
4,400	0.15
4,800	0.35
5,200	?
5,600	?

These are predicted to be the only possible outcomes, and the probability of sales of $5.2 million is exactly equal to the probability of sales of $5.6 million. The contribution to sales ratio of the product will be 35%. Fixed costs will be $196,000 per quarter.

6   The expected value of annual profit is [   ]

(3 marks)

7   The probability of the product at least breaking even next year is [   ], while the probability of the product earning a profit of at least $900,000 is [   ]   (3 marks)

8   A firm of financial consultants offers short revision courses on taxation and auditing for professional exams. The firm has budgeted annual overheads totalling $152,625. Until recently the firm had applied overheads on a volume basis, based on the number of course days offered. The firm has no variable costs and the only direct costs are the consultants' own time which they divide equally between the two courses. The firm is considering the possibility of adopting an ABC system and has identified the overhead costs as shown below.

	$
Centre hire	62,500
Enquiries administration	27,125
Brochures	63,000

The following information relates to the past year and is expected to remain the same for the coming year.

Course	No of courses sold	Duration of course	No of enquiries per course	No of brochures printed per course
Auditing	50	2 days	175	300
Taxation	30	3 days	70	200

All courses run with a maximum number of students (30), as it is deemed that beyond this number the learning experience is severely diminished, and the same centre is used for all courses at a standard daily rate. The firm has the human resources to run only one course at any one time.

Using ABC, what are the overhead costs for the two courses?

(Write your answer in the boxes below.)

Auditing [   ]

Taxation [   ]

(3 marks)

Objective test answer bank

1 C

	KK	DD	MM
Contribution per unit	$24	$18	$32
Litres required per unit	2	1	4
Contribution per litre	$12	$18	$8
Ranking	2nd	1st	3rd

2 D

Skilled labour for 60 units × 6 hours = 360 hours work must be replaced by unskilled labour, which must in turn be replaced by agency labour.

	$
Incremental costs	
Agency staff cost to do work of unskilled while they are doing work of skilled (360 hours × $12)	4,320
Agency staff cost to do unskilled labour part of job (60 units × 9 hours × $12)	6,480
	10,800

3 D

X requires 0.100 hours of labour grade A time.
Y requires 0.167 hours of labour grade A time.

720 hours are available.

∴ $0.1x + 0.167y \leq 720$

4 The correct answer is 13.04%.

Contribution per mix = ($22 × 6) + ($21 × 7) = $279

Breakeven point	=	fixed costs/contribution per mix
	=	$558,000/$279 = 2,000 mixes
	=	(2,000 × 6) 12,000 units of Y and (2,000 × 7) 14,000 units of Z
	=	(12,000 × $57) $684,000 revenue from Y and (14,000 × $41) $574,000 revenue from Z
	=	$1,258,000 in total
Margin of safety	=	budgeted sales – breakeven sales
	=	$(1,446,700 – 1,258,000)
	=	$188,700
Margin of safety (%)	=	($188,700/$1,446,700) × 100%
	=	13.04%

5 The correct answer is 1.95 years.

You should always use cash flows to calculate the payback period and so you need to subtract depreciation from running costs.

Cash flow in years 1 and 2

	$
Contribution (6 million x $180 per 1,000)	1,080,000
Cash running costs ($(828,000 – 210,000))	618,000
	462,000

Cash flow in years 3 and 4

	$
Contribution (5 million x $180 per 1,000)	900,000
Cash running costs ($(828,000 – 210,000))	618,000
	282,000

Residual value of the machine = $(900,000 – (4 × 210,000)) = $60,000. This is the estimated disposal value at the end of year 4.

Net cash flows

Year		$	Cumulative $
0		(900,000)	(900,000)
1		462,000	(438,000)
2		462,000	24,000
3		282,000	306,000
4	$(282,000 + 60,000)	342,000	648,000

Payback therefore occurs during year 2. Assuming even cash flows throughout the year, interpolation can be used to find the exact period.

Number of years = 1 + (438,000/462,000) = 1.95 years

6   The correct answer is $931,000.

We need to know the probabilities of the two highest sales values. Since the sales levels given are predicted to be the only possible outcomes, the sum of the probabilities must be equal to 1. The probabilities of the two highest sales values are therefore (1 – 0.1 – 0.15 – 0.35)/2 = 0.2.

EV of sales = $m(4 × 0.1 + 4.4 × 0.15 + 4.8 × 0.35 + 5.2 × 0.2 + 5.6 × 0.2) = $4.9m

	$
EV of contribution = $4.9m × 35%	1,715,000
Fixed costs ($196,000 × 4)	784,000
EV of annual profit	931,000

7   The correct answers are 100% and 40%.

To break even the contribution must be equal to the fixed costs.

Annual contribution required = $784,000
Contribution/sales = 35%
$784,000/sales = 35%
Sales = $2,240,000

The probability of achieving sales of at least $2,240,000 is 100%.

To earn a profit of at least $900,000, contribution required = fixed costs + profit = $784,000 + $900,000 = $1,684,000

Contribution/sales = 35%
$1,684,000/sales = 35%
Required sales = $4,811,429

The probability of achieving sales in excess of this amount is 0.2 + 0.2 = 0.4 = 40%.

8 **The correct answers are auditing $1,995.40 and taxation $1,761.85.**

	Auditing	Taxation	Total
Number of courses sold	50	30	
Duration of course (days)	2	3	
Number of course days	100	90	190

Centre hire cost per course day = $\dfrac{\$62,500}{190}$ = $328.95

Enquiries administration cost per enquiry = $\dfrac{\$27,125}{(50 \times 175) + (30 \times 70)}$ = $2.50

Brochure cost per brochure printed = $\dfrac{\$63,000}{(50 \times 300) + (30 \times 200)}$ = $3

Overhead costs per course using ABC

		Auditing $ per course		Taxation $ per course
Centre hire at $328.95 per day	(× 2)	657.90	(× 3)	986.85
Enquiries admin at $2.50 per enquiry	(× 175)	437.50	(× 70)	175.00
Brochures at $3 per brochure printed	(× 300)	900.00	(× 200)	600.00
		1,995.40		1,761.85

Exam question bank

1 Restaurant

18 mins

Learning outcome: A(vi)

W has operated a restaurant for the last two years. Revenue and operating costs over the two years have been as follows.

	Year 1 $'000	Year 2 $'000
Revenue	1,348,312	1,514,224
Operating costs		
Food and beverages	698,341	791,919
Wages	349,170	390,477
Other overheads	202,549	216,930

The number of meals served in year 2 showed an 8% increase on the year 1 level of 151,156. An increase of 10% over the year 2 level is budgeted for year 3.

All staff were given hourly rate increases of 6% last year (in year 2). In year 3 hourly increases of 7% are to be budgeted.

The inflation on 'other overheads' last year was 5%, with an inflationary increase of 6% expected in the year ahead.

Food and beverage costs are budgeted to average $5.14 per meal in year 3. This is expected to represent 53% of sales value.

Required

From the information given above, and using the high-low method of cost estimation, determine the budgeted expenditure on wages and other overheads for year 3.

(10 marks)

2 Webber Design

45 mins

Learning outcomes: A(i), (ii), (vi)

Webber Design had almost completed a specialised piece of equipment when it discovered that the customer who had commissioned the work had gone out of business. Another customer was found to be interested in this piece of equipment but certain extra features would be necessary.

The following data is provided in respect of the additional work.

Direct materials costing $2,500 would be required. Webber Design have these in stock but if not used to manufacture the specialised equipment they would be used on another contract in place of materials which would cost $4,500.

The company has three departments, welding, machining and assembly, within which the extra features would incur the following additional work to be undertaken. In the welding department one worker would be needed for three weeks. The wage rate is $280 per worker per week. The welding department is currently operating at only 50% of normal capacity, but two workers must be kept on the payroll to ensure that the department can respond instantly to any increase in demand.

Two workers would be needed for five weeks in the machining department, which is working normally and the wage rate is $240 per worker, per week.

The assembly department is always extremely busy. Its wage rate is $200 per worker, per week and is currently yielding a contribution of $5 per $1 of direct labour. The additional requirements for this job would be two workers for eight weeks.

Overtime would need to be sanctioned in order to finish the job for the customer. This would cost $1,500. Such costs are normally charged to production overhead.

Variable overhead is 15% of direct wages and a special delivery charge of $3,400 would be incurred. Fixed production overhead is absorbed in each department on the basis of a fixed percentage of direct wages as follows.

Welding at 120%
Machining at 80%
Assembly at 40%

The costs of the equipment as originally estimated and incurred so far are as follows.

	Original quotation $	Work to date $	Work to complete $
Direct materials	13,075	10,745	2,300
Direct wages	7,500	6,700	1,050
Variable overheads	1,125	1,050	150
Fixed production overhead	6,500	5,250	1,200
Fixed administration	1,250	1,050	200

The price to the original customer allowed for a profit margin of 20% on selling price. An advance payment of 15% of the price had been received on confirmation of the order.

If the work of the new customer is not carried out some of the materials in the original equipment would be used for another contract in place of materials that would have cost $4,000 but would need two workers weeks in the machining department to make them suitable. The remaining materials would realise $5,200 as scrap. The design for the equipment, which would normally be included in the selling price could be sold for $1,500.

Required

(a) Calculate the minimum price that Webber Design should quote to the new customer. **(10 marks)**

(b) State any further considerations you think Webber Design should take into account in setting the price. **(7 marks)**

(c) Define 'relevant cost', 'opportunity cost' and 'discretionary cost', and state their use to management. **(8 marks)**

(Total = 25 marks)

3 AB

45 mins

Learning outcome: A(i)

AB produces a consumable compound X, used in the preliminary stage of a technical process that it installs in customers' factories worldwide. An overseas competitor, CD, offering an alternative process which uses the same preliminary stage, has developed a new compound, Y, for that stage which is both cheaper in its ingredients and more effective than X.

At present, CD is offering Y only in his own national market, but it is expected that it will not be long before he extends its sales overseas. Both X and Y are also sold separately to users of the technical process as a replacement for the original compound that eventually loses its strength. This replacement demand amounts to 60% of total demand for X and would do so for Y. CD is selling Y at the same price as X ($64.08 per kg).

AB discovers that it would take 20 weeks to set up a production facility to manufacture Y at an incremental capital cost of $3,500 and the comparative manufacturing costs of X and Y would be:

	X $ per kg	Y $ per kg
Direct materials	17.33	4.01
Direct labour	7.36	2.85
	24.69	6.86

AB normally absorbs departmental overhead at 200% of direct labour: 30% of this departmental overhead is variable directly with direct labour cost. Selling and administration overhead is absorbed at one-half of departmental overhead.

The current sales of X average 74 kgs per week and this level (whether of X or of Y if it were produced) is not expected to change over the next year. Because the direct materials for X are highly specialised, AB has always had to keep large inventories in order to obtain supplies. At present, these amount to $44,800 at cost. Its inventory of finished X is $51,900 at full cost. Unfortunately, neither X nor its raw materials have any resale value whatsoever: in fact, it would cost $0.30 per kg to dispose of them.

Over the next three months AB is not normally busy and, in order to avoid laying off staff, has an arrangement with the trade union whereby it pays its factory operators at 65% of their normal rate of pay for the period whilst they do non-production work. AB assesses that it could process all its relevant direct materials into X in that period, if necessary.

There are two main options open to AB:

(a)   to continue to sell X until all its inventories of X (both of direct materials and of finished inventory) are exhausted, and then start sales of Y immediately afterwards;

(b)   to start sales of Y as soon as possible and then to dispose of any remaining inventories of X and/or its raw materials.

Required

(a)   Recommend with supporting calculations, which of the two main courses of action suggested is the more advantageous from a purely cost and financial point of view.   **(13 marks)**

(b)   Identify three major non-financial factors that AB would need to consider in making its eventual decision as to what to do.   **(5 marks)**

(c)   Suggest one other course of action that AB might follow, explaining what you consider to be its merits and demerits when compared with your answer at (a) above.   **(7 marks)**

(Total = 25 marks)

4 BB Company

45 mins

Learning outcome: A(vii)

For some time the BB company has sold its entire output of canned goods to supermarket chains which sell them as 'own label' products. One advantage of this arrangement is that BB incurs no marketing costs, but there is continued pressure from the chains on prices, and margins are tight.

As a consequence, BB is considering selling some of its output under the BB brand. Margins will be better but there will be substantial marketing costs.

The following information is available.

	Current year's results – 20X2 (adjusted to 20X3 cost levels)	Forecast for 20X3 (assuming all 'own label' sales)
Sales (millions of cans)	18	19
	$ million	$ million
Sales	5.94	6.27
Manufacturing costs	4.30	4.45
Administration costs	1.20	1.20
Profit	0.44	0.62

For 20X3 the unit contribution on BB brand sales is expected to be $33\frac{1}{3}$% greater than 'own label' sales, but variable marketing costs of 2p per can and fixed marketing costs of $400,000 will be incurred.

Required

(a)   Prepare a contribution breakeven chart for 20X3 assuming that all sales will be 'own label'.

(9 marks)

(b)   Prepare a contribution breakeven chart for 20X3 assuming that 50% of sales are 'own label' and 50% are of the BB brand.   **(9 marks)**

Note. The breakeven points and margins of safety must be shown clearly on the charts.

(c)   Comment on the positions shown by the charts and your calculations and discuss what other factors management should consider before making a decision.   **(7 marks)**

Ignore inflation.   **(Total = 25 marks)**

5 X   18 mins

Learning outcome: A(vii)

X manufactures four liquids – A, B, C and D. The selling price and unit cost details for these products are as follows.

	A	B	C	D
	$/litre	$/litre	$/litre	$/litre
Selling price	100	110	120	120
Direct materials	24	30	16	21
Direct labour ($6/hour)	18	15	24	27
Direct expenses	–	–	3	–
Variable overhead	12	10	16	18
Fixed overhead (note 1)	24	20	32	36
Profit	22	35	29	18

Note 1. Fixed overhead is absorbed on the basis of labour hours, based on a budget of 1,600 hours per quarter.

During the next three months the number of direct labour hours is expected to be limited to 1,345. The same labour is used for all products.

The marketing director has identified the maximum demand for each of the four products during the next three months as follows.

A   200 litres
B   150 litres
C   100 litres
D   120 litres

These maximum demand levels include the effects of a contract already made between X and one of its customers, Y Ltd, to supply 20 litres of each of A, B, C and D during the next three months.

Required

Determine the number of litres of products A, B, C and D to be produced/sold in the next three months in order to maximise profits, and calculate the profit that this would yield.

Assume that no inventory is held at the beginning of the three months which may be used to satisfy demand in the period.

(10 marks)

6 Research director

18 mins

Learning outcome: A(vii)

After completing the production plan in question 5 above, you receive two memos.

The first is from the research director.

'New environmental controls on pollution must be introduced with effect from the start of next month to reduce pollution from the manufacture of product D. These will incur fixed costs of $6,000 per annum.'

The second memo is from the sales director.

'An overseas supplier has developed a capacity to manufacture products C and D on a sub-contract basis, and has quoted the following prices to X.

C $105/litre
D $100/litre'

Required

Using the information from *both* of these memos, state and quantify the effect (if any) on X's plans.

(10 marks)

7 RAB Consulting

45 mins

Learning outcomes: A(vii), (viii)

RAB Consulting specialises in two types of consultancy project.

- Each Type A project requires twenty hours of work from qualified researchers and eight hours of work from junior researchers.

- Each Type B project requires twelve hours of work from qualified researchers and fifteen hours of work from junior researchers.

Researchers are paid on an hourly basis at the following rates:

Qualified researchers	$30/hour
Junior researchers	$14/hour

Other data relating to the projects:

Project type

	A	B
	$	$
Revenue per project	1,700	1,500
Direct project expenses	408	310
Administration*	280	270

* Administration costs are attributed to projects using a rate per project hour. Total administration costs are $28,000 per four-week period.

During the four-week period ending on 30 June 20X0, owing to holidays and other staffing difficulties the number of working hours available are:

Qualified researchers	1,344
Junior researchers	1,120

An agreement has already been made for twenty type A projects with XYZ group. RAB Consulting must start and complete these projects in the four-week period ending 30 June 20X0.

A maximum of 60 type B projects may be undertaken during the four-week period ending 30 June 20X0.

RAB Consulting is preparing its detailed budget for the four-week period ending 30 June 20X0 and needs to identify the most profitable use of the resources it has available.

Required

(a) (i) Calculate the contribution from each type of project. **(4 marks)**

    (ii) Formulate the linear programming model for the four-week period ending 30 June 20X0.

        (4 marks)

    (iii) Calculate, using a graph, the mix of projects that will maximise profit for RAB Consulting for the four-week period ending 30 June 20X0.

       (Note: projects are not divisible.) **(9 marks)**

(b) Calculate the profit that RAB Consulting would earn from the optimal plan. **(3 marks)**

(c) Explain the importance of identifying scarce resources when preparing budgets and the use of linear programming to determine the optimum use of resources. **(5 marks)**

    (Total = 25 marks)

8 Zaman
18 mins

Learning outcome: A(viii)

Zaman Ltd manufactures two products, the Qa and the Mar. Details of the two products are as follows:

	Qa	Mar
Selling price per unit	$200	$109
Labour required per unit	20 hours	8 hours
Raw material required per unit	4 kgs	5 kgs
Variable overheads per unit	$20	$15
Maximum annual demand	1,000 units	4,000 units

Both products require the same grade of labour (costing $3 per hour) and the same type of raw material (costing $10 per kg).

In the coming year, Zaman Ltd expects to have available a maximum of 40,000 labour hours and 20,000 kgs of raw material. The company has no stocks of either Qa or Mar, and does not wish to have any stocks of either product at the end of the coming year.

Required

(a) Prepare calculations to show the quantities of Qa and Mar that should be manufactured and sold in the coming year in order to maximise the profit of Zaman Ltd; and **(7 marks)**

(b) Discuss the limitations of your calculations. **(3 marks)**

    (Total = 10 marks)

9 XYZ

45 mins

Learning outcomes: A(vii), (viii)

(a)   The following details are taken from the forecasts for 20X1 of XYZ.

Thousands of units

	Sales demand per annum, maximum
Super deluxe model (x_1)	500
Deluxe model (x_2)	750
Export model (x_3)	400

Two production facilities are required, machining and assembly, and these are common to each model.

Capacity in each facility is limited by the number of direct labour hours available.

	Direct labour, total hours available in millions	Direct labour hours per unit		
		x_1	x_2	x_3
Machining	1.4	0.5	0.5	1.0
Assembly	1.2	0.5	0.5	2.0

Contribution is estimated as follows.

Model	Contribution per thousand units $
x_1	1,500
x_2	1,300
x_3	2,500

Required

Prepare formulae for this problem using the Simplex method of linear programming.   **(10 marks)**

(b)   Interpret the following tableau, given that it is the final solution to the above problem. The s variables (s_1, s_2, s_3, s_4, s_5) relate to the constraints in the same sequence as presented in (a) above.

x_1	x_2	x_3	s_1	s_2	s_3	s_4	s_5	
1	0	0	1	0	0	0	0	500
0	0	0	0.25	0.25	1	0	-0.5	112.5
0	0	1	-0.25	-0.25	0	0	0.5	287.5
0	0	0	-0.25	-0.25	0	1	-0.5	487.5
0	1	0	0	1	0	0	0	750
0	0	0	875	675	0	0	1,250	2,443,750

(15 marks)

(Total = 25 marks)

10 PN Motor Components

18 mins

Learning outcome: A(iii)

(a) In an attempt to win over key customers in the motor industry and to increase its market share, PN Motor Components plc have decided to charge a price lower than their normal price for component WB47 when selling to the key customers who are being targeted. Details of component WB47's standard costs are as follows.

Standard cost data

	Machine group 1 $	Machine group 7 $	Machine group 29 $	Assembly $
Materials (per unit)	26.00	17.00	-	3.00
Labour (per unit)	2.00	1.60	0.75	1.20
Variable overheads (per unit)	0.65	0.72	0.80	0.36
Fixed overheads (per unit)	3.00	2.50	1.50	0.84
	31.65	21.82	3.05	5.40
Setting-up costs per batch of 200 units	$10	$6	$4	-

Component WB47
Batch size 200 units

Required

Compute the lowest selling price at which one batch of 200 units could be offered, and describe the other factors to consider when adopting such a pricing policy. **(6 marks)**

(b) The company is also considering the launch of a new product, component WB49A, and have provided you with the following information.

	Standard cost per box $
Variable cost	6.20
Fixed cost	1.60
	7.80

Market research – forecast of demand

Selling price ($)	13	12	11	10	9
Demand (boxes)	5,000	6,000	7,200	11,200	13,400

The company only has enough production capacity to make 7,000 boxes. However, it would be possible to purchase product WB49A from a sub-contractor at $7.75 per box for orders up to 5,000 boxes, and $7 per box if the orders exceed 5,000 boxes.

Required

Prepare and present a computation which illustrates which price should be selected in order to maximise profits. **(4 marks)**

(Total = 10 marks)

11 DX

18 mins

Learning outcome: A(iii)

DX manufactures a wide range of components for use in various industries. It has developed a new component, the U. It is the practice of DX to set a 'list' selling price for its components and charge this price to all customers. It sells its components directly to customers all over the UK and abroad.

DX has surplus capacity available to enable it to produce up to 350,000 units per year without any need to acquire new facilities or cut back on the production of other products.

Market research indicates that:

(a) If demand is 100,000 units or less, marginal revenue is $9 - 0.06x$, where x is demand in thousands of units.

(b) If demand is above 100,000 units, marginal revenue is $10 - 0.08x$, where x is demand in thousands of units.

Research into production costs indicates that the marginal costs for a unit of production in any given year are as follows.

(a) **Labour**. Initially $2.00 per unit but falling by 2.5p per unit for each extra 1,000 units produced, thus upto the first 1,000 units produced incurs a labour cost of $2,000, the second 1,000 incurs a labour cost of $1,975, the third 1,000 incurs a labour cost of $1,950 and so on until output reaches 80,000; output can be increased beyond 80,000 units per year without incurring any additional labour costs.

(b) **Materials**. 50p per unit constant at all levels of output.

(c) **Overhead**. Initially $1.00 per unit and remaining constant until output reaches 100,000 units per year; the overhead cost per unit of producing at above that level rises by 0.25p for each extra 1,000 units produced, thus the 101st thousand units produced incur an overhead cost of $1,002.50, the 102nd thousand units produced incur an overhead cost of $1,005 and so on.

Required

Calculate the output level that will maximise DX's profit from U production.

(10 marks)

12 Plastic tools

18 mins

Learning outcome: A(ii)

A small company is engaged in the production of plastic tools for the garden.

Subtotals on the spreadsheet of budgeted overheads for a year reveal the following.

	Moulding department	Finishing department	General factory overhead
Variable overhead $'000	1,600	500	1,050
Fixed overhead $'000	2,500	850	1,750
Budgeted activity			
Machine hours (000)	800	600	
Practical capacity			
Machine hours (000)	1,200	800	

For the purposes of reallocation of general factory overhead it is agreed that the variable overheads accrue in line with the machine hours worked in each department. General factory fixed overhead is to be reallocated on the basis of the practical machine hour capacity of the two departments.

It has been a long-standing company practice to establish selling prices by applying a mark-up on full manufacturing cost of between 25% and 35%.

A possible price is sought for one new product which is in a final development stage. The total market for this product is estimated at 200,000 units per annum. Market research indicates that the company could expect to obtain and hold about 10% of the market. It is hoped the product will offer some improvement over competitors' products, which are currently marketed at between $90 and $100 each.

The product development department have determined that the direct material content is $9 per unit. Each unit of the product will take two labour hours (four machine hours) in the moulding department and three labour hours (three machine hours) in finishing. Hourly labour rates are $5.00 and $5.50 respectively.

Management estimate that the annual fixed costs which would be specifically incurred in relation to the product are supervision $20,000, depreciation of a recently acquired machine $120,000 and advertising $27,000. It may be assumed that these costs are included in the budget given above. Given the state of development of this new product, management do not consider it necessary to make revisions to the budgeted activity levels given above for any possible extra machine hours involved in its manufacture.

Required

Prepare full cost and marginal cost information which may help with the pricing decision.

(10 marks)

13 Costs and pricing

18 mins

Learning outcomes: A(ii), (iii)

(a) Comment on the cost information in question 12 above and suggest a price range which should be considered. **(5 marks)**

(b) Briefly explain the role of costs in pricing. **(5 marks)**

(Total = 10 marks)

14 PPA

18 mins

Learning outcome: B(i)

Discuss the advantages and disadvantages of post-project appraisal.

(10 marks)

15 Payback

18 mins

Learning outcome: B(vii)

Explain the uses, limitations and merits of the payback period method of investment appraisal.

(10 marks)

(b) Explain how the use of target costing would assist in the achievement of the required return where a year 1 launch price of $60 is used.
(8 marks)

(c) Quarefel plc wishes to consider the optimum sales volume for each of years 1 to 3 where the restrictions of a year 1 price of $60 per unit and the linking of market share in years 2 and 3 to that obtained in year 1 are removed.

Calculate the strategy (units and selling price) for each of years 1 to 3 which will maximise the return achievable over the life of the product (where MR = 70 – 0.3Q).
(5 marks)

(Total = 25 marks)

20 Elsewhere

45 mins

Learning outcomes: C(iv), (v)

Rubbish Records Ltd are considering the launch of a new pop group, Elsewhere.

If the group is launched without further market research being carried out it is thought that demand for their records and the present value of profit earned from record sales will be as follows.

Demand	Probability	Present value of profit $'000
High	0.5	800
Medium	0.2	100
Low	0.3	(300)

It is possible, however, to commission a market research survey which will forecast either a successful or unsuccessful career for Elsewhere. The probability of an unsuccessful career is 0.3.

Probabilities of high, medium or low demand for Elsewhere's records under each of the two market research results are as follows.

	High	Demand Medium	Low
Successful chart career	0.7	0.1	0.2
Unsuccessful chart career	0.1	0.3	0.6

So, for example, if the research indicated an unsuccessful chart career, then the probability of medium demand for the group's records would be 0.3.

The survey would cost $50,000.

Required

(a) Calculate the expected value of profit if Rubbish Records do not commission a market research survey.
(5 marks)

(b) (i) Draw a decision tree to show the choices facing Rubbish Records.
(10 marks)

(ii) Briefly explain whether or not the record company should commission the survey.
(3 marks)

(c) (i) Determine the maximum the company should pay for the survey. (Often referred to as the value of the imperfect information provided by the survey).
(2 marks)

(ii) Establish the disadvantages of using expected values and decision trees as decision-making tools.
(5 marks)

(Total = 25 marks)

21 Dench

18 mins

Learning outcome: D(iv)

Dench Manufacturing has received a special order from Sands Ltd. to produce 225 components to be incorporated into Sands' product. The components have a high cost, due to the expertise required for their manufacture. Dench produces the components in batches of 15, and as the ones required are to be custom-made to Sands' specifications, a "prototype" batch was manufactured with the following costs:

Materials		$
	4 kg of A, $7.50/kg	30
	2 kg of B, $15/kg	30
Labour		
	20 hrs skilled, $15/hr	300
	5 hrs semi-skilled, $8/hr	40
Variable overhead		
	25 labour hours, $4/hr	100
		$500

Additional information with respect to the workforce is noted below:

Skilled -   virtually a permanent workforce that has been employed by Dench for a long period of time. These workers have a great deal of experience in manufacturing components similar to those required by Sands, and turnover is virtually non-existent.

Semi-Skilled - hired by Dench on an "as needed" basis. These workers would have had some prior experience, but Dench management believe the level to be relatively insignificant. Past experience shows turnover rate to be quite high, even for short employment periods.

Dench's plans are to exclude the prototype batch from Sands' order. Management believes an 80% learning rate effect is experienced in this manufacturing process, and would like a cost estimate for the 225 components prepared on that basis.

Required

(a)   Prepare the cost estimate, assuming an 80% learning rate is experienced; and   **(6 marks)**

(b)   briefly discuss some of the factors that can limit the use of learning curve theory in practice.

(4 marks)

(Total = 10 marks)

22 Cost reduction

45 mins

Learning outcome: D(i)

It has been suggested that much of the training of management accountants is concerned with cost control whereas the major emphasis should be on cost reduction.

Required

(a)   Distinguish between cost control and cost reduction.   **(7 marks)**

(b)   Give *three* examples *each* of the techniques and principles used for (i) cost control and (ii) cost reduction.   **(8 marks)**

(c)   Discuss the proposition contained in the statement.   **(10 marks)**

(Total = 25 marks)

23 Life cycle costing

18 mins

Learning outcome: D(vii)

Explain life cycle costing and state what distinguishes it from more traditional management accounting techniques.

(10 marks)

24 ABC

18 mins

Learning outcome: D(v)

(a)   It is sometimes claimed that activity based costing (ABC) simply provides a **different** picture of product costs to traditional absorption costing, rather than a more accurate picture.   **(5 marks)**

Explain the concepts that underlie ABC and discuss the claim above.

(b)   Some advocates of ABC claim that it provides information which can be used for decision making. Critically appraise this view.   **(5 marks)**

(Total = 10 marks)

25 ABC systems

18 mins

Learning outcome: D(v)

'ABC systems are *resource-consumption models.* That is, they attempt to measure the cost of *using* resources, not the cost of *supplying* resources.'

Colin Drury, *Management Accounting Business Decisions*

Required

Discuss the statement above using figures, if you wish, to illustrate the points made.

(10 marks)

26 Just-in-time

45 mins

Learning outcome: D(ii)

Many organisations believe that a key element of just-in-time (JIT) systems is JIT production.

Required

(a)   Discuss five main features of a JIT production system.   **(20 marks)**
(b)   State the financial benefits of JIT.   **(5 marks)**

(Total = 25 marks)

27 CPA

18 mins

Learning outcome: D(x), (xi)

As the management accountant of XY Ltd you have undertaken an analysis of the company's profitability in relation to the number of customers served. The results of your analysis are shown in the graph below.

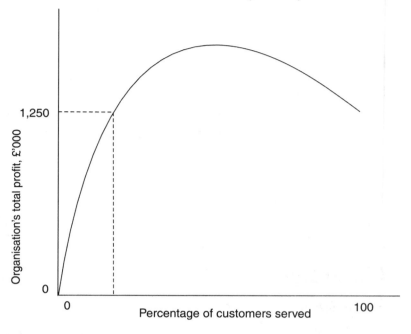

Required

Write a report to management which:

(a)   explains the general concept that is encapsulated by the graph   **(4 marks)**

(b)   advises management on the actions that are open to it to improve the profitability of the organisation.   **(6 marks)**

(Total = 10 marks)

28 Outsourced services

18 mins

Learning outcome: D(viii)

Explain how control can be exercised over the cost of outsourced services.

(10 marks)

Exam answer bank

1 Restaurant

Wages

> **Top tip**. You need to work out the variable wages cost using the high-low method. There are only two years, so one is taken as 'high' and one as 'low'.

	Year 1	Year 2	Increase
Number of meals	151,156	(× 8%) 163,248	12,092
	$	$	$
Wages cost	349,170	390,477	41,307

We must account for inflation, however, by adjusting year 1 to year 2 costs. The figure used is the 6% hourly rate increase.

	$	$	$
$349,170 \times 106\%$ =	370,120	390,477	20,357

In year 2, the variable wages cost of a meal is $\dfrac{\$20,357}{12,092} = \$1.68$

	$
Variable wages cost (year 2) ($1.68 × 163,248)	274,257
Fixed wages cost (year 2) (balance)	116,220
Total wages cost (year 2)	390,477

	$
So, in year 3, variable cost = (163,248 × 110%) meals × $1.68 × 107%	322,800
Fixed cost = $116,220 × 107%	124,355
Total wages cost (year 3)	447,155

Overheads

	Year 1	Year 2	Increase
Number of meals	151,156	163,248	12,092
	$	$	$
Overhead costs	202,549	216,930	14,381
Adjusting year 1 costs to year 2 cost (× 105%)	212,676	216,930	4,254

Variable overhead cost in year 2 is $\dfrac{\$4,254}{12,092} = \$0.352$ per meal

	$
∴ In year 2, variable overhead cost ($0.352 × 163,248)	57,463
Fixed overhead cost (balance)	159,467
Total overhead cost (year 2)	216,930

	$
∴ In year 3, variable cost = (163,248 × 110%) meals × $0.352 × 106%	67,002
Fixed cost = $159,467 × 106%	169,035
Total overhead cost (year 3)	236,037

2 Webber Design

Top tips. This is a relevant costing question so don't get led astray by the references to pricing.

Part (c) is a standalone question that can be answered independently of the rest of the question. It also asks for **definitions** so you should be able to answer this using knowledge rather than application.

(a)   Incremental costs and revenues of altering equipment

	Note	Alter $	Scrap $	Difference $
Materials	1	4,500	–	4,500
Welding	2	–	–	–
Machining	2	–	–	–
Assembly	3	3,680	(16,000)	19,680
Overtime	4	1,500	–	1,500
Variable overhead	5	–	–	–
Delivery	6	3,400	–	3,400
Fixed overheads	7	–	–	–
Original costs	8	–	–	–
Advance	9	–	–	–
Original materials	10	–	(4,000)	4,000
Scrap	10	–	(5,200)	5,200
Design	10	–	(1,500)	1,500
				39,780

The minimum price to be charged is $39,780, but this is subject to clarification of a number of matters which could significantly affect the figure given. See the notes for details.

Notes

1   The cost of proceeding is the $4,500 which will have to be spent on materials for the other contract.

2   Although additional work is required in the welding and machining departments there is no indication that workers can be taken on or laid off at will: we assume that all workers involved in the alteration work will be paid their weekly wages whether or not the work proceeds.

3   Assembly department workers appear to be in short supply and they can generate $5 for every $1 of direct labour. By redeploying 2 workers for eight weeks at $200 per worker the company will forgo $2 \times \$5 \times \$200 \times 8 = \$16,000$ contribution. Contribution is earned after having covered labour and variable overhead costs and therefore wages of $(2 \times 8 \times \$200) = \$3,200$ and variable overheads of 15% ($480) are also included in this case. Total reduced cost is $19,680.

4   Overtime is incurred as a direct result of the alteration work and will not be paid otherwise.

5   Variable overhead, like direct wages, will be incurred whatever decision is taken.

6   The special delivery charge is directly relevant to the new customer.

7   Fixed overheads do not change as a result of the decision to proceed and so no extra cost is included.

8   We do not know whether the 'additional work' is in place of or in addition to the work required to complete the equipment to the original specification. We do not know whether the completion costs are 'estimated' or already 'incurred'. We do not know whether direct wages costs are committed or not. Fixed costs are not relevant, since presumably they will not be saved whatever decision is taken.

None of the completion costs are included in our calculation but further information would have to be obtained before finalising the minimum price.

9   The advance can be calculated as follows.

		$
Original quotation – cost		29,450.00
– margin (20/80)		7,362.50
		36,812.50

Advance (15%) = $5,522

However, we do not know whether this is to be returned to the original customer or not – this will depend upon the terms of the contract. If it were returnable only in the event that the equipment were sold to another customer it would be a relevant cost of proceeding; we have assumed that this is not the case.

10   Savings of $4,000 in materials (ignoring machining costs (see note 2)) would be made if the original equipment were scrapped, and disposal proceeds of $5,200 for other materials and $1,500 for the design would be forgone.

(b)   In addition to the queries raised in the notes above, Webber should consider the following matters in setting the price.

(i)   Whether any of the costs incurred to date can be recovered from the original customer under the terms of the contract.

(ii)   If not, whether the price should attempt to recover costs incurred to date as well as future costs.

(iii)   Whether repeat work is likely from the new customer, in which case it might be worthwhile to grant favourable terms on this order.

(c)   Relevant costs are 'costs appropriate to a specific management decision. They are future cash flows arising as a direct consequence of a decision.

Opportunity cost is 'the value of the benefit sacrificed when one course of action is chosen, in preference to an alternative'.

Discretionary cost is 'expenditure whose level is a matter of policy', for example advertising costs or research and development expenditure.

Relevant costs are (or should be) used by management to make decisions, as stated above. Opportunity costs are a type of relevant cost. The concept is particularly useful where resources are scarce. Discretionary costs do not have to be incurred in order to continue in business: it is thus useful to management to know which costs can be so classified where cost reductions are necessary or when budgeting.

3 AB

> **Top tips.** This question has four ingredients of a good and testing problem on decision making.
>
> - It tests your ability to grasp the **nature of a decision problem**, and think about the assumptions you may have to make. It is assumed that inventory in hand of finished X, valued at $51,900 at full cost, is valued at the full cost of production and not at the full cost of sale. This would be in keeping with SSAP 9, although the wording of the question is ambiguous on this point.
>
> - It tests your knowledge of **relevant costs**. For example, the $3,500 capital cost of Y will be incurred whatever course of action is taken, although with the alternative recommendation we have made the spending could be deferred by 33 weeks. Selling and administration overhead has been assumed to be a fixed cost and so is irrelevant to the decision.
>
> - It includes a consideration of **non-financial factors**. We looked at the workforce, customers' interests and competition – you may have focused on different areas.
>
> - Part (c) of the question introduced the very practical issue **of searching for alternative opportunities**. For example, the alternative course of action we have suggested seems the most obvious one, but you might think otherwise, and a sensible alternative would be equally acceptable as a solution.

(a) **Full cost of production per kg of X**

	$
Direct materials	17.33
Direct labour	7.36
Production overhead (200% of labour)	14.72
	39.41

The quantity of stock-in-hand is therefore $51,900/$39.41 = 1,317 kg

At a weekly sales volume of 74 kg, this represents 1,317/74 = about 18 weeks of sales

It will take 20 weeks to set up the production facility for Y, and so inventory in hand of finished X can be sold before any Y can be produced. This **finished inventory** is therefore **irrelevant** to the decision under review; it will be sold whatever decision is taken.

The problem therefore centres on the inventory in hand of direct materials. Assuming that there is no loss or wastage in manufacture and so 1 kg of direct material is needed to produce 1 kg of X then inventory in hand is $44,800/$17.33 = 2,585 kg.

This would be converted into 2,585 kg of X, which would represent sales volume for 2,585/74 = 35 weeks.

If AB sells its existing inventories of finished X (in 18 weeks) there are **two options**.

(i) To produce enough X from raw materials for 2 more weeks, until production of Y can start, and then dispose of all other quantities of direct material – ie 33 weeks' supply.

(ii) To produce enough X from raw materials to use up the existing inventory of raw materials, and so delay the introduction of Y by 33 weeks.

The relevant costs of these two options

(i) **Direct materials**. The relevant cost of existing inventories of raw materials is $(0.30). In other words the 'cost' is a benefit. By using the direct materials to make more X, the company would save $0.30 per kg used.

(ii) **Direct labour**. It is assumed that if labour is switched to production work from non-production work in the next three months, they must be paid at the full rate of pay, and not at 65% of normal rate. The *incremental* cost of labour would be 35% of the normal rate (35% of $7.36 = $2.58 per kg produced).

Relevant cost of production of X

	$
Direct materials	(0.30)
Direct labour	2.58
Variable overhead (30% of full overhead cost of $14.72)	4.42
Cost per kg of X	6.70

Relevant cost per kg of Y

	$
Direct materials	4.01
Direct labour	2.85
Variable overhead (30% of 200% of $2.85)	1.71
	8.57

(*Note.* Y cannot be made for 20 weeks, and so the company cannot make use of spare labour capacity to produce any units of Y.)

It is cheaper to use up the direct material inventories and make X ($6.70 per kg) than to introduce Y as soon as possible, because there would be a saving of ($8.57 – $6.70) = $1.87 per kg made.

AB must sell X for at least 20 weeks until Y could be produced anyway, but the introduction of Y could be delayed by a further 33 weeks until all inventories of direct material for X are used up. The saving in total would be about $1.87 per kg × 74 kg per week × 33 weeks = $4,567.

(b) **Non-financial factors that must be considered in reaching the decision**

(i) **The workforce**. If the recommended course of action is undertaken, the workforce will produce enough units of X in the next 13 weeks to satisfy sales demand over the next year, (with 18 weeks' supply of existing finished goods inventories and a further 35 weeks' supply obtainable from direct materials inventories). When production of Y begins, the direct labour content of production will fall to $2.85 per kg – less than 40% of the current effort per kg produced – but sales demand will not rise. The changeover will therefore mean a big drop in labour requirements in production. Redundancies seem inevitable, and might be costly. By switching to producing Y as soon as possible, the redundancies might be less immediate, and could be justified more easily to employees and their union representatives than a decision to produce enough X in the next 3 months to eliminate further production needs for about 9 months.

(ii) **Customers' interests**. Product Y is a superior and 'more effective' compound than X. It would be in customers' interests to provide them with this improved product as soon as possible, instead of delaying its introduction until existing inventories of direct materials for X have been used up.

(iii) **Competition**. CD is expected to start selling Y overseas, and quite possibly in direct competition with AB. CD has the advantage of having developed Y itself, and appears to use it in the preliminary stage of an alternative technical process. The competitive threat to AB is two-fold:

(1) CD might take away some of the replacement demand for Y from AB so that AB's sales of X or Y would fall.

(2) CD might compete with AB to install its total technical process into customers' factories, and so the competition would be wider than the market for compound Y.

(c) **Alternative course of action**

 (i) Produce enough units of X in the next 13 weeks to use up existing inventories of direct materials.

 (ii) Start sales of Y as soon as possible, and offer customers the choice between X and Y. Since X is an inferior compound, it would have to be sold at a lower price than Y.

Merits of this course of action

 (i) The workforce would be usefully employed for the next 13 weeks and then production of Y would begin at once. Although redundancies would still seem inevitable, the company would be creating as much work as it could for its employees.

 (ii) AB's customers would be made aware of the superiority of Y over X in terms of price, and of AB's commitment to the new compound. AB's marketing approach would be both 'honest' and would also give customers an attractive choice of buying the superior Y or, for a time, an inferior X but at a lower price. This might well enhance AB's marketing success.

Demerits of this course of action

 (i) It is unlikely to be a profit-maximising option, because selling X at a discount price would reduce profitability.

 (ii) Customers who get a discount on X might demand similar discounts on Y.

 (iii) Some customers might query the technical differences between X and Y, and question why AB has been selling X at such a high price in the past – this might lead to some customer relations difficulties.

 (iv) AB must decide when to reduce the price of X, given that Y cannot be made for 20 weeks. The timing of the price reduction might create some difficulties with customers who buy X just before the price is reduced.

4 BB Company

Top tips. In the old syllabus, multi-product CVP analysis only appeared in the MCQ section of the exam paper, albeit on quite a few occasions. The P2 exam could include a full question on the topic, however, so ensure you make a good attempt at this one.

To draw up a **contribution breakeven chart** you need to **know** three things.

- Selling price per can
- Variable cost per can
- Fixed costs

These can all be calculated from information in the question with varying degrees of difficulty/ease.

As CVP analysis is based on **marginal costing principles** and given that information in the question is provided for two time periods, you have a rather large hint that you need to split the manufacturing costs into fixed and variable components using the **high-low method**. It is safe to assume that the **administration** costs are **fixed** as they are the **same** in both time periods. Selling price per unit is a straightforward calculation.

You then have enough information to draw up the chart. You can always calculate breakeven point and margin of safety and compare them with your chart to ensure that you have marked them on the chart correctly. (Did you actually see the note in the requirements asking you to show them on the chart?)

Part (b) involves **multi-product** CVP analysis. The data for the chart is not difficult to derive, but the calculation of breakeven point must be based on contribution per mix, **the standard mix being one own label, one BB brand**.

An exam question will invariably ask for some written analysis, and this question is no exception. The points you need to make are not particularly technical, but are simply grounded in common sense. If option 2 shows the higher profit, **lower breakeven point** (so that **not so many sales are required to cover costs**) and **a higher margin of safety** (which means that the **difference between expected sales and breakeven sales is likely to be higher**), it should be the better option. There are, of course, **other factors** that might affect that decision.

Assumption. Manufacturing costs for the BB brand will be the same as for own label brands.

Initial workings

Manufacturing costs

We need to analyse the cost behaviour patterns by separating the manufacturing costs into their fixed and variable elements, using the high-low method.

	Sales Millions	Costs $ million
20X3	19	4.45
20X2	18	4.30
	1	0.15

Variable manufacturing cost per can = $0.15

Fixed manufacturing cost = $4.45 million – (19 million × $0.15)
= $1.6 million

Selling prices

Selling price per can in 20X3	= 6.27/19	= $0.33
∴ Unit contribution per can	= $0.33 – $0.15	= $0.18
∴ Contribution per can of BB brand	= $0.18 × 133 1/3%	= $0.24
Variable cost per can of BB brand	= $0.15 + $0.02	= $0.17
∴ Selling price per can of BB brand	= $0.17 + $0.24	= $0.41

(a) **Data for chart**

	$ million	$ million
Variable costs (19 million × $0.15)		2.85
Fixed costs: manufacturing	1.60	
administration	1.20	
		2.80
Total costs		5.65

Breakeven point $= \dfrac{fixed\ costs}{contribution} = \dfrac{\$2.8m}{\$0.18}$
= 15.55 million cans
= $5.13 million sales

Margin of safety = 19m – 15.55m = 3.45 million cans = $1.14 million sales

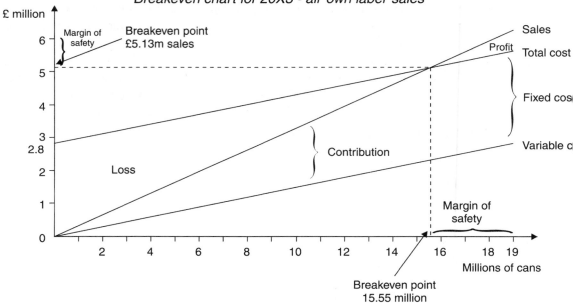

Breakeven chart for 20X3 - all 'own label' sales

(b) **Data for chart**

		$ million	$ million
Variable costs:	own label (9.5m × $0.15)		1.425
	BB brand (9.5m × $0.17)		1.615
			3.040
Fixed costs:	manufacturing	1.600	
	administration	1.200	
	marketing	0.400	
			3.200
Total costs:			6.240
Sales value:	own label (9.5m × $0.33)		3.135
	BB brand (9.5m × $0.41)		3.895
			7.030

Our standard mix is 1 own label, 1 BB brand.

$$\text{Breakeven point} = \frac{\text{fixed costs}}{\text{contribution per mix}} = \frac{\$3.2m}{\$(0.18 + 0.24)} = \frac{\$3.2m}{\$0.42}$$

$$= 7.62 \text{ million mixes} = 15.24 \text{ million cans}$$

$$= 7.62 \times (\$(0.33 + 0.41)) \text{ million sales} = \$5.64 \text{ million sales}$$

Margin of safety $= 19m - 15.24 \text{ million} = 3.76 \text{ million cans} = 1.88 \text{ million mixes}$
$= 1.88 \times (\$(0.33 + 0.41)) \text{ million sales}$
$= \$1.39 \text{ million sales}$

Profit $= \$7.03 \text{ million} - \$6.24 \text{ million} = \$790,000$

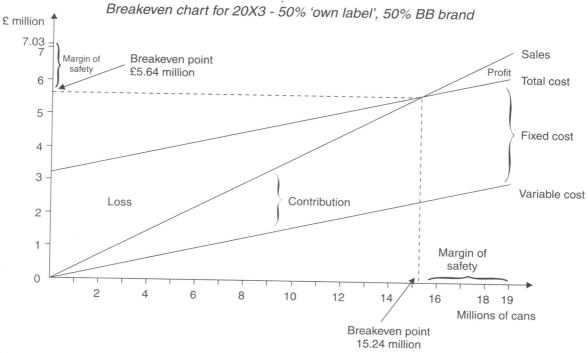

Breakeven chart for 20X3 - 50% 'own label', 50% BB brand

(c) The **first chart** shows a breakeven point of 15.55 million cans ($5.13m sales value) and a margin of safety of 3.45 million cans ($1.14m sales value). Forecast profit for sales of 19 million cans is $620,000.

The **second chart** shows a breakeven point of 15.24 million cans ($5.64m sales value) and a margin of safety of 3.76 million cans ($1.39m sales value). Forecast profit for sales of 19 million cans is $790,000.

Option 2 therefore results in a higher profit figure, as well as a lower breakeven point and increased margin of safety. On this basis it is the better of the two options.

Other factors which management should consider before making a decision

(i) The supermarket chains may put the same pressure on margins and prices of the BB brand as they do on the own label brands.

(ii) Customers may realise that the BB brand is the same product as the own label brand and may not be willing to pay the premium price.

(iii) If the mix of sales can be changed in favour of the BB brand then profits will improve still further.

5 X

> **Top tips.** The ranking of the products is relatively straightforward, provided you adopt a systematic approach.

	A $/litre	B $/litre	C $/litre	D $/litre
Selling price	100	110	120	120
Variable cost	54	55	59	66
Contribution	46	55	61	54
Labour hours used per litre	3	2.5	4	4.5
Contribution per labour hour	$15.33	$22	$15.25	$12
Ranking	2	1	3	4

The available **labour hours** should be allocated **first** to the **contract already made** with Y Ltd. The **remaining hours** should then be allocated to **products according to this ranking**, and **subject to the maximum demand**.

	Product	Litres		Hours used	Cumulative hours used
Y Ltd	A, B, C, D	20 each	(× 14)	280	280
Ranking	B	130	(× 2.5)	325	605
	A	180	(× 3)	540	1,145
	C	50	(× 4)	200	1,345

Summary of recommended production for next three months

Product	Litres
A	200
B	150
C	70
D	20

Calculation of profit for next three months

Product	Litres	Contribution $ per litre	Contribution $
A	200	46	9,200
B	150	55	8,250
C	70	61	4,270
D	20	54	1,080
Total contribution			22,800
Fixed overhead (see working)			12,800
Profit			10,000

Working

Calculation of fixed overhead per quarter

Using product A, fixed overhead per hour = $24/3 = $8 per hour

∴ Budgeted fixed overhead = 1,600 hours × $8 = $12,800

Note. The calculation of the hourly rate of $8 per hour could have been based on any of the four products.

6 Research director

> **Top tips**. The information provided changes the ranking compared with question 5, and so you will need to recalculate the production plan. Don't forget that the minimum quantity of D has to be produced.

Products **C and D** can both be **sold** for a **higher price than that offered by the overseas supplier**. The **unsatisfied demand** should therefore be **met** by using the **overseas supplier** next quarter.

	C	D
	$ per litre	*$ per litre*
External supplier's price	105	100
Internal variable cost of manufacture	59	66
Saving through internal manufacture	46	34
Labour hours used per litre	4	4.5
Saving per labour hour	$11.50	$7.56

Even when the extra cost of the pollution controls for product D is ignored, **it is therefore preferable to manufacture product C internally and purchase D from the overseas supplier.**

The capacity which would have been used to manufacture 20 litres of product D can now be allocated to product C (20 litres × 4.5 hours = 90 hours).

Summary of revised recommended production for the next three months

Product		Hours	Litres	Litres
A	Internal manufacture	600		200
B	Internal manufacture	375		150
C	Internal manufacture	370	92.5	
C	External purchase		7.5	100
D	External purchase			120
		1,345		570

Calculation of revised profit for next three months

Product			Contribution	
	Litres		*$ per litre*	*$*
A	200.0		46	9,200.00
B	150.0		55	8,250.00
C	92.5		61	5,642.50
	7.5	(120 – 105)	15	112.50
D	120.0	(120 – 100)	20	2,400.00
				25,605.00
Fixed overhead				12,800.00
Revised profit				12,805.00

Reasons that profit will increase by $2,805 per quarter are as follows.

(a) Production of product D is subcontracted and the time saved is used on production of product C.
(b) The additional fixed cost is not incurred because Product D production is subcontracted.
(c) Maximum demand for products C and D can be met.

A number of factors should be considered, however, including the following.

(a) The reliability of the supplier, which is particularly important in the case of an overseas supplier
(b) The quality of supply
(c) Any other sources of sub-contract supply

7 RAB Consulting

> **Top tips**. This is a straightforward linear programming question from the pilot paper under the old syllabus.
>
> The best way to approach graphical linear programming questions is to work through the **six steps** we recommend in the text.
>
> - Define variables
> - Establish objective function
> - Establish constraints
> - Graph the problem
> - Define feasible area
> - Determine optimal solution
>
> Notice the approach we have taken to choosing our sample **iso-contribution line**. This is something that students often find difficult, so choose easy **numbers (related to the coefficients of the variables)**, making sure that the line then falls within the feasible area.
>
> Don't forget that there will always be **marks** in the exam for **presentation** of the **graph**, so remember to label your axes, use a ruler and so on.

(a) (i)

		Type A $ per project		Type B $ per project
Revenue		1,700		1,500
Variable costs				
Labour				
– qualified researchers	(20 hrs × $30)	600	(12 hrs × $30)	360
– junior researchers	(8 hrs × $14)	112	(15 hrs × $14)	210
Direct project expenses		408		310
		1,120		880
Contribution		580		620

(ii) **Step 1** **Define variables**

Let a = number of type A projects
Let b = number of type B projects

Step 2 **Establish objective function**

Maximise contribution (C) = 580a + 620b, subject to the constraints below.

Step 3 **Establish constraints**

Qualified researchers time:	$20a + 12b \leq 1{,}344$
Junior researchers time:	$8a + 15b \leq 1{,}120$
Agreement for type A:	$a \geq 20$
Maximum for type B:	$b \leq 60$
Non-negativity:	$a \geq 0, b \geq 0$

(iii) **Step 4**   **Graphing the problem**

Constraints

Qualified researcher time:	if a = 0, b = 112
	if b = 0, a = 67.2
Junior researcher time:	if a = 0, b = 74.67
	if b = 0, a = 140
Agreement for type A:	graph the line a = 20
Maximum for type B:	graph the line b = 60

Step 5   **Define feasible area**

Iso-contribution line

580a + 620b = 35,960 (where 35,960 = 58 × 62 × 10) goes through the points (62, 0) and (0, 58)

Graph to show profit-maximising mix of projects

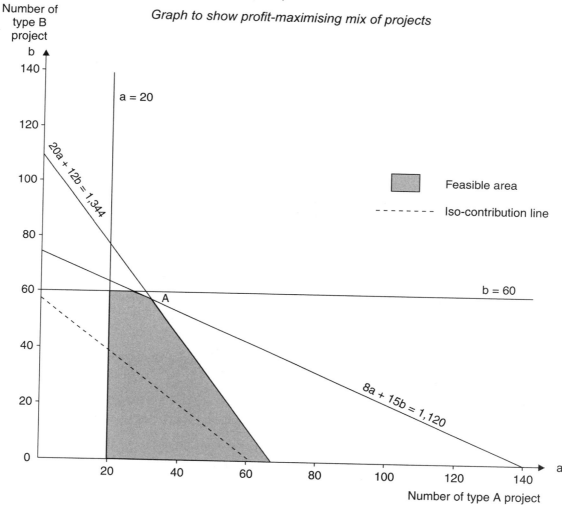

Moving the iso-contribution line away from the origin, we see that it leaves the feasible area at the intersection of the two time constraints (point A).

Step 6 — *Determine optimal solution*

Find the coordinates of A

20a + 12b	= 1,344	(1)	
8a + 15b	= 1,120	(2)	
20a + 37.5b	= 2,800	(3)	(2) × 2.5
25.5b	= 1,456		(3) − (1)
b	= 57.09		
20a + 685.08	= 1,344	substitute into (1)	
a	= 32.946		

The profit-maximising mix of projects is 33 of type A and 57 of type B.

(b) **Profit for profit-maximising mix**

		$
Contribution from type A:	33 × $580	19,140
Contribution from type B:	57 × $620	35,340
Total contribution		54,480
Less: fixed costs		(28,000)
		26,480

(c) **The importance of identifying scarce resources when preparing budgets**

Scarce resources restrict the activity level at which an organisation can operate. For example, a sales department might estimate that it could sell 1,000 units of product X, which would require 5,000 hours of grade A labour. If there are no units of product X in inventory, and only 4,000 hours of grade A labour available in the period, the company would be unable to make and sell 1,000 units of X because of the shortage of labour hours. Management must choose one of the following options.

- Reduce budgeted sales by 20%.
- Increase the availability of grade A labour by recruitment or overtime working.
- Sub-contract some production to another manufacturer.

If the fact that grade A labour is a **scarce resource** is **ignored** when the **budget** is prepared, it will be **unattainable** and of **little relevance for planning and control.**

Most organisations are **restricted** from making and selling more of their products because there would be **no sales demand for the increased output** at an acceptable price. The organisation should therefore budget to produce and sell the volume of its product(s) demanded.

The **scarce resource** might be machine capacity, distribution and selling resources, raw materials or cash.

(i) If an organisation **produces just one product**, the **budget for the scarce resources is usually the starting point in the budget preparation process**.

(ii) If an organisation **produces two or more products** and there is only **one scarce resource**, **limiting factor analysis** must be used to determine the most profitable use of the scarce resource.

(iii) When there is **more than one scarce resource**, **linear programming** must be used to identify the most profitable use of resources.

The use of linear programming to determine the optimum use of resources

Linear programming is a technique which **determines the most profitable production mix, taking into account resource constraints and limitations** faced by an organisation. **All costs are**

assumed to be either fixed or variable in relation to a single measure of activity (usually units of output).

The **problem is formulated** in terms of an **objective function** and **constraints** are then **graphed**. This process **highlights all possible output combinations given** the resource constraints and limitations and allows for the **identification of the output combination which would maximise contribution (the optimal solution).**

If there are **more than two types of output**, the graphical approach is not possible and the **simplex method** must be used instead.

8 Zaman

Top tips. The question does not ask for a graph but we have sketched one here. It helps you to find the optimal production level if you plot your axes correctly and use a rule to find the optimal point in the feasible region.

(a)   Let q = number of Qa units produced next year

and m = number of Mar units produced next year

Contribution per unit:

Qa = $\$200 - (20 \times \$3) - (4 \times \$10) - \$20 = \$80$
Mar = $\$109 - (8 \times \$3) - (5 \times \$10) - \$15 = \$20$

Objective function is to maximise contribution $\$80q + \$20m$.

Constraints:

Labour: $20q + 8m \leq 40{,}000$ (hours)
Material: $4q + 5m \leq 20{,}000$ (kgs)
Sales: $q \leq 1{,}000$ & $m \leq 4{,}000$ (units)
Non-negativity: $q \geq 0$ & $m \geq 0$

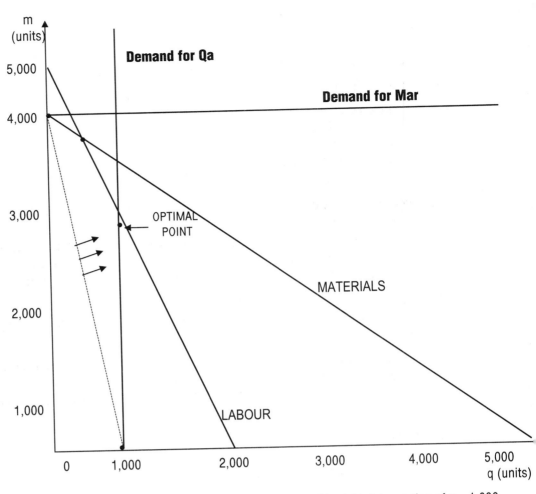

From the graph it will be seen that the optimal production level is at the intersection of q = 1,000 and labour 20q + 8m = 40,000, i.e. where q = 1,000 and m = 2,500.

Optimal production plan is 1,000 units of Qa and 2,500 units of Mar.

(b) The following limitations are inherent in the calculations:

(i) the model assumes linear relationships between the variables. This assumption may not always be true. For example, it may be possible to charge a higher price when production is at a restricted level. Similarly at higher levels of production, costs may be reduced either by mass production techniques, the learning effect and faster performance of employees or bulk discounts on materials.

(ii) All information is taken as certain which is unlikely to be the case in practice. Sensitivity analysis may be applied to deal with this problem.

(iii) The sale of Qa and Mar may be in markets with different debt collection patterns – this has been ignored in the solution.

(iv) It is assumed that there is no latitude in the availability of resources. In practice it will almost certainly be possible to obtain extra labour by payment of an overtime premium.

(v) The products may be complementary or substitutes. This may impose other limitations on the demand.

9 XYZ

Top tips. The formulation of a problem using the simplex method of linear programming (part (a)) involves **five key stages**.

- Define variables
- Establish objective function
- Establish constraints
- **Introduce slack variables**
- **Express constraints as equations**

The method only really differs from the graphical approach in the fourth and fifth stages. A **slack variable** is **needed for each constraint** (other than non-negativity constraints), and so five will be needed in this solution. The **constraints are then turned into equations** by **including the relevant slack variable** (which represents the amount of resource unused, the difference between actual production and maximum possible production and so on) so that the **two sides of the equation are equal.**

Interpretation of a final tableau may appear daunting at first, but once you have done a few questions you will find it becomes far easier. Honestly! Read through our solution and ensure that you really understand the meaning of the figures in the tableau.

The **optimal solution** is determined by looking for **variables** that have a **zero in every row of their column except for one row that has a figure 1**. This is the **solution** for that variable. The figure 1 in the x_2 column is in the same row as the 750 in the solution column, and so 750,000 units of the deluxe model should be produced.

By the way, did you notice that **the figures** were in **thousands**?

(a)   **Define variables**

Let x_1 be the number of Super deluxe produced
Let x_2 be the number of Deluxe produced
Let x_3 be the number of Export produced

Establish objective function

Maximise contribution (C) = $1,500x_1 + 1,300x_2 + 2,500x_3$ (subject to the constraints below).

Establish constraints

$$
\begin{array}{rcll}
x_1 & \leq & 500 & \text{(super deluxe demand)} \\
x_2 & \leq & 750 & \text{(deluxe demand)} \\
x_3 & \leq & 400 & \text{(export model demand)} \\
0.5x_1 + 0.5x_2 + x_3 & \leq & 1,400 & \text{(machining capacity)} \\
0.5x_1 + 0.5x_2 + 2x_3 & \leq & 1,200 & \text{(assembly capacity)} \\
x_1, x_2, x_3 & \geq & 0 &
\end{array}
$$

Introduce slack variables

Slack variables are introduced as follows.

s_1 is the amount by which demand for x_1 falls short of 500
s_2 is the amount by which demand for x_2 falls short of 750
s_3 is the amount by which demand for x_3 falls short of 400
s_4 is the unused machine capacity in thousands of hours
s_5 is the unused assembly capacity in thousands of hours

Then $x_1 + s_1 = 500$
$x_2 + s_2 = 750$
$x_3 + s_3 = 400$
$0.5x_1 + 0.5x_2 + x_3 + s_4 = 1,400$
$0.5x_1 + 0.5x_2 + 2x_3 + s_5 = 1,200$

and $C - 1,500x_1 - 1,300x_2 - 2,500x_3 + 0s_1 + 0s_2 + 0s_3 + 0s_4 + 0s_5 = 0$

(b) (i) Produce   500,000 units of the super deluxe model $(x_1 = 500)$
                     750,000 units of the deluxe model $(x_2 = 750)$
      and   287,500 units of the export model $(x_3 = 287.5)$

(ii) This means that demand for the export model will be 112,500 units short of the maximum demand $(s_3 = 112.5)$

(iii) There will be 487,500 unused direct labour hours in machining $(s_4 = 487.5)$

(iv) The total contribution will be $2,443,750.

(v) The shadow price of s_1 is $875 and that of s_2 is $675.

     (1) Contribution would therefore increase (or decrease) by $875 for each one thousand units by which the demand constraint for the super deluxe model increased (or decreased). For example if the maximum demand for the super deluxe fell to 490,000 $(x_1 \le 490)$, maximum contribution would fall by $10 \times \$875 = \$8,750$ to $2,435,000.

     (2) Similarly, contribution would increase (or decrease) by $675 for each one thousand units by which the demand constraint for the deluxe model increased (or decreased).

(vi) The shadow price of assembly time is $1,250 per thousand hours. This means that for every thousand hours extra (or less) of assembly time available, provided that the cost of this time remains at its normal variable cost per hour, maximum contribution would be $1,250 higher (or lower). This is readily apparent in this particular problem, because the extra time would have to be used to make the export model (since the other two models are already being produced up to maximum demand). One thousand extra hours of assembly time would be sufficient to produce 500 units of the export model, to earn a contribution of 50% of $2,500 = $1,250. This shadow price is only valid up to the point where demand for the export model is satisfied (an extra 112,500 units, or 225,000 hours), given that sufficient machining capacity does exist to produce all of these extra units.

10 PN Motor Components

Top tips. In part (a) you should have disregarded the information about fixed costs. You should have taken into account the setting-up costs, however, as they do vary with the volume of production and so are marginal costs.

Many candidates find the discussion parts of questions the most difficult and so don't worry if your list of 'factors' in part (a) is far shorter than ours.

(a) The **lowest selling price** of one batch of 200 units is **one which covers the marginal cost of production**. This comprises the variable costs of materials, labour, overheads and setting up.

Marginal cost per unit calculation

	Machine group 1 $	Machine group 7 $	Machine group 29 $	Assembly $	Total $
Materials	26.00	17.00	–	3.00	46.00
Labour	2.00	1.60	0.75	1.20	5.55
Variable overheads	0.65	0.72	0.80	0.36	2.53
Setting-up costs (÷ 200)	0.05	0.03	0.02	–	0.10
	28.70	19.35	1.57	4.56	54.18

The lowest selling price per batch is therefore $54.18 × 200 = $10,836.

The calculations show that the marginal cost of one batch of 200 units is $10,836 and this is therefore the lowest possible price that can be offered. However, to sell at such a price would mean that the component would make no contribution to fixed costs and such costs must be covered if the company is to make a profit.

Other factors to be considered when adopting such a pricing policy include the following.

(i)   It is inappropriate to set prices with reference only to an organisation's internal cost structure. Of equal **importance** is the **wider market environment** and the **pricing strategy of competitors**.

(ii)   The organisation must **take into account the likely reaction of competitors**. For example, such a policy could trigger off a price war in which the company could lose more than it gains.

(iii)   The organisation **cannot continue to sell at the minimum price indefinitely**. It must therefore decide its future plans for the component. Will it reduce costs or increase prices? It may, however, take longer than the organisation imagines to be able to charge the full price for the component.

(iv)   The organisation should consider the approach to be taken if existing customers for the component discover the 'special price' being offered to other customers. **Will the organisation gain a few new customers at the expense of alienating existing valuable customers?**

(b)   **We begin by calculating the contribution per unit at different sales prices and sales volumes.**

Outputs and sales up to 7,000 units

Total demand	Selling price $	Variable cost $	Contribution $
5,000 boxes	13.00	6.20	6.80
6,000 boxes	12.00	6.20	5.80
7,200 boxes	11.00	6.20	4.80
11,200 boxes	10.00	6.20	3.80
13,400 boxes	9.00	6.20	2.80

Outputs and sales above 7,000 units

Total demand	Supplied by sub-contractor	Selling price $	Variable cost $	Contribution $
7,200 boxes	200 boxes	11.00	7.75	3.25
11,200 boxes	4,200 boxes	10.00	7.75	2.25
13,400 boxes	6,400 boxes	9.00	7.00	2.00

The total contribution at different sales levels can now be found.

Selling price $	Demand $	Own boxes sold	Unit contrib'n $	Sub contr's boxes	Unit contrib'n $	Total contrib'n $
13.00	5,000	5,000	6.80	0		34,000
12.00	6,000	6,000	5.80	0		34,800
11.00	7,200	7,000	4.80	200	3.25	34,250
10.00	11,200	7,000	3.80	4,200	2.25	36,050
9.00	13,400	7,000	2.80	6,400	2.00	32,400

The calculations show that contribution and therefore profit are maximised at a selling price of $10 with sales of 11,200 boxes.

11 DX

> **Top tips**. The way to tackle this sort of question is to read through the information twice and then to formulate it mathematically, taking care to define your variables as you go. You should then find that you have condensed all the information into a few simple equations.

Profit will be maximised when marginal cost (MC) equals marginal revenue (MR).

Let x = the number of thousands of units sold

For values of x up to 80,

$$MC = 2 - 0.025x + 0.5 + 1$$
$$MC = 3.5 - 0.025x$$

For values of x between 80 and 100,

$$MC = 0.5 + 1 = 1.5$$

For values of x above 100,

$$MC = 0.5 + 1 + 0.0025(x - 100)$$
$$MC = 1.25 + 0.0025x$$

If the profit-maximising output is below 80,000 units, it is at

$$9 - 0.06x = 3.5 - 0.025x$$
$$5.5 = 0.035x$$
$$x = 157.14$$

This is above 80,000 units, so the profit-maximising output is not below 80,000 units.

If the profit-maximising output is between 80,000 and 100,000 units, it is at

$$9 - 0.06x = 1.5$$
$$7.5 = 0.06x$$
$$x = 125$$

This is above 100,000 units, so the profit-maximising output is not between 80,000 and 100,000 units.

The profit-maximising output is therefore at

$$10 - 0.08x = 1.25 + 0.0025x$$
$$8.75 = 0.0825x$$
$$x = 106.061$$

The profit-maximising output is 106,061 units.

12 Plastic tools

> **Top tips.** The techniques required in this question are extremely **straightforward** (calculation of overhead absorption rates for example) so beware of making a silly arithmetical error.

Calculation of overhead absorption rates

	Moulding dept $'000	Finishing dept $'000	General factory overhead $'000
Variable overhead			
Initial allocation	1,600	500	1,050
Reapportion general overhead (800:600)	600	450	(1,050)
Total variable overhead	2,200	950	–
Budgeted machine hours	800	600	
Variable overhead rate per hour	$2.75	$1.58	
	$'000	$'000	$'000
Fixed overhead			
Initial allocation	2,500	850	1,750
Reapportion general overhead (1,200:800)	1,050	700	(1,750)
Total fixed overhead	3,550	1,550	–
Budgeted machine hours	800	600	
Fixed overhead rate per hour	$4.44	$2.58	

Information to assist with the pricing decision

	$ per unit	$ per unit
Direct material		9.00
Direct labour: moulding dept (2 × $5)	10.00	
finishing dept (3 × $5.50)	16.50	
		26.50
Variable overhead: moulding dept (4 × $2.75)	11.00	
finishing dept (3 × $1.58)	4.74	
		15.74
Variable manufacturing cost		51.24
Fixed overhead: moulding dept (4 × $4.44)	17.76	
finishing dept (3 × $2.58)	7.74	
		25.50
Full manufacturing cost		76.74

A **full-cost plus price** will be **based on this cost** of $76.74 **plus a mark-up** of between 25% and 35%. Taking a high, low and average mark-up, the potential prices are as follows.

	25% mark-up $ per unit	30% mark-up $ per unit	35% mark-up $ per unit
Full manufacturing cost	76.74	76.74	76.74
Mark-up	19.19	23.02	26.86
Full cost-plus price	95.93	99.76	103.60

Certain incremental or specific fixed costs have been identified, however, and these should be borne in mind for a well-informed pricing decision.

Product cost based on incremental fixed costs

	$'000	$ per unit
Variable manufacturing cost		51.24
Incremental fixed costs: supervision	20	
depreciation	120	
advertising	27	
	167	
Incremental fixed cost per unit (÷ 20,000 (W))		8.35
Incremental total cost per unit		59.59

Working

Total market = 200,000 units per annum

Ten per cent market share = 20,000 units per annum

13 Costs and pricing

Top tips. In part (a), there is a lot of information in question 12 that you can use when suggesting a suitable price range. Your **higher-level skills** are required, however. Make sensible comments on the various possible prices.

The most important point to make in (b) is that **cost is not the only factor to consider** when setting prices, although of course it must be considered. This part of the question is only worth 5 marks, so you should only spend a maximum of **9 minutes** on it. It would have been very easy to wander from the point and discuss the various pricing approaches in detail.

(a)   The cost information provides a range of bases for a pricing decision.

Variable manufacturing cost

The variable manufacturing cost is $51.24 per unit. At a price below this level there would be no contribution to fixed overheads. Since the prevailing market price is between $90 and $100 each, such a low price might suggest that the product is of inferior quality.

Incremental total cost

The incremental total cost per unit is $59.59. Management must select a price above this level to be sure of covering all costs associated with this product. This unit rate depends on achieving an annual volume of 20,000 units.

Full manufacturing cost

The full manufacturing cost per unit is $76.74. A price based on this cost will ensure that all costs are covered in the long run, if the annual volume of 20,000 units is achieved. Since competitors' prices range between $90 and $100 it seems possible that the company can compete with a price calculated on a full cost-plus basis.

The range of prices suggested, using the company's usual mark-up of between 25 per cent and 35 per cent, is $95.93 to $103.60 per unit.

Given the current price range of the competitors' products and the fact that the product is expected to offer some improvement over competitors' products, a price towards the upper end of the suggested range would be appropriate.

(b)   In general, the **price charged** for a product should **exceed its cost**. There are a number of different cost-based approaches to pricing, however, and each is appropriate in different circumstances.

Full-cost plus pricing involves adding a profit margin to the fully absorbed total cost of a product. In certain situations, for example if an organisation has spare capacity, it may be appropriate to use **marginal cost** as the basis for pricing. Alternatively if the lowest possible price is sought, perhaps for strategic reasons, a **minimum** price based on **relevant costs** may be used as the basis for a pricing decision. Management must not lose sight of the need to cover fixed costs in the long run, however.

Whichever cost basis is used, it is important to appreciate that a cost-based price merely provides a **starting point for informed management decisions and pricing negotiations.**

Cost is **only one of the factors to bear in mind** when making a price-setting decision. Other factors to consider will include the organisation's objectives, the market in which the organisation operates and the effect which price has on the volume of demand for its goods.

14 PPA

> **Top tips.** Although a significant proportion of this answer is simply regurgitation of text book knowledge, this *was* part of an old syllabus question and was worth 10 marks. Questions on this topic could well centre on such an appraisal's advantages and disadvantages.

What is post project appraisal and audit?

Post project appraisal and audit (PPAA) involves **measurement of the success of a capital expenditure project** in terms of **the realisation of anticipated benefits**. PPAA should cover the **implementation** of the project from authorisation to commissioning and **its technical and commercial performance** after commissioning. The information provided by the appraisal and audit can also be used by management as **feedback** to help with the implementation and control of future projects.

Advantages of PPAA

PPAA cannot reverse the decision to incur the capital expenditure, because the expenditure has already taken place. It does have **advantages in terms of control**, however.

(a)   The threat of a PPAA will **motivate managers** to work to achieve the promised benefits from the project.

(b)   If the audit takes place before the project life ends, and if it finds that the benefits have been less than expected because of management inefficiency, steps can be taken to **improve efficiency**. Alternatively, it will **highlight those projects which should be discontinued**.

(c)   It can help to **identify** those managers who have been **good performers** and those who have been poor performers.

(d)   It might identify weaknesses in the forecasting and estimating techniques used to evaluate projects, and so should help to **improve** the discipline and quality of **forecasting** for future investment decisions.

(e)   Areas where improvements can be made in methods which should help to achieve **better results in general from capital investments** might be revealed.

(f)   The **original estimates may be more realistic** if managers are aware that they will be monitored, but PPAAs should not be unfairly critical.

Disadvantages of PPAA

There are a number of **problems** with PPAA.

(a)   There are many **uncontrollable factors** which are outside management control in long-term decisions, such as environmental changes.

(b)   It may **not be possible to identify separately** the costs and benefits of any particular project.

(c)   PPAA can be a **costly** and **time-consuming** exercise.

(d)   Applied punitively, PPAA may lead to **managers becoming over cautious and unnecessarily risk averse.**

(e)   The **strategic effects** of a capital investment project may **take years to materialise** and it may in fact never be possible to identify or quantify them effectively.

15 Payback

> **Top tip.** This is an easy question which you should be able to answer using material in the Study Text. Don't waffle and just put down the main points. Half a page will do for ten marks.

The payback period is the **time taken for the cash inflows from a project** to **equal the cash outflows**. A **maximum payback period may be set** and if the project's payback period exceeds this then it is not acceptable.

The payback method has the **advantage** of being **easily understood** and this may be important to the landowner who might not be a financial specialist. A further advantage is that it **focuses on early cash flows**, thereby **indicating projects likely to improve liquidity positions**. Again this may be important if the management does not wish to tie up cash any longer than necessary.

It is also claimed that the payback method **reduces risk by ignoring longer-term cash flows** occurring further into the future which may be subject to higher risk. The main risk element in a project might stem from the unpredictability of the weather. This risk does not increase in later years and so a shorter payback would not necessarily reduce this risk. There is, of course, a risk that demand could change in the future because of a fashion change or technological change. Use of a shorter payback period would reduce this risk, but it may not be as important as the unpredictability of the weather.

A **disadvantage** of payback is that it **ignores the timing of cash flows** within the payback period, the cash flows after the end of the payback period (which may sometimes be considerable) and therefore the total project return. It also **ignores the time value of money**. Furthermore it is **unable to distinguish between projects with the same payback period**, the **choice of the payback period is arbitrary**, it may lead to excessive investment in short-term projects and it takes no account of the variability of cash flows. Finally, it **does not distinguish between investments of different sizes**.

16 Two projects

> **Top tips.** This is an easy, very useful question, covering some of the key issues and techniques which are required in Paper 2 investment appraisal questions.
>
> When calculating the **IRR by interpolation**, you should aim to work with a **positive NPV** and a **negative NPV**. If the **NPV** at the cost of capital is **positive**, you need to **use** a **higher** cost of capital for the next calculation so as to produce a **negative** NPV. The **interpolation formula** is not provided in the exam so you need to **learn it**.
>
> If the NPV and IRR rules give **conflicting** results, it is generally accepted that the recommendation of the **NPV rule** should be **followed**.

(a)   **Project X**

Year	Cash flow $'000	Disc factor 10%	PV $	Disc factor 20%	PV $
0	(200)	1.000	(200,000)	1.000	(200,000)
1	35	0.909	31,815	0.833	29,155
2	80	0.826	66,080	0.694	55,520
3	90	0.751	67,590	0.579	52,110
4	75	0.683	51,225	0.482	36,150
5	20	0.621	12,420	0.402	8,040
			29,130		(19,025)

IRR = 10% + [(29,130/(19,025 + 29,130)) × 10]% = 16.05%

NPV at 10% = $29,130

Project Y

Year	Cash flow $'000	Disc factor 10%	PV $	Disc factor 20%	PV $
0	(200)	1.000	(200,000)	1.000	(200,000)
1	218	0.909	198,162	0.833	181,594
2	10	0.826	8,260	0.694	6,940
3	10	0.751	7,510	0.579	5,790
4	4	0.683	2,732	0.482	1,928
5	3	0.621	1,863	0.402	1,206
			18,527		(2,542)

IRR = 10% + [(18,527/(18,527 + 2,542)) × 10]% = 18.8%

NPV at 10% = $18,527

(b)   **Both** projects are **acceptable** because they generate a positive net present value at the company's cost of capital.

The company should **undertake project X**, because it has the **highest forecast net present value**. Although the internal rate of return for Y is greater, the NPV is generally accepted to be the better performance measure for maximising company wealth.

(c)   The **inconsistency** in the ranking of the two projects – ie the conflicting results obtained with IRR and NPV – has **arisen because of the difference in timing of the cash flows** of the two projects. Project X cash flows occur mainly in the middle three years, whereas project Y generates most of its forecast cash flows in the first year, resulting in a higher IRR.

17 NPV and IRR

> **Top tips**. Make sure you get down the key points (those in bold) when you answer a short ten-mark question. You only have eighteen minutes and expect to write round half a page.

(a) **Net present value (NPV)**

This method **takes account of the timing of cash flows and the time value of the money** invested in the project. Future cash flows are discounted back to their present values. These present values are then summed to derive the net present value of the project. If the result is **positive** then the project is **acceptable**. If **two or more projects** are being compared then the **project with the higher NPV should be chosen**.

The major **difficulty** in calculating the NPV is in **determining the most appropriate discount rate** to use. An organisation may have alternative investment opportunities and the discount rate may be the expected return forgone on these investments. This is therefore the opportunity cost of capital. Alternatively an organisation may have raised a loan to cover the project in question, in which case the discount rate may be the interest rate payable on the loan.

A problem with the use of NPV relates to the **difficulty of explaining it** to a (possibly) non-financial manager. The NPV is **preferable to the payback period**, however, since it quantifies the effect of the timing of cash flows and it takes account of the different magnitudes of investments.

(b) **Internal rate of return**

The internal rate of return (IRR) is the **discount rate which produces a zero net present value** when it is applied to a project's cash flows. If the IRR exceeds the cost of capital then the project is acceptable.

The IRR has the **advantage** of being **more easily understood** than the NPV and it does **take account of the time value of money**.

However the IRR may be confused with the accounting return on capital employed and it **ignores the relative size of investments**. Furthermore, when cash flow patterns are non-conventional there **may be several IRRs**. More importantly, the IRR is **inferior to the NPV for ranking mutually exclusive projects** in order of preference.

Lastly, the IRR **assumes that cash flows from a project can be reinvested to earn a return equal to the IRR of the original project**. The organisation may not have this opportunity.

18 HP

> **Top tips**. In part (a) set out your proforma as we have done for the calculation of capital allowances and the tax effect of those allowances. This keeps workings clear. Do separate workings for payback and NPV as both of these are referred to in the question.

(a)   **Initial workings**

   1   **Capital allowances**

	Tax @30%	Year 1	Year 2	Year 3	Year 4	Year 5
	$	$	$	$	$	$
Machine cost	520,000					
WDA year 1, 25%	130,000	39,000	19,500	19,500		
	390,000					
WDA year 2, 25%	97,500	29,250		14,625	14,625	
	292,500					
WDA year 3, 25%	73,125	21,938			10,969	10,969
	219,375					
Sale for scrap, year 4	50,000					
Balancing allowance	169,375	50,813			25,406	25,407
Tax payable on contribution (working 2)		(40,320)	(80,640)	(80,640)	(40,320)	
Tax relief on training costs ($5,000 × 30% × 0.5)		750	750			
Total tax recoverable/(payable)		(20,070)	(45,765)	(55,046)	(3,945)	25,407

   2   **Incremental contribution**

Demand per week	12,000	units
Demand per hour (12,000/40)	300	units
Current capacity per hour	200	units
Incremental units per hour (300 – 200)	100	units
Contribution per unit	$1.40	
Hours available (40 hours × 48 weeks)	1,920	
Contribution per annum (100 × $1.40 × 1,920)	$268,800	
Tax @ 30%	$80,640	

Cash flows from profit

Year	Acquisition/ disposal	Contribution (W2)	Tax (W1)	Total cash flow	Discount factor	Present value
	$	$	$	$	10%	$
0	(525,000)			(525,000)	1.000	(525,000)
1		268,800	(20,070)	248,730	0.909	226,096
2		268,800	(45,765)	223,035	0.826	184,227
3		268,800	(55,046)	213,754	0.751	160,529
4	50,000		(3,945)	46,055	0.683	31,456
5			25,407	25,407	0.621	15,778
Net present value						93,086

Payback period

Year	Cash flow	Cumulative cash flow
	$	$
0	(525,000)	(525,000)
1	248,730	(276,270)
2	223,035	(53,235)
Payback period	= 2 years + ($53,235/$213,754)	
	= 2.25 years, or approximately 2 years 3 months	

The net present value (**NPV**) of the project is **positive** at $93,086 and on that basis it is recommended that the **project should go ahead** after consideration is given to the following.

(i)   The company expects a **payback within two years**. In this instance payback is only reached after approximately 2 years and 3 months but this should be over-ridden by the positive NPV.

(ii)   The $50,000 **recoverable value** should be reconsidered in light of the fact that the current machine would be scrapped at a cost of $20,000.

(iii)   Consideration should be given to **alternatives** such as working overtime on the old machine as a way of alleviating the bottleneck, thus eliminating the need for this investment.

(iv)   It is noted that the new machine would be **operating at 60% capacity**. Is there an alternative machine with a capacity matched to our needs of 300 units per hour at a correspondingly lower price? Alternatively, are there actions we could take which would stimulate demand to be closer to our potential 500 unit capacity (assuming there would be no other bottlenecks) which would make this a more attractive investment?

(b)   There are a number of **reasons why investment decision making will be different when the investment involves a marketing or IT project rather than tangible manufacturing equipment**.

(i)   Although most projects will have specific outflows of cash in the investing period, neither IT nor marketing will necessarily give rise to the same sorts of **identifiable and easily measurable cash flows** as manufacturing equipment. In the case of marketing it may be possible to forecast an expected value of additional revenues as an estimate of future cash inflows, but for IT projects there may not be any easily attributable cash inflow.

(ii)   The **estimation of the expected future** life of an IT investment is made difficult by the rapid rate of technological change in this area, and estimating the time that a marketing campaign's impact may be felt is even more problematic.

(iii)   In terms of approach it is often recommended that NPV is used as a way of assessing IT investments. A **high discount factor** should be used to reflect the fact that any identified cash inflows are subject to a high risk of obsolescence.

(iv)   It is possible that a **negative net present value** will be generated from an IT project. The investment decision will be based on management's assessment of whether the negative present value is a price worth paying for the intangible benefits of the system (increased user-friendliness, faster processing and so on).

(v)   For marketing investments the decision-making approach will depend on the **value of marketing spend**.

(1)   For small marketing campaigns it should be adequate merely to consider whether there are sufficient profits available to absorb the cost of the campaign and still leave an acceptable level of reported profit.

(2)   For larger proposed expenditure an expected value of revenue increases should be calculated and compared to the campaign cost. The length of the campaign and its expected impact will often be so short that no discount factor will need to be applied to calculate the net present value of the campaign.

19 Quarefel plc

Top tips. Set out your workings clearly as we have done in part (a) so that the answer is easy to mark. In part (b) you will need to discuss target costing in the context of your findings in part (a).

Part (c) is a standard optimal pricing calculation.

(a) **Net present value calculations**

	Year 0 $'000	Year 1 $'000	Year 2 $'000	Year 3 $'000	Year 4 $'000
Cost of equipment/residual value	(2,000)	-	-	-	400.0
Advertising	(1,200)	(1,000.00)	(800.0)	-	-
Fixed costs	-	(600.00)	(600.0)	(600.0)	-
Variable costs (W2)	-	(1,666.68)	(2,500.0)	(1,250.0)	-
Sales revenue (W3)	-	4,000.02	5,500.0	3,125.0	-
Net cash flow	(3,200)	733.34	1,600.0	1,275.0	400.0
Discount factor at 12%	× 1.000	× 0.893	× 0.797	× 0.712	× 0.636
Present value	(3,200)	654.87	1,275.2	907.8	254.4

Net present value $= -3{,}200 + 654.87 + 1{,}275.2 + 907.8 + 254.4$
$= -107.73$ ie $-\$107{,}730$

Additional calculations for IRR

Year	Cash flow $'000	Discount factor 10%	PV $'000
0	(3,200.00)	1.000	(3,200.00)
1	733.34	0.909	666.61
2	1,600.00	0.826	1,321.60
3	1,275.00	0.751	957.53
4	400.00	0.683	273.20
			18.94

Using IRR $= a\% + \left[\dfrac{A}{A-B} \times (b-a)\right]\%$

where   a and b are interest rates
A = NPV at rate a
B = NPV at rate b

then **IRR** $= 10\% + \left[\dfrac{18.94}{(18.94 + 107.73)} \times 2\right]\%$

$= 10.299\%$, say **10.3%**

Workings

1   **Year 1**

P $= 70 - 0.15Q$
P $= \$60$ in year 1
∴60 $= 70 - 0.15Q$
∴Q $= 66{,}667$ units

Year 2

Change in size of overall market from year 1 to year 2 = ((1,200,000 − 800,000)/800,000) × 100% = 50% increase

∴ Q = 66,667 × 150% = 100,000 units

Year 3

Change in size of overall market from year 2 to year 3 = ((600,000 − 1,200,000)/1,200,000) × 100% = 50% decrease

∴Q = 100,000 × 50% = 50,000 units

2 **Variable costs** (using results of working 1)

Year 1: 66,667 units × $25 = $1,666,675
Year 2: 100,000 units × $25 = $2,500,000
Year 3: 50,000 units × $25 = $1,250,000

3 **Year 1**

Revenue = 66,667 units × $60 = $4,000,020

Year 2

$P = 70 − (0.15 \times 100) = \$55$
Revenue = 100,000 units × $55 = $5,500,000

Year 3

$P = 70 − (0.15 \times 50) = \$62.50$
Revenue = 50,000 units × $62.50 = $3,125,000

(b) **Target costing** is a term that has been defined in a number of ways. The essence of the concept is that a **product should cost less than the price that can be obtained for it on the market.**

Given a launch price of $60, the **costs of the product over its life cycle exceed the expected cash inflows** (revenue plus residual value of equipment) at the organisation's cost of capital of 12%. If Quarefel plc's market share has been accurately forecast and the price/demand function is realistic, **efforts must be made to reduce costs** from the level at which they are currently forecast if the product is to be viable at the organisation's cost of capital.

The application of target costing will involve a **comparison of the current forecast cost levels with the target cost levels** that have to be achieved. Any difference between the two must then be eliminated. **Cost elimination** is most successful at the **design stage** of a product, before unnecessary costs have actually been incorporated into the product and the associated production process.

There are a number of **cost elimination techniques** which can be used.

(i) **Cutting out non-value-added activities**, perhaps using techniques such as activity analysis (which will identify cost drivers and their root causes and allow a reduction in their incidence and cost).

(ii) **Implementing a programme of total quality management**. TQM emphasises continuous improvement which is essential if an organisation is eventually to get its costs down to a target level. Quality circles, for example, could generate cost reduction ideas.

(iii) **Carry out a value engineering exercise**. Value engineering is an activity which helps to design products which meet customer needs at **lowest cost** while assuming the required standards of quality and reliability. Such an exercise might highlight the following possibilities for cost reduction.

    (1)   Reducing the number of components
    (2)   Using different materials

(iv) **Other cost-cutting techniques** include the following.

    (1)   Using standard components wherever possible
    (2)   Training staff in more efficient techniques
    (3)   Using cheaper staff
    (4)   Acquiring new, more efficient technology

(c)   **Return will be maximised** at the point where **marginal cost (MC) = marginal revenue (MR)**.

MC = 25 (as the unit variable cost is $25)

Return is maximised where   MC = MR
        ie where $25 = 70 - 0.3Q$
        ie where $Q = 150$ ie 150,000 units

If $Q = 150$, $P = 70 - 0.15 (150) = \$47.50$

The **strategy which maximises return** is to sell 150,000 units in each of years 1 to 3 at a unit selling price of $47.50.

20 Elsewhere

Top tips. This question is split into five parts so you have plenty of opportunity to earn marks. Part (a) uses information straight from the table in the question. Part (b) is a lot harder but you will need to practise these decision trees as they have been examined recently. Refer back to our tips in the chapter for drawing a tree if you have forgotten. Look at how we answered part (c)(i) as a simple equation.

(a)   The expected value of profit is calculated as follows.

Profit $'000	Probability	Expected profit $'000
800	0.5	400
100	0.2	20
(300)	0.3	(90)
		330

(b)   (i)

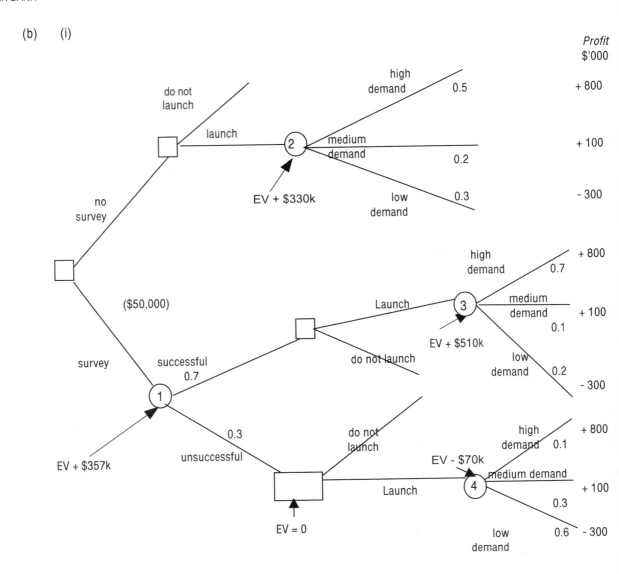

Key: ☐ - decision point   ◯ - outcome point

Expected value of profit

Profit	Probabilities outcome point			EV of profit outcome point		
	2	3	4	2	3	4
$'000				$'000	$'000	$'000
800	0.5	0.7	0.1	400	560	80
100	0.2	0.1	0.3	20	10	30
(300)	0.3	0.2	0.6	(90)	(60)	(180)
				330	510	(70)

(ii)   The record company should not commission the survey because the expected value of profit without the survey is $330,000. This is greater than the expected value of profit of $307,000 ($357,000 - $50,000) with the survey.

(c)   (i)   To find the maximum the company should pay for the survey, solve:

EV (survey) = EV (no survey)
$357K - survey cost = $330K

The maximum that the company should pay for this survey is $27,000.

(ii) Whenever a decision is made when the outcome of the decision is uncertain, there will always be some doubt that the correct decision has been taken. If a decision is based on selecting the option with the highest EV of profit, it can be assumed that in the long run, that is, with enough repetition, the decision so selected will give the highest average profit. But if the decision involves a once-only outcome, there will be a risk that in retrospect, it will be seen that the wrong decision was taken.

A decision tree is a simplified representation of reality, and it may omit some possible decision options, or it may simplify the possible outcomes. For example, in this question, 'success' and 'failure' are two extreme outcomes, whereas a variety of outcomes between success and failure may be possible. The decision tree is therefore likely to be a simplification of reality.

21 Dench

Top tips. Part (a) uses a table to calculate the cumulative average time per batch. This is based on output doubling (cumulative batches) and the time taken reducing by 0.80 for each doubling of batches. You can also use the formula $Y_x = aX^b$ to work out the cumulative average time per batch.

(a) Cost estimate for 225 components is based upon the following assumptions:

(1) the first batch of 15 is excluded from the order (and total cost for first batch is likewise excluded); and

(2) the 80% learning rate only applies to the skilled workforce (and related variable overhead), due to their high level of expertise/low turnover rate.

Cumulative batches	Cumulative units	Total time (hrs)	Cum. ave time/batch (hrs)
1	15	20	20
2	30	32	16
4	60	51.2	12.8
8	120	81.92	10.24
16	240	131.072	8.192

Total cost for 16 batches (240 components):

		$
Material A:	$30/batch	480
Material B:	$30/batch	480
Labour:	Skilled 131.072 hr @ $15/hr	1,966
	Semi-skilled $40/batch	640
Variable O.H.:	131.072 hr @ $4/hr	524
	5 hr/batch at $4/hr	320
		4,410
Less: cost for 1st batch (15 components)		(500)
... cost for 225 components		$3,910

(b) The limited use of learning curve theory is due to several factors:

(i) the learning curve phenomenon is not always present;

(ii) it assumes stable conditions at work (e.g. of the labour force and labour mix) which will enable learning to take place. This is not always practicable (e.g. because of labour turnover);

(iii) it must also assume a certain degree of motivation amongst employees;

(iv)   extensive breaks between production of items must not be too long, or workers will 'forget' and the learning process would have to begin all over again;

(v)   it is difficult to obtain enough accurate data to decide what the learning curve rate is;

(vi)   there will be a cessation to learning eventually, once the job has been repeated often enough.

22 Cost reduction

Top tips. Parts (a) and (b) shouldn't have given you major problems. Or did you find it difficult to think of three **cost control techniques**? As you will see from our answer, however, these include some of the principal **conventional management accounting techniques**, only it is not always usual to explicitly describe them as such!

Part (c) required a little more thought. Try to give **reasoned arguments** that look at **both sides** of the proposition. Don't be afraid to be vaguely critical of management accounting training, but be extremely polite about it, as we have been. Always provide some sort of **conclusion** to your discussion.

(a)   **Cost control** is the regulation of the costs of operating a business and is concerned with keeping costs within acceptable limits.

In contrast, **cost reduction** is a planned and positive approach to reducing expenditure. It starts with an assumption that current or planned cost levels are too high and looks for ways of reducing them without reducing effectiveness.

Cost control action ought to lead to a reduction in excessive spending (for example when material wastage is higher than budget levels or productivity levels are below agreed standards). However, a cost reduction programme is directed towards reducing expected cost levels below current budgeted or standard levels.

Cost control tends to be carried out on a routine basis whereas cost reduction programmes are often ad hoc exercises.

(b)   **Three examples of cost control techniques**

(i)   **Budgetary control**. Cost control is achieved by setting predetermined absolute levels for expenditure. If flexible budgeting is used then the budget cost allowance can be flexed in line with changes in activity. Control action is taken if actual expenditure differs from planned expenditure by an excessive amount.

(ii)   **Standard costing**. Designed to control unit costs rather than absolute levels of expenditure, the use of standard costing depends on the existence of a measurable output which is produced in standard operations. Control action is taken if the actual unit costs differ from standard unit costs by an excessive amount.

(iii)   **Limits on authority to incur expenditure**. Many organisations restrict the authority for their managers to incur expenditure. For example a budget manager may have an overall budget for overheads in a period, but even within this budget the manager may be required to seek separate authorisation for individual items of expenditure which are above a certain amount.

Three examples of cost reduction techniques

(i) **Value analysis**. CIMA defines value analysis as 'a systematic inter-disciplinary examination of factors affecting the cost of a product or service, in order to devise means of achieving the specified purpose most economically at the required standard of quality and reliability.' The aim in a value analysis exercise is to eliminate unnecessary costs without reducing the use value, the esteem value or the exchange value of the item under consideration.

(ii) **Work study**. This is a means of raising the production efficiency of an operating unit by the reorganisation of work. The two main parts to work study are method study and work measurement. Method study is the most significant in the context of cost reduction. It looks at the way in which work is done and attempts to develop easier and more effective methods in order to reduce costs.

(iii) **Variety reduction**. This involves standardisation of parts and components which can offer enormous cost reduction potential for some manufacturing industries. Variety reduction can also be used to describe the standardisation or simplification of an organisation's product range.

(c) The **statement suggests** that the training of management accountants should place the major **emphasis on cost reduction**.

This is true to some extent because of the changes in the competitive environment and the globalisation of markets. In order to remain competitive an organisation must provide goods and services of the right quality at prices which are attractive to the customer.

The **Japanese** in particular view costs as a **target** which must be reached rather than as a limit on expenditure. They employ cost reduction techniques to bring costs down below a target price with the result that prices dictate costs and not vice versa.

If companies are to compete effectively then they must adopt a similar philosophy. The management accountant needs to be trained to provide information which is useful for cost planning and cost reduction. An emphasis on cost control might create a tendency to concentrate effort and resources on the mechanics of recording and reporting historic costs, rather than on the planning and reducing of future costs.

On the other hand it is **still necessary to control costs** and to record and report actual costs so that management can take control action if necessary. An efficient plan will ensure that the organisation is starting out with the most effective cost targets, but only by recording the actual costs and comparing them with the targets will management know whether those targets have been achieved.

Despite the implied criticism of management accounting training, an increasing awareness of the need for a **more strategic approach to management accounting** does exist, both among trainee and qualified management accountants. Active discussion is also taking place on the need to adapt information systems to be more useful in an advanced manufacturing technology environment.

In **conclusion** while there may be a case for a **slight change in emphasis** in the training of management accountants, this should not lead to the total abandonment of cost control principles and techniques.

23 Life cycle costing

> **Top tips**. See how we have set out our answer with two headings addressing the two requirements in the question.

Life cycle costs

Life cycle costs are the **costs incurred on products and services from their design stage, through development to market launch, production and sales, and their eventual withdrawal from the market**. A product's life cycle costs might therefore be classified as follows.

(a) Acquisition costs (costs of research, design, testing, production and construction)

(b) Product distribution costs (transportation and handling)

(c) Maintenance costs (customer service, field maintenance and 'in-factory' maintenance)

(d) Operation costs (the costs incurred in operations, such as energy costs, and various facility and other utility costs)

(e) Training costs (operator and maintenance training)

(f) Inventory costs (the cost of holding spare parts, warehousing and so on)

(g) Technical data costs (cost of purchasing any technical data)

(h) Retirement and disposal costs (costs occurring at the end of the product's life)

Life cycle costing versus traditional management accounting systems

(a) **Traditional management accounting practice**

This is, in general, to report costs at the physical production stage of the life cycle of a product; costs are not accumulated over the entire life cycle. Such practice **does not, therefore, assess a product's profitability over its entire life but rather on a periodic basis**. Costs tend to be accumulated according to function; research, design, development and customer service costs incurred on all products during a period are totalled and recorded as a period expense.

(b) **Life cycle costing**

(i) Using **life cycle costing**, on the other hand, such **costs are traced to individual products over complete life cycles**. These accumulated costs are compared with the revenues attributable to each product and hence the **total profitability of any given product can be determined**. Moreover, by gathering costs for each product, the relationship between the choice of design adopted and the resulting marketing and production costs becomes clear.

(ii) The **control function** of life cycle costing lies in the **comparison of actual and budgeted life cycle costs for a product**. Such comparisons allow for the refinement of future decisions about product design, lead to more effective resource allocation and show whether expected savings from using new production methods or technology have been realised.

Life cycle costing and AMT environments

Research has shown that, for organisations operating within an **advanced manufacturing technology environment**, approximately **90% of a product's life-cycle cost is determined by decisions made early within the life cycle**. In such an environment there is therefore a **need to ensure that the tightest cost controls are at the design stage**, because the majority of costs are committed at this point. This necessitates the need for a management accounting system that assists in the planning and control of a product's life cycle costs, which monitors spending and commitments to spend during the early stages of a product's life cycle and which recognises the reduced life cycle and the subsequent challenge to profitability of products produced in an AMT environment. Life cycle costing is such a system.

Summary

Life cycle costing **increases the visibility of costs such as those associated with research, design, development and customer service**, and also enables **individual product profitability to be more fully understood** by attributing all costs to products. As a consequence, more **accurate feedback** information is available **on the organisation's success or failure in developing new products. In today's competitive environment, where the ability to produce new and updated versions of products is of paramount importance to the survival of the organisation**, this information is vital.

24 ABC

> **Top tips.** Requirements such as these are just the sort of thing you might encounter as parts of questions in the exam. You are expected to be able to critically appraise the management accounting techniques and methods included in the syllabus so don't be afraid to be critical of a view used as the basis for a question.

(a)   **ABC** attempts to **relate all costs**, with the possible exception of facility sustaining costs, to **cost objects** such as products, services or customers. It does this by **collecting costs/resources and relating them to either primary or support activities via resource cost drivers. Support activity costs are then spread across primary activities**. Finally the **costs of the primary activities** are **related** to **cost units using activity cost drivers**.

It is likely that ABC will **provide a different picture of product costs than that produced using traditional absorption costing**. This is because different assumptions are made because the costs are spread across the activities, etc. As both methods make assumptions about the behaviour and cause of costs, it is impossible to say categorically that ABC results are more accurate than those produced using traditional absorption costing.

Nevertheless there are usually more activities than cost centres and this should make the process **more accurate**. Furthermore it is **easier to justify the selection of cost driver rates** with ABC than the absorption rates used with traditional absorption costing. ABC also allows costs to be accumulated per batch or per number of products made, as well as per unit.

These factors all suggest that in most cases ABC will produce a more accurate answer.

(b)   Some commentators argue that only marginal costing provides suitable information for decision making. This is untrue. Marginal costing provides a crude method of differentiating between different types of cost behaviour by splitting costs into their variable and fixed elements. **Marginal costing** can only be used for **short-term decisions** and usually even these have longer-term implications which ought to be considered.

ABC spreads costs across products or other cost units according to a number of different bases. The analysis may show that one activity which is carried out for one or two products is expensive. If costs have been apportioned using the traditional method prior to this the cost of this activity is likely to have been spread across all products, thus hiding the fact that the products using this activity may be loss making. If these costs are not completely variable costs but are, for example, batch costs, marginal costing would not have related them to the products at all. Therefore **ABC** can be used to make **decisions about pricing, discontinuing products**, and so on.

25 ABC systems

Top tips. This old syllabus pilot paper question was not easy, in that you may have had difficulty in finding enough to write about to justify 10 marks. To get close to full marks you should expand your argument to include ABM.

To a certain extent Drury is correct when he states that ABC systems are resource-consumption models.

When ABC systems were first discussed companies were using other systems, usually absorption-based, for the purposes of inventory valuation. ABC analysis and supporting calculations would be carried out using actual data to see what the 'actual' costs of products were as a way of improving decision making and operational control.

In this retrospective context ABC starts with the processes of allocating costs to cost pools and determining an appropriate cost driver. For example $250,000 may have been spent on labour and materials for the packing department which processed 25,000 customer orders. This results in a cost of $10 per order to trace back to products, where 'number of orders' is the identified cost driver.

Clearly, in this context, ABC is looking at the **cost of using resources** within the packing department.

Increasingly, however, companies are using ABC as their main costing system but as part of a broader system of **activity based management** (ABM). Here an **activity based budget** (ABB) will be prepared, using budgeted costs and levels of activity, and compared to the ABC figures over the period for the purposes of exercising control.

It is likely that when the ABB is being prepared it will start with expected sales volumes and from there consider what activities will be required in order to generate the required volume of product. Thus the example above would shift emphasis from 'we spent $250,000 in packing last year' to 'how much resource should we supply the packing department with so as to have them pack the expected volume?' If the ABB is accurate then the ABB figure for packing will be the same as the figures obtained through ABC.

Hopefully companies that are using ABC are using it in the broader context of ABM so as to be able to obtain a broader range of benefits. Although ABC in isolation does focus on resource consumption, **ABM will consider both the consumption and the supply of resources.**

26 Just-in-time

Top tips. What a nice, straightforward old syllabus pilot paper question. No ambiguities in the requirements, simply discuss features and state benefits. In the exam you would probably only need to provide five (relevant) financial benefits in part (b) to gain the full five marks.

(a)   JIT production systems will include the following features.

Multiskilled workers

In a JIT production environment, production processes must be shortened and simplified. **Each product family is made in a workcell based on flowline principles**. The variety and complexity of work carried out in these work cells is increased (compared with more traditional processes), necessitating a group of dissimilar machines working within each work cell. **Workers must therefore be more flexible and adaptable, the cellular approach enabling each operative to operate several machines**. Operatives are trained to operate all machines on the line and undertake **routine preventative maintenance**.

Close relationships with suppliers

JIT production systems often go hand in hand with JIT purchasing systems. **JIT purchasing** seeks to **match the usage of materials with the delivery of materials** from external suppliers. This means that **material inventories can be kept at near-zero levels**. For JIT purchasing to be successful this requires the organisation to have confidence that the supplier will deliver on time and that the supplier will deliver materials of 100% quality, that there will be no rejects, returns and hence no consequent production delays. The **reliability of suppliers is of utmost importance** and hence the company must **build up close relationships** with their suppliers. This can be achieved by doing **more business with fewer suppliers** and placing **long-term orders** so that the supplier is assured of sales and can produce to meet the required demand.

Machine cells

With JIT production, factory layouts must change to reduce movement of workers and products. Traditionally machines were grouped by function (drilling, grinding and so on). A part therefore had to travel long distances, moving from one part of the factory to the other, often stopping along the way in a storage area. All these are non-value-added activities that have to be reduced or eliminated. **Material movements between operations are therefore minimised by eliminating space between work stations and grouping machines or workers by product or component** instead of by type of work performed. Products can flow from machine to machine without having to wait for the next stage of processing or returning to stores. **Lead times and work in progress are thus reduced**.

Quality

Production management within a JIT environment seeks to both **eliminate scrap and defective** units **during production and avoid the need for reworking of units**. Defects stop the production line, thus creating rework and possibly resulting in a failure to meet delivery dates. Quality, on the other hand, reduces costs. Quality is assured by **designing products and processes with quality in mind, introducing quality awareness programmes and statistical checks on output quality**, providing **continual worker training** and implementing **vendor quality assurance programmes** to ensure that the correct product is made to the appropriate quality level on the first pass through production.

Set-up time reduction

If an organisation is able to **reduce manufacturing lead time** it is in a better position to **respond quickly to changes in customer demand**. Reducing set-up time is one way in which this can be done. Machinery set-ups are non-value-added activities which should be reduced or even eliminated. **Reducing set-up time** (and hence set-up costs) also makes the manufacture of **smaller batches more economical and worthwhile**; managers do not feel the need to spread the set-up costs over as many units as possible (which then leads to high levels of inventory). Set-up time can be reduced by the **use of one product or one product family machine cells**, by **training workers** or by the use of **computer integrated manufacturing (CIM)**.

(b)   JIT systems have a number of financial **benefits**.

- Increase in labour productivity due to labour being multiskilled and carrying out preventative maintenance

- Reduction of investment in plant space

- Reduction in costs of storing inventory

- Reduction in risk of inventory obsolescence

- Lower investment in inventory

- Reduction in costs of handling inventory

- Reduction in costs associated with scrap, defective units and reworking

- Higher revenue as a result of reduction in lost sales following failure to meet delivery dates (because of improved quality)

- Reduction in the costs of setting up production runs

- Higher revenues as a result of faster response to customer demands

27 CPA

Top tips. This is a fairly straightforward question. You can pick up marks straight away by using a report format as requested.

REPORT

To: Management of XY Ltd
From: Management accountant
Date: 20/05/X0
Title: **XY Ltd's profitability in relation to the number of our customers served**

1   **Concept encapsulated by the graph**

1.1   The graph illustrates what is often referred to as the 80:20 rule, that is that 80% of our profits are generated by a core 20% of our customer base.

2   **Application of the principle**

2.1   The same principle (known as Pareto analysis) can be applied in other spheres. For example, in information systems, 20% of systems design effort may provide systems meeting 80% of business requirements, with 80% of the effort being expended to meet the final 20% of requirements.

2.2   In the case of profitability in relation to the customer base, those 20% of customers who buy our standard product, pay invoices in full and on time and in all other respects conform to our procedures will be the ones who generate 80% of our profits. The other 80% of our customers will generate further costs through their non-compliance with our processes.

3   **Improving the profitability of the organisation**

3.1   To build upon the principles of the 80:20 rule there are a number of steps which can be taken.

3.2   **Conduct a survey of Customer Profitability**. It may be possible to identify specific customers who, as a result of particular requirements they have regarding the product they buy or special ordering or payment procedures they demand, are not being fully charged for the costs which they generate.

3.3   If this is the case a new selling price should be established which does cover the additional costs they generate and if they are not willing to pay this higher price it may be necessary to consider discontinuing supply. Although this may reduce sales revenues it will increase profits because dealings with these customers are likely to be generating losses.

3.4   **Review internal processes**. It may be possible to align these more closely to those of our customers, thus increasing our overall profit.

3.5   The 20% most profitable customers need to be recognised and steps taken to ensure that they are retained and, if possible, sales to them are increased. Marketing need to ensure that these customers' needs are continually being identified and met. Investigations should be conducted to see whether it is possible to increase sales to these customers, for example by encouraging them to use XY Ltd as their sole supplier.

Signed: Management accountant

28 Outsourced services

The **most significant controls** will need to be **implemented at the planning stage of the process of outsourcing a service**.

(a)   The organisation should **document details** of the level and quality of the service it requires from the external organisation.

(b)   External organisations should then be invited to **tender** for providing the service. A documented policy as to the tendering process is required and should cover factors such as the number of bids required, whether the bids should be sealed and so on.

(c)   The organisation must confirm a **price** for the service with the successful bidder.

(d)   **On-going control** involves ensuring that the service delivered is actually of the contracted level and quality.

(e)   The organisation must also give consideration to drawing up **policies** to deal with problems which could arise in the following areas.

- Judging the quality of service provided

- Approving any costs in excess of those agreed

- Including a get-out clause in the contract (to be used if the contractor becomes complacent following a desire by the organisation to build up a long-term relationship)

- Including a price increase clause in the contract

- Reducing prices if the level of service is lower than anticipated

Index

BPP
LEARNING MEDIA

Note: **Key Terms** and their references are given in **bold**

Review Form & Free Prize Draw – Paper P2 Management Accounting Decision Management (5/07)

All original review forms from the entire BPP range, completed with genuine comments, will be entered into one of two draws on 31 January 2008 and 31 July 2008. The names on the first four forms picked out on each occasion will be sent a cheque for £50.

Name: _____   Address: _____

_____

_____

How have you used this Text?
(Tick one box only)

☐ Home study (book only)

☐ On a course: college _____

☐ With 'correspondence' package

☐ Other _____

Why did you decide to purchase thisText?
(Tick one box only)

☐ Have used BPP Texts in the past

☐ Recommendation by friend/colleague

☐ Recommendation by a lecturer at college

☐ Saw information on BPP website

☐ Saw advertising

☐ Other _____

During the past six months do you recall seeing/receiving any of the following?
(Tick as many boxes as are relevant)

☐ Our advertisement in *Financial Management*

☐ Our advertisement in *Pass*

☐ Our advertisement in *PQ*

☐ Our brochure with a letter through the post

☐ Our website www.bpp.com

Which (if any) aspects of our advertising do you find useful?
(Tick as many boxes as are relevant)

☐ Prices and publication dates of new editions

☐ Information on Text content

☐ Facility to order books off-the-page

☐ None of the above

Which BPP products have you used?

Text	☑	Success CD	☐	Learn Online	☐
Kit	☐	i-Learn	☐	Home Study Package	☐
Passcard	☐	i-Pass	☐	Home Study PLUS	☐

Your ratings, comments and suggestions would be appreciated on the following areas.

	Very useful	Useful	Not useful
Introductory section (Key study steps, personal study)	☐	☐	☐
Chapter introductions	☐	☐	☐
Key terms	☐	☐	☐
Quality of explanations	☐	☐	☐
Case studies and other examples	☐	☐	☐
Exam focus points	☐	☐	☐
Questions and answers in each chapter	☐	☐	☐
Fast forwards and chapter roundups	☐	☐	☐
Quick quizzes	☐	☐	☐
Question Bank	☐	☐	☐
Answer Bank	☐	☐	☐
OT Bank	☐	☐	☐
Index	☐	☐	☐
Icons	☐	☐	☐

Overall opinion of this Study Text	Excellent ☐	Good ☐	Adequate ☐	Poor ☐

Do you intend to continue using BPP products?   Yes ☐   No ☐

On the reverse of this page are noted particular areas of the text about which we would welcome your feedback. The BPP author of this edition can be e-mailed at: helendarch@bpp.com

Please return this form to: Nick Weller, CIMA Publishing Manager, BPP Learning Media Ltd, FREEPOST, London, W12 8BR

Review Form & Free Prize Draw (continued)

TELL US WHAT YOU THINK

Please note any further comments and suggestions/errors below

Free Prize Draw Rules

1   Closing date for 31 January 2008 draw is 31 December 2007. Closing date for 31 July 2008 draw is 30 June 2008.

2   Restricted to entries with UK and Eire addresses only. BPP employees, their families and business associates are excluded.

3   No purchase necessary. Entry forms are available upon request from BPP Learning Media Ltd. No more than one entry per title, per person. Draw restricted to persons aged 16 and over.

4   Winners will be notified by post and receive their cheques not later than 6 weeks after the relevant draw date.

5   The decision of the promoter in all matters is final and binding. No correspondence will be entered into.